The MAGNIFICENT HEEL

The Life and Films of
RICARDO CORTEZ

by DAN VAN NESTE

THE MAGNIFICENT HEEL
THE LIFE AND FILMS OF RICARDO CORTEZ
©2017 DAN VAN NESTE

ALL RIGHTS RESERVED.

No part of this book may be reproduced in any form or by any means, electronic, mechanical, digital, photocopying, or recording, except for in the inclusion of a review, without permission in writing from the publisher.

Published in the USA by:

BEARMANOR MEDIA
P.O. BOX 71426
ALBANY, GEORGIA 31708
www.BearManorMedia.com

ISBN: 978-1-62933-128-7 (alk. paper)

DESIGN AND LAYOUT: VALERIE THOMPSON

HEEL (NOUN)

"A contemptibly dishonorable or irresponsible person"
— *Webster's Collegiate Dictionary*

"A despicable or unscrupulous person, cad"
— *Your Dictionary*

"A criminal, a double crossing sneak thief, a despicable person"
— *Oxford Dictionary of Modern Slang*

" A loser, a jerk"
— *Alpha Dictionary.com*

TABLE OF CONTENTS

DISCOVERING CORTEZ — INTRODUCTION & ACKNOWLEDGMENTS ... 1

PART I — THE LIFE OF RICARDO CORTEZ

CHAPTER ONE — BIG DREAMS IN LITTLE HUNGARY (1900–22) ... 7

CHAPTER TWO — THE LATIN FROM MANHATTAN (1923–24) ... 31

CHAPTER THREE — FLYING WITH THE SNOWBIRD (1925–26) ... 51

CHAPTER FOUR — CRASH AND BURN (1927–29) ... 83

CHAPTER FIVE — ENDINGS AND BEGINNINGS (1930–31) ... 109

CHAPTER SIX — UP FROM THE ASHES (1931–32) ... 131

CHAPTER SEVEN — PROFESSIONAL SCOUNDREL (1933–35) ... 169

CHAPTER EIGHT — VON STROHEIM OF THE B'S (1936–40) ... 209

CHAPTER NINE — ONCE A HEEL, ALWAYS A HEEL (1941–49) ... 237

CHAPTER TEN — A LAST HURRAH (1950–59) ... 259

CHAPTER ELEVEN — A COMFORTABLE PLACE (1960–77) ... 273

CHAPTER TWELVE — RICARDO CORTEZ, ONE AUTHORS VIEW — SUMMARY THOUGHTS AND CONCLUSIONS ... 283

PART II — THE FILMS OF RICARDO CORTEZ

THE FEATURE FILMS ... 295

SHORT FILMS, RADIO, TELEVISON APPEARANCES ... 500

SELECTED BIBLIOGRAPHY ... 507

END NOTES ... 521

PHOTO CREDITS ... 563

ABOUT THE AUTHOR ... 565

INDEX ... 567

DISCOVERING CORTEZ

INTRODUCTION

"Listen, sister, if you wasn't such a dumb dame, you'd know you gotta be nice to me before you leave here!"
— as Goldie Gorio in *Bad Company*.

"Ok kid. You don't owe us a thing. You can go whenever you want to, but just remember this. You'll come back crawling and maybe I let you in."
— as Leo Darcy in *Midnight Mary*.

"Hey, Bee. Take this out in the hallway and open it. It might be a bomb. And if it is, I'll write you a nice epitaph, 'Here lies Bee. She was a good girl, but she went to pieces!'"
— as William Poster in *Is My Face Red*.

"The trouble with you is you have a guilty conscience. I haven't!"
— as Nolan in *The Walking Dead*.

"I hope you're not angry with me. See, you sort of had me on the spot, and I had to do a little double-crossing."
— as Gordon Creed in *West of Shanghai*.

Think you know which 1930's actor delivered those colorful lines on film? If you guessed Cagney, Robinson, Raft, Bogart or Muni, you'd be wrong. The above lines were delivered by a good looking, raven haired, olive-skinned, athletically built man with heavy-lidded dark brown eyes, an ever present smile, and a mouthful of pearly white teeth. The actor who recited them was a popular movie star for more than five decades; the only actor to ever receive top billing over Greta Garbo; the first to play Sam Spade in the cinema. During his heyday, in the late silent and early sound eras, this actor played opposite a majority of the greatest actresses of the silver screen, and worked with many of the most acclaimed directors and filmmakers in cinematic history. He was considered one of the handsomest, best dressed male movie stars of his era, renowned for his dependability, professionalism, and knowledge of all aspects of his craft. He was also one of Hollywood's most versatile thespians, a favorite of critics and studio heads alike; an actor who persuasively played all types of characters in all genres, but was particularly adept at playing charismatic scoundrels. A list of this star's villainous characterizations is a veritable rogue's gallery, from smiling heels, philanderers, wastrels and troublemakers, to double-dealing businessman, crooked gamblers, small-time hoods and gangsters, to killers and ruthless maniacal monsters. Each bore the particular stamp of this suave debonair actor's unique artistry. Still perplexed? His name was Ricardo Cortez, and in spite of all of these accomplishments, he has largely been forgotten.

In fact, when he died in 1977, most key newspapers and important film magazines and journals covered his death only briefly. In one or two paragraph summaries, they mentioned his beginnings as a cinematic Latin lover, listed a few of his screen credits, a few of his famous costars, and his subsequent work in the financial world. There were no in-depth discussions of his career, no analysis of his impact on the industry, no celebrations of his lifetime of achievement. In more recent years, whenever his name comes up at all (usually in the context of others), he is more often than not unfairly dismissed as a mediocre talent; a second string Valentino or a second rate Sam Spade. How could this be? **Who was Ricardo Cortez? Why has he been forgotten? What is his true legacy?** This book is an attempt to answer these questions, to shed light on the life and career of this unique, long-neglected star, whose significant contributions to the entertainment industry encompassed appearances on the stage, radio, television, and in over 100 feature films as well as seven motion pictures he directed.

ACKNOWLEDGMENTS

In case we've never crossed paths, let me introduce myself. My name is Dan Van Neste. I'm a freelance writer and biographer, and have been writing about classic movies for almost 30 years. My articles have appeared in a variety of newspapers, film magazines and journals. In 1994, one of my pieces was published in the acclaimed monthly magazine, *Classic Images*. Since then I have penned over 50 major articles for *CI*, its sister quarterly, *Films of the Golden Age*, and many other publications. Many of my pieces contain original interviews with vintage movie stars and other filmmakers. In 2011, I won acclaim for my book, *The Whistler: Stepping Into the Shadows*, about the groundbreaking Columbia film series.

This volume has been a long time coming. It seems I've been intrigued by Ricardo Cortez for much of my life. I don't recall the first time I saw him in films, but it was undoubtedly on the small screen years ago, when I was a kid growing up in rural south central Michigan. I was fascinated by villainous actors, and Cortez always stood out.

Since I began writing about classic movies and vintage filmmakers, I've encountered him many times in my research on others, and discovered time had not tarnished my admiration for him. Given his versatility, camera-friendly charisma, and prominence during the late silent and early sound eras, I found it surprising no one had ever written about him in-depth before. After embarking on this project in 2012, I soon discovered why. Cortez was an excessively private person. He didn't leave diaries, didn't trust the press, granted very few interviews, and when he did, they were rarely substantive. He had few intimate friends and his contemporaries are all deceased. As a consequence I was forced to scour the country, assembling pieces of his story bit by bit over time.

My four year quest to discover Cortez has involved lots of leg work, and lots of help from many fine individuals across the United States, without whom this volume would certainly not have been possible. For exemplary service beyond the call of duty, let me thank Janet Lorenz and the librarians at the Academy of Motion Picture Arts and Sciences (A.M.P.A.S. — Margaret Herrick Library); Mary Huelsbeck, Assistant Director, Department of Communication

Arts, Wisconsin Center for Film and Theater Research; Julie Graham, Archivist, RKO Archives, Charles E. Young Research Library, University Of California, Los Angeles; Susan Abler, Information Science Representative, Charles E.Young Library, University of California, Los Angeles; Benjamin Formaker-Olivas, Charles E. Young Research Library, U.C.L.A.; Jonathon Auxier, Warner Brothers Archives, University of Southern California; Richard Foster, Research Coordinator, Digital Collections, New York Public Library; **and** various librarians and archivists at the Library of Congress, Museum of Modern Art, New York City, and Brigham Young University in Provo, Utah.

Many other individuals also contributed mightily. In particular, I'd like to express my deep appreciation to Jan Taylor Garfield, Nancy Randle, Jim Manago, Tony Greco, G.D. Hamann, Karen Burroughs Hannsberry, Gary Moran, Farran Smith Nehme, Marylyn Noh, Brian Taves, Scott O'Brien, Kayla Sturm, D'Arcy More, and Steven Miller. Special thank yous to several distinguished individuals who granted me interviews including Ricardo Cortez's nephew, Don Kranze, Christine Cortez's great niece, Diedre Hart, Margaret Cortez's sister-in-law, Carol Bell, and the late actors Karen Morley, Edward Norris, and Jean Parker. I would also like to take this opportunity to thank the great people at BearManor Media: Ben Ohmart, Sandy Grabman, designer Valerie Thompson, and editor, Brian Tedesco for being so helpful and kind AND for doing so much to help writers preserve vintage entertainment history.

Finally, my gratitude goes out to my family for their love and encouragement, and to my late mom for being my rock. I would never have achieved anything in my life if not for her unconditional love, sacrifice, support, and encouragement. This particular volume is dedicated to another irreplaceable influence: my late sister, Caroline Marsh, who passed away in 2014. A wonderful, loving mother, sister, aunt, and friend, Carol set an example for all of us through her love and sacrifice, and by her valiant decade long battle against a demon called cancer. We should all be so brave!

Before beginning to relate Ricardo's story, I want to take a few moments to briefly outline and explain the structure of the book. It is divided into two main parts. The first half covers Cortez's personal and professional lives with the emphasis on the personal. There are

12 chapters, 11 of which cover a main phase of his life. Each chapter begins with a Cortez portrait and quote from the period in question. Chapter Twelve, entitled, "Ricardo Cortez, One Author's View," is a summary overview of Cortez the actor, the man, his personality, and decisions, and an overall assessment of his impact and importance in film history. In it, I attempt to answer the specific questions posed above.

The second half of the book is devoted to Mr. Cortez's most important legacy: his films. Each of the 100+ feature-length motion pictures and short films in which he appeared, and/or directed, has a separate section. Under each movie section are multiple subsections consisting of relevant production and credit information (i.e., genre, studio, producer, director, cast, length, prominent reviews, plot summaries, and significant taglines). Also included under each movie heading is a subsection entitled "availability," which includes information on the film's survival, and its availability on DVD or VHS. If the motion picture exists, but is not commercially available, I have endeavored to point out where a copy is stored. This subsection is particularly important with regard to the films of Cortez, because so many (including a majority of his silents and a handful of his sound films) apparently have not survived the ravages of time.

The final subsection under each movie heading is devoted to interesting facts and trivia. All types of items related to the particular film are included here from original titles, production notes, casting decisions, salaries, and box office receipts, to short summary biographies of prominent filmmakers involved in each production. Much of the information contained in this subsection was taken from various archives and has never been published.

CHAPTER ONE
"BIG DREAMS IN LITTLE HUNGARY" (1900–22)

"Ever since I can remember, I wanted to be an actor. When the opportunity came my way, I became a super at twelve dollars a week."

— RICARDO CORTEZ

The extraordinary life of filmland's "magnificent heel" began on a cool, cloudy, late summer day, amidst the hustle and bustle of turn of the century New York. A big, dynamic city of exquisite wealth and dire poverty, in 1900, the "Big Apple," as it came to be known, was a teeming hotbed of innovation and frenetic activity. Total inhabitants: 5,000,000 — 3.8 million citizens, 1.2 million aliens.

America's population had literally exploded during the latter portion of the 1800's, mainly due to the millions of immigrants who crossed the Atlantic to escape the poverty, political unrest, and tyranny of 19th century Europe. The immigrant hordes were a disparate lot, with all shapes, sizes, ages, ethnicities, origins, languages, and religions represented. All shared one thing in common; to them, America was a land of dreams, a place where they would have the freedom and opportunity for a better life denied to them in their home countries.[1]

Unfortunately, many would find life in the land of dreams a nightmare. For many immigrants, daily existence in America was as difficult, or more so, than the places from which they came. They were literally strangers in a strange land. Many were poverty stricken, had little or no education, few marketable skills, and worse yet, knew little or no English. Many ended up in big city slums, in poor, often filthy, crime-ridden neighborhoods. In their dingy tenements, daily survival so preoccupied their lives, there was little time for anything else. For them, hope was virtually all they had to hold on to.[2]

If Hollywood would eventually become known world-wide as the "city of dreams," it was New York which served that purpose for most Americans and world visitors at the turn of the century. One of the immigrant dreamers was Ricardo's father, a young Hungarian Jew named Morris Krantz, who arrived in New York from his home in Galicia (in what is now western Ukraine). A rich agricultural area coveted by many European powers, Galicia had been variously controlled by Russia, Poland, and Austria-Hungary over the years. When Morris Krantz was born in April, 1877, the province was part of Austria-Hungary. By then, the Austro-Hungarian Empire had milked it of its resources, and refused to provide funds for its development. Consequently, it was considered one of Europe's poorest areas. Many who lived there desperately wanted to leave and come to America where they might have some chance to succeed.[3]

Little is known about Morris Krantz. Whether by accident or design, neither Ricardo, his brother Stanley, or any other member of the family shared many details about him. Sadly, historical records are also sketchy. What we know about his early life could be stated in a short paragraph. Apparently, Morris was one of the younger children in a very large family. His parents, Jacob and Hannah Swartz Krantz were middle class Orthodox Jews (of both Hungarian and Austrian heritage) living in Galicia. Morris learned how to read and write, but had little formal education, and spoke Yiddish. During the late 1880's, his older brother Herman immigrated to America and settled in New York City. Seventeen-year-old Morris followed in 1894.

For a time, Morris lived with Herman (b. 1869) and his wife Yetta (b. 1867), and their expanding family in a crowded tenement apartment on Manhattan's Lower East Side, in an area near the famed Hester Street. By the late 1890's, Morris had learned enough English to become employed in New York City's burgeoning garment industry. While working as a "shirt maker," he appeared to have learned a trade. In her autobiography, Ricardo's first wife, Alma Rubens, claimed Morris had been a kosher butcher, but there is no evidence of that. U.S. Census records throughout the early part of the 20th century identify Morris as a "shirt maker" and/or a "tailor."

Morris was still living with his brother's family when he was introduced to Sarah Lefkowitz, a young Jewish girl whose parents were Austrians. Born in February, 1878, in Hungary, the daughter of Samuel and Rose Lefkowitz, Sarah and her family, including two siblings, Morris (b. 1876) and Pauline (b. 1881), emigrated to America in 1887. A fourth child, Joseph was born in 1900. By all accounts, Sarah was better educated and more worldly than her future husband. Some movie magazine articles suggested she had been a concert singer prior to coming to the United States. While it is true she did sing and love music, and passed that love on to her children, her singing career appears to be a colorful fabrication conjured up by inventive movie magazine writers.

No information is known about the courtship of Morris and Sarah, or if there even was a courtship; marriages were frequently arranged at the time. Whatever the truth, 22-year-old blonde haired, blue eyed Morris Krantz married 21-year-old dark haired, brown-eyed, olive- complexioned Sarah Lefkowitz in 1899. By then, Morris was earning enough money, so the newlyweds could have their own small apartment in a better area of Manhattan. The year 1900 census records indicate the Krantzs lived in Ward 16 near the Hudson River on Manhanttan's Lower East Side. Herman Krantz's eldest son, eight-year-old Maxim "Max" took up residence with his uncle and new aunt during this time.

Census records also reveal the couple's next door neighbor was Mary Lefkowitz (b. 1836). Who Mary was is not known, although she was likely a relative of Sarah. Because of her birthdate, she could have been Sarah's grandmother or an elderly aunt. It is only a guess, but perhaps the young couple took the apartment at her suggestion, and/or to be close to her. By the early weeks of 1900, they had a reason to want a relative nearby; Sarah was pregnant.[4]

Named for his grandfather, Jacob Krantz, the young man who would eventually become known around the world as Ricardo Cortez, took his first bow on September 19, 1900, somewhere on New York's Lower East Side. Like so many things about Ricardo's life, there has always been confusion and a bit of mystery associated with his place and date of birth. Surprisingly, up until recently, most biographies of Ricardo (contained in well-respected encyclopedias, books, and scholarly articles) incorrectly listed his birthdate as 1899, and his birthplace as Austria-Hungary. Many also contain a story about his parents bringing him to the United States when he was three years old. None of these stories are true. These falsities undoubtedly originated with the Paramount Pictures publicity department which, in an attempt to create a new Latin heartthrob, concocted the early details of his life to make him appear foreign and exotic. Why the misinformation persisted even after Ricardo publicly admitted the true facts of his birthplace and heritage during the early 1930's is anyone's guess.

Ricardo told the press he was born on Hester Street with relatives and a midwife in attendance.[5] Jacob would be the eldest of five children. His four siblings (two brothers and two sisters) were born in roughly two-year intervals: Malvina in 1902; Bernard in 1904; Helene in 1907; and Samuel a.k.a. Stanislaus in 1908. In an attempt to accommodate their expanding family, the Krantzs moved several times during the first decade of the 20th century. By 1910, they lived in a larger apartment on East Houston Street in what was known then as "Little Hungary," an area in Manhattan between Houston Street and East 10th Street where many Hungarian immigrants lived and worked. (** Please note: Eventually "Little Hungary" was relocated to Yorkville on the Upper East Side.) Sometime in the early 1900's, Morris opened his own wholesale clothing and tailoring shop nearby.[6]

While the first 10 years of young Jacob's life were relatively uneventful in a formal sense, they were important to the formation of the character and personality traits that would shape his life. Morris a.k.a "Papa Krantz" was kindly but strict, teaching all his children, most especially his eldest son, the value of thrift, discipline, hard work, and responsibility. Morris told Jacob, since he was the oldest, he had a special responsibility to look after his younger siblings and set a good example. Young Jacob whom family and friends called "Jack," took his father's admonitions to heart, especially when it came to making money and taking personal responsibility. His gentle mother, Sarah, also exerted a powerful influence on his life through her love for music and the arts. It is not an exaggeration to say her eldest son would never have aspired to become an actor if Sarah had not sparked his interest.

CHAPTER ONE: "BIG DREAMS IN LITTLE HUNGARY" (1900–22)

Hester Street on Manhattan's Lower East Side, circa. 1900.

Young Jacob "Jack" Krantz, circa. 1905.

Ricardo told interviewers he remembered little about his early years except they were filled with loneliness and unhappiness. Life for young Jack Krantz, growing up in the poor immigrant areas of Lower Manhattan, was hard. His innate sensitivity and love for the arts were often repressed out of necessity, masked behind a veneer of toughness and invulnerability. Gangs ruled the streets of these areas, and young boys who were deemed weak, different, or didn't belong to a group, found daily existence challenging if not intolerable. Ricardo later recalled some of the boys he knew at the time became the city's most notorious gang leaders.[7]

Jack employed multiple coping mechanisms. While he was a natural loner who kept his innermost feelings to himself, trusted very few, and didn't fit well in groups, early on he recognized he would need a few friends and certain survival skills if he were to get along. One of the advantages young Jack Krantz had, which many loners did not, was athleticism. Although of medium build, he was quick, strong and coordinated — a natural athlete adept at playing a variety of sports, including football, basketball, and baseball. One of the handiest skills he learned on the streets of New York was self-defense. Jack became an exceptional fighter. After several provocations and demonstrations of his skill, eventually the toughs learned to leave him alone. Later in junior high and in high school, he would work with coaches and trainers to develop this ability. By the time he entered pictures in his late teens, Jack was an expert amateur boxer and a physical fitness devotee.

Despite athletic prowess, Jack mainly coped by retreating into his own shell, however. Whenever possible, he would go somewhere alone where he could think, plan, and dream. While innately intelligent and a quick study, Jack was not a good student in school. His grades were fair to poor, more a reflection of lack of interest, than any intellectual deficiency. By the time he was 12 he was more interested in making money and getting into show business, than going to school to learn math or grammar. He would eventually regret his lack of a formal education, but that would come later.

According to the actor, when he was 11 years old, a transformative event occurred in his life; one which shaped his character and revealed much about his inner strength. He had been experiencing pain in his abdomen. When his mother took him to the doctor, she was informed the youngster had a hernia.

"I remember being told the night before that I was to go to the hospital in the morning. I took the news calmly—as I did everything else. I went to bed without further talk on the subject and arose in the morning ready to go. Mother went with me and I remember that the rest of the family felt awfully sorry to see me go but I thought their fears were childish. I wasn't afraid . . . Nor was I frightened when we actually got to the hospital and entered the elevator. But on the way to the fourth floor, it suddenly occurred to me that I hadn't thought this thing out for myself. So when the elevator stopped and we got out, I sneaked back into the car without mother's seeing me and went to the ground floor once again and out of the building. I believe I walked entirely around the hospital on the outside. I must think this over calmly by myself! Hadn't I always studied out everything alone? And here I suddenly find myself in a hospital about to have an operation. . . And I hadn't made up my mind about the thing! By the time I had circled around the hospital I was fully convinced that mother was right about the operation and that it would help me in the long run. So I decided to have it! When I re-entered the foyer, my mother was waiting for me. She smiled and asked if I was ready to go upstairs. When I had explained my reason for disappearing, she told me that she understood and we went to my room."[8]

As a result of the surgery, Ricardo said he learned valuable life lessons.

"I remember too, that after the operation was over, it suddenly occurred to me that I was being a terrific expense to the family. I recall asking my mother how much the operation would cost. She told me it wasn't important what the bill was—just so long as I hurried and got well. It was then that I came face to face with the thing called mother love. I had been so much to myself all these years that it never occurred to me before. I tried to sit up in bed as I told my mother she shouldn't worry— that I was certainly going to get well. Soon I would be grown-up, I assured her, and then I could get out and make a lot of money and take care of her. When she started to cry, it was I who turned into the adult as I attempted to dry her tears and tell her she shouldn't cry."[9]

Jack never forgot the experience, and soon began devising ways of making money to help his parents, and care for his own needs. In addition to assisting his father at the shop, he began doing odd jobs after school. One of the first was selling chewing gum in Van Cortlandt Park, which was a considerable distance from where the Krantzs resided. He would buy it for three cents a pack, and sell it for a two-cent profit. Ricardo recalled street gangs would often steal the money before he could get home to turn it over to his father.[10]

On the way home from his jobs, he would pass multiple concert halls and theaters, and pause to stare at the colorful marquees. While still in grammar school, Jack became obsessed with the theatre, opera, stage shows, and huge concert orchestras. Unbeknownst to his parents, with some of his earnings, he began buying theatre or opera tickets, and sitting in the gallery, mesmerized by the actors and performers. It didn't take long for Jack to decide he wanted to be part of that glamorous and exciting world. As a youngster, one of his most treasured possessions was a frayed scrapbook containing poems and theatre advertisements from newspapers and magazines.[11]

There is some confusion about the next events of young Jack's life, with differing accounts offered at various times. Some 1920's newspaper stories, and 1930's magazine articles, stated the Krantz family was living on New York's Upper East Side when Jack enrolled in high school in the fall of 1914. This is incorrect. While it is true 14-year-old Jack Krantz became a student at Dewitt Clinton High on the Upper East Side, the New York State Census of 1915 indicates he and his family were still living at 516 Houston Street in Lower Manhattan.[12]

During his first semester in high school, young Krantz quickly made a name for himself as a star athlete on the school's championship basketball team. Yet, despite the glory, school became a private hell for Jack. His grades were poor and his attitude toward his studies poorer still. He was particularly self-conscious and sensitive about receiving poor grades, feeling as if he were not intelligent or able to compete.[13] After only one semester, Jack decided to quit school to pursue his main interests: making money and becoming an actor, but not before receiving some questionable advice that he would never forget. In a 1931 interview, Jack (who by then had become Ricardo Cortez) recalled the advice came from an unlikely source, his bespectacled math teacher, who equated sensitivity and self-consciousness with weakness and cowardice.

"I'll never forget that teacher. He was a little man with big glasses. Andersen was his name. He told me without mincing matters that it was downright cowardly of me to be self-conscious. I remember I was very sensitive on the subject of bravery and when he made me see his point of view, he helped me immensely" [14]

Whether Papa and Mama Krantz attempted to dissuade their eldest son from quitting school is unknown, but it is unlikely they would have been able to change his mind. Even at 14 years of age, Jack had an iron will and a relentless determination to succeed in life.

The resolute young lad soon landed his first job, as a messenger boy, board operator, and copy boy for *The New York World*, one of the city's leading newspapers. After work, he began frequenting Broadway theaters, making acquaintances, and offering his services as a manual worker. His perseverance was rewarded sometime in late 1914, when he began doing various odd jobs at theaters. A few weeks later, a Broadway stage manager hired the strong youngster as a part-time fly boy. A dangerous job which required coordination and strength; Jack was positioned high above the stage among the ropes, assisting crew members in the operation of the rope riggings that lifted curtains, and various props.

Jack attempted to keep his part-time theater jobs a secret, but eventually his parents learned the truth. According to Ricardo, his father expressed disappointment when he learned his eldest wanted to become involved in show business. Morris did not forbid his son's involvement, but made it clear he was not happy. Jack worshipped his father, and his father's opinion mattered, but so did his love for the arts. [15]

In an attempt to placate his dad, who wanted him to become a merchant or an accountant, Jack eventually gave up his job with *The New York World*, and found one as a brokerage clerk, "a runner" on Wall Street paying $4.00 a week. [16] One of his main responsibilities was to deliver securities to various individuals. This took the youngster to all parts of the city and put him in contact with many influential people. During the morning and early afternoons, he worked on deliveries; in the late afternoons and evenings, he attended theater matinees, screenings of the latest motion pictures, and continued to search for entertainment work. Although he liked making money, the young man continued to dream of fame and fortune in the theater or movies. "Somehow, I never had much interest in the work," he recalled in 1932. "I sat beside the ticker tape and went through all the motions of being a young Morgan, but as I sat there I day-dreamed of stardom . . ."[17]

By 1915, motion pictures were fast becoming an important new medium of entertainment in America. The nickelodeons, which had showcased the crude, simplistic early movies, were beginning to disappear, and in their place were huge ornate movie palaces showing more sophisticated product. The combination of technical and business innovations was quickly transforming the motion picture industry. Important new companies devoted to the production and distribution of films were being created, which in turn, were hiring talented craftsmen and signing players who would soon become nationally recognized celebrities known as movie stars. In just the two-year period 1914-15 alone, such diverse, innovative, technically and artistically important motion pictures as *The Perils of Pauline, Tillie's Punctured Romance, The Exile, The Cheat,* and D. W. Griffith's groundbreaking *The Birth of a Nation* were released. That same period also saw the emergence of the first movie stars, including such fan favorites as Dustin Farnum, Mary Pickford, Theda Bara, Hoot Gibson, Tom Mix, Marie Dressler, Charlie Chaplin, Milton Sills, Norman Kerry, etc. Young Jack was mesmerized by the movies, and became a devoted fan of many of the actors who made them.

In 1915, Jack became employed as a supernumerary for a Shakespeare company. For those unfamiliar with the term, supernumeraries or "supers" are amateurs in training who do non-speaking roles, and appear in crowd scenes in order to enhance the realism of stage and operatic productions. Ricardo remembered being thrilled to finally work as an actor, but embarrassed to tell others the exact nature of his job. "I had no lines to speak—was merely given a flag to carry across the stage. . ." he laughingly recalled.[18]

In September, 1915, Jack scored his first minor breakthrough when he secured a role as a sailor for $15 a week in the flag-waving

15 year-old aspiring actor Jack Krantz, had one of his first stage roles as a sailor in the patriotic musical extravaganza, *Hip! Hip! Hooray!* staged at the legendary Hippodrome Theatre.

musical revue, *Hip! Hip! Hooray!* staged at New York's famed Hippodrome.[19] Featuring John Phillip Sousa and his band, operatic baritone Orville Harrold, ice skating rinks, and ski slopes, *Hooray* was a spectacular extravaganza that thrilled theatergoers who lined streets to see it. Jack had a small, non-speaking part, but was pleased

The Hippodrome in Midtown Manhattan was the largest and most successful theatre in New York during the early years of the 20th century, hosting circuses, massive stage productions, operas, and sporting events. It was demolished in 1939.

to be involved; excited to have such a prestigious production on his resume. Perhaps more importantly, he took advantage of the opportunity to begin learning how actors, dancers, and other performers practiced their crafts; not only how they worked, but how they dressed and conducted themselves when they were not on stage.

Sadly, when the production ended in October 1916, young Mr. Krantz was back among the ranks of the unemployed, but only temporarily. In February, 1917, he was cast in another minor non-speaking part (five-month run at $12 a week) as a soldier in Edmund Burke's acclaimed stage comedy, *Johnny Get Your Gun,* starring Louis Bennison at the Criterion Theater. The producer, John Cort, told Jack he won the role of a French soldier, whose main duty was to march on stage and wave a flag, because he looked French and looked good in the uniform.[20]

Indeed 16-year-old Jack Krantz (now sometimes spelled Kranze) did look good. During the last two years, he had developed from an awkward teen into a handsome young man. Although he was not particularly tall (either 5 foot 11 inches or 6 foot tall, depending on the source one consults), Jack's dark hair, olive skin, heavy-lidded brown-black piercing eyes, and muscular physique made him stand

CHAPTER ONE: "BIG DREAMS IN LITTLE HUNGARY" (1900–22) | 19

By the time he was in his late teens, young Jack Krantz had matured from an awkward adolescent to a good looking young man.

out in a crowd. Even as a French soldier waving a flag, he exuded a certain charisma that was noted by many, particularly members of the feminine gender.

After the run of *Johnny Get Your Gun*, in an attempt to stay connected to the theater world, Jack went to work at a ticket agency. There he met several notables, including future film producer Walter Morosco (son of stage impresario Oliver Morosco), who advised him to seek employment in the movies. During the fall of 1917, Jack began appearing as a movie extra at $2 a day for various movie studios in Fort Lee, New Jersey, and across the city of New York.[21]

Many are surprised to learn during the cinema's formative years, the East Coast was the hub of activity. In 1917, Hollywood was not much more than an orange grove, and Fort Lee, New Jersey, was the center of the movie-making industry. During the next two years, Jack would make scores of uncredited film appearances as a movie bit player, ordinarily viewed in crowd scenes, or as a bystander to the action. The pay was miniscule, but for the young Jewish boy with the big dreams, the experience was priceless. Not only was he continuing to learn the acting craft and discovering how movies were made, he was meeting professionals, including many of the film industry's main movers and shakers who possessed the power to make his dreams a reality.

The aspiring film actor would learn that finding fame in the movies would not come without a struggle, however. In late fall, 1917, Jack, who had now taken the stage name, Jack Crane (so as not to embarrass his family), was convinced he had taken a giant step toward making his film acting dream come true when he landed a featured role in director Robert Ellis' drama, *The Fringe of Society*, starring Milton Sills and Ruth Roland, to be produced by Pathe at the Talmadge Studios in New York City. Jack was ecstatic! Sills was his idol, and to be appearing with him was more than thrilling. Jack's small role as the renegade brother of Miss Roland required him to lead a group of toughs up a flight of stairs, and confront the heroic Sills, who would then knock him down.[22] As was his custom, Jack carefully studied all aspects of the part, knew every move he was to make, trying his best to ensure that his official film debut would be a success; but it was not to be. The rehearsals went well, but on the day of the actual filming, as he rushed up the stairs, the stalwart Mr. Sills delivered an uppercut that did not miss its mark as planned. The punch sent the youngster reeling, falling back down the flight. The bloodied victim required six stitches and a head bandage. The studio required another actor to play the part.[23]

Profoundly disappointed but undaunted, Jack returned to Fort Lee, and took non-show business jobs on the side. Life for an aspiring movie actor was hard, but Jack possessed three advantages many of his competitors did not: camera-friendly good looks, an eagerness to learn, and even more importantly, an overpowering will to succeed, which, as most successful people would attest, is one of THE most important secrets of success.

In late fall of 1918, Jack finally caught a break, securing a small featured role as a golfer in entertainer Elsie Janis' film, *The Imp*, all about a young woman who believes she is a notorious criminal after being hit by a golf ball. The director was again Robert Ellis. Ellis remembered the earnest, ambitious young Jack, and awarded him the part (and a $90 paycheck) to make up for having to replace him on *The Fringe of Society*.[24]

Jack Krantz, who took the stage name Jack Crane, made his official film debut as a golfer in the comic melodrama, *The Imp* (Selznick Pictures, 1919), starring entertainer Elsie Janis, seen here holding a golf club. Young Crane is on the far left.

This time all went as planned and Jack made his official film debut, but not before tragedy intervened to rob the youngster of his triumph. In late December, Jack's 16-year-old sister, Malvina contracted the flu that was sweeping New York. She died a few days later on December 30, 1918. For the close-knit Krantz family, Malvina's death was a stunning blow, particularly for her grieving parents and older brother Jack, whose bond with his kid sister had always been strong.[25]

Shaken, Jack forged ahead. With a portion of his earnings from *The Imp*, he purchased a suit. It seems rather preposterous today, but back in 1919, possessing a proper suit of clothes was often one of the deciding factors in whether or not an individual would be cast in a motion picture, especially for a bit role. Jack was extremely proud of his new suit, and engaged a photographer acquaintance to take pictures of him to use for publicity. In January 1920, one of the photos found its way to actor Johnny Walker who secured Jack an audition with director E.W. Griffith (a distant relative of D.W.), who was casting one of the leading roles in *Thimble Thimble*, a Vitagraph short adapted from an O'Henry story about a pair of lookalike cousins. Jack won the role because of his resemblance to the film's star, Rod LaRoque.[26]

Winning his first leading film role was another personal triumph for Jack, marking the attainment of a goal he had set for himself when he began appearing in movies in 1917. Once again, tragedy intervened, however. On February 20, 1920, a few days before Jack was to begin work on the picture, his father, Morris, died. The cause of death remains unknown. Years later, articles about Cortez's early life stated the deaths of his sister, Malvina, and his father, Morris, were days apart, both attributed to the flu epidemic. U.S. Census records contradict these versions. While the dates of their deaths were relatively close, Morris' came almost 14 months after his daughter's.[27]

The loss of both Malvina and Papa Krantz left a tremendous void. In addition to being a well-respected and beloved father, brother, and friend, Morris was the main breadwinner for his family. Unlike many immigrants, the Krantzs had never been without food or lodging, but they were not wealthy. Morris had a little savings, but not enough to pay the doctor and funeral expenses. The Krantzs now faced both a psychological and financial crisis, and Morris' eldest son, Jack inherited the responsibility. Ricardo recalled that on the day of his father's death, his Uncle Herman took him aside, put his hand on his shoulder, and said, "Young man, you're the head of the family now." The extended families (both the Krantzs and Lefkowiczs) did what they could to help, but they too were poor, and the extent of their assistance was limited.[28]

Grief-stricken and weighed down with financial obligations, and the responsibility for his mother and three younger school-aged siblings, Jack decided he would give up acting after completing work on *Thimble, Thimble*. Show business was just too volatile a career for a young man supporting a family. When he informed his mother of his intentions, she would have none of it. She told Jack in order to honor his father, he must continue to do what he loved. The family would find a way to make ends meet.

Although times were rough, and more often than not, the Krantz family's cupboard was almost bare, the family did indeed get by. Sarah took in sewing, Bernard "Bernie" and Helene found after-school jobs. Jack did not abandon his acting aspirations entirely, but did take several part-time jobs to help provide for the family. His old friends on Wall Street helped by kindly taking him back as a runner, while he worked as a traffic manager for the Fleet Shipping Company, and as a theatre doorman. During this time, the coordinated young man also took what would eventually become a controversial job as a taxi dancer at a New York night spot, dancing with feminine patrons for a small fee. When he wasn't on the job, he continued to look for acting assignments.[29]

During the summer of 1920, while Jack was working as an extra on D. W. Griffith's blockbuster melodrama *Way Down East*, starring Lillian Gish, the director noticed the charismatic young man, and told the cameraman he'd like to test him. A few days later the excited youngster arrived for the test wearing his prized suit. After the test was completed (which required him to don a costume), Jack returned to the dressing room to find his suit had been stolen. Years later, Ricardo recalled the panic he felt.

"I don't know about other extras, but when that dress suit was gone I was just about bankrupt. A dress suit is very nearly indispensable to an

extra's livelihood. It is almost impossible to obtain work without this equipment because an extra must furnish his own clothes in the pictures, except costume pictures of course—a dress suit is in demand perhaps more than any other bit of apparel. To say the least, I was not an opulent extra, and I couldn't see where another dress suit was coming from. I appealed to the studio, but was told clothes were left where they might disappear at the owner's responsibility. Well, I didn't know what to do. Then I just happened to see Mr. Griffith coming out of the studio. I summoned all my nerve and stopped him and told him my predicament. The next day I received a check for the dress suit." [30]

The would-be film actor didn't end up with a movie contract as he hoped, but Griffith did remember him, and that would become important in years to come.

Jack continued to burn the candle at both ends during the following months. The proverbial "wolf" was clawing at the Krantz's family door, and Jack knew he had to keep going to keep the beast from getting in. Some days he went all day without eating. In early summer, 1921, he secured what would be his second feature length screen role in the Fox melodrama, *Perjury*, starring William Farnum. It was a relatively small part, but important. In addition to giving him more screen time than *The Imp*, and $100 pay, it provided a much-needed psychological boost; a renewed hope he might still have a chance to make it in the business he loved.[31]

Shortly after filming *Perjury*, Jack received a more lucrative film offer; one with physical strings attached. The director, Tod Browning, needed two young men to stage a real fight scene with no punches pulled, for his new picture, *Outside the Law*, starring Priscilla Dean and Wallace Beery. Charles Furthman, assistant general manager at Universal, was assigned the duty of finding them. Furthman immediately thought of two young athletic types he'd seen playing bits, and summoned them to his office. One was young Jack Crane; the other was an aspiring actor named George O'Brien. The two had met while competing for bit roles around New York. When Furthman asked them if they would like to earn $1000 a piece, both jumped at the chance. Furthman recalled their responses in a 1934 article. "As well as I like Crane, I would kill him." said O'Brien. "The same goes for me," said Crane. Arrangements were made and the fight was filmed. According to Furthman, it was one of the most thrilling ever staged.

> *"On a hot afternoon—between two box cars, filmdom's greatest fight scene in history—and that still goes was staged. O'Brien and Crane (Cortez) fought for nearly three hours and 4000 feet of film was shot. Crane dropped first from exhaustion, bleeding, cut, and bruised. O'Brien picked him up to carry him to a seat. He too, fell, exhausted and covered with blood. I am here to tell you it was the most thrilling fight I ever saw in my life, and is still regarded by picture people as that. From the time of that fight to this day, O'Brien and Cortez have been intimate friends. Few people know the story behind their pairing."*[32]

Young Jack wore permanent scars over both eyes because of the battle, but it had been worth it. Due to his sacrifice, his family could now pay off their bills and, put ample food on the table, and he could quit the hated job at the Fleet Shipping Company. The experience also began a lifelong friendship between himself and George O'Brien, one on which he would rely on in years to come.

As fate would have it, Jack was still delivering securities during the early summer months of 1922. Among his clients was Emmanuel H. "Manny" Goldstein, treasurer of Universal Pictures Corporation. Jack had known Manny for a long time and they had forged a friendship. Manny admired the young lad's ambition to succeed in the movies. When Jack made deliveries, the two would often enter into conversations about the industry. One day, Goldstein confided he was having problems casting one of Universal's next big projects, *The Merry-Go-Round*, a romantic drama about a dashing young count in love with an organ grinder. The director, Erich Von Stroheim wanted Lew Cody for the lead, but Goldstein and the producers thought Cody unsuitable. When Jack suggested Norman Kerry, with whom he'd become acquainted on the set of one of his films, Goldstein appeared intrigued. He told the enterprising young man he'd check with other Universal executives and get back to him.[33]

The next day when Jack arrived at Goldstein's office, the executive had a surprising offer for him. Universal would hire Kerry for the role if Jack would find him and see to it he arrived in Hollywood on time to begin. Despite being a prominent star, Kerry had a well-deserved reputation as a wild man—a heavy drinker and partier who could not always be counted on to show up for assignments. For an all-expenses paid trip to Hollywood and $300, Jack would become a temporary employee of Universal, essentially acting as Kerry's bodyguard. Jack jumped at the chance and located Kerry, who accepted the offer. Together they boarded a train bound for the West Coast.[34]

In 1922, young Jack Crane got an all-expenses paid trip to Hollywood when he was hired as a bodyguard for mustachioed actor Norman Kerry (pictured here), slated to appear in *The Merry-Go-Round* (Universal) directed by Erich Von Stroheim.

Kerry and his youthful bodyguard arrived in Hollywood on August 1, 1922. For 21year-old Jack, who'd never been more than a 20-minute train ride away from New York, it seemed a dream world. Upon arrival, he and Kerry were installed in the luxurious Beverly Hills Hotel. A short time later they were chauffeured to Universal Studios where they met Von Stroheim and the studio's general manager, Irving Thalberg. After Kerry was ushered away to the wardrobe department, Jack informed the Universal executive he intended to remain in Hollywood and seek work in the movies. He presented Thalberg with a letter of recommendation from Manny Goldstein. Apparently impressed with the young man's drive, Thalberg informed Jack the studio had a small part open for a villain in Hoot Gibson's next movie, for a $125 a week.[35]

Two weeks later, filming began on the picture entitled, *The Gentleman from America*. Helmed by former screen comedian turned director Edward Sedgewick, it was the humorous tale of two American Army buddies (Gibson, Tom O'Brien) who end up spending their furloughs in Spain, where they have numerous adventures. Gibson falls in love with a Spanish senorita (Louise Lorraine) and pretends to be a bandit to rescue her from marrying a wealthy landowner's son (Crane), whom she doesn't love. Thanks to an excellent performance by western star Gibson, the 50-minute comic adventure won enthusiastic reviews. For the star struck Jack (still being billed as Jack Crane), making a picture with western hero Gibson was a treat. The film also proved historically important to the young man's movie career for multiple reasons. It not only marked his first appearance in a Hollywood film, but his first role as a Latin, and as a villain. Little did he know how significant those firsts would be![36]

If Jack imagined he would be able to find more film work after completing the Gibson movie, he was mistaken. For weeks he haunted casting offices each morning, to no avail. Eventually, in order to save money and meet people who might be able to aid his career, he moved from the ritzy Beverly Hills Hotel to a modest room at the Christie Hotel. Known around town as THE place to be seen for young aspiring talent, many of the film capital's most influential filmmakers, including directors, writers, actors, etc., either lived in, or frequented the Christie.

As time progressed, Jack developed a routine. Each day, after making the rounds of the studios, he would work out at the gym, and then take a streetcar to the beach. Just before 6 p.m. he would return to the hotel when the directors and writers came back from the studios, in order to see them in the hotel lobby. He didn't ask them for work, but was hoping if he got to know them, he might be discovered. His nights were ordinarily spent alone in his room. On the rare occasion he went out, it was usually to a restaurant or to the Cocoanut Grove in the Ambassador Hotel, where he could listen to the bands, see celebrities, and occasionally dance with one of the pretty girls who frequented the night spot. Although he never had any formal lessons, Jack was an excellent dancer. Athletic and poised, he could literally glide across the floor.[37]

By early November, 1922, Jack's financial status had reached a crisis. He'd managed to make a few bucks working as a bit player in two films in October, including one in which he danced the tango with star Mae Murray, but his room rent was $30 a week, and he had to eat at least one meal a day. His money was running out. In late November he ran into Herbert Somborn, former husband of Gloria Swanson, and president of Eagle Pictures, now owner of the Brown Derby restaurant. Somborn had known Jack in New York. He liked the youngster and offered to help promote him. He told Jack he knew Warner Bros. studio was looking for a "Latin type," and would intercede to help. Unfortunately, when the two arrived at the studio, Warner Bros. had already signed another young aspiring actor to be the company's "Latin heartthrob"—Don Alvarado.[38]

Before they parted, Somborn wrote a letter of recommendation for Jack to give to Jesse Lasky, powerful production head of Famous Players Lasky and Paramount Pictures. Somborn had known Lasky for years, and was convinced the letter would help the young man. For a brief few hours, Jack had hope again, but when he appeared at the executive's office, Lasky's secretary refused to let him see her boss. She said she would deliver the letter. Disheartened, Jack returned to the hotel. For the first time since he'd arrived in Hollywood, he felt totally defeated. Despite his best efforts, perhaps he would end up like so many before and after him, a has-been who never was—just another young aspiring actor who tried and failed to achieve success in the cinema. Perhaps he would have to abandon his lifelong ambition and return to New York in hopes his Wall Street friends would take him back yet again. He had survived hunger, disappointment, and the deaths of his beloved sister and father, but could he survive the death of his dream? He would have the answer soon.

CHAPTER TWO
THE LATIN FROM MANHATTAN (1923–24)

"I now know there can be no second anybody. All that billing as a second Valentino ever got me was bad will and sneers."
— RICARDO CORTEZ

The exact origins of the old proverb, "It's always darkest before the dawn" have been the subject of speculation for countless years. Some insist the saying came from an old Irish song; others maintain it's a traditional bit of folk wisdom dating back to ancient times. Still others attribute it to historian and theologian Thomas Fuller, who utilized the phrase in a 1650 religious travelogue.

Whatever the source, the old saying certainly seems apropos when describing the life of Jack Krantz, a.k.a Jack Crane, circa December, 1922. Out of money and ideas, and too proud to ask for a loan, Jack was desperate. He knew he would have to return home to his family in New York if he didn't catch a break soon. The darkness was about to end, however, and destiny would soon rescue the youngster and alter the course of his life forever.

The historical circumstances of Jack's first major break in the movies are almost as elusive as the origin of the old saying. A story furnished by Paramount's publicity department as part of Ricardo's first studio biography was repeated so many times it took on a life of its own, and eventually was more or less accepted as fact. The problem with this scenario is the facts stated appear to be only partially true. The basic story had young Jack and a female partner entering a dance contest at the Cocoanut Grove at the Ambassador Hotel, judged by celebrities including Jesse Lasky. According to the tale, the couple's dancing was so impressive they not only won the contest, but the handsome, debonair Jack caught the attention of Lasky, who was looking for a Rudolf Valentino lookalike to promote. Jack won a Paramount contract as a result. A variation of the tale (which appeared in a few movie magazines) had Lasky's wife judging the contest and discovering Jack, then recommending him to her husband.[39] A legend also arose around how Jack Crane got the name Ricardo Cortez. One popular version said he was named after two cigar brands. In her autobiography, Ricardo's first wife, Alma claimed screen comedian Joe Frisco named him. Yet another version stated Lasky's secretary came up with the name.[40]

One of the unfortunate by-products of film stardom was the misinformation that all-too frequently cropped up around successful players. Many of these "legends" had some basis in fact, but the most interesting aspects were often fabricated by the imaginative minds of studio publicity employees, and/or by the actors or filmmakers themselves. In this case, the truth is probably a combination of fact and fantasy. Ricardo probably did dance for Lasky, and did get a contract as a result, but it seems highly fantastical the events were quite the way they were described. Considering his calculating nature and the way things worked in Hollywood, there's a good probability the dance contest was an audition of sorts. Regarding the etiology of his name, Ricardo attempted to clear up the matter in 1933, telling columnist Sidney Skolsky that Lasky's secretary, "Miss Mowbarry," gave him his first name, and Mr. Lasky came up with "Cortez."[41]

However it happened, on January 1, 1923, six foot, 190-pound, darkly handsome Jack Crane signed a long-term contract with the most prestigious movie studio in Hollywood, and became Ricardo Cortez, the newest cinematic incarnation of the "Latin lover," so popular at the time.

The actual document the young actor signed is believed lost, but it was likely a standard movie contract in most respects. We do know there were at least two fairly unique provisions having to do with the young man's personal life, however. One clause prohibited him from revealing his true background and heritage, and another forbade him to marry during the initial term. His pay was to begin at $150 per week.[42]

One can only imagine the complex set of emotions flooding the brain of the 22-year-old actor as he affixed his name on the document.

His parents' sacrifice, his father's and sister's deaths, his own years of hard work and bitter disappointment had culminated in this—the achievement of the dream first conceived when he was a small boy in grade school. It was a magic moment to be sure, one rightly filled with a sense of triumph and satisfaction, but only a moment. For becoming a Famous Players Lasky/Paramount contract player named Ricardo Cortez had come at a price. The young man would soon learn that gaining fame and fortune had a downside, particularly if one is forced to live a lie, and become a carbon copy of someone else.

In 1923, becoming a Famous Players Lasky/Paramount contract player was a very big deal. Originally formed in 1916 by the three-way merger of Adolph Zukor's Famous Players, Jesse Lasky's Lasky Feature Play Company, and William Hodkinson's distribution company, Paramount Pictures Corporation, by 1920, the new film production entity had attained great prestige after releasing such audience favorites as *Oliver Twist* (1916), *Snow White* (1916), *Rebecca of Sunnybrook Farm* (1917), *Seven Keys to Baldpate* (1917), *Uncle Tom's Cabin* (1918), *Dr, Jekyll and Mr. Hyde* (1920), and *Treasure Island* (1920). By 1923, Famous Players Lasky/Paramount was well on its way to dominating the film industry thanks to the business acumen and eye for talent of Zukor and Lasky; the innovative brilliance and hard work of directors like Cecil B. DeMille, Marshall Neilan; etc., and an impressive roster of contract players that included Mary Pickford, Douglas Fairbanks, Wallace Reid, Gloria Swanson, William S. Hart, Dorothy Gish, Agnes Ayres, Pola Negri, Bebe Daniels and Betty Compson. In 1922 alone, the studio released multiple acclaimed hits such as *The Loves of Pharaoh* (1922), *Blood and Sand* (1922), and *The Sheik* (1922). Although the company continued to make films on the East Coast, by 1923, the majority of its production was originating in Hollywood.[43]

The biggest male star under contract to Famous Players Lasky/Paramount in 1923 was Rudolph Valentino. Of French and Italian heritage, born in Italy in 1895, Rodolfo (Rudy) was a pampered child who dropped out of schools and the Navy prior to spending time begging on the streets of Paris. A talented dancer, the darkly handsome and athletic Rudy was nevertheless considered a failure when he spent a small inheritance to cross the Atlantic in 1913.

When Famous Players Lasky/Paramount became Cortez's professional home in 1923, it was considered the most prestigious motion picture studio in Hollywood.

While living in New York, the penniless young man soon got into trouble with the law, accused of blackmail and petty theft. By early 1914, he was making his living as a taxi dancer in night spots. Eventually, he worked his way up in the ranks, and began dancing for society elites in posh nightclubs.

Thanks to a friendship with Norman Kerry (the same Norman who Ricardo accompanied to the West Coast), Valentino landed in Hollywood, where he initially began playing rogues, gigolos, and various good-for-nothings in several lower budget pictures. In 1921, screenwriter turned Metro executive, June Mathis, chose him for the lead in her adaptation of Vincente Blasco Ibanez's bestselling anti-war novel, *The Four Horseman of the Apocalypse*. The film was a sensational critical and box office smash that made Valentino a major star known as the cinema's "Latin lover." He followed this with three Metro pictures, two of which Mathis penned: *The Conquering Power* (1921), and *Camille* (1921). During the filming of the latter, Valentino became smitten with interior and costume designer Natacha Rambova who would eventually become his second wife.

In 1921, Valentino left Metro in a salary dispute, and signed a pact with Famous Players Lasky, which immediately cast him in his most iconic role as Sheik Ahmed Ben Hassan in the silent classic, *The Sheik*. In this story of a western-educated Arabian sheik who abducts and falls in love with an independent minded British woman (Agnes Ayres), Valentino's smoldering sexuality, exoticism, athleticism, and tenderness set feminine hearts aflutter. Particularly thrilling to female audiences was the way he gazed at his heroines; a combination of passion and melancholy. In a short biography of Valentino in his *Film Encyclopedia*, author Ephraim Katz summed up Valentino's appeal to the American female movie fan. He said to women, Valentino "represented a symbol of mysterious forbidden eroticism, a vicarious fulfillment of dreams of illicit love and inhibited passions . . ."[44]

Valentino followed the enormous success of *The Sheik* with another gigantic hit, *Blood and Sand* (1922), but when his next picture, *The Young Rajah* (1922), failed at the box office, relations with Famous Players Lasky began to sour. Encouraged by Rambova, Valentino demanded more creative control over his film assignments. When the studio resisted, ordering him to report to work on a film entitled, *The Spanish Cavalier*, he refused, embarking on a "one man strike." A court order was issued forbidding him to work, but sometime later the order was reduced, allowing him to work only in films. In the meantime, Valentino was off the screen, writing a book of poems and doing a dance tour.[45]

With the "Latin lover" craze at its peak, and the extremely profitable relationship between the studio and Valentino in jeopardy, Jesse Lasky realized he might need a person to take Rudy's place if he became unmanageable and/or departed. When he saw the darkly handsome Jack Crane dancing, and noted his olive-skinned, Latin look, the career of Ricardo Cortez was born.

For Ricardo, along with a new name and movie pact, came a new biography. Almost before the ink dried on his contract, Paramount's publicity machine hopped in motion to transform the poor Jewish lad from Manhattan into an exotic, sophisticated young gentleman of the European upper class. His studio bios would evolve over time, but the earliest of them (published in early 1923), described him as a "young Castilian" (from Castile in Spain) who came to the United States with his wealthy parents.[46] As early as May, 1923, a snippet from a newspaper story about Hollywood's ongoing obsession with "Latin lovers" described Ricardo Cortez as "a six foot languorous Castilian."[47] Still another article from later that year claimed he was French, born in the Alsace-Lorraine region of northeastern France, and that his mother was a renowned opera singer.[48] As they created his background and furnished him a new wardrobe, the studio rushed Ricardo into photo shoots in which he was posed to look as much like Valentino as possible.

Young Mr. Cortez was so grateful to have the contract and be able to work in films, he cooperated fully with all demands. According to Ricardo, he wasn't comfortable taking on a false identity, but deferred to the powers that be. "I figured I'd better follow their advice, since they ought to know about this business, so I became Ricardo Cortez," he said.[49] He would soon learn there were two major problems with this new scenario: 1) Too many people knew the biography being circulated across the country was untrue, and 2) Valentino was liked and admired in Hollywood and across America, and his many friends resented someone brought in to replace him. Instead of focusing their resentment on those responsible, the two groups took it out on the poor young man who was taking orders trying to make it in the business he loved so much.

It's doubtful Ricardo understood the full ramifications of his new bogus biography, and the resentments it inspired, when he began work on his initial Famous Players Lasky films in 1923. He would

CHAPTER TWO: THE LATIN FROM MANHATTAN (1923–24)

In 1923, Famous Players Lasky/Paramount signed 22-year-old Jack Crane, whom they named "Ricardo Cortez," because of his resemblance to the company's most popular male star, Rudolph Valentino, known as the cinema's "Latin lover." The resemblance was striking! This is Cortez as he appeared in *The Spaniard* (Paramount, 1925).

Rudolph Valentino in *Blood and Sand* (Paramount, 1922).

make five films during the year. The studio introduced him in small, relatively unimportant supporting roles, as a slick, well-heeled manipulator in *Sixty Cents an Hour* and *The Call of the Canyon*. The former cast him as a real estate salesman who takes advantage of a hapless bank employee (Walter Hiers), both of whom are vying for the affections of a banker's pretty daughter (Jacqueline Logan). Originally envisioned as a vehicle for the studio's top comic, Fatty Arbuckle, the rotund Hiers, was brought in after scandal permanently tainted the funnyman. The result was pleasant, but tepid. The outdoor adventure drama, *The Call of the Canyon*, filmed on location in Sedona, Arizona, and helmed by young, talented, Victor Fleming, presented Ricardo as a superficial city slicker who visits the rugged West to lure his former lady love (Lois Wilson) back from the arms of a rugged World War I veteran (Richard Dix). Ricardo's role was unremarkable, but making the picture became memorable when the cast and crew became stranded for an entire week after severe thunderstorms washed away trails out of the remote area.[50]

Ricardo appeared as himself in the star-studded Famous Players Lasky comedy, *Hollywood*, before playing the first of many Valentino-type parts as a Latin lothario who tries to break up the marriage of a bored society woman in the drama, *The Next Corner*. Perhaps his best film of the year was the comic drama, *Children of Jazz* starring Theodore Kosloff and Eileen Percy. In this picture, Ricardo portrayed a playboy who competes with the older, more serious Kosloff for the affections of jazz baby Percy. Like *The Call of the Canyon*, the picture turned out to be memorable to the new contract player, but for a very different reason. From the outset of the production, costar Kosloff and several crew members treated the young actor with rudeness and contempt. Ricardo decided to ignore their slights at first and go about his business, but as time progressed, the insults grew more frequent and impactful. Toward the end of the three-week shooting schedule, Cortez was seething with anger. One of the final scenes to be filmed was a fight between the romantic rivals. According to multiple sources, amateur boxer Ricardo delivered a punch to Kosloff that knocked him temporarily unconscious. Miss Percy, who witnessed the event, was said to have fainted.[51]

Unfortunately for Ricardo, this incident was not an isolated event. His initial euphoria regarding his new contract was short-lived.

Making movies was hard work, but his long apprenticeship had prepared him for the extended hours and the pressure. What he was not prepared for was the indifference and outright hostility he encountered from some of his fellow actors, filmmakers, and certain crew members. He was perplexed by it at first, but as time progressed, he came to realize at least some of the animosity came from friends and partisans of Valentino, who were upset by the way their friend had been treated by Famous Players Lasky, and resentful of the young man brought in as a replacement. Another source of the enmity came from certain acquaintances the former Jack Crane met while competing for bit roles in Fort Lee, and working multiple jobs in New York. Many of these individuals were aware that the extravagant bios and newspaper articles about his background were phony. They were envious of his success, and eager to take him down a peg.

During his first few months as a studio contract player, several stories began circulating about the young man, the sources of which were undoubtedly these two disaffected groups. The tales varied, but all were uncomplimentary. Some of the least destructive portrayed Ricardo as egotistical, self-absorbed, high hat, or ruthless. The more ornate stories painted him as a predator, a person so ambitious to succeed he would literally do anything. One of the most popular tales among Ricardo's various detractors had to do with young Jack's time working as a taxi dancer in New York. Supposedly he got into trouble with the law several times for selling his body to clients, both female and male. According to the story, he was hired by Famous Players Lasky because he was blackmailing someone at the studio whom he had serviced.[52]

It didn't take long for the stories to spread. Some more discriminating people at the studio and elsewhere instantly recognized them for what they were, malignant lies circulated by those with an agenda to destroy the young man's infant career. For whatever reason, however, others chose to believe them. Even people who did not necessarily accept the stories as fact became suspicious of the young man. There is absolutely no evidence whatsoever Ricardo was ever a male prostitute, ever engaged in homosexual activities, was involved in blackmail, or ever was in trouble with the law anywhere. It is certainly true he *could be* selfish and self-absorbed at times, but Jack Kranze a.k.a Ricardo Cortez was a conservative young man brought up with the conservative values of his father. By and large, he stayed true to those values throughout his life.

It is not known if Ricardo was aware of all the details of the vicious whisper campaign being conducted against him, but he certainly knew there were those at the studio who regarded him with contempt. Besides the insults and cutting remarks, he was effectively being ostracized. Whenever he entered the studio café for lunch, his entrance was met with whispers and dirty looks. When he found a table, he was often left to dine alone. Years later, he vividly recalled his difficulties.

"I was new, I thought, of course, I must leave it to the studio, that they knew their business. I now know there can be no second anybody. All that billing as a second Valentino ever got me was bad will and sneers. But I had never been a good mixer. I didn't know how to undo the impression; all I could think was to become as good an actor as possible, treat everyone as well as possible, and live everything down." [53]

Ricardo's own self-consciousness and lack of self-confidence were barriers, keeping him from letting others know him for who he really was. In his mind, all he could do was keep his nose to the grindstone, continue to learn his craft, do as he was told, and hope things would get better, but he underestimated the power of lies, and the gossip continued.

By the end of 1923, the studio had apparently gotten wind of the tales, and tried to put out some of the fires by inventing a romance between Cortez and the beautiful, recently divorced Famous Players Lasky contractee, Agnes Ayres.[54] It appeared to work, at least to some degree. Soon many of the gossipers and/or movie magazines were abuzz regarding the budding romance of the handsome, unattached Cortez and the lovely Agnes, who were photographed dining together and at night spots. Although Ricardo liked Agnes, he barely knew her. All the time the two were supposedly involved in a torrid romance, Agnes was dating someone else. The press was bound to learn the truth. Luckily for Ricardo, his fortunes would soon improve thanks to the efforts of an important and unexpected new ally, and a genuine romance of his own.

In late fall, 1923, Ricardo or "Ric," as he came to be known around the studio and elsewhere, learned he was to play a supporting role in Gloria Swanson's next film, *She Who Laughs Last*, a comedy drama based on Alfred Sutro's acclaimed stage success, *The Laughing Lady*, which had starred Ethel Barrymore on Broadway. Cortez was excited by the opportunity for two reasons. The movie was to be made at the Paramount Studio in New York, which would allow the homesick young man to see his family, and it's star, Miss Swanson, was one of the cinema's hottest, most prestigious actresses, since she had scored several box office hits at Famous Players Lasky/Paramount, including *Male and Female* (1919) and *The Affairs of Anatol* (1921).

Production on the picture retitled *A Society Scandal*, began in January, 1924, with Miss Swanson's favorite director, Allan Dwan, at the helm. Swanson played a young society woman who attempts to exact revenge on her husband's attorney (Rod La Rocque) after he ruins her reputation during a divorce battle. She falls in love with him in the process. Cortez played the handsome young rogue who gets Swanson's character in trouble.

Articles published during the production reported the film was shot on location across New York, including in the famed Ritz Hotel ballroom, and in a Brooklyn courtroom. In her memoirs, *Swanson on Swanson*, Gloria recalled working on the picture.[55]

"Allan knew I was at my best playing opposite very strong actors, and in this picture he was able to cast not one, but two actors who were both beyond a doubt destined for stardom. They were both Valentino types, as handsome Latins were called in the wake of 'The Four Horseman of the Apocalypse' and 'The Sheik', although Rod La Rocque was French-Canadian and Ricardo Cortez was from Brooklyn . . ."[56]

Gloria came to know and like young Ricardo during the filming, and when she heard the vicious stories being circulated about him, she became determined to help.

"Shortly after our picture together was finished, I began to hear vicious rumors about Ricardo, similar to those that had circulated for years about Rudy. People said he was a gigolo, an operator, involved in shady, even crooked doings. I decided he was too talented to be destroyed by such rumors if they were untrue, so one day I called up the Los Angeles

district attorney, whom I had met, and asked him to check through his files and find out if there were any indictments against Ricardo. He called me back the next day and assured me that all the stories were completely baseless. Therefore, I made Ricardo my escort for a few weeks and always made sure we were in the company of the most respectable and sophisticated people I knew. Within a month all the fires were out. It was a wonder, however, that new ones didn't spring up about me, who was seen everywhere for a short dazzling period with not one, but two of the most handsome men in the world—both Valentino types." [57]

Unfortunately, the "fires" stoked by jealousy and innuendo were not as easily extinguished as Miss Swanson hoped. In January, 1924, *Variety* reported Cortez's sudden return to the West Coast after being confronted by old acquaintances in New York. The report said he "ducked" to avoid a "flock of eggs."[58] Still, Miss Swanson's

One of Ricardo Cortez's claims to fame was his ability to hold his own when paired with strong actors, including many of the cinema's most famous and dominant leading ladies, including Gloria Swanson whom he supported in the drama, *A Society Scandal*. (Paramount, 1924).

assistance and the studio-invented Cortez/Ayres romance did help the young man to manage the crisis, and distract the gossipers. Ricardo would never forget Gloria's kindness, and they remained lifelong friends.

On the strength of good reviews generated by *A Society Scandal*, and Miss Swanson's positive public pronouncements about him, Ricardo became a busy young actor at Famous Players Lasky in 1924. This despite the fact Rudy Valentino had returned to the studio to finish out his contract. During the spring, Cortez appeared in three respectable, if minor, films: as a man falsely accused of the murder of his fiancé's father in the William DeMille directed mystery, *The Bedroom Window*; as a dashing crook who takes up with the snobbish daughter of a saloon keeper in James Cruze's drama, *The City That Never Sleeps*; and as a handsome troublemaker who tries to blackmail a talented singer in Phil Rosen's soap operatic drama, *This Woman*.

In May, 1924, Ricardo received a promotion of sorts when he learned he was to have a major supporting role in acclaimed director Cecil B. DeMille's upcoming film, *Feet of Clay*, a drama starring Rod La Rocque and Vera Reynolds as a young couple whose lives are forever altered when the young man becomes disabled during a shark attack.

Elaborate preparations preceded the actual filming, much of which was done on location on and around Catalina Island, from May to July, 1924. According to Simon Louvish's book, *Cecil B. DeMille, A Life in Art*, the noted director completely transformed the rocky beach of Catalina Island, "into a lovely crescent of white sand, imported from Hawaii at great expense."[59] Several elaborate, time-consuming, and potentially dangerous scenes were staged there, including one that featured Cortez and others operating boats with women (including Vera Reynolds) on surf boards.[60] The highlight of the picture was an elaborate sequence in which the young marrieds attempt to take their own lives, and cross "the bridge between the worlds" —DeMille's imaginative visualization of death, in which those who die cross a bridge that takes them to the "Book Keeper," who determines if they are to go to heaven or hell. In the cases of the LaRocque and Reynolds' characters, they are sent back to right their lives.[61]

Cecil B. DeMille's drama, *Feet of Clay* (Paramount, 1924) gave Cortez one of his strongest early roles as a sexy, young playboy, who tempts a young woman (Vera Reynolds) who is estranged from her spouse.

Cortez played Tony Banning, a young man who woos Vera Reynolds' Amy during an estrangement from her husband. The role was clearly subordinate, but the young actor had some good dramatic scenes that showed him to advantage. Critics disagreed about the overall merits of the picture, but audiences loved it. Famous Players Lasky/Paramount pocketed a tidy profit, and Cortez and the other actors picked up scores of new fans. For Ricardo, his excellent notices couldn't have come at a more opportune time, deflecting attention from the negative personal stories, while impressing his bosses and several writers and columnists who began championing his cause. Among them was Tamar Lane, who wrote a column entitled, "That's Out" for *Motion Picture* magazine. In an impassioned column in the March, 1924 issue, (published before the release of *Feet of Clay*) Lane berated Famous Players Lasky for not appreciating young Cortez's talent, by assigning him parts commensurate with his abilities. Lane boldly predicted "Cortez will one day spring a surprise to everybody by proving himself a strong personality and a splendid actor."[62] In January, 1925, after viewing Ricardo's performance in

Director DeMille filmed *Feet of Clay* (Paramout, 1924) on and around Catalina Island off the California coast. He required Cortez and cast to perform several potentially dangerous scenes, including this one which had Cortez (in foreground) operating a speedboat with costar Vera Reynolds (a stuntwoman) on a surfboard.

Feet of Clay, Lane reminded his readers of the prediction.

> "In *Feet of Clay*, Ricardo springs the surprise and makes good our prediction. To us, he scores the outstanding hit of the film and proves beyond a doubt that in neglecting Cortez, the Lasky outfit has missed an opportunity to develop a promising star. . ."[63]

If Cortez's employer had been ignoring his potential, as Mr. Lane claimed, the studio soon began trying to right the wrong, assigning the youngster two high-profile new projects that had the potential to make him an important new movie star.

Things began looking up on the personal front as well. After fabricating a torrid romance between Ricardo and Agnes Ayres that reached ludicrous levels on March 19, 1924, when *Variety* reported the couple had married over the previous weekend, by early summer both Paramount and the Hollywood press began dialing back the coverage.[64] This was necessary when Agnes became engaged to, and married, another man. By then, Ricardo, too, had become involved for real with an actress he'd met on the Warner Bros. lot in 1923. Her name was Alma Rubens, and the couple's love affair would soon become a hot topic for every gossiper, movie magazine writer, and journalist in Hollywood and across America. The complete story of the relationship of Alma and Ric is related in chapters three and four.

Professionally, young Cortez spent the remainder of 1924 working diligently on two big-budget Paramount films with mixed results. The first, *Argentine Love*, was from a Vincente Blasco Ibanez novel. Ibanez had penned the original stories on which both *The Four Horseman of the Apocalypse* and *Blood and Sand* were based. Although Rudolph Valentino returned to Paramount and completed the two films he owed the studio (*Monseiur Beaucaire* and *The Sainted Devil*), by the end of summer, 1924, he had departed. Paramount was determined Cortez would inherit the Valentino mantle.

Argentine Love was intended as the vehicle in which the novice would prove himself worthy. Filmed at Paramount's Astoria studio on Long Island, director Allan Dwan presided over a cast that included Cortez and Bebe Daniels, who had recently received kudos as Valentino's leading lady in *Monseiur Beaucaire* (1924). The melodramatic plot, set in Argentina, had Cortez as a hot-blooded Argentinian nobleman whose arranged marriage to a poor mayor's daughter (Daniels) is complicated when she falls in love with an American engineer (James Rennie). A sad ending is averted when Cortez's character steps aside and is conveniently killed.

Dwan kept a tight rein over his leads. Miss Daniels was technically the star of the picture, but much of the film's success or failure rested on the believability of Cortez's character, Juan Martin. According to Ricardo, he was very uncomfortable playing the part, and with Dwan's attempt to make him look and act like Valentino. The backlash against him was finally beginning to subside, and although he was a loyal soldier, Cortez told an interviewer he did not want to further antagonize Rudy's loyal fans.

"The worst thing that happened to me was getting off to a start as an imitator. I didn't want it, I didn't like it. But the studio insisted that I

Ricardo was amused and sometimes irritated by the exaggerations, half-truths, and outright lies written about him in the press. Among the hundreds of clippings contained in his personal silent film scrapbook is this one, dated March 18, 1924, which claimed he and actress Agnes Ayres were wed.

Famous Players Lasky/Paramount hoped to promote Cortez as the "new Valentino" when they assigned him the role of a hot-blooded Argentine nobleman in the big budget melodrama, *Argentine Love* (Paramount, 1924) costarring Bebe Daniels.

was a perfect Latin type . . . I was the goat in the argument of the studio with Valentino." [65]

Unfortunately, the young man's discomfort was painfully apparent on the screen, further weakening an overwrought and cliché-ridden screenplay. His dramatic tango scene with Miss Daniels was persuasive, but it was not enough. The movie was an expensive commercial and artistic flop.

Luckily, Cortez had a stronger follow-up. Hungarian-born dramatist, Ferenc Molnar's romantic comedy-drama, *The Swan*, had been adapted for the stage by Melville Baker, and presented on Broadway in October, 1923 with Eva Le Gallienne and Basil Rathbone in the leads. The acclaimed play's success caught the eye of Paramount Pictures, which purchased the property, and assigned Dimitri Buchowetzki to direct and write the screenplay, based on Molnar's story about a young princess who falls for her tutor in spite of the fact she is betrothed to a womanizing prince. The Russian-born German Buchowetski had won acclaim as a director in his native country before accompanying Pola Negri to Hollywood to helm her pictures at Paramount.

Thanks to a witty, literate script, and charming performances by Adolphe Menjou, Ricardo, and young stage actress Frances Howard, the film version of *The Swan* was a winner.[66] Despite his inexperience, Cortez was persuasive as the lovestruck tutor, Dr. Walter. Especially impressive were his love scenes with Miss Howard, which were both tender and romantic. Much of the credit was due to Buchowetzki, who liked Cortez, and took the youngster under his wing, helping him with his acting and camera techniques. Buchowetzki placed particular emphasis on the importance of acting with one's eyes; the proverbial "windows to the soul." His advice and guidance are apparent in Cortez's performance in *The Swan*, and throughout the remainder of his movie career.

Today *The Swan* is of interest to fans of Molnar's work as the first of two film adaptations, the last being director Charles Vidor's 1956 version starring Grace Kelly, Alec Guinness, and Louis Jourdan. The film is also of note as an example of the work of the underappreciated Buchowetzki (who would die just seven years later at the age of 42), and as one of only 17 Ricardo Cortez silent films to have survived the ravages of time. (He made 36!)

After filming *The Swan* in New York in early December, 1924, Cortez hurried back to the West Coast. Unlike the previous year, he was in a positive frame of mind as the holidays approached. Professionally, it had been a good year. He'd had the privilege of working with and learning from superb directors like DeMille and Dwan. He had made a positive impression in films like *A Society Scandal, Feet of Clay*, and *The Swan*, and acquired valuable friends including Gloria Swanson, and Dmitri Buchowetzki. He had also managed (with help) to weather the storm of gossip and innuendo that threatened to derail his career before it could get off the ground. Perhaps most notably, he'd met a young actress who appeared to be the person he'd been looking for all his life, the perfect partner—beautiful, loving, someone he could talk to and relate to.

CHAPTER THREE
FLYING WITH THE SNOWBIRD (1925–26)

"I saw her pale face and dark luminous eyes. I'll admit I was overcome. I walked back and forth watching her—trying not to be too apparent in my admiration."
— RICARDO CORTEZ (DESCRIBING ALMA RUBENS).

By 1925, things had begun falling into place for Ricardo Cortez. Since signing with Famous Players Lasky/Paramount; he had suffered isolation and rejection from his peers, but he had worked hard and persevered, and his tenacity was at last paying dividends. Aided by Gloria Swanson, various columnists and writers who championed him, and buttressed by good reviews, many of his skeptics and detractors were beginning to come around. With each additional feature film, Ricardo was gaining experience and popularity, not only with the public and the Hollywood press, but more importantly, with his studio bosses who began showing increased confidence in his ability. On a personal level, Ricardo had met and found the love and companionship of a woman whom he adored and respected; one who appeared to understand and appreciate him. Life was grand, or so it seemed.

When contemplating the relationship and love affair of Ricardo Cortez and Alma Rubens, one is reminded of another old saying, "Falling in love is like jumping off a really tall building. Your brain tells you it's not a good idea, but your heart tells you, you can fly!" Alma Rubens: spoiled, temperamental, quirky, free-spirited, out of control, paired with the inhibited, self-conscious, calculating, totally in control Ricardo Cortez. They say love is blind and conquers all, but surely even love couldn't possibly be powerful enough to bridge the gargantuan gulf between these two personalities, at least not for long.

During the mid 1920's (1924–25), much was made of the romance of Ricardo and Alma. During their courtship, the Hollywood press issued breathless reports detailing every twist and turn in their relationship. The truth was romantic (at least at first), but not nearly as idyllic as the gossip mongers and promoters wanted fans to believe. Ricardo and Alma did indeed fall in love, and their affection was genuine, as was the pain each eventually inflicted on the other, but when discussing their relationship, it is important to note that they were both self-absorbed individuals whose devotion to one another was tempered by their own personal needs and ambitions.

Alma Genevieve Reubens was born in San Francisco on February 19, 1897. Her parents, John B. and Theresa Hayes Reubens were Catholics, and educated Alma and her elder sister, Hazel, at the Sacred Heart Convent in the city by the bay. While only an adolescent, Alma began exhibiting the character traits that would define her life. In her heartrending autobiography first published in serialized form in the *New York Daily Mirror* and various other newspapers in 1931, then published as a book, *Alma Rubens, Silent Snowbird*, by Gary D. Rhodes and Alexander Webb in 2006, Alma was frank about her personality.

"I have already mentioned that I was of the idealistic, dreamer type, like my father, with an intensely inquiring and retrospective moodiness accompanied by an abnormal impulsiveness and sense of intuition. Added to these characteristics was a vivid imagination and an almost uncontrollable desire to do the forbidden." [67]

Despite their poor health and often precarious financial circumstances, Alma's parents indulged their youngest daughter whom they called "Baby." They tried to give her everything she desired. In her teens, "Baby" decided she wanted to become an actress. A petite, lovely, raven-haired girl with an oriental type beauty, and expressive, dusky eyes, her demure good looks and poise, helped secure her first stage job from actor/producer Bronco Billy Anderson. She began doing small parts in movies as early as 1914, but her first major break in films came one year later, when Vitaphone director, Roland Sturgeon engaged the angelic-looking youngster to play the title role in his film, *Lorelei Madonna* (1916). Alma's excellent reviews helped launch her film career, which began in earnest in 1916 when she signed a contract with Triangle Pictures, formed by D.W. Griffith, Mack Sennett, and Thomas Ince.

By 1920, Alma Rubens (the "e" was dropped from her last name in 1918) had amassed an impressive resume of 35 motion picture credits, including a small part in D.W. Griffith's monumental drama, *Intolerance* (1916). She'd appeared to advantage in several other films including *The Half Breed* (1916), and *The Americano* (1917), *The Regenerates* (1917), *The Ghost Flower* (1918), and *Humoresque* (1920). In just a handful of years, Alma became one of the cinema's foremost young female stars, one who inspired a devoted following and commanded a large salary. Along the road to success she married twice, briefly to actor Franklyn Farnum (1918–19), and to best-selling novelist, physician, film producer/director Daniel Carson Goodman (1923–26), who headed William Randolph Hearst's Cosmopolitan Pictures. Tragically, by the mid 1920's, she'd also acquired an addiction to narcotic drugs that would eventually overpower her.[68]

If one believes the tale regaled by multiple movie magazine writers and newspaper gossip columnists, the love story of Rubens and Cortez began years before they started dating, sometime during the early 1920's, when the young, would-be actor, part-time shipping clerk Jack Crane caught a glimpse of lovely Alma in a store window in New York, but didn't have the nerve to introduce himself. Ricardo told *Photoplay* it was an experience he would never forget.

"It was across from St. Patrick's Cathedral, near Kirpatrick's Jewelry Store in New York—I think the shop is still there. She was looking at a photographer's display. I saw her pale face and dark luminous eyes. I'll admit I was overcome. I walked back and forth watching her—trying not to be too apparent in my admiration. I thought she was wonderful then—I am convinced she is now!"[69]

Whether the story was true is irrelevant. Clearly the poor young Jewish immigrant's son from Lower Manhattan admired, perhaps even idolized, the noted movie beauty who symbolized a world of glamour, fame, and celebrity he had long dreamed of entering.

By the time he caught a glimpse of those "dark luminous eyes" in person again, the young man didn't have to admire Alma from a distance; that came in December, 1923. By then, lowly Jack Crane had become a rising star named Ricardo Cortez. He was visiting First National studio to discuss a possible movie project. Alma had just returned to Hollywood from New York after completing her contract with Cosmopolitan Pictures, and was at First National preparing to film a supporting role in the romantic drama, *Cytheria*, based on novelist Joseph Hergesheimer's book, *Cytheria, Goddess of Love*.

Alma always maintained Ricardo was also in the cast of *Cytheria* when she met him, but this is untrue. Apparently *Cytheria* director George Fitzmaurice did formally introduce the pair in the studio lunch room, however. For both, it would be a life altering event. "As far as I was concerned," said Alma, "it was a case of love at first sight . . . Tall, dark, slender, and with a Greek god profile, the more I saw of him the more I loved him."[70] As for Ricardo, he was similarly smitten. Soon he was actively pursuing Alma despite the fact she was a married woman, and the Famous Players Lasky publicity department had him romantically linked to Agnes Ayres at the time.

Purportedly the first dates of Alma and Ricardo were discreet dinners at her apartment and clandestine meetings at parties. Ricardo instantly liked Alma. Unlike other women he had known both before and after he came to Hollywood, she was easy to talk to. She seemed to relate to his experiences and understand him like no one ever had. On a strictly surface level, the two did have things in common. Both had risen from modest backgrounds to become film stars; both were ambitious actors dedicated to their professions; both had suffered the frustrations and instability inherent in the film acting business and were hypersensitive, sometimes temperamental individuals who had experienced the envy and resentment of others; both also felt misunderstood; but that is where the similarities ended. Alma was a very different kind of person than Ricardo, and that would soon become apparent.

The two began a torrid affair sometime in the spring of 1924. Estranged from her intellectually inclined husband, whom she called, "Dr. Goodman," the free-spirited Alma immediately invited her young lover to move in to her rented patio apartment. Her reputation be damned! Cortez demurred. Ever cognizant of his public image,

A 1920's portrait of Alma.

and fearful the affair might generate scandalous headlines that could anger his Paramount bosses and discourage his rapidly expanding (mainly feminine) fan base, the cautious Cortez was not about to do anything to sabotage his burgeoning career. Both he and Alma initially denied rumors of their relationship, and insisted they were only friends.

All changed in the summer of 1924. If "Ric," as Alma and many of Ricardo's friends and acquaintances preferred to call him, harbored any illusions of keeping the affair from the prying eyes of the press, they were soon shattered. Ever the loose cannon, Alma confided to friends the true nature of the relationship, and one of them shared the confidence with the media. By July, the Cortez/Rubens relationship was on the minds and tongues of every Hollywood gossiper, both of the formal and informal kind. In an August, 1924 column, one of the queens of the Hollywood rumor mill, Grace Kingsley, reported the engagement of Agnes Ayres to Manuel Reachi, attache to the consulate general of Mexico. She said Ricardo "was drying his eyes and looking with admiration in the direction of another pretty Hollywood actress, who, however, denies she is going to marry him."[71]

Things were progressing for Ricardo professionally as well. Famous Players/Lasky was so pleased with his previous film appearances, the studio rewarded him with his first starring role. The vehicle: *The Spaniard* (1925), the story of a Spanish bullfighter's (Cortez) romantic pursuit of a young Englishwoman (Jetta Goudal), based on a best-selling novel by Juanita Savage. Despite an absurdly melodramatic plot, and a lead part that was more than a little "Valentino-esque," the movie proved a showcase for Ricardo, who handled the physical requirements of his scenes admirably, and looked dashing in his period costumes. Director Raoul Walsh was particularly impressed with the young man's athleticism and skill as a horseman. One difficult scene required Cortez to put his mount over streams and fences, and then take a spectacular fall when approaching a ruined wall. Walsh bought Ricardo a free dinner after he performed the stunt-filled scene three times in perfect form.[72]

A success at the box office, *The Spaniard*'s positive reception inspired newspapers across the country to conduct polls to determine which of Hollywood's two favorite "sheiks" (Valentino or Cortez) was the "sheikiest!"[73] The results of the ludicrous survey were never formally published, but *The Spaniard* proved a stepping stone for the ambitious young actor's ascension to stardom. He had proven he could carry a film, which he knew could pay dividends. Now if he could shed the exotic Latin lover/sheik screen image. There was only one Valentino, and the public did not need another. His resemblance to the great star had opened the studio gates to

A Spanish nobleman/bullfighter's love for an Englishwoman formed the storyline of *The Spaniard* (Paramount, 1925), Cortez's first prominent starring role, directed by Raoul Walsh.

Ricardo was an accomplished horseman who often spent his free time riding alone in the Hollywood Hills. In this 1924 candid, he is seen with his four-legged friend, Don Juan.

Cortez, but it was now imperative he develop his own distinct screen persona.

His next two projects, *Not So Long Ago* (1925) and *In The Name of Love* (1925), were changes of pace. Both were moderately entertaining, modestly successful romantic comedies that presented Cortez as attractive, heroic lead characters, but the films were not strong enough to help him substantively alter his screen image. In fact, the latter movie again presented him as a European, this time as a French immigrant who returns to his birthplace in search of his childhood sweetheart, who has become a wealthy social climber.

While making *In the Name of Love*, Ricardo saw an opportunity to break free of the sheik straightjacket when he learned Paramount was making elaborate plans to film an epic western, a quasi-sequel to its enormously popular, critically acclaimed 1923 adventure, *The Covered Wagon*. The new motion picture, saluting the brave exploits of the famed Pony Express, was slated to begin production at the end of the summer. By late spring, 1925, the studio was searching for the right actor to play the lead character, Frisco Jack Weston, a debonair gambler who becomes a Pony Express rider during the 1860's, and helps thwart the nefarious plans of an unscrupulous U.S. senator to have California secede from the union. Ricardo saw the part of Frisco Jack as a way to show acting versatility, and mounted an aggressive campaign to win it. He met with director James Cruze (who helmed *The Covered Wagon*) on multiple occasions, and did at least one screentest. Several other actors were seriously considered, but in the end, Ricardo's good looks, athletic prowess, AND skill as a horseman (so apparent in *The Spaniard*) worked to his advantage. In April, 1925, Paramount announced Cortez would have the plum role.[74]

Three months earlier, in January, Alma boldly announced she would divorce Dr. Goodman, whom she asserted "cursed and swore" at her, and "struck her in the face and body with his clenched fist." She also claimed the bespectacled Goodman knocked her unconscious during a trip to the Adirondacks.[75] Alma's mother, Theresa corroborated her daughter's stories adding, "He (Goodman) pulled her hair and slapped her. I asked him to get out of the house." After initially declining to comment, Goodman told *The Los Angeles Times* he had been extremely busy during the last year, and had seen Alma only occasionally. "So, if Miss Rubens suffered from pugilistic complications, it must have been at the hands of some other sparring partner," he quipped. Goodman initially vowed to contest the divorce, and the truth would be revealed at the trial, but in the end, the potential negative publicity must have convinced him to reconsider.[76]

In April, 1925, Alma declared she and Ricardo would be married when she could satisfy the legal requirements pertaining to her divorce, and he "could talk his way out of a movie contract that prohibits him from marrying."[77] The press initially got wind of the plans after someone noticed Alma sporting a beautiful new ring. Ricardo was not consulted prior to the announcement, and could not have been pleased. He was deeply enamored of the actress and clearly wanted to marry her, but he did not want to announce their plans before consulting Paramount, particularly after the studio had given him a part he felt might make him a box office star. Alma had broken the news anyway. To Cortez's relief, Paramount said it would not fight the marriage. Upon receiving the good news, he told the *L.A. Times*, "I want to do the thing that is best for Miss Rubens. It seems to me though, that the announcement will do no harm. It is true we are engaged and will be married soon after her divorce becomes final. We are very happy."[78]

Basking in the glow of his romance, and apparently oblivious to signs of his fiancé's volatile behavior, Ricardo was content during the summer of 1925. He and Alma were spotted in various nightspots and parties hand and hand, happy and in love. In July, both took part in the Greater Movie Season celebration in Oakland, California, posing with fans, riding together in a parade. Alma confided to her pals she was the happiest she'd ever been, and Ricardo was her "dream man" — "handsome, loving, and understanding."[79] Professionally, both were busy with their projects. Alma was slated to begin filming the comedy-drama *Fine Clothes* for First National, and Ricardo was preparing to play the most demanding role of his career thus far.

Realizing he might not have another opportunity like *The Pony Express* again, young Cortez was determined not to fail. In the weeks leading up to the production, he spent all available free time studying the history of the 1860's, pouring over the script in an effort to understand and interpret all aspects of his character.

According to the press, he spent at least three hours each day in the saddle, "perfecting his horsemanship technique" to perform the dangerous stunts required.[80]

For their part, Paramount spared no expense to make the new picture a worthy successor to *The Covered Wagon*. In addition to acquiring the services of the talented Cruze, and assembling a top-notch cast headed by Cortez, Betty Compson (director Cruze' wife), George Bancroft, Wallace Beery, and Ernest Torrence, the studio hired multiple technical and historical experts to authenticate aspects of the picture, including famed author Henry James Forman, who was tapped to pen a novel to be published when the film was released. The studio spent several weeks constructing a replica of the town of Julesburg, Colorado (known in old West days as the "toughest town west of the Missouri"), near Cheyenne, Wyoming, utilizing several square miles of buffalo grass land. They hired over 500 Sioux Indians and hundreds of extras, and even managed to borrow several period artifacts for use in the picture.[81]

Production officially began in July, 1925. After spending the first few weeks filming scenes on location in Sacramento, Cruze took a company of 130 actors, technicians, etc., to Cheyenne with a coterie of Hollywood reporters not far behind.[82] Cortez was both thrilled and apprehensive as production progressed. Could he handle the part? Would he be able to perform up to the expectations of his celebrated director and please his employers? He told a gossip columnist years later he did not sleep for days prior to the production. His nervousness was apparent during the initial days of filming, and noted by several reporters. One humorous story recorded by a pushy fan magazine writer named Myrtle Gebhart noted the young actor's unease after she brazenly demanded to have her picture taken with him on his mount. When the nervous Cortez politely declined, telling her the horse had been unsaddled, the red-haired Myrtle upbraided the picture's husky hero. "I'd be ashamed if I were six feet tall and as brawny as you if I couldn't saddle my own horse," she exclaimed. Humiliated, Cortez rose from his chair and saddled his horse, "posing with the smiling Myrtle for the photo."[83]

Luckily the young star's apprehension eventually melted away. Cruze was an excellent craftsman and a fast worker, renowned for his knowledge of the filmmaking process. He was a former actor who understood the pressures and responsibilities of his cast, allowing his players freedom to interpret their parts. Cortez respected Cruze, and trusted him on all matters relating to his role. Like Raoul Walsh, Cruze came to admire his 24-year-old star, who endured the difficult rehearsals and performed the movie's complicated and strenuous stunts with considerable finesse. Cruze was particularly impressed with Ricardo's work ethic and willingness to please, publicly marveling at his ability to ride his mount at 10 miles an hour, and then make an abrupt stop. Ricardo took a serious spill while filming one of the complicated riding sequences, but got up and finished the scene without complaint.[84]

With much fanfare, the film was released on September 4, 1925, to both public and critical applause. Throughout the country, theaters reported full houses and delighted film goers. In New York, the movie packed both Paramount's Rialto and Rivoli theaters with first day ticket sales in excess of $11,000.[85] In smaller towns, from Hattiesburg, Mississippi, to Galveston, Texas, to Steubenville, Ohio, lines to view the picture ran for blocks, forcing theaters to extend its run, and add show times. In many towns like Davenport, Iowa, front page news stories hailed "the sensational enthusiasm" that greeted the picture.[86]

Critics were equally awed. Producer/writer, Wid Gunning, billed as the "severest critic on the West Coast" cited the movie's "virile sweep that impresses." As its star, Cortez was showered with praise. *New York Times* critic Mordaunt Hall called his performance "capitol." *The Steubenville Herald Star* reviewer stated, "Had Mr. Cortez been made to order for the picture, he could not have suited his part more, or the part to him. He undoubtedly adds a flavor of realism to an already realistic picture."[87]

In an effort to promote the film as an artistic achievement faithfully depicting an important aspect of American history, Paramount opted to coincide the film's premiere with California's Diamond Jubilee, commemorating the state's 75th birthday. In fact, *The Pony Express* was designated California's official Diamond Jubilee production, and was screened in theaters throughout the state as part of elaborate multi-day celebrations. Cortez had a special place in the events. He and Alma attended several screenings and presentations, gave short speeches and press briefings, and rode in multiple parades. For the

Ricardo (right) attempted to shed his "Latin lover" image, playing Frisco Jack Westin, a gambler who becomes a Pony Express rider to foil a nefarious plot in James Cruze's epic western, *The Pony Express* (Paramount, 1925), costarring Betty Compson (on left).

intensely ambitious actor, the reception was a triumph. His performance as the tough, two-fisted, gun-slinging Jack Weston was impressive, winning him respect both in and out of Hollywood. Clothed in rags and a growth of beard for much of the picture, Cortez couldn't have been more "un-sheik like."[88]

Today many critics belittle *The Pony Express*, unfavorably comparing it to *The Covered Wagon*, decrying its episodic nature, old-fashioned staging, and lack of movement. They also assert the film was a dismal failure at the box office. These critiques appear unfair and inaccurate. Since so much of the movie's original footage has been lost (almost half of its original 110 minutes—including several key scenes), it is impossible to fairly judge it by what remains of the print. Clearly 1920's critics who actually viewed the entire movie thought it an achievement. As for box office receipts, the film was said to have made a profit after multiple re-releases, but it was certainly not as large as Paramount had hoped, primarily because of its immense production costs.[89]

Clothed in rags for much of the picture, the rough and tumble Frisco Jack in *The Pony Express* (Paramount, 1925) was a far cry from the "Latin lovers" Cortez had become associated with.

1925 *Saturday Evening Post* ad promoting three of Paramount's prominent actors.

In all the excitement surrounding the filming and release of the epic Western, Ricardo almost forgot how tired and physically hurt he was. During the previous two years he had made multiple physically taxing films in rapid succession, often putting in 12+ hour work days, sustaining multiple injuries. He was a young man, but even a young body couldn't take this kind of punishment. In early October, while on a brief vacation, Ricardo woke up with limited mobility on his left side. He was admitted to a Fresno hospital with a combination of exhaustion and what doctors termed "neuritis" (probably a result of all the injuries). He was confined to bed and ordered to "rest or else."[90]

All through the ordeal, Alma was at his bedside holding his hand and cheering him on. Upon his release from the hospital she insisted he recuperate at her mother's ranch in Madera, California, where she was staying after completing work on three pictures, including the acclaimed melodrama, *East Lynne*, costarring Edmund Lowe.[91] Ricardo was deeply moved by her concern, and the couple grew closer as he regained his strength. They announced they would marry in January, 1926, as soon as the waiting period was over for Alma's divorce. Alma told columnist Russell Birdwell she intended to abandon her movie career after the marriage to become a housewife and mother. "With Ricardo I know I shall always be happy. His business career will be my career. We will fight together and make him the big man of the house," she said.[92]

It was a moving declaration inspired by Alma's love for her conservative young fiancé who wanted a stay-at-home wife, but in her heart of hearts, the ambitious Alma undoubtedly knew she could never give up her career, not even for love and a family. By the middle of October, both she and Ricardo were once again examining scripts, planning their next screen projects. Alma was the initial choice to play the lead in Cosmopolitan's big budget filmization of Vincente Blasco Ibanez's dramatic novel, *Entre Naranjos*, chronicling the doomed romance between an aristocrat's son and a poor peasant girl who becomes a famous opera singer. Alma desperately wanted to play the showy, dramatic lead role of Leonora, a.k.a. La Brunna, but there was a problem. The distributor, Metro-Goldwyn-Mayer, and director, Monta Bell, thought her undependable. She had caused problems and delays during the filming of her previous pictures, which had harmed her reputation. A month before the production commenced, Alma was replaced by MGM's newest contract player, a beautiful and talented young Swedish actress who had impressed Bell in a screentest helmed by her mentor, Finnish-born director Mauritz Stiller. Her name was Greta Garbo.

Ricardo, too, became interested in the Ibanez project after reading Alma's script. While the film was set in Spain and the lead role of Raphael Brull, (an aristocratic Spaniard who falls in love with one of his family's tenants) was another Latin part, Ricardo became convinced it had superb dramatic potential. To top it off, making the picture would afford him the opportunity to work with Alma. As fate would have it, his campaign to play Raphael was successful at the very time Alma was replaced. By early November, an agreement was struck between Paramount and Metro-Goldywn-Mayer to loan his services for the film retitled, *Torrent*, a.k.a. *Ibanez's Torrent*.

Production commenced in late November, 1925. Tension ruled the set. Young Miss Garbo was a bundle of nerves. Lonely and frightened, she desperately needed the aid and reassurance of her mentor Stiller, whom she originally thought would be her director. She was polite to all, but as soon as scenes were filmed, she sat with her assistant and interpreter, never interacting with anyone. According to biographer Karen Swenson in her book, *Greta Garbo, A Life Apart*, the young actress approached the making of her first Hollywood film "with all the excitement of a condemned person walking to the electric chair."[93]

For Cortez, making *Torrent* was no less an ordeal. Profoundly disappointed when Alma was replaced, his attitude deteriorated after meeting his inexperienced leading lady, whom he deemed remote and unworthy. After the first few days' shooting, when it became apparent his costar was becoming the movie's focus and would be garnering the lion's share of attention from producers, director, and press, Ricardo began showing his frustration—a lapse of good judgement from a man who prided himself on maintaining his professional cool.

Relations between the two leads worsened as the elaborate production continued into the middle of December. Increasingly resentful, Cortez made it known on the set he was the top-billed star of the picture, and demanded to be treated as such. According to Swenson, after filming the movie's spectacular flood scene, a jealous and frustrated Cortez "took the blankets Borg (Garbo's assistant/interpreter) was holding for Garbo as she came out of a studio-manufactured rainstorm." When Borg protested, Garbo stopped him. "Let him have them," she said. "You mustn't let yourself be bothered about a pumpkin like that."[94]

Ricardo Cortez (left) and young Greta Garbo being directed by Monta Bell in a scene from MGM's production, *Torrent* (1926).

Ricardo and Marion Davies were almost unrecognizable when they posed for this candid on the set of *Torrent* (MGM, 1926). Cortez was playing the aging landlord's son, Raphael Brull, and Miss Davies was in costume for the title role in *Beverly of Graustart* (MGM, 1926) about a young woman who impersonates her male cousin.

Fortunately for Cortez, no one outside of the cast and crew of *Torrent* seemed to be paying much attention to his unprofessional tantrums. Everyone, including the movie magazine press, was too mesmerized by the overnight transformation of the inexperienced young Swedish actress from a shy young girl into a genuine movie star, one who possessed the rare combination of beauty, screen charisma, and acting talent.

When the film was released in February, 1926, critics and public responded in unison. Reviews were unanimously positive. The largest share of kudos was awarded to Miss Garbo, whom *Variety* called "the find of the year," and whom the *New York Times* said "steals most of the thunder in this vehicle." Filmgoers concurred, and the movie was a box office success.

What was largely missed in all the hoopla surrounding Miss Garbo's sensational American movie debut was the praiseworthy performances of some of the other cast members, notably her leading man. Despite everything, Cortez had contributed an excellent performance as the mother-dominated Raphael who, during the course of the picture, transitions from Garbo's handsome young suitor to a successful politician and, later, to a bespectacled middle-aged man. For a young lead actor who won fame as a romantic idol, Cortez's willingness to appear bloated, old, and unattractive in the latter scenes was a genuine risk; one he deserved to be recognized for.

Cortez surely regretted his antics on the set of *Torrent* soon after filming wrapped and the picture became a success. While his disappointment was understandable given his hopes for the picture, he had unwisely let his ego and emotions get the best of him, making him appear difficult and ungrateful. It was a costly mistake he hoped never to repeat. As years passed he would often list *Torrent* (and his star billing over the great Greta) among the highlights of his career, and in a bit of "revisionist history," told interviewers he enjoyed working with the great diva. In a June, 1932 *Chicago Daily Tribune* article, he said he liked Garbo and understood her aloofness.

"I don't make friends easily myself, and I knew the feeling of being misunderstood and sneered at, and I was drawn to Miss Garbo. I have since run into her on the boulevard, at a store, and found her very pleasant. She chats, and always remembers one she has known." [95]

While Ricardo finished work on *Torrent*, Alma finalized plans for their wedding. Press reports indicated it would be a grand affair, but in the end, Ricardo, Alma, and Alma's mother, Theresa (who participated in all important decisions her daughter made) opted for a small private ceremony to take place on January 30, 1926, the day after Alma's divorce became final. As the big day approached, Alma's behavior appeared particularly erratic. She seemed agitated one minute, and strangely calm the next. One night in mid-January, two weeks before the proposed nuptials, as the couple dined at Alma's rented home in Cerritos, the actress created a scene after her cook mistakenly ate one of three ducks prepared for dinner, thinking the extra duck was for her consumption. When Cortez asked for more and there was none, Alma flew into an abusive rage, locking the frightened woman out of the house without her clothes. The following week, the servant (Mrs. Frucht) filed a complaint with the city prosecutor, and the unfortunate incident found its way to newspapers.[96]

Ricardo's reaction is unknown, but it is unlikely he thought it significant. Alma was an emotional person to begin with, and wedding jitters and studio pressures had probably set her off. Sadly, there was a much more serious explanation, one which young Mr. Cortez couldn't have imagined; Alma was addicted to morphine. First prescribed as a temporary remedy to combat gynecological pain two years before, gradually the "soothing white drops" became a crutch on which she relied to alleviate all her ailments both physical and emotional, real and imagined. By the time she married Ricardo, Alma's daily "fix" had become THE priority of her life. In her autobiography, she provided a blunt assessment of herself, and the demon that possessed her.

"Alma Rubens was a dope fiend. A weak, worldly girl, who hadn't sufficient will power to cast aside the treacherous needle, the insidious liquid, responsible for my loathsome yearning. Oh, God. No one knows how ashamed I was. No one will ever believe when I say that I spent hours, days, weeks, during that period, on my knees, praying, imploring God to save me, to give me strength to break away; and that failing, to let me die!"[97]

With a major assist from multiple unscrupulous doctors who

greedily provided dope to the movie actress in exchange for handsome fees and gifts, Alma somehow managed to keep her increasing reliance on drugs a secret even from those closest to her, including her mother, sister, and fiancé.

On January 30, 1926, Alma and Ricardo were married by Justice of the Peace L. J. Difani in Riverside, California. In attendance were Alma's mother and five family friends. After spending the night at the Glenwood Mission Inn in Riverside, the couple rushed back to Los Angeles where they hoped to celebrate their union with friends, before resuming work on their respective film projects. Upon their return however, instead of best wishes, and congratulatory notes, they were greeted by scandalous headlines. An enterprising reporter had checked court records and found Miss Ruben's divorce would not be legally final until February 6. He accused the actress of bigamy.[98] The news spread like wildfire. On February 7, Riverside District Attorney Albert Ford launched an investigation. A panicked Alma blamed her divorce attorney for the problem. She claimed she had consulted him prior to the wedding and he had signed off on the date. The attorney disputed this and threatened to sue. Caught in the middle, Ricardo backed his wife. "What has happened," he said, "is her attorney did not take the papers down and have them entered until February 6, 1925."[99]

The ordeal dragged on for a week before an agreement was reached with the D.A. The couple would remarry, and Mr. Ford would drop the investigation. On February 9, Alma and Ricardo returned to Riverside and were remarried by a local pastor.[100] On the way back to the hotel room, Alma collapsed in her husband's arms, from what she later described as a combination of "nervous strain" and the fact she had not had her "daily shot." Alarmed, Ricardo carried her back to their hotel room and put her to bed, while keeping a watchful eye on the swarm of reporters camped out in the hotel. What should have been a joyous celebration of their love and commitment had turned into a nightmare, and that was just the beginning.[101]

A day after their remarriage, the popular couple was off to their respective movie projects. With some "medicinal help," Alma regained her composure and boarded a train bound for Idaho, where she would film the final scenes for the Fox melodrama, *Siberia*. In demand as never before, Ricardo flew to the Caribbean island of

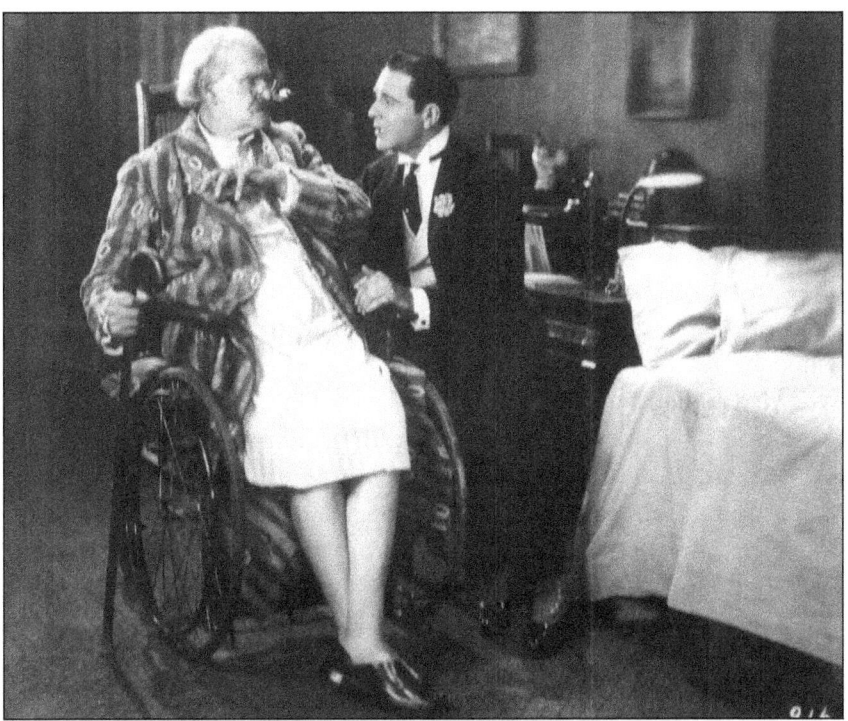

Cortez (right) and veteran character actor Theodore Roberts (in wheel chair) enact a scene from the comic drama, *The Cat's Pajamas* (Paramount, 1926) directed by William Wellman.

Martinique to shoot the melodramatic *Volcano*, the first of three Paramount pictures he would make during the early months of 1926. A silent era version of a modern day disaster movie, *Volcano*, set in the French Caribbean in 1902, presented him as a French aristocrat who conducts a "scandalous" romance with a girl (Bebe Daniels) believed to be biracial. Despite an overblown plot with misogynistic and racial overtones, the film was lifted by good performances and sensational special effects, notably a spectacular climax that featured the eruption of Mt. Pelee.[102] Audiences flocked to the picture. Cortez enjoyed his short stay on the island, where much of the filming was done at night to maximize the impact of the eruption scenes.[103]

He returned to Los Angeles to appear as an eccentric opera singer in love with his mother's seamstress in the serio-comic romance, *The Cat's Pajamas*. Like *Volcano*, it was basically an undistinguished picture with redeeming elements; in this case, skillful direction, and charming performances. Today *The Cat's Pajamas* is notable for marking the return to the screen of veteran character actor Theodore Roberts after a bout of illness, and for its up-and-coming director, talented William Wellman.[104]

Cortez's third 1926 assignment was by far the most ambitious—a film version of Marie Corelli's best-selling 1895 novel, *The Sorrows of Satan*, about a struggling writer's attempt to resist the temptations of Lucifer, the sad fallen angel of God who longs to find an incorruptible human so he can spend an hour in heaven. Cortez was excited when he learned his director would be the iconic D. W. Griffith, who had signed with Paramount in 1924. Unfortunately, the project would be a troubled one from beginning to end—a prime example of the immorality and underhandedness of studio politics.

The fascinating saga of *Sorrows* began during the early 1920's. Paramount wanted to make a picture based on the Corelli book, but couldn't come to terms with the eccentric author, who refused to accept Cecil B. DeMille as the director. Her death in 1924 paved the way for an agreement with her heirs. When DeMille suddenly departed the studio due to a contract dispute, Griffith inherited the production.[105] Initially skeptical (due to Corelli's negative reputation among serious literary scholars), the famed director eventually became convinced the project had enormous dramatic and romantic possibilities. According to Richard Schickel's biography, *D. W. Griffith, An American Life*, the director was especially interested in presenting an elaborate visual depiction of the struggle between the forces of light and darkness in order to "wow audiences into a suspension of belief, rewarding them for the advanced prices they would be expected to pay."[106]

The powers that be (both top and mid-level executives) at Paramount did not share Griffith's vision. They allotted him an ample budget ($650,000) and an expert cast (headed by Cortez, Griffith protégé Carol Dempster, the exotic Lya De Putti, and debonair Adolphe Menjou in the title role), but insisted Griffith concentrate on the romantic aspects of the tale, and de-emphasize the elaborate fantastical elements which would require costly special effects. Griffith remained determined to make the picture as he saw fit, and the matter was still unresolved when principal photography commenced in February, 1926 at Paramount's Astoria studio in New York.[107]

In D. W. Grifith's acclaimed drama, *The Sorrows of Satan* (Paramount, 1926), Cortez (left) portrayed a young writer tempted by Lucifer masquerading as a debonair count (Adolphe Menjou, right).

The filming was arduous. The movie had no formal script. Each morning, Griffith summoned his cast to a hall outside Keen's Chop House where they rehearsed scenes over and over before shooting and reshooting them in the afternoon. In his memoirs, *It Took Nine Tailors*, Adolphe Menjou recalled Griffith's "big ideas," which he described as "exciting to talk about but unpractical." Menjou said he felt foolish executing many of the elaborate sequences only to have them exorcised from the picture, and summed up the many months he spent making *The Sorrows of Satan* as "the unhappiest I have ever experienced in this business I love."[108]

For young Ricardo Cortez, filming *Sorrows* was exhilarating. He, too, was frustrated by the interminable retakes, but he liked the role of the idealistic scrivener, Geoffrey Tempest, was inspired by Griffith's style and technique, and knew he could learn a great deal about moviemaking by working with the screen legend. He also appreciated being back home in New York where he could spend

From left to right: Cortez, D.W. Griffith, Darryl Zanuck, and Adolphe Menjou pose for this candid photo on the set of *The Sorrows of Satan* (Paramount, 1926).

time with his family. With Griffith's permission, Ricardo invited his brothers to visit the set. Soon, thanks to the intervention of their elder brother, both Stanley and Bernard would become employed in the film industry. Eighteen-year-old Stanley, who was working as a photographer's assistant in New York, was fascinated by the filmmaking process and the photographer's role. Later he adopted his brother's stage name and migrated to Hollywood, where Ricardo helped arrange apprenticeships for him with such noted cinematographers as Hal Mohr, Arthur Miller, and Lee Garmes. Eventually he became one of the premier cinematographers in motion picture history. In his later years, Stanley often credited his visit to the set of *The Sorrows of Satan* as one of the key events that shaped his movie career. In a 1990 interview, he recalled the experience. "I walked into the studio and saw hundreds of lights. It was a big set with 300 people. A great orchestra played a great waltz, and there stood the director, D.W. Griffith,—holding a megaphone. I stood watching, transfixed by the magic of it all."[109]

Ricardo completed what he thought were his final scenes in April. Before filming wrapped, Alma joined him in New York, where the two finally had a brief honeymoon, and Alma shopped for antique furniture and draperies to furnish the couple's new home, a six-room bungalow at 1745 Wilton Avenue in Los Angeles, which she had purchased for them during Ricardo's absence. To celebrate their union, Cortez gifted his young bride with several pieces of jewelry, including a sapphire ring, a brooch, and a diamond bracelet that Alma referred to as a "slave chain."[110]

In July, 1926, after months of painstaking work and multiple weeks of editing, Griffith finally screened *The Sorrows of Satan* for Paramount president, Adolph Zukor. Present were several Paramount production executives including Jesse Lasky, William Le Baron, and Walter Wanger. Zukor liked the picture, but when he made suggestions for how it might be improved, studio politics became involved. In an attempt to ingratiate themselves with the boss, unbeknownst to Griffith, Wanger and Le Baron hired Broadway designer Norman Bel Geddes to write an additional sequence for *Sorrows*. When the financially-challenged Griffith learned of the interference, he was furious, but ultimately accepted the revisions, requiring members of his cast to return to work.[111]

By the time he was informed he would be needed back in New York to shoot additional scenes for *The Sorrows of Satan*, Ricardo was back in California filming Paramount's big-budget swashbuckler, *The Eagle of the Sea* (1926), adapted from Charles Tenney Jackson's celebrated novel, *Captain Sazarac*. Set in New Orleans and on the Spanish Main just after the War of 1812, it was a tale of adventure, intrigue, and romance on the high seas chronicling the exploits of pirate John Lafitte (a mustachioed Cortez), who foils a diabolical plot to rescue Napoleon from St. Helena, while romancing an aristocratic southern belle (Florence Vidor). Directed by Frank Lloyd, who had helmed the acclaimed action adventure *The Sea Hawk* (1924), the picture featured spectacular sea battles and much derring-do. To duplicate the cloud and water effects of the West Indies, Lloyd took his company and crew several miles off the southern California coast where the ships' battle scenes were filmed, utilizing old-time windjammers.[112]

During the weeks he spent making the immensely popular *The*

Set in New Orleans in 1817, director Frank Lloyd's fanciful seafaring adventure, *The Eagle of the Sea* (Paramount, 1926), cast Cortez as dashing pirate, Jean LaFitte, who disguised as Captain Sazarac, helps to foil a diabolical plot to rescue Napoleon from St. Helena.

Eagle of the Sea, Ricardo was at last able to spend time with his new bride. Outside of the two weeks they spent in New York, Ricardo had seen little of Alma since their marriage. He was very pleased with the simple yet elegant home she had purchased in his absence, and looked forward to their future. At the outset, both seemed committed to their union and naively determined to make it work. Alma renewed her vow to give up her career to become a homemaker and mother, and Ricardo resolved he would make her needs a priority. At his wife's urging, one of the first things he did upon arriving back in California was to renegotiate his Paramount contract, ostensibly so he would make enough money to support her when she gave up her career. The critical and box office success of his last pictures apparently inspired studio bosses to acquiesce to his demands, raising his salary to $1,000 per week for the first year, "with a renewal option of $1,500." [113]

As Ricardo prepared to head back east to shoot additional scenes for *The Sorrows of Satan*, he was stunned to learn of the passing of the man who had been indirectly responsible for his career. On August 23, 1926, Rudolph Valentino succumbed to an infection as a result of an operation for perforated ulcers. Although Rudy and Ricardo were often described as rivals, Ricardo knew and admired the actor and was saddened to learn of his demise. In a statement issued on the day of Valentino's death, Cortez expressed his sentiments. "In the passing of Valentino the picture industry has lost one of its true geniuses. Always happy and good natured, news of his death is to me one of the most tragic notes in the history of the screen."[114]

If Ricardo thought Rudy's death might end the comparisons and allow him to escape the "Latin lover/sheik" image once and for all, he would be disappointed. Although Ricardo made several image changes and/or transformations during the many years he made movies in Hollywood, Valentino would cast a very large shadow over the Cortez career, made even larger by his early death and the legend that grew around him.

In early September, 1926, Ricardo boarded a train for New York to film additional scenes for *The Sorrows of Satan*. During this stay, the young actor would have a unique chance to spend time with Griffith, an opportunity he would forever cherish. In a 1960's interview conducted by film historian Kevin Brownlow for his silent film volume, *The Parade's Gone By*, Cortez recalled the celebrated director.

"Griffith was a strange sort of man—very quiet. There seemed to be an invisible barrier around him. You couldn't get near him. I was under the impression that he was a very lonely man—although I got to know him quite well. I felt terribly sorry for him and would visit him at his hotel,— the Astor. He would go out for a walk and end up at the Pennsylvania railroad station, where he'd sit on a bench and just watch people." [115]

Griffith's travails on *Sorrows* continued even after he obligingly filmed the additional footage. When preview audiences reacted poorly, Zukor (unaware of the interference of subordinates) demanded Griffith restore the picture to its original form. Once again Griffith complied, only to have the movie tampered with yet again prior to its release in October, 1926. Critics were largely kind to the "corporate version" of *Sorrows*, but moviegoers stayed away. In the end, the film's enormous cost ($971,000) was prohibitive. The studio suffered a huge monetary loss (some $300,000), which was blamed on the frustrated, scapegoated Griffith, who departed Paramount months later.[116]

In spite of all the difficulties, the career of Ricardo Cortez was positively impacted by Griffith's *Sorrows*. His portrayal of Tempest, who is temporarily corrupted by Satan's temptations, was widely hailed. He told interviewers the film was one of his favorites.

"Only a Griffith would have had the temerity to cast me as a starving English author. It was a splendid role, and working for Griffith, and with an artist like Carol Dempster was incentive such as I never felt before." [117]

Among those impressed with Cortez was influential columnist Louella Parsons, who found the overall production wanting, but was unreservedly enthusiastic about Ricardo's portrayal, which she called "an event."[118] In a subsequent column, she cited him as "one of the most talked about leading men on the screen," one who rose "from apparent obscurity during the year, from a self-conscious actor to a player who has had no failures attached to his name."[119]

```
                    RICARDO CORTEZ
                      LOS ANGELES
```

Dear Fan:

    Your note arrived okay and here's the photo you ask for. It comes with my best to you.

    I am back in Hollywood after finishing "New York" in New York, and I've started already with Miss Negri in "The Woman on Trial." We're having a terrible time trying to figure out whether I'm hero or villain, but folks here at Paramount tell me that with all my badness there seems to be at least one spark of good in me at the grand finale. That's some comfort anyway.

    I must close. Wish it were possible for you to watch us "shoot" the big set we have up today. I guess there are at least a thousand people working.

    Adieu and all kinds of good wishes

        Sincerely,

        Ricardo Cortez

RC:LH.

After several successful films, Cortez's popularity grew as evidenced by his fan mail. This is a letter he sent to one of his admirers in 1927.

Cortez (left) played a songwriter wrongly accused of murder in the melodrama, *New York* (Paramount, 1927), costarring Lois Wilson, William Powell, and Estelle Taylor (seen here).

With influential critics and columnists like Parsons singing his praises, several critical and box office successes on his resume, and fan letters now rivaling Paramount's top stars, the ascendant young contract player was assigned another showy starring role in a big budget picture: *New York*, the melodramatic story of four poor boys whose disparate fortunes lead to death and despair. Filmed on location on the streets of Manhattan and at Paramount's Astoria studio, *New York* had a fine all-star supporting cast, and a good director, Luther Reed. Cortez was in his element as the protagonist, Michael Cassidy, one of the "sons of the bowery" who becomes a successful songwriter, only to be accused of murder. In newspaper interviews conducted during the filming (Nov.–Dec., 1926), Ricardo expressed great confidence in the production, believing it to be THE film that would solidify his status as a top-ranked movie star. As proof of his growing popularity, he was literally mobbed by fans when he filmed the movie's wedding scene at New York City Hall. A half-dozen police officers were eventually summoned to control the crowd and free the frightened actor from aggressive fans.[120] Due to delays caused by adverse weather conditions and illnesses, the film's four-week shooting schedule had to be lengthened, pushing the production into the holiday season. Consequently, Cortez's plans to return to California to celebrate the New Year with his wife were postponed, and Alma joined him in New York. Although exhausted, Ricardo was in excellent spirits. Life was very good! What could go wrong?

CHAPTER FOUR
CRASH AND BURN (1927–29)

"If an artist paints a great picture, he may not get recognition while he lives, but his work lives on and inspires after he is gone ... But an actor—he is soon forgotten. He does a good piece of work in one picture and if he doesn't get a chance in another good part for six months, he is forgotten."
— RICARDO CORTEZ

Ricardo's contentment was short-lived. Too soon, his hard won achievements, the very foundation of his life and career would begin to disintegrate bit by bit, piece, by piece. The period of 1927–29 would be the most turbulent of Cortez's life; a sad, tumultuous time that would leave permanent scars on his personal and professional lives. The most frustrating part of it all for the control-conscious Ricardo Cortez had to have been his utter lack of power over the events that were about to shape his future.

His difficulties began in January, 1927, when *New York* premiered to mixed notices. Small-town reviewers and theater patrons liked the sweep and realism of the picture, but big city critics and audiences were unimpressed. *Variety* spoke for elite critics when it lamented "so much good acting goes into a shoddy little yarn."[121] Despite respectable box office numbers, the film was a disappointment to Cortez, who had hoped it would be a triumph. His mood worsened when he learned the follow-up projects Paramount had in mind for him, which he felt would further diminish his momentum. By mid-January, multiple trade papers were reporting Paramount's intention to cast him in three pictures: as the titled hero in director Malcolm St. Clair's wild comedy, *The Cross Eyed Captain*; as a ruthless underworld kingpin in *Underworld*, by former Chicago newspaperman turned scenarist Ben Hecht; and as a sickly artist in the courtroom melodrama, *Confession*.[122]

Cortez did not want to play any of these roles, and uncharacteristically voiced his displeasure. In late fall, 1926, he had been approached by Metro-Goldwyn-Mayer to play Count Vronsky opposite Greta Garbo in the studio's upcoming adaptation of Tolstoy's classic novel, *Anna Karenina*. Cortez desperately wanted to play the part, but Paramount said no. For a time he thought perhaps the studio might reconsider after the St. Clair project was mercifully shelved, and *Underworld* delayed. "I was never late on the set. I didn't smoke on the lot. I left the girls on the lot and off, alone. They didn't have a more conscientious worker. I knew it," he told an interviewer.[123]

In February, 1927, Ricardo was ordered to report for work on *Confession*. Of the three projects, his least favorite was *Confession*, based on Erno Vadja's melodramatic play chronicling the life and loves of a Parisian stage actress. Cortez hated the script (which focused on the feminine lead), despised the one-dimensional part of a tubercular painter, and wanted to avoid working with the leading lady, the notoriously temperamental German film star, Pola Negri.[124] Filming began on the courtroom drama (made in Hollywood) in early February. It was inevitable there would be trouble. Miss Negri was her demanding self, Cortez had a chip on his shoulder, and the director, Mauritz Stiller (Garbo's celebrated mentor hired by Paramount after Metro-Goldwyn-Mayer terminated his contract), seemed distracted. After three days, filming was suspended when Negri and Cortez supposedly suffered "injuries." In her column dated February 22, Louella Parsons stated Negri had "slipped and skinned her knee," and Cortez had suffered a fall that left him "walking with a limp."[125] What exactly happened is uncertain, but four days later, Cortez was removed from the picture, and Swedish-born actor, Einar Hanson substituted.[126]

One version stated Negri had thrown "a fit of temperament." Another had Cortez storming off the set in a huff, and yet another, stated Negri and Stiller concluded Cortez was too husky to play a sickly artist. The latter version became the official reason for Cortez's departure, after Negri issued a statement expressing "regrets" at losing Cortez.[127] The explanation might have made sense if not for the fact

Hanson was as stocky and "healthy looking" as Cortez. Whatever the reason, Ricardo was relieved to be rid of Miss Negri and her *Confession*. He was right to want out. The film, retitled *The Woman on Trial*, would be a major flop and a jinx for its main participants. The coming of sound soon ended Miss Negri's career, Einar Hanson would die in a fatal car accident before the film was released, and director Stiller would make only one more Hollywood movie before returning to Sweden, where he died a broken man in 1928.

The Negri/Stiller fiasco had proven a turning point for Ricardo. He was deeply appreciative of Paramount's support of his career, but now it seemed as if they were uninterested in his artistic development. He was a good soldier who'd always complied with their requests, sometimes to the detriment of his career and at the expense of incurring the wrath of others, BUT he wanted to play Vronsky in *Anna Karenina*, slated to begin filming in April. His contract was due to expire in March; and he was determined to have the role even if it meant leaving Paramount.

When the studio insisted he begin work on *Underworld* in March, Ricardo walked.[128] It was a momentous decision for the conservative Mr. Cortez who was giving up a lucrative pact with a top studio for a one-film deal. It was a decision he would soon regret. *Underworld* would become a major critical and box office hit that aided the careers of all involved in its production. *Anna Karenina*, too, would be a success but, unfortunately, Cortez would never share in the glory.

Ricardo was certainly not anticipating any problems when he arrived at Metro-Goldwyn-Mayer's Culver City lot to shoot the studio's version of the Tolstoy classic in mid-April, 1927. Shortly after commencing the movie, it was retitled *Love* to better suit the Frances Marion script, which had substantially altered the massive novel. What remained, emphasized the tragic love affair of Anna Karenina, a Russian nobleman's wife, and Alexei Vronsky, a young officer. MGM spared no expense in bringing the Tolstoy novel to the silver screen, employing director, Dmitri Buchowetzki (Cortez's friend from *The Swan*), set designer Cedric Gibbons, and young, talented cinematographer Merritt Gerstad, who'd recently worked with Lon Chaney on *The Unknown*. In an effort to enhance the authenticity of the production, they hired members of the Russian aristocracy and Tsar Nicholas's White Guard to appear as extras. This was in addition to assembling a top notch supporting cast headed by Lionel Barrymore and Helene Chadwick.[129] Everyone seemed upbeat as work commenced. Miss Garbo appeared to be in excellent spirits on the heels of successfully renegotiating her Metro contract, receiving a huge raise and greater creative control. Cortez was also in a good mood, determined not to repeat the mistakes he'd made while working with Miss Garbo on *Torrent*. For the first two weeks, filming proceeded without a glitch. Things quickly changed in late April however, when Garbo suddenly fell ill, and failed to report for work. The studio initially thought her illness a power play, but gradually softened its stance after her personal physician delivered a diagnosis of "intestinal infection," possibly "pernicious anemia," an extremely serious condition.[130] For a time, filming continued without her, but by early May, her absence necessitated a halt in production.

Understandably concerned, Ricardo initially remained optimistic. With the exception of a few key scenes involving the eccentric star, the majority of the picture had already been finished. When she returned, it could be completed in short order, but Garbo didn't return, and by the end of May, Cortez became anxious. His fears were confirmed the first week in June when he received devastating news. After investing over $200,000, MGM head of production Irving Thalberg opted to scrap the existing footage of *Love* and change its director and cast including its leading man. On June 10, 1927, *Motion Picture News* reported Norman Kerry would take over the Vronsky role and Edmund Goulding would direct. The short article said the selection of Kerry had been "made necessary because of the casting of Ricardo Cortez for the romantic lead in *Terror*." A week later, Kerry was out, and Garbo's friend and "lover" John Gilbert was in, along with a new supporting cast, and Thalberg favorite, William H. Daniels as photographer.[131]

Speculation ran rampant regarding the nature of the dismissals. Many thought Garbo had made up the illness in order to replace Buchowetzki with Goulding, and allow Gilbert (who had been working on another picture) to be free to costar. Evidence provided by Garbo biographer Karen Swenson suggests Miss Garbo WAS genuinely ill, but may also have urged changes.

This is a rare original photo from the aborted first version of *Love* (MGM, 1927) featuring from left to right: Cortez, Lionel Barrymore, and Miss Garbo.

For Ricardo Cortez, the news was a bitter pill. The part he was given by MGM in the Lon Chaney vehicle, *Terror* (retitled *Mockery*), was a non-descript supporting role, in no way comparable to the one he had been forced to relinquish. He had sacrificed a great deal to be free to appear in *Love*, and felt betrayed. He would not forget the slight, forever remaining cautious to a fault. Surprisingly, none of his bitterness was ever focused on Garbo, who may have been the real instigator behind his dismissal.

Cortez's growing professional woes were not his only difficulties. In fact, his troubles with MGM were a veritable "walk in the park" compared to the challenges he now faced at home. The union of Alma Rubens and Ricardo Cortez would last only 71 months—a relatively brief period in the grand scheme of life, but into those six turbulent years, filled with disputes, accusations, breakups, reconciliations, and scandalous headlines, a lifetime of suffering, heartache, and humiliation were crammed. Alma endured unimaginable tortures in her battle with her demons, yet those who loved her were also severely impacted. He was in no way responsible for her ruinous addiction, but Ricardo Cortez became one of its chief victims, both personally and professionally.

Ricardo and Alma's "troubles" began in earnest when they actually began living together. They loved one another, but soon discovered they didn't much like married life. Like so many young couples, both were temperamental, self-absorbed individuals who found compromise and accommodation difficult. Mr. and Mrs. Cortez's problems were more fundamental, however, relating to their overall level of maturity and commitment, family issues, and Alma's increasing chemical dependency.

Despite having married twice, Alma had never really lived with her husbands. Both Franklyn Farnum and Dr. Goodman had been too busy with their professional lives to play much of a part in her life, and neither had placed any demands on her of any kind. She'd essentially led a "single" existence, doing exactly what she wanted when she wanted. Perhaps it was partially due to the increasingly dense, drug-induced fog under which she operated, but at the time she wed Ricardo, Alma harbored highly romantic notions of marriage. She not only thought a husband should be a lover, friend, and bread winner, but a selfless protector; one who would tolerate all her eccentric whims, and would pamper and enable her as her mother and family always had.

Twenty-six-year old Ricardo was ill equipped to fill the bill. He had grown up considerably as a result of his father's death and years of hardship trying to make it in acting, but his relationships with women had always been fleeting and immature. Like his wife, he too could be self-indulgent, sometimes arrogant, with unrealistic notions of marriage and the demands and responsibilities placed on him as a husband. Ricardo viewed his parents as the ultimate role models when it came to marriage. During their union, his father had been the breadwinner and protector; his mother the homemaker and nurturer. True to their Eastern European roots, Sarah Krantz always submitted to Morris, and submerged her needs in favor of those of her husband and family. Ricardo somehow expected his wife would do the same. The fact he had married a pampered, self-possessed actress who exhibited highly erratic behavior doesn't seem to have occurred to the young man, at least until January, 1927.

On this shaky ground, Mr. and Mrs. Cortez essentially began their life together. Throughout their courtship and marriage, the couple's arguments were numerous, covering a broad range of topics, from money and family, to matters of personality. Alma became furious when Ricardo refused to take her with him to clubs and sporting events, including weekly fight nights. She was hurt and offended by this slight, which she said in her autobiography, "went on for months and months during which my craving for the drug grew stronger and stronger."[132] Ricardo *was* indeed selfish at times, and stubbornly independent, but there were legitimate reasons he preferred leaving her home. He could never be certain how Alma would act at any given time. One minute she would be loving and understanding; the next, irritable or angry. The Cortez's battles would frequently end with Ricardo storming off in disgust. Sometimes he would not return for a day or two. A jealous Alma wondered where he'd gone, but by necessity cared more about her daily fix, the "soothing white drops" she needed to function.

A temporary lull in hostilities between the fighting Cortezes occurred when each would go back to making movies. In the late spring, 1927, Alma started shooting what would be her final Fox film, the far-fetched romantic melodrama, *The Heart of Salome*. A heavy-hearted Ricardo commenced MGM's *Mockery*, a melodrama set in Siberia during the Russian Revolution, featuring Lon Chaney as a dim-witted peasant who saves the life of a Russian princess (Barbara Bedford), then turns on her after she makes him a servant in her household. Helmed by Danish director Benjamin Christiensen (*The Mysterious X*, 1914, and *Haxan*, 1922), the film was a well-made, modestly entertaining star vehicle for the great Chaney, but second-billed Cortez had little to do as the heroic Russian officer the princess loves. Ricardo rightly considered it a demotion. His follow-up film, the 57-minute thriller *By Whose Hand?* (Columbia), which cast him as a brilliant investigator out to solve a baffling jewel theft, continued his slide down the ladder of success. He had the lead role, but the picture was a B movie made on Poverty Row with inferior production values and a second-string cast. Columbia didn't become a major studio until the mid-1930's.

While making *Mockery*, the resourceful Ricardo (now functioning as his own agent) was approached to appear in a foreign production he felt had the potential to get his acting career back on track. It was an opportunity to work with noted French auteur Leonce Perret, who had established a stellar reputation on both sides of the

Atlantic as a producer and director of stylish movies featuring innovative camera and lighting techniques. In hopes of presenting French films to a worldwide audience, Perret and others had formed Franco Films, operated out of the Rex Ingram studios in Nice, and were looking for established American stars to act in their movies. Perret asked Cortez to appear in one of his next productions, the romantic melodrama, *La Danseuse Orchide* a.k.a. *The Orchid Dancer*, about the life and loves of a poor young Frenchman who becomes a French film star. Cortez had never worked overseas and saw the project as a golden opportunity to demonstrate his ability. He also thought it might be a wonderful way for he and Alma to get away together and renew their relationship. She, too, liked the idea, so Cortez signed on.

As preparations were being made for the Perret picture to be filmed in October, 1927, Ricardo learned First National was casting key parts for one of its most prestigious projects, a film version of novelist John Erskine's best-selling book, *The Private Life of Helen of Troy*, a historical satire that put a contemporary, humorous spin on the classic Greek tale. Cortez had read and enjoyed the book and wanted to play the key role of Paris. To his surprise and delight, he won the role over dozens of Hollywood's most celebrated actors.[133]

Lavishly produced (certainly by First National standards), *The Private Life of Helen of Troy* commenced filming in late summer. In addition to Cortez and Hungarian-born actress Maria Corda in the title role, First National hired Alexander Korda (husband of Maria) to direct, gifted cinematographer Lee Garmes, a top-notch supporting cast, and over a thousand extras as soldiers, chariot drivers, wives, Nubian slaves, etc.[134]

Ricardo was thrilled with the elaborate sets, the costumes, the witty script by Gerald Duffy and Casey Robinson, and gratified he had won the part so many had coveted. He thought his wife would be excited for him, but she was not. In her autobiography, Alma described two events that occurred during the filming of *The Private Life of Helen of Troy* which further complicated the couple's burgeoning problems. Apparently, Alma felt Ricardo was getting too cocky during the making of the movie, and decided to bring him back down to earth. The first incident involved the couple's trip to a Spanish restaurant in Los Angeles. There, they encountered an older waiter who admired Ricardo and attempted to ingratiate himself with the actor by speaking in Spanish. In spite of his studio-created nativity, Ricardo knew almost no Spanish, and quickly became flustered. Alma became amused and burst into laughter, remarking, "What's the trub? No spikka da Espanole?" She said Ricardo became enraged and rushed out of the place without her. Although the facts appear to contradict her contention, Alma claimed she never knew the truth about her husband's ancestry prior to this event. She said a friend told her soon afterward. "At first I was very much upset," she recalled, "but later I didn't take this so seriously. Anyway, I probably was imposing on him as much, or more by my secret use of dope, as he had imposed on me."[135]

The other event occurred when a proud Ricardo, in full Greek *Helen of Troy* garb (including toga and wig), came home to show Alma his costume. She was entertaining a group of female friends for tea. Instead of complimenting him as he expected, she cruelly derided him in front of them. She candidly recalled the afternoon this way.

"He looked gorgeous. There was no question about that. But I simply couldn't resist the temptation to make a dirty little dig at his egoism. 'Oh,' I said, in the presence of everybody. 'Doesn't my little Jakie Kranz look magnificent!' Thinking back over the time, I really believe I must have been unusually exhausted by the drugs that afternoon, although no other woman present was an addict."[136]

According to Alma, Ricardo became "livid and he trembled in his anger. The other women tittered . . ." She said she enjoyed his "discomfiture." In spite of their differences and Alma's mercurial behavior, Ricardo had always thought she was on his side, his booster. Having her humiliate him in these ways must have been a blow to the appearance-conscious Ricardo.

Once again, the Cortez marriage was temporarily rescued by work assignments. While Ricardo completed *The Private Life of Helen of Troy*, Alma headed east to make the MGM drama, *The Masks of the Devil* (1928), starring John Gilbert. Despite her growing reputation for unreliability, she had the feminine lead and received second billing. Determined to maintain control of her life and hide her

In the midst of career downturn, Cortez (seen here) won the coveted role of Paris in Alexander Korda's witty, sophisticated satire, *The Private Lives of Helen of Troy* (First National, 1927).]

Cortez in full costume as Paris in *The Private Life of Helen of Troy* (First National, 1927).

growing addiction, she reported for work, but in the end, she couldn't handle all the demands of her role and director Victor Seastrom was forced to shorten her scenes.[137] In her book, *Without Lying Down: Frances Marion and the Powerful Women of Early Hollywood*, author Cari Beauchamp quoted screenwriter Marion as noting Alma's "drifting speech and glassy eyes."[138] Perhaps hoping to somehow repair their deteriorating relationship, Ricardo and Alma set off for Europe aboard the *Ile de France* for a three-month "second honeymoon" in October, 1927.[139] Filming on *The Orchid Dancer*, costarring French film stars, Louise LaGrange and Xenia Desni, began in Paris and proceeded on schedule to Berlin. Ricardo loved Europe, thought Perret a genius, and the movie a work of art. Convinced it would be a critical and box office smash in the U.S., he agreed to accept the film's distribution rights in exchange for his services and $2,000 for expenses.[140]

Sadly, his second honeymoon was not as pleasurable as making the movie. Alma referred to the trip as "weird." She said she and Ricardo barely spoke, but posed for pictures as if all was well. She recalled contemplating an annulment of their marriage at the time, but hesitated, fearful her morphine habit would be exposed. She insisted at this point no one outside of her doctor/suppliers yet suspected her drug usage.[141]

That changed in early 1928 after the couple's return to America. Alma had a near fatal reaction when one of her doctors accidentally gave her another medication instead of the morphine, then informed her mother and Ricardo he "suspected" she was a drug addict. The psychological impact of the news on Ricardo is unknown, but Alma said he initially treated her with kindness and compassion. Alma's severe withdrawal symptoms eventually landed her in a Hollywood hospital, and later, a sanitarium where she was sent to kick her habit. She said she wanted desperately to free herself from the "dope monster," but after she returned home, her usage resumed. In spite of the fact they did not get along, Ricardo and Alma's mother, Theresa, combined forces, trying valiantly to keep her sober and keep her addiction from becoming public knowledge, but they didn't understand the monster and its powerful hold over their loved one.

While dealing with his wife's crises, Ricardo was also facing major financial and career challenges. During his three and one half month stay in Europe, Hollywood changed. The sensational October, 1927 premiere of Warner Bros.' *The Jazz Singer* (which contained sound sequences) had set off a revolution in the film capital that left the studio heads scrambling to bring voices and music to the silver screen. By the time the first All-talkie, Warner Bros.' *Lights of New York*, premiered in the spring of 1928, all the majors were busy converting their production facilities and theaters to accommodate sound. As the revolution quickly gained steam, all who worked in films knew they would have to adapt to the new reality or face unemployment. For actors, from the lowliest bit players to the most celebrated Hollywood superstars, having a voice pleasing to film audiences would determine their fate in the industry.

During the early months of 1928, Ricardo came to the realization he would once again have to prove himself (his vocal ability) to remain employed, but until then, he had to keep the bill collectors at bay. Upon his return from abroad, he was surprised to find few acting offers greeting him—none from big studios. Convinced he was being blackballed by Paramount, and fully aware making low-budget movies might be a recipe for disaster, Cortez decided to take the only acting offers currently on the table—from B movie studio, Tiffany-Stahl.

Originally founded as Tiffany Productions in 1921 by actress Mae Murray, her husband at the time, director Robert Z. Leonard, and motion picture executive, Maurice Hoffman, the company eventually acquired the Reliance/Majestic Studios on Sunset Boulevard and became Tiffany-Stahl after director John M. Stahl was named head of production. A small studio with big aspirations, by the late 1920's Tiffany-Stahl was busy producing multiple films on its four sound stages, and booking its productions in over 2,000 theaters across the country. Like filmmakers in Europe, the company was looking for established stars who would add class and distinction to its output, thus giving the company legitimacy. One of the stars they were interested in was Ricardo Cortez.

Initially signing to make two pictures, Ricardo would eventually play leads in seven Tiffany-Stahl productions during the period 1928-29 at a salary less than half what he was making at Paramount. None were of enduring import, but all had meritorious elements and afforded Cortez a chance to play many types of characters in a broad range of genres. There were adventures: *Prowlers of the Sea* (1928); *The Gun Runner* (1928); *The Lost Zeppelin* (1929); comedies: *Ladies of the Night Club* (1928); dramas: *The Grain of Dust* (1928); melodramas: *New Orleans* (1929); even science fiction: *Midstream* (1929). Two of the pictures had singing and/or talking sequences, but only *The Lost Zeppelin* was strictly a sound film. Tiffany-Stahl did not begin producing all-talking pictures until the end of 1929.

The two most interesting of Cortez's Tiffany-Stahl productions were two of the last, *Midstream* and *The Lost Zeppelin*. The former, a science fiction drama, was a variation of the familiar story of *Faust*. The script, penned by Bernice Boone and Frances Guihan, related the tale of an older man (Cortez) so desperate to remain young in order to attract his beautiful neighbor (Claire Windsor), he travels abroad, undergoes a rejuvenation operation, fakes his death, and returns as his nephew. His elaborate scheme is almost successful, but fate deals him a crushing blow ironically as he and his fiance attend an operatic performance of *Faust*. Directed by James Flood, who would do acclaimed work for Warner Bros. during the early 1930's, including the dramas *The Mouthpiece* (1932) and *Life Begins* (1932), *Midstream* contained both intense dramatic and science fiction elements, as well a sound sequence. For Ricardo, in the midst of a career downturn, the movie was notable for providing him a meaty starring role, playing both young and older versions of the same character (a la *Torrent*). If one believes those who saw the film, his performance as the desperate Jim Stanwood in *Midstream* was even better than his Raphael in *Torrent*, yet it was largely ignored by major newspapers and Hollywood trades, who turned up their noses at low-budget movies. One of few major industry journals doing a thorough review of *Midstream* was *Harrison Reports*. Critic P. S. Harrison found fault with certain aspects of the movie, but heaped praise on its star, emphatically stating, "In becoming an old man again after a breakdown during the performance of 'Faust,' Cortez does the best acting of his career..."[142]

Another unusual and worthy Tiffany-Stahl picture was *The Lost Zeppelin*, an adventure drama about two romantic rivals whose mental and physical strengths are tested when they set out on an Antarctic expedition aboard a Zeppelin. Burdened with a clichéd script, stilted dialogue, and crude sound, *Zeppelin* (which was also made as a

Cortez (right) had one of his meatiest roles as an old man who undergoes a rejuvenation operation in order to woo his beautiful young neighbor in the low-budget melodrama, *Midstream* (Tiffany-Stahl, 1929), costarring Claire Windsor and Helen Jerome Eddy (on left).

silent) was nevertheless redeemed by attractive art deco sets and imaginative special effects, including the inventive use of miniatures. Cortez's role as a young officer in love with the captain's wife was nothing special, but the picture had an expensive look and feel, and performed well at the box office. Most importantly, it showed off Cortez's pleasant sounding baritone speaking voice in an all-talking production.

Amid all the professional upheaval, and an unenviable work schedule which frequently had him on the set from dawn to dusk making multiple films at the same time, Ricardo faced even more daunting responsibilities: to somehow keep his wife clean and sober while preserving his marriage. Perhaps he was too distracted by career woes, or too naïve to realize it yet, but it was an impossible situation. To effectively loosen dope's ever tightening grip over every aspect of her existence, Alma had to want to break free, and for whatever reason, she did not.

In May, 1928, Alma received an important new job offer: the key supporting role of Julie in Universal's upcoming production of Edna Ferber's novel, *Show Boat*, to begin filming sometime in early summer. A musical version of the bestseller with a score by Oscar Hammerstein and Jerome Kern was currently packing them in on Broadway, and the new film was much anticipated. It was a wonderful opportunity for Alma, whose career had been slipping. Both she and her family desired her participation for different reasons. While Alma saw the role as a great vehicle, in her clouded mind, she was more concerned about escaping the watchful eyes of her family, so she could take the morphine unhindered. Her husband and family wanted her to accept the part in order to focus her energies on something creative in hopes it might help her.

Production on *Show Boat* began in July on the Sacramento River, where exteriors were filmed by director Harry Pollard and crew. In August, filming shifted to the Universal lot in Hollywood. Somehow, Alma managed to remember her lines and finish her early scenes, but appeared on the edge of losing control. In an interview published in 1937, Ricardo recalled how hard he and her family worked to see her through. For a time, he employed someone to follow her and keep a log of her visitors, but when Alma learned she was being surveilled, she became furious, leading to ugly verbal battles.[143]

Things came to a head during the summer of 1928, when Ricardo learned Alma had exchanged jewelry for a few days' worth of drugs. Among the pieces she relinquished was the bracelet he had given her as a wedding present. Several versions of the story (with some variations) surfaced during the early 1930's, but apparently when Ricardo learned what Alma had done, he became apoplectic, demanding to know who the doctor/supplier was. Eventually Alma relented, and Ricardo confronted the physician, who relinquished the jewelry to keep the irate actor/former amateur boxer from attacking him.[144]

On August 30, 1928, Ricardo and Alma announced a trial separation.[145] Ricardo moved into an apartment, while Alma remained at their residence. When asked to comment, he told reporters it was "just one of those things."[146] A gossip columnist hinted the break-up was due to Alma's infidelity during the location shooting for *Show Boat*.[147] The likelier explanation was the jewelry incident, combined with her drug abuse. Ricardo and Alma would reconcile and live together for short periods of time after their initial separation, but things were never the same between them again. Ricardo eventually forgave Alma, but it's doubtful he ever forgot she had given up a symbol of their love for a few dollars' worth of dope.

Throughout his two-year stint making low budgeters for Tiffany-Stahl, Cortez continued his quest for suitable roles in A-level pictures. His efforts were largely unsuccessful. As true in the 1920's as today, once an established actor started making B's, it became extremely difficult to mount a comeback. In 1928, he managed to secure two parts outside of Tiffany-Stahl, and only one of them was a higher budget production. That was MGM's *Excess Baggage*, a silent comedy/drama directed by James Cruze starring William Haines. Cortez's sixth-billed role as a famed movie actor and romantic rival of a struggling juggler/acrobat (Haines) was small and forgettable.

A better opportunity came from B studio, Columbia Pictures. The project was *The Younger Generation*, a hard-hitting drama based on a Fannie Hurst play about Morris Goldfish, a poor but industrious Jewish immigrant's son (Cortez), who hides his humble heritage and his family in order to become a successful businessman and ascend the social ladder. Filmed as a silent, after production wrapped in December, 1928, Columbia decided to add sound. Since it was in the process of converting its stages to sound, it became necessary for the studio to rent the facilities of Al Christie's Metropolitan Studios to make the revisions, which included sound effects, dialogue sequences, and an orchestral score.[148]

Weakened by awkward dialogue, crude sound, and a certain disjointed quality (the result of the juxtaposition of both silent and sound sequences), the film was nevertheless memorable, thanks mainly to expert performances, and the intelligence of its director, young Frank Capra, who took a soap operatic storyline and crafted an effective morality tale. Its lesson—money does not always buy happiness—is hammered home powerfully in the final scenes in which Morris' heartbroken father dies, his mother leaves, and he is left dispirited and alone.

In his autobiography, *The Name Above the Title*, director Capra recalled the many difficulties he faced making his first sound picture, most having to do with the production of the sound sequences. He made no mention of tensions on the set, but they apparently existed. Cortez, whose personal problems were multiplying during the making of *The Younger Generation*, was distracted and irritable, and sometimes took it out on those around him, including fellow cast members. In her memoirs, entitled *Lina, DeMille's Godless Girl*, actress Lina Basquette (who portrayed Cortez's sister) said Ricardo was "rude, nasty, pompous, and everybody hated him." She described him as one of the first temperamental male stars.[149]

Did Ric Cortez dislike Miss Basquette as much as she disliked him? We will probably never know, as the discreet star never commented on the making of *The Younger Generation*, except to compliment its director. In an interview conducted for the Victor Scherle and William Turner Levy book, *The Films of Frank Capra* (1977), Cortez heaped praise on the famed director, stating " I thoroughly enjoyed working with Frank Capra; he is and was a warm, friendly man, and a very fine director. I never heard him raise his voice to anyone. He is an actor's director. We need more of his kind."[150]

Ricardo and Alma reconciled in October, 1928. Whatever caused their break-up was overcome temporarily by genuine affection, and by Ricardo's notions of responsibility to his wife and marriage. In early November they told the press they had "let bygones be bygones." Alma joined Ricardo and costar Buster Collier on a train bound for Louisiana where exteriors were to be filmed for the Tiffany-Stahl melodrama, *New Orleans*.[151] For a brief few days, Mr. and Mrs. Cortez appeared happy again as they toured the city, and enjoyed the famed Latin Quarter night spots. Little did they know it would be one of the last times they would enjoy each other's company. Alma was still using. Up until this time, she had somehow managed to hold her life together, albeit precariously, but the morphine was taking a toll on the fragile beauty and would soon take total control. All hell was about to break loose!

Alma's condition deteriorated markedly in mid-November, 1928. She had been asked by United Artists to add sound sequences to her supporting role in the World War I drama, *She Went to War*, originally shot as a silent. Alma had undoubtedly taken her daily shot, and was under the influence when she arrived on the United Artists lot for a meeting with U.A. president Joe Schenck on November 22, 1928. Two hours later, her chauffeur, and her personal maid were summoned to pick her up. While attempting to park outside of the U.A. lot, her driver accidentally collided with a parked vehicle. This led to a physical confrontation between Alma's maid, Edna Clayton, and the two women in the parked car. Eventually, the hubbub attracted the attention of studio employees, and Alma was summoned. According to published reports, the actress staggered out to the vehicle and verbally threatened both women in the parked car using abusive and profane language. Later, one of the women, Mrs. W.S. Schoelwer, filed a complaint, charging Alma's maid with battery, and Miss Clayton was arrested. In her affidavit, Schoelwer said when Alma arrived on the scene, the film actress was "extremely intoxicated," and threatened her with bodily harm. Alma posted her maid's bail and publicly declared herself innocent. "It is most amazing that they mentioned my name. I had nothing whatsoever to do with it . . ." she told reporters. She said both sides of the story would come out at the trial, and insisted her name had been dragged into the controversy because she was a famous motion picture star.[152]

News of the incident broke across the country. Perhaps in an effort to divert attention from the story, one week later, a smiling Alma posed for publicity photos alongside a Dodge coupe she'd supposedly purchased for her mother.[153] Before the dust settled, and the court case could be adjudicated, Mrs. Cortez was back in the news. On December 15, 1928, Alma filed a complaint with Los Angeles authorities alleging her apartment janitor had been "lurking outside her window."[154] Two weeks later, on January 1, 1929, her landlady and neighbors filed a formal complaint against Alma, charging her with disturbing the peace and peering into their windows at night with a flashlight. Among the complainants were actors LeRoy Mason and Rita Carewe. Once again, Alma denied the charges, threatening to hold "to strict accountability all persons making them."[155] In a January 3 court hearing, Alma pleaded not guilty, and a trial was set for mid-January. Mercifully, all three cases would eventually be dropped.

He was not directly involved in any of the above incidents, but clearly the publicity generated by his wife was not helpful to Ricardo, particularly at this critical time when he was struggling to make a comeback. While working on *The Younger Generation*, he hired a physician to follow his wife and report to him. When he wasn't working, both he and Alma's mother, Theresa, took turns accompanying her to the sets of *She Went to War* and *Show Boat* while she filmed sound sequences for each.[156] It was all for naught. To quote Alma, "I was slipping fast."

On January 25, 1929, Ricardo decided he must act. In consultation with doctors, he reserved a room in the Rosemead Sanitarium near Alhambra, and informed his wife she would have to go to a place where she could recuperate and rid herself of her addiction. There are several minor variations of what happened next, but apparently when Dr. E. W. Meyer and his assistant H. Barnett arrived to pick her up, Alma refused to go. Alma said Ricardo then lunged at her and they grappled "like a couple of frantic wrestlers," and she broke a tooth in the struggle.[157] Determined to commit suicide, Alma stuffed a paper knife in the sleeve of her fur coat before finally surrendering. As she was about to be loaded in the car, she suddenly broke free. For several blocks, crowds watched in amazement as the famous actress ran down Hollywood Boulevard screaming she was being kidnapped. Most thought she was making a movie. When the medical men caught up with her at last, Alma pulled out the knife, stabbed the doctor's assistant twice, and escaped. A short time later, after she was apprehended, she escaped from the vehicle and tried to hitch a ride with a passerby.[158] One version of the story says Cortez was then summoned. He called an ambulance and helped the medical crew subdue Alma and transport her to the sanitarium.[159] The official diagnosis: "complete nervous breakdown." In her autobiography, Alma blamed Ricardo for the entire episode. "Oh, if he had only been a little kind," she said. "I wanted to follow his wishes, but his manner irked me beyond measure."[160]

Beginning in 1928, Alma's morphine addiction began to take an increasing toll on the fragile beauty and those around her including her helpless husband.

ALMA REUBENS CREATES A BIG STREET SCENE

Leaps from Car Screaming En Route to Sanitarium; Stabs Doctor

HOLLYWOOD, Cal., Jan. 26.—(/P)— Alma Reubens, screen actress, was receiving treatment in a sanitarium near Alhambra, Cal., today after having attempted to escape a physician and his assistant by dashing through the crowds along Hollywood bolevard and later stabbing the assistant with a paper knife.

Needless to say the Hollywood press and headline writers across America had a field day, recounting every bizarre detail of the events of January 25. Luckily, the medical assistant was not severely injured in the melee, but if Ricardo had hoped Alma could somehow solve her problems before the media became fixated, it was too late. Alma remained at Rosemead for the next three weeks, during which she claimed one of her physicians, Dr. L. Jesse Citron (her chief drug supplier), visited her and administered a dose of morphine for a price. When she was released in February, Dr. Citron reportedly told her family she was cured. According to Alma, when she returned home, her grateful mother and husband greeted her at the door, all smiles. Alma said she was in no mood for congratulations. She proclaimed them fools. "I'm still an addict," she told them, "and now I'm going straight to hell." Upon hearing this, Ricardo walked out and did not return for days.[161]

Alma was right. She was far from cured. By mid-February, she was back in the hospital, the result of an infection she contracted after using a dirty needle. She created a ruckus in the hospital before being released in her mother's care. At her mother's ranch in Madera, she was visited by U. S. narcotics agents investigating Dr. Citron (famed in Hollywood as a "doctor to the stars") for prescribing drugs under fictitious names. Incredibly, it was only after the involvement of federal agents that news of Alma's drug use officially became public. On February 16, 1929, Alma's dark secret was finally revealed when her family formally announced Alma was, "fighting to reclaim herself from narcotic addiction." In a brief statement, Ricardo told reporters he had been unaware of Alma's addiction until the previous year. "I don't know how long Alma has been using narcotics," he said, "It has been only in the last few months that she has been so hysterical, that there could no longer be any doubt." [162] For his part, Dr. Citron denied the accusations of Alma and her family. "I did not know Miss Rubens was an addict when I took her case. Those prescriptions have been forged, by whom I do not know," he said. [163]

With Dr. Citron temporarily out of the picture, it became increasingly difficult for Alma to find dope suppliers. As her desperation mounted, she began relinquishing her remaining jewelry and most of her valuables to an ever more unscrupulous group of individuals willing to take advantage. Her family finally reached a point where they were simply unable to cope with her condition. A consultation was held with her doctors, who recommended her husband and mother commit Alma to the official care of the State of California so she could be admitted to the state Narcotics Hospital at Spadra. On Feburary 26, 1929, a special court session (attended by both Ricardo and Theresa) was held to make the arrangements. Since Spadra was an all-male facility, special permission had to be secured from the Governor of California so she could be admitted. Alma said this was accomplished through the intervention of one of her influential friends whom she did not name (more than likely, William Randolph Hearst). [164]

Alma spent roughly six weeks at Spadra, and proved a most uncooperative patient. She claimed she made at least two serious attempts to break out of the facility, the first of which landed her

ALMA RUBENS TO GO TO STATE INSTITUTION

Former Film Star Will Be Sent at the Discretion of Her Mother or Husband.

LOS ANGELES, Feb. 26 (*P*).—From the glitter of Hollywood's filmland, where she once reigned as a star Alma Rubens today will go to the Spadra State Hospital, a victim of the narcotic habit, as the result of complaints made by her husband and mother. She was under the care of physicians at her mother's home in Beverly Hills tonight and will be removed to the institution at the discretion of her husband or mother.

Judge McComb was called from a theatre to his court chamber by the mother, Mrs. Teresa Rubens and the actor husband, Ricardo Cortez. They asked that a warrant for the confinement of "Alma R. Cortez" be issued at once. Judge McComb complied, but refused to discuss the case. Earlier today a city official said she had already been sent to Spadra.

Miss Rubens left behind her a tangle of law suits and investigations. A Federal investigation is pending against Dr. L. Jesse Citron, alleged purveyor of narcotics to the actress; a threatened Federal investigation of the State Medical Board for alleged negligence in revoking licenses of physicians violating Federal narcotic laws hangs fire; a negro maid of the actress faces assault and battery charges, with Miss Rubens as an accomplice, for an alleged attack following an automobile collision, and Miss Rubens faces another action alleging disturbance of the peace in her Hollywood home for alleged "wild" parties.

In February, 1929, Ricardo and Theresa Rubens had Alma committed to the official care of the State of California, so she could be admitted to the State Narcotics Hospital at Spadra.

ALMA RUBENS SENT TO INSANE ASYLUM; HAD ATTACKED NURSE

Los Angeles, Cal., May 16.—[Special.]—After spending part of the day in the psychopathic ward at the general hospital, where she was quieted after a midnight outbreak at her mother's home, Alma Rubens, movie actress, was hurried today to the state hospital for the insane at Patton.

At the Hollywood home of Mrs. Theresa Rubens, her mother, the actress created an early morning uproar by a savage attack upon her nurse, armed with a knife. Miss Rubens also threatened to kill herself, her mother and others and fought deputy sheriffs who subdued her only after a struggle of ten minutes.

The actress was sent to Patton because of her status as a patient who violated parole from the state narcotics treatment hospital at Spadre, to which she was committed several months ago by Superior Judge Marshall McComb as a narcotic addict.

At Spadra she was placed under treatment for the drug habit, but was involved in some disturbing episodes and was later paroled to her mother and her husband, Ricardo Cortez, who removed her to a secluded place at Pomona, Cal.

Miss Rubens escaped from this place and then was taken to a private sanitarium in South Pasadena from which she was removed to her mother's home last week.

Last February Alma Rubens attacked a doctor with a knife on Hollywood boulevard.

In May, 1929, Alma's condition became so unmanageable, her desperate family had her committed to the Patton Insane Asylum where she remained for six months.

in solitary confinement. When she was paroled on April 14, the Superintendent of Spadra, Thomas Joyce told the press she had achieved "a marked improvement in her condition."[165] Alma was placed under a nurse's care in a Pomona sanitarium, and then sent home.

On May 16, 1929, while Alma was recuperating at home in Los Angeles, authorities were summoned by a distraught Theresa Rubens, who reported her daughter had tried to attack her nurse and was threatening suicide. When officers arrived, Alma, brandishing a butcher knife, kept them at bay for three hours, threatening to stab them if they approached. They eventually overpowered her, and transported her to a local hospital, where she was admitted to the psychopathic ward.[166] One day later, her desperate family had Alma committed to the Patton Insane Asylum, where she would remain for the next six months. Alma catalogued her experiences there in great detail. She described Patton as, "a city of the living dead," a snake pit of horror and misery. "I was just another animated ghost in the grim, grey, graveyard . . ." she said.[167]

If morphine addiction had left Alma one of "the living dead," her family was not much better off. Ricardo was emotionally drained by Alma's problems, bizarre behavior, and violent outbursts. He was mortified by the headlines she generated. He loved her, but couldn't help her. He could only watch as she destroyed herself. Over time, he came to realize he must watch from a distance, as he found it impossible to live with her this way. He rented an apartment not far from the Tiffany-Stahl studio and continued to work, but by the fall of 1929, he had become increasingly isolated and disheartened. Instead of reaching out to his family and friends who might have provided much needed advice and support, Ricardo retreated into himself.

The Ricardo Cortez career was in decline before Alma's problems became public, but the negative publicity was nonetheless devastating. Ricardo continued to feel he was being blackballed by Paramount, but Alma's headline making struggles made him virtually unemployable. He had never been a beloved figure in Hollywood, and now all who disliked and resented him seized the opportunity to circulate negative stories, blaming him for Alma's addiction, for deserting her in a time of crisis, and for sending her to the insane asylum. They pronounced his career over.

Ricardo tried his best to ignore all the rumors and press ahead. He managed to land a small fourth-billed part as a cowardly lothario in Metro's musical western, *Montana Moon* (1929), starring Joan Crawford, and the lead in an uninspiring talkie melodrama, *The*

Phantom in the House (1929), produced by the newly formed indie studio, Continental Pictures, but by the end of 1929, the phones stopped ringing. Even the B movie studios were not interested. To make matters worse, *The Orchid Dancer*, which Ricardo had made in France, and for which he'd accepted the U.S. distribution rights as salary, was not released in America. Exhibitors were no longer interested in showing silent pictures.[168] In October, 1929, yet another blow was delivered, when Cortez lost a considerable sum in the New York stock market crash. Just two short years ago, Ricardo had been on top of the world, certain he had established a firm foundation for personal happiness and professional success. Now his entire life was in shambles.

CHAPTER FIVE
ENDINGS AND BEGINNINGS (1930–31)

"I could not bear looking on and watching her deliberately destroying herself."

— RICARDO CORTEZ
(SPEAKING ABOUT HIS WIFE, ALMA RUBENS)

The beginning of the new decade found Ricardo Cortez facing an uncertain future. Alone, dispirited, and unemployed, multiple reports suggested he was on the verge of a nervous breakdown. With bills mounting and no job offers on the horizon, Ricardo knew he would soon have to make another life-altering decision. He loved being an actor and making motion pictures more than anything, but he had made a promise to himself during the hungry years in New York and Hollywood that he would never be poor and needy again.

This snippet from the 1930 issue of the *Hammond Calumt City Times* (Indiana), notes Cortez's precarious mental state as a result of his personal and professional challenges.

> **EXTRA!**
>
> (BULLETIN)
> HOLLYWOOD, Cal., Feb. 16.—
> (I.N.S.)—Ricardo Cortez, film actor and husband of Alma Rubens, today was reported on the verge of a breakdown as the result of the disclosure of the plight of his beautiful actress wife, who is in a hospital struggling to liberate herself from narcotic addiction.
> Miss Rubens' mother, Mrs. Theresa Rubens, also was said to be on the brink of a nervous collapse.

Such decisions were being made across Hollywood. Ricardo's situation was extreme, but his professional woes were not unique. With the coming of sound, many formally prominent silent film stars found themselves unemployed. Some opted to give up their careers; others made due taking whatever acting work they could find. One of the avenues the latter group utilized was vaudeville. By the late 1920's, the popularity of vaudeville was rapidly waning, but in 1927 and 1928, several formally popular silent film actors, including Tom Mix, Ralph Graves, Snub Pollard, Agnes Ayres, and Claire Windsor, signed to do vaudeville tours in hopes of resurrecting their flagging careers, and proving they had the vocal chops to remain relevant in motion pictures.[169] While filming *Midstream*, Ricardo's friend and costar Miss Windsor suggested he consider giving vaudeville a try. He initially ignored the suggestion, but as his options became increasingly limited, vaudeville (which was considered by some to be the last resort for washed up actors) became more and more viable.

In November, 1929, Ricardo contacted the newly formed Radio-Keith-Orpheum company (soon to be known simply as RKO) with an idea he had for a vaudeville tour. He would perform the lead role in Edwin Burke's melodramatic playlet, *Wanted*, about two brothers who end up on opposite sides of the law. The company was enthusiastic, and by the end of the month, Ricardo had signed a contract and was in rehearsals.

After a consultation of her doctors, in November, 1929, Alma Rubens was released from Patton Insane Asylum. Early Jensen, Director of State Institutions; Superintendent G.M. Webster of Patton; and Thomas Joyce of Spadra, all pronounced her completely cured.[170] She was released into the custody of her mother, who took her to the family ranch to recuperate. Alma recalled the day of her release as "the happiest I shall ever experience." She said the only thing missing was her husband's presence. "Dear Ric. How I loved him. Even though he had sent me but two crisp notes and a picture post card throughout the eight torturous months I had endured while in 'The Crazy House.'"[171] At the ranch, she claimed she sent him letters and left a phone message, which were unanswered. In her version of events, she made no mention of the fact her husband was in the final days of rehearsals for the vaudeville tour that would help pay the bills accrued during her hospital stays.

Was Ricardo a neglectful, uncaring husband, guilty of abandoning his wife in her hour of need, in order to rid himself of the taint of her scandal, or a devoted spouse trying to pay the bills she was racking up? The truth will probably never be entirely known. All the public had was Alma's version; for the most part Ricardo remained silent.

Certainly Hollywood did not abandon its errant daughter. Unlike many others whose scandalous, self-destructive behavior grabbed headlines, Alma received a rapturous embrace from colleagues upon her return to the film capital in January, 1930. Several articles reported visits from friends like Marion Davies and Marion's sister, Reine, and mountains of letters welcoming her back. Even the notoriously tough Hollywood press got into the act, publishing articles describing how lovely and healthy Alma looked, and forecasting a bright future. In late January, she was invited to perform a short play at the Writer's Guild. Newspaper columns and stories indicated the event was well attended, and her performance well received.[172]

In February, Alma decided to go to New York to see her husband. By then, Ricardo had commenced his multi-week vaudeville tour, which began at New York's 58th Street Theatre, followed by performances in New Jersey, Connecticut, Massachusetts, and Rhode Island, then back to New York. Radio-Keith-Orpheum gave the actor considerable freedom over the appearances. He not only selected the playlet (staged by Robert Glecker), but had a choice of supporting casts. In interviews published during the early 1930's, Ricardo admitted being petrified prior to his initial appearances in New York. He'd had a bit of stage experience in his youth, but had never been a headliner, and wasn't sure he was up to the task. All his insecurities were fully exposed on the tour, including his self-consciousness, his unease with exposing weakness and vulnerability, and his phobic reaction to being touched or grabbed by fans and admirers. It is a testament to his iron will and work ethic, that he not only embarked on the tour, but finished his bookings, meeting all expectations.[173]

Alma arrived in New York in mid-February, 1930. Ricardo greeted her at the train station. She had high hopes for their reunion, but recalled it as uncomfortable. Ricardo smiled sweetly and posed admiringly for the inevitable press photos, but according to Alma, he treated her coldly when the cameras were gone. She said,

After her release from **Patton Insane Asylum**, Alma visited Ricardo in **New York** where he was beginning a multi-city East Coast vaudeville tour.

"The moment I was alone with my husband I knew that everything was over between us. He had nothing to say to me, except what he would have said to a stranger. He was playing at a Broadway Theatre and he asked that I come and sit in a box, and see the performance . . . We had decided to 'put up a front' for the sake of the business, but we were never happy together for one minute again."[174]

Alma apparently assumed nothing had changed during the months she endured the horrors of Patton, and now that she was sober, all the pain and humiliation she had inflicted on her husband would magically be forgiven and forgotten. Her actions had consequences, however, and things *had* changed. Rightly or wrongly, Ricardo couldn't forget. In her autobiography, a hurt and angry Alma lashed out at Ricardo, consistently presenting him in an unflattering light as cold, calculating, and self-serving. Many would attest he could be all those things from time to time, but he could also be kind and thoughtful. Certainly, he attempted to be kind and helpful to Alma. For instance, she conveniently made no mention of the fact Ricardo was instrumental in helping her obtain a contract with Radio-Keith-Orpheum for an 18-week vaudeville tour that she hoped would help reestablish her acting career, and it was Ricardo who was undoubtedly responsible for arranging the screen test she was given by Tiffany-Stahl studio during the spring of 1930.[175]

When Ricardo departed New York for the next stops on his tour, he and Alma bid each other adieu. Unlike many of their goodbyes, this one was polite, cool, and passion-less; a goodbye that might have been exchanged by casual friends, not the loving farewell of a husband and wife. Two months later, Ricardo met Alma in Chicago where she was performing her vaudeville act. There, she angrily informed him she intended to file papers for a legal separation and demanded a $75,000 settlement for their joint holdings on the West Coast. She later told the press he disappeared before the final settlement details could be arranged.[176] After the Chicago meeting, Ricardo was only mentioned a few more times in Alma's autobiography, but apparently, they remained in touch. In 1932, he told a reporter he and Alma planned to meet in person again later in the year to iron out details of their final break-up, but the meeting never took place.

In spite of his trepidations, Ricardo's vaudeville tour was a success. His appearances were well attended and enthusiastically received. His choice of the dramatic playlet, *Wanted*, proved inspired. The story of a criminal (Cortez) who attempts to atone for his crimes by committing suicide after he is captured by his policeman brother; it had great dramatic power, providing a superb showcase for Ricardo's acting and vocal abilities. Critics were uniformly positive. The *Providence Journal* called the playlet "powerful and fast moving."[177] The *Boston Globe* characterized it as "thrilling . . . Cortez succeeds admirably."[178]

The demands of the tour made Cortez extremely uncomfortable. In articles published in Boston, Providence, and New York, interviewers tried in vain to penetrate the façade of the ever-smiling, sophisticated, composed Mr. Cortez, but he had become skilled at avoiding their questions, often manipulating interviews to discuss other things like literature and sports. Once in a while, his dedicated attempts to avoid talking about himself, or sharing details of his private life were illuminating. One article published in the *Boston Post* during the tour in early March, was particularly revealing. Although the author, Grace Davidson, portrayed Ricardo as "pleasant, affable, suave, and more than gracious," she also described him as "very reticent and difficult to interview . . . ." She said "His manner is very serious and even when he laughs or smiles, it is always with a note of restraint." She documented an incident which perfectly illustrated this astute observation. She said on the day of the interview, a crowd of young women gathered around the stage entrance to meet the actor. A press agent forced Cortez to greet them and pose for a picture with them. When one girl hid behind him so she could put her arms around him, Davidson said "he looked so distressed and uncomfortable that the press agent asked the girl, who could have been no more than 15, to desist . . . ."[179]

The RKO company was extremely pleased with Ricardo's work. When he arrived back in New York to play the legendary *Palace Theatre* in March, 1930, they presented him with a scrapbook of his appearances which included photos, letters, press clippings, and reviews. Cortez was gratified by the tour and kept the scrapbook as a treasured memento, a symbol of his triumph over fear, but by the time he completed the run in late March, he was worn out and extremely discouraged. He was proud of his vaudeville work, but hated the grueling schedule and the expectations placed on him. Worst of all, his successful tour did not immediately impact his movie career as he'd hoped. There were no job offers waiting for him at the end of the run. "It wasn't until the New Yorkers had been imported, and the studios had discovered that after all, it was pictures and not plays that were being made, that we of the silents were given a hearing," he told columnist Wood Soanes in 1932.[180]

This ad from Ricardo's vaudeville tour was one of many clippings found in a scrapbook presented to him by the Radio-Keith-Orpheum company at the end of the run.

This fascinating article dated March 3, 1930, (found in Ricardo's vaudeville scrapbook) notes Cortez's reluctance to talk about himself and his private life, and his discomfiture dealing with fans.

RADIO-KEITH-ORPHEUM-CORPORATION
EXECUTIVE OFFICES
1560-1564 BROADWAY   NEW YORK

E. F. ALBEE THEATRE
(R. K. O. RHODE ISLAND CORPORATION)

PROVIDENCE
RHODE ISLAND

OFFICE OF RESIDENT MANAGER

THESE ARE THE PEOPLE YOU MET AT A DINNER HELD IN YOUR
HONOR IN THE BILTMORE HOTEL

    Mayor James E. Dunne of Providence
    Foster Lardner, Manager of the RKO Albee Theatre
    William Brown, Secretary to Providence Mayor
    Charles Reed Jones, Novelist
    "Suds" Abbott, Announcer at Station WJAR
    Jack Sullivan, Dramatic Editor News-Tribune
    Alfred Marcello, Local Newspaper man and Variety correspondent
    Garret Byrnes, Movie Critic Evening Bulletin
    Chet Worthington, Movie Cirtic Providence Journal
    Guy Langley, Dramatic Editor Pawtucket Times

THE FOLLOWING PEOPLE DROPPED IN AFTER THE DINNER:

    Edward Fitzgerald, Radio Editor, News-Tribune
    Gene Bresson, Radio Corporation of America
    Larry Healy, owner of Healy's Hotel
    Harry Storin, Manager of the Victory Theatre

                                                                          Dick Farrell

This letter found in Cortez's vaudeville scrapbook describes a dinner held in his honor at the Biltmore Theatre in Providence, Rhode Island.

RKO attempted to re-sign him for a new tour, but Ricardo resisted. He had only done vaudeville to prove to movie producers he was marketable, and it apparently had not worked. Exhausted, his marriage crumbling, his career in ruins, for the first time in his life, Ricardo sank into a deep depression. Years later, he described the period immediately following his vaudeville tour as the low point of his life. He said he contemplated suicide.[181] His concerned family urged him to get away from Hollywood and New York, and get some rest. On April 18, he spent a portion of the money he made on the tour and headed for Europe aboard the *Ile de France*. In France, he rented a cottage outside Paris, seeking refuge from the crowds, the grasping fans, the prying eyes of the press, and his angry wife; a place where he could be alone, sort his thoughts and read. He informed his brother Stanley of his whereabouts, but remained essentially incognito for the next two months.[182]

Sadly, there was no permanent escape from his problems. In May, 1930, Stanley informed him Alma had filed papers for a legal separation, charging him with desertion.[183] By June, a defeated, despairing Ricardo returned home to face the music. He would give up acting and attempt to find work elsewhere. Once again, in his desperate hour of need, the fates would be kind to Ricardo Cortez. Waiting in his mailbox in New York was a personal and professional lifeline, and it came to him via an evil, dagger-wielding pimp, named Johnnie.

"BEEN LOOKING ALL OVER FOR YOU. HAVE GOOD SPOT IN PICTURE TITLED 'HER MAN' WITH TWELVETREES. WIRE ME IMMEDIATELY. SIGNED: CHARLES ROGERS"

Arriving back in New York on June 1, 1930, Ricardo found the above cable, dated May 26.[184] Overjoyed, but fearful the part might already be cast, Ricardo immediately contacted Rogers, Pathe's head of production, who gave him the good news—the part was still available. The studio had been holding it for him based on the success of his vaudeville tour, but time was of the essence and filming was about to commence. He would have to come to Hollywood immediately if he wanted the part. Uncharacteristically, Cortez didn't bother to inquire all the details of the role, negotiate his salary, etc., before accepting and boarding a train for the West Coast. During the trip, he received a copy of the script. For the first time in months, he saw a glimmer of hope. In a public pronouncement, Cortez declared "It's a privilege to be given a screen role offering such colorful possibilities as that of Johnnie in *Her Man*."[185] He later admitted "The moment I set eyes on the story of *Her Man*, I knew my day had come. Here was the kind of stuff I'd wanted to play all along. . ."[186]

Described by Pathe as "a dynamic underworld drama," *Her Man* was based on the classic American ballad, "Frankie and Johnnie." Set in a seedy waterfront nightclub in Havana, it related the tale of a young prostitute, Frankie (Helen Twelvetrees), whose unhappy, hopeless life is brightened when she meets a young sailor (Phillips Holmes) who promises to take her away. Complications arise when her lover and pimp, a murderer named Johnnie (Cortez), objects, and becomes determined to eliminate his competition.

Pathe assembled a talented group of actors and filmmakers to breathe life into the story. An interesting mix of newcomers and old pros, the cast included such veterans as Cortez, James Gleason, Harry Sweet, Stanley Fields, and stage star Marjorie Rambeau, opposite young up and comers Helen Twelvetrees, Phillips Holmes, and Thelma Todd. To direct came 36-year-old Tay Garnett, who'd only recently begun helming motion pictures after stints as a scenarist and gag writer for Mack Sennett and Hal Roach.

Both the subject matter and setting presented problems for Pathe before and after the film was released. Censors, represented by the Studio Relations Committee headed by Colonel Jason S. Joy, demanded several changes to the Tay Garnett and Howard Higgin script before filming could begin.[187] Among other things, they objected to the heroine's prostitution, the violence, and the excessive drinking to be depicted. While Pathe (currently a separate entity under the umbrella of the new RKO company), ignored many of their demands, records indicate the studio did tone down some of the sexuality and violence in the script prior to production.[188]

Shooting began on the RKO/Pathe lot in late June, 1930. By the time Cortez reported for work, director Garnett and photographer Eddie Snyder had been in Cuba where they'd filmed exterior "process" shots including the famed Morro Castle. The cast and crew worked well together and production proceeded on schedule. Everyone appeared aware of the significance of the project and its potential impact on their professional livelihoods, and went the extra mile to make it the best it could be. Cortez was particularly dedicated, knowing the movie constituted perhaps his last shot at resurrecting his career. "When I was working on *Her Man*, they had to shoo me home at night . . ." he told *Modern Screen*.[189]

The group effort paid off. Garnett, who would later make his mark helming such memorable motion pictures as *One Way Passage* (1932), *China Seas* (1935), *Slave Ship* (1937), and *The Postman Always Rings Twice* (1946), crafted a minor classic in *Her Man*. An effective blend of skillful narrative and colorful action with major doses of comedy and pathos; it was 83 minutes of top-notch entertainment. Garnett's imaginative use of the camera and his emphasis on movement were impressive. Of particular note was the concluding fight scene (between Holmes and Cortez)—a five-minute, no holds barred free-for-all which, in 1930, was considered the most thrilling ever filmed.

The performances were another of the film's major assets. Thanks to persuasive acting, both Twelvetrees and Holmes scored their first major hit, which propelled their careers. Rambeau, Gleason, and Todd also registered in lesser parts. Third-billed Ricardo was a revelation as Johnnie. Although essentially a despicable character, Cortez somehow managed to infuse Johnnie with enough charm and charisma to make him both fascinating and believable. Even before filming wrapped, news of his convincing performance was making the rounds of Hollywood studios. By August, both Warner Bros. and Columbia had signed him for new pictures.

Released in September, *Her Man* was a critical and box office hit. *The Film Daily* declared, "Pathe has an honest to goodness lulu in this corking melodrama." According to *The New York Daily News*, the picture inspired an enthusiastic response from filmgoers. "A crashing finish reaches the top mark in film thrills. The audience simply had to shout and yell to ease tension."[190] In her book, *Joseph P. Kennedy Presents: The Hollywood Years*, author Cari Beauchamp reported ticket sales totaling more than $800,000, which was enormous money in 1930 dollars.[191]

Not everyone was entertained, though. The film continued to spark controversy in small towns and rural areas where local censor boards and citizen groups objected to multiple aspects of it. Another brouhaha erupted when the Cuban government lodged a complaint, citing the movie's negative depiction of Havana. Pathe attempted to address the concerns by changing the film's setting in their advertising (to Paris), but did not alter the finished movie.[192]

As big city dwellers and small townspeople across the country argued the virtues of *Her Man*, for Ricardo Cortez, there was no

Cortez had decided to give up acting, when out of the blue came an offer from RKO of an important role (as a pimp named, Johnnie) in director Tay Garnett's crime drama, *Her Man*, costarring young Helen Twelvetrees.

debate. Like a shot of adrenalin administered to a dying patient, the film literally resuscitated his acting career as it gasped its last breath. The movie would be a benchmark for the actor in two important respects. It proved once and for all he had a speaking voice filmgoers responded to, and, it marked the beginning of a new phase of his career. His acclaimed portrayal of the morally corrupt Johnnie proved a prototype for the villains Cortez would often play during the 1930's. Like Johnnie, many of the characters Ricardo portrayed were slick, charismatic dandies, whose easy smile and soft voice masked corruption and treachery.

While Ricardo was basking in the applause generated by his performance in *Her Man*, fielding offers from a variety of studios and studying his lines for a new picture he was about to begin for Warner Bros., entitled *Illicit*, his estranged wife was preparing to rain on his parade. Sometime in the summer, during her grueling multi-week, cross-country vaudeville tour in which she did impressions and sang songs accompanying herself on a ukulele, an exhausted Alma began using drugs again. Earlier in the year, she had granted several interviews in which she recounted the trials and tribulations she endured as a result of her drug usage, and proclaimed herself cured. She said she'd been given a new chance and intended to make the most of it, but apparently the lure of morphine was just too strong. In her autobiography, she placed much of the blame for her relapse on her suppliers.

"My imitations were a great success, but when I got back to New York flushed with my triumphs, I met another well-known and highly-respected doctor. And in no time at all he had me trapped into dope—again!... Love cults, devil worship, drug madness—I got to know them all. That was how I stayed 'cured.'" [193]

By mid-September, 1930, Alma was telling intimates she would soon initiate the process to end her marriage. On September 23, 1930, just two days after the official nationwide release of *Her Man*, she forwarded a petition of divorce to Los Angeles, charging her husband with desertion. She told the press the real reason she was seeking the divorce, however, was her husband's behavior after her release from Patton. She said Ricardo adopted a "hero pose," taking too much credit for her rehabilitation. "It was my own battle," the actress declared. "My husband contributed very little toward helping me. Most of the money came from women friends." She said Ricardo maintained the pose strictly for publicity. She asked for attorney and court fees, and a $50,000 settlement.[194]

Her husband did not respond, but the publicity was potentially damaging. Just as Ricardo was beginning to emerge from past disasters, Alma's controversies and his personal character were again placed under the microscope. During the autumn of 1930, portraits of the troubled Cortezes adorned front pages across the country. Several newspapers and magazines ran in-depth stories rehashing all the scandals and presenting various versions of events. In early October, *The Nevada State Journal* published a long story entitled, "Alma's Suit Puts Cortez in Strange Enigma Role." In it, they speculated, "Is he (Cortez) the world's most underappreciated husband, or just another 'sheik' lover?" Later in the piece they described Ricardo as "the most criticized and praised, pitied and misconstrued screen star," and called differing versions of events "a game of pitch and toss in the arena of public opinion."[195]

Film fans took sides in the marital dispute. Both camps had dedicated partisans, but if it was Alma's intent to derail her husband's comeback and sabotage his career for good, she would fail. Luckily for Ricardo, he now had the enormous success of *Her Man* on his resume, and the studios, who might have paid attention to the negative publicity months ago, now elected to ignore Alma's contentions. On October 13, 1930, RKO production head William LeBaron announced the company had signed Ricardo to a term contract at a starting salary of $1,250 a week.[196]

Alma planned her own big time comeback. In early October, 1930, *The New York Times* reported she would take over the role originated by Edith Broder in the drama, *With Privileges*, playing at the Belmont Theatre on Broadway. Alma had long wanted to play on the Broadway stage, and the role of Rachel, a tragic young girl who commits suicide when she is jilted by her lover, was right up her alley. She took over the part as planned on October 13, but apparently, things did not go well, and the play closed nine days later on October 22.[197] An effort was then made to take it to Paterson, New Jersey, on October 27, but it, too, failed. There were rumors of Alma's erratic behavior and "temperament issues," but a *Syracuse Herald* article cited poor ticket sales as the reason for the closure.[198] According to Alma, she also received an offer of a role in a stage adaptation of D.E. Lawrence's novel, *Lady Chatterley's Lover*, at this time, but was unable to do the part because she couldn't remember her lines. The version of the play was never produced.

Unfortunately, Alma's descent into drugs (which now included cocaine and heroin) progressed after the closure of *With Privileges*. "I lived in a world peopled with ghosts. Parties, parties, parties, orgie, orgie, orgie—a few hours of sanity and then down into the dirt and slime of degradation again . . ." she said. She recalled the drug parties she attended, populated with wealthy, respectable-looking abusers who lost all inhibitions when under the influence. Alma detailed her relationship with one of them, a rich, older married man, fellow drug addict named, "Mr. Dee" with whom she became romantically entangled until his wife put an end to the affair.[199]

Alma admitted to squandering a fortune and sacrificing many of her prized possessions in her continuing quest to get, and remain, high. In late autumn, 1930, with her money rapidly dwindling and her functioning level deteriorating, she arranged with *The New York Daily Mirror* to sell her life story. Alma had been keeping notes on her life experiences for years, and planned to write an autobiography to be titled, *This Bright Road Again*. Her immediate financial needs now forced her to make the new arrangement. She claimed there were two main motivations for publishing her life story:

"The first is I hope that reading them may guide some—even one— poor unfortunate away from the dark cavern where King Dope has set his trap. The other reason is to earn money . . . Except for the money my mother has invested for me and which she will not turn over to me, for fear I'll squander it, as no doubt I would—I am absolutely broke." [200]

According to her biographers, Rhodes and Webb, Alma likely dictated the contents of *This Bright Road Again* to an unknown writer (at the *Daily Mirror* or elsewhere) who converted the material into a serial.[201] The publication date was set for January, 1931. How much she was paid is unknown, but apparently it was enough to purchase a ticket to the West Coast. When Ricardo learned of the eminent publication of his estranged wife's autobiography, it could not have made him happy. Given their recent acrimony, he knew she would not paint a positive portrait of him.

Alma returned to California in December. Her immediate need for money undoubtedly precipitated the December 7 property settlement agreement she reached with her husband, in which Ricardo agreed to pay legal and court fees, and give Alma $35,000 as her portion of the Wilton Avenue property and other joint holdings.[202] She had contacted him immediately after her arrival in Hollywood to set up a meeting and work out final details, but he was making a film, so the agreement was settled via telephone. Ricardo recalled the circumstances in a 1931 interview.

"I didn't know what was really happening in New York—that Alma had begun using drugs again," he told an interviewer in 1931. *"I was working hard, and didn't know she was coming back to Hollywood until she telephoned me she was here. I was in the midst of a picture. You know what that means. I explained the situation and urged her to go to her ranch for a rest. When she returned we could see each other. . ."* [204]

Alma did not heed Ricardo's advice. On January 5, 1931, she and a companion were arrested while staying at the U.S. Grant Hotel in San Diego, charged with possession of 100+ grams of narcotics. Alma, her friend, former chorine, Ruth Palmer (who'd been her roommate in New York prior to accompanying her to Los Angeles), and chauffeur Edward Tholman, had just returned from a three-day stay in Agua Caliente, Mexico, financed by funds from the Cortez divorce settlement. During the motor car trip back, Alma and Miss Palmer had an altercation and the police were summoned. Palmer charged Alma with assault, and Alma claimed her chauffeur stole an $8,000 brooch. When police investigated, they not only found the brooch (still attached to one of Alma's dresses), but 40 tubes of morphine sewn into the lining of one of her evening gowns, and a small amount in her purse. Alma, Miss Palmer, and Mr. Tholman were then charged. After a night in jail and arraignment on counts of smuggling, conspiracy to smuggle, and unlawful possession of narcotics, Alma was freed on $5,000 bail (believed to have been provided by her friend Marion Davies).[204] Sobbing hysterically but defiant, she maintained her innocence. "I've been framed!" she claimed. "They haven't given me a chance. I'm making a hard fight, but if the newspapers, the public, and officers won't give me a square deal, what can I do? I'm not taking drugs and never shall. I'm off the hop for good . . ."[205]

On January 13 (ironically the same day as *The New York Daily Mirror* published the first installment of her autobiography), Alma was bound over to the federal grand jury to face investigation on the charge she violated narcotics laws by possessing more than an ounce of morphine. During the initial court proceeding, Commissioner Henry C. Ryan dismissed the conspiracy charges against her, Palmer, and Tholman for lack of evidence, but the other charges remained.[206]

After steadfastly maintaining her innocence, vowing to fight the charges, and supplying investigators with several doctors' statements proclaiming her clean and cured, Alma returned to Los Angeles. During her night in jail, she'd caught a bad cold. Her prolonged drug usage had severely compromised her immune system, and the cold quickly progressed to pneumonia. Fearing she was too ill to be placed in a hospital, she was moved to the home of one of her physicians, Dr. Charles F. Phleuger, where she lapsed into a coma.

On January 21, Theresa Rubens issued a statement informing the public of her daughter's dire health status. "Alma's condition is extremely critical. She is receiving the best of medical aid but we know she is waging an uphill battle against great odds."[207]

The "best medical aid" was not enough. On January 22, 1931, at 7:25 p.m., surrounded by her mother, Theresa, sister, Hazel, a few friends, doctors, attending nurse, and Ricardo's brother, Stanley (who'd been called in), 33-year-old Alma Rubens died peacefully. Her estranged husband was not present.[208] A few hours before Alma's death, Ricardo had issued a statement, telling the press he had just learned of her illness. "I knew nothing about Miss Rubens being ill of pneumonia," he said. "The family did not inform me. I have not seen Miss Rubens in months."[209] His claim not to have been notified of Alma's illness would soon become a source of great controversy, one that would impact Ricardo's reputation and those who defended him.

Whether he was aware of her illness or not, Alma's unexpected death hit Ricardo hard. Although their marriage had been traumatic and unhappy, and Alma had all but declared war on him in recent months, she had been his first true love, and her passing was a great shock. In the early morning hours of January 23, a stunned, shaken Ricardo rushed to the Gates, Crane, and Smith Funeral Home on Highland Avenue in hopes of having a few moments alone with Alma before the rush of visitors arrived. He was turned away. He would not be allowed to see her until regular visiting hours, the latest salvo in the ongoing conflict between him and his in-laws.[210]

After visiting hours began, Ricardo lead the mourners who filed past the casket. Multiple celebrities were spotted among the roughly 2,000 people who paid their last respects to the screen beauty. Several fans became hysterical. One woman created a scene inside the funeral home when she shrieked "She's breathing! I saw her breathe!"[211] Various published reports indicated Marion Davies and her sisters helped the Rubens family arrange a Christian Science funeral service held at the Little Church of the Flowers, located in Forest Lawn Cemetery in Glendale, on January 24. A loudspeaker system was installed outside the chapel so fans could hear the service. Burial was the next day in a mausoleum in the Ararat Cemetery in Fresno.

Alma Rubens, Movie Star, Dies Suddenly

(Picture on back page.)

Los Angeles, Cal., Jan. 21.—[Special.]—Alma Rubens, not so long ago a starred beauty of the films, died tonight of pneumonia. It was the aftermath of a three year battle against addiction to the use of narcotics. She had been gravely ill for days and in a coma for many hours.

Death came to the brunette beauty of the screen at the home of friends. At the bedside were her mother, a sister, Mrs. Alma Lerch, and a few friends.

Drs. Carl J. Pflueger and Carl Conn gave typhoid asthenic pneumonia as the cause of death.

Cortez Is Not Present.

Ricardo Cortez, film actor and husband of Miss Rubens, was not present when she died. They had separated months ago in New York after Miss Rubens had returned there after dismissal as a narcotics addict from the Patton Asylum for the Insane in California and it had been announced that a suit for divorce would be filed.

"I know nothing about Miss Rubens being ill of pneumonia," Cortez said earlier in the evening. "The family did not inform me. I have not seen Miss Rubens for months."

FUNERAL RITES FOR ALMA RUBENS WILL BE HELD TOMORROW

Hollywood, Cal., Jan. 22.—[Special.]—Ricardo Cortez, estranged husband of Alma Rubens, was among the first at the undertaking parlor on North Highland avenue, Hollywood, this morning, when the body of the dead actress was removed following her death of pneumonia at the home of friends last night.

Cortez was not permitted to view the body of his wife, who recently had talked of divorcing him, until the casket had been prepared. He left a basket of American Beauty roses. Baskets, blankets and bouquets of flowers followed Cortez's offering in profusion.

Arrangements for the funeral were announced by Mrs. Hazel Large of Madera, Cal., sister of Miss Rubens.

Miss Rubens' body is to lie in state from 8 o'clock Friday morning until 11 o'clock Saturday in Hollywood.

Funeral services by a Christian Science reader are to be held in the Little Church of the Flowers, in the suburb of Glendale, at 1 o'clock Saturday afternoon. The church holds only 250 persons, so arrangements were made today to have loud speakers installed outside. The casket will then be taken to Fresno, Cal., where it will be placed in a mausoleum Monday.

Miss Rubens' sister stated today that some reports of the actress' parentage were incorrect. Her mother was Irish and her father Alsatian, Mrs. Large said.

Alma's sudden death on January 22, 1931, shocked Hollywood and movie lovers around the world. This was the headline from *The Chicago Daily Tribune*.

The headlines and controversies surrounding Alma Rubens did not end with her death. Even her funeral, noted here by *The Chicago Daily Tribune*, became a source of dispute, ending in a sensational 1932 libel trial against the *Photoplay* magazine, in which Cortez would be one of the star witnesses.

Accounts of Alma's funeral service varied, and those variations sparked more controversy. The majority of press reports listed attendance inside the small chapel at approximately 50 people, including the Davies (Douras) sisters (Marion, Reine, and Ethel), Claire Windsor, and the Cortez brothers. Notably, Stanley arrived with the Rubens family, and Ricardo alone in a separate automobile.[212] Not all the accounts agreed, however. In his monthly "Hollywood Goings On" column in the April, 1931 issue of *Photoplay*, noted gossip reporter Cal York chastised the Rubens family for not informing Ricardo of Alma's condition, and claimed there was practically no one at her funeral service. "To me it was one of the most pathetic things I ever heard of," he said.[213] The Rubens family was outraged. A few months later, Theresa Rubens filed a million-dollar lawsuit against the *Photoplay* publishing company, alleging it made several false claims regarding the circumstances of Alma's death and funeral. Ricardo would eventually be called as one of the prime witnesses.[214]

Alma's untimely death provided more dramatic fodder for the disputes between her fans and those of Ricardo. Her admirers seized the opportunity to blame him and her doctors for her demise. The Ric Cortez camp insisted Alma was the captain of her fate and had blown a second chance at life and a career.

As he gazed at his beautiful Alma lying lifeless, gone too soon, a complex set of conflicting emotions must have flooded Ricardo. Like Valentino, Alma would cast a very long shadow over him after her physical death. Her legacy reached into every aspect of his life and career, both for good and for ill. On the positive side, his love affair and stormy six-year union with Alma had taught him many important things like tolerance, compassion, perseverance, and courage. He had grown up. While her addiction and associated scandals had caused him considerable pain and embarrassment, which became so acute he contemplated suicide, ultimately the experience made him stronger, more resilient. If he could weather this adversity and humiliation, perhaps he could get through anything by working hard and never giving up. The negative aspects of the relationship also had a lasting impact, leaving permanent scars.

Ricardo had idolized and trusted Alma, and whether under the influence or not, she had betrayed and belittled him both publicly and privately. When he was somehow able to revitalize his career, she attempted to sabotage his comeback by charging him with lying about his part in her rehabilitation. Ricardo had always had trust issues, and Alma's actions reinforced them. Then, of course, there was Alma's autobiography—published in weekly installments during 1931. Like Alma herself, her version of events was controversial, a mixed bag of courage, wit, and charm, combined with irresponsibility, and no small amount of self-pity and revenge. It was likely embellished considerably by one or more cowriters, but as a documentation of the horrors and degradation of drug abuse, particularly among wealthy elites, it was powerfully persuasive and immensely valuable. It took genuine courage to expose one's private life to such scrutiny, and one would have to have a heart of stone not to be incredibly moved by the torture Alma endured.

Still, for Ricardo, his fans, and others (including many historians and writers who examined the text), there were problems with her memoirs. As a historical document, it left a lot to be desired. There was relatively little coverage of her career, and few dates. Also, the sequence of events depicted did not always match up with the historical record. Toward the end of her story, there's a preoccupation with the drug culture, which borders on glamourizing the orgies, self-indulgence, and debauchery she witnessed and participated in.

To Ricardo, perhaps the cruelest, most unfair thing Alma attempted to do in her version of events was point the finger of blame at him for her drug abuse. She said:

> "I was quite willing to retire. He was making sufficient money to support us in regal style and I really wanted a home, a real home, which I wanted to take care of myself, and which, if I had gotten it, might have so occupied my time that I might have forgotten about my daily shot. Ric would have none of this. He went out every night, going to his club here or there and never offering to take me along. Things went along this way for months, during which my craving for the drugs grew stronger and stronger..."[215]

Ricardo rightly sensed it would do no good to refute Alma's contentions; to essentially argue with a dead woman. It was best to keep silent. Whether intentional or not, Alma's experiences and untimely death had taught him an invaluable life lesson. She'd been given a second shot at life and a career, and had not seized it. Thanks to RKO and *Her Man*, Ricardo, too, had a second chance, and he was determined to make the most of it.

CHAPTER SIX
UP FROM THE ASHES (1931–32)

"I am a Jew... I am as tired as anyone of the sham. For nearly ten years I have been a man without a country—without a race—without a history..."
— RICARDO CORTEZ

In his Pulitzer Prize-winning novel, *The Road*, author Cormac McCarthy made a simple, yet profound comment about resilience and rebirth. He said, "All things of grace and beauty, such that one holds them to one's heart, have a common provenance in pain. Their birth in grief and ashes." Although written in 2006, over seven decades after the period in question, certainly those universal words of wisdom could have been written to describe the life of Ricardo Cortez during the years 1931 and 1932.

In the early months of 1931, it was by no means a sure thing Cortez could rise from the ashes. He had appeared in a hit movie, inked a new contract with RKO, and immediately begun work on a number of new productions, but the new films had not been released, and much had happened since he signed the contracts. Alma's sudden death and the controversies surrounding it, including revelations in her autobiography were generating great publicity, much of it negative for Ricardo. Would it affect his comeback? Would RKO assign him good parts in first rate productions? Many questions remained.

Ricardo did not know it yet, but his career would indeed survive and thrive. Through a combination of talent, professionalism, sheer determination, and hard work, he would not only solidify his comeback, but achieve his greatest cinematic success. The RKO years (1931-32), which coincided with Hollywood's more sexually liberal pre-Code era, would be the peak period of his career, during which he contributed many of his best, most acclaimed performances in several fondly remembered motion pictures—all this while essentially establishing a new screen persona.

To say Ricardo Cortez was a busy film actor during this time would be a gross understatement. He would make a mind boggling 21 motion pictures in the two-year period; 11 releases in 1931 alone. He played all sizes of roles: leads, second leads, and supporting parts in both grade A productions and low budgeters. He played multiple types of characters: heroes, scoundrels, and fascinating combinations of both, but during this time, he became most associated with villainous impersonations. With his dark good looks, olive complexion, heavy lidded bedroom eyes, and New York accent, Cortez exuded a sexy, dangerous quality that made him perfect for playing gangsters, criminals, gigolos, and various rascals. To this mix, he added an impeccably groomed appearance, perpetual smile, and soft voice, which served as an effective mask for cinematic corruption. Also of particular note during this period, and in the years immediately following, were his frequent appearances in movies opposite many of the era's most popular and dominant leading ladies; names like Stanwyck, Francis, Davis, Lombard, Dunne, Colbert, Young, Twelvetrees, and Astor.

Cortez's determination to make the most of his "second chance" was more than evident by mid-January, 1931. After the release of *Her Man*, the busy actor completed two films: *Illicit* and *Ten Cents a Dance*. Neither were great pictures, but both were sophisticated, competently produced, modern dramas whose themes challenged traditional codes of conduct. Both contained strong acting highlighted by refreshingly earnest, totally committed lead performances by former Ziegfeld girl, turned stage and film actress, Barbara Stanwyck.

Billed as a "smart, sophisticated, story of ultra-moderns," Warner Bros.' *Illicit* was the tale of a young couple (Stanwyck, James Rennie) whose live-in relationship undergoes stress when they succumb to societal pressures and wed. Tame by today's standards, the script, based on an Edith Fitzgerald/Robert Riskin play about the pros and cons of "living in sin," was considered daring at the time. The M.P.P.D.A. (Motion Picture Producers and Distributors of America headed by Will Hayes and its arm, The Studio Relations Committee, headed by Jason Joy) and local censor boards demanded changes before and after the film was made, but lacking real power to enforce them, they were ignored. Filmgoers flocked to see what all the hoopla was about, making the movie a big box office winner. Largely wasted in a small, sixth-billed assignment as Price Baines, Stanwyck's troublemaking former beau, Cortez's appearance was nonetheless important. Not only did it help pay his mounting bills (he received $2,500 for his services), but it gave his comeback another boost as installments of Alma's autobiography were being published.[216]

Ricardo fared better in the second billed role of a business tycoon involved in a romantic triangle with a self-sacrificing taxi dancer (Stanwyck) and her selfish, irresponsible lover (Monroe Owsley), in Columbia's *Ten Cents a Dance*. Like *Illicit*, it, too, was a box office winner that benefited the Cortez career, but unlike its predecessor, it was beset with problems. Its director, Lionel Barrymore (who'd just earned an Oscar nomination for helming *Madame X* in 1929), was suffering severe arthritic attacks that necessitated strong medications. Costly retakes and delays became necessary when Barrymore kept falling asleep during the filming, and when Miss Stanwyck became temporarily paralyzed after falling while filming a scene. Fears surfaced the production might have to be scrapped after the latter mishap, but luckily Stanwyck recovered quickly and, like the trooper she was, returned to the set and finished the picture. Years later, Cortez expressed considerable admiration for his leading lady, with whom he would work three times. Of Stanwyck he said, "She was no nonsense. She came to the studio to work. I admired her for her dignity and professionalism. She was the perfect lady at all times."[217]

Perhaps one of the reasons Ricardo so admired Barbara Stanwyck was her dedication and work ethic, which was similar to his own. He, too, was a no-nonsense, hard worker who arrived on the set totally prepared, even when he was literally working around the clock making multiple films at once. Such was the case in January, 1931, at the time of Alma's death. When he learned the news of his wife's desperate condition, Cortez was making two pictures concurrently: *Behind Office Doors* (RKO) and *Big Business Girl* (Warner Bros.). Typical of the pre-Code period, each featured a clever, ambitious, modern female main character attempting to make her way in a world ruled by men. Both paired Cortez with talented leading ladies (Mary Astor

Cortez made three films with former Ziegfeld girl, turned stage and film actress, Barbara Stanwyck, including the dramatic *Ten Cents a Dance* (Columbia, 1931).

and Loretta Young, respectively), but neither picture was particularly distinguished. While filming *Big Business Girl*, Warner Bros. head of production, Darryl Zanuck, approached Ricardo with an intriguing offer—one which the actor rightly surmised had considerable potential. It was a lead role in a crime film based on a popular and acclaimed novel about a private dick on the trail of a priceless black bird.

The story of the production of Ricardo Cortez's most famous film, Warner Bros.' 1931 adaptation of Dashiell Hammett's crime classic, *The Maltese Falcon*, began with the publication of the novel in serialized form in *Black Mask* magazine, beginning in September, 1929. The tale of a tough, cynical private eye (Sam Spade) who encounters multiple unscrupulous and murderous characters on a quest to acquire a grail-like artifact, it was a big hit with crime/mystery aficionados who admired both Hammett's style and the story. In February, 1930, the Alfred A. Knopf company published the novel. By April, its popularity had come to the attention of Warner Bros., who saw potential in the property. It was an exciting story with intriguing characters, and could be simply and inexpensively produced. By the end of June, the studio had acquired the film rights to *The Maltese Falcon* from Knopf for $8,500.[218]

A few days before the contract was drawn up, Hammett's agent offered his services for a prospective adaptation, but the tight-fisted studio brass declined. They had writers on the payroll who would do the job for less, and would do it according to the studio's strict specifications. In July, a tentative filming date was set for January, 1931, with a budget of $300,000 (an A -level production at Warner Bros.). Casting began in late summer, 1930. Initially, both Zanuck and production head Jack Warner envisioned *Falcon* as a vehicle for the studio's top-tier star, John Barrymore. Studio contract scenarists Maude Fulton and Brown Holmes were instructed to make Spade a strong, yet suave ladies' man in keeping with Barrymore's screen image. Plans changed, however, when Barrymore became preoccupied with another A-level Warner Bros. production, *Svengali*, and after rumors began circulating the "Great Profile" might soon leave the studio when his contract expired in 1931. In late autumn, the studio opted to revise the script to make it a vehicle for another of its top stars, Bebe Daniels, who'd recently signed a six-picture Warner Bros. pact after completing work on the drama, *My Past*.[219]

Zanuck's assistant, producer/writer Lucien Hubbard, was brought in to help Fulton and Holmes revise the screenplay. The trio worked for two months to make revisions emphasizing the Daniels' character, Ruth Wonderly, as a sexy, manipulative, and crafty criminal. Her romantic/sexual relationship with Spade was to be one of the film's key elements. According to author Kyle Dawson Edwards in *Corporate Fictions: Film Adaptations and Authorship in the Classic Hollywood Era*, "With the focus of the film now on the cagey criminal Wonderley, the male lead would now need to satisfy the romantic melodrama elaborated even further in the script drafts." When the screenplay (retitled *All Woman*) was finally completed in December, 1930, the role of Spade still had not been cast.[220]

With production looming in early January, 1931, the studio began a concerted effort to find their Sam Spade. For Cortez, landing the important part involved being in the right place at the right time. He was on the Warner Bros. lot working on *Big Business Girl*, when he received a call from Zanuck's office informing him of the studio's interest. Both Warner and Zanuck admired Cortez's work and thought he would be perfect for the role of Spade as they envisioned him. Casting Cortez had another distinct advantage. Warner Bros. could acquire his services for less money than one of their own top stars. By mid-January, an agreement had been crafted between RKO and Warner Bros., loaning Cortez for a salary of $1,250 per week (his earnings at RKO) plus a $3,750 bonus to his studio bosses.[221]

Two weeks before production commenced, Cortez received the definitive word he would have the part of Spade in *The Maltese Falcon*, joining a cast headed by his former *Argentine Love/Volcano* costar Daniels, supported by Dudley Digges, Una Merkel, Robert Elliott, Otto Mathieson, Dwight Frye, and Thelma Todd. His director would be Roy Del Ruth. Just prior to filming, Del Ruth received the final script from Hubbard and company along with a note from Zanuck making clear the hierarchy of authority, and the studio's wishes for the project. It read as follows: "This script is final and the dialogue is not to be changed or altered on the set, unless authorized by the production office."[222]

Production began on the Warner Bros. lot (4000 Warner Boulevard in Burbank, CA) on January 26, 1931, and lasted exactly one month. A former newsman, scriptwriter, and two-reel comedy director, Del Ruth was both a skilled craftsman and an obedient employee. Under the strict supervision of Zanuck, he and cinematographer William Rees shot the scenes as written. Three weeks into production, Del Ruth, Cortez, Elliott, and crew were sent to San Francisco for location shooting. During their stay, Cortez was briefly embarrassed when a young fan turned up on the set and started speaking to him in excellent Spanish. When he explained he didn't speak the language, she began "chattering on" in French, leading a frustrated Cortez to exclaim, "Won't someone tell this lady that the only language I know is English!"[223]

Despite the temporary humiliation, everything went smoothly for the actor. In fact, Cortez was playing the role too well to suit the studio brass. Written communications between Zanuck and Del Ruth reveal the studio's concern about the rough cuts of the picture. Both Zanuck and Jack Warner were unhappy Cortez's Spade was dominating the footage in spite of their efforts to emphasize Miss Daniels. Certain retakes and added sequences were ordered, including the film's concluding scene, in which Cortez visits Wonderly in

While working on the Warner Bros. lot making *Big Business Girl* in 1931, Cortez was selected to play his most famous role, private detective Sam Spade, on the trail of a priceless black bird in the first film version of Dashiell Hammett's iconic crime story, *The Maltese Falcon*.

prison and expresses genuine affection for her. In addition, the film underwent another title change to *Woman of the World*.[224]

Even with all the rewrites and edits, the finished motion picture was a successful adaptation of the popular novel. A tantalizing mix

Ricardo Cortez (right) won rave reviews and a testimonial from the author, Hammett, as Sam Spade in *The Maltese Falcon* a.k.a. *Dangerous Female* (Warner Bros., 1931), costarring Bebe Daniels and Una Merkel (on left).

of mystery, intrigue, humor, sex, and romance, Del Ruth's *Falcon* was highlighted by effective sequences, an adult approach to sexuality, and credible performances. The film suffers at times from a certain stagy quality, sound deficiencies, and the lack of a musical score, but it was solid entertainment that pleased critics and ticket buyers. Even devotees of the Hammett book expressed enthusiasm. After soliciting preview audience reactions, Warner Bros. executives became so enthused with the picture and Cortez's work, they opted to return to the movie's original title, *The Maltese Falcon*, and hire Hammett to craft a sequel to star Cortez (which was never produced). In his *New York Times* review, critic Andre Sennwald declared "The adventures of Sam Spade, private detective of the firm Spade and Archer, are here reported smoothly, fluidly, with cultivated humor and keen intelligence . . ."[225]

As usual, there *were* dissenting voices. Most of the movie's critics, including church groups, moralists, and censor boards, were upset with the sexual aspects of the film, namely its portrayal of the relationship between Spade and Wonderly. Particular objections centered on two scenes. The first had Wonderly (Daniels) nude in Spade's bathtub in full view of the detective, and the other, the famous kitchen strip scene, had Spade forcing Wonderly to disrobe in order to make sure she had not stolen a missing thousand dollar bill. In a June 9, 1931 missive from Colonel Joy to Zanuck, Joy declared both scenes objectionable, and said they MUST be removed. Zanuck ignored him.[226]

Both the film's supporters and detractors appeared in agreement on one subject—Ricardo Cortez was a smashing success as Sam Spade. He was exactly what Warner Bros. and the scriptwriters ordered: a handsome, smiling, likeable womanizer who, under his slick, well-coiffed façade, is a robust, unsentimental, money grubbing opportunist, as amoral as the clients he represents. Critics were positively giddy about his performance. *The New York Times* Sennwald complimented the "disarming ease and warmth" of his portrayal. In her June 6, 1931 column, Louella Parsons went one step further, terming the Cortez performance "brilliant and dominant."[227] In less than six months, the former silent film Latin lover, who was considered "washed up" at the dawning of the new sound era, had beaten the odds, scoring his second critically acclaimed triumph. His employer, RKO took note. Before *Falcon* was officially released, the studio announced its intention to star Cortez in his own vehicles.[228]

The "waste not, want not" brothers Warner would continue to utilize the filming rights to Hammett's classic novel for the next decade, during which they produced two remakes. In 1936, they renamed all the characters, and released an offbeat comic version entitled *Satan Met a Lady*, starring Warren William and Bette Davis in pursuit of an 8th century jewel-filled ram's head. Five years later, in 1941, the studio again remade the picture, this time with young John Huston as scriptwriter and director. In this case, the third time was definitely the charm, as most consider the Huston version, starring Humphrey Bogart, Mary Astor, Sydney Greenstreet, and Peter Lorre, to be the definitive one.

During the last two decades, film historians, mystery enthusiasts, and classic movie fans have produced endless articles and essays comparing Warner Bros.' three *Falcon* adaptations, weighing in on the merits and flaws of each. Most have rightly concluded the 1941 version to be the best. It is justifiably revered as one of the greatest film classics; a masterful blend of excellent production, direction, script, and cast. Opinions are mixed with regard to its 1931 ancestor. Unfortunately, in their enthusiasm for Huston's achievement, in recent times many professional and non-professional critics have chosen to dismiss Del Ruth's *Falcon* as totally trivial and crude, and Cortez's performance as off base and inappropriate (proof positive of his limitations as an actor). To many classic film enthusiasts, these critiques appear overly harsh.

Huston's version IS a more compact, effective retelling of the story, but could he have produced it so successfully without its 1931 antecedent? It's doubtful. Huston certainly watched and was influenced by the 1931 version prior to writing the script and making his picture. In fact, many of the scenes are duplicates of Del Ruth's. Furthermore, it is true Bogart *was* a more perfect embodiment of Spade as envisioned by author Hammett in the novel, but Cortez was nevertheless excellent, and deserves respect for his pioneering portrayal. With almost no time to prepare, Ricardo had performed exceptionally well, superbly interpreting the role of Spade according to the specifications laid out by Warner Bros. and his director. Those who refer to Cortez's work as "second rate" should read the opinion of the author, Hammett, the ultimate authority. In Warner Bros.' promotional package released with the picture, the former Pinkerton private detective offered his views of Cortez as Spade.

"Cortez is just right for the part. He evidences keen judgement and cool courage—making Spade human under temptation and altogether normal in his reactions to all sorts of trying situations. He is hard enough and yet human too. He is smart but not heroic. He puts over the qualities I have generally found in private detectives worthy of the name." [229]

Buttressed by the acclaim he garnered for his performance in *The Maltese Falcon* and the box office successes of both *Illicit* and *Ten Cents a Dance*, Ricardo Cortez was feeling more confident about the trajectory of his career when he finally reported to work for his new employer, RKO Radio Pictures.

The Radio Keith Orpheum (RKO) company was a relatively new entity—a child of the sound revolution set in motion in 1927. To take advantage of the public demand for sound films, the Radio Corporation of America (RCA) developed an optical sound-on-film system called Photophone, which they hoped would be competitive with A.T&T's sound technology (E.R.P.I.—Electrical Research Products Inc.) utilized by Warner Bros. and Fox. There was a problem, however. RCA was not affiliated with a studio. In 1927, RCA general manager David Sarnoff attempted to remedy the situation by reaching an agreement with Joseph P. Kennedy, the head of the medium-sized, FBO (Film Booking Offices) studio to purchase a substantial interest in FBO. In 1928, the Keith-Albee-Orpheum circuit of theaters and the legendary Pathe studio were also brought under the umbrella of RCA, and the Radio-Keith Orpheum company was born with Sarnoff as Chairman of the Board. In 1930, more acquisitions were made including the formal purchase of Pathe with its Culver studios, backlot, and contract players. When Ricardo Cortez signed with RKO, he was joining an impressive roster of actors that now included Irene Dunne, Richard Dix, Joel McCrea, Dolores Del Rio, Mary Astor, the comedy team of Wheeler and Woolsey, and former Pathe stars, Constance Bennett, Ann Harding, and Helen Twelvetrees, with Charles D. Rogers as head of production. By 1931, RKO was producing over 40 feature films per year.[230]

Cortez's initial post *Falcon* RKO assignments, *White Shoulders* and *Transgression* had been planned previously, thus did not reflect his improved status. Both movies were mediocre pot boilers that cast him in secondary roles as destructive, good-for-nothing playboys out to break up boring marriages. In *Transgression*, a remake of Ricardo's silent vehicle, *The Next Corner*, he reprised the role of Don Arturo, a womanizing Spanish nobleman who successfully lures a bored wife (Kay Francis, borrowed from Paramount) away from her neglectful husband (Paul Cavanaugh, borrowed from Fox), only to be killed by the father of one of his other romantic conquests.

Throughout his first months at RKO, Ricardo tried to maintain a low profile, concentrating his energies on mounting a career comeback and trying to forget the past. By mid-year he appeared to be making professional progress, but forgetting the past proved a more intractable problem. The publication of his late wife's autobiography kept the pain of her death fresh in his mind, and their marital disputes in public view. In addition, during the spring, the

Cortez would make six motion pictures with lovely Mary Astor (seen here), including *White Shoulders* (RKO, 1931), about a young woman who marries a rich older man, but is tempted by a corrupt womanizer played by Cortez.

California State Medical Board began taking testimony and examining records to answer complaints filed against famed Hollywood physician, Dr. L. Jesse Citron, to determine whether he should lose his medical license for dispensing drugs to Alma. To top it off, in August, 1931, his former mother-in-law, Theresa, filed a million dollar libel suit against *Photoplay* magazine, alleging they had perpetrated falsehoods in their coverage of Alma's death and funeral.[231]

For a time, Cortez suffered in silence and buried himself in work. He took a room at the Wilshire Hotel and let his brother Stanley (now working as an assistant cameraman) live in the Wilton Avenue house. When he had a day off, Ricardo would often be found in his apartment reading and smoking his pipe. He also liked to take long walks alone, go horseback riding, or go for a swim. Once a week, he attended the fights in Los Angeles with studio colleagues, and occasionally played tennis or polo. He avoided partying, preferring to get his rest and learn his lines for the next day's shooting. Much to the dismay of Hollywood gossipers, there was no sign of romance.

Cortez told a columnist that keeping a relatively low profile was not hard for him.

"Apparently the chatter writers expect me to become a polygamist. I can't take anyone to the theater, go into a restaurant for a bite to eat or escort an acquaintance to a party without being heralded as on the verge of matrimony . . . Actually, I live a pretty quiet life. Especially is this true while I am working. This is one business where you can't burn the candle at both ends . . . Give me a first class book, new or old, a pipe and sufficient tobacco, and my bachelor apartment is perfect . . ."[232]

Because of the increasing demand for his services, particularly after the release of *The Maltese Falcon*, the Hollywood press exhibited a renewed interest in Ricardo, his career, and private life. He had scrupulously avoided reporters at the time of Alma's last arrest and at the time of her death, but now RKO advised him to accept invitations for interviews and address all questions asked. During the summer and fall of 1931, he spoke to several newspaper and magazine reporters and columnists on a variety of topics. The most revealing of the interviews was conducted by writer Harry D. Wilson and published in *Modern Screen*. In it, Cortez broke his silence on the subject of his late wife, attempting to answer lingering questions regarding their relationship and her drug addiction and death. He sidestepped Alma's unkind remarks and uncomplimentary contentions. Also taking part in the interview (likely at the request of Cortez and/or RKO) was one of Alma's physicians, Dr. Charles F. Phleuger, who had taken her to his home and cared for her during her final hours.[233]

Cortez told Wilson much of the strife between he and his late wife was due to her condition. He refused to enable her habit and take part in her social life, because in his words "many of her friends catered to her weaknesses." Cortez maintained he did all he could to help her, sometimes restraining her with physical force, which incurred the wrath of her family and friends who misunderstood his motives.

"I couldn't bear looking on and watching her deliberately destroying herself. I tried to restrain her. Who wouldn't? One doesn't sit by and

watch those one loves expose their weaknesses. If you know anything at all about the self-will and determination of people who crave stimulants of any kind, you know what a fight it was.[234]

He noted several breakups and reconciliations. He said just prior to her hospitalization at Patton, he, Dr. Pfleuger, and others tried valiantly to help Alma complete her scenes in her final films: *Show Boat* and *She Went to War*. He said she was "insane with dope" the day of the Los Angeles premiere of *Show Boat*, so much so, he and a servant set the clocks back so she would miss the festivities. Dr. Pfleuger corroborated Cortez's version of events.

"We were with her every minute during those awful days(during the filmings). If I wasn't there, Ricardo was at her side . . . Ric did everything—everything a man could do under such terrible circumstances. If he appeared harsh at times, it was because of his love for Alma. She herself made this necessary so often."[235]

On the subject of their pending divorce, Ricardo was uncharacteristically blunt.

"I think if her mother had liked me better things might have been different. I never understood why she disliked me so intensely. She loved Alma and sacrificed a great deal for her, but she could never reconcile herself to the fact that I too loved Alma . . . ."[236]

When asked if he regretted his relationship and marriage to Alma, Cortez was adamant.

"Alma was adorable—one of the finest women I've known. Lovable, generous, and talented beyond words, in fact I think she was a genius. Is it any wonder I became beside myself when I realized what was happening to her. . . I feel sure she loved me to the end in spite of rumors to the contrary. I know I loved her dearly through it all. She was blameless for her actions when at the mercy of that wretched drug. During those periods I tried to remember the Alma she really was."[237]

Ricardo had little time to analyze public reaction to the interviews.

He was loaned to Universal to play a crooked bookmaker who utilizes a young couple's abode as his headquarters, in the minor-league drama *Reckless Living*, costarring Mae Clarke and Norman Foster; then returned to his home studio to take on one of the most colorful roles of his career in the crime drama *Bad Company*.

Based on former *New York Daily News* reporter Jack Lait's 1930 novel, *Put On the Spot*, *Bad Company* was a crime thriller purportedly inspired by the gang wars in Chicago during the 1920's. The Tom Buckingham and Tay Garnett script chronicled the struggles faced by a young woman (Helen Twelvetrees) experiencing a life crisis when she discovers both her young attorney husband (John Garrick) and brother (Frank Conroy) are mixed up in organized crime.

Her brother heads one of two big city criminal gangs battling for dominance, while her husband works for the other gang, led by Goldie Gorio (Cortez), an eccentric, excessively violent megalomaniac. RKO initially intended Harry Joe Brown to direct the picture and Lily Damita to have the feminine lead opposite Cortez, but had a change of heart. Hoping to repeat the commercial success of *Her Man*, the studio ultimately decided to utilize the project as a reunion vehicle for *Her Man*'s winning team of Twelvetrees, Cortez, and director Tay Garnett. For a variety of reasons, they were unable to recreate the magic, but still managed to produce a respectable, frequently riveting motion picture which looks better today than when it was made.[238]

Bad Company's main weakness was the basic storyline. Audiences didn't believe an intelligent, perceptive young woman could possibly be so ignorant of her family's associations, yet the movie was an effective pre-Code era thriller thanks to admirable direction, fluid camerawork, and some expert performances. One of the highlights was a powerful Garnett-created sequence 3/4 of the way through the picture, which harkened back to the 1929 St. Valentine's Day Massacre. In it, crazy Goldie traps his rivals (Conroy and six associates) in his apartment, lines them up, and executes them. Garnett's cameraman, Arthur C. Miller recorded the rapidly growing panic in the faces of each man as he approaches his death. Also memorable was the surprisingly violent shootout scene at the film's finale between Goldie's gang and the police.

Garnett and Miller were aided by persuasive acting from a gifted cast. Conroy was a standout as Twelvetrees' repentant brother, but acting honors belonged to Cortez, who dominated the picture as Gorio, a crazy, evil Al Capone clone whose wealth and lavish lifestyle cannot conceal the fact he is a boorish lout. Under the guidance of Garnett, Cortez skillfully captured the essence of a magnetic, yet repulsive mass murderer. Ricardo was particularly effective in an early scene in which he renders his elderly tailor unconscious when the old man advises him against wearing a two button coat. The camera lingered on his facial expressions, which transitioned from anger to confusion to sadness. Eighteen years later, one of Ricardo's costars, James Cagney, would further refine and perfect the psycho criminal genre, winning enormous acclaim as the "Goldie-like" gangster Cody Jarrett in Warner Bros. crime thriller, *White Heat.*

Critics reserved commendations for Garnett and Cortez, but encouraged the public to save their money. Ricardo told the press he enjoyed playing Goldie and working with Garnett, who respected his ability and professionalism enough to allow him to direct a couple of the film's scenes. For a long time, Cortez had voiced interest in trying his hand at directing, and Garnett gave him his first opportunity. When asked about the experience, Ricardo told *Los Angeles Examiner* columnist Marquis Busby, he hoped to become a director one day. "The acting game is fascinating. But it is usually kind to you only when you are young. Youth doesn't matter to a director, and directing fascinates me."[239] The project was also notable as Ricardo's first chance to make a picture with his brother, Stanley, who was an assistant cameraman on *Bad Company.*

In October, 1931, Ricardo celebrated his one-year anniversary at RKO. Professionally, it had been a positive, productive year. He had managed to revitalize his film acting career, but like so many of his accomplishments, it came with strings attached. To remain popular and relevant in the new sound era, it had been necessary for Ricardo to change his screen image. He was so good at roguish impersonations, by 1932, he felt he was in danger of being typecast as a villain. Cads and blackguards were colorful parts, but were ordinarily supporting roles. Cortez still retained aspirations of playing leads in big budget productions, and he knew he would need to become proactive to make that happen. Time was definitely of the

Ricardo had a colorful role as megalomaniacal gangster, Goldie Gorio, opposite Helen Twelvetrees in the crime drama, *Bad Company* (RKO, 1931). directed by Tay Garnett.

essence. The movie industry had always been the domain of the young, and at 31 years old, Cortez knew if he was ever to have his "moment in the sun," it would have to materialize soon.

Among the literary properties RKO optioned for movie adaptation at this time was *Night Bell*, novelist Fannie Hurst's dramatic tale of a poor young Jewish boy from Manhattan who becomes a successful Park Avenue surgeon, but must address the moral dilemmas of his success. The first time Ricardo read the rough script, he knew he wanted to play the lead role of Felix Klauber. The more he thought about the part, the more determined he became to play it. The problem was that RKO's newly installed production head, young

One of the most memorable sequences in Tay Garnett's *Bad Company* (RKO, 1931) harkened back to the famed St. Valentine's Day Massacre. In the stunningly effective scene photographed by cinematographer Arthur Miller, crazy Goldie (Cortez with gun in hand) lures his opponents to his apartment, then lines them up and executes them.

This jewelry tray engraved "Rico, September 19-31" was part of a grooming set believed to have been given to Ricardo by RKO in recognition of his 31st birthday, and to commemorate his one year anniversary as a studio contract employee. It was among countless pieces of Cortez memorabilia placed on the market after his widow's death.

Director Tay Garnett gave Cortez his first opportunity to direct during the production of *Bad Company* (RKO, 1931). This rare candid photo, shows Cortez (with hat and pipe) helming a scene assisted by his younger brother, Stanley (far left), who was an assistant cameraman on the picture.

David O. Selznick, and the prospective director, Gregory La Cava, did not think Cortez was suited for the role.[240]

Casting began in late autumn. The trades reported several actors as "in the running" for Felix, but Cortez's name was not on the list. Undeterred, Ricardo came up with a plan. Adapting a small portion of the rough script, with his own money, he hired a cameraman, electricians, lighting and sound men, and filmed the scene he'd written in an unused corner of one of RKO's sound stages. He presented the footage to his skeptical bosses and waited. Apparently, they were impressed. In November, multiple entertainment journals reported Cortez as one of the finalists.[241]

While he awaited word, Ricardo made two films. Both had respectable components but were largely unremarkable. He was back in familiar form as a two-timing wastrel in the Paramount drama *No One Man*. The story of a cynical, irresponsible socialite's quest for romantic fulfillment, had a good cast (Cortez, Carole Lombard, Paul Lukas) and decent production values, but lacked dramatic punch. It was notable as an early demonstration of the talent and versatility of Lombard, who would soon become a huge star, and for being Cortez's first Paramount picture since he left the studio in 1927. RKO's racetrack drama, *Men of Chance*, also had a winning cast (Ricardo, Mary Astor, and John Halliday) and some great footage of the legendary Tanforan Racetrack in San Bruno, but was likewise unexceptional. Cortez gave it his all as a bejeweled master gambler named Diamond Johnny Silk who is victimized by crooked rivals, but the part had no real substance, and the script was unoriginal.

In December 1931, Cortez learned he would have the coveted role of Felix in the newly named *Symphony of Six Million* ("Six Million" being a reference to the number of souls in New York City). Ricardo was elated; determined not to disappoint. In the weeks leading up to production, he carefully studied the script and conferred with director La Cava on his interpretation. Upon La Cava's suggestion, he visited a local L.A. hospital where he witnessed several operations in order to understand the procedures of the operating room, and how surgeons like Klauber used their hands.[242]

Symphony of Six Million was one of the first projects on the plate of new RKO production head David O. Selznick, upon assuming his position in October, 1931. The project had been in the planning stages for months. Selznick's predecessor, Bill LeBaron, had originally hired Hurst to produce the story, and had overseen the initial script written by Bernard Schubert and J. Walter Ruben. Just prior to Selznick's appointment, Le Baron dispatched writer/director/casting director Lynn Shores and a film crew to New York City to shoot footage of the Lower East Side, and to scout out actors for the key roles of Felix's parents. Both Gregory Ratoff (a Broadway actor, former star of the Moscow Art Theater) and Anna Appel (from the Yiddish Art Theater) were located during Shores' stay.[243]

For both personal and professional reasons, Selznick was determined to make *Symphony* a success. Like Cortez, he was Jewish. Jews had been depicted in several pictures (including *The Jazz Singer* and Capra's *The Younger Generation*), but Selznick never felt they had been portrayed realistically. One of his first decisions was to have the *Symphony* script rewritten to emphasize Jewish traditions and values, and to portray the warm, nurturing family life of the Jewish characters. In consultation with his assistant Pandro Berman, Selznick brought together a gifted group of filmmakers. To helm the film, illustrator and two-reel comedy director Gregory La Cava was chosen. Known around Hollywood for his fondness for the bottle, La Cava was nevertheless an innovative perfectionist with a thorough knowledge of all aspects of moviemaking, and a dedication to quality product. The highly respected cinematographer Leo Tover was also engaged. Rounding out the main cast were three RKO contract players: Noel Madison, Lita Chevret, and, on the heels of her Oscar nomination as the sturdy Sabra Cravat in the studio's mega western, *Cimarron*, young Irene Dunne (selected to portray Jessica, the physically disabled school teacher for the blind whom Felix loves). In an effort to maximize realism, Selznick hired a medical doctor as a technical advisor, registered nurses and interns to help enact the surgery scenes, and blind children to play themselves in Jessica's class. RKO set the budget at $270,000 (sizeable for the studio).[244]

All participants were cognizant of the intense preparation and money invested, and went the extra mile to make the project a success. This was particularly true of Ricardo, who literally poured his heart and soul into the part of Felix. He had always given his best to his work, but this picture and part were special. For multiple reasons, he felt a deep personal connection to Felix and his story. Felix's religion, his humble beginnings in a poor Lower Manhattan neighborhood, and his loving parents and family were uncannily similar to his own. Ricardo also related to the pressures, challenges, and guilt faced by Felix, who achieved success. His dedication to the film inspired both Miss Dunne (who became a lifelong friend) and his director. While making *Symphony*, La Cava developed a close personal and productive working relationship with his star. Like so many others who lived and worked in the film capital, he had read Alma's memoir, and heard Cortez described as cold, distant, and unfriendly. In an interview, La Cava attempted to put these rumors to bed, describing Cortez's reserve as a defense mechanism.

"Riccy is a very sensitive person. In a society such as Hollywood, when anyone has sensitivity, he throws out a defense. He can't be fully himself because he is dealing with people who are never themselves. The so-called inferiority complex is eventually a stimulus. It urges expression. But you must reach a point where you drop that complex. Riccy has not reached

that point yet. But he is grasping for it. He is as tender as a woman. All of his instincts are toward tenderness. Due to a series of circumstances over which had no control, he was forced to adopt his armor or he would have been trampled. What seems like indifference is merely compensation." [245]

Despite all the effort, Selznick was not entirely satisfied with *Symphony* after he and La Cava edited the picture. Convinced it needed improvement, they engaged composer Max Steiner to write original music for a segment. They were so pleased with Steiner's work, they hired him to write the theme music and underscore the entire feature, thus making it one of the first films to have original music throughout. By the time the movie was completed in mid-March, 1932, all involved were convinced it would be an enormous hit. Enthusiastic preview audiences confirmed their hopes. At the

Ricardo Cortez's most personal film was *Symphony of Six Million* (RKO, 1932), about a young Jewish doctor who becomes a famous surgeon and must deal with the moral dilemmas of his success. The promotional photo features Cortez, with his supporting cast, from left to right: Gregory Ratoff, Lita Chevret, Irene Dunne, Anna Appel, and Noel Madison.

Cortez and his screen mother, famed Yiddish Art Theatre actress, Anna Appel enact a tense, emotional scene in *Symphony of Six Million* (RKO, 1932).

L.A. preview, several moviegoers were seen visibly weeping during the climactic scenes in which Felix operates on his father. Critics echoed preview audience's enthusiasm. John S. Cohen Jr., critic for *The New York Sun* called the picture "One of the best cinematic feats I have ever seen. Brilliant performances by the whole cast . . ." [246]

Massive publicity accompanied the film's official release. All seats were reserved when *Symphony of Six Million* opened at New York City's *Gaiety Theatre* on April 14, 1932.[247] The *Film Daily* reported the movie sold out for several successive nights and most of its four-week run. Weekly reports noted brisk ticket sales in big cities across the country. Unfortunately, small town and rural America did not share the enthusiasm. Perhaps they were unable to relate to a story about a Jewish family in Manhattan. When all was said and done, *Symphony* made a modest profit, but was not the monster hit so many had envisioned.

Ricardo would never forget *Symphony of Six Million*. He would always consider it one of the highlights of his professional career. For the first time since the advent of sound, he had been given THE starring role in a grade A movie, one which allowed him to play an appealing, sympathetic character audiences could relate to. Judging from public and critical reaction, he had made the most of it. Fans flooded RKO mailboxes with letters of praise for Cortez and the cast. Critics rewarded him with superb reviews, lauding his "gentle empathetic performance." They pointed to his scenes with his screen parents, Ratoff and Appel, and to the operation sequences. Donning his surgical mask, without words (utilizing only his eyes), he ably conveyed the gradual transformation in Felix's demeanor from confidence to despair.

Cortez followed *Symphony* with another successful lead role in a very different kind of movie, RKO's comic melodrama, *Is My Face Red?*, purportedly inspired by the colorful machinations of noted Broadway columnist Walter Winchell. The title was a reference to one of Winchell's favorite catchphrases. By the early 1930's, Winchell had become an American household name, exposing the peccadillos and indiscretions of the rich and famous in his famed column. When a comic play based on him, *Blessed Event*, became a hit on Broadway in February, 1932, Hollywood took note. Three separate studios, RKO, Warner Bros., and Universal began projects more or less inspired by Winchell. RKO's version was said to be based on an original play by Allen Rivkin and Ben Markson.[248] At the behest of David O. Selznick, Markson and Casey Robinson converted the original work into a humorous, fast-paced movie script about an egotistical, acid-tongued hotshot (Cortez) whose influential "Keyhole to the City" column lands him at odds with almost everyone, including a murderous gangster who vows revenge. The sure-handed William A. Seiter was brought in to direct.

To assist Cortez, Selznick hired an expert supporting cast lead by Robert Armstrong, Arline Judge, ZaSu Pitts, and leading lady Helen Twelvetrees. Since she and Ricardo had first appeared together in *Her Man* in 1930, Helen had made quite a name for herself as a tragedienne in multiple RKO dramas. Cortez was delighted to learn of Helen's selection. He not only respected her ability, but considered her a lucky charm. Their two previous pictures had given him two of his best cinematic opportunities.

This movie proved no exception. *Is My Face Red?* was a witty, minor movie gem, a salacious, pre-Code showcase for all the filmmakers involved, especially its star actor. Cortez shined in the colorful, multi-faceted role of William Poster, whose brashness, braggadocio, professional ruthlessness, and unethical behavior masks a tender heart and a genuine affection for his best girl, Helen. The part allowed the actor to show off his best qualities: his innate charisma, roguish charm, sex appeal, underutilized ability to play comedy, recite complicated dialogue at a breakneck pace, and importantly, his unexploited ability to project kindness and intimacy. Cortez's exceptional work again won universal praise. The critic for *Variety* admitted being surprised and impressed by the versatility and durability of the former faux Latin heartthrob: "It's a cracking acting job by Cortez, and following '*Symphony*' brings the actor front and center again . . . Right now he's proving himself a better performer than anyone previously imagined."[249]

Cortez continued his string of acclaimed performances as an amoral gossip columnist who gets himself in trouble with a murderous gangster in the comic melodrama, *Is My Face Red?* (RKO, 1932), costarring Helen Twelvetrees, Robert Armstrong, and Arline Judge (pictured here).

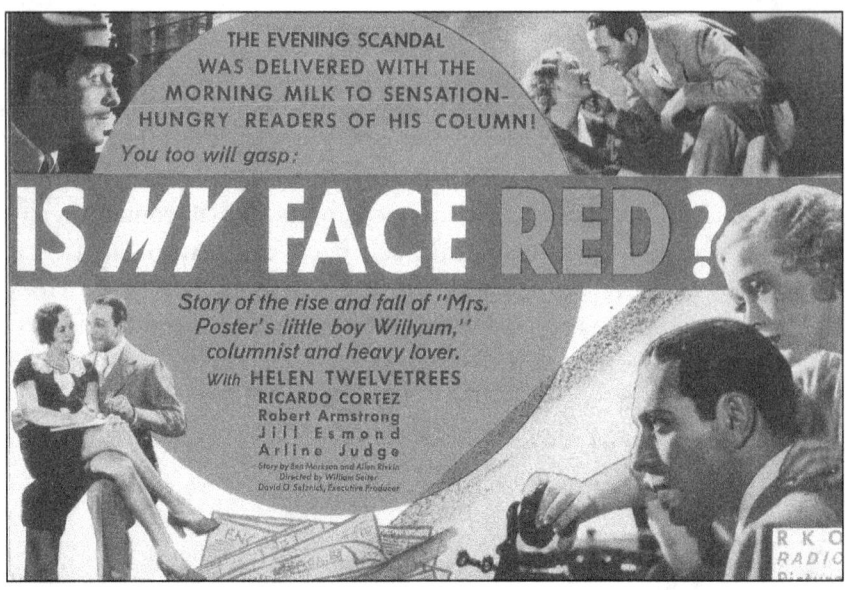

Promotional ad for *Is My Face Red?* (RKO, 1932).

Is My Face Red? was a hit with ticket buyers when it was released in June, 1932, but its ultimate success was tempered by the subsequent release of the two similarly themed movies later that year: Universal's *Okay America* with Lew Ayres (released in July), and particularly by the success of Warner Bros.' screen adaptation, *Blessed Event* (released in September), starring another talented fast talker, Lee Tracy.

In the spring and summer of 1932, on the heels of multiple successful starring roles, Ricardo was at the top of his game, and as fate would have it, the peak of his movie career. To accompany the release of *Symphony of Six Million* and *Is My Face Red?*, RKO again instructed Cortez to make himself available for multiple newspaper and magazine interviews, and tell journalists the truth about his background. Some of the articles generated at this time were typically superficial, but a few were substantive, containing heretofore unknown details of Cortez's life, personality, relationships with others, approach to his work, and thoughts about his image. The best of them contained brief, extremely rare glimpses of the man behind the charming, polite facade; a man full of insecurities and self-doubt who, in his short 32-year life span, had endured enormous adversity, but managed to survive.

Chapter Six: Up from the Ashes (1931–32)

One of the important things Cortez disclosed during this period was his ancestry and heritage. Although it was widely known around Hollywood and New York, and Alma had certainly exposed Ricardo's Jewish background in her serialized autobiography, many filmgoers were unaware of his true heritage before he formally addressed the matter of his faith and his birthplace in both newspapers and fan magazines. One of the best, most prominent of these interviews was conducted by columnist Jack Grant, published in *Movie Classic Magazine*. When asked about rumors regarding his background, Cortez didn't beat around the bush.

"I am a Jew . . . I am as tired as anyone of the sham. For nearly ten years I have been a man without a country—without a race—without a history. My birthplace has been variously reported as Vienna, Madrid, Rio de Janeiro and heaven knows where else. Stories of my life have been so contradictory, even I am confused . . . I know people have believed that I want to continue the masquerade—that I am ashamed to admit what is true . . . I am proud of my ancestry. I revere my mother and the memory of my father. I honor the blood of the Jewish race that flows in my veins . . . My name was Jacob Kranz. It was legally changed to Ricardo Cortez when I entered pictures. But it was Jacob Kranz when I was born in Hester Street on the East Side of New York City . . ."[250]

Perhaps the most revealing of these pieces was published in *Hollywood Magazine* during the summer of 1932. In it, Cortez told reporter Harry Lang as much about himself and his personality as he ever told another interviewer. According to Lang, Cortez smiled when asked about his screen image as a suave, sophisticated, overly confident villain.

"It hands me a laugh because it's all a veneer. I'm not like that at all. In everyday life, believe me, I'm the most timid man in any roomful of people . . . On the screen, I look like the most self-possessed person in the world. But that's a bluff too. Actually, the night before I start work in a picture, I can't sleep a wink. But the next morning, in spite of my sleepless night, when I step on the set, I become just the workman doing his job, full of confidence. . ."[251]

When asked about playing love scenes with some of the most glamorous actresses in Hollywood, Cortez admitted discomfort.

"Nobody'll ever know how utterly embarrassed, self-conscious, and awkward I appear when I have to play a hot love scene with some beautiful leading woman. Do you know—more than once, honestly, I've been afraid to play the scene the way the script called for because I'd be afraid the actress would think I was trying to get fresh and go on the make for her." [252]

And what about his reputation for being remote and arrogant, sometimes unfriendly or rude to coworkers, fans, and acquaintances?

"Inside, despite the screen position I've attained and the screen roles I play, I'm still a schoolboy. When I meet people, when I'm in crowds who expect me to be, 'the Ricardo Cortez,' I feel like a lump of ice had landed in my stomach. I'm always afraid I'll be a boob—and so I just force myself to be Ricardo Cortez. If I get away with it, it's merely by reason of good acting. I'm always wearing this veneer of nonchalance . . . People think I'm terribly conceited. They don't know that it's the contrary—that it's just self-consciousness, and that this outside appearance is just an inferiority complex going to work and making itself misunderstood for a superiority complex. When I enter a room full of people and overhear remarks like, 'Here comes that sheik'. 'Here comes that viper!' I become as self-conscious as a schoolboy making his first recitation. Before the camera, it's different. There it's my work, and I simply do it . . . People put me down as a high-hat man, often because I don't stop to talk to everybody. In the studio café, for instance, I'm so self-conscious that instead of stopping at each table to pass a hello and a how-do-you do with everybody I know, I just look straight ahead and make a quick dash through the room. It's because I feel awkward and embarrassed." [253]

Several interviewers asked about Alma and the current state of his love life, including recent speculation of a romance with costar Loretta Young. Cortez chalked up the Young rumors to studio publicity. He said the tragedy of Alma and all the publicity surrounding their relationship, and all the negativity voiced towards him, had made him a better, more sensitive actor. He told *Chicago Tribune* journalist

George Shaffer, he harbored no bitterness toward anyone who said unkind things about him.

"I'm one actor that feels he has no kicks or grudges. I've been through plenty. I'm not worried about trying to get more money. I have no secretaries, chauffeurs, swimming pools, or engagement rumors to worry me. I have a few friends, and I am able to keep a horse and go riding-by myself along that seventeen mile bridle path into the Bel-Air foothills. I ride on mornings when I am not working on a picture. I play golf in the afternoons . . . I'm 32 years old and I'm still hoping to get farther along. I want to make everyone forget I was ever launched as a synthetic Spaniard and a 'second Valentino,'"[254]

Cortez appeared to be well on his way to getting "farther along." RKO publicly announced its intention to star him in several more high-profile productions with challenging lead roles that would further demonstrate his versatility. Among the prestige projects were: the hard-hitting drama *Chain Gang*, in which Cortez was to portray a convict in a brutal prison camp; and *Phantom Fame*, a comic musical based on noted publicist's Harry Reichenbach's book, in which Cortez would play a slick, fast-talking promoter.

Ric Cortez must have felt a keen sense of satisfaction with his progress, but was wise enough to know the movie business was much too volatile to ever take anything for granted. Of course he was right to be cautious in his optimism. Amongst the joy and satisfaction of the present, were shadows from the past. On June 23, 1932, Ricardo was called as one of the star witnesses in Theresa Rubens' million-dollar libel suit against James R. Quirk and *Photoplay* magazine. One of Mrs. Rubens' main allegations was that a *Photoplay* article published at the time of Alma's death contained multiple untruths, the most prominent being her estranged husband (Ricardo) had not been informed of her illness. It had been widely reported Cortez would corroborate the Rubens family's version of events, but in his surprise testimony (which elicited audible gasps in Judge H. Parker Wood's courtroom), the actor declared he knew nothing of Alma's fatal pneumonia until his brother Stanley informed him she was near death. After the jury deadlocked, the matter was settled out of court for an undisclosed amount, but the trial kept the dark past alive. A few weeks later, James R. Quirk collapsed and died. A contributing factor was said to have been the stress of the trial.[255]

As he was forced to relive the pain in his personal life, things began to unravel professionally when Ricardo learned fellow RKO contract player Richard Dix would have the showy lead role in *Chain Gang*, retitled, *Hell's Highway*. In late summer came more disappointing news when the trades revealed he had also been replaced in *Phantom Fame* (retitled *The Half Naked Truth*) by Lee Tracy. Ricardo was particularly disheartened to lose the latter project to freelancer Tracy, who had a reputation for being unreliable. Cortez's admirers are left wondering how these projects might have impacted his career had he been given a chance to play them. His "consolation prizes" were costarring roles in two suspense thrillers: *The Phantom of Crestwood* and *Thirteen Women*. Both were entertaining examples of the genre, but Cortez's assignments were at best routine and colorless. Neither provided the hardworking star a suitable vehicle to maintain his hard-won momentum, and his career suffered as a result.

The mystery whodunit, *The Phantom of Crestwood*, chronicling the events leading up to, and following the mysterious murder of a glamorous blackmailer at a spooky country estate, was an intriguing project that attempted to marry the film and radio mediums. As conceived by RKO and scripted by Bartlett Cormack and scenarist/director J. Walter Ruben, the story began on radio as a mystery serial, entitled *The Phantom*. Six fifteen minute episodes were broadcast on NBC's "Hollywood-On-The Air" program for six weeks. The story ended in a cliffhanger.

As part of a clever promotional strategy, listeners were asked to submit possible conclusions for the thriller. Prior to releasing the movie, six thousand dollars in prizes were awarded to worthy solutions to the cinematic question "Who Killed Jenny Wren?"[256] (** Please note the script for the film's conclusion was already written, so the winning solutions were not used in the picture.)

A distinguished cast of suspects was chosen to enact the mystery. To portray the showy lead feminine role of the gold digging Jenny, RKO borrowed talented young Karen Morley from MGM. The result was a well-made thriller, which was a big hit. Produced for $187,000, box office receipts were reported in excess of $400,000,

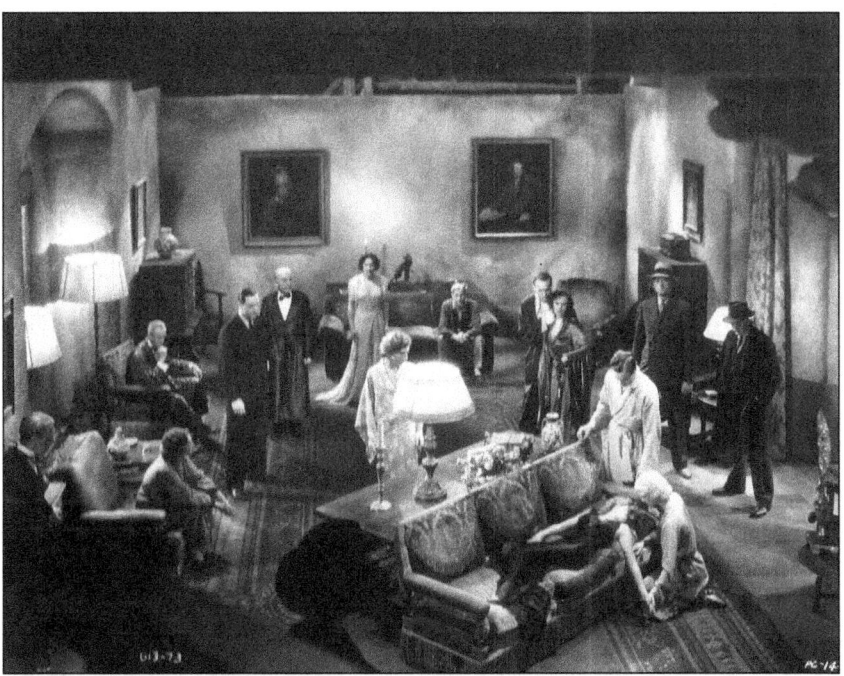

An overhead shot of the cast filming the mystery thriller, *The Phantom of Crestwood* (RKO, 1932).

giving a much-needed boost to RKO's sagging bottom line.[257] Cortez was pleased by the positive public reception and the massive publicity campaign for the film, but felt the part of Gary Curtis, a criminal who attempts to solve the baffling murder of Jenny, to keep authorities from accusing him of the crime, was nothing special.

He was even less enthused with his role as a dogged police investigator charged with solving the mysterious deaths of a group of sorority sisters in the chiller, *Thirteen Women*, based on novelist Tiffany Thayer's popular 1932 book. Like *The Phantom of Crestwood*, the movie was a bit of an experiment. RKO's attempt to combine the suspense genre with psychological drama, it was unsuccessful. It had an interesting premise, decent production values, excellent camerawork by Leo Tover, and a first-rate cast headed by Cortez, Myrna Loy (as a Eurasian villainess), and Irene Dunne, but roughly 20% of the picture (14 minutes) was left on the cutting room floor to placate Colonel Joy of the Hayes office, who complained of excessive violence and a lesbian relationship originally portrayed in the script.[258] What remained seemed disjointed. Critics savaged *Thirteen Women* as overly violent and silly, and audiences stayed away. The picture garnered more unwanted publicity on September 16, 1932, when one of the actresses featured, British-born stage star Peg Entwistle committed suicide by jumping off the famed Hollywoodland sign cliff in the Hollywood Hills.

As for Cortez, he considered the movie a demotion, proof RKO was uncommitted to its stated goal of making him a top-ranked star. Of late he'd also become concerned about the studio's financial future, after hearing rumors and reading articles detailing its monetary woes. Some doleful prognosticators suggested RKO was about to go bankrupt. Others suggested the company would soon institute severe cost containment measures to address the crisis, including trimming its roster of stars. Cortez's name was among those listed for possible termination. The studio insisted he was not on any list, but the loss of the plum leads in *Hell's Highway* and *The Half Naked Truth* suggested otherwise. His contract was due to expire in October, and by August, 1932, Ricardo was convinced RKO did not intend to renew it. On August 18, columnist Jimmy Starr reported Cortez had been cast for a lead role in the RKO adventure melodrama, *Secrets of the French Police*, but four days later, another columnist, Elizabeth Yeaman stated the part would be played by John Warburton. Clearly, something was up.[259]

Cortez's suspicions proved well founded. By 1932, the effects of the Great Depression, and RKO's spending sprees of the late 1920's and early 1930's combined to produce severe financial trouble for the studio, jeopardizing its survival. Since its formation in 1928, RKO had endeavored to become a major studio by investing freely. With the financial assistance of RCA, the new company had converted the FBO lot for sound, and acquired more properties to produce films and theaters to exhibit them. In addition, during the period of 1929-31, under the leadership of production chief Bill LeBaron, the studio spent lavishly on various productions, mainly musicals that featured Technicolor sequences. Some were hits; some were expensive misses. In 1931, LeBaron also oversaw the production of the mega adventure/western, *Cimarron*. Although a critical success, and an Academy Award winner for Best Picture, the box office receipts didn't come close to recouping production expenses. David O. Selznick replaced LeBaron in 1931, but even his brilliant movie making strategies could not keep the studio in the black as the American economy foundered and ticket sales plummeted.

By the summer of 1932, things had become bleak. New RCA president Merlin Aylsworth informed both Selznick and RKO treasurer, B. B. Kahane, that RCA could no longer afford to contribute funds to the studio, leaving it to fend for itself. The situation called for immediate action. In multiple missives exchanged between Aylsworth and Kahane, RKO's dire financial situation was discussed in detail, along with various cost containment strategies.[260] One of the strategies involved trimming the studio's roster of stars, particularly those making the highest salaries, and others who the studio determined had not performed up to expectations. In a July 25 memo to Aylsworth, Kahane provided candid assessments of RKO's contract players. Some were judged too valuable to let go, while others were considered dispensable. Cortez was seen as somewhere in the middle. Kahane thought him an overall asset, but deemed the actor's $1,750 a week salary too high, and expressed the studio's concern that Cortez "had failed to develop a box office following." Kahane's recommendation to Aylsworth was to postpone a final decision on Cortez's contract until just before it expired in October.[261]

As fate would have it, RKO would be spared the tough decision of whether or not to let Ricardo go. Sometime in late August, Cortez confronted his RKO bosses. This time, they leveled with him. They appreciated his ability and service enough to give him a contract extension, but only if he agreed to take a substantial pay cut. Cortez declined the offer, and an agreement was reached to release him from his contract. Unlike many similar situations involving the severing of professional ties between actor and studio, there was no acrimony or rancor involved in this break. RKO genuinely valued Cortez's ability and professionalism, and Cortez was grateful to RKO for throwing him a lifeline when his career was dying. On August 30, *Variety* reported Cortez's amicable departure.[262] Unfortunately, all the cost containment measures would not be enough to save RKO from bankruptcy. In early 1933, the studio was put into equity receivership with the Irving Trust Company, and Selznick packed his bags.[263]

Up until recently, there was confusion regarding the circumstances of Ricardo's participation in his next film, the MGM drama, *Flesh*.

In its original article detailing the Cortez/RKO break-up, *Variety* reported the actor would film *Flesh* for MGM as the last obligation under his RKO contract, but three weeks later, *Hollywood Citizen News* columnist Elizabeth Yeaman appeared to contradict this assertion, stating, "In the two or three weeks since he severed his connections with Radio Pictures, he (Cortez) has been signed for important roles at three different studios." She noted one of the pictures was *Flesh*.[264] RKO archival records contain no information on this matter, so the facts remained unknown until 2012 when the original contract for Cortez's services for *Flesh* (signed by both Selznick and Louis B. Mayer) turned up for sale online. *Variety* was correct. Ricardo completed work on *Flesh* as his last assignment for RKO, and the studio pocketed a tidy profit on the deal. According to the document, Mayer agreed to pay Cortez his RKO salary of $1,750 per week, billing him "as a featured player on the main title of all positive prints . . ." In addition, MGM paid RKO a lending fee of $5,250. Further confirmation was found in Cortez's sound film scrapbook, which contains a clipping regarding his departure from RKO.[265]

After several heroic and/or semi-heroic impersonations, Ricardo returned to familiar form, portraying a scoundrel in director John Ford's drama, *Flesh*. The Edmund Goulding-penned tale of an oafish, soft-hearted German wrestler (Wallace Beery) played for a chump by a manipulative parolee (Karen Morley) and her lover (Cortez), the project was originally planned as an immediate follow-up to Beery's acclaimed Oscar-winning performance in *The Champ*, but script rewrites and personnel changes necessitated delays. Goulding was Metro's original choice to direct, but when his involvement in a sex scandal necessitated a temporary stay in England, Metro brought in Raoul Walsh, then Robert Z. "Pop" Leonard, before eventually borrowing Ford from Fox. The leading lady also changed hands more than once. Both Colleen Moore and Madge Evans were announced to play the anti-heroine Laura Nash before Miss Morley was ultimately selected just two days before filming began.[266]

The difficulties did not end after production commenced. Exhausted from attempting to learn her part on such short notice, and by long hours of filming, Miss Morley fell down a flight of stairs, which caused another delay.[267] It was an omen of things to come. According to Ford's various biographers, the director did not like the material, and only agreed to do the movie for the money ($35,000), and as a "work study project," to see what the environment was like at MGM.[268] Apparently, the "environment" was not to his liking. According to Miss Morley, Ford resented the top heavy authority exercised by MGM, who forbid him to change the script. His displeasure made the set a tense, unhappy place. Miss Morley remembered being put off by Ford's manner and his disdain for the production. She told Ford biographer Scott Eyman "Ford was mad at everyone, especially the producer . . . It's not that he didn't care. He wanted it charming, and Wallace Beery had a rough sort of charm."[269] The director's attitude was not the only problem. Beery was notoriously difficult to work with, and Cortez appeared preoccupied by contract negotiations with his old bosses at Paramount.

Given all the personalities and difficulties, the picture turned out surprisingly well. Overlong and verbose in places (problems that could have been solved by judicious editing), *Flesh* was nevertheless an effective drama, showcasing three excellent performances. In less skillful hands, both male leading roles might have been cartoonish stereotypes, but with Beery as the self-sacrificing, child-like Polokai and Cortez as the charming but thoroughly selfish and ruthless Nicky, they were completely believable—real "flesh" and blood humans. Miss Morley's portrayal of the tough, yet sensitive Laura, was also extraordinary. The script clearly favored her character, but her multi-faceted work was proof positive of her singular gifts. In a 1999 interview with the author, Miss Morley basically echoed the comments she made to Ford biographer, Eyman, describing the making of *Flesh* as "unpleasant, but ultimately satisfying." Regarding Cortez, the outspoken actress had qualified praise. "I didn't know him personally, but I thought he was a decent actor. I'd heard he'd be difficult to work with, but that was not my experience. He was always prepared, knew his lines, and performed the scenes in a professional manner."[270]

In the summer of 1932, just prior to severing his professional relationship with RKO, Cortez began actively looking for employment opportunities elsewhere. Among the first calls he made was to an old friend who had helped rescue his career once before: Charles R. Rogers. After a brief stint as head of Production at RKO-Pathe

Cortez had another showy bad guy role as a petty crook who reunites with his ex-lover/partner (played by Karen Morley) in order to fleece a naïve, kindly wrestler, in director John Ford's dramatic, *Flesh* (MGM, 1932).

(where he produced several of Cortez's films, including *Her Man* and *Bad Company*), Rogers became an independent producer at Paramount. Rogers liked and respected Cortez, and signed him for the lead in one of his upcoming productions, tentatively titled *Bedfellows*, a crime drama about a gangster and the woman who loves him. He also paved the way for contract negotiations between Cortez and

Paramount, culminating in Cortez signing a long-term pact with his former employer on October 4, 1932.[271] Ricardo was thrilled to affix his name on a new contract with the studio that had given him his start. Even though he felt Paramount had assigned him what he termed "suicide roles," then blackballed him, all was forgiven.

As part of the new pact, Paramount agreed to pay Cortez his last RKO salary ($1750 per week), and allow him to complete work on *Flesh*, and Fox's *The Giant Swing* (which he had signed to do prior to the negotiations).[272] The latter film, an underworld story culled from a play penned by *Little Caesar* author W.R. Burnett, was slated for production in November. Everything seemed in readiness to begin work when Fox unexpectedly shelved the production for script revisions. On December 1, Fox informed Cortez, instead of portraying an underworld boss in *The Giant Swing*, he would replace Ralph Morgan as a benevolent Wall Street financier in the minor league romantic drama, *Broadway Bad*, costarring Joan Blondell.[273] Filmed in December, 1932, the 59-minute program picture contained expert performances and competent direction from Sidney Lanfield, but the positives were outweighed by a tired mother-love plot and a substandard script.

While working on *Broadway Bad*, Cortez began preparing to shoot two Paramount films. Besides *Bedfellows* to costar Nancy Carroll, Paramount chose Cortez to replace George Raft as a wisecracking, womanizing surgeon in the criminal division of an Emergency hospital in the melodramatic, *Police Surgeon*.

CHAPTER SEVEN
PROFESSIONAL SCOUNDREL (1933–35)

"There's always more color, more magnetism, more fascination in the villain's role, if it is properly written, than in the hero's."
— RICARDO CORTEZ

The preceding quotation from Ricardo, in 1935, provides a strong indication that sometime in the mid 1930's, whether voluntarily or out of necessity, Ricardo Cortez abandoned his dreams of mega stardom, and embraced his screen image as a movie bad guy: a heel, a second lead, or a character player who might dominate scenes or even an entire film, but wouldn't receive top billing or get the girl at the fadeout. This significant attitude adjustment was only one of the impactful changes occurring during the period of 1933-35. Even in a life as topsy-turvy as Ric Cortez's, the constant upheaval during this extremely volatile, yet pivotal time must have left his head spinning.

The rollercoaster ride began in the first weeks of 1933, with Cortez's involvement in an old- fashioned scandal. Since the Alma-related controversies, Ricardo had kept a low profile in romantic matters. This was not overly difficult for a natural loner who took refuge in his work. When the press inevitably inquired about his romantic life, the actor admitted occasional loneliness, but maintained his preference for solitude. Eventually he bowed to pressure and began dating again. During the latter months of 1932, the Hollywood gossip machine noted his occasional presence at nightclubs, charity events, premieres, and parties, on the arms of attractive women both inside and outside of the movie business. The majority were unknowns, but a few of the famous names included Lupe Velez,

Dorothy Dare, Una Merkel, Doris Warner (daughter of WB mogul, Harry), and Joan Crawford. Most were strictly casual dates. One of the possible exceptions was Miss Crawford who, at the time, was Mrs. Douglas Fairbanks Jr. Ricardo was friends with both Doug and Joan, but tongues began wagging in January, 1933, when Ricardo was seen alone with Joan at several restaurants and night spots. It was common knowledge Mr. and Mrs. Fairbanks were not getting along, so the gossipers had a field day.[274] Cortez's detractors insinuated he was responsible for the breakup of the Fairbanks marriage, which officially ended four months later in May, 1933. There is no evidence to support their contentions, although Joan and Ricardo may well have had a sexual tryst during the making of *Montana Moon* (when Ricardo was at the low point of his life). A likelier explanation for their "dates" in 1933 was the warm friendship between them, which endured. It is not a stretch to believe Ricardo was acting as a supportive friend for Joan during a difficult time.[275]

There IS ample evidence Ricardo remained hopeful regarding the trajectory of his career in the first months of 1933, after signing with Paramount. For its part, the studio seemed pleased to have him back, assigning him two new projects that appeared to have potential: *Strange Bedfellows* and *Police Surgeon*. The former, retitled *I Love That Man*, was slated to begin filming the first week in February. It had been delayed twice to accommodate leading lady Nancy Carroll, who had been working on James Whale's melodramatic *The Kiss Before the Mirror* at Universal. After a month-long hiatus due to the delays, Cortez was anxious to return to work. Unfortunately, his body was not. Mental stress and physical exhaustion had left his immune system compromised, and during the holidays, he'd contracted a virus that appeared to be getting worse. On February 5, 1933, Ricardo became so ill he was unable to get out of bed. An ambulance was summoned, which transported him to Cedars of Lebanon Hospital, where he was diagnosed with pneumonia as a result of a severe case of the flu.[276] For four days, his condition appeared to deteriorate. On February 7, columnist Elizabeth Yeaman reported his status as "extremely critical." Because of the absence of modern antibiotics (which did not come into common use until the early 1940's), similar conditions were often fatal.[277] Daily reports on his medical status were issued. His helpless family could only watch and wait, hoping

Gossipers had a field day when Joan Crawford (whose marriage to Douglas Fairbanks Jr. was said to be crumbling), turned up in the company of her old friend (perhaps lover) Ricardo Cortez during the early months of 1933.

he would not succumb to the flu as his sister had.

On February 11, their prayers were answered, and Ricardo's condition was upgraded. Newspapers reported his chances of recovery much improved. By the following week, he was said to be "gaining strength," and barring any unforeseen circumstances, would be released from the hospital in a few days. That couldn't come soon enough for the very weak, anxious actor who had been hounding the doctors to leave the hospital. His friend Charlie Rogers had been forced to replace him on *I Love That Man* (with Edmund Lowe), and Cortez was concerned about his other film assignment. While hospitalized, one of the trades reported fellow Paramount player George Raft would take over the lead in *Police Surgeon*, retitled *Girl in 419*, if Cortez was not well enough to begin filming. Cortez assured Paramount that would not be necessary.

Ignoring doctors' advice, on March 7, 1933, a gaunt, extremely weak, yet determined Ricardo reported for work on *Girl in 419*, costarring Gloria Stuart and David Manners. In her column, Louella Parsons reported encountering the actor on his way to the studio, and said "he looked far from well."[278] The third day of filming (March 10), a 6.3 magnitude earthquake shook the set. The screams of cast and crew members were recorded by Paramount sound engineer Earl Hayman, who remained in his sound booth. These recordings of the famed Long Beach earthquake were later sent to seismological scientists all over the world.[279] For Ricardo Cortez, the "trembler" was a portent of things to come. Five days later, he collapsed on the set, and was transported back to Cedars of Lebanon. He had returned to work too soon and suffered a major relapse.[280]

This time, his hospital stay was an extended one, and physicians were adamant. If he were to make a full recovery and be able to resume film work, he would need at least a month of complete rest. Cortez followed orders, but in the process, became increasingly despondent. He had always been a strong, athletic, independent individual who excelled in sports and enjoyed exercise. His extended illness had left him feeling vulnerable and alone. His negativity was compounded by anxiety over his career; more specifically his new Paramount contract. It seemed each day brought more negative news. Not only did he lose the role in B. P. Schulberg's *Girl in 419* (to James Dunn), but additional key parts in two other projects for which he had been the first choice for the male lead: *Supernatural* and *Gambling Ship*.

In an effort to combat his negativity, doctors advised Cortez to leave the isolation of his room and interact with other patients. He later recalled that his experiences with others helped him recover both physically and psychologically.

"When I was wheeled out in the sunshine and could talk with other patients, I soon discovered how well off I was. Poor legless fellows were overjoyed if they were given cigarettes. They were immeasurably grateful if someone sent them a book. I thought of the hundred books I have in my own bedroom, and remembered that I was physically whole. I may have had tough moments but I have no right to complain. I'm just glad I'm not destitute . . . ." [281]

In late March, Ricardo was finally strong enough to leave the hospital, with a long list of recommendations. His physician, Stanley Immerman, strongly advised him to take regular vacations, focus more on non-work related activities, and most importantly, seek out new friendships and relationships, especially feminine companionship. Cortez agreed to make an effort. His health crisis had been an eye opener.

From a professional standpoint, Ricardo's work release in mid-April didn't come a minute too soon. Earlier in the month, MGM had requested permission from Paramount to borrow his services for a crime drama they were about to produce based on an Anita Loos story, *Midnight Lady*, about a poor young woman who becomes a gangster moll. It was another bad guy role, but Ricardo liked the script. Paramount was amenable to the loan provided MGM would cover his salary and pay a bonus. When it was determined Cortez was physically able to do the part, a loan agreement was drawn up.

Looking weak and wan, and 14 pounds lighter, Ricardo arrived on the MGM lot in late April, 1933 to portray the small-time gangster, Leo Darcy, in the film retitled *Midnight Mary*, costarring Loretta Young, Franchot Tone, and Una Merkel. MGM had an experienced roster of its own first tier stars, directors, and craftsmen under contract, but chose to borrow several filmmakers from other studios to maximize the film's impact. In addition to Cortez, leading lady Loretta Young was borrowed from Fox. Cinematographer James Van Trees and director William Wellman came from Warner Bros.

A former salesman, ambulance driver, and World War I fighter pilot, the ruggedly handsome Wellman, known as "Wild Bill," first became involved in the film business as an actor, but eventually moved behind the camera, rising in the ranks from messenger boy, to assistant director, then director. In 1927, Paramount hired him

Cortez and costar Loretta Young enact a scene from the acclaimed melodrama, *Midnight Mary* (1933), directed by William Wellman.

to helm one of its major productions, *Wings*, an epic story of World War I fighter pilots. The film, which featured exceptional aerial combat and flight sequences, was a rousing success, netting the studio the first Academy Award for Best Picture, and its director rave reviews. Wellman followed with a succession of well-made, critically acclaimed pictures including *The Public Enemy* (1931), *Frisco Jenny* (1932), and *Heroes for Sale* (1933). By the time he arrived at MGM to direct *Midnight Mary*, he was considered one of the top up and coming directorial talents in Hollywood.

Cortez had enjoyed working with Wellman on *The Cat's Pajamas* in 1926, and was eager to do so again. Wellman ran a tight ship, but Cortez was impressed by the camaraderie and congeniality he fostered on the *Midnight Mary* set. Wellman had worked with Loretta and many of the other cast members before, and appeared eager to show everyone to advantage. Cortez appreciated the atmosphere and the opportunity to work with Miss Young and supporting actress Una Merkel again. He and Una had gone out on a dinner date during the making of *The Maltese Falcon* and exchanged memories of the experience in between takes on *Midnight Mary*. In a 1934 interview, Cortez recalled how self-conscious he felt on that date.

"It was one of Una's first pictures, and she was obviously frightened. I felt sorry for her for I thought her one of the sweetest girls I had ever met. I wanted to invite her out, but hesitated. I thought she would expect me to make violent love to her and live up to my screen reputation. I hated to disillusion her by telling her I was just a man who happened to desire the company of a very charming young lady for an evening. Well, finally I did take her to dinner and we spent a delightful evening together. But I would never ask her out again, for I was sure she was disappointed in me. When we met later on the MGM lot (for Midnight Mary), I brought up the subject. Imagine our amusement when Una informed me that she had tried so hard to act sophisticated. She didn't want me to think she was just a "nice girl" as she put it. She thought I expected her to be exotic and glamourous!" [282]

Midnight Mary won excellent reviews upon its release in June, 1933. Wellman overcame an unoriginal storyline to craft a fast-paced, engrossing pre-Code era motion picture. Of particular note was his skillful use of montage and flashback, his clever utilization of Depression-era themes intermingled with escapist fare, all while eliciting expert performances. Stunningly beautiful, 19-year-old Loretta surprised critics with an exceptional performance as Mary, the hapless victim of circumstances who becomes a hardened, world-weary, yet still sensitive moll. It was clearly Miss Young's picture, but Cortez also shined. By 1933, he had perfected his approach to playing scoundrels. While Cortez's villains, like Leo Darcy, were more often than not exceedingly malicious and thoroughly despicable, the good-looking actor consistently infused them with enough charm, vulnerability, and sex appeal to make them compelling.

Keeping a solemn promise to his physician to take periodic rests, the exhausted, not fully recovered Cortez boarded the *Malalo* for Honolulu for an extended rest after filming wrapped on *Midnight Mary*.[283] It would be an exceedingly short stay. Only two days after his arrival, he received a cable from Paramount summoning him back to Hollywood to replace Cary Grant in the Claudette Colbert vehicle, *Torch Singer*. A few days later, he was informed he would also inherit Grant's starring role in the drama, *Big Executive*; costar with George Raft in the bullfighting adventure, *The Trumpet Blows*; and be tested for the male lead in MGM's big budget production of *Queen Christina*, starring Greta Garbo. So much for rest and relaxation![284] Only two of the four films materialized with Cortez in them. Adolphe Menjou eventually played Raft's elder brother and rival in *The Trumpet Blows*, and once again John Gilbert ultimately won the plumb role of Spanish envoy, Antonio, the object of the famous monarch's affection in *Queen Christina*. The latter was particularly disappointing to Cortez, who was encouraged when MGM called him in for a second test.

The two pictures Cortez made at Paramount did little for his career. The soap operatic *Torch Singer*, about a young woman who becomes a successful saloon singer and children's radio host after giving up her illegitimate daughter, was strictly a star vehicle for the gifted Miss Colbert. Transcending an unbelievable plot, she contributed a standout performance, singing her own songs guided by musical advisor Bing Crosby. As the self-sacrificing radio executive who loves Colbert from afar, second-billed Cortez had little to do.[285] His role as a married Wall Street financier in love with his elderly partner's daughter in *Big Executive* was more substantive, but ultimately, no better. Burdened by a poor script and lack of chemistry between Ricardo and his inexperienced leading lady, Elizabeth Young (the future Mrs. Joseph L. Mankiewicz), Cortez failed to register. Even critics who regularly applauded him expressed disappointment, and audiences stayed away. One wonders how the film might have turned out had Helen Twelvetrees played the feminine lead as initially envisioned.

In spite of its flaws, *Big Executive* would leave a lasting imprint on the life of Ricardo, however. During its production, he was invited to a dinner party given by the film's director, Erle C. Kenton. Among the invited guests was an attractive young divorcee, Christine Conniff Lee, whom the director had known in New York. She'd recently come out to the West Coast to visit relatives, and Kenton wanted Cortez to meet her. Despite his hatred for matchmaking and blind dates, Cortez put in an appearance, and was surprised to find he enjoyed the company of the pretty, blue-eyed, auburn-haired Chris. They began dating, and soon became seriously involved.[286]

Born January 6, 1907, the third of six children of Mr. and Mrs. Andrew Conniff, a prominent Danbury, Connecticut couple, Christine's father was an Associated Press telegrapher, her mother, the former Lucy Costello, an influential state politician. Elected to the Connecticut state legislature as a Democrat, Lucy was highly regarded, eventually becoming recognized as the "First Lady of Connecticut Politics." Two of Chris' younger brothers became prominent as well. Frank Conniff became a noted journalist and editor, winning a Pulitzer Prize in 1955 for an interview he conducted with Russian Premier Nikita Khrushchev. Younger brother Vincent made a name for himself as a casting director for Hal Roach Studios in Hollywood.[287]

Early on in her life, Christine also aspired to be in show business. After graduating from high school, and briefly working as a bookkeeper in Danbury, she moved to New York City in 1926, where she worked as a model and dabbled in acting. According to her great niece, Diedre Hart, Christine eventually secured a job as a "Ziegfeld Girl" in the famous Follies staged at the newly constructed Ziegfeld Theatre on Sixth Avenue. Ms. Hart says her great aunt met Ricardo Cortez briefly during this period. In 1931, Christine married Lester Lee, a prominent stock broker on Wall Street and gave up the Follies. Christine enjoyed financial security with Lee and traveled in New York society circles, but the marriage was unhappy, and ended in divorce in 1933.[288]

It was brother Vincent's work in the film capital that originally brought his sister out to visit. For the recently unattached Christine, Ricardo appeared to be a breath of fresh air, seemingly so different from her ex-husband. Darkly handsome, impeccably dressed and mannered with an athletic build and a movie star profile, Ricardo must have cut quite a dashing figure to Christine. It would not be an exaggeration to say she was instantly smitten and star struck.

To Ricardo, Chris, too, was extraordinary. Per his physician's advice, he was seriously looking for a wife, and Christine seemed to be just what the doctor ordered. Unlike many of the women he had been dating, she expressed no further interest in show business. After his disastrous experience with Alma, the conservative Ricardo was determined to never marry an actress again. He wanted a traditional, stay-at-home wife who would manage their residence, serve as a hostess and, most importantly, respect his position as head of the household. During their courtship, Christine assured him that was the kind of future she wanted as well. In a 1934 interview, Cortez stated the reasons he was initially attracted to Christine.

"She is vitally interesting without being precocious. Has a mind of her own, but fortunately enjoys living as quietly and unostentatiously as I do. She is decidedly attractive rather than beautiful in the screen way. Strictly beautiful women have always bored me . . . She doesn't wear an armful of diamond bracelets or bizarre clothes, and insists a wife's place is in the home." [289]

Cortez's involvement with Mrs. Lee coincided with major changes in his professional life. His pact with Paramount wasn't due to expire until November 1933, and the studio claimed it was searching out starring roles for him, but by the summer, he was becoming discontented. Similar to his feelings regarding RKO, he was not angry or bitter, just disappointed. It seemed as if his second stint at Paramount had been jinxed from the start. His serious illness had delayed the beginning of his employment with the studio for several months, and by the time he was finally able to commence work, Paramount seemed to have lost interest. In late summer, Ricardo learned an agreement had been reached to loan his services to Warner Bros. to replace Adolphe Menjou as the male lead in *The House on 56th Street*, a drama originally planned as a vehicle for Menjou and Ruth Chatterton. When Miss Chatterton refused to play the part, the role was inherited by Kay Francis, marking the second of four pairings of Cortez with the dark-haired fashion plate.

Filming began in August, 1933, and proceeded through September. Ricardo excelled in his role as the slick, unscrupulous gambler, Bill Blaine, who teams up with a glamorous down-on-her-luck ex-con (played by Francis) to fleece patrons of a gambling casino operated in a house, formerly the abode of Miss Francis. Both director Robert Florey and Jack Warner (a personal friend and golf buddy of Cortez) were pleased by the rushes. Over the past several years, Warner Bros. had often borrowed the services of Cortez, who never failed to exceed their expectations. When Ricardo confided he was unhappy at Paramount, Jack Warner became determined to have him as an employee. Before the film was completed, an agreement was reached with Paramount to release Cortez from his contract so he could sign with Warner Bros. It is worth noting Paramount wanted to retain Cortez, and reportedly offered to star him in their upcoming production of *Counselor At Law* (a role eventually played by John Barrymore), but Ricardo wanted out.[290]

On August 25, 1933, Cortez signed a long-term pact with Warner Bros. at an initial salary of $1500 a week, to be raised to $1750 on November 1, after he completed the term of his Paramount pact. Basically, it was a standard studio contract that gave Warner Bros. the option to renew annually. Cortez was to receive a raise of $250 per week for each additional year he remained an employee. Contrary to rumors and press reports insinuating Warner Bros. intended to sign Cortez to both act and direct, there was no mention of directing in the document. The most notable provision was item #13, which stated Cortez was to be a featured actor. This was significant because it was the first time Ricardo had ever signed a contract to be a supporting player, thus abandoning his most cherished dream, to become a major star actor of motion pictures.[291]

With his signature on the dotted line, Ricardo officially joined the famed Warner Bros. repertory company, a rough, ready, and exceedingly able group of actors who shared many things in common beyond working for the same film factory. By 1933, the studio had established a reputation for producing quality, cutting edge motion pictures at a relatively low cost. Its employees were a reflection of the studio philosophy. Its contract actors were versatile, hardworking, conscientious professionals, most of whom readily completed assignments on time without complaint at relatively low salaries (in comparison to other top studios). Considering his versatility, knowledge of his craft, exceptional work ethic, and willingness to accept assignments in lesser vehicles, not to mention his friendship with the boss, the ever-reliable Ricardo Cortez seemed to have found the perfect home at Warner Bros. Alas, it was not. Ricardo would make a total of 15 films for the studio during the period 1933-36, playing leads, second leads, and character parts. There were a couple of A-level pictures along the way, but the vast majority were B's or B+'s. Some were exceptional B movies with multiple distinguishing qualities, and several provided the veteran star with colorful roles, but none substantively enhanced his reputation.

During his long career, Cortez was paired with many of the most famous and formidable female stars of the silver screen. Among them was Kay Francis, with whom he made four films, including the dramatic *The House of 56th Street* (Warner Bros., 1933), directed by Robert Florey.

Unlike many fellow actors, Ricardo (second from left) maintained friendly relations with studio moguls throughout his career. Among his golfing buddies was Jack Warner (far right), who in 1933, hired him as a contract actor.

Ricardo began his Warner Bros. tenure with three memorable bad guy roles. In each film his villainy was punished by a gruesome death. In the melodramatic *Mandalay*, costarring Kay Francis and Lyle Talbot, he was at his most charismatically despicable as Tony Evans, a gun runner in Rangoon who pays off a debt by selling his girlfriend (Francis) into white slavery. Of course, in the wonderful world of the movies, there was a heavy price to be paid for Riccy's ruthlessness. When he attempts to reenter her life to do more damage, Francis poisons him, and he falls into the ocean. Its patently absurd plot and eccentric dialogue notwithstanding, Hungarian-born director Michael Curtiz managed to fashion an exceedingly entertaining B+ potboiler that was fast moving and visually impressive. Curtiz guided both Ricardo and Miss Francis to memorable performances that inspired critics, even persnickety ones like the *New York Times'* Andre Sennwald, who called the film "a good deal better than adequate." He reserved particular praise for Cortez, whom he said "generates so much sympathy as the villain that his demise removes the one character for whom the audience feels anything like affection . . . ."[292] After viewing the picture, one small town critic and Cortez fan dubbed the actor "the cinema's magnificent heel." Indeed!

Cortez continued his scandalous ways as a racketeer who gives up bootlegging for phony pharmaceuticals in the melodramatic *The Big Shakedown*, costarring Charles Farrell and young Bette Davis. A ho hum, basically forgettable motion picture with an exaggerated plot and unbelievably naive characters, *Shakedown* was partially redeemed by the dynamic supporting performances from bad guy Ricardo and his fast-talking moll played by Glenda Farrell. In this film, Cortez had perhaps his most memorable and inventive death scene, in which he falls into a vat of acid.

Cortez ended the year of 1933 by joining an all-star cast of heavyweights to film Warner Bros.' mega musical, *Wonder Bar*. Along with *The Pony Express, The Sorrows of Satan, Symphony of Six Million*, and *The Last Hurrah*, it would be one of the most ambitious films of Cortez's career; one which he might have been able to point to with pride were it not for the inclusion of an overlong, totally tasteless musical number that permanently marred an otherwise exceptional motion picture.

Originally adapted from a book written by Hungarian-American authors Geza Herczog and Karl Farkus, *Die Wunderbar* was turned into a successful European stage production in 1931. That same year, Irving Caesar and Aben Kandel translated the German work, added their own songs, and produced an American version titled *Wonder Bar*, which opened on Broadway at the Nora Bayes Theater.[293] Its star Warner Bros.' contractee Al Jolson, purchased the film rights to the original and pitched the idea of a *Wonder Bar* film to the studio as a star vehicle for himself. Jolson's last film, *Hallelujah, I'm a Bum* had been a critical and box office disappointment, and his movie career was in a rut. New Warner Bros. production head Hal Wallis liked Jolson's idea, and pulled out all the stops to make the project a top-tier film musical in the distinguished tradition of *42nd Street* (1933), *Golddiggers of 1933* (1933), and *Footlight Parade* (1933). In addition to assembling a sure-fire cast headed by Jolson, Kay Francis, Dolores Del Rio, Cortez, and Dick Powell, Wallis tapped ace choreographer Busby Berkeley to stage elaborate musical numbers, the award-winning team of Al Dubin and Harry Warren to write original songs, and gifted Sol Polito to photograph.

The studio's all-purpose director, Lloyd Bacon, was eventually tapped to helm the project. Already a proven commodity at the studio, Bacon seemed the perfect choice. A former actor and director of two-reel comedies, he graduated to feature films after he signed with Warner Bros. in 1926. During his initial years at the studio, he proved his worth, helming several notable pictures, including Jolson's hit musical, *The Singing Fool* (1928), *Moby Dick* (1930), and two acclaimed all-star musical extravaganzas: *42nd Street* (1933) and *Footlight Parade* (1933). Not only was Bacon a capable director and worked well with Jolson, Berkeley, and several of the other craftsmen, he was adept at integrating musical numbers and plot, and keeping his films on schedule and under budget. Perhaps most importantly, he knew how to handle large casts and keep oversized, fragile movie star egos in check. He would have the challenge of his life on the set of *Wonder Bar*.

Warner Bros.' musical answer to MGM's Academy Award winning drama *Grand Hotel*, *Wonder Bar* chronicled one eventful night at a posh Parisian night club where a colorful assemblage of performers and patrons gather for an evening of entertainment. Filming began in mid-November, 1933. It was apparent from day one it would not be smooth sailing on the set. Most of Bacon's principal cast were unhappy and edgy for various reasons, both personal and professional. Among the professional reasons was the gigantic media buildup that preceded the making of the movie. Newspapers and magazines across the country promised an unprecedented extravaganza, and all involved were acutely aware they were expected to make good on the promise. Outside of director Bacon, perhaps the most pressure was born by the film's star, Jolson, who was nervous as a cat as shooting commenced. He owned a piece of the motion picture, and suspected his film career hinged on its success. In order to succeed, he was determined to make the movie as he saw fit. Constantly in conference with Bacon, Jolson not only offered ideas on his own contributions, but attempted to micromanage how other characters would be portrayed. This placed him in the crosshairs of the other major stars, who resented his interference. At one time or another, all four blew off steam, but none more than Ricardo Cortez.[294]

The filming of *Wonder Bar* would bring out the best and worst qualities of Ricardo's character. He, too, was on edge and feeling pressure on multiple fronts. *Wonder Bar* was a grade A picture, his first important assignment for his new employer, and a real test of his ability. He was cast as one of the club's star dancers, and was apprehensive about performing the elaborate dances planned. He had been working with a dance instructor to make sure he would not fail. He was also feeling pressure on the personal front. In November, he and Chris announced their engagement and pending nuptials. They purchased a brand new home still under construction at 1707 Tropical Avenue, in Beverly Hills, and Christine began purchasing furnishings. An elaborate wedding was planned by Christine and her parents to take place in her hometown of Danbury, just before Christmas. By early December, preparations were well under way.[295]

Jolson and Cortez shared several key scenes in the picture. When Al began giving him orders, Ricardo became angry. Although he would often make suggestions to directors on how he thought a role should be played, Cortez recognized producers and directors as the ultimate decision makers, and he was particularly sensitive to violations of protocol and any hint of disrespect. He did not appreciate another actor telling him how to play his part, and became even more frustrated when director Bacon failed to intervene.

According to a bystander, Jolson and Cortez almost came to blows one day during the filming of a discordant scene between Cortez's character, Harry, and Jolson's Al Wonder (the proprietor and star entertainer of the club). Just before cameras rolled, Jolson requested the scene be changed. When Cortez balked, Jolson informed him he owned a piece of the picture, which gave him a say on how all parts would be played. A furious Cortez complied, but at the end of the tense sequence, (while in character), he blew smoke in Jolson's face. Bacon was delighted by the intensity of the scene, but Al was incensed. Louella Parsons was the first to break the story of "the feud" in a November column. A subsequent Parsons' column detailed another Cortez outburst, after he learned his young costar actor/singer Dick Powell had been given a larger portable dressing room than his. Ricardo suspected this slight to be the work of Jolson, but his temper tantrums reflected badly on his own character and reputation, making him appear arrogant and petty.[296]

Apparently Bacon or Wallis (or both) eventually intervened, and the open hostility between Al and Ricardo was reduced to pranks and smart alecky comments. An article included in Warner Bros.' promotional materials for *Wonder Bar* recalled the Jolson/Cortez "rivalry," and related another entertaining incident that occurred while the two were filming a scene near the finale, after Ricardo's character Harry is stabbed to death by his dance partner, Inez (Dolores Del Rio). The scene required Al Wonder (Jolson) to carry Harry's body out to a car. According to the piece, as Al attempted to carry him across the sound stage, the 6 foot tall, 192 pound Cortez bore down hard on the 142 pound Jolson, making himself a dead weight. Bacon required eight takes of the scene, and by the last, Jolson was on the verge of physical collapse.[297]

Unfortunately, the "feud" was not the only problem Ricardo and the other filmmakers encountered. Temper tantrums aside, the film featuring Berkeley's elaborate musical numbers proved exceedingly difficult to make, and despite the expertise of Bacon, Berkeley, and company, production went over schedule. The filming of the musical numbers was still under way throughout the holiday season, necessitating the postponement of Cortez's wedding. Christine and her family had spent considerable time and money planning the event, and were not pleased about the change in plans. It was a harbinger of things to come.

The grueling production of *Wonder Bar* was finally completed in early January, 1934. Like Warner Bros. other high-end musicals, the finished film was an interesting hodge-podge of music, comedy, drama, and melodrama; a marriage of the traditional with the modern, the sentimental with the sophisticated. This particular film also married the sublime with the cringe worthy. Among the sublime elements was a Berkeley-directed musical number combining the dramatic "Valse Amoreuse" with an original Dubin/Warren song, "Don't Say Goodnight" sung by Dick Powell. Berkeley pulled out all the stops to make the sequence a standout, constructing special sets made of huge octagonal mirrors and columns. He supervised the construction of special platforms to hold overhead cameras, which tracked the action. Utilizing over 200 dancers, the number (partially performed by Ricardo and Miss Del Rio) was both elegant and dramatic, a testimony to the choreographic and filmmaking genius of its creator, aided by an accomplished technical crew and the expertise of cinematographer Polito.[298]

For the most part, the performances were also of a high caliber. Jolson was at his charismatic best as Al Wonder, the host, star, and ace problem solver at the *Wonder Bar*. Del Rio also had some good dramatic scenes as Inez, a woman torn between two lovers, as did Powell, who was earnest and appealing as a nightclub singer and bandleader who pines for Inez. Some superb comic moments were furnished by several Warner Bros.' stalwarts, including Ruth Donnelly, Guy Kibbee, Hugh Herbert, and Louise Fazenda. As the talented yet morally bankrupt gigolo, Harry, who continues to romance his dance partner while conducting an illicit affair with the married Liane (petulantly portrayed by Francis), Cortez excelled. He had originally won a Hollywood movie contract partially due to his poise and ability on a dance floor, but *Wonder Bar* was surprisingly his first major film role as a dancer.

Sadly, all of the film's superior elements (and its ultimate reputation) were negatively impacted by an unfortunate 13-minute musical sequence built around an original Dubin/Warren song entitled "Goin to Heaven on a Mule." Much has been written about the

One of the most ambitious films Cortez made was the mega musical, *Wonder Bar* (Warner Bros., 1934), which featured an all-star cast of heavyweight talents with oversized egos.

sequence through the years, and, unfortunately, most of it is true. Although technically brilliant, and beautifully filmed, the images presented were patently racist and overwhelmingly offensive,

This candid photo on the set of *Wonder Bar* shows Cortez and Dolores Del Rio holding hands before completing a complicated and controversial sado-masochistic dance number, directed by Busby Berkeley.

presenting every black stereotype imaginable. Supposedly a parody of *Green Pastures*, the sequence was in extremely poor taste.

Since it had nothing to do with the plot, for decades many have wondered why it was included. Studio records do not provide a definitive answer. Most likely Jolson and the Warner Bros. brass decided moviegoers would be disappointed if Al did not appear in one of his signature black-face numbers, and inserted the sequence. Apparently there was an initial effort to cast black actors in the "Mule" number, but that was shot down by the studio's business office. In a memorandum from production head Wallis to Busby Berkeley dated January 6, 1934, Wallis said he and Jack Warner had discussed the matter with the sales office, and concluded, "There was too much sales resistance against a thing of this kind, and we have too big a property to take a gamble. It is definitely understood that we will use white people made up through the entire number and not a single negro is to be used."[299]

There were protests by some organizations and citizen groups regarding the "Mule" number after the film's release in March, 1934, but they were largely drowned out by outrage expressed by censor boards who were incensed, not by the blatant racism, but by the "immoral" activities depicted. Several scenes were deemed inappropriate for public viewing, notably a flashy, sado-masochistic dance entitled "Tango del Rio" in which Cortez (as Harry), attired as a gaucho, whips dance partner Inez into submission. Another, even more famous scene, which caused considerable consternation, features a couple dancing. As they make their way around the floor, a mustachioed man asks to cut in. When he receives a yes, instead of taking the hand of the woman, he dances away with the man prompting Jolson to mincingly exclaim "Boys will be boys. Woooo!" Since the film was released prior to the rigorous enforcement of the Production Code (in the summer of 1934), the studio ignored the censors.[300]

In spite of the controversies, or perhaps because of them, *Wonder Bar* was an enormous critical and popular success—one of the biggest box office hits of 1934. Everyone involved celebrated, particularly its star. Jolson was jubilant. On March 8, he took out a full-page ad in *Variety* to express his appreciation to cast and crew. The public undoubtedly viewed Jolson's ad as a grand gesture of magnanimity, but those who participated suspected it was an apology of sorts for his antics during the filming.[301] Cortez apparently accepted Jolson's indirect apology, and subsequently appeared on his radio program.

Just prior to completing production on *Wonder Bar*, Warner Bros. informed Cortez he would be reteamed with Joan Blondell as stars of *Hit Me Again*, a comedy based on a play by F. Hugh Herbert, which debuted off Broadway in 1927. Cortez agreed to report for work on January 10, despite the fact it would mean putting off his wedding yet again. On January 5, the *Los Angeles Times* reported the Cortez/Lee nuptials were indefinitely postponed.[302] The decision started tongues wagging. Hollywood wondered out loud whether Cortez was afraid of saying no to his new employer, or having second thoughts about marriage. Whatever the reason, when he informed his fiancé, she issued an ultimatum. Either the wedding was now, or it was off!

Apparently that was a game changer. On Sunday, January 7, the couple flew to Phoenix and checked into a hotel just outside the city. Ricardo contacted Maricopa County Sheriff J. R. McFadden, who helped arrange the details of a simple double ring wedding ceremony to be held at the hotel, officiated by Justice of the Peace, Nat T. McKee. On Monday January 8, 1934, at 11 a.m., accompanied by a handful of witnesses, including Ricardo's friends, American Tobacco Company vice president Arthur C. Mower and wife, 33-year-old Ricardo and 26-year-old Christine finally tied the knot. Ricardo was so nervous, he forgot the ring, which caused a brief delay in the ceremony while he retrieved it from his hotel room.[303] After spending the night in Phoenix, the new Mr. and Mrs. Cortez rushed back to Hollywood so Ricardo could begin work on *Hit Me Again*, retitled *Smarty*. As it turned out, the hurried return was unnecessary. When Warner Bros. executives learned of the wedding, they replaced Cortez with Warren William, thus enabling him to have a honeymoon. A grateful Ricardo and Chris headed to New York.

Ricardo's second marriage would be as unsuccessful as his first; a huge mistake by two people who were old enough and experienced enough to have known better. It was another of those familiar instances in which the heart rules the head, when high hopes and wishful thinking trump hard-nosed reality. One can only guess the exact motivations of Ricardo and Christine, but both had to have had doubts and misgivings prior to their marriage.

By all accounts, Christine was an attractive, intelligent, articulate, and personable young woman who had much to offer as a spouse. She was fond of Ricardo and might have been the perfect match for him had they met a decade later when he was truly

CORTEZ WEDDING PARTY
The climax of a five-months' romance--the marriage of Ricardo Cortez, motion picture actor, and Mrs. Christine Lee. Photo shows the bridal party at Phoenix, Ariz. L to R: Justice Nat. T. McKee, who performed the ceremony; Mr. and Mrs. A. C. Mower, attendants; Mrs. Cortez; Ricardo Cortez; Sheriff McFadden and Harry Boyle

Ricardo met 26-year-old divorcee Christine Conniff Lee in 1933. They were married in Phoenix on January 8, 1934 by Justice of the Peace, Nat T. McKee.

"ready" to remarry. She certainly tried to make the marriage work in the beginning. Having heard his horror stories regarding his life with Alma, and having been disappointed in love and marriage herself, she appeared initially determined to be what Ricardo told her he wanted: a "traditional" stay-at-home wife, a supportive mate who would oversee the couple's home. What she wasn't willing to do, however, was stay at home alone while he did whatever he pleased. If one accepts her version of the story (related years later), she was unaware of Ricardo's selfishness and unwillingness to compromise before their marriage, but it's hard to see how she could have been so blind.

Ricardo appeared no less delusional. He liked Chris and liked the idea of being married, but was not prepared to alter his lifestyle to accommodate his new bride. He wanted to follow Dr. Immelman's advice to find a wife and have a home, but was too self-absorbed and set in his ways at the time to make the necessary effort. Since his breakup with Alma, he'd established a routine which he enjoyed

Cortez attends a dinner given by Warner Bros., saluting the Rose Bowl winning Columbia football team, who were featured in the studio's short, *Hollywood Newsreel 1934*. Seated next to Cortez is Warner Bros. general manager, William Koenig, and across from him, Joe E. Brown.

and did not intend to give up. Apparently, Ricardo operated under the impression Chris would somehow be content to be his housekeeper, hostess, and part-time companion and lover, but it's difficult to fathom how he could have deluded himself into believing this set-up could possibly work. The unpleasant realities of the new Mr. and Mrs. Cortez's relationship would become apparent in the coming months, but during the spring of 1934, optimism ruled the day.

Much to Ricardo's surprise and delight, Jack Warner and company extended his vacation/honeymoon by several weeks so he would be available to attend multiple East Coast film premieres. While in New York, the studio informed him he would be cast in another top tier movie. This time he would play a sympathetic part as a Broadway producer in love with a married actress in an adaptation of the George S. Kaufman and Alexander Woolcott black comic play, *The Dark Tower*, which debuted on Broadway in November, 1933. Despite a farfetched plot and a certain "stagey" quality, the movie, titled *The Man With Two Faces*, was a hit, redeemed by witty Kaufman/Woolcott dialogue supplanted by studio scriptwriters Niven Busch and Tom Reed, and by superb performances from Edward G. Robinson, Mary Astor, and Louis Calhern. Sadly, the film would be Ricardo's last A-level picture while a contract player at Warner Bros.[304]

During the remainder of 1934, Cortez churned out five films and began a sixth. Only one was genuinely notable, and it was made for another studio. Warner Bros.' *A Lost Lady*, directed by Alfred E. Green, reunited Cortez with the equally prolific Barbara Stanwyck for the third and final time. An adaption of Willa Cather's Pulitzer Prize-winning novel about a woman's disillusionment, scriptwriters Kathryn Scola and Gene Markey (who had penned Stanwyck's popular 1933 vehicle, *Baby Face*) opted to de-emphasize the spiritual qualities of Cather's story and make it a traditional drama. They even decided to change the ending, as Markey put it "to avoid the low key depressing effect of the last half of the novel."[305] The result looked hurried and pleased no one. After filming wrapped, Miss Stanwyck reportedly told associates she thought her Warner Bros. pictures were "getting lousier and lousier."[306] No one was unhappier with *A Lost Lady* than the author, Miss Cather. After seeing it, she added a stipulation to her will forbidding any further movie adaptations of her work.

Cortez, too, voiced disappointment with his part as a dashing pilot who tempts the protagonist, but insisted he enjoyed playing villains and "other men." In an interview with columnist Reine Davies (Marion's sister, Alma's old friend), Ricardo expressed contentment with his villainous screen image.

"There's always more color, more magnetism, more fascination in the villain's role, if it is properly written, than there is in the hero's. If it were not so, he couldn't engage and hold the interest of the leading lady during five-sixths of the picture, as he usually does. That goes for the people of the audience too. They may not admit it, because it seems so obviously logical for good people to like other good people, but subconsciously, they know that all heroes are monotonously alike, but the villain has dash and individuality. So I'd rather be an interesting screen villain than a stainless Galahad. A heavy, with a few redeeming qualities is remembered long after the average hero is forgotten."[307]

Cortez and costar Anita Louise are photographed in between takes on the set of *The Firebird* (Warner Bros., 1934).

Mr. Cortez alternated between heroes and heels in his remaining 1934 Warner Bros. features. In *The Firebird*, he was a narcissistic American actor who is murdered while carrying on affairs with multiple women in Vienna. The movie had a capable cast, an exceptional director, William Dieterle, and first tier cinematography and art direction, but an inferior script (based on a popular Hungarian play) doomed the motion picture to mediocrity. A similar problem plagued the melodramatic *I Am a Thief*, about jewel thieves aboard

Ricardo acquired a mustache to play the hero in *I Am a Thief*, about killers and thieves in pursuit of rare jewels. It was the fifth of six pairings of Cortez with costar, Mary Astor.

the *Orient Express*. It, too, had a gifted director, Robert Florey (*The House on 56th Street*), a charming leading lady, Mary Astor, and some clever plot twists, but the basic storyline (competing criminals aboard a luxury train) was unexceptional. Ditto *The White Cockatoo*, an entertaining whodunit featuring a mustachioed Cortez as a man who gets caught up in a convoluted scheme to kill heirs to a fortune.

Notably, Cortez's best 1934 opportunity came outside Warner Bros., when RKO borrowed his services to play a talented defense attorney whose unique conflicts of interest complicate his attempt to defend a young man accused of murder in *Hat, Coat, and Glove*. The conflicts included his wife's romantic entanglement with the defendant and, incredibly, his own involvement in the crime. John Barrymore had been the original choice to play the flawed hero, Robert Mitchell, but he was unable to remember his lines or complete even the simplest tasks. The studio was finally forced to replace him. Several actors were considered before RKO settled on one they knew they could count on. That someone was Ricardo Cortez, who, with Warner Bros. consent (see movie section for contract), accepted the assignment with only a few days to prepare.[308]

Production was completed four weeks later. *Hat, Coat, and Glove* was not a great motion picture, but a good one thanks to young director Worthington Miner, who crafted realistic and compelling scenes from a fanciful script based on an unbelievable story. He was aided by excellent acting, particularly by his star, who was surprisingly subdued and effective as the attorney whose love and yearning for his estranged spouse (Barbara Robbins) inspires him to take the case of her young lover (John Beal) and eventually be willing to give her up. Cortez's scenes with supporting actress Dorothy Burgess (who portrays the young man's ex-girlfriend) were particularly strong. When Burgess' character asks Mitchell about his love for his wife, he tenderly replies "To me, she's beautiful. But then she's all I've got, part of me. Wife, daughter, dream, and reality." Cortez was also excellent in the courtroom scenes in which he manages a range of emotions while forcefully defending his client. It is not an overstatement to say *Hat, Coat, and Glove* contains some of Cortez's best, most compelling film acting. His portrayal of a character so unlike the slick, polished villains film audiences so often associated him with, was additional proof he could effectively handle a broad range of characterizations. In his review in *The Hollywood Citizen News*, columnist James Francis Crow said it best. "Barrymore is not missed . . . Cortez dominates the picture. His is a most unusual portrayal, marked by studied peculiarities which serve to make his characterization all the more engrossing . . . ."[309]

Ricardo was justifiably proud of his work on the picture. Among his personal effects, which eventually were put up for sale in 2008, were three personal scrapbooks containing clippings, reviews, and various ephemera that Cortez kept as treasured mementoes of his five-decade-long movie acting career. One was devoted to the silent era, one to vaudeville, and, the other to his sound motion pictures. In the sound scrapbook were multiple reviews of five motion pictures that Cortez apparently considered his best. They were: *The Maltese Falcon, Symphony of Six Million, Is My Face Red? Hat, Coat, and Glove,* and *Her Husband Lies.*[310]

Sadly, the unconditional love and touching devotion of the character

Cortez had one of his best roles as an attorney whose conflicts of interest complicate his defense of a young man falsely accused of murder in *Hat, Coat, and Glove* (RKO, 1934), costarring John Beal (pictured on the stand). This original photo came from the late Mr. Beal's personal collection.

Among the items included in Ricardo's sound film scrapbook was this set of clippings of reviews he received for *Hat, Coat, and Glove* (RKO, 1934).

Robert Mitchell had for his spouse, that Ricardo had so beautifully portrayed onscreen in *Hat, Coat, and Glove*, did not apply to his own wife. Christine found being Mrs. Ricardo Cortez a rough go. Problems surfaced soon after the nuptials, and became more pronounced over time. When their new home was not ready for occupancy in January, 1934, Ricardo and Chris rented a furnished house on Foothill Road in Beverly Hills. The house was large and roomy, so much so that the ever frugal Ricardo invited his brother, Stanley (still a poor aspiring cinematographer), to move in and share expenses. As it turned out, all the extra room came in handy. According to Christine, within a week after they moved in, her husband informed her he wanted his own room where he could be alone. He insisted on complete freedom to come and go as he wished. In addition to long hours at the studio, his regimen included daily sports and exercise activities, including daily rides on his thoroughbred race horse, "Little Joe," Wednesday night wrestling matches, Friday night fights with his pals, and Saturdays at the Santa Anita or Hollywood Park racetracks. His wife was rarely invited along.[311]

When he wasn't occupied with the aforementioned, Ricardo was often busy preparing for his film roles, (researching parts, learning his lines), doing interviews and publicity for his films, appearing on radio, working on and/or checking on his many investments, or reading his favorite books, newspapers, and magazines. All this left little time for his wife. The couple did entertain occasionally and attend formal functions, but when they were together, Christine complained her husband treated her with coldness and indifference. "He said he did not feel any affection for me; and when I tried to show affection for him, he repulsed me,"[312] she said. The new Mrs. Cortez soon came to the realization she was the junior partner in this union, and if it were to endure, she would have to accept Ricardo as he was and be content with the proverbial "crumbs" he threw her.

Ricardo's employer, Warner Bros., was doing some adjusting as well, adapting its business model, personnel, and production practices to comply with the new strict enforcement of the Production Code. Originally established by movie studios and distributors in 1922 as a trade association, the M.P.P.D.A. (Motion Picture Producers and Distributors Association, headed by Will Hays) was given the authority to handle industry relations with various entities. One of its branches, the S.R.C. (Studio Relations Committee), was set up to monitor the moral content of motion pictures. To combat sin and corruption in the movies, a set of guidelines was issued in 1930. Known as the "Hays Code," it included 11 objectionable topics. Because it had no real authority to enforce its will, the studios often ignored the S.R.C.'s recommendations.

That changed in 1934. In response to unrelenting pressure from civic, religious, and political groups upset about corruption and immorality in movies, an amendment to the original Code was passed by the studios creating the Production Code Administration (P.C.A.). Effective July 1, 1934, former Catholic layman Joseph Breen was appointed head of the P.C.A. and given the authority to enforce strict adherence to what was described as "standards of good taste"—a requirement that "no picture shall be produced which will lower the standards of those who see it."

Breen said, "The sympathy of the audiences should never be thrown to the side of crime, wrongdoing, evil, or sin." Precise regulations prohibited the onscreen portrayal and/or suggestion of various activities deemed immoral or unethical. Among them were miscegenation, homosexuality, promiscuity, seduction, rape, profanity, excessive and lustful kissing, and suggestive postures or gestures. In addition, specific methods of crime could not be presented, and criminal activities could never be seen to succeed. Breen's enforcement mechanism was certificates of approval issued to all films that adhered to the provisions of the Code.[313]

The new code enforcement would have a profound effect on the film industry from top to bottom. Pre-Code freedoms to portray life in a more realistic fashion were severely curtailed, and the careers of many of the early sound era's most successful stars and filmmakers, including Ricardo Cortez, were impacted. Since the advent of sound, Cortez had become one of the screen's most charismatic antiheroes. A significant part of the attractiveness and peculiar charm of Ricardo's roguish screen persona, was based on the salacious relationships and criminal activities his characters were free to carry on during the early sound period. The new, strict enforcement of the Production Code severely altered the equation, sanitizing Cortez's sin and, in the process, making his characters (particularly his villains) less intriguing.

This fact was born out during the remainder of Cortez's tenure at Warner Bros. (1935-37), in which he alternated between heroes and villains, leads and supporting roles. Although he continued to bring his own unique combination of skill, charm, charisma, and professionalism to bear on each part, beginning in the summer of 1934, something was missing. There were a few respectable opportunities during this time, including a chance to portray Erle Stanley Gardner's famed attorney/sleuth Perry Mason, but the magic was all but gone, "Lysolled" away by Joe Breen and his P.C.A.

The incredibly busy Mr. Cortez would make six motion pictures in 1935, often shuttling between movie studios, doing more than one picture at a time. He began the year with two loan outs. The first was MGM's *Shadow of Doubt*, a movie mystery with a high gloss look and A-level cast. Both Metro-Goldwyn-Mayer head Louis B. Mayer and his production chief Irving Thalberg were longtime admirers of the dependable Cortez. In December, 1934, they negotiated a contract with Jack Warner to loan Cortez for his $2,000 a week salary, plus a bonus of $6,000 for the studio.[314] The result was a respectable B+ movie lifted by MGM's high-end production values (notably art direction from the legendary Cedric Gibbons) and an impressive cast.

Adapted from an Arthur Somers Roche novel originally serialized in *Colliers* magazine, Cortez was in his element as a wealthy ad man who is implicated in the murder of his girlfriend's (Virginia Bruce) ex-lover. All appears lost until his eccentric Miss Marple-like aunt (Constance Collier) intercedes to solve the crime and save the day. Ricardo's follow-up film, Universal's grade Z romantic musical comedy, *Manhattan Moon*, wasted him in the ill-defined part of a night club owner anxious to gain entrée into high society.

Back at Warner Bros., Ricardo supported James Cagney and Bette Davis in two middling program pictures with respectable elements. *Frisco Kid*, a period melodrama set in 1850's San Francisco, gave Cortez a substantive character role (and a showy death scene) as a crooked gambler who helps a lowly sailor (Cagney) become a political powerhouse, amid the corruption and violence of the Frisco waterfront. For whatever reason, the movie was made at the same time as another similar picture, United Artists' *Barbary Coast*, written by the acclaimed duo of Ben Hecht and Charles MacArthur, and suffered for it. While *Frisco Kid* contained superb direction from Lloyd Bacon (*Wonder Bar*), first-rate art direction from John Hughes (who brilliantly recreated the vintage setting), and a stalwart cast, critics and audiences rated it a poor imitation of *Barbary Coast*. An even harsher judgement was rendered by its star, Mr. Cagney, who described it as" a stinking piece of junk made on tissue paper and spit." [315]

Similar sentiments were expressed by Bette Davis regarding the melodramatic *Special Agent*, about a treasury agent (George Brent) who goes undercover as a newspaperman to help the federal government nab a notorious Capone-like crime kingpin (Cortez) for tax evasion. Based on a story by noted New York newsman, Martin Mooney, and directed by William Keighley, with a good script by Abem Finkel and Laird Doyle, the picture was not nearly as bad as Miss Davis claimed, but it was not particularly memorable. This, despite a tour-de-force portrayal from Ricardo, who, sans smile and salacious activities, delivered a cool, calculated, and thoroughly chilling performance as the cold-blooded Carston, who skillfully evades the long arm of the law until his trusty secretary (Davis) cooperates with the Feds to do him in.

An ad for *Frisco Kid* boldly proclaimed Ricardo Cortez had been killed more times in the movies than any other major actor. Fact or fiction, the screen veteran was aware of the distinction, and amused by it. In 1935, he told a journalist he was often intrigued by the creative ways writers found to rid the world of his menace.

"I believe I have been subjected to every possible death torture conceived by the civilized and uncivilized world! I died so often that I am willing to discount the ordinary garden variety demise, such as being stabbed, choked, shot, or other simple methods of dispatch. What really fascinates me is the more novel methods, such as dying in an acid bath!" [316]

Ricardo followed the Cagney and Davis projects in quick succession with two low-grade thrillers from ace Warner Bros. producer Bryan Foy's newly created B unit. He was a doctor/murder suspect in the formulaic mystery, *The Murder of Dr. Harrigan*, and a fugitive gangster hiding out in a small town in the melodrama, *Man Hunt*. The former was notable as the last of six movies Cortez made with versatile

Cortez supported the dynamic James Cagney in the period melodrama, *Frisco Kid* (Warner Bros., 1935). Front row from left to right, Cortez, Cagney, and George E. Stone.

Up and coming actress Bette Davis (right) played the secretary of a murderous gangster (Cortez, far left) who cooperates with authorities to nab her boss for tax evasion in the crime drama, *Special Agent* (Warner Bros., 1935).

Mary Astor. During its production, a journalist asked Ricardo if he ever viewed "the daily rushes" of his films (i.e., the film record of what was shot the previous day). In a rare bit of self-revelation, he admitted he had long ago ceased watching them due to self-consciousness and a self-described inferiority complex.

"Any mistake that I would make would prey on my mind so much that my performance on the next day suffered. I figured it wasn't worth it, and now I spend that time relaxing, which I formally spent squirming on the edge of a seat in the projection room." [317]

Ric Cortez's discomfiture with the daily rushes coincided with his increasing displeasure with his professional career at Warner Bros. Because of his own intense interest in the financial world, Ricardo had always understood his studio bosses' motives. He was sensitive to their desire to increase profits and satisfy stock holders, but by the mid 1930's, he had become convinced his employer was taking advantage of his ability and work ethic. For the first time since he signed with the studio, Cortez began refusing film assignments, including nondescript roles in two B dramas: *Housewife*, and the Jackie Cooper vehicle, *Dinky*. When he declined the assignments, the studio promptly suspended him. A week after his suspension for *Dinky*, someone noticed Cortez milling around the studio lot and notified production head Hal Wallis. Responding to an inquiry from Wallis, in an inter-office memo dated March 1, 1935, Warner Bros. legal executive, Roy Obringer sought to clarify Cortez's status. In a highly revealing note, Obringer told Wallis the studio had no right to keep Cortez away from the lot because (unlike many of their contract players) his contract did not contain a clause to "keep him on suspension until the player substituted to portray the role which he refused to do, has entirely completed it." [318]

In September, 1935, Ricardo reportedly complained to his bosses about the lack of quality film roles, and reminded them they had made him an informal, unwritten promise to give him an opportunity to direct. The Warner Bros. bosses promised to address these issues, but little came of it. Cortez was tested for parts in two of the studio's big-budget epic adventures: *Anthony Adverse* and *Captain Blood*, but the roles went to others. [319] It was then announced he would reprise the role of pirate Jean Lafitte (whom he had portrayed in Paramount's *The Eagle of the Sea*) opposite George Brent in an A level adventure, *Black Ivory*, based on Polan Banks' popular novel, but the project never saw the light.[320]

Ricardo's growing professional woes were mirrored in his home life. After only a year, his marriage was on the rocks. Christine was becoming increasingly discontented with her husband's selfishness, neglect, and half-hearted commitment to their marriage, and began voicing her displeasure. This led to frequent arguments that were usually patched up by apologies from Ricardo and promises to do better, but he never did.

By 1935, the hyper-active film star was literally becoming a money-making machine. During his suspension, Ricardo accepted engagements to appear on radio. The most notable of his radio gigs was as substitute master of ceremonies (February–May, 1935) on Guy Lombardo's popular NBC musical program, *Pleasure Island* (temporarily originating from Hollywood while Lombardo and his band fulfilled an engagement at the Cocoanut Grove in Los Angeles.)[321] Cortez also accepted offers from various clothiers to sponsor lines of apparel. Always counted among Hollywood's best dressed men, several key men's clothing merchants were eager to have his name attached to their products. Cortez was flattered, and only too happy to accede to their requests, and cash their substantial checks.[322]

Also of considerable note during this period (and throughout his Hollywood career and beyond) was Cortez's interest in financial matters. Multiple newspaper stories and columns during the period of 1933-37 chronicled his personal and financial involvement in several real estate and business ventures, including land, rental homes, an investment firm, a cafeteria style restaurant, and various creative properties and projects. For instance, in June 1935, columnist Wood Soanes noted the sale of the screen rights to author-playwright Roi Cooper Megrue's comic play, *Honors Are Even*, to Paramount Pictures "by co-owners Ricardo Cortez and Broadway producer Arch Selwyn." Paramount purchased the play as a vehicle for Carole Lombard and Herbert Marshall, but for unknown reasons, never made the movie.[323]

In spite of his growing frustrations, Ricardo's last year as a Warner Bros. contract player, 1936, saw the release of two of the

In addition to making motion pictures, Cortez made several appearances on radio. The most prominent was a four-month stint (February-May, 1935), as substitute host of Guy Lombardo's popular NBC musical program, *Pleasure Island*.

In addition to acting and his many investments, the dapper Cortez became a spokesman for various clothiers. This ad for Sturdevant's Department Store, published in the September 28, 1935 issue of *The Zanesville Signal*, notes of the sale of "Ricardo Cortez shirts."

most memorable films of his tenure. Both were program pictures made to fill the bottom half of a double bill, but both were skillfully produced, and gave the veteran actor roles that showed him to advantage.

The first chronologically, and undoubtedly the best of the pair, was *The Walking Dead*, which was a highly unusual mix of the horror, crime, and dramatic genres. The idea for the picture had originated with Hal Wallis in August 1935. After attending a showing of the Columbia melodrama, *The Black Room*, starring Boris Karloff as twin brothers, Wallis came away so impressed by the actor's work, he purchased one of Scottish-born writer Ewart Adamson's stories, commissioned Adamson to construct a rough script, and contacted agent Myron Selznick in hopes of acquiring Karloff's services for Warner Bros.[324] Scenarist Joseph Fields was eventually brought in to help Adamson fine tune his screenplay about a musically inclined parolee who is brought back to life by a noted doctor/scientist, after his execution for a crime he didn't commit. Later, inspired by a higher power, the man sets out on a quest to find the reason for his death by confronting those responsible.

By early November, Wallis was well on his way to making his vision a reality. Karloff was signed to a one-picture deal, an exceptional supporting cast (including Cortez) had been assembled, and the studio's top director, Michael Curtiz, was slated to helm the picture. The movie was not considered one of Warner Bros.' prestige projects, but particular care was utilized to make it top notch. Prior to filming, art director Hugh Reticker supervised the construction of an elaborate laboratory set that included an exact replica of the headline-making "Lindbergh heart," a mechanical circulating system invented by Nobel prize winning scientist Dr. Alexis Carrel and aviator Charles Lindbergh, which figured prominently in the plot.[325]

When all appeared to be in readiness for the production to proceed, problems surfaced when Karloff expressed grave concerns regarding the screenplay. In the original Adamson/Fields script, the protagonist, John Ellman, was an inarticulate addict named "Dopey," who spoke few words and possessed a Tarzan-like physical strength. Karloff was unhappy with the lack of humanity and realism portrayed in the character. Anxious to please the popular star, Wallis promptly halted plans to begin filming, and brought in three more writers to address concerns. It took two extra weeks, and cost the studio almost $50,000, but the time and money proved well spent. By the time production was completed in December, 1935, *The Walking Dead* had been transformed into a beautifully constructed B+ movie, a testament to the talents of its director and star, and, proof positive an excellent motion picture could be made on a modest budget.[326]

The perpetually undervalued Curtiz brilliantly interpreted an average script, giving it depth and dimension while keeping the action moving. With the able assistance of Hal Mohr's knowing camera, the Hungarian-born director brought his expressionist influences to bear through skillful use of lighting and shading. Apparently, Curtiz also kept his infamous dictatorial personality in check in deference to his star, whom he admired. This allowed Karloff considerable latitude to interpret his character, resulting in a virtuoso performance, one of the best of his long career.

The film was both a critical and financial success. Even reviewers who routinely dismissed horror films were largely enthusiastic. The lion's share of the acclaim was rightly shared by Curtiz and Karloff, but the film was a plus for all involved, including Ricardo Cortez who received kudos for his portrayal of the slimy mob lawyer, Nolan, who represents Ellman at his trial, and helps railroad him to the electric chair.

Cortez's reward for his success in *The Walking Dead* was the unemployment line. In November, 1935, Warner Bros. chose not to pick up his option.[327] His refusal to accept certain assignments was undoubtedly a factor, but not the deciding one. In the end, money appeared the primary reason. Production records reveal Cortez had been paid $12,000 for six weeks' work on *The Walking Dead*, second only to Karloff's $18,750. The studio apparently felt his salary was becoming too high, and decided to cut ties.[328]

Once again, Ricardo Cortez was without a job, or offers of a job. When it happened initially in 1930, he had contemplated suicide, but not this time. Things were different now! Back then he was facing a perfect storm of personal, professional and financial woes. There was a good chance he might end up back on the poverty-stricken streets of Lower Manhattan, but not now! During the last five years, he had worked steadily, tirelessly, often at the expense of his own health and well-being, and saved much of his earnings.

Through thriftiness and savvy investments, Ricardo Cortez could now take comfort in the knowledge he'd never be poor again. Still, the decision by Warner Bros. to drop him from their roster was a blow to Cortez's fragile ego, one that left the actor smarting and wondering. He had managed to endure the ups and downs of the dog-eat- dog world of the movies for 14 years; but would he be able to resurrect his career yet again? Only time would tell, but Ricardo knew one thing, he would survive.

CHAPTER EIGHT
"VON STROHEIM OF THE B'S" (1936–40)

"I'd like to go into the production end when I'm through acting. But when that day comes, my outside interests may be of such importance to me that I shall be able to forget all about the screen."
— RICARDO CORTEZ

As the newly unemployed Ricardo contemplated his professional future, he and Christine boarded a train for New York for a brief holiday. For Mrs. Cortez, it was a much-needed break from her unhappy life in California. She missed her friends and her parents in the East. A chance to spend time with them was akin to a lifeline. For Ricardo, it was a time to plot a second comeback. Since his first had involved the stage, he decided to try the theatre a second time. While doing a few radio gigs, he contacted a booking agency, who arranged for him to do a series of personal appearances in which he performed a brief skit, answered questions, and signed autographs. The appearances began in New York in late January, 1936, and continued along the East Coast, ending in Washington, D.C., in March, 1937. The majority of the events (held in prominent theatres) were sellouts. Cortez had always been popular with audiences, and his fans savored a chance to see him in person. One two-day (Friday and Saturday) booking in Cumberland, Maryland, in late February was so popular, a special session of the city council was called so the theatre could stay open on the Sabbath to give patrons another chance to see one of their favorite actors.[329]

Ricardo was pleased by the interest, but unenthused about the appearances. During a two-week run in Washington, D. C.'s Earle Theatre, he took time to tour the nation's capital. According to

After Warner Bros. dropped him from their roster in November, 1935, Ricardo embarked on a series of East Coast stage performances in which he performed a skit, answered questions and signed autographs. Many of his personal appearances were sellouts.

personal letters Cortez kept in his possession until his death (which were sold online in 2008), he and two associates were taken on a guided tour of FBI headquarters at this time by lieutenants of director, J. Edgar Hoover. The letters reveal a personal friendship between Hoover and Cortez, apparently initiated at the time of the release of *Special Agent*.

As his vaudeville tour had in 1930, Ricardo's theater appearances ultimately proved a fruitful investment of time, reminding Hollywood his name still carried weight with the public. By the end of his run, Ricardo had a new film offer from his old friend, Charlie Rogers, newly installed as head of production at Universal Pictures. The offer was the title role in the Universal melodrama, *Postal Inspector*, about criminals involved in the theft of mail. For a change, Cortez would play the hero, a post office policeman whose job was to protect the U.S. mail. Production was slated to begin in June, 1936.

Ricardo and Christine returned to California in mid-April so he could prepare. In early May, he received yet another film offer, this one from a most unexpected source, his old boss, Jack Warner.

> JOHN EDGAR HOOVER
> DIRECTOR
>
> FEDERAL BUREAU OF INVESTIGATION
> U. S. DEPARTMENT OF JUSTICE
> WASHINGTON, D. C.
>
> February 11, 1936.
>
> Mr. Ricardo Cortez,
> The Earle Theatre,
> Washington, D. C.
>
> Dear Mr. Cortez:
>
> I have just returned to my office and am terribly sorry that I was unable to be here when you and your party called. The Appropriations Hearings before the Committee of the House of Representatives have been in session for the last two days and I just completed my testimony late this afternoon, though I had hoped to complete it yesterday, in which event I was looking forward with the greatest of pleasure to personally showing you the Federal Bureau of Investigation.
>
> I do hope, though, that you had a very pleasant visit and that it will be my good fortune to at least see you and say hello before you leave the city.
>
> With expressions of my very best regards, I remain
>
> Sincerely yours,
>
> J. Edgar Hoover

While performing in Washington D.C., Cortez was given a tour of FBI headquarters by a lieutenant of director J. Edgar Hoover. This letter found in Cortez' personal files, indicates a friendship between Cortez and Hoover, which was initiated during the production of *Special Agent* (Warner Bros., 1935).

Warner needed an actor to take over the role of brilliant attorney/sleuth Perry Mason in the studio's popular series based on Erle Stanley Gardner's bestselling books. Longtime Warner Bros. contract player Warren William, who had successfully played Mason in four films, was leaving the studio for RKO, and both Warner and Bryan Foy felt Cortez would be the best possible candidate to replace him. Ricardo was still smarting from the studio's decision to drop him, but his old golfing buddy, Jack Warner, was persuasive, and the part of Mason was intriguing.

On May 14, 1936, Cortez signed a second term contract with Warner Bros. as a featured player to commence July 1, after *Postal Inspector* was completed. In all but two respects, the pact was similar to its predecessor. This contract contained the studio's new layoff clause, which gave Warner Bros. the right to lay Cortez off without pay for 12 weeks a year, including one four-week period. The other notable difference was salary. Cortez would now make $1250 a week, to be increased to $1500 after 26 weeks. This was a demotion of sorts, as Cortez had been making $2000 a week on *The Walking Dead*.[330] Cortez swallowed his pride and accepted the pay cut. At this stage in his career, he undoubtedly felt becoming Perry Mason was the best he could hope for.

Production began on *The Case of the Caretaker's Cat* (retitled *The Case of the Black Cat*) one week after *Postal Inspector* wrapped. Because he had been working at Universal, Cortez had little time to prepare. Playing the role of Mason proved more challenging than first anticipated. The Gardner books were enormously popular. Virtually everyone was familiar with them, and had an opinion on how the famed attorney should be played. Perhaps most importantly, another actor (Warren William) had become identified with the character. Although the last two Mason films had drastically altered the character's traditional persona, from a serious attorney/sleuth, into a lighthearted comic figure in the mold of Nick "*The Thin Man*" Charles, William was a gifted actor, and replacing him would not be easy.

According to Cortez, by the time he arrived on the Warner Bros. lot he had already received countless letters from across America offering him advice on how to play Mason. In an interview conducted for the *The Case of the Black Cat* press book (distributed to theaters), Cortez recalled some of the advice.

"They wrote in and suggested how I should walk, how I should talk, and how I should part my hair. A woman in Memphis who said she was the mother of ten children, all of whom were potential Perry

Masons, advised me to go to bed early on the nights before I was to work on the part. She said I could think more clearly in the morning if I did... If I took my fans collective advice, my Perry Mason would be a remarkable person indeed. He'd be thin and fat, tall and short—and clean shaven with a moustache and a goatee."[331]

Even more guidance was offered by producer Foy, director Alan Crosland (who had worked with Cortez on *The White Cockatoo*), and scriptwriter F. Hugh Herbert (not to be confused with Warner Bros. contract comedian Hugh Herbert). All agreed Cortez should not attempt to copy William's portrayal, but leave his own stamp on the character. The script, based on Gardner's 1935 book, *The Case of the Caretakers Cat* (about murder and mayhem involving quarrels over an elderly millionaire's estate), was helpful. In essence, scenarist Herbert returned to basics by abandoning the comic aspects of the previous films and making Mason more as Gardner envisioned: a sophisticated, serious-minded attorney and criminologist whose brilliant mind and legal expertise helps him solve complex murder cases and free his clients. Herbert also returned Mason to bachelor status. With no explanation, Mason's marriage to his indispensable secretary/assistant Della Street, which took place in *The Case of the Lucky Legs*, was abandoned.

In spite of the tragic accidental death of director Crosland (killed in an auto mishap on Sunset Boulevard midway through production), *The Case of the Black Cat* met expectations, mainly due to expert direction by Crosland's successor William McGann, and a superb lead performance. His pre-production worries notwithstanding, the role of Mason appeared to fit Cortez like an old shoe. Charming and sophisticated with a keen mind and a compassionate heart, Cortez's Mason was all a poor, unfortunate, wrongly accused defendant could ask for. "Ricardo Cortez acts the part as though it was tailor-made," said *The New York Times*; "Ricardo Cortez as the lawyer-detective Perry Mason delivers a standout job" said *Variety*.[332]

Studio executives were exceedingly pleased. By late fall 1936, Warner Bros. announced Cortez would star in another Mason picture, *The Case of the Stuttering Bishop*, but it was not to be.[333] Cortez would never play Perry Mason again. The reasons are a bit murky. In his book, *The Detective in Hollywood*, author Jon Tuska said novelist

Erle Stanley Gardner's objection to "a Latin" playing Mason was the deciding factor.[334] While it is true Gardner WAS unhappy with the entire Warner Bros. film series, particularly the portrayal of Mason, AND was continually voicing complaints, there is no evidence in archival records indicating his objections were the reason Cortez was replaced. In fact the opposite is true. The studio routinely ignored Gardner's complaints. The primary reason Cortez never portrayed Mason again likely had to do with money. After he finished work on *The Case of the Black Cat*, Warner Bros. received two lucrative offers for Cortez's services that were just too good to pass up.

In 1936, Warner Bros. re-signed Cortez to a term contract to take over the role of famed attorney/sleuth Perry Mason in the studio's popular series based on Erle Stanley Gardner's stories. Ricardo would play the part only once: in *The Case of the Black Cat* (Warner Bros., 1936), costarring June Travis as Della Street.

The first came from across the pond. In 1935, English flour magnate J. Arthur Rank and building tycoon Charles Boot formed a partnership which eventually became known as J. Arthur Rank Organization. In hopes of competing with the American film industry, they transformed a large country estate Boot owned at Iver Heath, Buckinghamshire, into a movie studio with state- of-the-art equipment.

Despite his preoccupations with various endeavors, Mr. and Mrs. Ricardo Cortez would occasionally entertain in their lovely two-story Tropical Avenue home. Among their illustrious guests were many Hollywood luminaries, including Carole Lombard, seen here with Cary Grant, Clark Gable, and Cortez.

Nine months later, Pinewood Studios was born with five sound stages that could be rented out. By late fall of 1936, all was in readiness to begin filming at the new facility, and an effort was made to attract famous American actors to appear in the initial productions.[335] On the recommendation of Universal's Charles Rogers, one of the first stars contacted was Ricardo Cortez. Ricardo was pleased and excited about the invitation, but Warner Bros. remained unenthusiastic until monetary details were discussed. British and Dominions Film Corporation was prepared to pay handsomely for Cortez's appearance in a motion picture tentatively titled *The Man With Your Voice*, and the studio was only too happy to take their money.[336]

On September 16, 1936, Mr. and Mrs. Ric Cortez and actress Sally Eilers (Cortez's costar) were among the passengers sailing from New York to Southampton aboard the French liner, *Normandie*.[337] Ricardo was in a festive mood throughout the trip. He loved to travel and was pleased by the enthusiastic reception he received in England from British filmmakers and dignitaries who greeted him like a foreign monarch, giving him a special guided tour of the beautiful new facilities. He and Christine stayed in a luxurious suite at the Pinewood Actor's Clubhouse, formerly the estate's mansion. On September 30, he was one of the special guests at a luncheon celebrating the official opening of the studio. Among the over one thousand dignitaries attending was Parliamentary Secretary of the British Board of Trade, Leslie Burgin, who gave the keynote speech declaring "With studios such as these, we have no excuse for not producing films which should be world winners."[338]

Unfortunately, *The Man With Your Voice*, retitled *Talk of the Devil*, was not close to being in the "world winner" category. Director Carol Reed, who would eventually become one of his country's premier filmmakers by helming such classics as *The Fallen Idol* (1948) and *The Third Man* (1949), was still a novice in 1936, and his inexperience showed. The storyline, involving a rogue shipbuilder's (Basil Sydney) attempt to take over his brother's business by hiring a mimic (played by Cortez), was intriguing, but many of the scenes Reed created were weak and overly melodramatic. The movie did respectable business in Britain, but for a variety of reasons (both critical and financial), was unsuccessful in the U.S.

Despite the movie's box office failure, Cortez thoroughly enjoyed the experience of making it. He had a showy role, was paid well for his work, and loved the Pinewood facilities. Even more importantly, after suffering recent career setbacks, the respect and attention

Ricardo and Christine Cortez pose for photos in England where Cortez made the melodrama, *Talk of the Devil* (Rank, 1936), directed by Carol Reed.

afforded him in Britain gave his fragile ego a much-needed boost. Just prior to his departure, he told British reporters he intended to make more films in England.

Meanwhile, during his absence, back in Hollywood, Warner Bros. had scheduled Ricardo's appearances in two more upcoming productions. In addition to the Perry Mason movie, *The Case of the Stuttering Bishop*, he was slated to costar in two Bryan Foy produced low-budget comedies: *Public Wedding* and *The Go-Getter*. Preparations were well under way for the latter picture to be directed by Busby Berkeley when Warner Bros. received another outside offer for Cortez from B. P Schulberg Productions (distributed by Paramount). The proposed project was a film remake of Oliver H.P. Garrett's story, *Street of Chance*, based on the life of gangster Arthur Rothstein. Paramount had previously filmed the story in 1930 with William Powell, Jean Arthur, and Kay Francis.

Warner Bros. was not initially eager to loan Cortez again. Another loan would mean yet another postponement of the Mason series, and possibly the other two films, but Paramount's offer of $3,000 a week for a minimum of five weeks convinced them to reconsider. On December 10, 1936, signatures were affixed to a contract between Schulberg Productions and Warner Bros., sending Cortez to Paramount for a minimum fee of $15,000. In exchange, Warner Bros. agreed to pay Cortez's salary ($1250 per week). Notably, this agreement contained no bonus for Cortez.[339]

Production on the medium-budgeted *Street of Chance*, retitled *Her Husband Lies*, was completed in just three weeks by efficient director Edward Ludwig. Cortez handled the substantive lead role admirably, aided by a fine script that gave him several showy scenes, and a multi-dimensional character to play. He had portrayed morally challenged professional gamblers in several other pictures, but the family-centric crook, Spade Martin, gave Cortez added opportunities to demonstrate the breadth and range of his acting ability. He was particularly fine in the quiet scenes with his screen wife and brother, well played by Gail Patrick and Tom Brown. With subtle gestures and his expressive eyes, he conveyed wisdom, sensitivity, and compassion. Sadly, his excellent reviews and the profit Warner Bros. netted from his appearance in *Her Husband Lies* did not improve his standing at the studio. After he completed the picture, Cortez learned Warner Bros. had recast all of his proposed parts, including the role of Perry Mason (inherited by Donald Woods). To top it off, on January 29, 1937, he received a layoff notice.[340]

Cortez was livid, but there was nothing he could do for now, except bide his time and hope things might improve. Such was the life of an actor in Hollywood. Just weeks ago, he had been treated like a king in Britain, then made an acclaimed picture in Hollywood; now he was unemployed! Ricardo enjoyed many aspects of acting, and took great pride in his work, but by 1937, he was becoming increasingly frustrated with the profession. For years he had wanted to try directing. Jack Warner and Hal Wallis had made him verbal promises to make it happen, but never made good on them.

On February 17, *Variety* reported Cortez's next movie appearance (after he completed his four-week layoff) would be a supporting role in a new Warner Bros. Boris Karloff vehicle entitled *China Bandit*, based on a Broadway play. Ricardo liked working with Karloff and had heard positive things about the proposed director John Farrow, but he was unenthusiastic. His villainous role as a greedy oil man who crosses paths with a Chinese warlord was relatively small and unremarkable.

The project, retitled *West of Shanghai*, was the third film adaptation of Porter Emerson Brown's successful Broadway play, *The Bad Man*, about an ethical Mexican bandit named Pancho Lopez. To write the new version, producer Hal Wallis tapped scenarist Crane Wilbur, who made the story unique, while mining the current fascination with the Orient, by changing the setting to China and making Pancho Lopez a Chinese warlord named Wu Yen Fang. In addition to Farrow, Wallis hired noted cinematographer L.W. "Lu" O'Connell (who had photographed the groundbreaking melodrama, *Scarface*, in 1932) to lens the picture.

With the help of some witty Crane Wilbur dialogue, Karloff was able to create a full-bodied characterization, infusing the brutal, violent warlord with humor and humanity, as indicated in this memorable quote from General Fang—"Sorry, my friend, in one hour, you die. But I not let you die alone. I come watch." Karloff's scenes with the mercenary Gordon Creed (Cortez) were riveting. *West of Shanghai* would be the fourth and final collaboration of the two screen veterans.

Warner Bros. hoped to release the picture sometime in late spring or early summer of 1937, but unexpected complications surfaced. While they were editing the movie in March, the studio received a letter from the Chinese Consulate in Los Angeles protesting the film's depiction of "Chinese life and customs."[341] A fascinating series of missives between the two entities followed, which detailed the lengths and limits of a studio's willingness to change a creative work to address concerns and satisfy censors. (For more information, see *West of Shanghai* film section in Part II.)

Considering all the furor, it is surprising *West of Shanghai* did only modest box office business. Perhaps audiences were swayed by critics, who found the movie wanting. Opinions of the picture have evolved over time, however. Today, many writers, film historians, and buffs are enthusiastic about *West of Shanghai*, often rating it a B movie classic, citing its superb dialogue and colorful performances, particularly Karloff's memorable turn.

While working on the picture, Cortez received an intriguing offer from his old friend/boss Darryl Zanuck, now head of 20th Century Fox Pictures. Zanuck wanted him for the title role in his upcoming production of *The Gentleman from California*, an old west tale of a Spanish-style Robin Hood set against the backdrop of 1850's California. Ricardo wanted to accept, but the film was slated to begin immediately, and he was still a Warner Bros. employee until May, 1937. He doubted the studio would attempt to renew his contract; but he was also certain his bosses would never agree to another loan. They had already scheduled his appearances in more productions, and to recast them at this late date would be difficult. Cortez knew he had to make a decision soon. He could finish his contract or ask for a release to accept Zanuck's offer. In early April, he chose to leave Warner Bros. The studio's precise reaction is unknown, but they agreed to set him free. A termination agreement effective April 10, 1937, released Cortez along with a payment of $6,000.[342] With the stroke of a pen, Ricardo's tenure at Warner Bros. came to an unceremonious end after three and one half years, two contracts, and 15 films. Relations had been strained from time to time, but by and large, it had been a long, productive, and mutually beneficial relationship. While the studio had not given Cortez the A level vehicles he hoped for, or allowed him an opportunity to direct, it had provided many colorful and interesting characters for him to play.

Judging strictly from an artistic viewpoint, why Ricardo chose to leave Warner Bros. to take the role of Ramon Escobar in *The Gentleman from California*, a.k.a. *The Californian*, is not entirely clear. Granted, the movie gave him a rare romantic hero role, and allowed him to do another Western (his first since *The Gunner Runner* in 1928), but the hour-long adventure was a B movie all the way, entertaining stuff on its own terms, but trivial and forgettable.

In May, 1937, Cortez opted to leave Warner Bros. to accept the role of Ramon Escobar, a Spanish-style Robin Hood in the 20th Century Fox B western, *The Gentleman from California*, a.k.a. *The Californian*.

Mr. and Mrs. Cortez headed back to New York after the film was completed. Chris had made many new friends in California and had been able to spend time with two of her brothers, Vincent and Maurice, while in Hollywood, but she was miserable. Relations between the couple continued to deteriorate. Ricardo attempted to placate her from time to time, taking her on trips and buying her gifts, but he was unwilling to give Chris what she longed for most—a devoted full-time husband.

The breaking point came during the argument-filled New York trip. In early September, columnist Walter Winchell announced the couple would part. On September 11, 1937, Ricardo's personal business manager, Milton L. Cashy, confirmed Winchell's story and read a prepared statement from his client. In typical Cortez fashion, the statement sought to present the separation as amicable, thus muffle any possible bad publicity. "Mr. Cortez has commissioned me to say that the disagreement is just one of those things, and that he and his wife are still very good friends," said Cashy.[343] The Cortezes would eventually reconcile, but the basic problems between them persisted. Whether out of pride, fear of bad press, or other reasons, Ricardo kept trying to breathe life into something already dead.[344]

Cortez's career was not in the best of health either. After his departure from Warner Bros. he tried to land directing jobs with major studios, to no avail. Frustrated, in August, 1937, he signed a pact with Ambassador Productions, a small independent company specializing in the manufacture of ultra-low budget Westerns and action adventures. Formed in 1934, Ambassador was owned and operated by Maurice Conn and Sigmund Neufield, who rented facilities to make their pictures and contracted with other studios to distribute them. Ricardo's contract called for him to write, produce, direct, and act in Ambassador films. In late August, *The Film Daily* reported Conn's intention to produce 36 pictures in the coming months. Among them were: *The Ghosts Run Wild* and *Crime Takes a Holiday*, to star Ricardo Cortez.[345]

As fate would have it, Cortez would make neither film, nor would he work for Conn and Neufield. In September he received what he considered a better offer from Darryl Zanuck and Sol Wurtzel, executive producer of 20th Century Fox's B unit. Wurtzel wanted Cortez to costar with up and coming actress Phyllis Brooks in a crime drama tentatively titled *Blonde Moll*, about a poor young woman whose dreams of living in luxury lead to bad choices with tragic consequences. Cortez saw potential in furthering a professional relationship with Wurtzel and 20th Century Fox, so he signed on.

Undeniably low-budget fare, *Blonde Moll*, retitled *City Girl*, was nevertheless a compelling film thanks to a taut, dramatic script, the skill and expertise of Sol Wurtzel's crew of filmmakers, lead by director Alfred Werker, and an excellent lead performance by young Miss Brooks, who had been making B movies for 20th Century Fox since 1934. Cortez's performance was also convincing, although the role of a handsome gangster who leads the young protagonist astray was hardly a stretch.

Shortly after completing *City Girl*, Ricardo entered into negotiations with Wurtzel to follow in the footsteps of his old pal and costar, Norman Foster, and become a director. Both Wurtzel and Zanuck considered Ricardo a solid professional, and were sufficiently impressed by his knowledge of filmmaking to give him a shot. In February, 1938, Cortez inked a three-way pact with 20th Century Fox to act, write, and direct, thus fulfilling his dream to step behind the camera.[346] During the next two years (1938-40), Ricardo would helm seven low-budget films for Wurtzel, and in so doing, learn that directing a movie, particularly a program picture, was more challenging than he could possibly have imagined.

Cortez's new employer, 20th Century Fox Pictures was a relatively new entity. Its formation in 1935 came as the result of the merger of the old Fox Film Corporation and the new Twentieth Century Pictures. It was a marriage born of convenience and economic need. The Fox Film Corporation was originally formed in 1915 by legendary mogul William Fox, who began buying nickelodeons during the early 1900's. By 1920, Fox had amassed an impressive empire that included film production facilities, a distribution company, and theater chains. Under the brilliant management of Fox and his team, the aggressive, innovative corporation continued to grow during the boom of the1920's. One of its most impressive achievements was the invention of a sound on film process it called Movietone, which soon swept the industry. By 1929, Fox claimed his holdings were worth over $300 million.[347]

Things began to go south for Fox and his company in 1929, however, thanks to the stock market crash, an anti-trust investigation, and Mr. Fox's ill-advised attempts to acquire multiple filmmaking-related companies, including the Loewe's Theater chain. In 1930, William Fox was forced to relinquish control over his beloved companies to various financial entities. Eventually, he was forced into bankruptcy and later went to prison for attempting to bribe a judge during his bankruptcy hearing. The Fox Film Corporation continued to operate under the management of former Paramount-Publix manager, Sidney Kent, with Winfield Sheehan in charge of production, but the company began to lose key talent and prestige. By 1935, it was lagging behind its competitors in both star and story power.[348]

The other half of the new company, Twentieth Century Pictures, was formed by Darryl Zanuck and Joe Schenck after Zanuck's departure from Warner Bros. in 1933. Already an experienced veteran film executive, Zanuck immediately set about hiring the best possible filmmakers and actors to ensure his new company's success. Among those he signed to contracts were such notable directors as Gregory

La Cava, Roy Del Ruth, and Rowland Lee, and cinematic luminaries including Loretta Young, Ronald Colman, Wallace Beery, and George Arliss. In spite of the fact that he had no production facilities and no distribution company during the period of 1933-35, Zanuck's company managed to turn out several key films, including *House of Rothschild, Folies Bergere,* and *The Call of the Wild.*[349]

The May 29, 1935 merger filled each company's needs. Twentieth Century Pictures gained production facilities and a distribution company, and Fox acquired a dynamic production supervisor. Under the aegis of Zanuck, by 1938, the new 20th Century Fox Pictures quickly reestablished the prestige of the old Fox Film Corporation by producing a quality product. Among the A-level films produced during the first three years (1935-38), were such acclaimed motion pictures as *Lloyds of London* (1936), *In Old Chicago* (1938), *Kentucky* (1938), *Alexander's Ragtime Band* (1938), and several Shirley Temple vehicles including *The Littlest Rebel* (1935), *Heidi* (1937), and *Rebecca of Sunnybrook Farm* (1938). Like other top studios, 20th Century Fox's high-end productions were supported by programmers, a.k.a. the B's, manufactured quickly and cheaply to fill the bottom half of the mandatory double bill. Longtime Fox executive Sol M. Wurtzel was placed in charge of the new company's B unit, headquartered in Fox's old Western Avenue Lot.[350]

A tough, no-nonsense taskmaster with a nervous facial tick (presumably from all the pressure he'd been under for decades), Wurtzel ran a tight ship; he had to. At the time Cortez began working for him, Wurtzel had a six million dollar annual allowance from which to make 24 motion pictures. While an average production budget for Wurtzel's B movies (made in two to three weeks) ranged from $150,000-$200,000, many were made for less than $100,000.[351] It is true that larger studios like 20th Century Fox tended to take more time and care producing their "low enders" than minor studios, but making B movies was extremely challenging. Some of Wurtzel's employees claimed one of the most difficult parts of their jobs was dealing with the boss, who had a well-deserved reputation for being crude, rigid, and unapproachable.[352]

To Darryl Zanuck, Wurtzel's crudeness was offset by his managerial ability and shrewd programming decisions. Among Wurtzel's wisest decisions during his long 20th Century Fox tenure (1935-49), was his emphasis on series films. Building on the popularity of Fox's Charlie Chan movies during the period of 1935-41, Wurtzel created several other series featuring continuing characters with whom filmgoers could identify.

One of the new series created in the crime/mystery category was *The Roving Reporters* (1938-39). Starring Michael Whalen and Chick Chandler, it chronicled the adventures of an eccentric newshound and his zany, dimwitted photographer sidekick. Their quest to obtain and publish news stories get them in all kinds of dangerous situations. Produced in 1938, the first two entries, *Time Out for Murder* and *While New York Sleeps* (both directed by H. Bruce Humberstone), were entertaining, fast-paced program pictures that got the new series off to a rousing start.

After serving an apprenticeship of sorts as a dialogue director on a few films, including *The Mysterious Mr. Moto*, in late spring, 1938, Cortez received his first directorial assignment: to helm the third installment of *The Roving Reporters* series. Tentatively titled *A Very Practical Joke*, the script had the two protagonists becoming involved with a beautiful clip joint hostess (Jean Rogers) whose boss (Douglas Fowley) is a murderous racketeer.[353]

Extremely anxious to please his new bosses, Ricardo approached the direction of the B movie as if he were about to helm *Citizen Kane*. He spent countless hours studying the script and planning each sequence in consultation with the involved filmmakers, especially producer Howard Green and unit manager Ben Wurtzel (Sol's brother). The executives liked his ideas and appreciated his interest, but deemed many of them impractical, given time and money constraints.

Controversy preceded the filming of the movie when the proposed leading lady, Phyllis Brooks withdrew from the picture and was promptly suspended. In her *Los Angeles Examiner* column, Louella Parsons reported Brooks' departure was not due to the role, but because she did not want to work with either director Cortez or leading man Whalen.[354] Four days later, after being contacted by Miss Brooks, Parsons clarified her initial report, stating, "Phyllis wants it known that she got along excellent with Riccy Cortez and Mike Whalen, but bowed out of the cast because she felt that at this point in her career, the story wasn't right for her." She was replaced by Jean Rogers.[355]

Filming began in mid-August, 1938, and proceeded on schedule without incident for two and one half weeks, until September 2. While shooting the movie, Cortez was hyper tense, obsessing over each sequence, even bits of dialogue. He poured his heart into the movie, and when a particular scene did not go as planned or was not completed to his satisfaction, he became visibly irritated or upset. How the actors handled this added pressure is unknown, but it couldn't have made for a contented set. As a consequence of his intense involvement, Cortez took it personally when Wurtzel (who was largely pleased with the finished movie) cut several minutes of footage, and insisted one of the scenes be reshot. To the studio, *A Very Practical Joke*, retitled *Inside Story*, was just another B movie; but to the overly earnest, self-conscious Ric Cortez, it was his artistic baby, an expression of his ability, his shot at proving himself worthy of being a Hollywood director. He would eventually lighten up, scaling back his obsessive, self-conscious, and ultimately unproductive approach to directing, but never his commitment to make his movies as good as they could be.[356]

Due to revisions, *Inside Story* was not released until March, 1939. Cortez had no time to be anxious about the reception of it. By the time the film came out to largely positive reviews, the actor/director had helmed two more B pictures and acted in another. The acting assignment came in *Mr. Moto's Last Warning*, the sixth installment of the popular series starring Peter Lorre as a brilliant Japanese Interpol (international police) investigator who battles crime around the world.

In *Warning*, Moto matches wits with a dedicated gang of international spies bent on causing conflict between France and England, by blowing up the French fleet as it approaches the Suez Canal. A good plot, a competent script, excellent direction from Cortez's old buddy Norman Foster, and a first-rate supporting cast headed by Cortez, George Sanders, and John Carradine made for a colorful, exciting low budgeter. Cortez was excellent as the head spy/saboteur who poses as a ventriloquist. The performance of his ventriloquist act is one of the film's unexpected highlights. Cortez was so good, several writers and reviewers openly speculated whether he'd had formal training.

Ricardo's second and third directorial efforts came in the last

After inking a three-way pact with 20th Century Fox as an actor, director, and writer, Cortez directed seven motion pictures and acted in several others, including *Mr. Moto's Last Warning* (20th Century Fox, 1939). Here, Cortez is seen enjoying a laugh with series' star, Peter Lorre.

quarter of 1938 and during the early months of 1939. *Chasing Danger* was the second entry in 20th Century Fox's *Camera Daredevils* series. Similar to *The Roving Reporters*, the *Daredevils* films were an interesting mix of the crime, adventure, and comedy genres, recounting the exploits of an international newsreel cameraman (Preston Foster) and his inept sound man (Wally Vernon). In this outing, the boys are

Ricardo portrayed a murderous spy who poses as a ventriloquist in *Mr. Moto's Last Warning* (20th Century Fox, 1939). In this candid photo, Cortez is seen with the youngest member of the supporting cast, child actress, Joan Carroll.

sent to cover an Arabian revolt in French Algeria, and get entangled in foreign intrigue thanks to a beautiful young spy (Lynn Bari).

Still upset over the alterations ordered to *Inside Story*, Cortez tried valiantly to prevent the need to make substantive changes to *Chasing Danger*. On the set, both his stars (Foster and Vernon) became amused by their director's dedication to the low-budget movie, and by the lengths Cortez would go to make clear how he wanted a scene played. During the shoot, two humorous anecdotes emerged illustrating Cortez's obsessive commitment. While filming a night scene that had Foster and Vernon escaping their Arab pursuers by jumping into a truck and speeding away, Vernon forgot to turn on the truck's headlights and ruined the footage. After being reprimanded by Cortez, Vernon reportedly quipped "I didn't think it would make much difference. Everything else is dubbed in, and I thought you could dub in the lights, too!" Another amusing anecdote recalled Cortez becoming "so absorbed in what he was doing that he worked his way onto the set in front of the camera, acting out Foster's role." This prompted Foster to step behind the camera, and when Cortez stopped acting, he yelled "Cut! That was perfect. Print it!"[358]

Cortez followed *Chasing Danger* by helming his first non-series picture. A serious crime drama based on an original screenplay by Robert Ellis and Helen Logan, *The Escape* chronicled the tragic story of an embittered young man (Edward Norris) whose poverty-stricken background and bad associations lead to a life of crime. Although the basic tenants of the storyline were unremarkable and the script not much more than an outline, director Cortez managed to shape an affecting low-budget motion picture. His years of experience as an actor in both high and low-end productions helped him create effective scenes. Critics found much to like in *The Escape*. *Variety* called it "an unusual and novel technique of celluloid story . . . Ricardo Cortez's direction is almost uniformly excellent . . ."[359]

Unlike others who found working with director Cortez amusing and/or challenging, *The Escape*'s star Edward Norris expressed admiration for the director, and gratitude for his interest in the picture. A former Metro-Goldwyn-Mayer contract player who became a B movie star, Norris worked with a wide array of low-budget directors during his long and productive career. According to Norris, many did not take an active interest in their program pictures. They did their jobs, nothing more. In a 1999 interview with the author, Norris recalled Cortez as one of the exceptions.

"I met Ricardo Cortez while I was at Metro. I thought he was one of the better B movie directors I worked with; and The Escape one of my better B movies . . . He [Cortez)] seemed to care about the overall quality of the picture, and I appreciated that. We were on a tight schedule and

Cortez is seen in the background standing on the city street with his cast members, including Henry Armetta (left), Edward Norris (wearing hat on right), and various child actors, while directing a scene cast in the taut melodrama, *The Escape* (20th Century Fox, 1940).

didn't have time for rehearsals, but he did take an active interest in the actors and our performances, and tried to help us, which he knew would help the movie. Probably because I had been around for a long time, he let me interpret my part as I saw fit, which to me, was helpful. As I recall the movie got pretty good reviews . . ."³⁶⁰

In between directorial efforts, Ricardo sandwiched in another acting assignment, as a suspect in *Charlie Chan in Reno*, the 21st entry in the popular, long-running series now starring Sidney Toler as the indefatigable Asian sleuth. It must have felt like the proverbial "old home week" for the 38-year-old Ricardo Cortez as he made the picture. He'd worked with virtually all of the principal cast and most of the crew during his many years in Hollywood. His pal and *Reckless Living* costar, Norman Foster, was again at the helm. Foster had been instrumental in Cortez fulfilling his dream to direct, encouraging him, and recommending him to his bosses at 20th

Century Fox. The former actor had found his calling behind the megaphone and hoped his friend would as well. Even-tempered and highly efficient, Foster navigated the difficult terrain of being a B movie director at 20th Century Fox effectively.

While the set of *Charlie Chan in Reno* was quiet and cooperative, Cortez's home life was in turmoil. Ricardo and Christine reconciled, but nothing changed. In fact, Ricardo's directorial responsibilities kept him away from home even more than in the past. When he was home, he was often irritable and distracted. By 1939, the couple's frequent arguments had turned into an icy silence. Both were unhappy and Chris had lost all hope. Encouraged by family and friends, she finally decided to end her marriage to Ricardo once and for all, and return to the East Coast.

Christine's move back East coincided with the commencement of production on Ricardo's fourth directorial assignment, *Heaven With a Barbed Wire Fence*, a comic drama chronicling the adventures of a department store clerk, a pretty refugee, and a hobo (played by Glenn Ford, Jean Rogers, and Nicholas Conte, respectively) riding the rails across the U.S. on a quest to fulfill their dreams in the American West. Based on a story by former newspaperman turned scenarist, Dalton Trumbo, the script by Trumbo, Leonard Hoffman, and Ben Grauman Kohn traced the challenges faced by the threesome and the interesting mix of characters they meet on their journey.

Overwhelmed by a combination of professional pressures and personal issues, Cortez was in a volatile frame of mind during the lensing of the picture. Sadly, his volatility came into play on the set of *Heaven With a Barbed Wire Fence*. Cortez was initially enthusiastic about the script and the craftsmen assembled to make the picture, but his mood changed when producer Sol Wurtzel refused to cast the actor he wanted in the lead. Instead, Cortez got 23-year-old Quebec-born, California-raised Glenn Ford—a stage actor who would be making his feature-length motion picture debut.

Extremely displeased, Cortez took out many of the frustrations he was feeling on the unfortunate novice. What should have been a triumph for the young man turned into a nightmare. In a biography entitled *Glenn Ford: A Life*, based on interviews with, and reminiscences of Mr. Ford, his son Peter Ford chronicled his famous father's experiences on the set of *Heaven With a Barbed Wire Fence* and the hostility his director heaped on him. Mr. Ford said it began on the first day and continued throughout the two-week production.

"Hurried through make-up and wardrobe, he [Ford] joined the crew and his fellow cast members on the soundstage. Trying to hide his nervousness, he stood around making small talk with the other actors. At last, flanked by flunkies, strutting and glowering like a summer stock copy of Erich Von Stroheim, Ricardo Cortez arrived. The director stopped before the line of gathered actors and looked them over then barked, 'Which one's Ford?' 'Mr. Cortez,' my father said clearing his throat. 'Uh. . . I'm Glenn Ford.' 'Yes, that's right,' said Cortez. The director backed up and raised his voice to address the entire cast and crew, 'I want you all to know,' he began, 'They have stuck me with this guy in the lead. I didn't want him. I wanted a real actor for this thing and not some unknown amateur. I'm disgusted, but there is nothing I can do, so I ask for your patience as we put up with him.'

My father stood there, almost sick with anger and humiliation. Before he could speak, Cortez clapped his hands and barked some orders and everyone went to work. Mortified but determined not to walk out on the biggest opportunity of his life (which he was sure was exactly what Cortez wanted), Glenn swallowed his pride and took his place on the set." [361]

Peter Ford said his father never forgot the way he was treated and never forgave Cortez. After the experience, Glenn vowed if he ever became an important actor, he would never allow anyone on the set to be treated in such a manner. Of course, he did become very important; he became one of the biggest box office stars of the 1950's and 1960's.

For his part, Cortez never spoke of the production during his lifetime. Given his own early experiences in Hollywood, and the abuse to which he had been subjected, it is more than surprising that Ricardo would ever have treated a young actor the way he treated Ford. While his behavior was indefensible, in all probability, Ricardo was so wrapped up in himself and his own personal and professional challenges, he was not fully aware of how cruel he was being.

How Cortez dealt with the other young cast members of *Heaven*, is not known, but it is unlikely he gave young Nicholas Conte (later known as Richard Conte) a hard time, especially after the young actor was responsible for saving his life. This was the result of a mishap that occurred during the filming of one of the outdoor scenes involving a truck and a trailer. While cinematographer Eddie Cronjager was busy setting up the shot from below a 12-foot embankment, director Cortez dragged his folding chair to sit near the camera. As Cortez was studying the script, suddenly the cable broke holding the trailer. As fate would have it, young Conte was standing nearby and saw the cable break. Bravely risking his own life to save Cortez, he tackled the director, hurling him to one side, just in time to miss the trailer, which catapulted down the steep embankment, crushing the chair Ricardo had been sitting in. A shaken Cortez thanked the actor and dismissed the filmmakers for the day.[362]

Considering the bad feelings and mishaps involved, it is a testament to the talented professionals assembled to make *Heaven with a Barbed Wire Fence* that the movie turned out well. Not particularly strong plot-wise, the film was nevertheless an effective Depression-era fable; a sweet, optimistic slice of Americana, extolling the virtues of the United States as a melting pot where citizens from around the world could come to find freedom and opportunity. Beautifully scripted by the talented threesome, superbly photographed by Cronjager, skillfully edited by Norman Colbert, and engagingly enacted by the three young leads aided by a veteran supporting cast including Raymond Walburn (memorable as a former professor who has fallen on hard times), Marjorie Rambeau, Paul Hurst, and Eddie Collins, the movie was a winner with critics and the public.

Of course much of the credit for its success should properly be awarded to Cortez. Of the seven movies he directed, *Heaven with a Barbed Wire Fence* best shows his creativity and overall potential. Like the others, it was a programmer with a limited budget, but *Heaven* had the look and feel of an A-level picture, in no small part due to memorable sequences Cortez crafted while guiding high-caliber performances. Mr. Ford apparently did not like his performance, and blamed Cortez for destroying his concentration, but he received excellent notices that undoubtedly helped him secure a Columbia contract later in 1939, which, in turn, eventually paved the way for his success.

During the next six months, Cortez would helm his final three

Cortez won rave reviews for his fourth film as a director, the heartwarming drama, *Heaven With A Barbed Wire Fence* (20th Century Fox, 1939), about three young people (from left to right: Nicholas (Richard) Conte, Jean Rogers, and Glenn Ford) on a quest to fulfill their dreams in the American West. The screenplay was co-scripted by Dalton Trumbo.

films for 20th Century Fox. The first two, *City of Chance* and *Free, Blonde, and 21* were comic melodramas that featured talented leading lady Lynn Bari. Both were pleasing to audiences and contained good scenes, but neither approached the quality and effectiveness of *Heaven With a Barbed Wire Fence*.

On December 26, 1939, during the production of *Free, Blonde, and 21*, another earthquake rocked the set of a Cortez picture, upsetting equipment, frightening the filmmakers, and disrupting the day's shooting.[363] Luckily, there were no injuries and no extensive damage done. A few hours later, production resumed. For Ricardo, the event probably seemed like just another daily irritation, an added pressure in what he had concluded was a thankless, increasingly intolerable job. He didn't know it yet, but like the earthquake that had disrupted the filming of Paramount's *Girl in 419* in 1933, this seismic disturbance would take on a strange significance in his life, becoming a metaphor for the challenges he would face and the life-altering decisions he would make in the coming months that would shake his life to its very foundations.

CHAPTER NINE
"ONCE A HEEL, ALWAYS A HEEL" (1941–49)

"By reestablishing myself as an actor, I hope to be able to pick and choose. If no good role is available, I will be able to pick a good story to direct and vice versa."
— RICARDO CORTEZ

January 1, 1940—the start of a new year, a new decade. Out with the old, in with the new; a time for "Auld Lang Syne," New Year's resolutions, fireworks displays, and joyous revelers. As in years past, worldwide celebrations marked the beginning of the new year, but in many world capitals in 1940, there was a sense of foreboding mixed with the revelry. In September 1939, Nazi Germany invaded Poland, plunging the European continent into war. Given the military power of the Nazis and their determination to extend their influence, another protracted and catastrophic world conflict seemed unavoidable. In January, 1940, America remained steadfastly determined to stay out of another European armed struggle, but among influential government officials and increasing numbers of Americans, there was a growing realization that might not be possible.

Like so many Americans, Ricardo Cortez was concerned for the future of his country and for the free world. He was also uneasy about his own future. For the first time since their marriage, he and Christine celebrated the new year apart. Just prior to the holidays, Ricardo had secured permission to take a few weeks off, fly to New York and try and salvage his crumbling marriage. The trip proved unsuccessful. Christine had finally had enough and would not be talked into a reconciliation. Ricardo apparently accepted her decision without incident, and both vowed to make the split amicable. In her November 29, 1939, column, Louella Parsons broke the news, telling her readers Ricardo and Chris had decided it was "best to go their separate ways."[364] One day later, Ricardo publicly confirmed Parsons' column. "We have not gone into the matter of divorce as yet," he said. "Mrs. Cortez prefers to live in New York City and my work requires I remain in Hollywood. I am truly sorry this condition prevails."[365] Even though his neglectfulness and selfishness had caused much of the couple's difficulties, Ricardo took the separation hard. He was not used to failing in anything so important as marriage, and he considered the break a personal failure.

His personal problems were not his only concerns. Overwhelmed and disillusioned with his job as a B movie director, Cortez was at another personal and professional crossroads as he began work on what would be his final directorial effort. Filmed in March, 1940, the third and last entry of 20th Century Fox's *Hotel For Women* series, *Girl in 313* was a crime drama about a young policewoman (Florence Rice) who goes incognito to bust a jewel smuggling gang headed by a prominent jeweler (Lionel Atwill) and his debonair assistant (Kent Taylor). Complications arise when the young woman falls in love with the handsome smuggler. Despite an unoriginal storyline and an innocuous title, *Girl in 313* was clever, well-scripted, and skillfully filmed. With a little more investment of time and money and 15 more minutes of footage, it might have become a well-regarded A-level picture. As is, it's a very good B movie, thanks to a superb cast, quality photography by Eddie Cronjager, and exceptional direction from Ricardo, who created effective scenes, particularly the unusual end sequence. With all the personal and professional issues weighing him down, his work on the picture seems all the more impressive.

After its completion, Cortez secured permission to accept acting assignments. During the summer and fall of 1940, he acted in two pictures: as president of an aircraft company and prime suspect in the murder of a British intelligence officer in the Charlie Chan mystery *Murder Over New York*; and as the money-hungry nephew of an elderly Spanish rancher in the Cisco Kid Western, *Romance of the Rio Grande*. Both were respectable if unremarkable entries in two popular series.

When his 20th Century Fox contract expired in November, 1940, Cortez opted against an extension. Press reports indicated

The absorbing B crime drama, *Girl in 313* (20th Century Fox, 1940), starring Florence Rice (second from left) and Kent Taylor (far left) was Cortez's seventh and final film as a director.

the studio was still interested. On the whole, Wurtzel and Zanuck were pleased with Cortez's work, both as an actor and director. They wanted to re-sign him, but Ricardo wanted his freedom. For the vast majority of his time in Hollywood, Cortez had been a studio contract employee, enjoying all the benefits and frustrations that entailed. 20th Century Fox had allowed him an opportunity to fulfill his dream of directing, but it appeared to Ricardo as if he shouldered all the responsibility for his productions, with little creative control over the content of the films and casting. In 1941, he explained his frustration with the studio and his decision to resume acting full time.

"If I'm going to direct, I want a free hand in picking my stories and in casting. I want no more of these castings because 'he is a swell fellow.' The actor may be a swell fellow, but he may be a rotten actor. By reestablishing myself as an actor, I hope to be able to pick and choose. If no good role is available, I will be able to pick a good story to direct and vice versa." [366]

> **The Gotham**
> 5TH AVE. AT 55TH ST.
> NEW YORK CITY
>
> Oct - 28 - 40
>
> Dick Hyman
> King Features
> East 45 St —
>
> My dear Dick —
>
> I am terribly grateful and delighted, to be a "Banshee" I've never met a finer bunch of men —
>
> Thank you so very much for your many kindnesses —
>
> "Sunset Towers"
> Sunset Blvd —
> Hollywood - Cal.

This is a handwritten note from Cortez, (sent in 1941 after his departure from 20th Century Fox), to Dick Hyman, longtime publicity director for King Features Syndicate, a distributor of comic strips, columns, and editorial cartoons to newspapers.

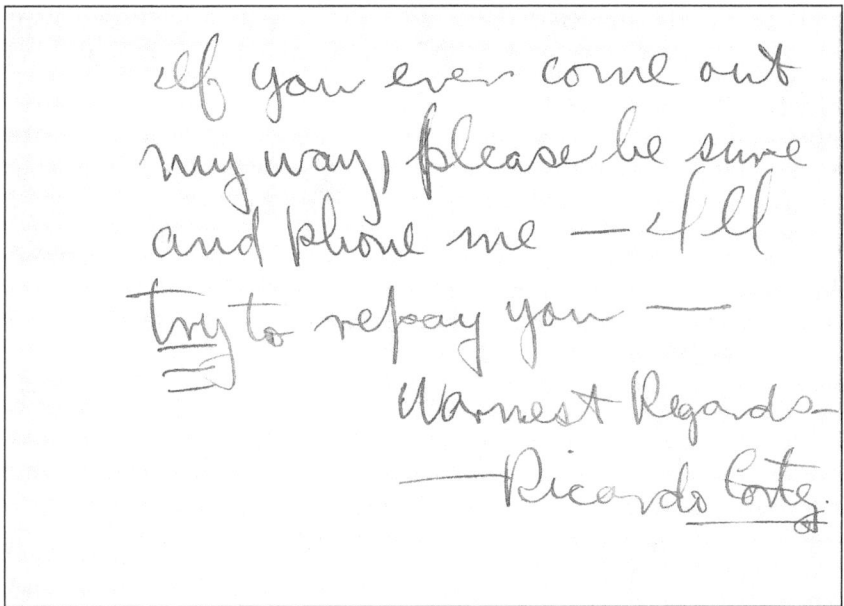

Part II of the letter.

Despite his stated intention to alternate between acting and directing, Ricardo Cortez would never take the megaphone again, AND would never be a contract player again.

On May 18, 1940, Christine Conniff Lee Cortez made good on her vow and filed for divorce from her husband of six and one half years, charging him with "extreme cruelty." At the divorce hearing, she was openly hostile to Ricardo. She told Superior Judge Lewis Smith that her husband was, "a very cold person"—unaffectionate, indifferent, sometimes abusive. She said within a week of their marriage, he rejected her. "He told a friend of mine he did not know why he had married, that he was not meant to be married and should have remained single."[367] She told the judge her husband was frequently absent. She said he would go away on trips "because he said he wanted to be away by himself for awhile." On three separate occasions, Christine testified that Ricardo became so angry, he struck her. "Once I was fixing dinner and he didn't like something and struck me . . ." she said. Christine's brother Vincent Conniff corroborated her testimony, and stated that his sister "tried her best in every way to make a go of their marriage, but it did not change Ricardo's attitude toward her."[368]

Ricardo did not defend himself or contest the divorce, but through his attorney Mickey Black, sought to revise the alimony agreement due to "changes in market conditions." Judge Smith appeared unmoved. Granting the divorce, the judge ordered Cortez to pay $500 a month in alimony for the first five years. In addition, he was ordered to give Christine $5500 in cash and surrender the deed to their home on Tropical Avenue in Beverly Hills. Since the breakup, Cortez had been renting the house to actor Herbert Marshall, and had taken an apartment at the Sunset Towers on Sunset Boulevard in West Hollywood.[369]

For the frugal, very private Ricardo Cortez, the divorce hearing and settlement were nothing short of a self-inflicted disaster. His reaction to the court proceedings and final settlement was likely a combination of sadness and outrage. He was sad to have made such a gigantic mistake, and outraged that his "dirty laundry" had been exposed. As for Christine, her sad, unhappy life would not improve after the divorce. She won her freedom and the chance to tell her side of the story, but it would be a Pyrrhic victory. Like the doomed Alma Rubens, Ricardo's second wife's story would soon end in tragedy.

As a freelance actor, the middle-aged Cortez would continue to make motion pictures throughout the 1940's. His productivity trailed off, mainly due to lack of decent parts and his waning interest in acting. Of the 13 movies he made during the decade, all featured him in character roles, and all but two were program pictures ranging from grades B through Z. Looking back at the entirety of the film career of Ricardo Cortez, the 1940's decade is notable for two reasons: it marked his return to predominantly roguish roles, and to making movies for second and third tier studios like Republic, Monogram, and PRC.

Ricardo made six motion pictures in the two-year period of 1941-42, all but one second features. The mysteries, *A Shot in the Dark* and *Who is Hope Schuyler?*, both presented the veteran actor as a guilty looking murder suspect. The minor-league crime dramas, *Rubber Racketeers* and *Tomorrow We Live*, both featured him as a ruthless, merciless racketeer. In the latter, filmed at PRC studio (considered the lowest of low on the totem pole of prestige), he played opposite lovely Jean Parker, who, like Cortez, had been a contract player for a major studio (Metro-Goldwyn-Mayer). Unlike some of Cortez's former costars and coworkers, Miss Parker remembered working with Ricardo as a pleasurable experience. In a 1996 interview with the author, she admitted being a fan of his.

"Oh, Ric Cortez, I liked him! I had a crush on him as a young girl. He was a real professional. I had been told he would be unfriendly and a scene hog, but the opposite was true. He was easy; perfectly charming to me. I don't really remember the film we did together except it was not very good, and it was directed by Edgar Ulmer, who I did not like. I was doing several B movies a year at that time and few, if any were particularly memorable." [370]

The other two motion pictures Cortez made at the time gave him less stereotypical parts. He was an assistant district attorney on the trail of a killer who murdered his victim with a poison dart in Monogram's unusual melodrama, *I Killed That Man*; and had a fifth-billed supporting role as a narcissistic actor in the raucous, anti-Nazi, pre-World War II comedy, *World Premiere* (Paramount), starring John Barrymore. The latter part almost didn't materialize. Singer/actor Rudy Vallee had been the first choice to play the egotistical, womanizing movie star Mark Saunders; but when he became tied up on another film, Paramount replaced him with Cortez. Ricardo jumped at the chance to do comedy and work with the great Barrymore.

For Ricardo, another perk associated with the production of *World Premiere* was a chance to meet and work with leading lady Frances Farmer. During the production, and in the immediate weeks following it, the two were seen together frequently, dancing and dining, many times hand in hand. Unlike his retreat from the world at the time of Alma's untimely death, after his divorce from Christine, Ricardo was seen almost nightly at parties, premieres, and nightclubs, etc., often in the company of attractive women. Among the ladies with whom he would be romantically linked during the early 1940's were names both inside and outside the filmmaking business, including actresses Miss Farmer, Lilian Bond, Virginia Bruce, Los Angeles socialite Liz Pierson, and model/heiress Constance Probert. It is not known how many of these relationships were serious, but

After his divorce from Christine in 1940, Ricardo dated a number of women both in and out of the film industry. Among them was Frances Farmer (seen here), whom Cortez met while making *World Premiere* **(Paramount, 1941).**

Ricardo was dating Miss Farmer in August 1941, when Louella Parsons announced the couple "were aflutter."

Cortez was preparing to begin filming *I Killed That Man* on September 20, 1941, when he received an unsettling call from his ex-inlaws with shocking news regarding his former wife, Christine. After the divorce, she had returned to California and was renting a cottage on Laguna Beach with a female friend. On the evening of September 19, Christine arose from bed, grabbed some blankets, went outside, and sat on a porch swing which faced the ocean. Sometime between 4 a.m. and 6 a.m., she apparently fell asleep while smoking a cigarette. When her friend, Mrs. Moorhead, was awakened by the smell of smoke, she found the swing in flames. After pulling Christine from the fire, she summoned the fire department, who extinguished the blaze and transported a conscious but extremely weak Christine to St Joseph's Hospital in Santa Ana.[372] Suffering second and third degree burns over much of her body, Christine was listed in critical condition. Ricardo rushed to her side, but by the time he arrived, she had lapsed into a coma. She died early the next morning, four hours before her distraught parents arrived from Connecticut to be with her.[373]

A requiem mass was said for her on September 24 at the Church of the Good Shepherd in Beverly Hills. Attendance was large, including many from the entertainment world. The warm, affable Christine had made many friends during her years in Hollywood. She was buried in the Conniff family plot in Danbury, Connecticut. In an eerie coincidence, the tragic deaths of Ricardo's first two wives, Alma and Christine, occurred one decade apart. Both were in their early 30's. Christine was 34, and Alma was 33, (one month shy of her 34th birthday).[374]

While their marriage had been a mistake, and their breakup messy, Christine's untimely death was a horrendous tragedy not only for her family and friends, but also for her ex-husband. Ricardo was not one to dwell on past mistakes, but there must have been regret intermingled with the grief he felt over her passing. It is doubtful he ever truly loved her as a husband should love his wife, but he cared for her; and to see her young life end this way must have been a tremendous blow.

In 1943, Ricardo returned to Warner Bros., the latest stop in what turned out to be an informal farewell tour. This time, his assignment was a small eighth-billed part in the B farce *Make Your Own Bed*, produced by Bryan Foy, and directed by 44-year-old, British-born Peter Godfrey. Critics dismissed the movie as a "a limp and labored endeavor," but audiences packed theatres to see the slapstick antics of the talented cast, headed by the dynamic duo of Jane Wyman and Ricardo's old friend, Jack Carson, who had acted in two of his directorial assignments, *The Escape* and *Girl in 313*.

Just prior to filming *Make Your Own Bed* in 1943, Ricardo became reacquainted with vivacious Billie Seward, a former B movie actress and ex-wife of William Wilkerson, a noted entrepreneur responsible for opening several famed restaurants, nightclubs, and hotels, including the Café Trocadero, Ciro's, and later, Las Vegas' famed Flamingo Hotel. Cortez first met Billie years before while working at Columbia Pictures, where she was employed as a contract player. The two happened to meet again at Hollywood's Mocambo nightclub and hit it off right away. Billie was a sweet, thoughtful, outgoing girl who, like Christine, was attractive, but not technically beautiful. What she didn't possess in beauty, she possessed in charm. She seemed to bring out the best in the sad, sullen Ricardo, who appeared happier, more positive, and less intense in her company. In June, 1943, columnist Dorothy Kilgallen cited the couple as a "perfect match," and said both were "sniffing orange blossoms."[375]

By July, Louella Parsons was speculating about marriage. In September, 1943, she said Miss Seward was expected "to tell the world some interesting news about herself and Ricardo Cortez."[376] A short time later, Parsons reported Ricardo and Billie might already be wed, but there would be no marriage. Sometime during the early months of 1944, the couple abruptly parted ways. Billie clearly wanted marriage, but Ricardo did not. He loved having her in his life, but at this point, he was not interested in a long-term commitment.

With his dalliance with Miss Seward at an end, Ricardo began another flirtation, this one of a professional nature. By the mid-1940's, with fewer movie offers coming his way, he began spending more time in New York. Most of his family, including his mother and sister Helene (who lived together), brother Bernie (who, thanks to Ricardo, now worked in the sales department of RKO studios in New York), and many other friends and business associates, lived in the "Big Apple." Ricardo loved his hometown. He loved the excitement, the hustle and bustle, the food, the shops, the sporting events and, especially, the theatre. Whenever he was in New York, he would try to attend at least one Broadway production. Throughout his long entertainment career, Ricardo publicly and privately expressed admiration for the stage and stage performers, and often voiced interest in someday returning to the "Great White Way" where his career began so many years ago.

Cortez's return to Broadway appeared as if it might materialize in the spring of 1944, when Broadway producer Jed Harris expressed interest in hiring him and Paul Lukas for key roles in Elmer Rice's dramatization of Ira Wolfert's novel, *Tucker's People*, about a notorious racketeer's lawyer whose greed compromises his search for justice.[377]
In July, the *New York Times* reported Harris had signed both Cortez and Lukas, but both denied the report. Cortez was interested, but his agent, Jules Ziegler, said no deal had been consummated.[378]

Unfortunately, Harris eventually abandoned the project, but Broadway's loss was Hollywood's gain. In 1948, Warner Bros. produced an acclaimed grade A film of Wolfert's novel entitled *Force of Evil*, starring John Garfield. Cortez's proposed stage role was played by Roy Roberts in the film version.

Ricardo's interest in the Broadway stage did not end with the buzz over *Tucker's People*. In August, 1944, *The Billboard* reported Cortez might take the role of an underworld kingpin who kidnaps critics in the Charles Washburn/Barney Girard comedy, *April in the Alley*.[379] This project was also abandoned, but in April, 1945, the veteran movie actor was back in New York in talks with famed producer Oscar Serlin (*Life With Father*), who wanted him for a key role in his production of Theodore Robert's play, *Beggars Are Coming to Town*, which was the story of a criminal who, after serving a long prison term, returns home to find his former partner (who didn't get caught) prospering from their stolen money. On April 27, 1945, *The New York Times* announced that Cortez had been signed for the role of Noll Turner (the partner). In May, the *Times* reported Cortez's costars would be film actors Paul Kelly and Dorothy Comingore.[380]

Preparations continued throughout the summer of 1945. In July, noted stage director, Harold Clurman was hired, with rehearsals slated to begin in September. The play was to be tested in Bridgeport, Connecticut, and Boston before opening night in New York City scheduled for late October. Everything appeared to be falling into place for Cortez's formal return to the Broadway stage after a 28-year absence.[381]

Ricardo was enthusiastic about the play when rehearsals began on September 10, but after the first few days, his attitude completely changed. What happened during the rehearsals is a mystery, but on September 26, the *Times* announced that Cortez had withdrawn from the play. According to the report, it was an amicable departure, and his role would be taken by veteran actor Luther Adler.[382] The given reason for his abrupt exit was his dissatisfaction with his part, but was that the whole truth? We'll probably never know, but his decision was fortuitous. *Beggars Are Coming to Town* did indeed open as planned on October 27 at Broadway's Coronet Theatre, but closed after only 25 performances. Walter Winchell reported that Cortez had a front row seat at every performance, and watched it flop.[383]

There were occasional whispers of Cortez's return to the stage after *Beggars*. In July, 1946, Hedda Hopper announced that he and Ella Raines were being sought for parts in Steve Fisher's play, *Winter Kills*.[384] In November, 1946, a column suggested that Cortez might take over the role of rich junk dealer Harry Brock in Garson Kanin's hit comedy *Born Yesterday* (Lyceum Theatre), but both were rumors, and nothing came of them.[385] In the end, Broadway producers apparently didn't appreciate abrupt departures like Cortez's, and it is highly unlikely the actor would have accepted any new stage offers if they had been proffered. Ricardo Cortez's flirtation with the stage was officially over.

His love and devotion for the cinema was another story. Even though film offers became less frequent and parts smaller, for a time Cortez retained the desire to make an occasional movie, and his many fans still turned out to see him. In late January, 1946, *Variety* reported Ricardo had signed for a key supporting role in RKO's crime drama, *What Nancy Wanted*, based on a Leonard St.Clair/Lawrence Taylor radio play. The film was to be directed by German-born John Brahm, who had recently won acclaim for his work on two taut 20th Century Fox thrillers, *The Lodger* (1944) and *Hangover Square* (1945).

Ricardo appeared as a night club owner and gangster in Republic's minor film noir, *The Inner Circle*, before returning to RKO to make his best film in years. A stylish thriller, *What Nancy Wanted*, retitled, *The Locket*, was a grade A picture all the way, with a first-rate cast, an accomplished director, and high-end production values. The unusual story of a young kleptomaniac named Nancy (Laraine Day) whose compulsion to steal (the result of an incident in her childhood) eventually leads to tragedy and murder; the project had a complicated, convoluted road to the silver screen. Penned by Norma Barzman (wife of blacklisted scenarist Ben Barzman), the screenplay was originally purchased by actor Hume Cronyn, who hoped to direct the film, with his wife Jessica Tandy as star. When the project didn't pan out, Cronyn sold the screenplay to RKO, who assigned Sheridan Gibney to tighten it up. Thanks to Gibney's work, the contribution of director Brahm, who effectively utilized multilayered flashbacks to tell the tale, the chiaroscuro photography of Nicholas Musuraca, and extraordinary acting from a great cast headed by Laraine Day and young Robert Mitchum, an unusual story was turned into an exceptional movie.[386]

Ricardo had only a small, sixth-billed part as a wealthy art patron with a wheelchair-bound wife who takes a keen "interest" in the troubled Nancy, but the role was key to fueling the plot, and Cortez was enthusiastic. He was impressed by Brahm's ability and gratified by the respect shown him by members of the cast, particularly Miss Day, who had idolized him since childhood, and had suggested him for the role of Andrew Bonner.[387] Reviews of *The Locket* were mixed at the time of its release in December, 1946, but its reputation has steadily increased over the last 50+ years. Today the movie is seen as a well-crafted, innovative example of film noir.

In spite of a marked decline in film appearances, Ricardo Cortez remained a very busy man throughout the 1940's. With all his foibles and weaknesses, Ricardo was a go-getter, a highly industrious individual with an enormous competitive drive and a variety of

In 1946, Cortez accepted a key supporting role in director John Brahm's nourish drama, The Locket (RKO), which starred Laraine Day (right) and Robert Mitchum (left).

The star of *The Locket* (RKO, 1946), Laraine Day, idolized Cortez and suggested him for the role. This promotional photo shows her adjusting his corsage in between takes.

interests. When he wasn't acting he was pursuing other money-making ventures both inside and outside the motion picture industry, and/or enjoying his myriad of hobbies. Ricardo continued his love affair with investing throughout the 1940's and beyond. His speculation in stocks, bonds, real estate, businesses, and creative entities were a source of constant fascination and great personal satisfaction to him, as well as making him a very wealthy man. Cortez was a savvy, talented investor who knew a good deal when he saw one. Many felt he might have made an excellent movie executive if he had not become an actor.

His multiple hobbies might well have kept him busy even without acting or investing. Always enamored of physical fitness and sports, even in middle age, Ricardo could often be found at the gym exercising, swimming, playing tennis, golf, or riding. He also continued to be an avid sports fan. Throughout the 1940's, columnists, and reporters noted his presence at various sporting events, including boxing matches, football and baseball games, and/or at the Santa Anita race track. Cortez was personal friends with many sports celebrities, and was often seen in their company.[388]

In addition to sports, Ricardo was an avid reader and collector. Because he had dropped out of school in ninth grade, he made a point of being well read. He was extremely sensitive about his lack of a formal education and considered it a must to be able to converse with friends and coworkers on any subject. Fans were often surprised to learn he was also a dedicated collector of books, cigarette cases, pipes, opera programs, etc. He sometimes denied it, but he kept memorabilia and scrapbooks containing various ephemera on his career and some of the luminaries he worked with. One of his scrapbooks contained newspaper and magazine clippings of the countless untrue things that had been published about him.[389]

If that wasn't enough, the dapper Mr. Cortez continued to be intensely interested in men's fashion. He had always been obsessed with looking his best; acting and dressing like he thought a movie star should. His immaculate appearance was consistently noted by coworkers, columnists, and fashion experts. Beginning in the 1930's, his name frequently turned up on "best dressed" lists, not only for Hollywood stars, but among worldwide notables.[390] His nephew, Donald Kranze, recalled his uncle as a "fastidious, sharp, stylish dresser."[391]

Because of his renown in the fashion world, his advice was often solicited. Beginning in the late 1920's, Cortez penned essays offering advice to fans and the general public. His personal files at the Motion Picture Arts and Sciences (Margaret Herrick) Library in Los Angeles, are filled with his treatises on a variety of men's fashion topics, from the purchase of suits, shirts, and ties, to accessories such as rings, watches, cufflinks, as well as proper exercise.[392] As mentioned previously, his expertise on these subjects was noted by several retailers who used him to market their product lines through the years. Long before there were Michael Jordan shoes and Martha Stewart home

Cortez and pal Bing Crosby playing the ponies at the Santa Anita Racetrack, circa. 1937.

Among Cortez's favorite pastimes was reading. In this 1940's photo, he is seen reading in his apartment in the Sunset Towers.

Cortez and typewriter, circa. 1940's.

products, there were Ricardo Cortez suits, shirts, ties, and cuff links. In the spring of 1945, Ricardo signed a contract with *Esquire* magazine and its affiliate, *Coronet*, to be their West Coast men's fashion consultant, offering essays and advice on all matters of men's attire, grooming, and exercise. Cortez would work for them for the next several years.

Ricardo often denied it, but he kept scrapbooks of his career including this one which chronicled his career in silent films.

A glimpse inside Ricardo's fragile 90+ year old silent film scrapbook.

Cortez's acclaimed appearance in *The Locket* temporarily revived interest in his career as a Hollywood character player. In 1947, he accepted offers to make two pictures, both low budgeters that presented him as suspicious, shady heels.

"You're Ziggy Cranston, entertainment tycoon with a Midas touch, a genius of show business, a partner of lady luck, the only man who's had five smash hits on Broadway simultaneously, and the owner of the Consolidated Radio Network." This colorful description of Cortez's character, a playboy financier and gambler who is being blackmailed, was a piece of eccentric dialogue delivered by the hero in Ricardo's next film, Republic's grade Z crime drama, *Blackmail*. A convoluted, intellectually challenged, unintentionally hilarious "bad movie we love," it was panned by critics and "serious minded" writers. In a blistering review, one critic asked why an experienced actor like Cortez would appear in such a mess. While the true answer was probably money, Cortez appeared to be enjoying himself playing the megalomaniacal Ziggy and reciting the ludicrous dialogue. RKO's melodramatic *Mystery in Mexico*, about missing jewels and disappearing investigators, wasn't nearly as entertainingly bad as *Blackmail*, but it wasn't particularly distinguished either. An unoriginal premise and a mediocre script defeated the best efforts of talented young director Robert Wise to create a compelling, entertaining suspense movie. Ricardo's familiar role as a criminal night club proprietor was unchallenging, but the production did have an upside. Much of the film was shot on location at RKO's Churubusco Studios in Mexico City; and Ricardo and fellow cast and crew members received all expenses paid trips.[394]

Another of the perks the middle-aged Cortez derived from working at RKO during the late 1940's was meeting Margarette Bell, (also referred to as Margaret Bell) an attractive 26-year-old brunette from Chicago who'd begun working at the studio as a secretary. Born to working-class parents and raised in Illinois, she moved to California in the 1940's to work in the motion picture industry. By all accounts, she was a friendly, quiet, sensitive individual who appeared to take pleasure in making others happy. According to Ricardo's nephew, Don Kranze, they met about the time his uncle was making *The Locket*.[395] Cortez was attracted to Margarette, and she to him, but the two didn't begin dating until many months later when they happened to see one another again. Like Billie Seward, Margarette seemed to bring out the best in Ricardo. Although she was 20 years his junior, Ricardo appeared relaxed and contented in her company, proud to be squiring such a young pretty girl around town. As months passed, the two became inseparable, but remained unmarried. Ricardo was a two-time loser when it came to marriage, and he was determined not to make another mistake.

After the completion of *Blackmail* and *Mystery in Mexico*, Cortez had only one film offer, a similar part in another B movie for a Poverty Row studio. He declined, telling a reporter he was tired of playing

When decent film offers became nonexistent, Cortez signed to do a recurring role on the radio soap opera, *The First Hundred Years*. This is the actual application for membership in the American Federation of Radio Artists Ricardo signed in September 1949.

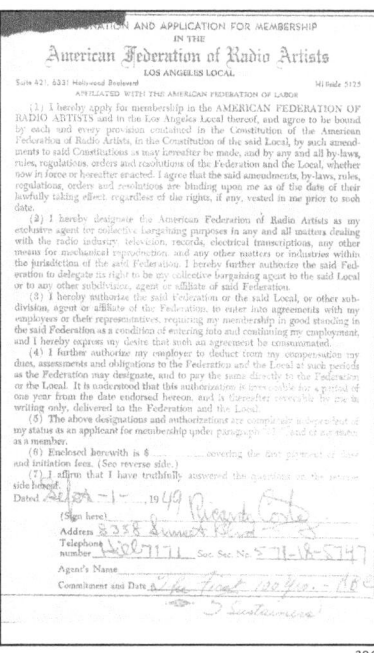

heels and gangsters, while alluding to other offers and opportunities.[396] Those "opportunities" were in radio. During the summer of 1949, Ricardo was offered a recurring role on a radio soap opera, *The First Hundred Years*, a serio-comic look at a young couple's newly minted marriage. Created by Nancy Holloway, the weekly 30-minute ABC Network broadcast starred Barbara Eiler, Sam Edwards, Joseph Kearns, and Bea Benaderet. Ricardo had done radio sporadically through the years, but this was a new and intriguing challenge. The hyperactive Mr. Cortez still wanted to act, and with no decent film offers on the table, radio seemed a way for him to keep working and keep his show business career alive. With high hopes, on September 1, 1949, Ricardo became a member of the AFTRA union (American Federation of Radio Artists) and joined the cast.[397] Sadly, his hopes were dashed three weeks later when ABC abruptly canceled the broadcast, citing poor ratings. Ironically, the Nancy Holloway story was not dead, however. In December, 1950, the program was resurrected—not on radio, but on television with a brand new cast. Broadcast on the CBS television network, *The First Hundred Years* would make history as the first ongoing daytime serial.[398]

CHAPTER TEN
A LAST HURRAH (1950–59)

"When I'm fifty, I'll retire. I'll make a round-the-world tour—a leisurely one occupying five or six years—I shan't miss anything. Being occupied is the only thing that can keep one happy late in life. The occupation can be work or play..."
— RICARDO CORTEZ

Ricardo was just 25 years old when he told an enterprising movie magazine writer what he'd be doing at age 50. It might have seemed like a fanciful dream to her and her readers back in 1925, but, true to his word, during the 1950's, Cortez would make the prediction a reality; all this while tying up the loose ends of his personal life and ending his acting career with a bang![399] They say history repeats itself. In the life and career of Ricardo Cortez, the old adage and many others certainly ring true. The dawning of each new decade saw Cortez facing a crossroads, a crisis, or both. In January, 1950, Ricardo was undeniably at another of life's "forks in the road." At 49 years old, he knew his life was about to change in a substantive way. He didn't know exactly how it might all play out, but he was wise enough to realize he must accept whatever happened. He had been acting and making movies for well over 30 years. Through a combination of talent, adaptability, industry, and sheer force of will, he'd manage to carve out a niche for himself in the movies when most of his contemporaries' careers had fallen by the way. When others had written him off, he had forged ahead, and fate had rewarded him time after time. Cortez was grateful to the industry, but he knew his days as a movie actor might well be numbered. He loved the business and he wanted to act, but was no longer willing to keep playing the same character over and over.

Ricardo also knew the coming months would be pivotal on a personal level. He had grown very fond of Margarette. They had been together for a long time, and she wanted to become his wife, but for both their sakes, he knew he had to be sure he was able to be the devoted, full-time husband she deserved. He had to get this right.

On February 20, 1950, entertainment columnist Wood Soanes announced that RKO had signed Cortez for a costarring role as the head of a phony fortune telling ring in the crime drama *Bunco Squad*, to be directed by Herbert I. Leeds.[400] The announcement came as a surprise given Ricardo's avowed disinterest in playing criminals. We'll never know why he took the role, but perhaps it was a final favor to the company that had provided him the best opportunities of his movie career.

During the late 1940's, RKO increased its budgets for its program pictures, and *Bunco Squad* reflected the improved quality of the studio's B product. Formerly an Oscar-nominated art director, producer Lewis Rachmil put together a first-tier team of professionals to breathe life into Reginald Taviner's story relating the efforts of law enforcement—namely L.A's "Bunco Squad," to break up a notorious criminal enterprise centering on phony mind reading, fortune telling, numerology, and séances. The result was a good low-budget crime drama, not a movie classic to be sure, but a respectable effort. Cortez received fine reviews for his work, but no substantive new offers.

Perhaps it was the knowledge he might never work as an actor again that prompted the veteran star to begin tidying up his personal life in the summer of 1950. According to Ricardo's version of the story, on August 24, he and Margarette were out driving around Los Angeles when "on an impulse," they dropped in on the county clerk and obtained a marriage license.[401] Since Ricardo rarely did anything "in the moment," this seems highly improbable. The more likely explanation for the sudden impulsiveness was his lifelong aversion to publicity.

Three weeks later, on Ricardo's birthday, September 19, the two were wed before a Justice of the Peace with a couple of friends in attendance.[402] The next day, they set sail on the *U.S.S. Lurline* for an extended honeymoon in Honolulu.[403] Upon their return, they

After vowing never to play a gangster and or criminal onscreen again, Ricardo surprised many by accepting the role of the head of a phony fortune-telling ring in RKO's low-budget crime thriller, *Bunco Squad* (1950) costarring Bernadene Hayes (center) and John Kellogg (right).

set up housekeeping in Ricardo's apartment at the Sunset Towers.

Unlike his first two unions, which could generously be described as mistakes, the Cortez/Bell alliance would last until death separated them. Like all marriages, there were a few rocky spots, but this union succeeded where the others had failed, primarily because both parties entered into it fully prepared and committed.

After two previous tries, Ricardo had made a very wise choice in a mate. Not much detail is known about her background, except her birth on November 23, 1919, in Hammond, Indiana, but Margarette was a gentle, unassuming young woman, a cooperative individual, perfectly willing to allow her husband to take charge of her life.[404] She can be likened to a piece of clay, which Cortez carefully molded into the kind of wife he had always wanted. According to Ricardo's nephew, Don Kranze, "They seemed happy, but she served him as an acolyte to his fame. He was in charge."[405]

On Ricardo's 50th birthday on September 19, 1950 he and 30-year-old Margarette Bell were married by a justice of the peace. The union would last until death separated them 27 years later.

While Margarette's accommodating nature was a major factor in the union's long-term success, Ricardo's own transformation was no less significant. With advancing age came wisdom. He remained a controlling, sometimes selfish person, but by the time he married Margarette, years of mistakes, hard knocks, and disappointments had taught him needed patience, understanding, and humility.

Certainly the veteran actor's newly minted humility came in handy during the 1950's, when film offers became scarce. For a time, during the early 1950's, he tried television, telling reporters he might be interested in doing a TV series if the part and project were right, but it never came to pass. He did make a handful of television appearances, including guest shots on *Four Star Revue* (1951), and *The Jack Carson Show* (1954), but he never really "took" to TV. By

Many people are surprised to learn Cortez was an avid collector. Among his prized collections were these framed antique opera programs, some of which he collected as a youngster in New York.

During their first decade together, Mr. and Mrs. Cortez lived in his apartment at the Sunset Towers where he had lived since 1940.

the mid-1950's, he had become increasingly content with a life removed from acting.[406] The new life contained a familiar variety of activities, both personal and professional. He remained busy managing his diversified financial affairs, enjoyed attending sporting events, plays, and movie premieres, and tried to remain physically fit; but for the first time in his life, Ricardo attended many of these events and outings with his wife. He was also content to spend time alone with her, smoking his ever-present pipe, reading books, listening to opera records, or partaking in his many hobbies.

During the early 1950's, the hardworking Ricardo decided he'd earned the right to do a few things he'd always wanted. One of his lifelong passions was travel. In the past, whenever he'd had an opportunity, whether work-related or not, he'd taken a number of foreign trips. He loved seeing new sites, experiencing new cultures. Beginning in 1954, he and Margarette took several extended vacations to various locations around the globe. They toured Mexico in 1954, England and France in 1955, the Caribbean in 1956, and spent four months touring seven European countries in 1957.[407]

Ricardo also took time to forge closer bonds with his immediate family during the 1950's. He'd always maintained a close relationship with his mother, Sarah, and visited her when he was in New York, but beginning in the 1950's, he made an extra effort to spend more time with her. Now well into her 70s, she lived in a modest, yet comfortable apartment on New York's Lower East Side, which her eldest son had always paid for. Ricardo tried to spend more time with his siblings as well. His two brothers had made substantive careers for themselves in the motion picture industry. By the latter 1950's, Stanley Cortez had become one of the preeminent cinematographers in Hollywood, famed for his mastery of chiaroscuro photography; for creating a particular look through the use of a fluid camera, deep focus, and unique framing. Among his notable credits were such diverse classics as *The Black Cat* (1934), *The Magnificent Ambersons* (1942), *Since You Went Away* (1944), *The Man on the Eiffel Tower* (1949), *The Night of the Hunter* (1955), and *The Three Faces of Eve* (1957).

After many years of working in the New York sales departments of various movie studios, including RKO and United Artists, Bernard "Bernie" Kranze also became notable as one of the executives and chief proponents of Cinerama. One of the cinema's attempts to compete with television, Cinerama was a widescreen process originally utilizing three cameras and three projectors synchronized to project a single image onto a curved screen, thus achieving the illusion of vastness. The first film to showcase the innovation, the 1952 travelogue, *This is Cinerama*, (featuring rollercoaster rides and flights over the

Grand Canyon), was such an enormous success, it prompted the production of similar projects. Due to technical problems, the three lenses were eventually replaced by a single lens 70mm process. The popularity of Cinerama reached its zenith in 1962 with the release of the all-star historically based adventure, *How the West Was Won*, the first full-length film featuring the process.[409] Bernie and his wife Daisy had two sons: Donald and Arthur Barry Kranze. Donald, a.k.a. Don Kranze became a highly successful second unit and assistant director and producer. Among his credits were such classics as *12 Angry Men* (1957), *A Face in the Crowd* (1957), *Splendor in the Grass* (1961), *Advise and Consent* (1962), *The Graduate* (1967), and *There Was a Crooked Man* (1970). He also won acclaim for producing the acclaimed television series, *East Side/West Side* (1963-64).[410]

During the 1950's, in order to maintain ties to friends and associates in the entertainment industry, Ricardo continued to purchase artistic properties, mainly plays and novels, for production in movies and/or television. Little was written about the particular works he acquired at this time, or the success of his speculations, but Cortez maintained these ventures were lucrative, and remained involved in them throughout the remainder of his life. In October 1959, *The Los Angeles Times* reported Cortez had acquired "ownership of all rights" to two novels, *East of Broadway*, a mystery by Octavius Roy Cohen, and the melodramatic *Stevedore* by Reed Fulton. It does not appear as if either novel was ever adapted for the big or small screens.[411]

Even though he wasn't making movies, and had for all intents and purposes, reentered private life, Ricardo wasn't completely out of the public eye, at least during the 1950's. As Hollywood pioneer filmmakers of the silent screen became old and began passing away, an era of nostalgia swept the film capital and spread across the country. Silent actors and filmmakers were suddenly in demand for tributes. As one of the era's survivors, Ricardo was often included in events commemorating the silent screen.

In April, 1956, he joined many of his old costars and contemporaries at a special reunion/party in honor of silent filmmakers hosted by Mary Pickford and her husband, Buddy Rogers at their estate, Pickfair. Among the attendees were such past and present luminaries as Buster Keaton, Harold Lloyd, Joe E. Brown, Vilma Banky, Chester Conklin, and Betty Compson.[412] In January, 1957, Ricardo was invited to appear on Ralph Edwards' popular nostalgic series, *This Is Your Life* (NBC), in an episode commemorating the life and accomplishments of his former costar and longtime friend, Gloria Swanson. Ricardo was undoubtedly honored to join the celebrated roster of stars who appeared on the episode, including Mack Sennett, Francis X. Bushman, Jesse Lasky, Allan Dwan, Lois Wilson, and Rod La Rocque.[413]

Just prior to these events, columnist Erskine Johnson asked Cortez, of all the famed actresses he had appeared with onscreen (a list that included many of the cinema's most beloved and acclaimed feminine stars), who was his favorite. Without hesitation he told Johnson it was a tie.

"At the peak of their careers Joan Crawford and Irene Dunne were the most glamorous of all—Joan the tigress; and Irene for her spiritual quality. There's never been anyone else like them!"[414]

When asked about the future, the aging star told the press he had not formally retired from show business, but was considering it. Whatever he decided, he said he would continue to buy properties for the screen. He said he intended to move back East to be close to his family and to pursue new business opportunities.

Cortez would eventually keep all his promises, but not before fate intervened to provide him with one last movie assignment; a chance to retire in style! That came in late fall, 1957, when Ricardo's agent, Lillian Small, asked if he would be interested in a supporting role in John Ford's upcoming film adaptation of Edwin O'Connor's best-selling novel, *The Last Hurrah*, about the final campaign of a colorful veteran East Coast Irish-American politician. For weeks Cortez had been reading press reports regarding the proposed production, to star Spencer Tracy, and was gratified to be considered. He was even more excited after he read the script and learned the names of some of the other supporting players in the all-star cast, a veritable who's who of old Hollywood: O'Brien, Carradine, Rathbone, Crisp, McHugh, Lowe, Brophy, Gleason, Darwell, etc. In January, 1958, a personal call from the veteran director (with whom Cortez had worked on *Flesh* in 1932) sealed the deal.[415]

Loosely based on the life of former Massachusetts governor and Boston mayor James Curley, *The Last Hurrah* was the tale of Frank

Skeffington (Spencer Tracy), a veteran city mayor, a machine politician, whose bid for one more term turns out to be more difficult than anticipated. While the novel's emphasis was on the intricacies and machinations of urban politics, the Columbia Pictures film adaptation, as written by *New York Times* movie critic Frank S. Nugent, was a full-bodied character study of a great, but deeply flawed man. Press reports and subsequent interviews indicate Ford considered both Orson Welles and James Cagney for the lead in *The Last Hurrah*, but in the end, opted for Tracy, with whom he had worked on the comic melodrama *Up the River* in 1930. It was an inspired choice.[416]

Shooting commenced on February 24, 1958, and continued for approximately two months. Fifty-seven-year-old Tracy, who had just completed the long, physically and psychologically taxing production of Hemingway's *The Old Man and the Sea* (during which he had running battles with both the director and the famed novelist), was exhausted and discouraged. He was looking forward to working with Ford again, but told reporters that, like Cortez, he was contemplating ending his long, successful career. "I've joked about retiring," he said, "but this could be the picture. I'm superstitious—you know that's part of being Irish—and I'm back with John Ford again for the first time since I started out 28 years ago. I feel this is the proper place for me to end. Even the title is prophetic."[417] Fortunately, Tracy's experience making *The Last Hurrah* would be a pleasurable one. Ford directed the picture at a leisure-like pace, relishing the Irish-American themes and characters, and the chance to work with Tracy and company.

Everyone involved seemed to know the project was special and to savor every moment. Ricardo Cortez was euphoric while making the movie. *The Last Hurrah* was a top-notch production in every way, the kind of movie he had wanted to make for a long time. He considered it a privilege to have the opportunity to work with Ford and his distinguished colleagues, and was determined to give it his all.

News dispatches emanated from the production on a regular basis. Columnist Erskine Johnson (who contributed daily progress reports) publicly wondered how director Ford would manage so many notorious scene stealers. After the first day of filming, which involved scenes featuring most of the veteran cast, Johnson asked Spencer Tracy "Who won the first round?" According to the columnist, Tracy knew exactly what he was referring to and grinned "I'll tell you who wins every round on this set. It's John Ford—and everybody is smart enough to know it."[418] Another amusing report stated that on St. Patrick's Day, 1958, a case of Irish whiskey was delivered to the set by someone. Tracy, O'Brien, and others were delighted, but director Ford ordered it removed. "Jesus Christ, what do you want to do, shut down the picture?" he reportedly quipped.[419]

There was some speculation, especially after Tracy's experience making *The Old Man and the Sea* (1958), there would be problems between him and Ford. None materialized. The opposite was true. Each went out of his way to accommodate the other. Informed sources reported Tracy's contentment, which showed in his performance.[420] According to actress Dianne Foster, who portrayed the young wife of Skeffington's nephew (Jeffrey Hunter), Ford treated the entire cast well and created an atmosphere in which actors strived for excellence. In an interview with author James Rosen, Foster recalled the production and the crucial contribution of the director.

"I always preferred a director who allowed me to contribute something on my own. Some directors don't want any contribution. They prefer to tell you exactly what to do and where to move. John Ford wasn't like that. He was very open. He gave his actors a lot of freedom and watched what they brought to the scene. Then he'd make his adjustments and shoot the scene in one or two takes. He felt it kept the actors fresh and spontaneous . . ."[421]

Ricardo echoed Ms. Foster's praise in interviews and discussions conducted after the film was released in October, 1958. Ford had allowed him considerable freedom to interpret his role as Skeffington's Jewish campaign advisor, Sam Weinberg. It was a small part, but Cortez shined. He was warm and humorous in his scenes with Tracy, Gleason, O'Brien, and Brophy (who played Skeffington's other lieutenants). Particularly memorable was the film's last sequence, in which all of Skeffington's trusted advisors gather to pay final respects to their dying boss. In these funny, touching scenes, filmgoers rightly sensed the genuine camaraderie between the characters and the great veteran movie actors who played them.

Cortez was overjoyed when director John Ford asked him to join the star-studded cast of *The Last Hurrah* (Columbia, 1958). Top row from left to right: James Gleason, Cortez; Bottom row from left to right: Edward Brophy, Spencer Tracy, and Pat O'Brien.

Reviews were almost universally enthusiastic. Ford was cited for creating a cinematic critique of the current state of American politics, and for establishing an atmosphere in which his actors could give their best. Tracy won kudos for his multi-dimensional characterization. The prestigious National Board of Review named the film one of the top 10 of the year, naming Ford as Best Director and Tracy as Best Actor. Surprisingly, the N.B.R. nod did not lead to Oscar recognition. Tracy received a Best Actor Academy Award nomination in 1958, not for the *The Last Hurrah*, but for *The Old Man and the Sea*. He would lose the award to David Niven for his work in *Separate Tables*.

Although the lion's share of critical praise was reserved for Ford and Tracy, *The Last Hurrah* was a feather in the cap of everyone involved, including all the exceptional members of the supporting cast. "The subordinate characters are sketched in a lower key," said *Motion Picture Daily*, "but each is a gem of characterization . . ."[422]

To promote *The Last Hurrah* (Columbia, 1958), cast members were sent out in pairs to various prominent theatres in bigger cities. Veteran actors Jane Darwell and Ricardo Cortez were among the celebrated duos who gave brief presentations, answered questions, and posed for photos.

Just prior to the film's official release, Columbia announced it had hired Ricardo and five other top cast members to fan out across America, attending premieres, luncheons, and press events promoting it. The six were sent in pairs: Donald Crisp with Wallace Ford, Pat O'Brien and Frank McHugh, and Ricardo Cortez and Jane Darwell. The tours consisted of 27 separate visits to 13 cities. Some of the cities, such as New York, Washington, Boston, and Philadelphia, were visited by all three groups. Ricardo and 79-year-old Miss Darwell were the busiest of the three pairs. Press reports noted their appearances at various events in at least 10 of the 13 cities. Basking in the embrace of the acclaimed film, both Ricardo and Jane seemed to revel in all the new attention, comforted by the fact that they were still remembered and admired.[423]

Unfortunately, the personal triumphs and positive experiences shared by the entire cast and crew of *The Last Hurrah* would turn out to be bittersweet—marred by lawsuits, monetary losses, and death. Four days into the filming, Columbia President Harry Cohn died. While Cohn was not a popular figure in many Hollywood circles, at Columbia, he was akin to a demigod. All production was halted for his funeral. His loss was a body blow to the company he founded.[424] A few months later, after *The Last Hurrah* had been completed, former Boston Mayor Curley sued Columbia, claiming he had not signed off on the project, and that the movie would, in essence, prevent a film being made of his upcoming autobiography. An out-of-court settlement was reached before the film's release, netting him $42,000.[425] Columbia Pictures also suffered a huge loss at the box office. Despite critical raves and huge crowds for the film's premieres in multiple cities, records indicate that the movie lost $1.4 million, which many industry insiders attributed to the film's downbeat ending and its immense production costs.

Saddest of all, the movie would be the last significant film assignment for several cast members who had impactful careers on the silver screen. Ricardo's old friend, Jimmy Gleason, whom he had met on the set of *Her Man* in 1930, would enter the hospital two months after the premiere of *The Last Hurrah*, for an operation from which he never recovered. He died four months later. Another old friend, veteran character actor Edward Brophy, who contributed an Oscar-worthy performance as Skeffington's dim-witted deputy, "Ditto," would make only two uncredited film appearances before his death in May, 1960. By the end of the 1960's, death had claimed six more of the cast members, including the two top-billed stars: Spencer Tracy and Jeffrey Hunter.

Ricardo Cortez didn't know it yet, but the film would also be his last. After the positive experiences of its production and the publicity tour, he briefly contemplated a resumption of his acting career, telling interviewers he would consider making more movies and/or acting on television, provided the roles suited him. He said he was particularly interested in TV drama.[426]

In the fall of 1959, Ricardo followed up his acclaimed return to the movies by accepting an offer to appear on the small screen, portraying a Spanish landowner in a serio-comic episode of the popular Western television series *Bonanza* (1960). The episode, entitled "El Toro Grande," chronicled the multiple problems encountered by the Cartwright boys (Hoss and Little Joe, portrayed by Dan Blocker and Michael Landon) when they are sent by their father,

Ben (Lorne Greene), to purchase a prize-winning seed bull from a wealthy California landowner, Don Xavier Lozaro (Cortez). A pleasant if uneventful episode that had the Cartwrights battling thieves, stowaways, and a cantankerous bull, it was nevertheless memorable for the appearance of the distinguished-looking Ric Cortez, who at 59-years-old, was still slim, trim, and physically fit. Reviewers noted the veteran star "still cut a dashing figure on a horse." Cortez told a reporter his waist size was exactly the same as when he signed his first movie contract in 1923.[427] Another notable thing had not changed as well. After 37 years as a professional film actor, Jack Krantz a.k.a. Ricardo Cortez, the Jewish boy from Lower Manhattan, was still playing Latins!

CHAPTER ELEVEN
A COMFORTABLE PLACE (1960–77)

"I have found my greatest happiness in my work, in giving my best to whatever I am doing . . ."
— RICARDO CORTEZ

As Ricardo Cortez began the sixth decade of his life, he had much to look back on with pride and satisfaction. He was now in a financial position to do as he wanted, and had found the perfect mate to share his life with. After countless years of turmoil and struggle, enduring the triumphs and bitter disappointments of a film actor's life, Ricardo Cortez was at last in a comfortable place.

The pleasurable experience of making *The Last Hurrah* in 1958, and the affectionate embrace the film engendered, temporarily prompted Ricardo to contemplate a return to acting. After his guest starring role on the popular *Bonanza* series, broadcast in January, 1960, he followed with an appearance as himself on columnist Hedda Hopper's all-star NBC television special, *Hedda Hopper's Hollywood*, which also featured many of his comrades from the olden days.[428] On February 8, 1960, Cortez attended a ceremony honoring him with a coveted star on the renowned Hollywood Walk of Fame (at 1500 Vine Street).[429] Although well-deserved and overdue, Ricardo was elated and deeply moved by the recognition, and by the realization that his contributions were appreciated.

In the early 1960's, while contemplating acting, he and Margarette divided their time between East and West Coasts, but by mid-decade, they had given up their apartment at the Sunset Towers in Los Angeles and taken up sole residence in Manhattan. Ricardo continued to maintain ties to the movie industry by acquiring

Ricardo loved to travel and see new cultures. During the last decades of his life, he and Margarette made innumerable foreign trips. This photo was taken in 1965, just after they arrived in London aboard the legendary *Queen Mary*.

creative properties (mainly books and plays) for movie adaptation. In addition, during the 1960's, he began utilizing important contacts in the financial world to help arrange financing for motion picture projects. This frequently took him to the European continent, particularly to France, of which both he and Margarette were particularly fond.

After making their permanent home in New York, Mr. and Mrs. Cortez became involved in various East Coast clubs and charitable organizations. Throughout the 1960's, the names of one or both Cortezs often turned up in society columns, noting their participation and/or attendance at various events, including sporting matches and tournaments, theater premieres, fashion shows, concerts, parties, charitable events, and club fundraisers.[430] Because of Ricardo's ties to the movers and shakers in both the financial and entertainment worlds, the couple traveled in elite circles, hobnobbing with some of the wealthiest, most influential people on the East Coast.

Living comfortably and socializing with influentials did not immunize Ricardo from life's disappointments and sadness, however. On February 22, 1965, his mother Sarah Lefkowwitz Kranze, died at the age of 87. A much beloved mother, sister, grandmother, and friend, her passing was deeply felt by her family, and all who touched her life. Gentle and loving, yet tough and resilient, she had passed on these qualities to her family. She was survived by four children, two grandsons, two great-granddaughters, and her brother and sister. She was buried next to her husband in Mt. Zion Cemetery in Queens.[431] Her grandson, Don Kranze, remembered her as "a lovely kind lady who loved all her children."[432] Less than three years later, on January 17, 1968, Don's father, (Ric's brother), Bernard "Bernie," died at age 64. A well-respected movie executive, Bernard was revered in the film industry as a creative professional who devoted his entire life (thanks to the initial intervention of Ricardo) to making movies.[433]

By the mid-1960's, Ricardo's love for, and expertise at investing, began taking on an even greater significance in his life when one of Wall Street's top financial and investment firms, David Greene & Company, offered him part-time employment. Although in his 60's and enjoying life in retirement, the ever industrious, energetic, physically fit, mentally sharp Ricardo wanted to be productive, and accepted the offer. His exact duties are not entirely known, but apparently he not only sold stocks and investment portfolios, but was involved in the financing of various creative ventures. While acting in films, he had always related to the business aspects of the industry almost as much as the creative. As a result of the new position, he was able to marry the two on a formal basis.[434]

According to published reports, Cortez loved his new job and was a model employee. During these years, he and Margarette lived in modest apartments near his office. He was often seen around Lower Manhattan commuting to and from work. One writer who spotted him said he looked more like a tycoon than a movie star, noting, "Cortez is so rich he only drops down to his Wall Street brokerage once or twice a week to visit his coupons."[435] In a 2013 interview, Ricardo's nephew Don Kranze corroborated the statement, attributing his uncle's riches to "shrewd stock investments and his acting salary, which was relatively high at a time when income taxes were low or non-existent."[436] While her husband worked on Wall Street, Margarette became more involved in charity work.

For the most part, beginning in the early 1970's, Ricardo's name effectively fell off celebrity radar screens. By then he had not appeared in films for over a decade and memories of his accomplishments were fading. Little is known about his last years, as they were almost entirely spent happily out of the public eye. One New York City society and celebrity writer, and longtime Cortez friend, Jack O'Brien, known for his column, "Voice of Broadway," mentioned seeing Ricardo from time to time at various restaurants, nightclubs, and hangouts, including the famous Lambs Club (a social and charitable organization whose membership included many veteran actors and entertainers), but by the late 1960's, the celebrity press stopped paying attention.[437] One of the few prominent sightings of Cortez was in a Manhattan restaurant during the late 1960's. According to an article in *The New York Times*, while dining, a longtime fan recognized him, came over to his table, and asked for an autograph. During his heyday, the fan-phobic Ricardo might have refused the request, but that was long ago. Now, kindly and mellow, a friendly, smiling Ricardo happily complied, seemingly grateful to be recognized.[438]

There are several bits of misinformation that have circulated through the years about Ricardo's Wall Street employment. Several short biographies claimed he worked for the investment firms, Solomon Brothers and Merrill Lynch. This is untrue. He only worked for David Greene & Company. His last passport, issued in 1975, lists Greene as his employer.[439] Another rumor stated he was a market analyst. The basis of the rumor was a well-publicized 1975 article forecasting the future of stocks and other investments, written by Ricardo Cortez, "a senior market analyst at Merrill Lynch."[440] The article was published across the country, and through the years many have understandably attributed its authorship to the former film actor. The truth is, Ricardo Cortez did write the piece, but it was another Ricardo Cortez.

The last prominent press sightings and/or mentions of Ricardo during his lifetime were in Jack O'Brien's column. In one early 1970's item, O'Brien said he saw Ricardo and Margarette in a London restaurant having dinner on their way home from a vacation in Rome. Another column noted Ricardo's presence at the opening of a new Manhattan eatery. When someone recognized him, O'Brien said the actor "took bows and signed menus . . . looking handsome, dapper, and fit as a fiddle."[441] Unfortunately, Ricardo was not as healthy as he appeared. According to Carol Bell, Margarette's sister-in-law, Ric was diagnosed with cancer sometime during the early 1970's. Despite the diagnosis, he carried on as before, remaining a very active, vital person up until just before he passed away. His last passport notes a trip abroad in the fall of 1976.

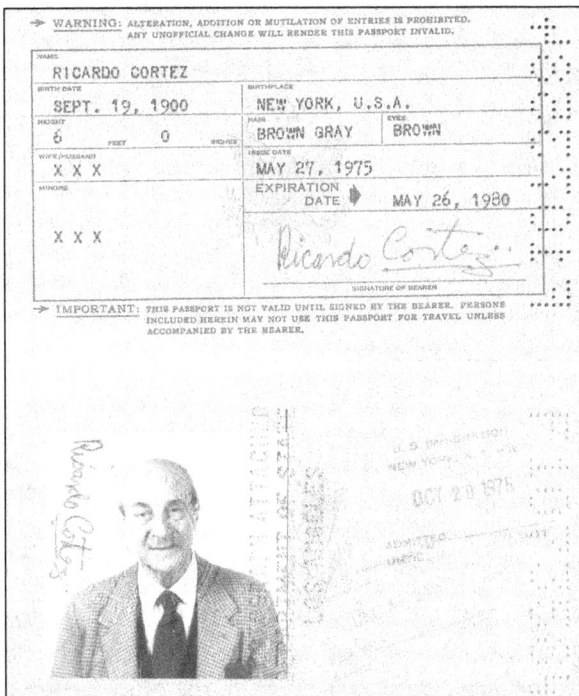

Cortez's last passport, dated May 27, 1975, notes a foreign trip in the fall of 1976.

A close-up of 74 year old Ricardo Cortez's passport photo.

Like so many events and issues in Ricardo's life, his death was a very private affair, the circumstances a bit mysterious. Cortez's lifelong obsession with privacy extended to all areas, including his health. Back in April, 1934, a year after he had been near death with pneumonia, Cortez checked back into Cedars of Lebanon hospital for what was termed "an operation." When the press expressed concern, he steadfastly refused to explain what was done.[442] Although Ricardo had changed considerably during the last 40 years, certain aspects of his personality never changed, including a desire to keep important private affairs private.

In mid-April, 1977, 76-year-old Ricardo Cortez was admitted to Doctor's Hospital in the Yorkville neighborhood of Manhattan, not far from where he had been born in 1900, suffering from an unknown ailment. Outside of his wife and a few intimates, his illness and hospitalization were kept from the public, even from family members.

His nephew, Don, said he never learned the cause of his uncle's final hospitalization, but noted that he didn't think Ricardo had been ill for a long time. Carol Bell, who married Margarette's brother Stanley a few years after Cortez's death, said Margarette told her Ric's cancer spread, thus prompting his admission to the hospital.

Cortez would remain hospitalized for approximately 10 days. One wonders if, during those last days, he ever had the opportunity to relive the old times, the triumphs, the tragedies, and recall all the remarkable people whom he had touched, and who had touched him. We will probably never know for sure, but there's a good chance he did.

Ricardo was still in the hospital when his condition took a substantial turn for the worse. At 3:50 in the afternoon of April 28, 1977, one of the cinema's best-loved rogues and scoundrels played his final death scene. There were no knives, guns, nooses, vials of poison, or vats of acid involved. In fact, this death scene was one of the most mundane, boring ones Ricardo had ever played, but one somehow befitting the distinguished old gentleman he had become. He simply closed his eyes and went to sleep.[443]

AFTERWORD

Although most important newspapers, magazines, and film journals across the country noted Cortez's death, many simply described him as a silent film star, noting his age, date of death, and nothing more. The cause of death was never publicly announced, but it was undoubtedly due to complications from cancer. His death certificate stated he died of "natural causes."

Of the formal obituaries that were published, most were exceedingly short, consisting of brief descriptions of his career, and a few of his film credits. The movies listed were often not his most significant. Not one described his career in any depth or noted his many contributions. Jack O'Brien was one of a handful of Cortez admirers to offer a brief tribute. In a portion of his regular column entitled, "Saying So Long to a Fine Old Friend," O'Brien recalled Cortez as "a New Yorker first and last with a great Hollywood career. He was a quality guy, genial and intelligent, full of enthusiasm, and sophisticated decency and witty companionship right up to his death at 77. His last movie was *The Last Hurrah* which drew fine notices for a fine actor and gentleman. . . ."[444] A month later, Mr. O'Brien mentioned missing his old pal, who he said "was bright and intellectually wise to the end."[445]

After an unpublicized private funeral held on May 1, 1977 at the Frank E. Campbell Chapel on Madison Avenue, in New York City, Ricardo Cortez was laid to rest in a mausoleum in Woodlawn Cemetery in the Bronx. He was survived by his widow, Margarette, sister Helene, brother Stanley and his wife Mildred, and two nephews: Don Kranze, and Arthur Barry Kranze (Bernard's sons). Helene died in 1986; Stanley's wife, Mildred in 1989; and Stanley in 1997.[446]

Cortez was buried in a mausoleum in the Woodlawn Cemetery in the Bronx.

Margarette Bell Cortez would survive her husband by over 30 years. She lived in New York for most of those years; then, near the end of her life, moved to Sebastian, a small town 92 miles southeast of Orlando on Florida's east coast near Vero Beach. She died there on November 6, 2007, at age 87.[447] Her sister-in-law, Carol remembers her fondly.

"For years Margaret lived in New York and would come to Florida for the holidays and stay with us. So many times she said she wished Ric had been alive to share that time as he longed for a peaceful family life in his later years. It is so sad that he had so much bad luck in earlier marriages. I know he was very fond of Margarette's mom and siblings. After Ric passed, Margarette went to Paris for a few months and every year until she was about 80. She loved Paris! We went once with her and it was wonderful. She knew the city well, the locals and the best little restaurants that tourists didn't know. She and Ric loved to travel. They never bought a house together.

Margarette had a stroke in New York, and we brought her to Florida during the last years of her life. I became her legal guardian as my husband who was older than I, wasn't well. Margarette didn't want to age. She didn't even apply for social security when she turned 65. She was beautiful and fun and loved to dress up and go out to lunch. She died here in Florida at 87. She had lots of life left, but broke an arm and had complications in the hospital. I still have her ashes. She asked me to keep them. It would seem she should be with Ric, but she never told me he was in New York. I found that out only a few years ago."[448]

Unfortunately, during her lifetime, Margarette never donated her late husband's papers to a library where they would have been preserved. Instead, at the time of her death, many of Ricardo's personal effects were placed up for sale, including family and other personal photos, scrapbooks, some important papers and letters, and other memorabilia from his 50-year movie career. Much of it was sold online on auction sites, thus scattered across the U.S. and the world.

CHAPTER TWELVE
RICARDO CORTEZ — ONE AUTHOR'S VIEW

SUMMARY, THOUGHTS, CONCLUSIONS

Although he continued to haunt late late shows on television, little has been written about Ricardo Cortez in the years since his death in 1977. On the rare occasions when his name has been brought up, it is almost always in reference to others, namely the illustrious directors and leading ladies with whom he worked. During the past decade or so, his name has also turned up in comparative analyses of the various versions of *The Maltese Falcon*. In the latter essays, he is almost always maligned and/or dismissed as an inferior, second-rate actor who misinterpreted the role of Sam Spade. For all intents and purposes, Ricardo Cortez's unique screen persona, his contributions, and legacy have been relegated to the dustbin of cinematic history. After carefully studying his career and his many cinematic contributions, I feel this oversight to be unjust and unacceptable. Hopefully, this biography is a significant first step in the process of righting this wrong.

In the introduction to this volume, I set forth the reasons I embarked upon this biography, and key questions I hoped to answer as a result of my quest to discover Cortez and relate his story. Since launching the project, thanks to help from several key individuals, I have managed to acquire and/or view several pieces from Ricardo's personal collection of career memorabilia. Among the interesting pieces are a grooming set he used, a trophy he received, three scrapbooks, multiple movie and other contracts, scripts, a variety of personal letters and correspondence, his last S.A.G card, his last passport, and several personal photos. Over the past four years I

Among Cortez's personal possessions was this treasured photo and corresponding trophy. The photo was taken on July 17, 1937, during a benefit baseball game pitting "The Leading Men" versus "The Comedians" to raise money for Mt. Sinai Hospital. The photo features "Leading Men" team members from left to right: George Raft, John Boles, Richard Arlen, Robert Armstrong, Unknown, and Ricardo Cortez.

The trophy presented to Cortez by comedian Benny Rubin reads as follows: "In appreciation to Ricardo Cortez, Screen Stars Classic Baseball Game for Mt. Sinai Hospital, July 17, 1937."

have scoured the country, searching key archives, major libraries, and countless books and articles in an effort to piece together Ricardo's life story, understand his personality and motivations, and assess his importance in film history.

As helpful as these resources have been, and as grateful as I am to have had a chance to examine them, what I coveted most eluded me. I refer to 50 years of movie memories that Ricardo apparently took with him to his grave. Regrettably, with a couple of exceptions, during his lifetime no one bothered to ask him about his treasure trove of personal and professional reminiscences, decades of recollections of all the legendary individuals he knew and worked with. What stories he could have told! One can only imagine what new information might have been gleaned or mysteries solved. Who knows? Maybe in old age, Ric Cortez might have revealed some of his own secrets; but we'll probably never know.

With this impediment in mind, I will share my findings and do my best to answer the questions posed. The first is, **"Who was Ricardo Cortez?"** In my opinion, this particular question can best be answered by separating the professional and personal Cortezes. Professionally, Ricardo Cortez was a very popular and successful movie actor whose career spanned five decades and encompassed over 100 feature length motion pictures. If one were to count the bits he contributed at the outset of his career in Fort Lee, New Jersey, and other studios across New York, the total number of his motion picture appearances is believed to be in excess of 275![448] He was never considered a superstar, but Cortez was an important actor of the late silent and early sound eras. Although he is often associated with villainous second leads and supporting parts, both the size and nature of his film roles ran the proverbial gamut, from leads to second leads and character assignments; from law loving, upstanding heroes, to vile murderers, and everything in between. He worked in all genres, and was a contract player for four major studios: Paramount, RKO, Warner Bros., and 20th Century Fox. At one time or another, he also worked for all the other majors and minors, including MGM, Universal, Columbia, and Republic, as well as Tiffany-Stahl, Monogram, and PRC. For a short, two-year period in the late 1930's, he graduated to directing, helming seven respectable low-budget films before opting to return to acting.

There were many reasons Cortez's professional career lasted when so many of his contemporaries did not: his innate intelligence, good instincts, and adaptability. The latter quality was particularly important. During his moviemaking years, he made several successful (and necessary) transitions that demonstrated versatility, flexibility, and dedication to his craft. Initially hired for his looks and poise, as a silent screen "Latin lover," a threat to Valentino, through hard work and perseverance, Cortez gradually learned the craft of movie acting, and all aspects of making motion pictures. As he learned, he expanded his repertoire of characters. By the middle 1920's, he was playing more diverse roles and campaigning for more complex, multi-dimensional assignments with some success. His lead performances in *The Pony Express, Torrent, The Sorrows of Satan, Midstream*, etc., during the mid to late 1920's proved he was more than just a pretty face; he could act.

He was clearly at the precipice of greater things when a series of bad decisions and financial and personal disasters (many associated with his marriage to actress Alma Rubens) combined to set Cortez back on his heels, derailing his progress and threatening his career's very survival. As a result of these setbacks and the sound revolution, Cortez was again called upon to prove himself. With the help of a stint in vaudeville and a pleasant baritone, he made a successful transition to sound films. Beginning in 1930, his career entered an important new phase. While he played all types of roles at the time, including memorable heroic turns like the morally challenged surgeon in *Symphony of Six Million*, and the conflicted attorney in *Hat, Coat, and Glove*, the darkly handsome Cortez reached new heights as a film actor portraying charismatic antiheroes, sexy screen villains, and heels. He brought a multi-dimensional quality to these roguish impersonations that made them both appealing and dangerous. His work in such films as *Her Man, The Maltese Falcon, Bad Company, Midnight Mary, Is My Face Red?, The House on 56th Street, Her Husband Lies,* etc. was impressive, winning him a dedicated fan base and critical kudos. He was so good in his treacheries, he eventually became closely associated with these characterizations, which proved limiting.

The combination of his typecasting as a screen rogue, his willingness to accept work in B movies, some unfortunate luck (including a health crisis), and the excessive censorship imposed by the Production Code Administration in 1934 negatively impacted Cortez's career yet again, as he seemed poised to ascend to the top echelon of stardom. By the mid 1930's, he had given up his quest for super-stardom and made another successful transition, this time to strictly character roles. As a featured actor and, later, as a B movie director, Cortez again distinguished himself with expert performances in such diverse productions as *The Walking Dead, City Girl, The Locket,* and *The Last Hurrah*; and by helming memorable low-budget movies including *The Escape, Heaven With a Barbed Wire Fence,* and *Girl in 313.*

While his adaptability was certainly one of the linchpins of his success, there were many other significant elements. Among them were his reputation, industriousness, and dedication to his craft. Cortez was highly regarded by most producers and directors as a total professional; a hard worker, always on time, always prepared, totally committed to contributing a polished performance. When others would fail to show up, refuse to play particular parts, or make unrealistic demands, producers and studio heads knew they could count on Cortez. He was literally one of their go-to guys. It is true he could be difficult and temperamental on occasion, but the instances of unprofessional conduct were relatively rare, many having to do with the antagonism of others and the overwhelming personal problems he was experiencing from time to time.

Perhaps one of THE most overlooked aspects of Cortez's long successful professional acting career was his ability. Over the years, some have claimed Cortez had little or no talent. Typical of these critics was Ohio-based writer Carmie Amata who, in a piece published in 1977, shortly after Cortez's death, referred to Ricardo as "not exactly a monumental star or for that matter, much of an actor . . . ." Later in the article, Amata said, "Obviously Cortez had no illusions, he had been tapped for stardom because of any great show of talent on his part, but rather for his uncanny resemblance to Paramount's biggest star, the greatest screen lover of all time, Rudolph Valentino. . . ." Near the end of the piece, Amata stated, "With plenty of money coming in from his business ventures, Cortez was secure. He could pick and choose his roles to suit his limited abilities . . . ."[450]

With all due respect, I STRENUOUSLY disagree with Mr. Amata and others who have denigrated or discounted Cortez's ability over the years. A thorough examination of his filmography reveals him to be an exceptionally fine, versatile actor, who learned his craft studying other actors and working with some of the best directors of the silent and sound eras. It is true he was given a Paramount contract because of his resemblance to Valentino, AND NO ONE is claiming he was one of the greatest actors who ever stepped in front of a camera. The partisans of Bogart, Edward G. Robinson, Walter Huston, Spencer Tracy, etc., can rest easy. BUT, he was VERY GOOD! From such silent masters as Griffith, DeMille, Cruze, Crosland, Buchowetski, Lloyd, and Christenson, he acquired the skill of acting with his eyes, conveying great emotion with the slightest glance. The skill served him well throughout his career.

After the advent of sound, under the guidance of such legendary directors as Capra, Ford, Curtiz, Wellman, etc., Cortez also learned to effectively utilize his voice. While his New York accent was pronounced (and was influential in his frequent casting as gangsters and villains), Ricardo skillfully utilized the loudness and tone of his voice to create full-bodied characterizations, further maximizing the impact of his performances. During the early sound era, he played opposite some of the screen's greatest feminine stars, holding his own with the likes of Stanwyck, Crawford, Davis, Lombard, Dunne, Young, Francis, Colbert, Astor, etc. Like all actors, the entirety of his career was impacted by the quality of scripts, budgetary issues, and the expertise of others with whom he worked, but those who question Cortez's abilities should reexamine his films of the late silent and early sound eras. They should read the reviews of important critics, columnists, and experts of the era, who were almost all enthusiastic about his work.

Before addressing Cortez's personality, there is one more thing I'd like to say—about his most famous portrayal. Regarding the critiques of his performance in *The Maltese Falcon*, it must be stated in his defense, Cortez played the role as written. As detailed in Chapter Five, after Warner Bros. determined Barrymore would not be available to play Spade, the part was rewritten to emphasize the Wonderly character to be played by Bebe Daniels. The rewrite portrayed Spade as a tough, wily, amoral womanizer, and that is exactly how Cortez played him. Few (certainly not this author) would argue the 1931 movie version of Hammett's novel is superior to John Huston's near-perfect 1941 remake, (with the masterful Bogart as Spade), but that does not mean the Cortez version and his performance were poor; quite the contrary. Incredibly, in the midst of an ongoing personal crisis, on two weeks' notice, Ricardo Cortez took over the part of Spade, contributing an excellent portrayal that dominated the film, wowed the critics, and even impressed the author, Hammett, who offered a testimonial.

Personally, Cortez was an enigma, a complex, insecure, self-conscious, extremely cautious, very private human being, the product of his humble beginnings and conservative upbringing, and, influenced by the positive and negative events of his life. As is true of every person, he had good and bad qualities, strengths and weaknesses.

Many of Cortez's positive attributes have already been mentioned in this chapter: his intelligence, superior work ethic, thriftiness, and single-minded dedication. From a poverty-stricken childhood on the poor, dangerous streets of Manhattan, with little formal education, Jack Krantz, a.k.a. Ricardo, relentlessly pursued his dream of becoming a successful actor. His personality was shaped during those early years. While only a young boy, in order to survive and pursue his goals, he learned to depend on himself. His tragedy-tinged childhood reinforced his independence and self-sufficiency. In interviews conducted during the early 1930's, Cortez admitted he was a loner who enjoyed solitude and valued his privacy. Early on, he concluded if he were to succeed, he would have to do it on his own. Consequently, young Jack had few friends and trusted fewer still. On the streets of Manhattan, he learned the importance of physical strength and fitness, and the necessity of knowing how to physically defend one's self, and from a high school teacher, he learned that showing vulnerability was a sign of weakness. By the time he arrived in Hollywood in the early 1920's, Jack's insecurities were masked behind a veneer of self-confidence and bravado.

His first 10 years in the film capital would test both his inner and outer strength to the max. After signing a contract with the most powerful studio in the movie industry, he was forced to endure a baptism by fire. In addition to learning his craft, and dealing with the responsibilities and pressures of his job, young Cortez was forced to mask his true background, while enduring the ridicule and destructive lies of those who resented his employment and success. His preference for solitude and inability to make friends easily inhibited his progress at times. The hostility shown him, and his first wife's betrayal of him, reinforced his insecurities and further exacerbated his isolation and trust issues. Yet, his ability to persevere and power through these crises was impressive. This was never better illustrated than during the latter 1920's, when he tried valiantly to help his wife deal with her ruinous addiction, while handling the psychological stress and professional challenges of his career.

In addition to his devotion to acting and the creative arts, Cortez displayed many other significant abilities, interests, and hobbies throughout his life that were reflections of his personality and character. The most prominent of these were sports and physical fitness, men's fashion, and financial speculations. While a youngster, Ricardo exhibited prowess as a boxer and developed his natural ability. According to several experts and various trainers, he displayed considerable talent. In addition, he was an avid sports enthusiast and physical fitness advocate, who, in his free time, would often be found at the gym working out; participating in his favorite sports including horseback riding, swimming, golf, and tennis; or enjoying sporting events as a spectator.

Men's fashion and grooming were also main interests. Likely influenced by the Broadway and stage actors he'd seen as a child, Cortez was obsessed with looking and acting like a star. During the 1930's and 1940's, he turned up on several best dressed lists, and in newspapers and magazine ads endorsing particular lines of clothing. He also penned dissertations on men's grooming and fashion; and during the mid-1940's, he became a formal fashion consultant for prominent men's magazines.

Of all his hobbies, the most important by far was investing. Inspired by his frugal father, and humble background, and influenced by his early years as a Wall Street runner, Cortez developed an intense interest in, and aptitude for investing. Throughout his life, he maintained close ties with investment professionals who wisely advised him on the purchase of stocks, bonds, and real estate. Newspaper and magazine stories reveal that Cortez's speculations also included various businesses and creative properties. Most of his business ventures netted him a tidy profit, which eventually made him a very wealthy man. He was so well respected as an investor, after his retirement from acting he was hired by a prominent Wall Street firm for whom he worked up until his death.

Ricardo's weaknesses and faults are well-documented in this volume and elsewhere. Under the ever-smiling, confident facade was an insecure man whose valiant attempts to conceal self-doubt and self-consciousness often inspired fits of temper and made him appear arrogant and distant. While he was a devoted son and a supportive brother who financially cared for his mother and sister throughout his life, and helped his brothers secure employment in the film industry, his periodic selfishness, self-centeredness, trust issues, and volatility appear to have been limiting to him both personally and career-wise. Several reference volumes, biographies and autobiographies of various filmmakers and costars paint Cortez as egocentric, humorless, and temperamental. Of particular note, were the memoirs of actress Lina Basquette, the biography of Glenn Ford written by his son, Peter, and a magazine interview with Cortez's *Murder of Dr. Harrigan* costar, Kay Linaker.

His first two wives also portrayed him in a negative light. There's barely a positive word about him in Alma's autobiography. In their divorce hearing, Christine claimed he was cold, controlling, and sometimes physically abusive. Ricardo never defended himself in any of these instances, and it is important to note, there may well have been hidden agendas and ulterior motives at play in some of these criticisms (particularly his wives'). However, there were too many critiques to simply chalk them all up to fabrications. When asked in 2013, Ricardo's nephew Don told me he had not known his uncle well. On the few occasions they met, Mr. Kranze said, "He was in charge. He was polite, wasn't kind or unkind." [451]

In recent years, some authors writing short summary biographies of Cortez for various books and articles have cited his conservative nature. One described his personality as "dull, colorless." Although the latter critique appears petty and unfair, it is certainly true Cortez was a conservative, serious-minded guy with traditional values and tastes in all aspects of life.

That brings us to the second major question posed in the introduction: **"Why has Ricardo been forgotten?"**

In my opinion, there are multiple reasons. His personality was a factor, but only one of many. Despite his long, productive movie career, perhaps THE most important reason Cortez has been all but forgotten until now is apparent if one takes a thorough look at a list of his films. The truth is, Ricardo Cortez never made what is considered a great classic movie. There are some very good ones in his filmography which showcase his ability as an actor, but most of his resume of motion pictures consists of routine features or low budgeters. The vast majority had redeeming qualities, including his performances, but most had serious deficiencies (e.g., poor scripts, lack of investment, other weaknesses) that detracted from them.

The typecasting of Cortez as a cinematic scoundrel during the early 1930's was another major factor impacting modern assessments of his career. There is no question he was a memorable malefactor, bringing weight and dimension to these portrayals, but villains were ordinarily subordinate roles. By and large, up until recently, film historians and writers have tended to only focus their attention on heroes and megastars, and ignore contributions of second leads and others, no matter how important their work was.

Also significant was Cortez's cooperativeness with studio executives; his willingness to accept all assignments, including routine second features. This kept him working in the business he loved for over five decades and helped pay the bills, but did nothing to enhance his historical standing. Unlike many of his fellow actors, Ricardo was friendly with many of the moguls and rarely defied them. As a businessman himself, he understood and related to them.

Cortez's obscurity can also be blamed on bad luck and bad timing. He died in 1977, seven years before a large scale renaissance of interest in classic films precipitated by the 1984 debut of the American Movie Classics Channel (AMC), which broadcast vintage movies uncut, and uninterrupted on cable television. This was followed in 1994 by the launch of Turner Classic Movies, which broadcast the vast film libraries of Metro-Goldwyn-Mayer (MGM), RKO, and Warner Bros., and various short films, trailers, etc., all uncut and uninterrupted. These two channels and several others rekindled a dormant interest in classic movies, vintage stars, and movie memorabilia, which in turn inspired authors to write books and articles on the subject, fans to collect classic films on video and DVD, and various other movie memorabilia. By the late 1980's and early 1990's, the living stars from the silent and "golden age" eras suddenly found themselves in demand for interviews and appearances commemorating their work. Sadly, Ricardo missed out on the attention.

In this author's opinion, the most unfair, unfortunate reason Cortez has never received the recognition his career merits has been discussed. It involves assessments of his acting ability. Over the years, certain film writers and "experts" have judged him harshly. Some of the harshest criticisms appear to be based on one or two of his film performances, and do not consider the large body of his work.

So, **"What is Cortez's true legacy?"** Why should we remember him? Many of his singular accomplishments were listed in the introduction and throughout this volume, including his long, successful career, his portrayals of Spade, Mason, etc., his versatility and adaptability, and his acclaimed collaborations with some of the cinema's most illustrious directors, craftsman, and players.

In addition, during the early 1930's, Cortez reached the zenith of his popularity as one of the cinema's premier villains, bringing multi-dimensional depth to his portrayals of cads, rascals, malefactors, and killers that few could match. This brought him considerable acclaim, and continuous offers of employment. His fame and popularity coincided with the pre-Code era (discussed in Chapters 5-7), a brief and fascinating period of film history from the late 1920's–to 1934, between the advent of sound and the strict enforcement of the Production Code, during which Hollywood producers enjoyed relative freedom to present mature, sophisticated themes in an adult manner. Cortez's acclaimed portrayals of lascivious, opportunistic, often violent characters, appeared to fit comfortably into the relaxed moral structure of this cinematic era. He was an important actor of this period and deserves recognition for it.

Upon reflection, perhaps the most important reason Cortez deserves to be remembered is his life story; one that could have been penned by Horatio Alger. It is a tale of a poor boy who made good, an inspiring saga of a lowly immigrant's son who set a goal for himself, and through talent, hard work, responsibility and thrift, achieved his dream. Along the way, he endured countless slings and arrows, triumphs and tragedies, but came out a winner by meeting every challenge with courage and an iron will. Because of all his hard work and sacrifice, when he formally retired, he was able to live the life he had envisioned as a youngster. Looking back, it seems Ricardo Cortez achieved something akin to the American dream; a most welcome and surprisingly happy ending for the cinema's magnificent heel who had suffered so many unhappy, often gruesome endings on the silver screen.

Many years after Ricardo's death, author James Bawden interviewed Stanley Cortez. When asked about his older brother, Stanley proudly recited Ricardo's many accomplishments, including his assistance in launching his own legendary Hollywood career. He said Ricardo was "a wonderful older brother to me. Always!" When Bawden wondered out loud, given his many achievements, why Ricardo was never mentioned in film histories, Stanley replied simply, "Well, he should be!" Yes, indeed!!

This is an original 1938 lithograph of a drawing of Cortez by the noted caricaturist Henry Major, featuring a caption by humorist "Bugs" Baer.

PART II
THE FILMS OF RICARDO CORTEZ

FEATURE FILMS (AS AN ACTOR)

The Imp (1919) (Crime Drama)
Selznick Pictures Corporation
Director: Robert Ellis
Screenplay: Elsie Janis, Edmund Goulding (story)
Length: 60 minutes
Taglines: "Love, romance, and a burglar's kit!"; "Do you think all criminals are mentally unbalanced?"
Status: Largely lost—A fragment survives at the Library of Congress in Washington D.C.

Cast: Elsie Janis (Jane Morgan), Joseph King (Joseph King a.k.a. "The Leopard"), Ethel Stewart (Jane's Mother), E. J. Radcliffe (Jane's Father), Duncan Pewarden (Dr. James), Arthur Marion (The Butler), John Sutherland (The Deacon), William Frederic (The Warden), Edith Forest (Maid), Joseph Granby (Hampden), Jack Ridgeway (Comedian), Jack Crane a.k.a. Ricardo Cortez (Golfer).

Summary: When she is struck with a golf ball, a crime obsessed young woman (Janis) emerges from a coma, thinking she is a notorious pickpocket. Her attempts to rob a bank inspire her parents (Stewart, Radcliffe) to hire an unconventional specialist (King) to try and save her from a life of crime.

Reviews:
Denton Record-Chronicle "A comedy drama with funny Elsie Janis at her best. A winning story with a winning star . . . ."

Syracuse Herald "Elsie Janis, who is 'the imp' has fulfilled every expectation motion picture lovers had for her in this latest Selznick photoplay. The excellent acting done by the little star and by her leading man is amplified by captions more than ordinarily apt."

PRODUCTION NOTES, INTERESTING FACTS, TRIVIA:
1. Billed as Jack Crane, Cortez's bit role as a golfer was not credited.

2. Columbus, Ohio native, Elsie Janis (1889-1956), enjoyed a long and varied show business career which began when she was a child in vaudeville, and included major theatrical productions and successful stage shows on Broadway. In England and France she entertained troops on the front lines in Europe in World War I, and wrote books, articles, and songs, while acting, writing, and supervising Hollywood films. She co-wrote the script for *The Imp* with future film director Edmund Goulding.

3. In what has to be one of the most bizarre promotional stunts of all time, *The Sandusky Star-Journal* chronicled the elaborate efforts of a local theatre owner, Mr. Schade, to publicize *The Imp* by sponsoring an essay contest. Prizes were awarded to the best, most concise answers (200 words or less) to the question "Do you think all criminals are mentally unbalanced?" Second prize was a $5 gift certificate. **First prize was a 10-week-old-baby**, not a doll, but according to the ad "one real live white baby." In small print at the bottom of the ad was the following quote. "Mgr. Schade also announces he will open a bank account at the Citizens Banking Company, Third National Exchange Bank, Commercial National Bank, and American Banking Co. for the baby. A Prominent Sandusky Attorney will give the baby away. — NOTE — Winner will be investigated and must be financially and morally satisfactory to Manager Schade."

4. At the top of the above ad was a request by star Elsie Janis that she be allowed to name the baby. Also included was a promise from J. Selznick, President of Select Pictures Corporation, to have the "prize baby" appear in one of his productions "when old enough to do so."

Do You Think All Criminals Are Mentally Unbalanced?

L. J. Selznick, President of the Select Pictures Corp. Announces His Intention of having this prize baby appear in Selznick Pictures when old enough to do so.

ELSIE JANIS

NOTE:—
MISS ELSIE JANIS, SELZNICK STAR IN—"THE IMP," FEMALE "JIMMY VALENTINE AND "RAFFLES" COMBINED, REQUESTS THAT SHE BE ALLOWED TO NAME THE BABY.

Star of Selznick Pictures Comes to Schade Theater, Tuesday and Wednesday, In the Startling, Thrilling, Dramatic Production

'THE IMP'

BUT—MANAGER SCHADE, OF THE SCHADE THEATER, WANTS SANDUSKIANS TO TELL HIM HOW THEY WOULD ANSWER THE ABOVE QUESTION, AND AS AN INDUCEMENT HE HAS ARRANGED

TO GIVE AWAY ONE 10-WEEK-OLD BABY

To the Person Writing the Best Essay of Not More Than 200 Words on the Subject of—
"ARE ALL CRIMINALS MENTALLY UNBALANCED?"

UNDERSTAND THIS—The baby will actually be given away! And to the person writing the best essay. All essays must be mailed to Manager Schade in care of the Schade Theater, to reach him not later than 3 P. M. TUESDAY, MARCH 9th.

THE BABY WILL BE GIVEN AWAY AT 9 O'CLOCK SHOW ON WEDNESDAY EVENING, THE SECOND DAY OF THE PICTURE

Do you want a baby? A real live white 10-week-old baby? Here is your chance! Write that essay or theme. You may not win the first prize, so there are others.

1st Prize—One Real Live White Baby   2nd Prize—$5 Due Bill Ticket to Big Store

Next ten prizes—Pair Theater Passes to see "THE IMP," starring ELSIE JANIS.

See window displays for the baby at Andres & Frey, Sacksteder Shoes, Wade Drug Store, Ueberle-Brengartner Shoe Store.

Mgr. Schade also announces he will open a bank account at the Citizens Banking Co., Third National Exchange Bank, Commercial National Bank and American Banking Co., for the baby. Prominent Sandusky Attorney will give baby away. NOTE:—Winner will be investigated and must be financially and morally satisfactory to Manager Schade.

The elaborate film promotion campaigns of today can't quite compare to this one initiated by a small theatre owner in Ohio for The Imp (1919).

PERJURY (1921) (MELODRAMA)
FOX FILM CORPORATION
PRODUCER: William Fox
DIRECTOR: Harry Millarde
SCREENPLAY: Ruth Comfort Mitchell (adaptation), Mary Murillo (scenario).
LENGTH: 90 minutes
STATUS: Lost

CAST: William Farnum (Robert Moore), Sally Crute (Marsha Moore), Wallace Erskine (John Gibson), Alice Mann (Helen Moore), Gilbert Rooney (Jimmy Moore), Grace La Vell (Mira), Jack Crane a.k.a.

Ricardo Cortez (Ralph Mills), Frank Joyner (Edward Williams), Frank Shannon (Phil Rourke), John Webb Dillon (District Attorney Choate).

SUMMARY: When a general manager (Farnum) for a wealthy businessman (Erskine) hears gossip regarding his wife (Crute) and his boss, he visit's the latter, and finds him dead. He is convicted of murder and sent to prison. The real murderer eventually confesses and the man is released. He is then persuaded to visit his ex-wife, who is now married to a man who abuses her.

REVIEWS:
Variety "It is right along the line of the usual Fox program picture and contains nothing that would warrant lifting it from the program class of production . . . ."

PRODUCTION NOTES, INTERESTING FACTS, AND TRIVIA:
1. Based on a 1920 play, *Guilty, a Modern Drama in Four Acts*, by Julius Steger, which in turn, was based on a story by Ruth Comfort Mitchell.

2. The film was previewed to a group of critics in August 1921, before its release in October. When the reviewers began laughing inappropriately during the film, the playwright, Mr. Steger (who was attending), became visibly upset, upbraiding the critics. According to *Variety*, his actions "solidified the entire newspaper group against the director and perhaps the picture as well."

THE GENTLEMAN FROM AMERICA (1923) (COMEDY)
UNIVERSAL PICTURES
PRODUCER: Carl Laemmle
DIRECTOR: Edward Sedgwicke
SCREENPLAY: George Hull (scenario), Raymond L. Shrock (story)
LENGTH: 5 reels (50 minutes)
TAGLINE: "This might be called the story of a fighting American in sunny Spain, with dashing senoritas and romance in the background!"
STATUS: Lost

CAST: Ed "Hoot" Gibson (Dennis O'Shane), Tom O'Brien (Johnny Day), Louise Lorraine (Carmen Novarro), Carmen Phillips (The Vamp), Frank Leigh (Don Ramon Gonzales), Jack Crane a.k.a. Ricardo Cortez (Juan Gonzales), Bob McKenzie (San Felipe), Albert Prisco (Grand Duke), Rosa Rosanova (Old Inez), Boris Karloff (bit as an outlaw).

SUMMARY: Two Army buddies (Gibson, O'Brien) find love, adventure, and trouble when they decide to take a furlough in Paris and end up in Spain. There, they meet a beautiful young woman (Lorraine) who is being forced to marry a man (Crane/Cortez) she doesn't love.

REVIEWS:
The Film Daily: "While *The Gentleman from America* isn't as funny as some of Gibson's other recent releases, it has a satisfying humor and enough comedy incident to make it register sufficiently well to get it over . . . ."

Variety: "The absurd contrast of two bonehead A.E.F.'s stumbling about in situations of hectic romance is a delightful bit of fooling, and it works out into a gorgeous comedy idea for five reels . . ."

PRODUCTION NOTES, INTERESTING FACTS, TRIVIA:
1. Nebraska-born Edmund "Hoot" Gibson (1892-1962) was an American rodeo champion before becoming one of the cinema's premier cowboy actors during the 1920's. His Westerns were unusual because of their emphasis on comedy.

2. *Gentleman*'s other lead actor was burly Tom O'Brien (1890-1947), who appeared in over 80 films in a career spanning 22 years. Primarily cast in comic supporting roles as "Irish types," he never graduated to top-tier parts despite his acclaimed appearance as Corporal Bull O'Hara in the King Vidor classic *The Big Parade* (1925).

3. *The Gentleman from America* marked the first of four joint film appearances of Cortez and a young British actor named Boris Karloff who played an uncredited villain in this picture.

Sixty Cents an Hour (1923) (Comedy)
Famous Players-Lasky Paramount
Director: Joseph Henaberry
Screenplay: Grant Carpenter (scenario), Frank Condon (story)
Length: 6 reels
Tagline: "It's a Bubbling, refreshing, gloom-chasing offering, with a laugh for every flicker of the film"
Status: Lost

Cast: Walter Hiers (Jimmy Kirk), Jacqueline Logan (Mamie Smith), Ricardo Cortez (William Davis), Charles Ogle (James Smith), Lucille Ward (Mrs. Smith), Robert Dudley (storekeeper), Clarence Burton, Guy Oliver, Cullen Tate (three crooks).

Summary: A soda jerk (Hiers) loves a banker's daughter (Logan), but her father (Ogle) does not approve. When the soda jerk finds money stolen from the father's bank, he must fight a two-front battle to claim the reward and win the hand of the daughter.

Reviews:
Motion Picture Guide: "Good comedy with fat funny man, Hiers . . ."

Time Magazine: "Ever since the recoil of a certain obese comedian from the comedy centers of California, a gentleman named Walter Hiers has been striving for the heavyweight custard pie championship. *Sixty Cents An Hour* is his latest. For that strange stratum of the commonwealth, which derives amusement from watching a ton lump of humanity at his wooing, the venture is doubtless entertaining."

Production Notes, Interesting Facts, and Trivia:
1. Cortez had a supporting role as a real estate agent (Hiers' romantic rival) in this broad comedy. It would be one of the first of countless films in which he would portray a heavy.

2. Rotund silent film comedian, Walter Hiers (1893-1933), made over 100 motion pictures during a 20-year span (1912-32).

After the career of funnyman Fatty Arbuckle was tainted by scandal, Paramount hired rotund comedian Walter Hiers to play similar parts. In the comedy *Sixty Cents an Hour* (1923), a soda jerk (Hiers, left) competes with a handsome real estate agent (Cortez, right) for the affections of a pretty banker's daughter.

Discovered by D. W. Griffith, he appeared for Biograph in bits and character roles mostly emphasizing his 235-pound girth to comic affect. Eventually signed by Paramount, he graduated to leads during the early 1920's, but his career waned with the coming of sound. Hiers died of pneumonia at age 39.

HOLLYWOOD (1923) (COMEDY)
FAMOUS PLAYERS-LASKY PARAMOUNT
PRODUCER: Jesse L. Lasky
DIRECTOR: James Cruze
SCREENPLAY: Frank Condon (story), Tom Geraghty (adaptation)
LENGTH: 8 reels
TAGLINE: "All the Stars in Hollywood Skies!"
STATUS: Lost

CAST: Luke Cosgrave (Joel Whitaker), George K. Arthur (Lem Lefferts), Hope Brown (Angela Whitaker). As themselves were:

Agnes Ayres, Mary Astor, Noah Beery, William Boyd, Betty Compson, Ricardo Cortez, Cecil & William DeMille, William S. Hart, Jack Holt, Leatrice Joy, Lila Lee, May McAvoy, Thomas Meighan, Owen Moore, Nita Naldi, Pola Negri, Anna Q. Nilsson, Jack Pickford, Will Rogers, Anita Stewart, Gloria Swanson, Lois Wilson, and many others.

SUMMARY: A would-be actress (Brown) moves to Hollywood to find a job in the movies, accompanied by her grandfather (Cosgrave). She is unsuccessful, but her grandfather is signed to a contract as a character player. When other family members and the girl's sweetheart (Arthur) decide to rescue the old man from the evil influences of the cinema, they are tempted themselves. While in Hollywood, they meet Paramount's roster of stars.

REVIEWS:
New York Times: "As a smart satire with sparkling wit, Hollywood, James Cruze's latest production, overwhelms all other screen efforts in its line."

The Paramount Story: "Frank Condon's slight story, adapted by Tom Geraghty, was spiced with satire on the film city's people and customs. James Cruze's direction had great panache and the movie was a big hit."

PRODUCTION NOTES, INTERESTING FACTS, AND TRIVIA:
1. Several noted movie magazines and columnists reported there were so many stars who appeared in cameo roles in the film, its producers were forced to hire unknown actors for the principle roles.

2. In a rare film appearance following the scandal that ruined his career, Roscoe "Fatty" Arbuckle had a bit in *Hollywood*, ironically as an unemployed actor.

CHILDREN OF JAZZ (1923) (COMEDY)
FAMOUS PLAYERS-LASKY PARAMOUNT
DIRECTOR: Jerome Storm
SCREENPLAY: Beulah Marie Dix (screenplay), Harold Brighouse (play)
LENGTH: 60 minutes
TAGLINE: "The Thrills of Yesterday Mixed With the Jazz of Today!"
STATUS: Lost

CAST: Theodore Kosloff (Richard Forestall), Ricardo Cortez (Ted Carter), Robert Cain (Clyde Dunbar), Eileen Percy (Babs Weston), Irene Dalton (Lina Dunbar), Alec B. Francis (John Weston), Frank Currier (Adam Forestall), Snitz Edwards (Blivens), Lillian Drew (Deborah), Julie Bishop.

SUMMARY: A dancer (Kosloff) becomes engaged to the daughter (Percy) of a wealthy man (Francis). Not ready to settle down, the high flying young woman becomes engaged to two more young men (Cortez, Cain), before she returns to her senses and comes to appreciate the more serious-minded dancer.

REVIEWS:
Hamilton Evening Journal: "A delightful, modern, melodramatic comedy having as its central figures the much discussed present-day miss and her hair-brained set of admirers, all devotees of jazz."

New York Times: "The novelty of this production makes it quite pleasing as entertainment, and the only pity is that such a serious looking individual as Theodore Kosloff should have been cast in this story of the defeat of jazz life."

PRODUCTION NOTES, INTERESTING FACTS, AND TRIVIA:
1. Based on Harold Brightouse's play, *Other Times*.

2. During the filming of a fight scene in *Children of Jazz*, between rival characters played by Theodore Kosloff and Ricardo Cortez, amateur boxer Cortez landed a punch which knocked Kosloff

unconscious. Press reports indicated he remained so "for quite some time—requiring much sponging to free himself of gore." Costar Eileen Percy reportedly fainted after the incident.

3. The athletic Cortez was required to do dangerous stunts during the filming of *Children of Jazz*. One of the scenes required him to land on top of a sailing vessel (containing the abducted Miss Percy) with a hydroplane. He and another actor had to parachute on to the vessel and rescue the damsel in distress. According to newspaper items, the stunt went off as planned and spectators were thrilled.

THE CALL OF THE CANYON (1923) (WESTERN)
FAMOUS PLAYERS-LASKY PARAMOUNT
DIRECTOR: Victor Fleming
SCREENPLAY: Edfrid A. Bingham, Doris Schroeder (script), Zane Grey (novel)
LENGTH: 7 reels
TAGLINE: "Jazz Mad New York and the Rugged West; Frivolous Society & the Mighty Realities of Nature—The Picture Shows Both!"
STATUS: Exists—A complete copy is held by the Library of Congress.

CAST: Richard Dix (Glenn Kilbourne), Lois Wilson (Carley Burch), Marjorie Daw (Flo Hutter), Noah Beery (Haze Ruff), Ricardo Cortez (Larry Morrison), Fred Huntley (Tom Hutter), Lillian Leighton (Mrs. Hutter), Helen Dunbar (Aunt Mary), Eddie Clayton (Tenney Jones), Dorothy Seastrom (Eleanor Harmon), Laura Anson (Beatrice Lovell), Charles Richards (Roger Newton), Arthur Rankin (Virgil Rust), and Mervyn LeRoy (Jack Rawlins).

SUMMARY: A young man (Dix) who is gassed during World War I, returns home to New York to find his fiance (Wilson) has changed, and has taken up with a fast crowd. To escape the situation and recover his health, he moves to Arizona and becomes a rancher.

REVIEWS:
Motion Picture News: "A picture that 'kills two birds with one stone.'" It has society life in the effete East, jazz dances of the '400,' and striking feminine fashions for the folks who like these ingredients in their film fare; and it has red blooded western scenes, thrilling physical combats, wonderful shots of the Arizona canyon country, and a terrific prairie storm."

PRODUCTION NOTES, INTERESTING FACTS, AND TRIVIA:
1. Two future film directors worked on the crew of *The Call of the Canyon*. Mervyn LeRoy was a wardrobe assistant and played a bit role in the film, and Henry Hathaway was a prop man.

2. The *Call of the Canyon* was among the first movies to be filmed on location in Oak Creek Canyon, near Sedona, Arizona.

3. The first few scenes of *The Call of the Canyon* were filmed in Flagstaff, Arizona, where locals were employed as extras.

4. During the filming (September, 1923), a devastating storm halted production for a week, stranding all cast members. Legendary cinematographer James Wong Howe photographed the event to spectacular effect.

5. Bebe Daniels was originally slated to play the part of Flo Hutter, but when she learned it was a supporting role, she refused to get off the train in Flagstaff, Arizona. Estelle Taylor was then brought in to replace her, but she too left the production after she became ill from becoming wet in the massive rainstorm. Marjorie Daw was eventually hired to play Flo, and all Taylor's footage had to be refilmed.

6. The film was considered lost until a copy was located in Russia, who presented a digital print to the Library of Congress in 2010.

7. According to the book, *Dolly and Zane Grey: Letters From a Marriage* by Pearl Zane Grey and Lina Elise Grey, the author Grey was contracted by Jesse Lasky to go to Arizona prior to

Cortez and Lois Wilson enact a scene from the adventure drama, *The Call of the Canyon* (Paramount, 1923) directed by Victor Fleming.

filming, and find locations contained in his books. Grey spent the next two months there while *The Call of the Canyon* was filmed.

8. For the film's spectacular windstorm sequence, special equipment was shipped via chartered express railroad car. Among the equipment were two automobiles outfitted with truck bodies to transport Stutz airplane motors to generate the wind. The sandstorm was shot approximately 14 miles from Flagstaff in Winona, Arizona.

9. *The Call of the Canyon* was one of very few Zane Grey stories to be filmed only once. In 1942, Republic Pictures paid $750 for the title to be used in a Gene Autry musical western. The story had no relationship to Grey's.

THE NEXT CORNER (1924) (MELODRAMA, ROMANCE)
FAMOUS PLAYERS-LASKY PARAMOUNT
PRODUCERS: Adolph Zukor, Jessie L. Lasky
DIRECTOR: Sam Wood
SCREENPLAY: Monte Katterjohn
LENGTH: 71 minutes
TAGLINE: "Wives, never put it in writing—It might happen to YOU!"
STATUS: Lost

CAST: Conway Tearle (Robert Maury), Lon Chaney (Juan Serafin), Dorothy Mackaill (Elsie Maury), Ricardo Cortez (Don Arturo), Louise Dresser (Nina Race, Elsie's mother), Remea Radzina (Countess Longueval), and Dorothy Cumming (Paula Vrain).

SUMMARY: A neglected wife (Mackaill) runs away with a Spanish nobleman (Cortez), then writes a goodbye note to her engineer husband (Tearle). The nobleman tries to prevent it from being mailed, but he is killed by the father of a young girl he has betrayed. After his death, the wife returns to her husband, and attempts to keep him from seeing the letter.

REVIEWS:
Motion Picture News: "Old fashioned in theme and characterization, and conventional in treatment is this picture, which carries very little entertaining qualities. . . . The best feature of the picture is Dorothy Mackaill's vital performance . . . ."

Variety: "All the surface elements of a fine picture are here assembled. Still, the production isn't worth the trouble, for the reason [that] it has a silly plot . . . ."

PRODUCTION NOTES, INTERESTING FACTS, AND TRIVIA:
1. Remade in 1931 by RKO as *Transgression*. In the later version, Cortez reprised the villainous role of Don Arturo, opposite Kay Francis and Paul Cavanaugh.

2. Based on Kate Jordan's novel, *The Next Corner* (1921).

3. Legendary actor, Lon Chaney (1883-1930), had a supporting role as Cortez's servant, Juan. *The Next Corner* was his only Paramount film during the 1920's. Unlike many of his movies in which he donned elaborate make-up and disguises, he wore almost no make-up for this picture. Cortez would make another film with Chaney three years later, the MGM adventure drama, *Mockery*, with the roles reversed. Chaney was the star and Cortez a supporting player.

A SOCIETY SCANDAL (1924) (COMEDY-DRAMA)
FAMOUS PLAYERS-LASKY PARAMOUNT
PRODUCERS: Adolph Zukor, Jessie L. Lasky
DIRECTOR: Allan Dwan
SCREENPLAY: Forrest Halsey (scenario), Alfred Sutro (play)
LENGTH: 7 reels
TAGLINE: "The Sensational Story Told Amid the Dazzling Splendor of a Society Ball"
STATUS: Lost

CAST: Gloria Swanson (Marjorie Colbert), Rod La Rocque (Daniel Farr), Ricardo Cortez (Harrison Peters), Allan Simpson (Hector Colbert), Ida Waterman (Mrs Maturin Colbert), Thelma Converse (Mrs. Hamilton Pennfield), and Catherine Proctor (Mrs. Burr).

SUMMARY: A society woman (Swanson) whose reputation is damaged by the efforts of a high-powered attorney (La Rocque) hired by her estranged husband (Simpson), exacts revenge by falsely accusing the attorney of a sexual attack. The attorney is then forced to endure the same humiliation and embarrassment he inflicted on her.

REVIEWS:
New York Times: "In some parts this story is undoubtedly frivolous, but it is produced so lavishly that it is always pleasing. Ricardo Cortez gives a pleasing performance of the love-smitten young man."

Variety: "A little better than the average program feature about sizes it up. Gloria Swanson is the wife. She plays intelligently and with a likeable repression. The wife's boyfriend is capably played by Ricardo Cortez."

PRODUCTION NOTES, INTERESTING FACTS, AND TRIVIA:
1. The original title of the film was *She Who Laughs Last*.

2. Paramount remade *A Society Scandal* in 1929, utilizing the play's original title, *The Laughing Lady*, but changed some of the character's names and altered the plot. The remake starred Ruth Chatterton, Clive Brook, and Nat Pendleton.

3. To satisfy the public's demand that she be dressed to the hilt, Miss Swanson wore 14 extravagant gowns and handful of elaborate headdresses in *A Society Scandal*.

4. Allan Dwan was Gloria Swanson's favorite director. After the success of *Manhandled* in 1924, (directed by Dwan), Gloria's employer, Paramount, demanded she should do one picture per year in which she would be glamorously coiffed and gowned. *A Society Scandal* was to be such a picture, but according to Gloria in her autobiography, *Swanson on Swanson*, Dwan saw to it the movie would be much more than a costumer.

5. During the filming of *Scandal*, Gloria admitted in her autobiography she had a brief love affair with La Rocque, but ended it when he became jealous of her other male friends.

6. When Gloria Swanson appeared on the comedy series, *The Beverly Hillbillies*, in 1966, the character of Granny (Irene Ryan) mentioned seeing *A Society Scandal*.

THE BEDROOM WINDOW (1924) (MYSTERY)
FAMOUS PLAYERS-LASKY PARAMOUNT
PRODUCERS: Adolph Zukor, Jessie L. Lasky
DIRECTOR: William DeMille
SCREENPLAY: Clara Beranger
LENGTH: 70 minutes
STATUS: Exists — Complete copies can be found at the Library of Congress in Washington D.C. and at the UCLA Film and Television Archive in Los Angeles.

CAST: May McAvoy (Ruth Martin), Malcolm MacGregor (Frank Armstrong), Ricardo Cortez (Robert Delano), Robert Edeson (Frederick Hall), George Fawcett (Silas Tucker), Ethel Wales (Matilda Jones, alias Rufus Rome), Charles Ogle (butler), Medea Radzina, (Sonya Malisoff), Guy Oliver (detective), and Lillian Leighton (Mammy).

SUMMARY: An innocent young man (Cortez) is accused of murdering his fiance's (May McAvoy) father and is imprisoned. Thanks to the efforts of his fiancé's eccentric novelist aunt (Wales), who is an amateur sleuth, the real guilty part is revealed.

REVIEWS:
Moviefone.com: "William DeMille, Cecil B DeMille's talented director brother, teamed with his favorite collaborator, Clara Beranger, for the 7 reel silent, *The Bedroom Window*. Essentially a by-the-book mystery tale, the film is lifted from the ordinary by the expertise of DeMille and the charm of the leading lady, May McAvoy."

New York Times: "Splendid entertainment, but we have seen better mystery stories . . . Ricardo Cortez has very little opportunity as he is in jail during most of the story, and scenes of his cell are only shown three times . . . ."

PRODUCTION NOTES, INTERESTING FACTS, AND TRIVIA:
1. The working title for this film was *The Inside Story*, based on an original story by Clara Beranger who also wrote the script.

2. Shown at the Cinecon Film Festival in Los Angeles in 2012.

THE CITY THAT NEVER SLEEPS (1924) (MELODRAMA)
FAMOUS PLAYERS-LASKY PARAMOUNT
PRODUCERS: Adolph Zukor, Jessie L. Lasky
DIRECTOR: James Cruze
SCREENPLAY: Walter Woods, Anthony Coldeway
LENGTH: 6 reels.
TAGLINE: "A story of New York's White Way, lights and bowery shadows!"
STATUS: Lost

CAST: Louise Dresser (Mother O'Day), Ricardo Cortez (Mark Roth), Kathlyn Williams (Mrs. Kendall), Virginia Lee Corbin (Molly Kendall), Pierre Gendron (Cliff Kelly), James Farley (Mike), Ben Hendricks (Tim O'Day), and Vondell Darr (Baby Molly).

SUMMARY: A bowery saloon owner (Dresser) sends her young daughter (Darr) away to live with a rich society woman (Williams). The girl becomes a snob and takes up with a crook (Cortez), but is eventually reunited with her loving mother and her childhood sweetheart (Gendron), who exposes the criminal.

REVIEWS:
Chicago Daily Tribune: "Taking it all in all, it's an enjoyable picture—you really can't kick about it! . . . Ricardo Cortez, of the wily smile and the faultless haberdashery, is the villain of the piece. He's rapidly becoming one of the smoothest gentleman crooks of the movies . . ."

Movie Weekly: "A picture called *The City That Never Sleeps* is only half as good as it ought to be, for if James Cruze could get that much out of the first three reels, he should have done better than he did by the last three . . . Ricardo Cortez is excellent as a sort of sleek villain who wins the hearts of the spectators as well as the ladies of the screen."

PRODUCTION NOTES, INTERESTING FACTS, AND TRIVIA:
1. The original titles for the film were *The Café of Fallen Angels* and *A Drama of the Night*.

2. Adapted by scenarists Walter Woods and Anthony Coldeway from LeRoy Scott's famous story, *Mother O'Day* (which was published in *McCall's* in July 1924).

FEET OF CLAY (1924) (DRAMA)
FAMOUS PLAYERS-LASKY PARAMOUNT
PRODUCERS: Adolph Zukor, Jessie L. Lasky
DIRECTOR: Cecil B. DeMille
SCREENPLAY: Beulah Marie Dix, Bertram Millhauser
LENGTH: 10 reels
TAGLINE: "The real story of the married flapper—."
STATUS: Lost

CAST: Vera Reynolds (Amy Loring), Rod La Rocque (Kerry Harlan), Ricardo Cortez (Tony Channing), Robert Edeson (Dr. Fergus Lansell), Julia Faye (Bertha Lansell), Theodore Kosloff (Bendick), and Victor Varconi (The Bookkeeper).

SUMMARY: A young wife becomes a fashion model (Reynolds) when her husband (La Rocque) is severely injured. This leads to temptation, tragedy, and ultimately, to the triumph of true love.

REVIEWS:
The Motion Picture News: "This is a typical Cecil B. DeMille picture. We have come to expect something different from this showman-director and he has not failed to work in surprising novelties in this instance. Here is a combination of all the ingredients used in modern film production."

Variety: "A whale of an audience picture that will tap money everywhere. It has a couple of thrills that are real thrills, and with it a society atmosphere with a full portion of sex stuff that will get over in great shape . . ."

PRODUCTION NOTES, INTERESTING FACTS, AND TRIVIA:

1. *Feet of Clay* was one of three motion pictures director Cecil B. DeMille completed shortly after his acclaimed epic, *The Ten Commandments* (1923). In his autobiography, he dismissed all three as "comparatively low-budget modern stories." He said he was obligated to make this type of picture in between ones he really wanted to make, to satisfy the studio's desire for "quicker returns."

2. Roy Pomeroy (1892-1947), the special effects genius who had parted the Red Sea in *The Ten Commandments*, handled the climactic scene in *Feet of Clay* in which Reynolds and La Rocque inhale gas in a suicide attempt. In an elaborate sequence, they cross the "bridge between the worlds" to the great beyond, but are turned back from death's door to complete their lives on Earth.

3. The release of *Feet of Clay* resulted in lawsuits, and censorship difficulties. In his book, *Cecil B. DeMille: A Life in Art*, author Simon Louvish said censor boards were upset with the use of the word, "passion." After the release of *Feet of Clay*, playwright Sutton Vane sued Paramount for plagiarism, and his lawsuit was settled out of court. In addition, novelist Tuttle was sued for $2500 by a woman, Laura D Wilck, who claimed she had been acting as Miss Tuttle's agent in order to sell the film rights to the novel, *Feet of Clay*. Wilck said she secured an agreement with Warner Bros. for $25,000, but Tuttle told her she had decided not to sell the rights. A short time later, Wilck learned Tuttle had sold the rights to Famous Players for the same amount. Wilck claimed Tuttle owed her a commission. It is not known how the suit was settled.

4. According to Louvish, in order to give the picture authenticity, DeMille transformed the rocky shore of Catalina Island (where much of the film was made) "into a lovely crescent of white

Rod LaRoque, Julia Faye, Ricardo Cortez, and Bill Boyd, in Cecil B. DeMille's dramatic, *Feet of Clay* (Paramount, 1924).

sand, imported from Hawaii at great expense." Each day, the cast was served fancy dinners "by white-coated servants, off tables loaded with solid gold, Spode and Wedgewood plate."

5. *Feet of Clay* is considered a lost film, although approximately two minutes of footage was seen in the Kevin Brownlow/Patrick Stanbury documentary, *Cecil B. DeMille: American Epic* (2004).

6. According to Robert Birchard's book, *Cecil B. DeMille's Hollywood*, Paramount netted over $390,000 profit from *Feet of Clay*.

7. Known for her "perfect legs" and a pair of the "prettiest feet and ankles" in America, actress Julia Faye (1893-1966) was among DeMille's favorite actresses, appearing in his productions through the years including many of his most celebrated. For a long time, she was said to be the director's mistress.

8. Estelle Taylor was originally cast in the role of Amy in *Feet of Clay*, but was pulled from the production so she could appear opposite Tom Meighan in *The Alaskan*. Vera Reynolds replaced her, and was signed to a long-term Paramount contract as a result of her work in the picture.

THIS WOMAN (1924) (DRAMA)
WARNER BROTHERS
DIRECTOR: Phil Rosen
SCREENPLAY: Hope Loring, Louis Duryea Lighton
LENGTH: 7 reels
TAGLINE: "She built a brilliant career with a secret past constantly threatening her destruction!"
STATUS: Exists—A complete copy is housed at Lobster Films Archive in Paris.

CAST: Irene Rich (Carol Drayton), Ricardo Cortez (Whitney Duane), Louise Fazenda (Rose), Frank Elliott (Gordon Duane), Creighton Hale (Bobby Bleeker), Marc MacDermott (Stratini), Helen Dunbar (Mrs. Sturdevant), Clara Bow (Aline Sturdevant), and Otto Hoffman (Judson).

SUMMARY: The loves and travails of a poverty-stricken singer (Rich) who is saved from suicide by a woman of the streets (Fazenda).

REVIEWS:
New York Times: "It is hardly conceivable that Phil Rosen, who triumphed with his artistic production, *Abraham Lincoln*, could have produced such a banal effort as *This Woman* . . . Mr. Rosen has emphasized the pathos and neglected many of the dramatic possibilities of the story . . ."

PRODUCTION NOTES, INTERESTING FACTS, AND TRIVIA:
1. Based on the 1924 novel, *This Woman*, by Howard Rockey.

2. Cortez plays the supporting role of the love-struck brother of a wealthy man (Elliott), who hires the aspiring vocalist to sing underneath the window of his lover (Bow).

3. According to a contract dated 7-31-24 (on file at the Warner Bros. Archives at the University of Southern California), Famous Players/Lasky Corporation loaned the services of Cortez to Warner Bros. for *This Woman*, for $375 a week. $300 of this went to Cortez, and the other $75 was a "studio carrying charge."

4. Three years before she became the "It" girl, young Clara Bow (1905-65) was among those featured in small roles in *This Woman*.

ARGENTINE LOVE (1924) (MELODRAMA)
FAMOUS PLAYERS-LASKY PARAMOUNT
PRODUCERS:	Adolph Zukor, Jessie L. Lasky
DIRECTOR:	Allan Dwan
SCREENPLAY:	Vincente Blasco Ibanez (story), Gerald C. Duffy, John Russell (script)
LENGTH:	6 reels
TAGLINE:	"A tale of warm tango nights, of Spanish beauties, and jealous lovers, of treachery, conflict, and unending thrills!"
STATUS:	Lost

CAST: Bebe Daniels (Consuelo Garcia), Ricardo Cortez (Juan Martin), James Rennie (Philip Sears), Mario Majeroni (Senator Cornejo), Russ Whital (Emanuel Garcia), Alice Chapin (Madame Garcia), Julia Hurley (La Mosca), Mark Gonzales (Raphael Cornejo), and Aurelio Coccia (Pedro).

SUMMARY: A headstrong Argentinian (Cortez) is in love with a beautiful senorita (Daniels) who prefers to spend her time with an American engineer (Rennie).

REVIEWS:
New York Times: "One of the best examples of a stereotyped picture . . . This production might have been made by a punctilious old drill sergeant, who had called upon the various actors and in stentorian tones instructed them as to their duties . . . Mr. Cortez gives a sorry imitation of Rudolph Valentino, narrowing his eyes and twitching his lips."

An Argentinian nobleman's affection for a woman who loves someone else was the storyline of *Argentine Love* (Paramount, 1924) starring Ricardo Cortez and Bebe Daniels.

Variety: "Decidedly a woman's picture, with enough men strolling by the camera who look like Valentino to make it appear as a musical comedy production dedicated to Rudolph . . . The work of Cortez as the villain, who finally gives his life for the girl as a saving grace, is distinctly spotty. His performance is particularly impaired through the inadequacy to withstand the ordeal of the close shots in other than a detrimental manner . . . ."

PRODUCTION NOTES, INTERESTING FACTS, AND TRIVIA:
1. Produced at Paramount's Long Island Studio, the film was based on a story by Vincente Blasco-Ibanez.

2. *Argentine Love* was the first of three films Cortez would make with Bebe Daniels.

3. One of the newspaper stories generated by the release of *Argentine Love* referred to Cortez as "the King of the Ballroom Dancers."

4. Alan Crosland was originally slated to direct, but was replaced by Allan Dwan.

5. In one of the most memorable moments in the film, BeBe Daniels and Ricardo Cortez do a very showy, spirited version of the tango. One critic, writing for *The Riverside Daily Press* (California) called the dance "one of the finest exhibitions of the tango as it is really done by the Argentinians ever done on the screen."

THE SWAN (1925) (ROMANTIC COMEDY)
FAMOUS PLAYERS-LASKY PARAMOUNT
PRODUCERS: Adolph Zukor, Jessie L. Lasky
DIRECTOR: Dmitri Buchowetzski
SCREENPLAY: Dmitri Buchowetzski
LENGTH: 6 reels
TAGLINE: "Her lips say NO — Her eyes say, YES!"
STATUS: Exists — Complete copies are housed at National Archives of Canada (Ottawa) and

George Eastman House (Rochester, New York). (DVD)

CAST: Frances Howard (Alexandra, The Swan), Adolphe Menjou (H. R. H. Albert of Kersten-Rodenfels), Ricardo Cortez (Dr. Walter, the tutor), Ida Waterman (Princess Beatrice), Helen Lindroth (Amphirosa), Helen Lee Worthing (Wanda von Gluck), Joseph Depew (Prince George), George Walcott (Prince Arsene), Michael Visaroff (Father Hyacinth), and Claire Eames (Princess Dominica).

SUMMARY: A princess (Howard) uses a handsome young tutor (Cortez) to make her betrothed (Menjou) jealous, but falls in love with the young man.

REVIEWS:
New York Times: "Liberties also have been taken with the story so as to meet with popular approval. However, no matter what changes have been made, there is no disputing the fact that it is a picture directed with artistry, skill, and imagination . . . ."

PRODUCTION NOTES, INTERESTING FACTS, AND TRIVIA:
1. Produced at Paramount's Long Island studio in New York, the film was based on the 1923 Melville Baker stage adaptation of the famed Ferenc Molnar play.

2. Paramount purchased *The Swan* as a vehicle for Gloria Swanson. When she wasn't able to do the picture, they replaced her with Broadway actress, Elsie Ferguson. After production commenced, Ferguson pulled out of the production to appear on Broadway, and she was replaced by young stage actress Frances Howard (1903-76). After making two more films, Miss Howard married producer Sam Goldwyn (in 1925) and retired from the movies.

3. Hollywood remade *The Swan* twice; in 1930 as *One Romantic Night* with Lillian Gish, Rod La Rocque and Conrad Nagel; and in 1956 with Grace Kelly, Alec Guinness, and Louis Jourdan.

Cortez won acclaim for his role as Dr. Walter, the tutor in *The Swan* (1925). Photo courtesy of Jan Taylor Garfield.

4. An *Oakland Tribune* item generated in conjunction with the release of *The Swan* referred to Ricardo Cortez as a "fiery Spanish swain" and proclaimed the film as his first starring role.

Cortez scored one of his first major screen successes in the Valentino-esque role of Don Pedro de Barrego in *The Spaniard* (Paramount, 1925), opposite Dutch-born actress Jetta Goudal.

THE SPANIARD (1925) (ROMANTIC MELODRAMA)
FAMOUS PLAYERS-LASKY PARAMOUNT
PRODUCERS: Adolph Zukor, Jessie L. Lasky
DIRECTOR: Raoul Walsh
SCREENPLAY: James T. O' Donohue
LENGTH: 70 minutes
TAGLINE: "'The woman does not exist whom I cannot tame!' Boasts the Spaniard!"
STATUS: Lost

CAST: Ricardo Cortez (Don Pedro de Barrego), Jetta Goudal (Dolores Annesley), Noah Beery (Gomez), Mathilda Brundage (Senora de la Carta), Renzo De Gardi (Count de Albaveque), Emily Fitzroy (Maria), Bernard Siegel (Manuel), and Florence Renart (Consuelo).

SUMMARY: A Spanish bullfighter (Cortez) visits England and falls for a young English girl (Goudal) who resists him. Later they fall in love when he rescues her from the clutches of his valet (Beery).

REVIEWS:
Chicago Daily Tribune: "The story as it continues is something of a steal on The Sheik . . . Mr. Cortez isn't Valentino, but he's quite as good an imitation as there is on the market."

Minneapolis Star: "This is the first starring picture of Ricardo Cortez, who plays the title role of the Spanish matador with fire and earnestness, that would do credit to the famous Rudolph Valentino . . . ."

PRODUCTION NOTES, INTERESTING FACTS, AND TRIVIA:
1. Based on the novel, *The Spaniard* by Juanita Savage.

NOT SO LONG AGO (1925) (ROMANTIC COMEDY)
FAMOUS PLAYERS-LASKY PARAMOUNT
PRODUCERS: Adolph Menjou, Jessie Lasky
DIRECTOR: Sidney Olcott
SCREENPLAY: Violet Clark (screenplay), Arthur Richman (play)
LENGTH: 70 minutes
STATUS: Lost

CAST: Betty Bronson (Betty Dover), Ricardo Cortez (Billy Ballard), Edwards Davis (Jerry Flint), Julia Swayne Gordon (Mrs. Ballard), Laurence Wheat (Sam Robinson), Jacqueline Gadsdon (Ursula Kent), and Dan Crimmons (Michael Dover).

SUMMARY: The romantic daughter (Bronson) of an inventor (Crimmons), works as a seamstress for a wealthy woman (Swayne Gordon). In an attempt to make one of her suitors jealous, she tells him she is being courted by one of her employer's sons (Cortez), who eventually falls in love with her.

REVIEWS:
Chicago Daily Tribune: "There are some interesting scenes of old New York, and the director has caught the spirit of the times, making the film a gentle, sweetly charming and old fashioned picture . . . Ricardo Cortez, with sideburns, top hat, and snappy cane, is a personable beau . . ."

New York Times: " . . . thoroughly delightful from start to finish . . . Ricardo Cortez is excellent as the young aristocrat who falls in love with the heroine, thus becoming the hero by marriage. . . ."

PRODUCTION NOTES, INTERESTING FACTS, AND TRIVIA:
1. Set in the 1850's.

2. During the production of *Not So Long Ago*, it was reported that Cortez and his longtime paramour, Alma Rubens, had split because they could not marry (due to the clause in his Paramount contract forbidding it). As most know, they did get back together and were married a few months later with the permission of Paramount.

IN THE NAME OF LOVE (1925) (ROMANTIC COMEDY)
FAMOUS PLAYERS-LASKY PARAMOUNT
PRODUCERS: Adolph Zukor, Jessie L. Lasky
DIRECTOR: Howard Higgen
SCREENPLAY: Sada Cowan (screenplay), Edward Bulwer-Lytton (story)
LENGTH: 6 reels
STATUS: Lost

CAST: Ricardo Cortez (Raoul Melnotte), Greta Nissen (Marie Dufrayne), Wallace Beery (M. Glavis), Raymond Hatton (Marquis de Beausant), Lillian Leighton (Mother Dufrayne), Edythe Chapman (Mother Melnotte), and Richard Arlen (Dumas Dufrayne).

SUMMARY: A successful businessman (Cortez) returns to the place of his birth in France to search for his former sweetheart (Nissen), who has become a social climber. When she turns his marriage proposal down because he is not titled, he masquerades as a prince to win her over.

REVIEWS:
Chicago Daily Tribune: "This is a light and airy little something calculated to furnish entertainment, but not thought for a summers day. The hero is the dark, dreamy eyed, romantically handsome

Ricardo Cortez. The heroine is the blonde Swedish bon bon of a Greta Nisson . . . Mr. Cortez' Raoul is a thrilling lover . . ."

New York Times: ". . . a curious mixture of highly improbable action, crude comedy, and a sympathetic heroine and hero . . . Mr. Cortez has evidently won his film spurs through his dreamy-eyed stare and not through his expansive smile, which is good natured and all that sort of thing, but a little more capacious than one imagines a hero's smile ought to be . . ."

PRODUCTION NOTES, INTERESTING FACTS, AND TRIVIA:
1. Based on the play, *The Lady of Lyon*, by Edward Bulwer-Lytton (1838).

2. *In the Name of Love* was director Howard Higgen's first film for Paramount, and marked the film debut of Norwegian star, Greta Nissen.

THE PONY EXPRESS (1925) (WESTERN)
FAMOUS PLAYERS-LASKY PARAMOUNT
PRODUCERS: Adolph Zukor, Jessie L. Lasky
DIRECTOR: James Cruze
SCREENPLAY: Walter Woods, Henry James Forman, Walter Woods (story)
LENGTH: 10 reels
TAGLINE: "Ten reels of matchless thrills, adventure, romance, and humor!"
STATUS: Exists—Incomplete versions are found at George Eastman House (Rochester), U.C.L.A Film and Television Archive (Los Angeles), and Pacific Film Archive, (Berkeley, California). (DVD)

CAST: Betty Compson (Molly Jones), Ricardo Cortez (Jack Weston), Ernest Torrence ("Ascension" Jones), Wallace Beery ("Rhode Island" Red), George Bancroft (Jack Slade), Frank Lackteen (Charles Bent), John Fox Jr. (Billy Cody), William Turner (William Russell), Al Hart (Senator Glen), Charles Gerson (Sam Clemens), and Rose Tapley (Aunt).

SUMMARY: When he speaks up against the nefarious plot of a power-hungry Senator (Hart), a debonair gambler (Cortez) flees to Colorado and becomes a Pony Express rider. He later competes for the affections of a young woman (Compson) with one of the corrupt Senator's agents (Bancroft), while foiling the latter's evil plans.

REVIEWS:
Alt Film Guide.com: "A rousing James Cruze western depicting the founding of the Pony Express with a backdrop of political ambitions . . . A great cast and Cruze's direction keep this one interesting—even though Ricardo Cortez in a period film seems woefully out of place . . ."

Chicago Daily Tribune: "You're going to be sorry if you miss seeing *The Pony Express*. It's one cracker jack of a movie! A more fascinating combination of thrill and humor rarely comes to the screen. Nor a picture better acted . . . Ricardo Cortez is the picturesque and brave young hero . . ."

New York Times: "The undying exploits of those fearless mail riders who urged their swift mounts from point to point across a vast stretch of this continent, braving the Indians and the weather, are vividly told in a picture entitled, *The Pony Express*."

PRODUCTION NOTES, INTERESTING FACTS, AND TRIVIA:
1. The Forman and Woods novel, *The Pony Express*, was published simultaneously with the release of the film.

2. A former teenage vaudevillian turned actress, beautiful blonde Betty Compson (1897-1974), became a top silent film star during the early 1920's. After making a smooth transition to sound, garnering an Academy Award nomination for her performance in *The Barker* (1928), she drifted into minor productions and small supporting roles. The first of her three marriages was to *The Pony Express* director, James Cruze, whom she wed on October 25, 1925. They were divorced in 1929.

Cortez as Frisco Jack Westin and his trusty pal, "Rhode Island Red" (Wallace Beery) in a scene from the big budget Western *The Pony Express*, (Paramount, 1925).

3. Betty Compson was making $2500 a picture at the time she made *The Pony Express.*

4. The film was considered so prestigious by Famous Players/Lasky at the time of its release, the studio presented it in two Broadway theaters instead of one (which was the custom).

5. To make some of the scenes more authentic, director Cruze borrowed several genuine artifacts from the 1860's era, including an antique fire engine known as "Broderick No. 1." Named for U.S. Senator Broderick of California, (a northern supporter who was shot in a famous duel with Judge Terry, a southern sympathizer), the engine was said to be the "pride of San Francisco."

This elaborate parade scene depicting a celebration for California volunteers leaving to join the Union cause at the outbreak of the Civil War, is one of many scenes which no longer appear in the severely edited version of James Cruze's epic Western, *The Pony Express,* (Paramount, 1925) which survives.

This photo featuring Frisco Jack (top-hatted Cortez on far right leaning against the post) is from another scene which does not appear in the 65-minute version of *The Pony Express* (Paramount, 1925).

Torrent (1926) (Drama)
Metro-Goldwyn-Mayer Corporation
Director: Monta Bell
Screenplay: Katherine Hilliker, H. H. Caldwell (title), Dorothy Farnum (adaptation)
Length: 7 reels
Tagline: "Spanish love!—Flaming, vibrant, soul stirring!"
Status: Exists—Complete copies at George Eastman House (Rochester), Institute Valenciano de Cinematografia (Valencia, Spain), and Filmoteca Espanola (Madrid, Spain). (DVD)

Cast: Ricardo Cortez (Don Raphael Brull), Greta Garbo (Leonora), Gertrude Olmsted (Remedios), Edward Connelly (Pedro Moreno), Lucien Littlefield (Cupido), Martha Mattox (Dona Bernarda Brull), Lucy Beaumont (Dona Pepa), Tully Marshall (Don Andreas), Mack Swain (Don Mattias), Arthur Edmund Carew (Salvatti), Lillian Leighton (Isabella), and Mario Carillo (King of Spain).

Summary: In Valencia, the son of a landed Spanish aristocrat (Cortez) falls in love with the daughter of one of his family's tenants (Garbo), but his domineering mother does not approve, and manages to break up the romance. Although their passion is rekindled sometime later when he saves his former lover's life during a flood, in the end his mother wins out. He marries another, and becomes a successful politician; she becomes an opera star.

Reviews:
The Film Daily: "Monta Bell comes to the fore with an outstanding production . . . At times quite impressive and again strangely lovely to look upon, in Greta Garbo there is almost a constant reminder of Nazimova in her appearance and manner of playing. Ricardo Cortez, the handsome hero, must sacrifice his fine looks for the climax disillusion . . . ."

New York Times: "Mr. Bell seems to have had too much action to work upon to make this a clear cut drama . . . Mr. Cortez acquits himself acceptably. . . . As a result of her ability, her undeniable taste in fur coats, she (Garbo) steals most of the thunder in this vehicle . . ."

PRODUCTION NOTES, INTERESTING FACTS, AND TRIVIA:

1. Based on the novel *Entre Naranjas*, a.k.a. *Among Orange Trees*, by Vincente Blasco-Ibanez.

2. *Torrent* was the only film in which Greta Garbo received second billing. Cortez was top billed.

3. Miss Garbo met cinematographer William H. Daniels while making this film. She considered him a genius and requested his services on her films. They would make 20 films together.

4. MGM spent $250,000 on the production, and posted gross receipts of $460,000.

5. Up and coming young actor, Joel McCrea performed stunt work in the film.

6. During the filming, supporting actress Gertrude Olmstead became friendly with the young, inexperienced Garbo, and helped her whenever she could. According to Anthony Slide's book, *Silent Players: A Biographical and Autobiographical Study of 100 Silent Film Actors and Actresses*, Olmstead claimed she taught the famous star how to wax her lashes.

7. A Spanish village was constructed on the Metro lot, solely to be demolished during the film's flood scene. According to a *New York Times* article "High in the air, above the angle of the cameras, were water pipes, perforated along their length like a great sprinkling system. Huge tanks of water on pivots stood at the head of the artificial river running through the twenty acres on which the village is said to have been constructed. Great pumps threw water under enormous pressure into the mains . . ."

Ricardo and Greta Garbo in *Torrent* (MGM, 1926).

8. Several years after making *Torrent*, Ricardo Cortez recalled his costar, Miss Garbo.

"She's a strange creature. Throughout our work together, I was always conscious of an indefinable barrier between us. She was gracious, polite, even cordial, but there was always that barrier that kept me from getting at all close to her—until we went into a scene. Then, immediately, that barrier startlingly disappeared, and I felt by her very side—almost part of her, full of confidence that seemed to emanate from her, warmth. Then the director would call 'cut'— and instantly, that barrier was up again. She was a different woman."

Volcano (1926) (Drama)
Famous Players-Lasky Paramount
Producers: Adolph Zukor, Jessie L. Lasky
Director: William K. Howard
Screenplay: Bernard McConville (scenario)
Length: 6 reels
Status: Exists — Incomplete copies (one reel missing) are housed in the Library of Congress (Washington D.C.), Museum of Modern Art, (New York City), and the U.C.L.A Film and Television Archive (Los Angeles).

Cast: Bebe Daniels (Zabette de Chauvalons), Ricardo Cortez (Stephane Sequineau), Wallace Beery (Quembo), Arthur Edmund Carew (Maurice Sequineau), Dale Fuller (Cedrien), Eulalie Jensen (Madame de Chauvalons), Brandon Hurst (Andre de Chauvalons), Marjorie Gay (Marie de Chauvalons), Robert Perry (Pere Benedict), and Snitz Edwards (auctioneer).

Summary: During the early 1900's, a young French woman (Daniels) leaves a convent to visit her father, who lives on the island of Martinique in the Caribbean. When she arrives, he has died. She is forced by his widow to endure harsh conditions in the island's mulatto quarter, where she is mistaken for a quadroon. Later, she gains the love of a French aristocrat (Cortez), who learns her true parentage.

Reviews:
Bangor Commercial: "Something absolutely different in screen entertainment has been achieved in *Volcano*, the Paramount picture featuring Bebe Daniels and Ricardo Cortez . . . The eruption of Mt. Pelee is shown with startling reality and provides one of the real thrills of the picture . . . ."

Motion Picture Guide: "Some spectacular special effects redeem this otherwise intolerant film . . ."

Production Notes, Interesting Facts, and Trivia:
1. Based on the play, *Martinique*, by Lawrence Eyre.

2. Partially filmed on location in Martinique, where the eruption of Mt. Pelee provided filmmakers with what one described as "an almost continuous Fourth of July celebration!"

THE CAT'S PAJAMAS (1926) (ROMANTIC COMEDY)
FAMOUS PLAYERS-LASKY PARAMOUNT
PRODUCERS: Adolph Zukor, Jessie L. Lasky
DIRECTOR: William Wellman
SCREENPLAY: Hope Loring, Louis D. Lighton, Ernest Vadja (story)
LENGTH: 6 reels
STATUS: Lost

CAST: Betty Bronson (Sally Winton), Ricardo Cortez (Don Cesare Gracco), Arlette Marchal (Riza Dorena), Theodore Roberts (Sally's Father), Gordon Griffith (Jack), and Tom Ricketts (Mr. Briggs).

SUMMARY: The romantic trials and tribulations of a poor seamstress (Bronson) who becomes infatuated with a famous opera singer (Cortez). Besieged by female fans, the singer makes a business arrangement with the seamstress to marry her, in order to escape his public, but she is determined to be a true wife to him.

REVIEWS:
Variety: "A strangely mishandled Cinderella theme that doesn't jell. At times it is in the spirit of the Brothers Grimm, and at others, it smacks of Sinclair Lewis. Pretty fantasy on the one hand, and on the other, something like tart satire. . . ."

PRODUCTION NOTES, INTERESTING FACTS, AND TRIVIA:
1. Best known for her portrayal of Peter Pan in Paramount's famed 1924 film adaptation of the James Barrie fantasy, Betty Bronson (1906-71) was an American film actress who made over 30 movies in a five-decade long acting career. Her elfin-like appearance and sprightly personality made her a popular film ingénue during the silent era, but as she matured, her popularity declined. She retired from the screen in 1937, but reemerged during the 1960's playing small parts in films and television.

The Cat's Pajamas was filmed just prior to the release of MGM's multi-million-dollar epic, *Ben Hur* (1925), in which Miss Bronson played the Virgin Mary.

2. *The Cat's Pajamas* was director William Wellman's first directorial assignment under contract to new Paramount production head, B.P. Shchulberg. In an interview published in Richard Schickel's book, *The Men Who Made the Movies* (1975), Wellman remembered being assigned the picture starring Betty Bronson and Ricardo Cortez.

"Now Betty Bronson, you remember, played kid things beautifully. And they sent word down to me that they wanted me to put some sex in her. I sent word back, "You don't want a director, you want a magician." Peter Pan—that's what she was. She was a delightful little actress, but that's what she was, and, to make a long story short, when she tried to be sexy she looked like a little girl that wanted to go to the bathroom . . . ."

3. Famed character actor Theodore Roberts (1861-1928), who played the heroine's crippled father in *The Cat's Pajamas*, made one of his last screen appearances in the picture before succumbing to uremic poisoning in December, 1928. In William Wellman's memoirs published by his son, William Jr., as part of the book, *William Wellman and the Making of the First Best Picture*, the noted director called the picture "indescribably atrocious." "Daddy (Theodore) Roberts was the great character actor of that era. He died shortly after the picture, and I often wondered if he had seen the finished product. It could well have caused it . . . ."

4. According to a Paramount press release, the final scenes in which Cortez appeared "were speeded up to allow him to depart for New York where he will play the hero role in D.W. Griffith's production, *The Sorrows of Satan*." It goes on to describe his *Satan* role as "the most important yet assigned to this promising young player who recently signed a new two-year contract with Paramount."

5. *The Cat's Pajamas* marked the American film debut of French actress Arlette Marchal (1902-84). Miss Marchal was hired for her role based on the recommendation of Gloria Swanson, with whom she had made a picture in France, *Madame Sans-Gene*, in 1925.

6. Playwright Ernest Vadja visited the set of *The Cat's Pajamas*, and presented director Wellman and stars Betty Bronson and Ricardo Cortez with ceramic cats.

THE SORROWS OF SATAN (1926) (DRAMA)
FAMOUS PLAYERS-LASKY PARAMOUNT
PRODUCERS:	Adolph Zukor, Jessie L. Lasky
DIRECTOR:	D.W. Griffith
SCREENPLAY:	Forrest Halsey (screenplay), Julian Johnson (title), John Russell, George Hull (adaptation)
LENGTH:	9 reels
STATUS:	Exists—Complete copies are held at Cinematheque Royale de Belgique (Brussels, Belgium), Museum of Modern Art (New York City), and George Eastman House (Rochester).

CAST: Adolphe Menjou (Prince Luico de Rimanez), Ricardo Cortez (Geoffrey Tempest), Lya De Putti (Princess Olga), Carol Dempster (Mavis Claire), Ivan Lebedeff (Amiel), Marcia Harris (The Landlady), Lawrence D'Orsay (Lord Elton), Nellie Savage (Dancing Girl), Dorothy Hughes (Mavis' Chum), and Josephine Dunn (Bit).

SUMMARY: Two struggling young writers who share the same boarding house (Cortez, Dempster) fall in love. When publisher rejections force them into extreme poverty, the desperate couple face their respective calamities in different ways. She maintains her faith, while the young man curses God, and is befriended by the devil masquerading as a debonair prince (Menjou). The devil helps him financially, while wreaking havoc on his life.

REVIEWS:
Chicago Daily Tribune: "An artful blending of legend, scripture,

and modern fiction; of poverty and pageantry. . . The captivating story glows and palpitates under the spell of that sorcerer D.W. Griffith . . . Ricardo Cortez, as Geoffrey Tempest, who writes and sins is a magnetic and intensely appealing character. A fine actor, this man; and if I know what "It" is, why he has got "It". . ."

Los Angeles Examiner: "*The Sorrows of Satan* is a decidedly unusual picture. There are times when it drags and other times when it makes up for any tediousness by its excellent technique and characterizations . . . The devil's victim, Geoffrey Tempest, poor struggling writer who gives up his career, his love, his all to Rimenez (the devil), gets a good break in the hands of Ricardo Cortez. I can even make it stronger, and say Mr. Cortez's performance is an event. His restraint is admirable, and his handling of all the big dramatic situations is really excellent . . . ."

PRODUCTION NOTES, INTERESTING FACTS, AND TRIVIA:
1. Based on Marie Corelli's bestselling 1895 novel, *The Sorrow of Satan,* or *The Strange Experience of one Geoffrey Tempest, Millionaire.*

2. Filmed on Long Island, Manhattan, and at Paramount's Astoria Studio in Queens, New York.

3. Minnesota-born, Carol Dempster (1902-1991), rose to stardom during the early 1920's after she became a protégé of D. W. Griffith. She appeared in several acclaimed pictures during the early to mid-1920's, including *Sherlock Holmes* (1922), *One Exciting Night* (1922), *Isn't Life Wonderful* (1924), and *America* (1924), but walked out on her movie contract when she married a wealthy banker. *The Sorrows of Satan* was her final picture, and considered by many to be her best.

4. Although hailed by critics, *The Sorrows of Satan* was a major box office failure. According to Richard Schickel, in his book *D.W. Griffith, An American Life*, the picture's negative cost was $971,260.

5. According to John T. Soister's book, *Up From the Vault: Rare Thrillers of the 1920's and 1930's*, Rod La Rocque was Paramount's first choice to play the protagonist, Geoffrey Tempest (eventually portrayed by Cortez).

6. In an interview with film historian Kevin Brownlow for his book, *The Parade's Gone By*, Cortez described Mr. Griffith this way:

"Griffith was a strange sort of man—very quiet. There seemed to be an invisible barrier around him. You couldn't get near him. I was under the impression that he was a very lonely man—although I got to know him quite well. I felt terribly sorry for him and would visit him at his hotel,— the Astor. . . During the making of the picture I was playing in one of the attic scenes. We'd been working for six weeks, not getting very far, and for just thirty seconds I lost my temper. He had said, 'If you knew anything about acting you wouldn't do that.' 'I don't know a thing about acting,' I snapped. 'which was why I wanted to be directed by you!'"

THE EAGLE OF THE SEA (1926) (ROMANTIC ADVENTURE)
FAMOUS PLAYERS-LASKY PARAMOUNT

PRODUCER:	B.P. Schulberg
DIRECTOR:	Frank Lloyd
SCREENPLAY:	Julien Josephson (scenario); Peter B. Kyne (adaptation)
LENGTH:	70 minutes
TAGLINE:	"Shades of Captain Kidd, what a thrill this one is!"
STATUS:	Exists—Incomplete copies are housed at George Eastman House (Rochester), U.C.L.A Film and Television Archive (Los Angeles), Filmoteca Espanola (Madrid, Spain), and the Danish Film Institute (Copenhagen, Denmark).

CAST: Florence Vidor (Louise Lestron), Ricardo Cortez (Captain Sazarac), Sam De Grasse (Colonel Lestron), Andre de Beranger

(John Jarvis), Mitchell Lewis (Crackley), Guy Oliver (Beluche), George Irving (General Andrew Jackson), James Marcus (Dominique), Ervin Bernard (Don Robledo), and Boris Karloff (bit as Pirate).

SUMMARY: In 1818 New Orleans, the pirate, Jean Lafitte, masquerading as Captain Sazarac (Cortez), falls in love with a New Orleans belle (Vidor) at a masked ball, but is ordered by General Andrew Jackson (Irving) to leave the country. When he learns the girl's treacherous uncle (De Grasse) has kidnapped her and is attempting to foment a war between England and Spain, which would endanger America, he steps in to foil the evil plan, and rescue his sweetheart.

REVIEWS:
Chicago Daily Tribune: "The picture has been splendidly staged and costumed. Frank Lloyd, who is a master hand at sea and pirate stuff, has directed with his usual skill and success . . . The smoldering-eyed Mr. Cortez is a romantic figure as the hero . . ."

Los Angeles Examiner: "Frank Lloyd has made some of his best productions with the sea and its men and ships for his tools. In this story, however, the producer evidently found little inspiration . . . Cortez in the pirate role was always meticulously dressed and affected the costume of the club man, rather than any garb indicative of his life before the mast . . . ."

PRODUCTION NOTES, INTERESTING FACTS, AND TRIVIA:
1. Based on Charles Tenney Jackson's swashbuckling novel, *Captain Sazarac*.

2. Boris Karloff played an uncredited bit as one of Sazarac's (Jean Lafitte's) pirate crew.

3. A candid photo Paramount used to promote *The Eagle of the Sea* depicts Frank Lloyd directing the climactic naval battle by the use of radio. The caption reads, "In this manner, Lloyd was able to direct the vessels at a distance of several miles."

4. Ricardo Cortez was a talented amateur boxer. According to a

Cortez played a dashing pirate in Frank Lloyd's seafaring swashbuckler, *The Eagle of the Sea* (Paramount, 1926) filmed off the California coast.

1926 Paramount press release during the filming of *The Eagle of the Sea*, Cortez did a 30 minute workout with former champion bantom weight boxer and fight referee, Gene Delmont. Afterward, Delmont told reporters if the screen star ever decided to leave films, he would be capable of vying for light heavyweight honors. "All this sounds like bunk," declared Delmont, "but I'm here to say, no one ever gave me a greater fight than Cortez."

5. According to press reports, star Ricardo Cortez took both fencing and polka lessons in order to film the role of Captain Sazarac.

NEW YORK (1927) (CRIME DRAMA)
FAMOUS PLAYERS-LASKY PARAMOUNT
PRODUCER: William LeBaron, Adolph Zukor, Jessie L. Lasky
DIRECTOR: Luther Reed
SCREENPLAY: Forrest Halsey (script), Becky Gardiner, Barbara Chambers (story)
LENGTH: 7 reels
STATUS: Lost

CAST: Ricardo Cortez (Michael Angelo Cassidy), Lois Wilson (Marjorie Church), Estelle Taylor (Angie Miller), William Powell (Trent Regan), Norman Trevor (Randolph Church), Richard "Skeets" Gallagher (Buck), Margaret Quimby (Helena Mathews), Lester Schariff (Izzy Blumenstein), and Charles Byer (Jimmie Wharton).

SUMMARY: In New York City, four young men (Cortez, Powell, Schariff, Gallagher) find friendship and camaraderie in a Bowery cabaret. One of them (Powell) becomes a gangster, and murders his girlfriend (Taylor). His boyhood friend, a successful songwriter, (Cortez), is falsely accused and convicted of the crime.

REVIEWS:
Chicago Daily Tribune: "The catchy label borne by this film is honest, appropriate, and aptly descriptive. The story is one that might plausibly occur any day in the city which achieves for itself more publicity than any other village on earth. . . Ricardo Cortez is quite personable as the modern musician . . ."

Los Angeles Examiner: "The best thing about New York is its title. . . Ricardo Cortez has had more suitable roles than that of Mike Cassidy, Eastside songwriter who becomes a famous composer . . ."

PRODUCTION NOTES, INTERESTING FACTS, AND TRIVIA:
1. Produced at Paramount's Astoria studio, with additional footage filmed on location in Manhattan.

2. Audiences responded positively to the exciting melodrama, which netted a tidy profit for Adolph Zukor's studio.

As part of their promotional campaign for the big budget melodrama, *New York* (1927), Paramount published the original Barbara Chambers/Becky Gardiner story (from which the movie was based), and filled it with photos from the film.

3. *New York* would turn out to be Cortez's last film done during his initial stint as a contract player at Paramount. In 1927 he would ask for his release from the studio.

4. According to a candid photo dated November 16, 1926, in preparation for his role as Mike Cassidy in *New York*, Cortez took trap drumming lessons from famed orchestra leader, George Olsen (1893-1971).

5. Actress Estelle Taylor was loaned to Famous Players/Lasky by the Joseph M. Schenk organization for her role in *New York*.

MOCKERY (1927) (DRAMA)
METRO-GOLDWYN-MAYER CORPORATION (MGM)

DIRECTOR:	Benjamin Christenson
SCREENPLAY:	Benjamin Christensen (story), Bradley King (continuity), Joe Farham (title), Stig Esbern (story)
LENGTH:	75 minutes
STATUS:	Exists—Compete copies are found at Cinetca Del Fruli (Italy), George Eastman House (Rochester), and the Danish Film Institute (Copenhagen, Denmark). (DVD)

CAST: Lon Chaney (Sergei), Ricardo Cortez (Dmitri), Barbara Bedford (Tatiana), Mack Swain (Mr. Gaideroff), Emily Fitzroy (Mrs. Gaideroff), Charles Puffy (Ivan), Kai Schmidt (butler), and Johnny Mack Brown (bit).

SUMMARY: During the Russian Revolution, a countess (Bedford) promises a hungry peasant (Chaney) a job if he will assist her in escaping the Bolsheviks. He helps her, and is rewarded with a menial job in her kitchen, where he comes under the influence of revolutionaries who hate her and her aristocratic class. During an uprising, the peasant attacks the countess, but a young army officer (Cortez) comes to her defense. Eventually the peasant proves his loyalty by risking his life.

REVIEWS:

Harrison's Reports: "Masterfully produced, but it is gruesome to the point of repulsive . . . The only bright spot in the picture is the presence of Miss Barbara Bedford; she takes the place of the duchess, and a duchess she looks . . . Ricardo Cortez makes a good hero, an officer of the Russian Army . . ."

Silentsaregolden.com: "Make no mistake, *Mockery* is an enjoyable film with a compelling performance by Chaney; however, admittedly, it will not fare well when compared to other Chaney films such as *The Hunchback of Notre Dame* (1923), *He Who Gets Slapped* (1924), *The Phantom of the Opera* (1925), *The Unholy Three* (1926), *Tell It to the Marines* (1926), or *West of Zanzibar* (1928), among others . . ."

PRODUCTION NOTES, INTERESTING FACTS, AND TRIVIA:

1. Originally titled, *Terror*, the script was adapted from an original story by Stig Esbern.

2. In his biography, *Lon Chaney, The Man Behind A Thousand Faces* (1997), author/make-up artist, Michael F. Blake described how Chaney created the face of Sergei in *Mockery*.

"He (Chaney) grew his own beard, penciled in heavy brows to the bridge of his nose, and widened his nostrils with the use of cigar-holder ends. A low forehead wig completed the look. The greasy texture of the face was accomplished by applying very little powder to the heavy greasepaint base."

3. Mr. Blake also reported the script went through several overhauls prior to production. One draft, which included comic relief during the violent denouement, was rejected by director Christiansen, who felt it would ruin the dramatic impact of the finale.

4. Danish-born director Benjamin Christensen (1879-1959) was an opera singer and actor on the Danish stage, before making an impressive debut as a film director in *The Mysterious X*

(1913). In 1922 he won worldwide acclaim for directing, writing, and appearing in the docudrama, *Haxan: Witchcraft Through the Ages* (Sweden). He later came to America where he directed a handful of mystery/horror films, before returning to his native land.

BY WHOSE HAND? (1927) (CRIME DRAMA)
COLUMBIA PICTURES
PRODUCER: Harry Cohn
DIRECTOR: Walter Lang
SCREENPLAY: Marion Orth (story, scenario)
LENGTH: 57 minutes
STATUS: Lost

CAST: Ricardo Cortez (Van Suydam Smith), Eugenia Gilbert (Peg Hewlett), J. Thornton Baston (Sidney), Tom Dugan (Rollins), Edgar Washington Blue (Eli), Lillian Leighton (Silly McShane), William Scott (Mortimer), John Streppling (Claridge), and De Sacia Moors (Tex).

SUMMARY: While investigating a well-known New York confidence man (Scott), a daring detective (Cortez) falls in love with a night club entertainer (Gilbert). Their romance is put to the test when he begins to suspect her involvement in a jewel robbery.

REVIEWS:
Motion Picture Guide: "Not too exciting society thriller has Agent X-9 (Cortez) with the help of insurance agent Baston, exposing notorious jewel thief Scott . . . ."

Moviefone.com: " . . . a swift little thriller assembled by up and coming Columbia Pictures . . . Art director Robert E. Lee does wonders convincing us that Columbia's decidedly economical sets are actually a lavish night club and a large mansion . . . ."

PRODUCTION NOTES, INTERESTING FACTS, AND TRIVIA:
1. According to a newspaper item published in the *Salt Lake Tribune*, lead actress Eugenia Gilbert was described as "one of

the best rifle shots in the film colony." Gilbert claimed she gained the expertise after filming a picture which showed her loading and unloading a rifle. She said the producers received several complaints about the authenticity of the scenes she did, so she decided to learn how to use a gun.

THE PRIVATE LIFE OF HELEN OF TROY (1927) (SATIRICAL COMEDY)
FIRST NATIONAL PICTURES
PRODUCER: Carey Wilson
DIRECTOR: Alexander Korda
SCREENPLAY: Carey Wilson (scenario, adaptation), Ralph Spence, Gerald Duffy, Casey Robinson (title)
LENGTH: 8 reels
TAGLINES: "Her beauty rocked a nation . . . Her loves shocked the world!"; "It's not HISTORICAL, It's HYSTERICAL!"
STATUS: Exists—A partial copy is held at the British Film Institute (London, England).

CAST: Maria Corda (Helen), Lewis Stone (Menelaus), Ricardo Cortez (Paris), George Fawcett (Eteonius), Alice White (Adraste) Gordon Elliott (Telemachus), Tom O'Brien (Ulysses), Bert Sprotte (Achilies), Mario Carillo (Ajax), Charles Puffy (Malapokitoratoreadetos), George Kotsonaros (Hector), Constantine Romanoff (Aeneas), Emilio Borgato (Sarpedon), Alice Adair (Aphrodite), Helen Fairweather (Athena), and Virginia Thomas (Hera).

SUMMARY: When her husband neglects her, a bored Queen Helen of Troy (Corda) flees with Paris (Cortez) to Sparta, thus sparking a war with her husband, Menelaus (Stone). Although she is forced to return to Menelaus who has a right to kill her, her beauty and seductive qualities restrain him.

REVIEWS:
National Board of Review: "We dare say that for the great mass of the public who will see this film, the story of Helen and of Troy will for the first time be made real . . ."

New York Times: "The combination of 1927 colloquialisms and ideals with the replicas of ancient settings and modes, makes this film most amusing . . . Ricardo Cortez makes Paris a lovelorn specimen . . ."

PRODUCTION NOTES, INTERESTING FACTS, AND TRIVIA:

1. Although he died before the film was released, writer Gerald C. Duffy's titles were nominated for an Oscar for Best Title Writing during the first year of the awards. He has the distinction of being the first person nominated posthumously.

2. French director George Fitzmaurice began the film, but was replaced by Alexander Korda.

3. Carey Wilson's script was based on the John Erskine novel, *The Private Life of Helen of Troy*, and Robert Sherwood's 1927 play, *The Road to Rome*.

4. In interviews completed after the production of the picture, director Korda complained that *Helen* should have been made as a sound film since dialogue was such an important part of it.

5. *The Private Life of Helen of Troy* is largely considered Korda's best Hollywood produced work, and was one of his personal favorite films.

6. First National studios utilized over half of its great Burbank lot for the production of *The Private Life of Helen of Troy* which had multiple elaborate indoor and outdoor sets.

7. First National's costumer, Max Ree was given the Herculean task of outfitting more than a hundred extras with early Grecian period costumes, jewelry, and sandals to match.

8. All of the extras had to be personally reviewed and approved by director Korda before they could appear in the production. When asked why, Korda said it was to keep his wife, Maria,

Cortez played Paris opposite Maria Corda as the titled heroine in Alexander Korda's acclaimed satirical comedy, *The Private Life of Helen of Troy* (First National, 1927).

from making a scene. "She is, like Helen of Troy, like all women, inclined to be tempestuous."

9. *Helen of Troy* star Maria Corda (1898-1976) was born Maria Farkas in Deva, Hungary. A former dancer on the Budapest stage, she came to the attention of producer/director Alexander Korda, who began utilizing her as an actress in his Hungarian films in 1919. They were married in 1919, and divorced in 1930. They had one son, Peter Vincent born in 1921.

WOMAN OF DESTINY A.K.A. ***THE ORCHID DANCER*** (1928)
(COMEDY-DRAMA) (FRENCH)
FRANCO FILMS
DIRECTOR: Leonce Perret
SCREENPLAY: Jean-Joseph Renaud
LENGTH: 120 minutes
STATUS: Exists

CAST: Louise Lagrange, Ricardo Cortez, Xenia Desni, Daniele Parola, Sig Arno, Ernest Chambrey, and Gilbert Roland.

SUMMARY: In a small French village in the Pyrenees, a young man (Cortez) becomes disillusioned when he learns his sweetheart (Lagrange) was an exotic dancer, and the mistress of a wealthy Parisian businessman. He eventually becomes a famous film actor, falls in love with a beautiful film star (Desni), then crosses paths with his former love.

PRODUCTION NOTES, INTERESTING FACTS, AND TRIVIA:
1. Filmed at Studios Riviera, 16 Avenue Edouard Grinda, Nice, France.

2. Based on a novel by Jean-Joseph Renaud (1873-1953), a famed French fencer who participated in the summer Olympics in 1900 and 1908. A great proponent of dueling, he refereed many duels. He was also a prolific author and playwright whose works often covered the subjects of honor, combat, and self-defense.

3. Leonce Perret (1880-1935) was an able French film actor, producer, and director. Referred to as "the magician of film," he was renowned for his innovative editing and use of light and

camera angles. After being employed by Gaumont and working briefly in America, he returned to France where he won acclaim. *A Woman of Destiny* (*The Orchid Dancer*) was his next to last silent film.

4. Xenia Desni (1894-1962) was a popular Russian-born silent film actress.

5. Newly restored in 2012, *A Woman of Destiny* a.k.a *The Orchid Dancer* was shown at the National Gallery of Art in Washington D.C., and also screened in Bristol England (the first time the film had been shown in Britain since its release in 1928).

6. Ricardo Cortez was a savvy investor who made a fortune on stocks and real estate during his lifetime, but he was involved in a few bad deals along the way. One of them was *The Orchid Dancer*. Cortez bought the American rights to the film in lieu of a large salary, but lost the money. By 1928, American film studios were committed to sound and were not interested in showing silent films like *The Orchid Dancer*. In a 1933 interview published in the *Joplin Globe*, Cortez claimed the advent of sound cost him between $50,000 and $100,000.

LADIES OF THE NIGHT CLUB (1928) (COMEDY)
TIFFANY-STAHL PRODUCTIONS
DIRECTOR: George Archainbaud
SCREENPLAY: Ben Grauman Kohn (story), Houston Branch, John Francis Natteford (continuity), Paul Perez (title)
LENGTH: 7 reels
STATUS: Lost

CAST: Ricardo Cortez (George Merrill), Barbara Leonard (Dimples Revere), Lee Moran (Joe Raggs), Douglas Gerrard (Cyril Bathstowe), and Cissy Fitzgerald (Bossy Hart).

SUMMARY: A wealthy night club owner (Cortez) falls in love with a young vaudevillian (Leonard) who works for him. They agree

From left to right: Barbara Leonard, Cortez, and Lee Moran in the Tiffany-Stahl comic drama, *Ladies of the Night Club* (1929).

to marry, despite the girl's love and devotion for her partner (Moran).

REVIEWS:
Uniontown Morning Herald: "George Archainbaud realizes that a director can't pull on the public's heartstrings if he doesn't make the characters genuine—and he has done this with a deft, but sure touch, in *Ladies of the Night Club* . . . ."

Variety: "Backstage story suggesting more than a little inspiration from *Excess Baggage* and *Broadway* . . . Ricardo Cortez gives his usual suave performance in the straight lead role . . ."

PRODUCTION NOTES, INTERESTING FACTS, AND TRIVIA:
1. Although primarily a silent film, *Ladies of the Night Club* contained a sound sequence.

2. At the time *Ladies of the Night Club* was playing in theaters,

both its stars Ricardo Cortez and Barbara Leonard were seen in ads for Baby Ruth Gum.

PROWLERS OF THE SEA (1928) (ADVENTURE-DRAMA)
TIFFANY-STAHL PRODUCTIONS
PRODUCER: Roy Fitzroy, John M. Stahl
DIRECTOR: John G. Adolfi
SCREENPLAY: John Francis Natteford (scenario), Leslie Mason (title)
LENGTH: 6 reels
TAGLINE: "To her he pledged his love—his faith—his life! And she betrayed him!"
STATUS: Exists—A complete copy can be found at Archives Du Film du CNC (Bois d'Arcy, France)

CAST: Carmel Myers (Mercedes), Ricardo Cortez (Carlos de Neve), George Fawcett (General Hernandez), Gino Corrado (The Skipper), Frank Lackteen (Ramon Sanchez), Frank Leigh (Felipe), and Shirley Palmer (Cuban maid).

SUMMARY: In Cuba, a brave young Spanish military officer (Cortez) is appointed captain of the coast guard when revolutionaries threaten the government. The insurgents counter by recruiting a beautiful Cuban girl (Myers) to distract him while they smuggle guns into the country.

REVIEWS:
Medicine Hat News: "John A. Adolfi directed this Tiffany-Stahl movie and injected tenderness with thrills . . . Ricardo Cortez is an appealing and manly captain of the guards, who very naturally falls victim to the clever trap set for him . . . ."

PRODUCTION NOTES, INTERESTING FACTS, AND TRIVIA:
1. Based on the Jack London story, *The Siege of the Lancaster Queen*, published in *Tales of the Fish Patrol* in 1905.

2. By 1928, Tiffany-Stahl was booking its films in over 2000 theaters.

3. Filmed on the Tiffany-Stahl studio lot at 4516 Sunset Boulevard. After Tiffany went bankrupt in 1932, the lot was eventually purchased by Columbia Pictures and given to Irving Briskin and Sam Katzman as a base for their B film units.

THE GRAIN OF DUST (1928) (DRAMA)
TIFFANY-STAHL PRODUCTIONS
PRODUCER: John M. Stahl
DIRECTOR: George Archainbaud
SCREENPLAY: Frances Hyland (continuity), Paul Perez (title), L. G. Rigby (adaptation)
LENGTH: 7 reels
STATUS: Lost

CAST: Ricardo Cortez (Fred Norman), Claire Windsor (Josephine Burroughs), Alma Bennett (Dorothea Hallowell), Richard Tucker (George), John St. Polis (Mr. Burroughs), and Otto Hoffman (chief clerk).

SUMMARY: A happily married man (Cortez) foolishly abandons his wife when he becomes infatuated with a vampish typist (Bennett) who is in his employ.

REVIEWS:
Billings Gazette: "It is an absorbing picture, a perfect combination of entertainment and dramatic values . . . Ricardo Cortez plays with feeling and understanding, the difficult role of the young engineer who meets disaster through a woman just as he is about to reach the heights . . . ."

The Motion Picture Guide: "All but forgotten now, second string vamp Bennett has her moments as the secretary who lures Cortez away from his wife, his best friend to suicide, and his business to ruin."

PRODUCTION NOTES, INTERESTING FACTS, AND TRIVIA:
1. Based on David Graham Phillip's bestselling 1911 novel, *The Grain of Dust*.

2. Legend has it MGM acquired Tiffany-Stahl's entire original nitrate film negative library and burned it during the burning of Atlanta sequences in *Gone With the Wind* (1939).

3. During the production of *The Grain of Dust*, Ricardo Cortez granted interviews in which he said he considered his role in the movie the best of his career thus far. In one, published in the *Hattiesburg American*, Cortez explained why.

"David Graham Phillips was the first American author to write serious social studies. Every one of his books has a basic problem on which he builds his premise, and the basic problem in The Grain of Dust is the overwhelming power of sex. In these days of tabloids and newspaper scareheads, we've got to admit fundamental human instinct is responsible for a good share of the predicaments that get into the papers."

EXCESS BAGGAGE (1928) (COMEDY, DRAMA)
METRO-GOLDWYN-MAYER PICTURES
DIRECTOR: James Cruze
SCREENPLAY: Frances Marion (continuity), Ralph Spence (dialogue, title)
LENGTH: 8 reels
STATUS: Exists—A non-circulating archival copy of *Excess Baggage* is housed in the Film and Television Archives at U.C.L.A.—

CAST: William Haines (Eddie Kane), Josephine Dunn (Elsa McCoy), Neely Edwards (Jimmy Dunn), Kathleen Clifford (Mabel Ford), Greta Granstedt (Betty Ford), Ricardo Cortez (Val D'Errico), and Cyril Chadwick (Crammon).

SUMMARY: An acrobat (Haines) falls in love and marries a dancer (Dunn), but their relationship is strained when she becomes a success in the movies and he remains in vaudeville. Further complications arise when he suspects her of infidelity with a handsome actor (Cortez).

REVIEWS:
Chicago Daily Tribune: "A commendable picture chockfull of

interest and charm, and most excellently produced."

New York Times: "Unless one is disposed to laugh at such antics as William Haines rolling a dill pickle down a ribbon attached to the neck of his wife's frock, one is apt to find the pictorial transcription of John McGowan's play, *Excess Baggage*, is at least lacking in a sense of humor . . . Ricardo Cortez and Cyril Chadwick, in minor roles, give impersonations more credible than those of the featured players. . . ."

PRODUCTION NOTES, INTERESTING FACTS, AND TRIVIA:
1. Based on John Wesley McGowan's play, *Excess Baggage* (1927).

2. The film contains one sound sequence (provided courtesy of Fox Movietone equipment), which according to reviewers, was "badly done and unnecessary."

3. In his biography of *Excess Baggage*, star William Haines entitled, *Firecracker*, author William J. Mann, stated the Hays Office had problems with multiple scenes. They objected to particular lines and spanking scenes between the vaudevillian (Haines) and his wife (played by Josephine Dunn).

4. Director James Cruze (1884-1942) was a former stage and film actor and a member of the prestigious Belasco acting company who appeared on Broadway several times. By 1918, he had switched to directing. A hardworking, prolific craftsman, his work covered a broad range from slapstick, to suspense thrillers, to epic adventures. Among his distinguished credits were The *Covered Wagon* (1923), *The Pony Express* (1925), *Old Ironsides* (1926), and two episodes of *If I Had a Million* (1934). Cortez worked with Cruze four times: *Hollywood* (1923), *The City That Never Sleeps* (1924), *The Pony Express* (1925) and *Excess Baggage* (1928).

5. According to an item in the *Muscatine Journal*, Ricardo Cortez first met William Haines in New York when they were both cast as extras in the Mae Murray film, *Zazzmania*.

The Gun Runner (1928) (Adventure Comedy)
Tiffany-Stahl Productions
Director: Edgar Lewis
Screenplay: J. F. Natteford (continuity), Paul Perez (title)
Length: 6 reels
Tagline: "A Life for a Life and All For Love!"
Status: Lost

Cast: Ricardo Cortez (Julio), Nora Lane (Inez), Gino Corrado (Garcia), John St. Polis (Presidente).

Summary: In South America, a carefree young man (Cortez) is enlisted to capture a notorious gunrunner (Corrado) plotting a revolution. He changes his mind after he meets the insurrectionist's beautiful sister (Lane).

Reviews:
The Film Daily: "Like all those stories of South American revolutions, it is pretty much musical comedy material. Director Lewis has contrived to invest it with an air of plausibility, and has built in some great atmospheric touches, but it is Ricardo Cortez that makes it a really entertaining number. He is really a romantic figure, and whether fighting or lovemaking, does both with telling effect . . . ."

Variety: "Mild comedy about one of those mythical Latin American republics with a comic opera president, cabinet, and army that will just about make the grade in the cheaper grinds . . ."

Production Notes, Interesting Facts, and Trivia:
1. Based on a 1909 story by novelist, poet, and scriptwriter Arthur Stringer (1874-1950). Among his other film scripts were: *The Perils of Pauline* (1914), *The Purchase Price* (1932) and *Buck Benny Rides Again* (1940).

2. After Tiffany-Stahl went bankrupt, the copyrights for their films were allowed to expire, thus most of their library is in the public domain.

THE YOUNGER GENERATION (1929) (DRAMA)
COLUMBIA PICTURES
PRODUCER: Jack Cohn
DIRECTOR: Frank Capra
SCREENPLAY: Sonya Levien
LENGTH: 75 minutes
STATUS: Exists in both silent and partial sound versions. Silent version housed at Cinematieque Royale de Belgique (Brussels, Belgium), George Eastman House (Rochester, New York), Filmoteca Espanola (Madrid, Spain), National Archives of Canada (Ottawa).Please note: The location of a master copy of the partial sound version of *The Younger Generation* is unknown, but this version has been shown on Turner Classic Movies multiple times.

CAST: Jean Hersholt (Julius Goldfish), Lina Basquette (Birdie Goldfish), Rosa Rosanova (Tildie Goldfish), Ricardo Cortez (Morris Goldfish), Rex Lease (Eddie Lesser), Marsha Franklin (Mrs. Lesser), Julia Swayne Gordon (Mrs. Striker), Julanne Johnston (Irma Striker), Jack Raymond (Pinsky), and Otto Fries (tradesman).

SUMMARY: The trials and tribulations of an upwardly mobile young Jewish man (Cortez) who uproots his family in an attempt to keep up appearances.

REVIEWS:
Los Angeles Examiner: "Frank Capra has directed with an understanding restraint, and although the cast numbers but five, each player gives a more than adequate characterization . . . ."

New York Times: "The film, which has a sound accompaniment, has several dialogue sequences which did not add to the story. In several of the talking scenes there were long, unnecessary pauses between the word passages . . ."

PRODUCTION NOTES, INTERESTING FACTS, AND TRIVIA:
1. Based on the Fannie Hurst play, *It Is to Laugh* (1927).

2. The movie contains four lip synchronized dialogue passages. Sources indicate this was the first partial sound film produced by Columbia and its young director Frank Capra.

3. In his autobiography, *The Name Above the Title*, director Capra recalled filming the picture and the many obstacles he faced.

"Shooting your first sound picture was an etude in chaos. First of all, no one was used to being quiet. Shooting of silent scenes had gone on with hammering and sawing on an adjacent set... Suddenly, with sound, we had to work in the silence of a tomb. When the red lights went on, everyone froze in his position—a cough or a belch would wreck the scene. To the nervous snit of the non-stage actors—over having to memorize lines for the first time—the funereal hush added the willies. They shook with stage fright. Then there were the cameras... To kill the camera noise, our wonderful mobile, moving cameras were mummified and entombed in thick padded booths—a soundproof window in the front, a padded door in the back. Of course, the cameraman was stuffed into the booth with his camera, and, of course, he couldn't hear a blessed thing about what was going on. But who cared about hearing when he was suffocating...."

4. Columbia employed the services of five-foot-five, 300 pound cinematographer Ben Reynolds for *The Younger Generation*. According to Capra,

"He looked like a whisky barrel walking on two fire plugs... Well, it took two huskies to shove Big Ben into the airless booth and sit him next to his camera, but it took half a dozen to pull him out. As soon as the camera-start bell rang, and his booth barred shut, Ben went peacefully to sleep. It didn't matter much to the scene because his camera was pre-set and locked into the position. But it meant Ben's life to get him out in a hurry at the end of the scene—and snatching three hundred pounds of limp, stuck flesh out of that hot box wasn't easy...."

5. Capra also noted the difficulties of working with the "hellish hot lights" required by sound, and the biggest "gremlin" of all, the sound man who inserted mikes in drawers and flower pots.

6. As tough as the production might have been for its director, working with Capra was apparently a pleasurable experience for *The Younger Generation* cast. In a magazine interview conducted during the filming, Jean Hersholt recalled "This man, Frank Capra, will emerge as a giant amongst the pygmy minds in Hollywood."

7. The story of the Goldfish family depicted in *The Younger Generation* was one with which Ricardo Cortez could identify. Like his character, he was a conscientious and penny-wise young Jewish man whose rise to fame impacted the standard of living of his poor family. Even his character's name, Morris, was ironic and significant as Ricardo's father's name was Morris.

NEW ORLEANS (1929) (CRIME DRAMA)
TIFFANY-STAHL PRODUCTIONS
DIRECTOR: Reginald Barker
SCREENPLAY: John Frances Natteford (story, continuity), Frederick Hatton (dialog-title)
LENGTH: 8 reels
STATUS: Exists—A complete silent copy is housed at George Eastman House (Rochester, New York). The status of a partial talkie version is unknown.

CAST: Ricardo Cortez (Jim Morley), William Collier Jr. (Billy Slade), Alma Bennett (Marie Cartier).

SUMMARY: A race track manager (Cortez) and a jockey (Collier Jr.) become bitter rivals over the affections of a beautiful, but corrupt young woman (Bennett).

REVIEWS:
Chicago Daily Tribune: ". . . unexpectedly interesting . . . To William Collier Jr. belongs most of the films honor and glory. He does far and away the best acting and you like him immensely throughout. Ricardo Cortez is all right, but his role of weakling is not an alluring one to audiences who have been used to Ricardo playing the strong man who can do no wrong . . . ."

[Cortez (center) was costarred with William Collier Jr. (left), as best friends who become rivals for the affections of an unprincipled young woman (Alma Bennett, right) in the crime drama, *New Orleans* (Tiffany-Stahl, 1929).]

Film Daily: "Program picture carries a sexy kick and has some good racetrack atmosphere . . . ."

PRODUCTION NOTES, INTERESTING FACTS, AND TRIVIA:
1. Both silent and partial talkie versions were released. The latter version has both talking and singing sequences.

2. Stars Ricardo Cortez, Alma Bennett, and William "Buster" Collier Jr. filmed part of the picture on location in New Orleans.

MIDSTREAM (1929)
TIFFANY-STAHL PRODUCTIONS
DIRECTOR: James Flood
SCREENPLAY: Frances Guihan (scenario), Frederick Hatton, Fanny Hatton (dialog, title), Bernice Boone (story)
LENGTH: 8 reels
STATUS: Exists—A complete copy can be found at the Archives Du Film du CNC (Bois d'Arcy, France).

CAST: Ricardo Cortez (James Stanwood), Claire Windsor (Helene Craig), Montagu Love (Dr. Nelson), Larry Kent (Martin Baker), and Helen Jerome Eddy (Mary Mason).

SUMMARY: When he falls in love with a much younger woman (Windsor), a middle-aged financier (Cortez) undergoes a "rejuvenation operation" in hopes of attracting her. He then telegraphs his death and returns as his nephew, who has inherited his estate, and begins to woo her.

REVIEWS:
Chicago Daily Tribune: "*Midstream* holds your attention and is intelligently produced in the main . . . Mr. Cortez does well with his peculiar role. Miss Windsor is charming, although not perfectly cast as the girl next door . . . ."

The Film Daily: "Very unusual love triangle story. Carries tense interest and film acting by three principles puts it over . . . Claire Windsor is as charming as ever and Ricardo Cortez as the youthful beau is convincing . . ."

PRODUCTION NOTES, INTERESTING FACTS, AND TRIVIA:
1. Originally shot as a silent, both speaking and singing sequences were added to *Midstream* after shooting was complete. One of the musical sequences, the operatic "Faust" scene, was the only portion of the film which was thought to have survived. Years later, a complete copy was located at the Archives Du Film du CNC in France.

2. According to a newspaper item published in the *Charleston Daily Mail*, Tiffany-Stahl engaged an opera company for the musical portion of the production, and recorded the sequence under the personal supervision of Hugo Riesenfeld, who composed the synchronized score for the picture.

3. The musical footage from *Midstream* was excised from the feature, and eventually released as a musical short.

4. Longtime Cortez friend, silent leading lady Claire Windsor, made her talkie debut in *Midstream*.

The Phantom in the House (1929) (Melodrama)
Trem Carr Productions, Continental Talking Pictures
Director: Phil Rosen
Screenplay: Arthur Hoerl (adaptation, continuity, dialog)
Length: 64 minutes
Status: Exists—Both talkie and silent versions have survived. The silent version is housed at British Film Institute (London, England). (DVD of talkie version)

Cast: Ricardo Cortez (Paul Wallis), Nancy Welford (Dorothy Milburn), Henry B. Walthall (Boyd Milburn), Grace Valentine (Peggy Milburn), Thomas A. Curran (Judge Thompson), Jack Curtis ("Biffer" Bill), and John Elliott (Police Captain).

Summary: While attempting to enlist the financial backing of a wealthy family friend, a struggling inventor's wife (Valentine) is attacked by the potential financier; she kills him. In order to protect their young daughter, her husband (Walthall) takes the rap and goes to prison for fifteen years. While he is incarcerated, his inventions become successful, and his wife changes her name and attempts to marry her daughter (Welford) into society, despite the girl's love for a poor young man (Cortez). More melodrama follows after the prisoner returns home, and another death occurs.

Reviews:
The Film Daily: "Strong dramatic story rides easily with good direction and acting . . . Cortez is fine as the young hero . . ."

Production notes, interesting facts, and trivia:
1. Based on Andrew Soutar's 1928 novel, *The Phantom of the House*.

2. Both silent and talkie versions of *The Phantom in the House* were released by Continental. The sound version was the studio's first all talking film.

3. According to an item in *Variety,* *The Phantom in the House* was the first independent, all-talkie movie booked by the Loew's chain.

THE LOST ZEPPELIN (1929) (ADVENTURE)
TIFFANY PRODUCTIONS
DIRECTOR: Edward Sloman
SCREENPLAY: Charles Kenyon (dialog), Frances Hyland, John F. Natteford (story).
LENGTH: 8 reels.
TAGLINE: "The Mightiest Thrill of All Time!"
STATUS: Both silent and sound versions were produced. Talkie version exists, but the silent has been lost. (DVD)

CAST: Conway Tearle (Commander Hall), Virginia Valli (Mrs. Hall), Ricardo Cortez (Tom Armstrong), Duke Martin (Lieutenant), Kathryn McGuire (Nancy), and Winter Hall (Mr. Wilson)

SUMMARY: As he prepares for a flight over the South Pole, a zeppelin commander (Tearle) learns his wife (Valli) is in love with his best friend and flying partner (Cortez). When the zeppelin crashes and a rescue plane (which can only hold one person) finds the pair, the husband insists his friend be saved. Later, his friend discovers the "widow" still loves her husband, who is miraculously rescued.

REVIEWS:
Los Angeles Evening Herald: "Tensely told, with exceptionally good dialogue and with realistic effects, *The Lost Zeppelin* reflects credit upon the Tiffany Company which made it, upon the cast which is uniformly good, and upon Edward Sloman, the director . . . ."

New York Times: "Presumably the producers of *The Lost Zeppelin*, an audible pictorial melodrama at the Gaiety do not believe in a very high order of intelligence among cinema audiences, for the best that can be said of the film is that it appears to have been fashioned with a view to appealing to boys from 8 to 10 years of age . . ."

Disastrous complications ensue when a zeppelin commander (Godrey Tearle) and his flying partner (Cortez) embark on a polar expedition in the adventure, *The Lost Zeppelin* (Tiffany-Stahl, 1929). From left to right: Duke Martin, Tearle and Cortez.

PRODUCTION NOTES, INTERESTING FACTS, AND TRIVIA:

1. After filming the feature entirely as a silent, entitled *Zeppelin*, in the fall of 1929, a decision was made to add sound effects and sound sequences. To make the major revisions, the producers replaced the original director, Reginald Barker, with Edward Sloman, and cast members Claire Windsor and Larry Kent with Virginia Valli and Ricardo Cortez. The talking footage was eventually spliced into the silent version. The title was also changed to *The Lost Zeppelin*.

2. The movie was loosely based on the crash of the airship Italia near the North Pole on May 25, 1928, and the rescue effort in which famed polar explorer Roald Amundson lost his life.

3. According to a March, 1930 article in *Motion Picture* magazine, actual shots of the Graf Zeppelin were cleverly inter-mixed with miniatures by the art directors and scenic designers.

Montana Moon (1930) (WESTERN, MUSICAL COMEDY)
METRO-GOLDWYN-MAYER PICTURES
DIRECTOR: Malcom St. Clair
SCREENPLAY: Sylvia Thalberg, Frank Butler (story, continuity), Joe Farnham (dialogue).
LENGTH: 71 minutes.
STATUS: Exists — Both silent and sound versions were produced. The sound version exists on DVD. The status of the silent version is unknown.

CAST: Joan Crawford (Joan), John Mack Brown (Larry), Dorothy Sebastian (Elizabeth), Ricardo Cortez (Jeff), Benny Rubin "The Doctor"), Cliff Edwards (Froggy), Karl Dane (Hank), and Lloyd Ingraham (Mr. Prescott).

SUMMARY: On her way out west to her father's ranch, an East Coast society girl (Crawford) meets a cowboy (Brown). They fall in love and marry, but he finds it difficult to adjust to her way of life. The marriage is further threatened when Joan's former beau (Cortez) arrives on the scene on the couples' wedding day.

REVIEWS:
New York Times: "An interminable, amateurish talking picture, with spasmodic snatches of music . . . Taking it all in all, the most pleasing features of this production are Miss Crawford's camel hair coat and her jodhpur riding outfit . . . ."

Variety: "Largely on the strength of snatches of clever dialog, carrying laughs, and some of the comedy situations and the music, *Montana Moon* has a chance for nice grosses around the country."

PRODUCTION NOTES, INTERESTING FACTS, AND TRIVIA:
1. Inexplicably, MGM released a silent version of this musical drama at the same time it released the sound one.

2. Many of the scenes in *Montana Moon* were filmed on location in the titled state.

3. Miss Crawford did her own singing in *Montana Moon*. She sprained her ankle during rehearsals, necessitating changes in the production schedule.

4. The script was co-written by Sylvia Thalberg, the sister of MGM production head, Irving Thalberg.

5. In an interview conducted years later, Miss Crawford said *Montana Moon* "was a bit of fluff that was supposed to help Johnny Mack Brown, but I think it hurt him instead."

6. Although the film met with mixed reviews, filmgoers apparently liked it. Total box office receipts topped $900,000, netting MGM a $326,000 profit.

7. Much footage was exorcised from the original movie to satisfy local censors. Since the country was still under Prohibition, among the censors' many demands was to cut all liquor drinking.

8. Ricardo Cortez and Joan Crawford became lifelong friends, and perhaps lovers, during the making of *Montana Moon*. Throughout the early to mid-1930's, they were often seen together with and without their spouses. The exact nature of their relationship would remain forever unknown, but certainly the Hollywood gossip machine thought there was a sexual component. In April, 1933, a *Chicago Tribune* article about the breakup of Miss Crawford and Douglas Fairbanks Jr., stated Joan had been spotted with Cortez several times during the previous months. Ironically, the two close friends would die within days of each other in 1977. Both had funerals at the Frank E. Campbell Chapel on Madison Avenue in New York City.

Her Man (1930) (DRAMA)
PATHE EXCHANGE
PRODUCER: E.B. Derr
DIRECTOR: Tay Garnett
SCREENPLAY: Thomas Buckingham (story), Howard Higgen, Tay Garnett (story)
LENGTH: 8 reels
STATUS: Exists

CAST: Helen Twelvetrees (Frankie), Marjorie Rambeau (Annie), Ricardo Cortez (Johnnie), Phillips Holmes (Dan), James Gleason (Steve), Harry Sweet (Eddie), Stanley Fields (Al), Mathew Betz (Red), Thelma Todd (Nellie), Franklin Pangborn (Sport), Mike Donlin (bartender), and Slim Summerville (The Swede).

SUMMARY: Based on the familiar "Frankie and Johnnie" theme, a prostitute (Twelvetrees) who works for a brutal pimp (Cortez) in a Havana waterfront dive, falls for a young sailor (Holmes) who vows to take her away to a better life.

REVIEWS:
Los Angeles Record: "Beautiful entertainment, sturdy, gallant and true . . . Helen Twelvetrees is wonderful, Phillips Holmes turns in a shining performance, and Ricardo Cortez makes a strong sinister impression . . ."

Los Angeles Evening Herald: "Her Man will prove a stepping stone to Ricardo Cortez, whose portrayal is a characterization of high order . . ."

Los Angeles Examiner: "Undeniably good entertainment, it puts Mr. Garnett into the front rank of capable directors . . . Ricardo Cortez, as the lawless Johnnie, dead to all decency and not even true to Frankie, gives one of the outstanding performances in the picture . . . ."

PRODUCTION NOTES, INTERESTING FACTS, AND TRIVIA:
1. Originally titled, *Frankie and Johnny*.

2. Censors objected to the script of *Her Man* in several respects. A note dated May 7, 1930, to Pathe from the office of Colonel Jason Joy, (head of The Studio Relations Committee, which monitored movies and advised producers on censorship issues during the Pre-Code era), noted, "close consultation" on the screenplay, but said the script still did not satisfy "the standards set by the Code." Of particular concern was the portrayal of the relationship of Frankie and Johnnie as that of a prostitute and pimp, Frankie's pick pocketing, and the brutal murder of the character of Red by Johnnie. Joy suggested the writers change the relationship between the main characters to one of "sincere attachment," and Frankie should be portrayed as different from the other girls; a victim of circumstance. Although they did not address all the concerns, there is evidence Garnett and Pathe did alter the film to satisfy censor boards. For instance, in the finished film, audiences never really see the murder of Red, only Johnnie throwing a knife.

3. After the film was released in September 1930, Colonel Joy's office received a complaint from The Cuban Charge de'Affaires about its unfavorable depiction of Havana. In a letter dated October 29, 1930, Pathe responded by claiming Havana had not been the setting, and that a person associated with the advertising of the film had mistakenly referred to the setting as Cuba, contrary to "our instructions." Since scenes of Morro Castle and scenes of Havana were filmed on location, this was clearly a lie.

4. In a Pathe inter-office memo dated April 10, 1930, (located in the *Her Man* file at the A.M.P.A.S. Library), an unknown person who reviewed scripts for Pathe summed up the screenplay of *Her Man* this way: "There is about as much moral value in this picture as there is in a five-week-old kippered herring . . . ."

5. A major box office hit, total box office receipts exceeded $800,000.

6. In his memoirs, *Light Up Your Torches, And Pull Up Your Tights,*

The chemistry between Cortez and leading lady, Helen Twelvetrees, is palpable in all three of the motion pictures they made together. *Her Man* (Pathe, 1930), directed by Tay Garnett, was the first and most famous of their pairings.

director Tay Garnett recalled being assigned to produce and direct *Her Man* during the initial months of 1928. According to Garnett, he and Tom Buckingham "whipped up the script" from one of his original stories and added one of his favorite comedy routines involving drunken sailors and slot machines (which was performed by actor/comedians James Gleason and Harry Sweet).

7. Garnett said he wanted Dean Jagger for the key role of Dan, but Pathe "had cooked up a deal with Paramount-Lasky to borrow one of their contract players, Phillips Holmes, in exchange for one of ours."

8. Garnett also said the cast of *Her Man* was excited when they learned the film was set in Havana, but were disappointed when they were told it wouldn't be necessary for them to film on location. "Only a cameraman, Eddie Snyder, and I were

to spend a few days in Cuba, picking up background footage for 'process' shots." MGM shared the cost of shooting for four days in exchange for the rights to use some of the exterior shots in their upcoming production, *Cuban Love Song*.

9. According to a *Tyrone Daily Herald* item, one of the stunt men who enacted the famous fight scene in *Her Man* (which was considered one of the most realistic scenes of its kind during the 1930's), was Jack Woody. Leading lady Helen Twelvetrees would marry Jack in 1931.

ILLICIT (1931) (DRAMA)
WARNER BROTHERS
PRODUCER: Darryl F. Zanuck
DIRECTOR: Archie Mayo
SCREENPLAY: Harvey Thew
LENGTH: 81 minutes
STATUS: Exists. (DVD)

CAST: Barbara Stanwyck (Anne Vincent), James Rennie (Dick Ives), Charles Butterworth (George Evans), Joan Blondell (Helen "Duckie" Childers), Natalie Moorhead (Margie True), Ricardo Cortez (Price Baines), and Claude Gillingwater (Ives Sr.).

SUMMARY: An independent woman (Stanwyck) is reluctant to marry her lover (Rennie) because she feels it will negatively impact their relationship. Social pressures eventually cause her to relent, only to learn she was right all along.

REVIEWS:
Los Angeles Examiner: "Barbara Stanwyck proves herself every inch a star in her portrayal . . . Ricardo Cortez as the disappointed. but still hopeful suitor, is outstanding . . ."

New York Times: " . . . an intelligent adaptation of a play by Edith Fitzgerald and Robert Riskin, the real conqueror is not marriage, but love . . . Ricardo Cortez does quite well in the minor role of Price Baines . . ."

Production notes, interesting facts, and trivia:
1. Based on the play *Illicit*, by Edith Fitzgerald and Robert Riskin, which was also the basis of Warner Bros. 1933 film, *Ex-Lady* starring Bette Davis and Gene Raymond.

2. Sources indicate multiple adjustments were made to *Illicit* to placate censors who objected to its depiction of cohabitation without marriage, excessive drinking, certain sexual references, and bits of dialogue. The New York censors even objected to the film's title.

3. *Variety* reported Barbara Stanwyck was borrowed from Columbia Studios for $7,000 a week.

4. According to his contract housed at the Warner Bros. Archives at University of Southern California, Ricardo Cortez was paid $2,500 to portray playboy Price Baines in *Illicit*.

5. In an interview published in the *Los Angeles Record, Illicit* director, Archie Mayo, ascribed the film's box office success to the intelligence of the picture audience. "We made no pretentions of describing a cure-all for marital dissension. We merely took two people through what might be called a general scenic tour of the matrimonial landscape . . . ."

6. In the biography, *The Life of Barbara Stanwyck: Steel True 1907-1940*, author Victoria Wilson, says in order to help the cast record their voices, director Mayo used a pitch pipe to test the note at which the words recorded best.

7. According to Al Di Orio's *Barbara Stanwyck A Biography*, *Illicit's* star worked well with director Mayo who "tended to allow Stanwyck to work out her own characterization. This resulted in a natural and gentle portrayal on Barbara's part . . ."

8. Barbara's sister, Mabel passed away a few days after production began on *Illicit*.

9. According to a *New York Times* tidbit, director Mayo ordered studio hairdressers to make Joan Blondell's hairstyle to be different in each of the 28 scenes in which she appeared, in order to emphasize her "ultra-modern" look.

TEN CENTS A DANCE (1931) (DRAMA)
COLUMBIA PICTURES CORPORATION
PRODUCER: Harry Cohn
DIRECTOR: Lionel Barrymore
SCREENPLAY: Jo Swerling (story, dialogue), Dorothy Howell (continuity)
LENGTH: 75 minutes
STATUS: Exists. (DVD)

CAST: Barbara Stanwyck (Barbara O'Neill), Ricardo Cortez (Bradley Carlson), Monroe Owsley (Eddie Miller), Sally Blane (Molly), Blanche Frederici (Mrs. Blanchard), Martha Sleeper (Nancy), David Newell (Ralph Sheridan), Victor Potel (Smith), and Sidney Bracy (Wilson)

SUMMARY: A taxi dancer (Stanwyck) attracts the attention of a wealthy man (Cortez), but loves a weak-willed social climber (Owsley) who mistreats her.

REVIEWS:
Chicago Daily Tribune: "A splendidly acted and produced movie . . . Barbara Stanwyck is, as always, appealing and convincing, and the men in the cast give real life performances . . ."

Los Angeles Examiner: "Perhaps it is a bit maudlin, the idea of a girl dancing for ten cents a customer while her heart is breaking to the tone of a jazz refrain. It isn't maudlin when Barbara Stanwyck does it. She gives this dance hall girl reality and humanness . . . Ricardo Cortez is very fine as the rich man who loves the dance hall girl . . ."

PRODUCTION NOTES, INTERESTING FACTS, AND TRIVIA:
1. Originally titled, *Roseland,* the eventual title was taken from the

Richard Rodgers, Lorenz Hart song, "Ten Cents a Dance" sung by Ruth Etting in the stage musical, "Simple Simon" (1930).

2. A Spanish language version of this film, entitled *El Triunfo de un Amor*, was released in Buenos Aires, and another titled *El Torbellino del Jazz* in Bilbao, Spain. The Spanish version was directed by William Cabana, a.k.a. William "Christy" Cabanne.

3. *Ten Cents a Dance* was the last film in which Lionel Barrymore received sole credit as a director. According to Al DiOrio in *Barbara Stanwyck A Biography*, he was ailing and "not at his best" during the filming. "Crippling arthritis confined him to a wheelchair and his medication caused him to fall asleep, even while directing." Although Ricardo Cortez recalled Barrymore's direction as being nonexistent, Stanwyck was kinder. She said "He tried his best. As a performer you just had to try harder."

4. Miss Stanwyck apparently lived by the motto "The show must go on." DiOrio says she was injured in a scene with actor Monroe Owsley during production. "She was rushed to the osteopathic hospital where it was apparent that she was partially paralyzed, and doctors feared that she had fractured her pelvis. Her recovery was quick though, and she returned to work the next day."

5. According to Victoria Wilson's book *The Life of Barbara Stanwyck: Steel True 1907-1940*, while making *Ten Cents a Dance* for Columbia, Barbara Stanwyck signed a letter of agreement with Warner Bros., to make three pictures for $100,000 to take effect August 1, 1931.

6. According to Victoria Wilson's book, *Barbara Stanwyck, Steel True 1907-1940*, Ricardo Cortez's professed admiration for Stanwyck was not mutual. Miss Stanwyck privately referred to Cortez as "old fish eyes." Regarding the filming of *Ten Cents a Dance*, Stanwyck stated "He (Cortez) gave me nothing to work with. I was on my own in every scene. And without a director to help out, playing against nothing was even more frustrating."

Behind Office Doors (1931) (Drama)
RKO Radio PicturesRKO Radio Pictures
Producer: William Le Baron
Director: Melville Brown
Screenplay: Carey Wilson (script), J. Walter Ruben
                (adaptation, dialogue)
Length: 82 minutes
Status: Exists. (DVD)

Cast: Mary Astor (Mary Linden), Robert Ames (Jim Duneen), Ricardo Cortez (Ronnie Wales), Catherine Dale Owen (Ellen Robinson), Kitty Kelly (Dolores Kogan), Edna Murphy (Daisy Presby), Charles Sellon (Ritter), and William Morris (Charles Robinson).

Summary: Largely responsible for the company's success, a loyal, hardworking, secretary (Astor) for a paper wholesaler uses her considerable influence over her elderly boss (Sellon) to urge the promotion of a young salesman (Ames) she's fallen in love with. After the young man assumes the top job, he treats her cavalierly.

Reviews:
Los Angeles Record: " . . . as perfectly cast as anything that has been filmed. The individual efforts of Mary Astor, Robert Ames, Ricardo Cortez and Kitty Kelly are all that you could ask . . ."

Variety: "Aimed squarely at the women and hits the target . . . Story gives Miss Astor her heaviest film job thus far. She plays it easily, smoothly, and pleasantly, coming out on top of the picture at the finish after keeping the lead all the way. Everything's a setup for her accomplishment, including some excellent foiling by the two men, Robert Ames and Ricardo Cortez . . ."

Production notes, interesting facts, and trivia:
1. The original title for the film was *Private Secretary*, based on a novel by Alan Brener Schultz (1929).

2. The first of six films Cortez would make with future Oscar

winning actress Mary Astor, who had the distinction of being his most frequent feminine costar.

3. The son of an accountant, Connecticut-born actor Robert Ames (1889-1931) had a significant career as a leading man on the New York stage prior to coming to Hollywood during the late 1920s, where he costarred in several significant movies, both silent and early sound. He is perhaps best known for his performance as Johnny Case in the 1930 version of the comic drama, *Holiday*, starring Ann Harding. Mr. Ames died of a heart attack at age 42, a few months after completing work on *Behind Office Doors*. An autopsy revealed he had died from delirium tremens brought on by alcohol withdrawl.

WHITE SHOULDERS (1931) (DRAMA)
RKO RADIO PICTURES
DIRECTOR: Melville Brown
SCREENPLAY: J. Walter Ruben (adaptation, dialogue), Howard Estabrook (continuity)
LENGTH: 80 minutes
STATUS: Lost

CAST: Mary Astor (Norma Selbee Kent), Jack Holt (Gordon Kent), Ricardo Cortez (Tommy Pierce a.k.a. Lawrence Marchmont), Sidney Toler (William Sothern), and Kitty Kelly (Marie Fontaine).

SUMMARY: When a wealthy mining engineer (Holt) becomes enamored with a penniless show girl (Astor), he persuades her to marry him hoping she will come to love him. Much to his dismay, she runs away with her womanizing ex-lover (Cortez). The multi-millionaire husband vows revenge.

REVIEWS:
Kansas City Star: "*White Shoulders* will hold your attention from the first reel to the last . . . Ricardo Cortez is all that could be asked for as the ladies' man who finally acquires one woman too many for him."

Variety: "One of the most elementary and episodic program pictures of the season, White Shoulders will fail to convince any lower degree of mentality."

PRODUCTION NOTES, INTERESTING FACTS, AND TRIVIA:

1. Originally titled, *Disillusioned*, the movie was adapted from a short story, *Recoil*, by Rex Beach, published in *Cosmopolitan* in November, 1922. A March, 1931 *The Film Daily* item notes that director Howard Estabrook "meticulously scanned and tightened" Beach's story prior to filming *White Shoulders*.

2. The Beach story was filmed previously in 1924 as *The Recoil* starring Mahlon Hamilton and Betty Blythe as stars.

3. RKO borrowed the services of Jack Holt from Columbia for this film.

4. *White Shoulders* was the first RKO picture Cortez completed for his home studio under his new contract.

5. When director Melville Brown took the company of actors to Santa Barbara for location shooting, he enlisted five of the city's wealthiest inhabitants to appear as extras in the picture, including Mrs. C. Ogden Armour (of the famed Chicago Armour family), Mike Dowley, vice president of J. L. Hudson Company, and A. Lincoln Filene, noted Boston merchant. They were each paid $1 for their work, and checks were mailed to each as a souvenir of their appearance.

6. A *The Film Daily* item noted Evelyn Brent was originally slated for the role played by Mary Astor.

7. Another item in *The Film Daily* stated Madame Iso Auabuki, the female tennis champion of Japan, visited the set of *White Shoulders* during production, and lunched with the cast.

8. According to an *Associated Press* report, during the filming of an important love scene between by Ricardo Cortez and Mary

Astor in *White Shoulders*, a house fly buzzed around and lit on Miss Astor's nose, which ruined hundreds of feet of film, forcing director Melville Brown to do a costly retake. Brown told the reporter he was not amused.

"There was nothing unusual about that scene. Some of the best shots and sequences ever made were spoiled by a fly. It happens every day at every studio. One can't just cut that part in which the fly decides to park on a lens or a nose. The whole thing has to be redone because a fly never lights except at the climax."

THE MALTESE FALCON (1931) (MELODRAMA)
WARNER BROTHERS
DIRECTOR: Roy Del Ruth
SCREENPLAY: Maude Fulton, Brown Holmes
LENGTH: 80 minutes
STATUS: Exists. (DVD)

CAST: Bebe Daniels (Ruth Wonderly), Ricardo Cortez (Sam Spade), Dudley Digges (Caspar Gutman), Una Merkel (Effie), Robert Elliott (Dundy), Thelma Todd (Iva Archer), Otto Matieson (Joe Cairo), Walter Long (Miles Archer), Dwight Frye (Wilmer), J. Farrell MacDonald (Polhaus), Oscar Apfel (District Attorney), and Agostino Borgato (Captain Jacobi).

SUMMARY: The mad search for a priceless falcon statue sets the stage for greed, thievery, revenge, and murder in this first screen adaptation of Dashiell Hammett's 1930 novel. In the middle of all the malevolence is a suave, indefatigable private eye, Sam Spade (Cortez), who becomes involved when a beautiful, but untrustworthy woman (Daniels) procures his services to locate her sister.

REVIEWS:
Chicago Daily Tribune: "*The Maltese Falcon* is ingeniously directed, excellently acted . . . You will be impressed by Ricardo Cortez's impersonation of a gay, unscrupulous, hardboiled detective . . . A brilliant and slightly pulse quickening characterization, Mr. Cortez!"

Los Angeles Examiner: "A gripping story, full of suspense and drama... Mr. Cortez gives a brilliant performance...."

Motion Picture: "Cortez steals this odd mystery... Bebe Daniels, as the adventuress is eclipsed by the highly colorful personality of Ricardo Cortez, who creates a new cinema character, a graceless but attractive heavy...."

New York Times: "Into the spacious silences and shadows of the *Winter Garden*, the Warners last night dropped a screen interpretation of Dashiell Hammett's 'The Maltese Falcon' that brought back the reassuring hum which is the hallmark of contented audiences... Played with disarming ease and warmth by Ricardo Cortez, the character of Sam Spade is enormously unique and attractive..."

PRODUCTION NOTES, INTERESTING FACTS, AND TRIVIA:

1. Based on the 1930 novel, *The Maltese Falcon*, by Dashiell Hammett. According to James Robert Parish and Michael Pitts in their book, *The Great Gangster Films*, both Hammett, and scenarist Lucian Hubbard made uncredited contributions to the script.

2. *The Film Daily* also noted some scenes which involved Cortez (but not Daniels) that were filmed on location in San Francisco.

3. A memo dated January 16, 1931, from Colonel Joy of the Studio Relations Committee to producer Darryl Zanuck, (found in *The Maltese Falcon* files at the A.M.P.A.S library) noted potential problems with the script from the standpoint of censors, including the famed strip scene, its depiction of Miss Wonderly in the bathtub, its suggestion that Spade and Wonderly slept together, and excessive drinking. In three later notes, Joy made specific complaints regarding the bathtub and strip scenes, and objected to the depiction of two $100 bills.

4. Also in the A.M.P.A.S Library files is a June 9, 1931 memo from Will Hays to Zanuck strenuously complaining about the

aforementioned sequences remaining in the picture after its release. Hays warned the studio it must start complying with the wishes of the censors "for the future development and the security of the system which has been put into effect by the producers in Hollywood." Warner Bros. ignored Hays. It is important to note that although the censors lost the battle on this picture, eventually they won the war. When the film was remade in 1941, the "strip scene" was not in the new version.

5. According to contracts found in the RKO Archives at U.C.L.A, in contrast to Miss Daniels who received star billing and a salary of $10,000 a week, Cortez was paid only $1250 a week. His employer, RKO, received a bonus of $3,750 for loaning his services. Separate records at the Warner Bros. Archive at the University of Southern California indicate Cortez earned a total of $9,375 for 7 ½ weeks work on the picture, in contrast to Miss Daniels who made $40,000.

6. An *Oakland Tribune* article noted Daniels' filmed her bathtub scene in a specially constructed bathroom set boxed off from prying eyes. The "monitor room," a glass cage occupied by a sound expert, was moved back about 50 feet from the set for the special scene. After the bathtub was filled by a property man, and suds added, a bathrobe clad Daniels emerged from behind the walled-in set with her maid. When Daniels was safely seated in the tub, the maid departed and the star announced she was ready to film. Out of sight from around a corner, director Del Ruth clicked a handheld gadget to signal "Action!" Cortez was seated in a chair out of view of the camera. Del Ruth required the scene be filmed twice. After he was satisfied, the maid returned with towels and bathrobe, and Miss Daniels returned to her dressing room.

7. *The Film Daily* reported actor Hale Hamilton was originally slated for the role of Dundy, but was replaced just prior to production by Robert Elliott.

8. When the film was released to television, it was retitled *Dangerous Female*.

BIG BUSINESS GIRL (1931) (DRAMA)
FIRST NATIONAL PICTURES (WARNER BROTHERS)
DIRECTOR: William A. Seitter
SCREENPLAY: Robert Lord (adaptation)
LENGTH: 79 minutes
STATUS: Exists. (DVD)

CAST: Loretta Young (Claire "Mac" McIntire), Frank Albertson (Johnny Saunders), Ricardo Cortez (Robert J. Clayton), Joan Blondell (Pearl), Frank Darien (Luke Winters), Dorothy Christy (Mrs. Emery), Oscar Apfel (Walter Morley), Nancy Dover (Sarah Ellen), Mickey Bennett (Joe), and Virginia Sale (Sally Curtis).

SUMMARY: An ambitious young, married woman (Young), temporarily casts her young boyfriend (Albertson) aside to pursue a career in a New York ad agency where she is pursued by her lecherous boss (Cortez).

REVIEWS:
Motion Picture: "A secret marriage revealed halfway through the picture makes a lot of rather naughty lines and undressing scenes perfectly proper in this blithe comedy of young love and office intrigue, directed by that sterling comedy director, William Seiter . . . Ricardo Cortez is excellent as the seasoned business philanderer and shows a comedy sense which increases the wonder that this really capable actor has not been given more chances on the screen . . . ."

Variety: "A fair programmer, but ranking as a lightweight for the big time . . . Cast neatly balanced with Loretta Young and Ricardo Cortez as the only two names who meaning anything. Cortez takes the playing cake. His work as the boss is very capable and well delivered . . ."

PRODUCTION NOTES, INTERESTING FACTS, AND TRIVIA:
1. Based on the story, *Big Business Girl*, by Patricia Reilly and H. N. Swanson, published in *College Humor* in 1930.

2. The picture was filmed at Warner Bros. studio in Burbank, CA, with exteriors lensed at the Glendale Amtrak Station.

3. Director William A. Seiter (1890-1964) was a former artist, scriptwriter, and bit player before graduating to film direction in 1918. A prolific, versatile, if sometimes rigid craftsman, Seiter helmed a wide variety of mostly minor motion pictures in a career spanning over 30 years. Among his best known vehicles were the all-star anthology *If I Had A Million* (1932), Laurel and Hardy's *Sons of the Desert* (1933), the Astaire, Rogers, Dunne musical, *Roberta* (1935), *The Little Princess* (1939) with Shirley Temple, and *You Were Never Lovelier* (1942), starring Rita Hayworth. Cortez worked with Seiter twice: *Big Business Girl* (1931) and *Is My Face Red?* (1932).

4. Cortez was working on *Big Business Girl* when he received news of the serious illness and death of his estranged wife, Alma Rubens, in January, 1931.

5. A contract dated December 24, 1930 (between RKO and First National productions), kept in Warner Bros. Archives at the University of Southern California, indicates Cortez's services were loaned to Warner Bros. in exchange for his salary of $1,250 a week, and a bonus to RKO of $3,750. Another document stated he was paid a total of $8,750 for his work on the picture.

Transgression (1931) (Drama)
RKO Radio Pictures
Producer: William LeBaron
Director: Herbert Brenon
Screenplay: Elizabeth Meehan (adaptation), Benn Levy (additional dialogue)
Length: 70 minutes
Status: Exists

Cast: Kay Francis (Elsie Maury), Paul Cavanaugh (Robert Maury), Ricardo Cortez (Don Arturo de Borgus), Nance O'Neil (Honora Maury), Doris Lloyd (Paula Vrain), John St. Polis (Serafin), Ruth Weston (Viscountess), and Adrienne d'Ambricourt (Julie).

Summary: Although she loves her neglectful English businessman husband (Cavanaugh), a woman (Francis) runs away with a wealthy playboy (Cortez). While at his Spanish villa, the playboy persuades her to write a letter to her husband asking for a divorce, but he is subsequently killed by a peasant exacting revenge for the seduction of his daughter. After the death of her lover, the neglected wife regrets her infidelity and becomes determined to intercept the letter before it reaches her husband.

Reviews:
The Film Daily: "Highly sophisticated drama with appeal to women. Direction good but story punchless..."

New York Times: "... for the most part an intelligently filmed story, parts of which are directed so admirably that one wonders why some of the weak spots were overlooked... Ricardo Cortez is acceptable as Arturo, but he is too much given to smiling through his part..."

Production notes, interesting facts, and trivia:
1. Based on Kate Jordon's 1921 novel, *The Next Corner*.

2. The working titles of this film were *The Next Corner* and *Around the Corner*.

3. *Transgression* was a remake of the 1924 Paramount melodrama, *The Next Corner*, costarring Dorothy Mackaill, Conway Tearle, Lon Chaney, and Ricardo Cortez (who reprised the villainous role of Don Arturo).

4. Kay Francis was borrowed from Paramount, and Paul Cavanaugh from Fox, to appear in the picture.

5. RKO production records reveal Cortez replaced Don Alvarado in the role of Don Arturo.

6. *Transgression* was the first of four pairings of the handsome Cortez with the glamourous Miss Francis, who worked well together. Cortez's characters were murdered in all four.

RECKLESS LIVING (1931) (CRIME DRAMA)
UNIVERSAL PICTURES CORPORATION
DIRECTOR: Cyril Gardner
SCREENPLAY: Courtenay Terrett (script), Felix Reisenberg (story), Cyril Gardner, Tom Reed (adaptation)
LENGTH: 65 minutes
STATUS: Believed Lost

CAST: Ricardo Cortez (Curly), Mae Clarke (Bee), Norman Foster, (Doggie), Marie Prevost (Alice), Slim Summerville (The drunk), Robert Emmett O'Connor (Ryan), Thomas Jackson (McManus), and Russell Hopton (Kid Regan).

SUMMARY: When an attractive proprietor of a speakeasy (Clarke) and her ne'er do well husband (Foster) experience a severe financial crisis, they are set up in business by a crooked bookmaker (Cortez) who has designs on the wife.

REVIEWS:
Los Angeles Examiner: "Being a "good" bad man all of the time must become rather monotonous for Ricardo Cortez. He's at it again in *Reckless Living* . . . While his performance is just as good as ever, he is not quite so sympathetic in his villainies as in other pictures . . ."

New York Times: "Played expertly and with some degree of truth by Ricardo Cortez, Mae Clarke, and Norman Foster, it makes fair enough entertainment that is revealing its atmosphere and meager in its story."

PRODUCTION NOTES, INTERESTING FACTS, AND TRIVIA:
1. Based on the 1930 play, *The Up and Up*, by Eva Kay Flint and Martha Madison.

2. Working titles for the film included, *The Up and Up* and *Twenty Grand*.

3. Press reports indicated Tod Browning was originally slated to direct.

4. *The Film Daily* reported Ricardo Cortez was loaned to Universal to portray the criminal, Curly, in *Reckless Living*, when Pat O'Brien withdrew from the project. Universal had insisted O'Brien sign a five-year contract in order to have the part. He refused.

5. Cortez's costar Norman Foster would become a lifelong friend. Both eventually would become movie directors at 20th Century Fox. Foster directed two of Cortez's later films: *Mr. Moto's Last Warning* and *Charlie Chan in Reno*, both produced in 1939.

6. During the mid 1930's Cortez, and his buddy, producer Charles Rogers were joint investors attempting to buy Universal Pictures. The deal fell apart.

BAD COMPANY (1931) (CRIME DRAMA)
RKO PATHE PICTURES
PRODUCER: Charles R. Rogers
DIRECTOR: Tay Garnett
SCREENPLAY: Tom Buckingham, Tay Garnett (screenplay, dialogue).
LENGTH: 65 minutes.
STATUS: Exists

CAST: Helen Twelvetrees (Helen King), Ricardo Cortez (Goldie Gorio), John Garrick (Steve Carlyle), Paul Hurst (Butler), Frank Conroy (Markham King), Harry Carey (McBaine), Frank McHugh (Doc), Kenneth Thomson (Barnes), Arthur Stone (Dummy), Emma Dunn (Emma), William V. Mong (Henry), Edgar Kennedy (Buffington), Wade Boteler (Monk), Al Herman (Pearson), Robert Keith (Prof), and Mike Donlin (Gladden James).

SUMMARY: A woman (Twelvetrees) has no idea both her husband-to-be (Garrick) and brother are involved in crime. Her fiancé works for a mentally unstable gangster named Goldie Gorio (Cortez), and her brother (Frank Conroy) is the head of a rival gang.

REVIEWS:
Los Angeles Evening Express: "If it hadn't been for Ricardo Cortez as the temperamental gang leader, Goldie Gorio, the film might have been a rather sad affair. Mr. Cortez is one of the screen's best menaces and he proves it by making something of a character which would undoubtedly have been laughingly absurd without his usual finesse . . ."

Los Angeles Examiner: "*Bad Company* doesn't offer Helen Twelvetrees many opportunities for big moments, but it is generous to Ricardo Cortez, who takes full advantage of all. This man is a fine actor . . . ."

New York Times: "One of the stragglers in the beer and murder procession has limped into the Mayfair, dragging in tow a truck-load of machine guns, a girl who has been spared the more brutal facts about life, and a paranoiac gang leader . . . Ricardo Cortez plays his part effectively, carrying his delusions well, making his audience believe that the unintentional humor in his lines and situations was carefully planned . . ."

PRODUCTION NOTES, INTERESTING FACTS, AND TRIVIA:
1. Working titles for the film were: *Mad Madness, The Gangster's Wife*, and *The Mad Marriage*.

2. According to RKO archival records housed at the Charles E.

Cortez and Helen Twelvetrees in a tense scene from *Bad Company* (RKO, 1931).

Young Library at University of California at Los Angeles, President Will Hayes of the M.P.P.D.A. (Motion Picture Producers and Distributors of America), recommended the gangster activities of the character played by Garrick be downplayed so as not to glorify crime.

3. The bust of Goldie Gorio (Ricardo's maniacal gangster character), prominently featured in the film, was created by Spanish-Filipino artist Charley Gemora, who designed and wore the famed gorilla costume in the film, *Ingagi* (1930).

4. A *Manitowoc Herald* article stated two hundred persons, including major cast members, director Garnett, fifty extras, boat crews, and mechanical crews, were transported from Hollywood to the isthmus at the north neck of Catalina Island to do location shots for *Bad Company*. Many of the scenes were filmed aboard the schooner yacht, *Gloria Dalton*.

5. According to Carlos Clarens and Foster Hirsch in their book,

Crime Movies, *Bad Company* may have been the first picture to feature the famous St. Valentine's Massacre, the gangland slaughter which took place in Chicago on Valentine's Day, February 14, 1929.

MEN OF CHANCE (1931) (MELODRAMA)
RKO RADIO PICTURES
PRODUCER: William LeBaron
DIRECTOR: George Archainbaud
SCREENPLAY: Louis Weitzenkorn (script), Louis Stevens (adaptation, dialogue)
LENGTH: 67 minutes
STATUS: Exists

CAST: Ricardo Cortez (Diamond Johnny Silk), Mary Astor (Martha Preston Silk), John Halliday (Richard Dorval), Ralph Ince (Joe Farley), Kitty Kelly (Gertie), James Donlan (Clocker), and George Davis (Provencial Frenchman).

SUMMARY: In Paris, a poor young woman (Astor) is saved from a jail term by a crooked gambler (Halliday) in an attempt to best his rival (Cortez).

REVIEWS:
Los Angeles Examiner: "A good, fast moving race track story... Ricardo Cortez gives one of his best performances to date, as the flashy, cocksure race track habitue. These strong, men-of-action roles are exactly right for Cortez, and how he has come up in the last year playing them."

New York Times: "Louis Weitzenkorn has shuffled the ancient and honorable ingredients of race track melodrama into two violent climaxes in *Men of Chance* ... The acting of Mary Astor and Ricardo Cortez in the principal roles is a triumph of mind over some pretty painful dialogue ..."

PRODUCTION NOTES, INTERESTING FACTS, AND TRIVIA:
1. The working title was *Exposed*.

2. The film was shot at the RKO ranch, with location shooting in San Francisco, and at the famed Tanforan racetrack in San Bruno. The racetrack became infamous in 1942 as the site of one of 17 temporary detention camps established by the U. S. Army, to hold Japanese Americans forcibly removed from the West Coast until concentration camps could be built.

3. Like his character "Diamond Johnny" Silk, Ricardo Cortez exhibited a lifelong love of horses and horse racing. During his years in Hollywood, he owned several horses. On his days off he could often be found riding, competing in polo matches, or "playing the ponies" at the Hollywood Park or Santa Anita racetracks.

4. *Men of Chance* scriptwriter, Louis Weitzenkorn (1893-1943), was a Pennsylvania-born news reporter turned playwright who penned the critically acclaimed, *Five Star Final*, which was produced on Broadway before being transformed into an acclaimed motion picture. After writing several other moderately successful plays, Weitzenkorn turned his attention to Hollywood, where he won acclaim for his adaptation of *Ann Vickers*. He died tragically in a fire at his home.

5. According to *The Film Daily*, Count Allan de la Falaise, brother of director Henry de la Falaise, was hired as a technical advisor on the picture.

NO ONE MAN (1932) (DRAMA)
PARAMOUNT PUBLIX CORPORATION
DIRECTOR: Lloyd Corrigan
SCREENPLAY: Sidney Buchman, Agnew Brand Leahy (script), Percy Heath (adaptation)
LENGTH: 73 minutes
STATUS: Exists

CAST: Carole Lombard (Penelope "Nep" Newbold), Ricardo Cortez (Bill Hanaway), Paul Lukas (Dr. Karl Bemis), Juliette Compton (Sue Folsom), George Barbier (Alfred Newbold), Virginia

Hammond (Mrs. Newbold), Arthur Pierson (Stanley Mellvaine), Frances Moffett (Delia), and Irving Bacon (License clerk).

SUMMARY: A beautiful but irresponsible young society woman (Lombard) rejects the professed love of a dedicated Viennese physician (Lukas), and marries a wealthy philanderer (Cortez). The marriage turns out badly, but her cheating husband has a heart condition. His convenient death paves the way for a reunion with the doctor.

REVIEWS:
Chicago Daily Tribune: "Sleazy yarn at best. Rupert Hughes wrote it. Carole Lombard, looking extraordinarily beautiful as she sashays about Palm Beach wearing clothes that fairly take your breath away, gives a sympathetic portrayal of a teeter-totter minded daughter of the rich. Ricardo Cortez is quite likeable as the sexy and domineering playboy to whom she is most powerfully drawn for a while . . ."

PRODUCTION NOTES, INTERESTING FACTS, AND TRIVIA:
1. Based on a Rupert Hughes magazine serial.

2. Cortez and Miss Lombard initiated a friendship during the making of this picture, which lasted until Carole's tragic death in 1942.

SYMPHONY OF SIX MILLION (1932) (DRAMA)
RKO RADIO PICTURES
PRODUCER: Pandro S. Berman
DIRECTOR: Gregory La Cava
SCREENPLAY: Bernard Schubert, J. Walter Ruben (script, dialogue), Fannie Hurst (story), James Seymour (additional dialogue).
LENGTH: 85 minutes.
STATUS: Exists. (DVD)

CAST: Ricardo Cortez (Dr. Felix Klauber), Irene Dunne (Jessica), Anna Appel (Hannah Klauber), Gregory Ratoff (Meyer Klauber),

Lita Chevret (Birdie Klauber), Noel Madison (Magnus Klauber), Helen Freeman (Miss Spencer), John St. Polis (Dr. Schiffen), Julie Haydon (Miss Grey), and Lester Lee (Felix as a boy).

SUMMARY: A poor but ambitious Jewish boy (Lester Lee) grows up to become a successful surgeon (Cortez), but in the process of attaining success, he loses track of his roots, his ideals, and neglects those he loves.

REVIEWS:
The Film Daily: " Strong human interest story highlighted by exceptional performances . . . Ricardo Cortez, as the doctor, gives the best performance of his career . . ."

Illustrated Daily News: " A beautiful, dignified, yet compelling picture . . . Unforgettable portrayals are offered by Ricardo Cortez and Gregory Ratoff. . ."

Los Angeles Record: "Symphony of Six Million contains all the elements of a genuine audience picture—humanness, drama, comedy, and romance. . . Ricardo Cortez delivers a grand performance."

PRODUCTION NOTES, INTERESTING FACTS, AND TRIVIA:
1. *Symphony of Six Million* was based on the story *Night Bell*, written expressly for the screen by novelist Fannie Hurst.

2. A *New York Times* article chronicled the preparations to make *Symphony*. In an effort to enhance the authenticity of the big city scenes, RKO sent former director and writer Lynn Shores to New York to photograph life in the metropolis. He came back to Hollywood with several reels, which featured Fifth Avenue and various congested arteries of the city. He also located and engaged the services of Anna Appel of the Yiddish Art Theater, and noted Moscow Art Theater actor Gregory Ratoff, to play the elder Klaubers in the picture. Producer Pandro Berman (assistant to studio head, David O. Selznick), had initially sought actor Maurice Moskovitch to play the father. Moskovitch was

the father of *Symphony* cast member Noel Madison.

3. *Symphony* marked the film acting debut of noted Russian born actor, producer, director, Gregory Ratoff (1897-1960), who had appeared on Broadway prior to his entry in films during the early 1930's. In 1936, Ratoff began directing and producing Hollywood motion pictures. Among his directorial credits were *Rose of Washington Square* (1939), (*Intermezzo—A Love Story* (1939), *Adam Had Four Sons* (1941), *The Corsican Brothers* (1941), and *Carnival in Costa Rica* (1947).

4. RKO records indicate much of the dialogue written for the film was cast aside by Selznick and director La Cava just prior to production. When producer Pandro Berman became concerned, Selznick reportedly told him to "forget about the dialogue. I can always spit that out at the last minute."

5. In a May, 1932 interview published in *Hollywood Citizen News*, director Gregory La Cava described several details of the production of the film. He said whenever possible he employed non-professionals players to achieve "the realism so important to the picture." Included were blind children who populated the school run by Jessica, as well as registered nurses, orderlies, anesthetists, and internes who assisted Cortez in the tense, operation scenes.

6. According to *The Film Daily*, in another effort to achieve authenticity, RKO hired Dr. Marcus Rabin as a technical advisor.

7. RKO archival records (U.C.L.A.) listed the budget for *Symphony* as $267,797. For 7+ weeks of work on the picture at $1500 a week, Ricardo was paid $11,750.

8. *Hollywood Citizen News* reported RKO executives, including David O. Selznick, were so pleased by director La Cava's handling of the picture, they offered him a brand new contract before it was released.

9. In marked contrast to many of the early sound era films Cortez appeared in, censors were quite pleased with the final script of *Symphony*. Among A.M.P.A.S. Library records for the picture, is a note dated January 14, 1932, from Colonel Joy of the Studio Relations Committee, who called the picture "splendid," noting only a few "oversights" which included the use of wine at a dinner, and one of the characters saying "For God's sake." After the film was released, RKO studio records indicate some Ohio censors did object to some of the operating scenes, which they termed "too realistic." Director La Cava insisted the film be left intact, and nothing was altered.

10. The *Variety* review of *Symphony* suggested the film was one of only a few to feature a Reform Rabbi.

11. According to a *Los Angeles Examiner* article, Ricardo Cortez was very superstitious. He bought a felt hat from a young man he met on the street just prior to filming *Symphony of Six Million*. When the movie turned out to be a success, Cortez considered the hat a lucky charm.

12. *Motion Picture* magazine reported, after the release of this picture, Ricardo Cortez celebrated his excellent reviews by buying a new horse.

13. Ricardo Cortez and Irene Dunne initiated a lifelong friendship on the set of *Symphony of Six Million*. In 1934, Miss Dunne expressed her admiration for Cortez and recalled an anecdote during the making of the picture.

"The scenes were in a blind school. I was the teacher and Ric was the doctor who came to call on the pupils. Real blind children were brought to the studio to work in this picture. We were asked not to pity them as they were perfectly happy. Still, it was heartbreaking to see their misfortune. The second day on the picture, one little boy went up to Ric and told him how well he looked. I'll never forget that look of his. I know he suffered agony working with those children. I could read pity all over his face, yet to everyone else, he seemed unfeeling and indifferent."

"RESTING — An off-stage portrait of Ricardo Cortez, taken as he was resting between scenes in RKO-Radio Pictures' *Symphony of Six Million* (1932)." The preceding caption was found on the reverse of this original still photo by photographer Fred Hendrickson.

Is My Face Red? (1932) (DRAMA)
RKO RADIO PICTURES
PRODUCER: David O. Selznick
DIRECTOR: William A. Seiter
SCREENPLAY: Casey Robinson, Ben Markson (script), Bartlett Cormack (dialogue).
LENGTH: 67 minutes
STATUS: Exists. (DVD)

CAST: Helen Twelvetrees (Peggy Bannon), Ricardo Cortez (William "Bill" Poster), Jill Esmond (Mildred Huntington), Robert Armstrong (Ed Maloney), Arline Judge (Bee), ZaSu Pitts (Telephone Operator), Sidney Toler (Tony Mugatti), Clarence Muse (Horatio), and Fletcher Norton (Angelo Spinetti).

SUMMARY: An aggressive and conceited gossip columnist (Cortez) pursues juicy stories for his column above honor, friendship, and his romantic relationship with a Broadway actress (Twelvetrees). This eventually lands him in hot water with his girl, and in considerable physical danger.

REVIEWS:
Chicago Daily Tribune: " . . . good entertainment . . . Mr. Cortez, who is proving to have quite remarkable versatility in the way of character drawing, depicts William Poster with humor and a nice feel for effect . . ."

Illustrated Daily News: "Ben Markson and Allen Rivken are authors of this lively, devil-may-care picture, which moves with a nerve and a snap . . . Again, the versatility of Ricardo Cortez is demonstrated in *Is My Face Red?* . . . Cortez makes his characterization the dashing, fascinating figure it is supposed to be . . .

New York Times: "It is a shrewd, witty, and scathing portrait, and Mr. Cortez plays the part to the hilt."

Variety: "*Is My Face Red?* is an entertaining picture that has the grace of not getting too serious in denouncing the press in general, or columnists in particular . . . Cortez, who is a long way from looking like any newspaperman outside a journalism school, succeeds in making the keyholer quite believable as the picture unreels. It's a cracking acting job by Cortez, and following 'Symphony' brings the actor front and center again . . . Right now he's proving himself a better performer than anyone previously imagined."

PRODUCTION NOTES, INTERESTING FACTS, AND TRIVIA:

1. *Is My Face Red* was filmed on RKO's Gower Street Studios.

2. In the original Markson/Robinson script, the brash, self-possessed William Poster's egotism and pursuit of a scoop gets him killed. When preview audiences reacted unfavorably, the unhappy ending was dropped, and a new one filmed.

3. Ricardo made four of his most memorable films: *Symphony of Six Million*, *Is My Face Red?*, *Thirteen Women*, and *The Phantom of Crestwood*, under the brief but notable tenure of David O. Selznick (1931-32) as head of production at RKO. Unhappy with the RCA leadership, who insisted he clear all decisions with them, Selznick resigned his position at RKO in December, 1932, and went to work for his father in-law, Louis B. Mayer, at MGM, who gave him his own production unit. By then Cortez had also moved on.

4. Screenwriter, director, and producer Casey Robinson (1903-79) was borrowed from Paramount to write the film's screenplay. A former English and journalism teacher, during the late 1920's, Robinson began penning titles for motion pictures including Korda's *The Private Life of Helen of Troy* (1927) starring Cortez. After trying his hand at directing, Robinson eventually settled into writing scripts. *Is My Face Red?* was one of his first major assignments as a scenarist. By the late 1930's, he had established a reputation as a top notch film writer whose credits included such well regarded motion pictures as *Captain Blood* (1935) (for which he was a write-in candidate for an Oscar), *The Old Maid* (1939), *Dark Victory* (1939), *Kings Row* (1942), *Now*

Voyager (1942), and *Days of Glory* (1944). Although he did his most prominent work at Warner Bros., he later moved to MGM and 20th Century Fox.

5. A memo dated April 4, 1932, (found in A.M.P.A.S Library) from Colonel Jason Joy (Studio Relations Committee) to producer, David O. Selznick, outlined some of the potential problems censors had with the script of *Is My Face Red?* Among them was the running gag of filling the water cooler with gin cocktails, various sexually suggestive lines, and its depiction "of a white man having an affair with a mulatto, which will be offensive to race-conscious people."

6. According to A.M.P.A.S. Library files, when the finished picture was screened by Will Hays (president of the Motion Picture Producers and Distributors of America) on June 13, 1932, he voiced dismay over its depiction of Italians. "I don't know how I can go ahead with the Italian Ambassador in the face of these kind of pictures, as we have promised him to try and lighten up on this." The changes he requested were never made.

7. *The Film Daily* reported Ricardo's brother, Stanley Cortez, was the assistant cameraman on *Is My Face Red?*

8. According to *The Film Daily*, for his audition for the role of columnist, William Poster's barber in the film, Austrian born comic actor, Billy Engle (1889-1966), had to give a close shave to an RKO employee.

9. As a result of his work on the acclaimed *Is My Face Red?*, scenarist Ben Markson was assigned to collaborate on Constance Bennett's new film, *What Price Hollywood?*

10. *Motion Picture* magazine reported Cortez was issued a speeding ticket during the filming of the picture. While in traffic court (to pay his fine), Ricardo also paid the fine of a poor Italian man who could not afford it. Several crew members heard of

Among the items in Ricardo Cortez's sound film scrapbook, was this page of rave reviews for *Is My Face Red?* At the bottom is a note from Ricardo's brother, Bernard, which reads as follows: "Dear Ric, You probably have seen this before, but I'm taking a chance you have not. Everybody is well in N.Y., Fondest Regards, Bernie."

the event and cooked up a scheme to play a joke on the actor. They wrote Cortez a phony note of thanks from the man, then a week later, sent the actor another note asking for $100 to pay for the upcoming birth of the man's child. Cortez's reaction was not recorded.

THE PHANTOM OF CRESTWOOD (1932) (MYSTERY)
RKO RADIO PICTURES
PRODUCER: David O. Selznick
DIRECTOR: J. Walter Ruben
SCREENPLAY: Bartlett Cormack (script, story), J. Walter Ruben (story)
LENGTH: 77 minutes
TAGLINE: "Now…The world will know who killed Jenny Wren!"
STATUS: Exists. (DVD)

CAST: Ricardo Cortez (Gary Curtis), Karen Morley (Jenny Wren), Anita Louise (Esther Wren), Pauline Frederick (Faith Andes), H. B. Warner (Priam Andes), Mary Duncan (Dorothy Mears), Sam Hardy (Pete Harris), Tom Douglas (Tom Herrick), Richard "Skeets"Gallagher (Eddie Mack), Ivan Simpson (Henry T. Herrick), Aileen Pringle (Mrs. Walcott), George E. Stone (The Cat), Robert McWade (Senator Herbert Walcott), Hilda Vaughn (Carter), and Gavin Gordon (William Jones).

SUMMARY: A blackmailer (Morley) summons all her former lovers to a large mansion where she plans to exact large sums of money from them to keep quiet regarding their relationships. When she is murdered, a former criminal who has been following her to retrieve letters for a client (Cortez), becomes determined to solve the complex case so he will not be charged with the crime.

REVIEWS:

Los Angeles Examiner: "If you like nice, hair-raising mystery stories with plenty of good bloodcurdling murders, and a white-faced spook thrown in, you'll like Phantom of Crestwood . . ."

Variety: "Radio's widely advertised mystery story, which has been on the air in connection with a prize contest, has been given a handsome production, offers a plot with ample motivation, carefully avoids clutching hands, and enlists the services of an exceptional cast."

PRODUCTION NOTES, INTERESTING FACTS, AND TRIVIA:

1. A prologue was inserted in the film originally, which identified the contest. It was later dropped.

2. Karen Morley was borrowed from MGM for *The Phantom of Crestwood*.

3. The picture was a big hit at the box office, netting RKO a much needed profit. Total box office receipts were in excess of $400,000. Production costs totaled $187,000.

4. *Phantom* marked the return of veteran stage and film actress Pauline Frederick (1883-1938) to the screen after a two year absence.

5. *The Phantom of Crestwood*'s director/co-scriptwriter J. Walter Ruben (1899-1942), was originally an actor and publicist prior to becoming a distributor for MGM during the mid-1920's. He graduated to screenwriting in 1927, then signed a contract to direct at RKO in 1931. He later returned to MGM where he directed such films as *Riff Raff* (1936) and *Bad Man of Brimstone* (1937), before becoming a producer, notably overseeing several Wallace Beery vehicles. He died of a heart ailment complicated by an infection at age 43. His widow was actress Virginia Bruce.

6. *The Film Daily* reported director J. Walter Ruben worked his cast in the evening whenever possible, in order to get them in the proper mood to play their parts in the murder mystery. In addition, Ruben opted to film on a stage which required actors to walk through the deserted studio after nightfall.

7. Comic actor Sam Hardy (1883-1935), who played a robber in *The Phantom of Crestwood*, made over 85 films between 1915-35. In addition to his movie appearances, he co-wrote the script for his friend W. C. Field's movie, *The Man on the Flying Trapeze* (1935). According to a *Hollywood In Person* column by Mollie Merrick, he always carried matches with the inscription, "Sam Hardy, America's Sweetheart" on the folders, and would

announce his first appearance on the set of any movie by stating "Director, I'm glad I'm here to save the picture." Mr. Hardy died of complications from emergency abdominal surgery performed after he collapsed on the set of the Eddie Cantor vehicle *Strike Me Pink* (1936). He was replaced by William Frawley.

THIRTEEN WOMEN (1932) (MELODRAMA)
RKO RADIO PICTURES
PRODUCER: David O. Selznick
DIRECTOR: George Archainbaud
SCREENPLAY: Bartlett Cormack, Samuel Ornitz
LENGTH: 74 minutes
STATUS: Exists. (DVD)

CAST: Irene Dunne (Laura Stanhope), Ricardo Cortez (Sergeant Clive), Jill Esmond (Jo), Myrna Loy (Ursula Georgi), Mary Duncan (June Raskob), Kay Johnson (Helen Frye), Florence Eldridge (Grace Coombs), C. Henry Gordon (Swami Yogadachi), Peg Entwistle (Hazel Cousins), Harriet Hagman (May Raskob), Edward Pawley (Burns), Blanche Frederici (Teacher), Wally Albright (Bobby Stanhope), Julie Haydon (Mary), and Marjorie Gateson (Martha).

SUMMARY: A mentally disturbed Eurasian woman (Loy) murders members of an exclusive sorority after she is rejected for membership. A dedicated police detective (Cortez) is brought in to solve the case.

REVIEWS:
Conference of Catholic Bishops: "Half-baked hokum . . . Stylized violence and Asian stereotyping."

New York Times: "It is horror without laughter; horror that is too awful to be modish and too stark to save itself from a headlong plunge into hokum . . . Ricardo Cortez, as the shrewd detective who is assigned to clear up the incomprehensible chain of deaths, gives an intelligent performance . . ."

PRODUCTION NOTES, INTERESTING FACTS, AND TRIVIA:
1. Several sources indicate producer Selznick delayed the release of this picture to capitalize on the expected publicity generated by the release of Irene Dunne's follow-up picture, *Back Street.*

2. Zita Johann was originally slated to play the villain, but was replaced by Myrna Loy just prior to production.

3. The script was revised several times just before, and during production on the picture, deemphasizing the roles of 3 of the 13 women. Only 10 were actually featured in the final film.

4. According to author Margie Schultz in her book, *Irene Dunne: A Bio-Bibliography*, "The producer of *Thirteen Women* hired an astrologer to make up charts for the stars of the film since the plot involved astrology." Dunne, a devout Catholic, reportedly bet the other cast members none of the charts would come true, and the women agreed to meet in five years to check. It is not known if they ever did.

5. *The Film Daily* reported over a dozen famous circus acts were employed for the circus scenes.

6. In a June 9, 1932 memo from Colonel Jason Joy (S.R.C.) to David O. Selznick (found in the *Thirteen Women* file in A.M.P.A.S. Library), Joy expressed concern about a scene between two women early in the picture, which he said could be interpreted by some as a reference to lesbianism. It was removed.

7. Ricardo Cortez first became friends with Irene Dunne on the set of *Symphony of Six Million*. They remained friends throughout their lives. Cortez so admired Irene, he penned a tribute article to her published in several newspapers and magazines in February, 1933, entitled, "The Story of Irene Dunne."

FLESH (1932) (DRAMA)
METRO-GOLDWYN-MAYER CORPORATION
PRODUCER: John Considine
DIRECTOR: John Ford
SCREENPLAY: Edmund Goulding (story), Leonard Praskins, Edgar Allan Woolf (adaptation), Moss Hart (dialogue)
LENGTH: 95 minutes
STATUS: Exists. (DVD)

CAST: Wallace Beery (Polakai), Karen Morley (Laura Nash), Ricardo Cortez (Nicky Grant), Jean Hersholt (Mr. Herman), John Miljan (Joe Willard), Herman Bing (Pepi, Head waiter), Vincent Barnett (Waiter), Greta Meyer (Mrs. Herman), Edward Brophy (Donlan, referee), Ward Bond (Wrestler Muscles Manning), and Nat Pendleton (Wrestler).

SUMMARY: When a dishonest and embittered young American woman (Morley) is released from a German prison, she is befriended by a kindly waiter (Beery) who becomes a champion wrestler. She eventually becomes his wife, but yearns for her ex-lover (Cortez), a scoundrel, who hatches a scheme to take advantage of her husband.

REVIEWS:
Los Angeles Examiner: "*Flesh* may not be the greatest motion picture ever produced, but when it comes to entertainment it comes near topping the 1932 output . . . Ricardo Cortez is even more coldly cruel than the girl. He is what is known in American parlance as a first-class rat. No one plays a rotter with more conviction than Mr. Cortez . . ."

Variety: "That it takes 95 minutes to get home is *Flesh*'s big fault. Quicker pace in and plot development might have meant another smash for Beery. This way it has a handicap to hurdle. That it makes the grade is due to three excellent lead performances and some natural plot strength that wasn't put into full play . . . Doing a perfect job of a 100% unsympathetic character, is Ricardo Cortez . . ."

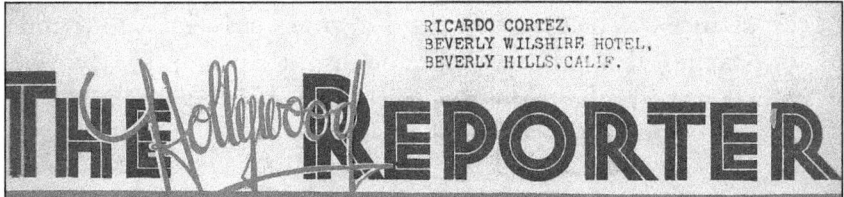

This front page from *The Hollywood Reporter* dated August 31, 1932, noting Cortez's amicable departure from RKO, was found in Ricardo's sound film scrapbook. Note the copy of the newspaper is addressed to: "Ricardo Cortez, Wiltshire Hotel."

PRODUCTION NOTES, INTERESTING FACTS, AND TRIVIA:
1. Archival records (A.M.P.A.S. Library) indicate production on the picture was delayed by several disputes between MGM and scriptwriter, Leonard Praskins. The disputes prompted MGM to hire several other scenarists, including William Faulkner and Moss Hart (who supplied dialogue).

2. A *New York Times* item stated that during the filming of *Flesh*, Cortez began negotiations with Paramount Pictures to return to his old home studio.

3. A *Syracuse Herald* article indicated MGM employed a crew of 20 noted wrestlers, fighters, weight lifters, football players, and others for the wrestling and gym scenes in *Flesh*. The most prominent was Wladak Zbysko, former World Heavyweight wrestling champion. Others included, "Wild Bill" Betts, future actor Nat Pendleton, and Jack Dempsey's former sparring partners, Jack Herrick and Larry Williams. According to a short *Variety* item, director Ford ordered 281 extras as prizefight spectators for a scene in *Flesh*.

4. Some of the early scenes in *Flesh* are set in Germany. According to a *Laredo Times* article, in order to avoid variations in accents, all members of the cast were given German dialogue drills by a technical expert during camera rehearsals.

BROADWAY BAD (1933) (DRAMA)
FOX FILM CORPORATION
DIRECTOR: Sidney Lanfield
SCREENPLAY: Arthur Kober, Maude Fulton (script), William R. Lipman, A.W. Pezet (story), William Conselman (revisions, additional dialogue)
LENGTH: 61 minutes
TAGLINE: "She was afraid Broadway would call her bluff!"
STATUS: Exists

CAST: Joan Blondell (Tony Landers), Ricardo Cortez (Craig Cutting), Ginger Rogers (Flip Daly), Adrienne Ames (Aileen), Allen Vincent

(Bob North), Francis McDonald (Charley "Tommy" Davis), Frederick Burton (Robert North Sr.), Ronald Cosbey (Big Fella), Donald Crisp (Darrall), Phil Tead (Joe Flynn), Spencer Charters (Lew Gordon), Margaret Seddon (Bixby), Victor Jory (Stone), and Eddie Kane (Eddie Berger).

SUMMARY: When her marriage falls apart due to her husband's jealousy, a chorus girl (Blondell) feels she must lie in order to retain custody of her beloved young son. She keeps the boy, but loses her reputation in the process.

REVIEWS:
Variety: "Nothing outstanding in this repetition of the undeserved reputation, but it's a well-made picture with some snappy backstage stuff for the men and the mother-love appeal for the women . . . Practically all of the acting falls to Joan Blondell and Ricardo Cortez both coming through with strong contributions."

PRODUCTION NOTES, INTERESTING FACTS, AND TRIVIA:
1. According to a *Hollywood Citizen News* item, Hamilton McFadden was originally slated to direct *Broadway Bad*, with Joan Bennett and John Boles to star.

2. Some scenes were shot at the Yale University football stadium.

3. Leading lady Blondell married the film's cameraman, George Barnes, in 1933.

MIDNIGHT MARY (1933) (DRAMA)
METRO-GOLDWYN-MAYER CORPORATION
DIRECTOR: William Wellman
SCREENPLAY: Gene Markey, Kathryn Scola (script), Anita Loos (original story)
LENGTH: 75 minutes
TAGLINE: "Her beauty a lure that men could not resist!"
STATUS: Exists. (DVD)

CAST: Loretta Young (Mary Martin), Ricardo Cortez (Leo Darcy),

Franchot Tone (Tom Mannerling Jr.), Andy Devine (Sam Travers), Una Merkel (Bunny), Frank Conroy (District Attorney), Warren Hymer (Angelo), Ivan Simpson (Tindle), Harold Huber (Puggy), Sandy Roth (Blimp), Martha Sleeper (Barbara Mannering), Charles Grapewin (Clerk), Halliwell Hobbes (Churchill), and Robert Emmett O'Connor (Cop).

SUMMARY: As she awaits the jury's verdict in her trial for murdering her longtime lover, in flashbacks, a young woman (Young) recalls her troubled past and how she reached this low point. Falsely accused of theft while only a girl, she fell in with thieves and became the mistress of a crime boss (Cortez). She tried to go straight thanks to the love of an earnest young attorney (Tone), but murders her gangster lover in order to save the attorney's life.

REVIEWS:
The Film Daily: "Well produced and directed drama-romance with fine cast and fair appeal."

Los Angeles Examiner: "Anita Loos' original story, William Wellman's direction, spirited performances by a sterling cast, and intelligent production by Cosmopolitan, combine to produce one of the year's best films . . . Credit Loretta Young with lifting this from the rank and file . . . Tone is charming, gracious, and restrained, and Ricardo Cortez offers fine contrast to Tone in a colorful menace role . . ."

PRODUCTION NOTES, INTERESTING FACTS, AND TRIVIA:
1. The original treatment by writer Anita Loos was titled *Nora, Girl Delinquent*, and based on stories written by a gang moll and her informant.

2. Working titles included, *Midnight Lady* and *Lady of the Night*. The latter was eventually rejected when the Hays office objected, calling the title obscene.

3. *Midnight Mary* was originally conceived as a vehicle for Jean Harlow and Clark Gable, but both rejected the project.

4. According to an *International Photographer* article, Wellman had worked with cameraman, James Van Trees (1890-1973), on several films and had enormous confidence in his ability. Although on a vacation, and resting on his ranch in the Santa Ynez Mountains, just prior to production on *Midnight Mary*, Wellman persuaded Van Trees to leave the ranch and work on the picture.

5. During and after the filming of *Midnight Mary*, it was widely reported Ricardo Cortez dated Loretta Young. In an interview conducted by author Edward Funk for his book, *Eavesdropping*, Miss Young denied she ever dated Cortez. She told Funk, "Ricardo Cortez was perfectly cast; He's tough, he's mean. He didn't have to act mean. He was!"

TORCH SINGER (1933) (DRAMA)
PARAMOUNT PICTURES

PRODUCER:	Albert Lewis
DIRECTOR:	Alexander Hall
SCREENPLAY:	Lenore Coffee, Lynn Starling
LENGTH:	72 minutes
TAGLINE:	"Give a man a break…and he'll break your heart!"
STATUS:	Exists. (DVD)

CAST: Claudette Colbert (Sally Trent), Ricardo Cortez (Tony Cummings), David Manners (Michael Gardner), Lyda Roberti (Dora Nichols), Baby LeRoy (Dora's baby), Charley Grapewin (Judson), Sam Godfrey (Announcer), Florence Roberts (Mother Angelica), Virginia Hammond (Mrs. Judson), Cora Sue Collins (Sally at five years old), Mildred Washington (Carrie), Helen Jerome Eddy (Miss Spaulding), Albert Conti (Carlotti), and Ethel Griffies (Agatha Alden).

SUMMARY: A poor chorine (Colbert) gives birth to an illegitimate baby girl, but must give her up when she is unable to provide for the child. Later, she becomes a famed New York night club singer and the host of a beloved children's radio show. After her success as a host, she sets out to find her long lost child.

REVIEWS:

Chicago Daily Tribune: "If *Torch Singer* doesn't make exhibitors patty cake with glee—I miss my guess . . . Miss Colbert gives a highly intelligent performance and is appealing in all the modes and tenses demanded of her role . . . Ricardo Cortez is a peach as the mainstay of Mimi Benton. You're not human if you don't hate to see him step out of the picture for David Manners . . ."

Hollywood Citizen News: "With Miss Colbert laboring under the handicap of a thoroughly hokum's role, most of the good acting is done by Ricardo Cortez, who moves smoothly through the picture as the singer's friendly radio manager."

PRODUCTION NOTES, INTERESTING FACTS, AND TRIVIA:

1. Based on the short story, *Mike*, penned by Grace Perkins and first published in *Liberty* magazine.

2. Miss Colbert sang her own songs in *Torch Singer*. She was coached by Bing Crosby, who acted as a technical advisor.

3. One of the supporting players, Polish-born, platinum blonde actress, Lyda Roberti (1906-38), was a former child trapeze artist turned vaudevillian and stage actress. She made her film debut in 1932 and established herself as an up-and-coming screen comedienne. Her promising film career ended abruptly in 1938 when she died suddenly of a heart attack at age 31.

4. Cary Grant relinquished the role of radio manager, Tony Cummings, in *Torch Singer*, to play the young investment banker in *Big Executive*. Ricardo Cortez ended up playing both parts.

5. An item in the *Connellsville Daily Courier*, noted while filming the scene at the orphanage, director Alexander Hall had to halt production several times because of the antics and crying of six babies who were appearing on camera.

6. Composer Ralph Rainger, who wrote torch songs, "Moanin

Low" and "Please" for Bing Crosby, penned the songs Miss Colbert performed in *Torch Singer*.

7. In a July. 1933 column, writer Harrison Carroll reported former silent screen leading lady, Elinor Fair (*The Volga Boatman* (1926), *The Yankee Clipper* (1927)) was slated to play a bit role in *Torch Singer*. Miss Fair was formerly married to western star, William Boyd.

BIG EXECUTIVE (1933) (DRAMA)
PARAMOUNT PRODUCTIONS, INC.
DIRECTOR: Erle C. Kenton
SCREENPLAY: Laurence Stallings
LENGTH: 70 minutes
TAGLINES: "Up to his neck in the market. . . and head over heels in love!"
STATUS: Believed lost.

CAST: Ricardo Cortez (Victor Conway), Richard Bennett (Commodore Richardson), Elizabeth Young (Helena Richardson), Sharon Lynne (Miss Dolly Healy), Dorothy Peterson (Sarah Conway), Barton MacLane (Harry), John M. Sullivan (Harrison), Charles Middleton (Sheriff), Pop Kenton (Coroner), Maude Eburne (Coroner's wife), Albert Hart (Reverand Oates), and Frank Darien (Richardson's secretary).

SUMMARY: In spite of profound reservations regarding the young buyer's character, a veteran businessman (Bennett) sells his interest in a bank to a Wall Street hot shot (Cortez). The elder man's concerns deepen when the young executive's wife (Peterson) is accidentally killed, and his daughter (Young) becomes romantically involved with the widower.

REVIEWS:
The Film Daily: "Mildly entertaining comedy-drama of stock market crashes with an unimpressive romance . . . Ricardo Cortez as the broker breezes through his part, smiling and laughing, as a foil to Richard Bennett's portrayal of a grouchy old man . . ."

Los Angeles Examiner: "*Big Executive* contrasts the Wall Street wizards of past generations with those of today . . . Written in a not very convincing manner, it doesn't offer much for Cortez or even Bennett . . ."

PRODUCTION NOTES, INTERESTING FACTS, AND TRIVIA:
1. According to a *Hollywood Reporter* item, Cary Grant and Helen Twelvetrees were originally slated for the leads. Grant withdrew because of illness, but it is not known why Miss Twelvetrees was replaced by Elizabeth Young.

2. Elizabeth Young (1913-2007) was the first wife of producer, director, screenwriter, Joseph L. Mankiewicz, who achieved his greatest fame directing the 1950 drama, *All About Eve*.

3. According to the *Waterloo Daily Courier*, in the original story entitled, *Big Executive* by Alice Duer Miller, Cortez's character, Victor Conway, deliberately shoots his wife, carries on an affair with his secretary, and makes love to the daughter of the scion of wealth. In the end, when everything falls apart, he leaves for parts unknown. Paramount executives refused to film it that way, preferring to make Conway a more sympathetic character who accidently shoots his wife, then starts a new life with his fiancé at the fadeout.

THE HOUSE ON 56TH STREET (1933) (DRAMA)
WARNER BROTHERS
DIRECTOR: Robert Florey
SCREENPLAY: Austin Parker, Sheridan Gibney (script), Joseph Santley (story)
LENGTH: 69 minutes
TAGLINE: "No girl can call her soul her own once she enters the house on 56th street!"
STATUS: Exists. (DVD)

CAST: Kay Francis (Peggy Martin), Ricardo Cortez (Bill Blaine), Gene Raymond (Monte Van Tyle), John Halliday (Lindon Fiske), Margaret Lindsay (Eleanor), Frank McHugh (Chester Hunt),

William "Stage" Boyd (Bonelli), Sheila Terry (Dolly), Hardie Albright (Henry Burgess), Phillip Reed (Freddy), Phillip Faversham (Gordon), Henry O'Neill (Baxter), Walter Walker (Dr. Wyman), Nella Walker (Mrs. Van Tyle), and Samuel S. Hinds (Curtis).

SUMMARY: The early 20th century travails of a show girl (Francis) who becomes the mistress of a businessman (Halliday), then falls in love and marries a wealthy young man (Raymond). They have a daughter and the future seems bright, until her former lover attempts to re-enter her life, and she accidentally kills him. She is convicted of murder and sentenced to 25 years in prison. During her prison term, her husband dies in World War I. After she leaves prison she meets a card shark (Cortez), and they operate a gambling house at her old abode on 56th Street. Complications ensue when her young, gambling-addicted daughter (Lindsay), loses a great deal of money on the premises.

REVIEWS:
New York Times: ". . . quite an original and intriguing drama . . . Ricardo Cortez gives an expert conception of a cardsharp . . ."

Variety: "Another rambling adaptation of a novel. This time they make two stories of it. The first half is laborious planting and dull to an extreme. . . Midway it perks up, and from that point to the finish gathers fair speed to a suspenseful closing sequence . . . Cortez never fails in the gentleman crook type."

PRODUCTION NOTES, INTERESTING FACTS, AND TRIVIA:
1. Cortez was borrowed from Paramount for the role of Blaine, after Adolphe Menjou was taken out of the film, and placed in *Convention City* (1933).

2. Warner Bros. archival records (U.S.C.) reveal the film was an enormous box office hit. Total gross receipts were over $483,000.

3. According to author/film historian, Brian Taves, in his biography, *Robert Florey, The French Expressionist*, the film was director Florey's favorite of all the movies he made for Warner Bros.

4. Author Taves, who knew and interviewed Florey, says the director was particularly enthusiastic about the early scenes in *House on 56th Street*, which recreated the café and restaurant entertainers of New York during the early 20th century.

5. *The Film Daily* reported the original choice for the feminine lead in *The House on 56th Street* was Ann Dvorak.

6. An item published in *The Salt Lake Tribune* stated cinematographer Ernest Haller and associates filmed footage at the famed Casino Theater at Sherry's and Delmonico's restaurants, in New York City, for inclusion in the picture.

THE BIG SHAKEDOWN (1934) (CRIME DRAMA)
FIRST NATIONAL PICTURES
DIRECTOR: John Francis Dillon
SCREENPLAY: Niven Busch, Rian James (script), Niven Busch, Sam Engel (story)
LENGTH: 64 minutes
TAGLINE: "It tears the heart out of chislers!"
STATUS: Exists. (DVD)

CAST: Charles Farrell (Jimmy Morrell), Bette Davis (Norma Nelson), Ricardo Cortez (Dutch Barnes), Glenda Farrell (Lily "Lil" Duran), Allen Jenkins (Lefty), Henry O'Neill (Sheffner), Dewey Robinson (Slim), John Wray (Gardinella), Philip Faversham (John), Robert Emmett O'Connor (Regan), Adrian Morris (Trigger), Ben Hendricks (Spike), George Cooper (Shorty), Earl Foxe (Casey), and Samuel S. Hinds (Kohlsadt).

SUMMARY: In order to help his clients and make enough money to marry his longtime sweetheart (Davis), a naïve druggist (Farrell) becomes involved in an illegal medicine racket masterminded by an ex bootlegger (Cortez).

REVIEWS:
Hollywood Citizen News: "The plot, as this outline indicates, is usually pretty obvious and always excessively melodramatic. There

are, however, some saving moments of comedy and drama in the picture. Most of the good dramatic bits are provided by Cortez, who has given some of the best gangster portrayals the screen has known..."

PRODUCTION NOTES, INTERESTING FACTS, AND TRIVIA:
1. Based on the Niven Busch, Sam Engel story, *Cut Rate*, the film's working title was *The Shakedown*.

2. According to multiple Bette Davis biographies, she was extremely unhappy with her role as the compliant wife in *The Big Shakedown*. She would have preferred playing the gangster's mistress (portrayed by Glenda Farrell).

3. Former two-reel comedy actor, turned movie director, John Francis Dillon (1884-1934), enjoyed considerable success during the silent era, but was relegated to helming mainly low budgeters after the coming of sound. Although he won acclaim for a handful of his early sound films, including *Millie* (1931), *The Reckless Hour* (1931), and especially Clara Bow's comeback film, *Call Her Savage* (1932), his later work consisted mostly of undistinguished movies and shorts. *The Big Shakedown* would be the last feature film of his career. On April 4, 1934, he succumbed to a fatal heart attack.

MANDALAY (1934) (MELODRAMA)
FIRST NATIONAL PICTURES
PRODUCER: Robert Presnell
DIRECTOR: Michael Curtiz
SCREENPLAY: Austin Parker, Charles Kenyon (script), Paul Hervey Fox (story)
LENGTH: 65 minutes
STATUS: Exists. (DVD)

CAST: Kay Francis (Tanya), Ricardo Cortez (Tony Evans), Warner Oland (Nick), Lyle Talbot (Dr. Gregory Burton), Ruth Donnelly (Mrs. Peters), Lucien Littlefield (Mr. Peters), Reginald Owen (Police Captain), Etienne Girardot (Mr. Abernathie), David Torrence

(Captain), Rafaela Ottiano (The Countess), Halliwell Hobbes (Col. Dawson Ames), Bodil Rosing (Mrs. Kleinschmidt), Herman Bing (Mr. Kleinschmidt), Hobart Cavanaugh (Purser), and Shirley Temple (Betty Shaw).

SUMMARY: In Rangoon, Burma, a Russian refugee (Francis) falls in love with a gun runner (Cortez) working for an underworld kingpin (Oland), who runs a notorious night club. The gun runner is forced to relinquish her to his boss to settle a debt, and she becomes a prostitute. Later, she makes enough money to escape. On the boat to Mandalay, she meets and falls in love with an alcoholic doctor (Talbot), but her ex-lover shows up, and attempts to make her return to Rangoon.

REVIEWS:
Los Angeles Evening Herald Express: "Make no mistake, you'll like Kay Francis in her clothes, her rich, exotic lure, her drama, no matter how you quarrel with the over-wrought story . . . To the hilt is played the role of the gun-runner by Ricardo Cortez."

New York Times: "A fundamental flaw with the film is that Ricardo Cortez generates so much sympathy as the villain that his demise removes the one character for whom the audience feels anything like affection . . ."

PRODUCTION NOTES, INTERESTING FACTS, AND TRIVIA:
1. In both *The House on 56th Street* and *Mandalay*, Ruth Chatterton and Adolphe Menjou were the first choices for the roles played by Miss Francis and Ricardo Cortez. The lead feminine role in *Mandalay* was turned down by both Chatterton and Bebe Daniels. Miss Chatterton said she declined it because she did not want to play another fallen woman. Her husband at the time, George Brent, also turned down one of the leads (the role of the doctor) due to "prior commitments." Donald Woods was then announced for the role, but was replaced by Talbot.

2. According to Rudy Behlmer's book, *Inside Warner Brothers*, the studio's production head, Hal Wallis, anticipated problems with

censors having to do with Miss Francis' character Tanya "Spot White." Wallis actively sought director Michael Curtiz's aid in toning down certain scenes, including those which portrayed her as a prostitute, but Curtiz ignored Wallis' pleas.

3. As Wallis predicted, censors and religious groups had multiple problems with the picture. Records housed at the A.M.P.A.S Library reveal their main objection was the heroine who they described as "an immoral woman" who "got away with murder." The Catholic Legion of Decency even took the extra step of banning their followers from seeing the movie.

4. Although it was produced before the Production Code was enforced in July, 1934, *Mandalay* did not escape the censors who refused to renew it for re-issue in 1936.

5. Warner Bros. archival records (University of Southern California) reveal the film was an enormous box office success enhancing the popularity of its cast, particularly star Kay Francis. It netted Warner Bros. profits in excess of $300,000.

6. According to *Mandalay* cast member Lyle Talbot, whose memories were recorded for posterity by his daughter, Margaret, and published in a biography entitled, *The Entertainer: Movies, Magic and My Father's Twentieth Century*, to create a tropical atmosphere, director Curtiz filmed on location on the Sacramento River.

"We lived on a boat called the Delta Queen. It was all mahogany and very beautiful. There were Chinese people living all along the river there at the time. The film crew didn't have to do much to make it look like a port in the Orient. The actors all slept on the Delta Queen and ate there . . ."

7. Fans and film historians have been arguing for years whether or not Kay Francis actually performed the lovely Irving Kahal/Sammy Fain ballad, "When Tomorrow Comes" in *Mandalay*, or if it was dubbed. In his book, *Kay Francis, I Can't Wait to Be*

Forgotten, Miss Francis' biographer Scott O'Brien quotes a reporter on the set of *Mandalay* who heard Kay singing accompanied by a piano.

8. In his book, *The Women of Warner Brothers*, author Daniel Bubbeo said Miss Francis was unenthusiastic about her part in *Mandalay*. She told an interviewer "If it does any better than my other films, it's because I parade thirty-six costumes instead of sixteen."

9. A *Lowell Sun* item revealed while filming *Mandalay*, Ricardo Cortez joined the Screen Actors Guild. He had been among the last holdouts.

10. According to a *Nevada State Journal* article, in April, 1934, a few months after the release of *Mandalay*, several columnists and newspaper stories declared Ricardo Cortez "the busiest major actor in Hollywood," with no less than seven films playing in theatres across the country.

WONDER BAR (1934) (MUSICAL DRAMA)
FIRST NATIONAL PICTURES
DIRECTOR: Lloyd Bacon
SCREENPLAY: Earl Baldwin
LENGTH: 85 minutes
STATUS: Exists. (DVD)

CAST: Al Jolson (Al Wonder), Kay Francis (Leane Renaud), Dolores Del Rio (Ynez), Ricardo Cortez (Harry), Dick Powell (Tommy), Guy Kibbee (Simpson), Ruth Donnelly (Mrs. Simpson), Hugh Herbert (Corey Pratt), Louise Fazenda (Mrs. Pansy Pratt), Hal LeRoy (Himself), Fifi D'Orsay (Mitzi), Merna Kennedy (Claire), Henry O'Neill (Richard), Robert Barrat (Captain Von Ferring), Henry Kolker (Mr. Renaud), Spencer Charters (Pete), and Jane Darwell (Buxton Grande Dame).

SUMMARY: The Parisian nightclub, "Wonder Bar," a popular gathering place of society types and various musical and dance artists, is owned and operated by a singer/performer (Jolson). The club serves as a melodramatic backdrop (a la *Grand Hotel*) for love, betrayal, revenge, murder, and suicide, along with some excellent singing, sprightly comedy, and lavish dance numbers.

REVIEWS:
Hollywood Citizen News: " *Wonder Bar* is variety entertainment on the screen, more handsomely mounted than anything of its kind could be . . . Jolson rises to an undisputed position . . . Delores Del Rio is dazzlingly beautiful, and Ricardo Cortez, cast as her philandering dancing partner, does some of his best screen work . . ."

Motion Picture Guide: "You can't help comparing this musical to *Grand Hotel*, because of the number of characters, plots, and subplots . . . Most of the Harry Warren/Al Dubin songs are only serviceable, but push the several plots along. One terribly tasteless production sequence has Jolson in his standard black-face singing . . ."

PRODUCTION NOTES, INTERESTING FACTS, AND TRIVIA:

1. Al Jolson was under great pressure to make *Wonder Bar* a success after his last picture, *Hallelujah, I'm a Bum* (1933), bombed at the box office. Just prior to filming, columnist Dan Thomas essentially pronounced Jolson a has-been, stating, "There isn't much doubt about the fact Al Jolson's name means little as a screen attraction today."

2. Warner Bros. archival records (U.S.C.) reveal Jolson demanded and received 10% of the gross receipts from Warner Bros. to star in the picture. It turned out to be one of the most lucrative moves of his career, as the movie was one of the top box office pictures of the year, grossing in excess of $2 million dollars. Profits exceeded $750,000.

3. Songwriters Harry Warren and Al Dubin composed the eight songs featured in *Wonder Bar*, and the legendary Busby Berkeley created and directed the lavish dance numbers, utilizing 300 dancers and others in the ensembles. A highlight of the film

was "Don't Say Goodnight," a visually impressive song and dance number featuring the singing of Dick Powell (who played a singing bandleader), scantily clad young female dancers of all shapes and sizes, and a mirrored set photographed from above, to resemble a kaleidoscope.

4. Several newspapers articles published at the time of the movie's release, including one in the *Sheboygan Press*, chronicled the many problems Berkeley encountered filming *Wonder Bar*'s musical numbers, including overseeing the construction of the sets, the equipment necessary to film the many overhead shots, the lighting, costumes, and actual dances. During the filming of her tango number, Miss Del Rio became so dizzy she collapsed. Multiple takes were necessary.

5. The final production number, the shockingly racist, "Going To Heaven On a Mule," featured a black-faced Jolson and Hal LeRoy, and multiple black-faced angels singing and dancing in a separate heaven which featured a pork chop orchard, a watermelon palace, and an "Uncle Tom tonight" neon sign. Although very little criticism was leveled at the time of the premiere, in recent times, the number has been deemed so offensive it has been exorcised from some later prints. Many stations refuse to broadcast the film because of it.

6. Actress Merna Kennedy, who played one of the women who attempt to entice and take advantage of two middle-aged businessmen played by actors Guy Kibbee and Hugh Herbert, was married to choreographer, Busby Berkeley.

7. One of the great dancing talents of his time, Hal LeRoy (1913-85) had a prolific (40+ year) career in film, television, and the stage. Some biographies of LeRoy list *Wonder Bar* as his feature-length film debut, while others list several other pictures as preceding it.

8. According to a short article in the *Tyrone Daily Herald*, when he announced his engagement and pending nuptials to

Christine Conniff Lee, Ricardo Cortez was given a pre-wedding shower on the set of *Wonder Bar*. His gift from screen nemesis/erstwhile rival, Al Jolson, was a ham in black face.

9. To meet the meticulous standards of dance director Busby Berkeley, the *Los Angeles Examiner* reported Cortez worked overtime on the dance routines seen in *Wonder Bar*. He eventually delayed his upcoming wedding to socialite Mrs. Christine Lee in December, 1933, so he could do retakes.

10. A *New York Times* piece dated October 29, 1933, noted Ann Dvorak was the original choice to play the part of Inez eventually essayed by Dolores Del Rio.

11. *The Film Daily* reported Kay Francis was in, out, and back in the cast of *Wonder Bar*. Warner Bros. archival records reveal when the shooting time for *Mandalay* was postponed, Francis was briefly replaced by Genevieve Tobin, whose name appears in the original Warner Bros. budget for the picture. However, when *Mandalay* was completed just prior to the beginning of production on *Wonder Bar*, Miss Francis was brought back in to give the film added star power.

12. According to a Warner Bros.' promotional article (Warner Bros. Archives), director Lloyd Bacon filmed the stabbing scene in which Harry (played by Cortez) is killed eight times. Bacon was dissatisfied with each of the first seven takes.

13. Although Al Jolson was the star of *Wonder Bar*, the contracts of both Kay Francis and Delores Del Rio required they be billed above Jolson in all advertising.

14. A *Moorhead Daily News* article stated that while finishing work on the film, Ricardo Cortez was named as one of the "23 best dressed men of the universe" by a group of tailors based in London, New York, and Hollywood.

15. According to sources listed in the *American Film Institute*

Cortez played one of his most famous scoundrel roles as a talented dancer who is two-timing his partner/lover (Dolores Del Rio) in the musical extravaganza, *Wonder Bar* (Warner Bros. 1934).

catalogue, Frank Borzage was the original choice to direct *Wonder Bar*.

HAT, COAT, AND GLOVE (1934) (MELODRAMA)
RKO RADIO PICTURES
PRODUCER: Pandro S. Berman
DIRECTOR: Worthington Miner
SCREENPLAY: Francis Faragoh
LENGTH: 66 minutes
STATUS: Exists

CAST: Ricardo Cortez (Robert Mitchell), Barbara Robbins (Dorothea Mitchell), John Beal (Jerry Hutchins), Dorothy Burgess (Ann Brewster), Paul Harvey (The prosecuting attorney), Sara Haden (The secretary), Margaret Hamilton (Madame Du Barry a.k.a. Mrs. Pansy Jones), David Durand (Thomas Sullivan), Murray Kinnell (The judge), and Frederick Sullivan (The court clerk).

SUMMARY: A defense attorney (Cortez) who witnessed the death of a young woman (Burgess) while visiting the apartment of his estranged wife's (Robbins) lover (Beal), is asked to defend the young man when he is accused of the murder. He agrees, with the stipulation his wife return to him.

REVIEWS:
Hollywood Citizen News: ". . . a well executed specimen of psychological courtroom drama . . . When the great John Barrymore left the cast, his followers, doubtless, were sharply disappointed. They may take consolation, however, in the excellent performance of Ricardo Cortez . . . Mr. Cortez dominates the picture. His is a most unusual portrayal, marked by studied peculiarities which serve to make his characterization all the more engrossing . . . ."

Variety: "Radio originally bought it for John Barrymore. Cortez proves a fine substitute as the great criminal lawyer who's torn between conscience and jealousy to defend his wife's lover against a murder charge of which he knows the lad is innocent."

PRODUCTION NOTES, INTERESTING FACTS, AND TRIVIA:
1. Based on the 1934 German play, *A Hat, a Coat, and a Glove*, by Wilhelm Speyer.

2. Playwright William Drake completed an English translation of Speyer's work, which debuted on Broadway in January, 1934. The play closed after only 13 performances.

3. According to the *New York Times*, RKO originally bought the Speyer play as a vehicle for John Barrymore. When Barrymore was unable to complete the film, Adolphe Menjou, Paul Lukas, Warner Baxter, and Otto Kruger were considered for the lead. In the end, RKO opted to borrow the dependable Cortez from Warner Bros.

4. According to the loan agreement between Warner Bros. and RKO, dated May 24, 1934, (kept in the Warner Bros. Archives—at the University of Southern California), Warner Bros. received a

Ricardo and screen wife (Barbara Robbins) in a dramatic scene in *Hat, Coat, and Glove* (RKO, 1934).

$5,250 bonus for the loan of Cortez, while the actor received his regular salary ($1,750 a week), for his work on *Hat, Coat, and Glove*.

5. RKO remade *Hat, Coat, and Glove* in 1944, as *A Night of Adventure* with Tom Conway in the lead.

6. 18-year-old New York stage actress Barbara Robbins (1915-93) made her one and only feature-length film appearance in *Hat, Coat, and Glove*. *The Chicago Daily Tribune* reported Miss Robbins held up production on the film when she spent too long sunbathing with friends on Santa Monica beach, and suffered "a broiling sunburn." She returned to the New York stage a few months after completing the picture.

7. *Variety* noted the picture was one of the first given the purity seal by Production Code Administration head Joe Breen after the new stricter Code was enforced.

8. *Hat, Coat, and Glove* director Worthington Miner (1900-82) was a multifaceted stage, film, and television actor, director, writer, and producer. Among his noted stage directorial credits were such respected plays as *Reunion in Vienna* with Lunt and Fontanne, *Jane Eyre* with Katharine Hepburn, and the Ray Bolger musical, *On Your Toes*. Miner was also highly regarded as one of the pioneers of television, as a writer, director, and producer of such noted series as *Studio One* and *The Ed Sullivan Show*. He was married to actress Frances Fuller. Their son, Peter, produced the memorable television series, *Dark Shadows*.

9. *The Film Daily* reported while working on *Hat, Coat, and Glove*, Ricardo Cortez visited his brother, Bernard Kranze, who was working in the sales office for RKO.

THE MAN WITH TWO FACES (1934) (MYSTERY)
FIRST NATIONAL PICTURES
PRODUCER: Robert Lord
DIRECTOR: Archie Mayo
SCREENPLAY: Tom Reed, Niven Busch.
LENGTH: 72 minutes
TAGLINE: "The greatest actor on Broadway! . . . Played the greatest role of his career OFF the stage!"
STATUS: Exists. (DVD)

CAST: Edward G. Robinson (Damon Wells/Jules Chautard), Mary

Astor (Jessica Wells), Ricardo Cortez (Ben Weston), Mae Clarke (Daphne Flowers), Louis Calhern (Stanley Vance), Arthur Byron (Dr. Kendall), John Eldredge (Barry), David Landau (Curtis), Emily Fitzroy (Hattie), Henry O'Neill (Inspector), Arthur Aylsworth (Morgue keeper), Anton Stengel (Morgue keeper), Margaret Dale (Martha Temple), Virginia Sale (Peabody), and Dorothy Tree (Patsy Dowling).

SUMMARY: As a mentally fragile Broadway actress (Astor) recovers from a nervous breakdown brought on by her unscrupulous husband, who is presumed dead, he suddenly reappears. The hypnotic hold he has on her causes her family and friends great concern, particularly her actor brother (Robinson), and producer beau (Cortez). When the would-be Svengali demands money to leave town, her brother decides to take matters into his own hands.

REVIEWS:
Motion Picture Guide: "Tight, tense mystery . . . Hard to believe the censors allowed this to get past them as Robinson got away with murder; and there was no retribution given to the character."

New York Times: "There may have been reasons for doubting the excellence of the original work, but only a diehard will deny that the motion picture has performed an effective translation . . ."

PRODUCTION NOTES, INTERESTING FACTS, AND TRIVIA:
1. Based on a play *The Dark Tower* by George S. Kaufman and Alexander Woolcott, which ran on Broadway from November, 1933 until January, 1934 (Morosco Theatre—57 performances). Character actors Margaret Dale (Martha) and Anton Stengel (Morgue keeper) reprised their Broadway roles in the film.

2. The film, as adapted by Reed and Busch, changed the play considerably. Stage audiences were left wondering who killed the husband until the end. Filmgoers know who the guilty party is from the outset.

3. In the film, the title of the play in which Miss Astor's character

Jessica is appearing is "The Dark Tower."

4. In his autobiography, *All My Yesterdays*, Edward G. Robinson said he liked the script for the movie and was looking forward to working with Mary Astor, but "I wasn't very happy with the way *The Man with Two Faces* turned out. You couldn't exactly say the brothers Warner were turning handsprings either. You'd think they'd have said 'That's it, brother. Good-bye. Good luck!'"

5. Leading lady Mary Astor conducted a torrid love affair with *The Man with Two Faces*' playwright, Kaufman, during the run of *The Dark Tower* on Broadway. That affair (chronicled in her infamous diary) would become the center of a sensational custody battle in 1936, which would be the talk of Hollywood.

6. A *Chicago Daily Tribune* article stated that immediately after finishing this picture, in early April, 1934, the secretive Ricardo Cortez entered a hospital for what was described as an "operation." The exact nature of the surgery was never revealed.

A LOST LADY (1934) (DRAMA)
WARNER BROTHERS

PRODUCER:	James Seymour
DIRECTOR:	Alfred E. Green
SCREENPLAY:	Gene Markey, Kathryn Scola
LENGTH:	61 minutes
TAGLINE:	"Four great stars…United to bring you Willa Cather's celebrated novel of a woman who tried to save herself from love by marriage!"
STATUS:	Exists

CAST: Barbara Stanwyck (Marian Ormsby), Frank Morgan (Daniel Forrester), Ricardo Cortez (Frank Ellinger), Lyle Talbot (Neil Herbert), Phillip Reed (Ned Montgomery), Hobart Cavanaugh (Robert), Rafaela Ottiano (Rosa), Henry Kolker (John Ormsby), Willie Fung (Cook), Walter Walker (Judge Hardy), Samuel S. Hinds (Jim Sloane), Edward McWade (Simpson), Jameson Thomas (Lord

Verrington), Colin Kenny (Butler), and Addison Richards (State attorney).

SUMMARY: After her fiance (Talbot) is killed, a woman (Stanywck) marries a kindly older man (Morgan) whom she does not love, then falls for another man (Cortez), whom she cannot have.

REVIEWS:
New York Times: "The particular charm of Miss Cather's work was her method, and that has been rather definitely lost in the process of transition to the screen.

Variety: "As the most fashionable one-woman fashion show to date, this will have some interest for the women, but beyond that, has little to offer. Sartorially, the picture's star, Barbara Stanwyck, was generously supplied, but otherwise left high and dry . . . ."

PRODUCTION NOTES, INTERESTING FACTS, AND TRIVIA:
1. The Willa Cather novel, *A Lost Lady*, was initially filmed in 1925 with Irene Rich playing the lead role of Marian, and Harry Beaumont directing.

2. A June. 1934 *Hollywood Reporter* item announced Kay Francis for the lead role of Marian. Clearly, the very large wardrobe budget for *A Lost Lady* reflects that fact.

3. Actor John Eldredge was to have had the role of Neil, but left the production when he was cast in Warners Bros. *Flirtation Walk*. He was replaced by Lyle Talbot.

4. Warner Brothers archival records reveal the total budget for *A Lost Lady* was $230,000. Miss Stanwyck earned $50,000 for her participation. Frank Morgan made $12,500 and third-billed Cortez was paid $5,250.

5. The picturesque outdoor scenes in *The Lost Lady* were filmed on location at Lake Arrowhead, California (80 miles northeast of Los Angeles).

THE FIREBIRD (1934) (MELODRAMA)
WARNER BROTHERS
PRODUCER: Gilbert Miller
DIRECTOR: Wiliam Dieterle
SCREENPLAY: Charles Kenyon (script), Jeffrey Dell (adaptation)
LENGTH: 74 minutes
STATUS: Exists. (DVD)

CAST: Veree Teasdale (Carola Pointer), Ricardo Cortez (Herman Brandt), Lionel Atwill (John Pointer), Anita Louise (Mariette Pointer), C. Aubrey Smith (Police Inspector Miller), Dorothy Tree (Jolan), Helen Trenholme (Mile. Mousquet), Hobart Cavanaugh (Emile), Robert Barrat (Halasz), Hal K. Dawson (Assistant stage manager), Russell Hicks (Stage manager), Spencer Charters (Max), Etienne Girardot (Professor Peterson), Nan Gray (Alice Van Attern), and Jane Darwell (Mrs. Miller).

SUMMARY: In Vienna, a respected diplomat's wife (Teasdale) conducts an affair with a handsome, egotistical actor (Cortez) who lives in the same apartment building. When he turns up dead, the affair becomes public, and suspicion falls on her.

REVIEWS:
Chicago Daily Tribune: "The Firebird is handsomely staged and cleverly directed . . . Ricardo Cortez with his sultry eyes makes Brandt convincingly erotic . . ."

New York Times: "Among the definite failings of the smoothly-filmed edition of Lajos Zilahy's play is the circumstance that, like the original, it conceals the actual murderer from the audience for such an extended period that the motivation for the homicide never becomes completely real . . . ."

PRODUCTION NOTES, INTERESTING FACTS, AND TRIVIA:
1. Based on the play, *Muvesz, Szinhaz*, by Lajos Zilahy (1932).

2. Jeffrey Dell's adaptation of the Zilahy play was a hit on the London stage.

3. The *New York Times* reported British actor, Colin Clive, was to play the role of the husband in this film, but was pulled from the production at the last minute and replaced by Lionel Atwill.

4. In her *Hollywood Citizen News* column, Elizabeth Yeaman reported Warner Bros. purchased *The Firebird* as a vehicle for Kay Francis, but when she was cast in another picture, her part was assigned to Veree Teasdale. This was Miss Teasdale's first starring role in a motion picture.

5. Shortly after completing work on *The Firebird*, leading lady Veree Teasdale married Ricardo's former costar, Adolphe Menjou. The marriage would last 29 years, ending with Mr. Menjou's death in 1963.

6. The *Firebird* file at the A.M.P.A.S. library reveals composer, conductor, pianist, Igor Stravinsky, sued Warner Bros. for 600,000 francs over the use of his composition, "The Firebird," in the movie, claiming it was used without his permission; Warner Bros. counter sued. The cases were eventually settled in Stravinsky's favor. His award was one franc.

I Am A Thief (1934) (Crime Drama)
WARNER BROTHERS
PRODUCER: Henry Blanke
DIRECTOR: Robert Florey
SCREENPLAY: Ralph Block, Doris Malloy
LENGTH: 64 minutes
STATUS: Exists

CAST: Mary Astor (Odette Mauclair), Ricardo Cortez (Pierre Londais), Dudley Digges (Col. Jackson), Robert Barrat (Baron Von Kampf), Irving Pichel (Count Trentini), Hobart Cavanaugh (Daudet), Ferdinand Gottschalk (M. Cassiet), Arthur Aylsworth (Francois), Florence Fair (Madame Cassiet), Frank Reicher (Max Bolen), and John Wray (Borricci).

SUMMARY: When a series of jewel robberies rock Paris, the authorities and insurance companies decide to offer up the famed Karenina Diamonds as bait to capture the culprits. At the auction of the diamonds, both legitimate buyers and thieves bid on the valuables. When the winning bidder (Cortez) boards the *Istanbul Express*, he is pursued by two criminal gangs and a beautiful jewel thief (Astor), who is working for the French police.

REVIEWS:
The Film Daily: "Fair entertainment chiefly by reason of a good cast and a certain amount of intriguing suspense and movement."

Variety: "Implausible story in which the authors endeavor to repeat the crime-on-a-train theme . . . Invention is replaced with lively movement, but it does not make for real interest as the story is too involved to be easily followed . . . Mary Astor is capital as the girl, and Cortez, Pichel, and Barrat help."

PRODUCTION NOTES, INTERESTING FACTS, AND TRIVIA:
1. Warner Bros. reportedly considered Paul Muni and Ann Dvorak for the leads roles eventually assigned to Cortez and Astor.

2. In his biography, *Robert Florey, The French Expressionist,* author Brian Taves says Mr. Florey enjoyed making *I Am a Thief* because of the technical challenges it presented. Mr. Florey told author Taves some of the ways he worked his magic on the movie.

"Convincing miniatures provided the necessary establishing shots. Full-size duplicates of Orient Express dining and sleeping cars were constructed on railroad tracks with sliding partitions to enable the cameras to photograph any necessary angle."

3. Interestingly, *I Am a Thief* brought together three actors who had prominent roles in two Warner Bros. versions of Hammett's *The Maltese Falcon*: Cortez and Digges from the 1931 version, a.k.a. *Dangerous Female*, and Miss Astor from the iconic 1941 version.

THE WHITE COCKATOO (1935) (MYSTERY)
WARNER BROTHERS
DIRECTOR: Alan Crosland
SCREENPLAY: Ben Markson, Lillie Hayward
LENGTH: 73 minutes.
TAGLINE: "Try to solve the riddle that stumped a million readers!"
STATUS: Exists. (DVD)

CAST: Jean Muir (Sue Talley), Ricardo Cortez (Jim Sundean), Ruth Donnelly (Mrs. Felicia Byng), Minna Gombell (Grete Lovscheim), Walter Kingsford (Marcus Lovschiem), John Eldredge (Francis Talley), Gordon Westcott (Dr. Roberts), Addison Richards (David Lorn), Pauline Garon (Marianne), and Arnaud de Bordes (Marcel).

SUMMARY: Murder ensues when an American girl (Muir) travels to an eerie hotel on the French coast to meet her long lost brother, and claim her inheritance. There, she meets several sinister, suspicious characters, and an American engineer (Cortez) who attempts to protect her from harm.

REVIEWS:
Los Angeles Examiner: "Those who like their murders complicated and logically unraveled will find much to enjoy . . . It isn't fair to give away the plot, but it may interest you to know that Ricardo Cortez is given a pleasant and very sympathetic role . . ."

PRODUCTION NOTES, INTERESTING FACTS, AND TRIVIA:
1. Based on the bestselling novel, *The White Cockatoo*, by Mignon G. Eberhardt (1933).

2. *The Film Daily* reported George Brent and Josephine Hutchinson were originally announced as leads for *The White Cockatoo*, but when Warner Bros. decided to cast them in another picture, Cortez and Margaret Lindsay were brought in as replacements. When Miss Lindsay became tied up filming *Bordertown*, Jean Muir replaced her.

3. *The White Cockatoo* files (A.M.P.A.S. Library) reveal that although production on the picture began on schedule the last week in September, 1934, it had to be suspended a week later when lead actor Cortez contracted the flu and couldn't report for work. In spite of several days' delay, thanks to Warner Bros. hardworking cast and crew, the film was finished just four weeks later (on October 27), on time and under budget.

4. According to Warner Bros. archival records, another temporary delay was caused by one of the film's other stars: the titled character, an Australian sulfur-crested cockatoo, who refused to play ball according to the script. The action called for the bird to be captured when it escaped from its cage, but it flew up in a tree on the set and would not come down. The director, Alan Crosland (who had once had a pet cockatoo), solved the problem by turning a hose on the bird. When its wings got wet, it came down.

5. For his work on the picture, Ricardo earned $11,885. In comparison, comedian Ruth Donnelly was paid $5,650, Walter Kingsford was paid $2,250, and interestingly, first-billed Jean Muir was paid only $1,550.

6. Ricardo's former leading lady, the exotic Jetta Goudal (*The Spaniard*), tested for the role of menacing innkeeper, Grete, in *The White Cockatoo*, but the part went to Minna Gombell.

7. Warner Bros. archival records indicate Miss Donnelly designed her own dresses for the *The White Cockatoo*.

Shadow of Doubt (1935) (THRILLER)
METRO-GOLDWYN-MAYER
PRODUCER: Lucien Hubbard
DIRECTOR: George B. Seitz
SCREENPLAY: Wells Root
LENGTH: 75 minutes
STATUS: Exists. (DVD)

CAST: Ricardo Cortez (Simeon "Sim" Sturdevant), Virginia Bruce (Trenna Plaice), Constance Collier (Aunt Melissa), Isabel Jewell (Inez Johnson), Arthur Byron (Morgan Bellwood), Betty Furness (Lisa Bellwood), Regis Toomey (Reed Ryan), Ivan Simpson (Morse), Bradley Page (Len Haworth), Edward Brophy (Fred), Samuel S. Hinds (Mr. Thomas Granby), Richard Tucker (Mark Torrey), Bernard Siegel (Ehrhardt), Paul Hurst (Lt. Jack Sackville), and Russell Hicks (Detective chief).

SUMMARY: Over the objections of his dowager aunt (Collier), a successful advertising man (Cortez) becomes romantically involved with a penniless actress (Bruce) who is engaged to a producer (Page). When the producer is murdered, both the ad man and his girlfriend become suspects. The disapproving aunt eventually has a change of heart regarding her nephew's romance, and is instrumental in helping to solve the case.

REVIEWS:
Film Daily: "Top notch murder mystery holding good blend of action and comedy with smart all around handling . . ."

Los Angeles Evening Herald Express: "Mystery story lovers, spook and thrill devotees, and the great army of cinema fans have a treat in store for them when *Shadow of Doubt* comes to town . . . The entire cast offers sharp, interesting portrayals."

PRODUCTION NOTES, INTERESTING FACTS, AND TRIVIA:
1. Based on the novel, *Shadow of Doubt*, by Arthur Somers Roche, first published as a serial in *Colliers* magazine in 1934-35. The popular Mr. Roche died of heart disease complicated

by pneumonia just two days after the film's premiere. He was 51 years old.

2. Veteran British-born stage actress Constance Collier (1878-1955), who made her film debut in Griffith's *Intolerance* (1916), marked her return to filmmaking in *Shadow of Doubt*, after a long absence. During the next 15 years, she would become of the cinema's premier character players typically appearing as dowagers and/or grande dames reminiscent of Edna May Oliver and Marie Dressler.

3. Charles Reisner was originally slated to direct the film, but was replaced just prior to production by Seitz.

4. A *Hollywood Reporter* item stated Rosalind Russell had been added to the cast, but never appeared in the film.

5. In a December 1934 article published in *The Chicago Daily Tribune* (while Ricardo was making this movie), critic Rosalind Shaffer proclaimed him "at the peak of his career." Three months later, the Academy of Motion Picture Arts and Sciences named him one of the 46 "Busiest Players in the Movie Colony."

6. According to the loan agreement which sent Cortez from Warner Bros. to MGM, dated December 11, 1934 (Warner Bros. Archives at the University of Southern California), Warner Bros. received a $6,000 bonus for loaning Cortez, and he received his salary of $2,000 a week, with a guaranteed minimum of $8,000.

7. During the long delays between scenes of *Shadow of Doubt*, Virginia Bruce taught Cortez how to knit. According to *Screenland* columnist, Weston East, the actor knitted his dog a sweater. The couple became friends during the production, and dated years later after the death of Miss Bruce's second husband.

8. *The Charleston Daily Mail* reported that Constance Collier had

to learn how to play a tune on a pipe-organ for her role in *Shadow of Doubt*.

MANHATTAN MOON (1935) (COMEDY)
UNIVERSAL PICTURES CORPORATION
PRODUCER: Stanley Bergerman
DIRECTOR: Stuart Walker
SCREENPLAY: Barry Trivers, Ben Grauman Kohn (script), Robert Harris (original story), Aben Kandel (adaptation), Robert Presnell, Harvey Gates, and James Mulhauser (contributed to treatment)
LENGTH: 65 minutes
TAGLINE: "He loves one of them, but doesn't know which one!"
STATUS: Unknown

CAST: Ricardo Cortez (Dan Moore), Dorothy Page (Yvonne/Doris "Toots" Malloy), Henry Mollison (Reggie Van Dorset), Hugh O'Connell (Speed), Regis Toomey (Eddie), Adrienne D'Ambricourt (Maid), Luis Alberni (Luigi), Henry Armetta (Tony), Irving Bacon (Hot dog man), and Jack Cheatham (Henchman).

SUMMARY: A wealthy New York night club owner from a poor background (Cortez) wishes to advance in society. To clear a debt, one of his society patrons (Mollison) agrees to help him gain social status, but when he falls for a beautiful opera singer (Page) and invites her on a date, the patron substitutes her lookalike. The lookalike is a commoner who rents an apartment from him.

REVIEWS:
Chicago Daily Tribune: ". . . neat little program picture . . . There are a number of seasoned players in the film, led by Ricardo Cortez, who always turns in a finished performance . . ."

PRODUCTION NOTES, INTERESTING FACTS, AND TRIVIA:
1. Working titles included, *Sing Me a Love Song* and *Lucky in Love*.

2. Universal obtained Cortez' services on loan from Warner Bros.

3. The *San Marino Tribune* reported that while on his way home from Universal Studios, where he was making *Manhattan Moon*, Ricardo Cortez was cited for speeding. Court records indicate he pleaded guilty and paid a $5.00 fine.

SPECIAL AGENT (1935) (CRIME DRAMA)
WARNER BROTHERS
PRODUCER: Sam Bischoff
DIRECTOR: William Keighley
SCREENPLAY: Laird Doyle, Abem Finkel (script), Martin Mooney (story idea)
LENGTH: 75 minutes
TAGLINE: "Now…See the 'T-Men' mop up the gangsters, g-guns couldn't reach!"
STATUS: Exists. (DVD)

CAST: Bette Davis (Julie Gardner), George Brent (Bill Bradford), Ricardo Cortez (Alexander Carston), Jack La Rue (Jake), Henry O'Neill (District Attorney), Robert Strange (Armitage), Joseph Crehan (Chief of Police), J. Carroll Naish (Durell), William Davidson (Young), Robert Barrat (Head of the Internal Revenue Department), Paul Guilfoyle (Secretary to the district attorney), and Irving Pichel (U.S. District Attorney).

SUMMARY: A treasury agent (Brent) poses as a newspaperman to help nab a tax-evading mobster (Cortez), whose financial records are kept in code. In his quest for justice, the agent enlists the aid of the racketeer's secretary (Davis), who is frightened she will be killed if she cooperates with the law.

REVIEWS:
Los Angeles Evening Herald Express: "If you liked all the thrills and chills of *G-Man*, then *Special Agent* is your dish . . . Although he enacts the "you'll-have-to-hiss-him" role, Ricardo Cortez is positively outstanding as the big shot of the racketeers. He gives the part a cool, menacing touch that is absolutely chilling. . . ."

New York Times: " . . . crisp, fast moving, and thoroughly entertaining melodrama . . . Ricardo Cortez is entirely convincing as the racket lord . . ."

PRODUCTION NOTES, INTERESTING FACTS, AND TRIVIA:
1. A.M.P.A.S Library records reveal the Hays Office demanded a scene involving Cortez's character be deleted or substantially altered due to offensive language. Producer Bischoff initially resisted, but eventually a compromise was reached which retained the scene with the Cortez dialogue muted.

2. At the time of the film's release, *The Oakland Tribune* profiled journalist Martin Mooney, whose original story was the basis of *Special Agent*. A reporter for *The New York American*, Mooney specialized in stories involving illegal activities and organized crime. One of his stories was also the basis of the 1940 Warner Bros. film, *Gambling on the High Seas*. Mr. Mooney faced jail several times for his refusal to violate the confidence of his sources.

FRISCO KID (1935) (DRAMA)
WARNER BROTHERS
PRODUCER: Sam Bishoff
DIRECTOR: Lloyd Bacon
SCREENPLAY: Warren Duff, Seton I. Miller
LENGTH: 77 minutes
TAGLINE: "Glittering with glamour . . . Seething with scum! Where living men asked no questions and dead men told no tales!
STATUS: Exists. (DVD)

CAST: James Cagney (Bat Morgan), Margaret Lindsay (Jean Barrat), Ricardo Cortez (Paul Morra), Lili Damita (Belle), Donald Woods (Charles Ford), Barton MacLane (Spider Burke), George E. Stone (Solomon "Solly" Green), Joseph King (James Daley), Addison Richards (Coleman), Robert McWade (Judge Crawford), Joseph Crehan (Maclanahan), Robert Strange (Graber), Joseph Sawyer (Sluggs Crippen), Fred Kohler (Shanghai Duck), and Edward McWade (Tupper).

SUMMARY: During the mid-1800's, a tough young sailor (Cagney) works his way up the ladder of success on San Francisco's notorious Barbary Coast. Eventually, he gains political power, opens a saloon, and battles rival gangs and killers. He falls in love with a cultured young woman (Lindsay) who owns and operates the local newspaper.

REVIEWS:
New York Evening Post: "*Frisco Kid* is a carbon copy of *The Barbary Coast*, and a muddled one. It plays with vitality and frenzy, but it never gets close to the core of its subject. . . ."

Variety: "So similar to UA's *Barbary Coast* as to be almost its twin, 'Frisco Kid' is nonetheless good entertainment . . . Cagney is, as usual, forceful and aggressive, which is what the role calls for. . . A light-hearted card shark assignment is a walk, well done by Ricardo Cortez."

PRODUCTION NOTES, INTERESTING FACTS, AND TRIVIA:
1. During the filming of *Frisco Kid*, Cortez admitted he was thinking of giving up acting for directing. In an item published in *Illustrated Daily News* in December, 1935, he told the interviewer he had been seriously considering the change for at least two years, but "hesitated because the demand for my services as an actor." He went on to cite several other actors who became directors, including Lowell Sherman, Cecil B. DeMille, Michael Curtiz, Archie Mayo, and William Dieterle. Two years later he would sign a contract with 20th Century Fox allowing him to achieve his long desired goal.

2. Several notable filmmakers of the silent era appeared as extras in *Frisco Kid*, including actors Helene Chadwick, Alice Lake, Vera Stedman, Jane Tallent, Bill Dale, and director Dick Kerr.

3. Veteran actress Estelle Taylor (1894-1958) (Cortez's former costar in *New York*), was another of the former silent screen stars to make an uncredited appearance in *Frisco Kid*. It was her first film in three years. She would make only two more movies before retiring during the mid 1940's. According to

records housed in the Warner Brothers Archives, she was originally slated to play the part of Belle, but was replaced by Lili Damita.

4. In his memoirs, *Cagney By Cagney*, the great star described *Frisco Kid* as:

"One of those catch-as-catch can affairs Warner's put out purely because they had to be put out. By that I mean Frisco Kid had already been sold to the exhibitors even before a foot of it had been shot or conceived. This will give you some idea of its inherent artistic flavor. The picture was built just the way a Ford sedan might have been."

5. Warner Bros. archival records reveal that despite his unhappiness with the *Frisco Kid* script, Mr. Cagney was likely pleased with his paycheck for his work on the picture. He was paid $32,000; Cortez netted $11,330; and Miss Lindsay $4,000.

6. According to a *Middleboro Daily News* item, in order to prepare for his role as slick gambler Paul Morra in *Frisco Kid*, Ricardo Cortez was given dealing lessons by veteran gambler, Dan Jones, who began his professional gambling career on San Francisco's Barbary Coast.

7. *The Lowell Sun* reported it took two days, countless extras, innumerable takes, and eventually, five fire trucks to film the climactic scenes of *Frisco Kid* in which vigilantes charge, then torch Bat Morgan's (Cagney's) Barbary Coast nightspot, "Bella Pacific."

8. According to the *Salt Lake Tribune*, the main character, Bat Morgan, was based on "an actual character in California history," and many of the original landmarks of the San Francisco waterfront were rebuilt (by art director John Hughes) to lend the production authenticity.

The Murder of Dr. Harrigan (1936) (Mystery)
WARNER BROTHERS
PRODUCER: Bryan Foy
DIRECTOR: Frank McDonald
SCREENPLAY: Peter Milne, Sy Bartlett
LENGTH: 67 minutes
STATUS: Exists

CAST: Ricardo Cortez (George Lambert), Kay Linaker (Sally Keating), John Eldredge (Dr. Harrigan), Mary Astor (Lillian Cooper), Joseph Crehan (Lieutenant Lamb), Frank Reicher (Dr. Coate), Anita Kerry (Agnes Milady), Phillip Reed (Simon), Robert Strange (Peter Melady), Mary Treen (Margaret Brody), Johnny Arthur (Wentworth), Gordon Elliott (Ladd Martin), and Don Barclay (Jackson).

SUMMARY: When a young surgical nurse (Linaker) is arrested for the murders of a prominent doctor (Eldredge) and a hospital official (Strange), a young intern who's in love with her (Cortez) attempts to determine those responsible among a plethora of suspects.

REVIEWS:
Chicago Daily Tribune: "If you're not hard to excite, *The Murder of Dr. Harrigan* should excite you."

New York Times: "*The Murder of Dr. Harrigan* occurs in a self-service elevator of one of the larger metropolitan hospitals. It is well to bear that in mind; otherwise you will be bound to suspect that it took place in a lunatic asylum filled with manic depressives pretending to be doctors and nurses . . ."

PRODUCTION NOTES, INTERESTING FACTS, AND TRIVIA:
1. Based on the Mignon B. Eberhard's 1931 novel, *From a Dark Stairway.*

2. The film marked the first directorial effort of Frank McDonald (1899-1980), a former dialogue director, who would go on to helm over 100 B movies for Warner Bros., Paramount, Republic, and other studios, from 1936 to 1965. During the 1950's and

beyond he would also do considerable work in series television.

3. The film was the sixth and final film pairing of Ricardo Cortez and Mary Astor.

4. Mary Astor was originally cast as the female lead in *The Murder of Dr. Harrigan*, but when she refused to play the part, she was demoted to a supporting player, and forced to make the picture.

5. *Dr. Harrigan* also marked the film debut of Broadway actress, Kay Linaker (1913-2008), who was signed to play Sally after Miss Astor refused the part. Miss Linaker would play over 50 screen roles in Hollywood. After marrying singer/writer turned TV executive, Howard Phillips, she retired from acting and moved to the East Coast. Later, she became a college teacher and a writer, penning the screenplay for the famed horror classic, *The Blob*, in 1958.

6. According to a latter day interview with Kay Linaker conducted by Leonard Kohl, published in *Scarlet Street* magazine, Cortez's leading lady in *Dr. Harrigan* thoroughly disliked him and hated making the picture with him.

"In all my time in Hollywood, I only met two people I didn't like. One was my leading man in my first picture, and Mary Astor took care of him for me. Ricardo Cortez was an ugly, ugly, man! Looking at it now, I realize that he was hired for the film because he had the Valentino look . . . He was a Jewish boy and he was groomed as a Spanish lover; and he had a very unsatisfactory life. Now I realize that's what made him so unpleasant, but at the time I didn't think about things like that . . ."

Man Hunt (1936) (crime comedy)
Warner Brothers
Producer: Bryan Foy
Director: William Clemens
Screenplay: Roy Chanslor
Length: 65 minutes
Tagline: "A sleepy village relives the days of Jessie James"
Status: Exists.

Cast: Ricardo Cortez (Frank Kingman), Marguerite Churchill (Jane Carpenter), Charles "Chic" Sale (Ed Hoggins), William Gargan (Hank Dawson), Dick Purcell (Skip McHenry), Olin Howland (Starrett), Addison Richards (Mel Purdue), George E. Stone (Silk), Anita Kerry (Babe), Nick Copeland (Blackie), Russell Simpson (Jeff Parkington), Eddie Shubert (Joe), Kenneth Harlan (Jim Davis), Cy Kendall (Sheriff at Hackett), and Maude Eburne (Mrs. Maria Hoggins).

Summary: A naïve small town schoolmarm (Churchill) whose romantic notions of notorious outlaws get her fired, helps a big city gangster (Cortez) hide from the police. Her boyfriend, a local newspaperman (Gargan), learns of her activities, and attempts to alert authorities, but she warns the gangster and he escapes. When the crook hatches a scheme to rob the local bank, the young woman comes to her senses and joins forces with her beau and the police to thwart his plans.

Reviews:
Murphysboro Daily Independent: "Sure-fire entertainment, exciting, funny, and romantic . . . Cortez gives his usual convincing performance as the suave, soft-spoken, and outwardly gentlemanly rascal . . ."

Variety: "There have been too many previous pictures similar in style and formula for *Man Hunt* to reach anything but minor rating as entertainment and at the box office . . . The gangster role doesn't deserve the trouping Ricardo Cortez gives it."

Production notes, interesting facts, and trivia:
1. The working title for the film was *Backfire*.

2. *Man Hunt* was a first for Cortez in two respects: It was the first of three films he would make under the aegis of producer Bryan Foy, known as "Keeper of the B's" (based on his work producing program pictures as head of Warner Bros. legendary B unit); it was also the first of three films he would make with his best friend's (George O'Brien) wife, Marguerite Churchill.

3. The movie was also a first for director William Clemens (1905-80). After many years as an editor at Warner Bros., he was promoted to director. During the next five years he would helm 24 low budget feature films for the studio, making a name for himself as an efficient craftsman.

4. According to a *Galveston Daily News* article, while doing publicity for *Man Hunt*, Cortez was asked to describe the movie's appeal. He said "*Man Hunt* is strong in all the elements which go to make up a good picture. It is essentially an action picture with a strong leavening of humor."

THE WALKING DEAD (1936) (HORROR)
WARNER BROTHERS

PRODUCER:	Hal Wallis
DIRECTOR:	Michael Curtiz
SCREENPLAY:	Ewart Adamson, Peter Milne, Robert Andrews, Lillie Hayward (script), Ewart Adamson, Joseph Fields (story)
LENGTH:	66 minutes
TAGLINE:	"He died a man…with a hunger to live! — Returned a monster with an instinct to kill!"
STATUS:	EXISTS. (DVD)

CAST: Boris Karloff (John Elman), Ricardo Cortez (Nolan), Edmund Gwenn (Dr. Beaumont), Marguerite Churchill (Nancy), Warren Hull (Jimmy) Barton MacLane (Loder) Henry O'Neill (Werner), Joseph King (Judge Shaw), Addison Richards (prison warden), Paul Harvey (Blackstone), Robert Strange (Merritt), Joseph Sawyer (Trigger), Eddie Acuff (Betcha), Kenneth Harlan (Stephen Martin), Miki Morita (Sako), and Ruth Robinson (Mrs. Shaw).

SUMMARY: On the road to rehabilitation, an ex-convict (Karloff) is framed for the murder of a judge by a group of gangsters aided by a corrupt attorney (Cortez). In spite of his innocence, the man is executed, but is brought back to life a by a brilliant scientist (Gwenn) utilizing an apparatus called the "Lindbergh Heart." Afterward, he is a changed man. Inspired by a higher power, and possessed with the knowledge of those who victimized him, he sets out to avenge his own death.

REVIEWS:
Motion Picture Guide: "While the story is basically just a variation on the Frankenstein themes, director Curtiz infuses the film with a moody visual style full of low-key lighting and interesting camera angles that make this the best of Karloff's many living dead movies."

Variety: "Those with a yen for shockers will get limited satisfaction from the story that has been wrapped around Boris Karloff's initial stalking piece under the Warner Brothers banner . . . As the head menace, Cortez is loaded down with no easy assignment. About all he can do is look wise, keep a sneer well-oiled, and give the living dead man stare for stare . . ."

PRODUCTION NOTES, INTERESTING FACTS, AND TRIVIA:
1. In his book, *Hollywood Cauldron,* author Gregory Mank revealed Karloff's contract specified his salary to be $3,750 a week with a four-week guarantee. His option was picked up before the film was completed. Between 1936-40, he would make five motion pictures for Warner Bros.

2. According to Warner Bros. archival records, Karloff earned a total of $18,750 for his work in *The Walking Dead*. Edmund Gwenn received $6,000, and second-billed Ricardo Cortez made $12,000.

3. *The Film Daily* reported Warner Bros., who had recently employed MGM contract player Edmund Gwenn for their epic adventure, *Anthony Adverse* (1936), again arranged to borrow his services to play the kindly doctor/scientist in *The Walking*

Dead. This was particularly pleasing to star Boris Karloff as the two were longtime friends.

4. Multiple reviews of *The Walking Dead* mentioned the real-life experiments of Dr. Robert Cornish and Dr. Alexis Carrel. In 1934, Cornish made several high-profile attempts to revive dead dogs in hopes of finding a way to restore human life. In 1935, Nobel Prize winner Dr. Carrel, along with famed aviator, Charles Lindbergh, developed a mechanical circulatory device called the "Lindbergh Heart" which turned up in the film. *The Film Daily* reported a duplicate of the famed Lindbergh mechanical heart, housed at the Rockefeller Institute in New York, was one of the many apparatuses constructed for the laboratory scenes in the movie under the supervision of art director, Hugh Reticker.

5. According to author Mank, production on *The Walking Dead* took place at both Warner Bros. studios: the original studio on Sunset, and the First National 135-acre lot in Burbank. Some key scenes were also filmed in L.A.'s Griffith Park in the Santa Monica Mountains.

6. In his book, *The Very Witching Time of Night*, author Gregory Mank revealed production problems on the picture ended up delaying its completion and costing the Warners an extra $47,000. The film turned out to be a box office hit, however. With domestic rentals of $273,000 and foreign rental proceeds of $316,000, the Warners ended up netting over $94,000 in profits.

7. Cinematographer Hal Mohr (1894-1974) worked in various capacities in the film industry before becoming a director of photography in 1921. An accomplished craftsman, Mohr won two Academy Awards for *A Midsummer Night's Dream* (1935) and *The Phantom of the Opera* (1943, shared with W. Howard Greene). His first Oscar for *Dream* came as a result of a write-in vote, the one and only time a write-in ended up victorious.

8. According to *The Film Daily*, famed writer H. G. Wells visited the set of *The Walking Dead* escorted by none other than Jack Warner. After seeing the "Lindbergh Heart" device used to revive the character, John Elman (Karloff), Wells reportedly looked at the actor and said "And I suppose *that* is your stand in?"

9. Famed producer, director, ace showman, William Castle, might well have been taking notes, when, according to *The Film Daily*, A. W. Sobler, managing director of the Spreckels Theater in San Diego, decided to pull out all the stops to promote *The Walking Dead*, which was playing at his theater. After setting up a mechanical robot in the theater lobby, Sobler sent a man in a robot suit to stalk the street with the name of the picture and theater name painted on him. In addition, he hired a girl to faint at the opening day matinee and a man to dress up in a medical uniform to be on duty in case someone else collapsed of "shock" during the picture.

10. According to memos on file in the Warner Bros. Archive (at U.S.C.), the studio received a missive from chief censor Joe Breen's office, dated May 28, 1936 (well after the premiere of the film in March). In it, Breen demanded deletions of specific scenes in *The Walking Dead*, including one in which criminals are standing around a billiard table discussing the murder of a judge, and another in which a priest appears in a cell. In addition, Breen demanded a sign be posted in all lobbies of theaters which showed the picture, with the following words: "CENSORSHIP WARNING: NERVOUS AND EXITABLE PEOPLE SHOULD AVOID THIS 'HORROR' PICTURE." Warner Bros. ignored Breen's demands.

11. Scottish-born author, Ewart Anderson (1882-1945), was a major in the Canadian armed forces prior to his migration to Hollywood in 1922. While in the film capitol, he gained fame as a screenwriter for multiple studios, including Warner Bros., RKO, Republic, and Columbia. Although he produced screenplays for such highly respected feature films as *Annie Oakley* and *The Walking Dead*, Adamson became best known

From left to right: Barton MacLane, Cortez, and Boris Karloff, in *The Walking Dead* (Warner Bros.,1936).

for penning scripts for shorts, the most notable being several *Three Stooges* comedies for Columbia.

POSTAL INSPECTOR (1936) (CRIME DRAMA)
UNIVERSAL PRODUCTIONS

PRODUCER:	George Owen
DIRECTOR:	Otto Brewer
SCREENPLAY:	Horace McCoy (script), Robert Presnell, Horace McCoy (story)
LENGTH:	60 minutes
TAGLINE:	"The Daring Exploits of Secret Agents of the Mail Service!"
STATUS:	Exists. (DVD)

CAST: Ricardo Cortez (William Davis), Patricia Ellis (Connie Larrimore), Michael Loring (Charles Davis), Bela Lugosi (Gregory Benez), Wallis Clark (Inspector Pottle), Arthur Loft (Inspector Richards), David Oliver (Butch), Guy Usher (Evans), Billy Burrud (The Boy), Harry Beresford (Ritter), and Hattie McDaniel (Deborah).

SUMMARY: A dedicated postal inspector (Cortez) must battle corruption, mail fraud, floods, and his naïve brother (Loring) who, with his girlfriend (Ellis), inadvertently assist mail thieves to steal a shipment of used $10 bills heading to Washington D. C.

REVIEWS:
Modern Screen: "This looks for all the world like a newsreel gone wrong . . . Ricardo Cortez gives his usual suave performance."

Variety: " Some highly capable talent and a novel, basic idea, are wasted in *Postal Inspector* . . . Ricardo Cortez is his usual suave self as the ace postal inspector."

PRODUCTION NOTES, INTERESTING FACTS, AND TRIVIA:
1. Actor Michael Loring and former Universal newsreel cameraman, David Oliver, made their screen debuts in *Postal Inspector*.

2. *The New York Times* noted Oliver's historic newsreel footage of the 1936 Pittsburgh floods which were utilized in the film.

3. According to Gregory William Mank's book, *Bela Lugosi and Boris Karloff: The Expanded Story of a Haunting Collaboration*, the total budget for *Postal Inspector* was $175,174. Bela worked on the film for three weeks and made $15,000.

4. A *Modern Screen* magazine publicity item revealed the filmmakers had a short laugh at the expense of star Ricardo Cortez during the production of a flood scene in the picture, when one of Cortez's knee-high boots sprung a leak and filled with water. The scene had to be halted, and Cortez was forced to wade into the ice cold water barefoot.

5. A native of Michigan, singer/actress Patricia Ellis (1916-70) migrated to Hollywood as a teen appearing in films in juvenile supporting roles beginning in 1932. By the latter 1930's, she had graduated to major character parts and second leads. Although she demonstrated a flair for comedy and was a talented vocalist who performed in many of her prominent films, she was largely

utilized in second features. A veteran of over 40 films, she opted to call it quits in 1940 after marrying a wealthy businessman. She died of cancer at age 53.

6. As the nightclub singer, Connie Larrimore, Miss Ellis performed two songs in *Postal Inspector*, both penned by the songwriting duo of Frank Loesser and Irving Actman.

7. According to *The Film Daily*, to publicize the movie, Universal Studios designed giant-sized letters addressed to the stars of *Postal Inspector*, to be delivered to theaters on opening nights. According to several theatre owners, these attracted considerable attention when mail delivery people carried them through towns.

THE CASE OF THE BLACK CAT (1936) (MYSTERY)
WARNER BROTHERS
PRODUCER: Bryan Foy
DIRECTOR: William McGann
SCREENPLAY: F. Hugh Herbert
LENGTH: 65 minutes
STATUS: Exists. (DVD)

CAST: Ricardo Cortez (Perry Mason), June Travis (Della Street), Jane Bryan (Wilma Laxter), Craig Reynolds (Frank Oafley), Carlyle Moore Jr (Douglas Keene), Gordon Elliott (Sam Laxter), Nedda Harrigan (Louise DeVoe), Gary Owen (Paul Drake), Harry Davenport (Peter Laxter), George Rosener (Ashton), Gordon Hart (Dr. Jacobs), Clarence Wilson (Shuster), Guy Usher (Burger), Lottie Williams (Mrs. Pixley), and Harry Hayden (Rev. Stillwell).

SUMMARY: Noted attorney/sleuth, Perry Mason (Cortez) becomes involved in an effort to unravel a complex conspiracy and murder case when one of his clients, a wealthy old man (Rosener), dies mysteriously in a fire after changing his will and disinheriting his granddaughter (Bryan).

REVIEWS:

The Film Daily: "A baffling murder mystery which keeps suspense mounting as thrills pile up . . . Very effective work is done by Ricardo Cortez and June Travis . . ."

New York Times: "Erle Stanley Gardner and the Warner Bros. have plotted a frugal, though somewhat complex mystery . . . And Ricardo Cortez who succeeds Warren William as the suave lawyer-detective Perry Mason, acts the part as though it were tailor-made . . ."

Variety: "Production, cast, and screenplay are all 100% . . . On the acting side, Ricardo Cortez as the lawyer-detective, Perry Mason, delivers a standout job . . ."

PRODUCTION NOTES, INTERESTING FACTS, AND TRIVIA:

1. Curiously, the cat used in the film was not black, but gray and white. It is likely the studio intended to use the original title (*The Case of the Caretakers Cat*), but changed its mind after the picture was filmed. The last minute title change was probably made because having a "black cat" in the title would help sell the film.

2. After starring in four Perry Masons, actor Warren William bought out his Warner Bros. contract so he could freelance. Cortez inherited the role, but played it only once.

3. Included in the publicity items for the film in the Warner Bros. Archives (at U.S.C.) was a story about legends surrounding black cats bringing bad luck. This became especially ironic when the movie's original director, Alan Crosland (1894-1936), was tragically killed in a car accident on Sunset Boulevard in the midst of making the picture. He was replaced by B movie director, William McGann (1895-1977).

4. Although P.C.A. administrator, Joe Breen, thought the basic story of *The Case of the Black Cat* met "the requirements of the Production Code," in a memo dated June 27, 1936 (found in A.M.P.A.S. Library), he expressed reservations regarding certain

aspects of the script, including its discussion of an attempted murder by carbon monoxide, fearing it might provide specific ideas and methods for murder or suicide. Other major areas of concern were the use of brand names and the portrayal of a minister as a comic character.

5. Warner Bros. archival records (at U.S.C.) also reveal production on *Black Cat* was suspended briefly when star, Ricardo Cortez, reported to work with the after effects of a sunburn. Since his forehead was peeling, director McGann opted to send him home and film around him, but not before extracting a promise from the actor he would not go sun bathing again until after the film was completed.

6. Eighteen-year-old actress, Jane Bryan (1918-2009), made her film debut in *The Case of the Black Cat*, as an heiress who owns a waffle house. According to A.M.P.A.S. Library files, she was required to carry a large load of plates for a scene. When she kept dropping them, director McGann brought in a waitress from the Warner Bros. restaurant to give her pointers.

7. Warner Bros. archival records indicate Ricardo Cortez was paid $6,667 for his role as Perry Mason, by far the highest salary of anyone who worked on the film (in front of, or behind the camera). Next closest was scenarist F. Hugh Herbert who was paid $2,700.

8. An article published in the *Cumberland Evening Press* noted an interesting coincidence regarding the cast of *The Case of the Black Cat*. Almost all the main cast members were investors; Craig Reynolds was part owner of a candy company; Carlyle Moore, a firm which manufactured gym equipment; Gordon "Bill" Elliott dabbled in real estate; June Travis was part owner of some California softball teams; and Cortez (among many other investments) was part owner of a New York City cafeteria.

TALK OF THE DEVIL (1936) (CRIME DRAMA) (BRITISH)
BRITISH & DOMINIONS FILM CORPORATION — GAUMONT-BRITISH
DIRECTOR: Carol Reed
SCREENPLAY: Anthony Kimmins (script), Carol Reed (story, script), George Barraud (dialogue)
LENGTH: 76 minutes
STATUS: Exists. (At least one complete copy is known to exist in Great Britain).

CAST: Ricardo Cortez (Ray Allen), Sally Eilers (Ann Marlow), Basil Sydney (Stephen Findlay), Randle Ayrton (John Findlay), Fred Culley (Mr. Alderson), Charles Carson (Lord Dymchurch), Gordon McLeod (The Inspector), and Margaret Rutherford (Housekeeper).

SUMMARY: In England, an honest shipbuilder (Ayrton) is victimized by his dishonest brother (Sydney), who in an underhanded attempt to seize control of the business, employs a mimic (Cortez).

REVIEWS:
New York Times: "We resent this English intrusion into our Class C market . . . For *Talk of the Devil* is an infernal shame; the kind of film which torments a competent cast with the weakest possible writing and utterly maladroit direction . . ."

Variety: "English-made melodrama, which will have a tough going at the box office . . . Surprise of the production is Ricardo Cortez as the American hero. Usually cast for heavy dramatic stuff, the actor cashes in on several comedy bits in the early scenes, but is subsequently buried under the script and direction . . . ."

PRODUCTION NOTES, INTERESTING FACTS, AND TRIVIA:
1. According to author Ed Sikov in his biography, *Dark Victory, The Life of Bette Davis*, after Miss Davis refused to appear in Warner Bros. production of *God's Country and the Woman* (1937) until she received a more lucrative studio contract, she flew to Great Britain to make a British film. While there, she initiated a lawsuit against Warner Bros., who enjoined her from making the picture in Britain. In the midst of the battle, in

September, 1936, the studio unexpectedly loaned Cortez to the London production company making *Talk of the Devil*. Miss Davis lost her court case, but ultimately got her contract, and went on to star in a long list of successes at Warner Bros.

2. *Talk of the Devil* was the third feature-length film directed by Carol Reed (1906-76), who also penned the original story and co-wrote the script. Reed would eventually make a name for himself in the film industry as a top-notch director, helming such noted productions as *The Fallen Idol* (1948), *The Third Man* (1949), *Our Man in Havana* (1959), and *Oliver* (1968).

3. *Talk of the Devil* holds the distinction of being the first feature film made entirely at the Pinewood Studios in Iver Heath, Buckinghamshire.

HER HUSBAND LIES (1937) (CRIME DRAMA)
PARAMOUNT PICTURES
DIRECTOR: Edward Ludwig
SCREENPLAY: Wallace Smith, Eve Greene (script), Oliver H. P. Garrett (story)
LENGTH: 74 minutes
TAGLINE: "He couldn't play straight with a woman!"
STATUS: Exists. (DVD)

CAST: Gail Patrick (Natalie Thomas), Ricardo Cortez (Spade Martin a.k.a. J. Ward Thomas), Akim Tamiroff ("Big Ed" Bullock), Tom Brown ("Chick" Thomas), Louis Calhern (Joe Sorrell), June Martell (Betty), Dorothy Peterson (Dorothy Powell), Jack LaRue ("Trigger"), Ralf Harolde (Steve Burdick), Bradley Page ("Pug"), Ray Walker (Maxie), Fuzzy Knight ("Ears" Norris), Robert Emmett O'Connor (Bartender), Noel Madison ("Jackie" Taylor), Thomas Jackson ("Omaha" Johnson), and George Lloyd ("Corker" Evans).

SUMMARY: An investment broker by day and crooked gambler by night, a man (Cortez) opts to go straight when his wife, a night club singer (Patrick), threatens divorce. Complications arise however, when his younger brother (Brown) decides to take up gambling, forcing the veteran to step in to save him from ruination.

Reviews:
Motion Picture: "Here's something you can sink your teeth into and take home with you. It's a good drama handled expertly by the players. Ricardo Cortez, a gambler, plays a character similar to the famous Arthur Rothstein and does a memorable job . . . ."

Variety: "Superb direction and expert acting make this familiar fable of big-shot gamblers hold more than passing interest . . . Ricardo Cortez takes full advantage of breaks given him in his characterization. Result is a finely polished portrayal of an honest gambler who wanted to quit the racket too late . . . ."

Production Notes, Interesting Facts, and Trivia:
1. The working title for this film was *The Love Trap*.

2. Adapted from a story by noted newsman, scenarist Oliver H. P. Garrett, the movie was a remake of the 1930 William Powell and Kay Francis film, *Street of Chance*, purportedly based on the headline-making events surrounding the murder of notorious gangster, Arthur Rothstein, in November, 1928.

3. Warner Bros. archival records (at U.S.C.) reveal Ricardo Cortez worked almost four weeks on *Her Husband Lies*, for a salary totaling under $5,000. In contrast, his employer, Warner Bros. pocketed approximately $10,000 for lending his services to Schulberg Productions (distributed by Paramount Pictures).

4. Gail Patrick (1911-80), who played a nightclub vocalist in *Her Husband Lies*, did her own singing in the picture, winning kudos for her two numbers, "No More Tears" and "You Gambled With Love," written by the songwriting team of Ralph Freed and Burton Lane. At the time she made the picture, she was married to Robert Howard Cobb, the owner of one of Ricardo Cortez's favorite restaurants, the Brown Derby.

5. The script for *Her Husband Lies* was co-written by reporter, author, artist, Wallace Smith (1888-1937), who migrated to Hollywood in the late 1920's, writing scripts for various studios. Among his screenwriting credits were such noted films as *The Lost Squadron* (1932) and *The Captain Hates the Sea* (1934). Roughly two months after completing work on *Her Husband Lies*, he suffered a fatal heart attack and died at his home in Hollywood. He was 48 years old. The script was his last work.

THE CALIFORNIAN (1937) (WESTERN)
PRINCIPLE PICTURES (20TH CENTURY FOX FILM CORPORATION)
PRODUCER: Sol Lesser
DIRECTOR: Gus Meins
SCREENPLAY: Gilbert Wright (script), Harold Bell Wright (story), Gordon Newell (adaptation)
LENGTH: 59 minutes
TAGLINE: "A phantom bandit . . . Leaving a haunting laugh behind as a token of his daring raids!"
STATUS: Exists. (DVD)

CAST: Ricardo Cortez (Ramon Escobar), Marjorie Weaver (Rosalia Miller), Katherine DeMille (Chata), Maurice Black (Pancho), Morgan Wallace (Tod Barstow), Nigel De Brulier (Don Francisco Escobar), George Regas (Ruiz), Helen Holmes (Josephine), Gene Reynolds (Ramon as a child), and Ann Gillis (Rosalia as a child).

SUMMARY: In 1850's California, a Mexican landowner's son (Cortez) returns from his schooling in Spain to find unscrupulous American officials robbing Spanish settlers for their personal aggrandizement. Donning a black mask, he sets out on a dedicated quest to return monies and property to their rightful owners and bring the plunderers to justice, while battling bandits who have joined his gang and kidnapped his best girl (Weaver).

REVIEWS:
The Film Daily: "Action filled, interesting, and entertaining outdoor drama with historical setting . . . Under Gus Meins' direction, a familiar plot is made enjoyable by a nice piece of balancing of

action with laugh material and well-handled romance. The cast, headed by Cortez, Marjorie Weaver, and Katherine DeMille perform in fine style . . . ."

Variety: "Around the character of Ramon Escobar, early Californian patriot of the days before and after annexation, when the land of sunshine, citrus groves, and Townsend plans passed from Mexican rule . . . Ricardo Cortez has the hero's role to which he brings a personable appearance and good deal of dash and earnestness, and very little comedy."

Production notes, interesting facts, and trivia:

1. The film is also known under the title, *The Gentleman from California.*

2. Based on an unpublished story, *The Californian*, purportedly inspired by the life and career of of "Mexican patriot," Joaquin Murrieta.

3. Sources indicate Richard Arlen was originally slated to play the title character, but left the picture one week before filming, and was replaced by Cortez.

4. Writer Gordon Newell (a pen name for Charles Arthur Powell) sued 20th Century Fox for $30,000 claiming he did not receive credit for his adaptation for *The Californian*. The case was reportedly settled out of court for an undisclosed sum.

5. In an interview conducted after the release of the picture, published in *The Medicine Bay Daily News*, veteran director Gus Meins claimed the actors, including star Ricardo Cortez, risked their lives during the making of the action-filled film. The director declared he had never made a picture "in which the element of danger was so constantly present."

6. Playing Ricardo Cortez's character, Ramon, as a child in *The Californian* was 13-year-old juvenile actor Gene Reynolds. After a long stint as an actor in films and television, Reynolds

Ricardo and leading lady Marjorie Weaver in *The Californian*, a.k.a. *The Gentleman from America* (20th Century Fox, 1937).

eventually began working behind the camera. During the 1960's and 1970's, he would make a name for himself by producing and/or directing episodes of such noted television series as: *My Three Sons, Hogans Heroes, Room 222, M*A*S*H**, and *Lou Grant*. Mr. Reynolds has won six Emmy awards, and has been nominated 24 times. He is currently 93 years old, at the time of publication of this book.

7. German born director Gus Meins (1893-1940) first made a name for himself in silent films directing the *Buster Brown* comedies, before being hired by Hal Roach in 1932 as a gag writer and director of Charley Chase and Patsy Kelly/Thelma Todd shorts. In 1934, he co-directed *Babes in Toyland* starring Laurel and Hardy. Between 1934 and 1936 he became known for helming the *Little Rascals* shorts, before leaving Roach and turning his attention to feature-length comedies in 1937. In 1940, he was arrested on a "morals charge" after three young boys age 10-15 claimed he molested them. Released on bail, he committed suicide before the cases were tried.

WEST OF SHANGHAI (1937) (ADVENTURE)
WARNER BROTHERS
PRODUCER: Hal Wallis
DIRECTOR: John Farrow
SCREENPLAY: Crane Wilbur
LENGTH: 65 minutes
TAGLINE: "The master of the sinister in a triumph of suspense!"
STATUS: Exists. (DVD)

CAST: Boris Karloff (Wu Yen Fang), Beverly Roberts (Jane Creed), Ricardo Cortez (Gordon Creed), Gordon Oliver (Jim Hallet), Sheila Bromley (Lola Galt), Vladimir Sokoloff (General Chow Fu-Shan), Gordon Hart (Dr. Abernathy), Richard Loo (Mr. Cheng), Chester Gan (Kung Nui), and Selmer Jackson (Hemingway).

SUMMARY: A Chinese warlord (Karloff) who controls much of northern China intervenes on behalf of an oil field operator (Oliver), who is fighting attempts by greedy Americans to foreclose on his oil interests. While in China, one of the mercenaries (Cortez) is reunited with his estranged wife (Roberts), a missionary, who is in love with the young oil man.

REVIEWS:
Motion Picture Guide: "An attempt to spruce up the Chinese backgrounds is only moderately successful, but at least they used actual Chinese extras, not a common practice at the time."

New York Times: "A mildly amusing restatement of the Porter Emerson Browne play . . ."

PRODUCTION NOTES, INTERESTING FACTS, AND TRIVIA:
1. Based on the play, *The Bad Man*, by Porter Emerson Browne (1920).

2. The film had four working titles: *China Bandit, The Adventures of Chang, Warlord,* and *Cornered*. Some of the titles were invented by Warner Bros. in an attempt to placate the Chinese

government, who was upset over the portrayal of the Chinese people and culture in the script.

3. Warner Bros. archival records (at U.S.C.) detail difficulties the studio encountered with the Chinese government as a result of the production. After filming was completed on the picture, the Warners received a letter from the Chinese Consulate in Los Angeles, protesting the depiction of Chinese characters and customs. A fascinating series of letters between the Consulate and Warner Bros. followed. Initial communications were polite and accommodating. To their credit, even though the film had been completed before the Chinese government's concerns were known, Warner Bros. made an effort to address them. They held up the release of the picture while several bits of dialogue were exorcised. The studio even altered the title of the film from *Warlord* to *Cornered*, but when the Chinese deemed the changes unsatisfactory, Warner Bros. accommodating attitude turned to annoyance. In a July 20, 1937 letter to T.K. Chang, Counsel of the Republic of China, an increasingly frustrated Jack Warner listed the alterations made, and expressed hope the two parties had "laid a foundation of cooperation in the future," but added "it is unfortunately not possible to achieve the ideal on this particular picture." He went on to say he felt sure the Chinese government would "recognize that they must meet us half way." The Chinese would not budge and Warner Bros. was not willing to re-film the objectionable scenes.

In fact, the studio actually chose to reverse one of its previous concessions. When the film was finally released around Halloween in 1937 (to take advantage of Karloff's horror reputation), its title was changed to the Chinese themed *West of Shanghai*. The last correspondence retained in the production files is a letter from the Chinese to Jack Warner, dated October 8 (after the film had been previewed), demanding the studio present the film for inspection according to "our understanding."

4. First National made two previous films entitled *The Bad Man*, based on the Browne play: in 1923, starring Clarence Binn,

and in 1930, with Walter Huston. In 1940, MGM also made a film based on the play, *The Bad Man*, starring Wallace Beery.

5. Crane Wilbur (1886-1973), who wrote the *West of Shanghai* script, wore many hats in his long and productive career in the entertainment industry. A former silent screen actor best known for his appearance in the famed serial *The Perils of Pauline*, during the mid-1920's, Wilbur transitioned from acting to writing and directing. Specializing in crime, mystery, and horror screenplays, Wilbur won acclaim for his scripts for *House of Wax* (1953) and *Mysterious Island* (1961). He was the first cousin of actor Tyrone Power.

6. *West of Shanghai* was the last of four films Cortez made with Boris Karloff. The first three were *The Gentleman from America* (1923), *The Eagle of the Sea* (1926), and *The Walking Dead* (1936). It was also the last film Ricardo would do under his second Warner Bros. contract.

CITY GIRL (1938) (CRIME DRAMA)
20TH CENTURY FOX FILM CORPORATION

PRODUCER:	Sol Wurtzel
DIRECTOR:	Alfred Werker
SCREENPLAY:	Frances Hyland, Robin Harris, Lester Ziffren
LENGTH:	63 minutes
TAGLINE:	"We'll bust up every racket in the city . . . But a girl tries the most daring racket of all!"
STATUS:	Exists.

CAST: Phyllis Brooks (Ellen Ward), Ricardo Cortez (Charles Blake), Robert Wilcox (Donald Sanford), Douglas Fowley (Ritchie), Chick Chandler (Mike Harrison), Esther Muir (Flo Nichols) Adrienne Ames (Vivian Ross), George Lynn (Steve), Marjorie Main (Ellen's mother), Charles Lane (Dr. Abbott), Lee Phelps (Sergeant Farrell), Paul Stanton (Ralph Chaney), Lon Chaney Jr. (Gangster), Pierre Watkin (District Attorney), Charles Trowbridge (Pearson), Robert Lowery (Greenleaf), and Gloria Roy (Girl in the café).

SUMMARY: A poor waitress (Brooks) who forsakes her attorney boyfriend (Wilcox) for a notorious crime boss (Cortez), comes to regret her choices.

REVIEWS:
B Movies: ". . . a taut and matter-of-fact hour, depicting the rise and fall of a pretty but greedy young waitress, well played by Phyllis Brooks. The story moved steadily to its tragic conclusion without making concessions to a typically Hollywood happy ending."

The Film Daily: "A realistic drama, excellently produced and directed. It has honest writing and reflects credit on all concerned in its making. Phyllis Brooks is splendid . . . Ricardo Cortez gives his usually dependable performance as his city's chief racketeer . . . ."

PRODUCTION NOTES, INTERESTING FACTS, AND TRIVIA:
1. The working title for the film was *Blonde Moll*.

2. The character of the special prosecutor character played by actor Paul Stanton, was reportedly based on presidential candidate, Thomas E. Dewey.

3. One of the three scenarists who collaborated on the screenplay of *City Girl* was Lester Zeffrin (1906-2007), a former reporter who won fame during the mid-1930's for his coverage of the Spanish Civil War. After he fled Madrid, Zeffrin relocated to California, where he met and became engaged to Edythe Wurtzel, niece of Twentieth Century-Fox producer Sol Wurtzel, who hired him as a scriptwriter. For the next several years, he wrote or co-wrote over a dozen screenplays, including some entries in the famed *Charlie Chan* series. Afterward, he was in and out of the movie business, but eventually became involved in diplomatic work and private industry. He died at the age of 101 years old.

Mr. Moto's Last Warning (1939) (Mystery)
20th Century Fox Film Corporation

Producer:	Sol Wurtzel
Director:	Norman Foster
Screenplay:	Philip MacDonald, Norman Foster
Length:	71 minutes
Status:	Exists. (DVD)

Cast: Peter Lorre (Mr. Moto), Ricardo Cortez (Fabian), Virginia Field (Connie Porter), John Carradine (Danforth), George Sanders (Eric Norvel), Joan Carrol (Joan Delacour), Robert Coote (Rollo), Margaret Irving (Madame Delacour), Leyland Hodgson (Hawkins), and John Davidson (Hakim).

Summary: Masquerading as an antique dealer, master criminologist/International Police agent, Mr. Moto (Lorre), attempts to expose and foil the sinister plot of a spy (Cortez—posing as a ventriloquist) to blow up the French fleet to foment discord between England and France.

Reviews:
The Film Daily: "Exciting crime thriller staged in the colorful atmosphere of Port Said, near the Suez Canal . . . Peter Lorre has one of his best Mr. Moto roles, for the plot is well conceived and logical. Ricardo Cortez is admirable as the foreign agent."

Variety: "This is one of the better 'Moto' pictures. With Peter Lorre in the title role, Moto in this film has more lives than a cat. It's a good dualer . . . Strong supporting cast is chiefly notable for excellent comeback by Ricardo Cortez . . ."

Production Notes, Interesting Facts, and Trivia:
1. Based on character Mr. Moto, created by John P. Marquand.

2. Working titles for the film included, *Mr. Moto No. 6, Mr. Moto in Egypt,* and *Winter Garden.*

3. Pre-production records reveal Virginia Bruce was originally cast in the role of Connie Porter, the girlfriend of Fabian, the spy

(Cortez). Miss Bruce was replaced shortly before filming commenced by Virginia Field.

4. *Mr. Moto's Last Warning* was the sixth of eight *Mr. Moto* films produced by 20th Century Fox starring Peter Lorre. An update of the character was produced in Great Britain in 1965. The film, titled, *The Return of Mr. Moto*, starred Henry Silva.

5. In his book, *The Complete Mr. Moto Film Phile: A Casebook*, author Howard M. Berlin points out there were two references to another 20th Century Fox film series, *Charlie Chan*, in this movie. One was a movie poster at the Sultana Theatre which advertised the film *Charlie Chan in Honolulu*. The studio also promoted its Fox Movietone Newsreels in the film. A segment of one is featured in a prominent scene toward the end of the picture.

6. According to author John Tuska in *The Detective in Hollywood*, George Sanders was so unhappy with his role in *Mr. Moto's Last Warning*, he took it out on director Norman Foster by running up a huge restaurant bill, charging it to Foster's account.

7. According to an *Oakland Tribune* tidbit, Cortez's role as Fabian the ventriloquist was one of his favorite parts in all of his movies.

CHARLIE CHAN IN RENO (1939) (MYSTERY)
20TH CENTURY FOX FILM CORPORATION
DIRECTOR: Norman Foster
SCREENPLAY: Frances Hyland, Albert Ray, Robert E. Kent (script), Philip Wylie (story)
LENGTH: 70 minutes
TAGLINE: "Her divorce is ready . . . But murder signs the decree!"
STATUS: Exists. (DVD)

CAST: Sidney Toler (Charlie Chan), Ricardo Cortez (Dr. Ainsley), Phyllis Brooks (Vivian Wells), Slim Summerville (Sheriff Fletcher),

Kane Richmond (Curtis Whitman), Sen Yung (James Chan), Pauline Moore (Mary Whitman), Eddie Collins (Cab driver), Kay Linaker (Mrs. Russell), Louise Henry (Jeanne Bently), Robert Lowery (Wally Burke), Charles D. Brown (Chief of Police King), Iris Wong (Choy Wong), Morgan Conway (George Bently), and Hamilton McFadden (night clerk).

SUMMARY: A love triangle and a quickie divorce provide the backdrop for a complex murder case, which only veteran master sleuth Charlie Chan can solve.

REVIEWS:
The Film Daily: "The performers are superior to the material. Sidney Toler handles the Chan role convincingly. Ricardo Cortez as the hotel doctor makes a strong suspect . . ."

Variety: "Pointed direction by Norman Foster, trim scripting by a trio of writers, and spirited action that never goes overboard, have made the Philip Wylie original, *Death Makes a Decree* an intriguing yarn . . . Besides Toler's clean-cut portrayal, supporting work is studded by fine performances. Cortez, as the Reno colony doctor, makes a solid semi-menace character . . ."

PRODUCTION NOTES, INTERESTING FACTS, AND TRIVIA:
1. Based on the novel, *Death Makes a Decree*, by Philip Wylie. The character of Charlie Chan was created by Earl Derr Biggers and Robert E. Kent.

2. After wrapping up directorial duties on *Chasing Danger* in December, 1938, Ricardo Cortez took time out to appear in this movie filmed during January-February, 1939.

3. Besides Sidney Toler as Chan, the film ironically included three other actors who played famed crime fighters on film during their careers: Ricardo Cortez (who played Sam Spade in *The Maltese Falcon* (1931) and Perry Mason in *The Case of the Black Cat* (1936), Robert Lowery (who was Batman in the serial, *The Adventures of Batman and Robin* (1941), and Morgan Conway

(who played Dick Tracy in two RKO feature films: *Dick Tracy* (1945) and *Dick Tracy vs Cueball* (1946)).

4. According to a *Washington Post* article, while reminiscing about their exploits as aspiring silent film bit players in Fort Lee, New Jersey, on the set of *Charlie Chan in Reno*, Morgan Conway and Ricardo Cortez discovered they had something else in common. It seems both were up for the same part in a Violet Mersereau silent film when they were just starting out in the business. Conway was originally cast in the picture, but when he was late arriving on the set because he didn't have money for transportation, Cortez was given the part.

5. According to an article in *The Film Daily*, a small controversy erupted on the set of *Charlie Chan in Reno* when superstitious actor Slim Summerville, who played an eccentric sheriff, refused to play a scene with a black cat. Director Norman Foster, who was also superstitious, liked black cats in all of his films, because he considered them good luck charms. A standoff ensued for a time. Eventually Summerville played the scene as written.

MURDER OVER NEW YORK (1940) (MYSTERY)
20TH CENTURY FOX FILM CORPORATION
PRODUCER: Sol Wurtzel
DIRECTOR: Harry Lachman
SCREENPLAY: Lester Ziffren
LENGTH: 65 minutes
STATUS: Exists. (DVD)

CAST: Sidney Toler (Charlie Chan), Marjorie Weaver (Patricia Shaw), Robert Lowery (David Elliott), Ricardo Cortez (George Kirby), Donald MacBride (Inspector Vance), Melville Cooper (Herbert Fenton), Joan Valerie (June Preston), Kane Richmond (Ralph Percy), Sen Yung (Jimmy Chan), Leyland Hodgson (Boggs), Clarence Muse (Butler), Frederick Worlock (Hugh Drake), John Sutton (Richard Jeffries), and Dorothy Dearing (Mrs. Percy).

SUMMARY: When his friend, a British Intelligence officer is murdered, noted crime solver Charlie Chan (Toler) becomes enmeshed in the case which involves spies, sabotage, and poison gas pellets.

REVIEWS:
The Film Daily: "Murder mystery with New York background is up to par for *Charlie Chan* series . . . There are two murders, a sufficient amount of assault and battery, and plenty of suspense until the culprits are disclosed. The cast is agreeable . . ."

PRODUCTION NOTES, INTERESTING FACTS, AND TRIVIA:
1. The 21st of 41 *Charlie Chan* films, and the eighth starring Sidney Toler, who replaced Warner Oland as the star of the successful 20th Century Fox series in 1938.

2. The plot of Biggers' 1928 novel, *Behind That Curtain*, was updated and served as the basis for this third film version.

ROMANCE OF THE RIO GRANDE (1941) (WESTERN)
20TH CENTURY FOX FILM CORPORATION
PRODUCER: Sol Wurtzel
DIRECTOR: Herbert I. Leeds
SCREENPLAY: Harold Buchman, Samuel G. Engel
LENGTH: 73 minutes
TAGLINE: "That charming rascal's here again!"
STATUS: Exists. (DVD)

CAST: Cesar Romero (Cisco Kid/Carlos Hernandez), Patricia Morison (Rosita), Lynne Roberts (Maria), Ricardo Cortez (Ricardo), Chris Pin Martin (Gordito), Aldrich Bowker (Padre Martinez), Joseph McDonald (Carlos Hernandez), Pedro De Cordoba (Don Fernando De Vega), and Inez Palange (Mama Lopez).

SUMMARY: The notorious bandit, "The Cisco Kid" (Romero), and his sidekick, Gordito (Martin), intercede on behalf of a wealthy Arizona landowner (De Cordoba) to foil the evil plot of his nephew (Cortez) to gain control of his vast holdings. The elderly man wishes to pass his land on to his grandson, who just happens to be a lookalike for Cisco.

REVIEWS:
The Film Daily: "Best *Cisco Kid* release to date . . . The film is replete with action and a colorful background, the pace is fast, the direction smooth, the story credible, and the players are all on the plus side of the ledger in performing ability. . . ."

New York Times: "With the *Romance of the Rio Grande*, which arrived yesterday at the Palace hardly two months after the preceding chapter, the Cisco Kid's adventures are beginning to resemble a continued-next-week serial. But not nearly so much as they resemble themselves."

PRODUCTION NOTES, INTERESTING FACTS, AND TRIVIA:
1. Based on the 1923 novel, *Conquistador*, by Katherine Fullerton, and suggested by the character, "Cisco Kid," created by William Henry Porter a.k.a. O'Henry. Originally filmed by Fox in 1929 as The *Cisco Kid*, it starred Warner Baxter.

2. According to the *American Film Institute Catalog*, the movie was filmed on location at Vasquez Rocks in the Angeles National Forest, in Chatsworth, California, and at Lone Pine, California.

3. The *A.F.I. Catalog* also stated Cesar Romero had just recuperated from a paratyphoid infection when he made this picture. It is notable he performed all his riding and stunt work.

4. Patricia Morison (1915-) was borrowed from Paramount to appear as the beautiful but dangerous Rosita. She is currently 101 years old.

5. A *New York Times* item revealed Ricardo Cortez received the supporting role of Ricardo, the evil nephew in *Romance*, after Gilbert Roland turned down the part.

A Shot in the Dark (1941) (MYSTERY, CRIME DRAMA)
WARNER BROTHERS
PRODUCER: William Jacobs
DIRECTOR: William McGann
SCREENPLAY: M. Coates Webster
LENGTH: 57 minutes
TAGLINE: "A nightclub where the menu is…Terror!"
STATUS: Exists.

CAST: William Lundigan (Peter Kennedy), Nan Wynn (Dixie Waye), Ricardo Cortez (Phil Richards), Regis Toomey (Bill Ryder), Maris Wrixon (Helen Armstrong), Lucia Carroll (Claire Winters), Noel Madison (Al Martin), John Gallaudet (Schaffer), Donald Douglas (Roger Armstrong), Frank Wilcox (Naval officer), Theodore Von Eltz (George Kilpatrick), and Emory Parnell (Marsotti).

SUMMARY: When a nightclub owner is murdered there appears to be a multiplicity of suspects, each with motive and opportunity. It falls to a police investigator (Toomey) and a reporter (Lundigan) to sort out the facts and identify the responsible party.

REVIEWS:
Variety: "Another slick 'B' feature to come from the Warner lot in recent weeks . . . Adroit scripting by M. Coates Webster and sparkling direction by William McGann lift a fairly familiar story . . . Ricardo Cortez is a suave nitery operator trying to quit the business despite objections of friends and enemies."

PRODUCTION NOTES, INTERESTING FACTS, AND TRIVIA:
1. *A Shot in the Dark*'s original title was *No Hard Feelings*. The source material for the film was a story written by Frederick Nebel, published in *Black Mask* magazine in February, 1936. The original main characters MacBride and Kennedy were a hard-nosed police investigator and a hard-drinking reporter.

2. Nebel's story, *No Hard Feelings*, was originally adapted by Warner Bros. in 1937 as *Smart Blonde*, the initial entry in the studio's *Torchy Blaine* series. In *Smart Blonde*, Kennedy became

wisecracking female reporter, Torchy Blaine, played by Glenda Farrell. In *A Shot in the Dark*, Kennedy reverted to being a man, (William Lundigan) vying with police lieutenant Bill Ryder (Regis Toomey) for the affections of a nightclub singer (Nan Wynn), while tracking a killer.

3. The 1941 version of *A Shot in the Dark* has no relationship to the 1935 Chesterfield film of that name starring Charles Starrett.

4. An item in *The Film Daily*, dated February 3, 1941, listed actor Edward Brophy in the cast of *A Shot in the Dark*. He never appeared in the film.

WORLD PREMIERE (1941) (COMEDY)
PARAMOUNT PICTURES
PRODUCER: Sol C. Siegel
DIRECTOR: Ted Tetzlaff
SCREENPLAY: Earl Felton (script), Earl Felton, Gordon Kahn (story)
LENGTH: 70 minutes
TAGLINE: "It's the great profile at his greatest! . . . his funniest . . . his romantic best!"
STATUS: Exists.

CAST: John Barrymore (Duncan DeGrasse), Frances Farmer (Kitty Carr), Eugene Pallette (Gregory Martin), Virginia Dale (Lee Morrison), Ricardo Cortez (Mark Saunders), Sig Rumann (Franz von Bushmaster), Don Castle (Joe Bemis), William Wright (Luther Skinkley), Fritz Feld (Muller), Luis Alberni (Signor Scarletti), Cliff Nazzaro (Peters), and Andrew Tombes (Nixon).

SUMMARY: To publicize his new anti-Axis picture, *The Earth's On Fire* premiering in Washington D.C., a tyrannical Hollywood Studio mogul (Barrymore) and his publicity man (Castle) decide to hire fake spies to threaten to disrupt the movie, in order to attract publicity. Problems arise when two real spies (Rumann, Alberni) are hired. The bumbling pair intend to sabotage the east and west coast premieres of the production, and show their own propaganda film. On the publicity trip from the California to Washington D.C., the stars of the picture, who are lovers (Cortez, Farmer), quarrel over his interest in a young ingénue (Dale).

REVIEWS:
The Film Daily: "Lots of factors go into making this an enjoyable farce. For one thing, the film has Hollywood poking fun at itself with little damage done. Then there's a novel idea carried off by a good cast with a great deal of relish and gusto . . . It affords Ricardo Cortez the opportunity for contributing a swell portrayal as the ham star . . ."

New York Times: "An utterly mad buffoonery which makes wild jokes about movie premieres, and it seems to be scrambled together like the tag end of a Mardi Gras parade. But the one surprising thing about it is that it pops with impulsive fun, and occasionally works itself into tangles which generate some side-splitting mirth."

PRODUCTION NOTES, INTERESTING FACTS, AND TRIVIA:
1. The film marked the directorial debut of Ted Tetzlaff (1903-95), who originally gained fame as a cinematographer, lensing many of Capra's early films at Columbia (including *The Younger Generation* starring Cortez), and later, many prestigious films for Paramount. After making this picture and serving in World War II, Tetzlaff briefly returned to cinematography before resuming his directing career in 1947 with *Riffraff*, starring Pat O'Brien.

2. Several published reports indicate Otis Garrett was the original director of the picture, but had to withdraw shortly after production commenced, after suffering a medical emergency requiring surgery. He was replaced bythe cameraman, Tetzlaff.

3. *World Premiere*'s legendary star, John Barrymore (1882-1942), would make only one more film before succumbing to bronchial pneumonia, hardening of the arteries, hemorrhaging ulcers, and cirrhosis of the liver on May 19, 1942.

4. In the film, Barrymore's character, Duncan DeGrasse, carries a monkey around with him. According to a *Las Cruzes Sun-News* report, the monkey used in the movie became so upset when he first heard Barrymore's voice, he grabbed a large cracker and hid his face behind it. Barrymore then glared at the monkey and quipped "How can you top an animal with routines like that!"

I Killed that Man (1941) (MYSTERY)
K-B PRODUCTIONS — MONOGRAM PICTURES CORPORATION

PRODUCER: Maurice King
DIRECTOR: Phil Rosen
SCREENPLAY: Henry Bancroft (script), Leonard Fields, David Silverstein (original story)
LENGTH: 71 minutes
TAGLINE: "Murder strikes in the death house!"
STATUS: Exists. (DVD)

CAST: Ricardo Cortez (Roger Phillips), Joan Woodbury (Gert Reynolds), Pat Gleason (Bates), George Pembroke (Lowell King), Iris Adrian (Verne Drake), Herbert Rawlinson (Warden), Ralf Harolde (Nick Ross), Jack Mulhall (Collins), Vince Barnett (Drunk), Gavin Gordon (J. Reed), John Hamilton (District attorney), and Harry Holman (Lanning).

SUMMARY: At his execution, a convicted hired killer (Harolde) informs spectators he intends to reveal the identity of the person who ordered the killing he was convicted of. Before he can do so, he is murdered by a poison dart. An Assistant District Attorney (Cortez), ably assisted by his reporter girlfriend (Woodbury), sets out on a quest to solve the complex crime and reveal the culprit.

REVIEWS:
B Movies: "The Kozinskis became the King brothers with their next film, with Maurice and Frank producing, and brother number three, Herman, as production assistant. They had moved to Monogram from PRC and took advantage of the slight upward step by using an old studio story property for their second movie

venture, *I Killed That Man* (1941), made by Monogram in 1933 as *The Devil's Mate*. It was a whodunit with a prison setting, well enough directed by Phil Rosen, and smartly acted by Ricardo Cortez, Joan Woodbury, and a carefully chosen cast. In the same budgetary category as the rest of the Monogram output, it nevertheless seemed an improvement, with the money well spent."

The Film Daily: "Swell mystery story packed with action and suspense is a natural for young and old alike . . . The cast, headed by Ricardo Cortez and Joan Woodbury is great . . . ."

PRODUCTION NOTES, INTERESTING FACTS, AND TRIVIA:
1. *I Killed That Man* was a remake of Monogram's 1933 melodrama, *The Devil's Mate*, starring Preston Foster and Peggy Shannon. In *The Devil's Mate*, Cortez's character played by Foster, was a police detective, not a prosecuting attorney. Both versions were directed by Phil Rosen.

2. During his career, Ricardo Cortez made four films under the direction of Phil Rosen: *This Woman* (1924), *The Phantom in the House* (1929), *A Lost Lady* (1934), and *I Killed That Man* (1941).

3. Ricardo Cortez began work on *I Killed That Man* roughly one week after the funeral of his ex-wife, Christine Conniff Lee Cortez, who died of burns suffered when she fell asleep while smoking.

WHO IS HOPE SCHUYLER? (1942) (MYSTERY)
20TH CENTURY FOX FILM CORPORATION
PRODUCER: Sol Wurtzel
DIRECTOR: Tomas Z. Loring
SCREENPLAY: Arnaud D'Usseau
LENGTH: 57 minutes
TAGLINE: "5 times she struck! 5 times she killed! But who is Hope Schuyler?"
STATUS: Exists.

CAST: Joseph Allen Jr. (Tom Mason), Mary Howard (Diane Rossiter a.k.a. Hope Schuyler), Sheila Ryan (Lee Dale), Ricardo Cortez (Anthony Pearce), Janis Carter (Vesta Hadden), Joan Valerie (Phyllis Guerney), Robert Lowery (Robert Scott), Rose Hobart (Alma Pearce), Paul Guilfoyle (Carl Spence), William Newell (Perley Seymour), Pat Flaherty (Nash), Charles Trowbridge (Judge Rossiter), Frank Puglia (Baggott), Ed Stanley (Gillian Stafford), Edward Keane (Judge), and Cliff Clark (Lieutenant Palmer).

SUMMARY: When the governor appoints a special prosecutor (Allen Jr.) to try a district attorney (Cortez) on corruption charges, the conviction hinges on a mysterious astrologer named Hope Schuyler, who accepted bribery payments from the crooked D.A. The intense hunt for the missing woman casts a wide and complicated net of suspects.

REVIEWS:
Variety: " Filled with obvious situations and not well told by scripter or director, picture is lightweight fare for dual filler spots in subsequent bookings . . . Allen and Miss Ryan provide most convincing performances, with able assistance of Ricardo Cortez in the heavy department . . ."

PRODUCTION NOTES, INTERESTING FACTS, AND TRIVIA:
1. Based on the novel, *Hearses Don't Hurry*, by Stephen Ransome (1941).

2. Several published reports indicate 20th Century Fox originally planned to utilize the story as part of its Michael Shayne detective series, but changed its mind.

3. According to a *The Film Daily* article, 20th Century Fox constructed a mini airfield on the grounds of the studio golf course for this picture because of the wartime prohibition on establishing commercial and military airports for "production purposes."

Rubber Rackateers (1942) (crime drama)
Monogram Pictures Corporation
Producer: Maurice King
Director: Harold Young
Screenplay: Henry Blankfort.
Length: 67 minutes.
Tagline: "Bootleg tires . . . Death on wheels!"
Status: Exists. (DVD)

Cast: Ricardo Cortez (Gilin), Rochelle Hudson (Nikki), Bill Henry (Bill Barry), Barbara Read (Mary Dale), Milburn Stone (Angel), Dewey Robinson (Larkin), John Abbott (Dumbo), Pat Gleason (Curley), Dick Hogan (Bert), Alan Hale Jr. (Red), Sam Edwards (Freddy Dale), and Marjorie Manners (Lila).

Summary: A young man (Henry) sets out to expose the criminals (Cortez, Stone, Abbott) operating a rubber bootlegging enterprise after the brother of his girlfriend (Hudson) is killed in an accident caused by a faulty tire.

Reviews:
B Movies: "Rubber Racketeers hopped on the topical headlines and made a timely expose of the traffic in black marketing of tires during wartime. Henry Blankfort wrote a compact script intelligently directed by Harold Young. Ricardo Cortez made the chief hoodlum a menacing figure, Rochelle Hudson added her own figure to the proceedings . . ."

Variety: "Current activities of tire bootleggers provide a topical basis for this meller of gangdom, with defense plant workers in the roles of heroes. Following familiar melodramatic trails, the picture is neatly set up to accent the adventurous angles, and will provide good dual support in the secondary and family bookings . . . Ricardo Cortez, Bill Henry, and Rochelle Hudson carry the leads along in good style . . ."

Cortez portrayed a crime boss who oversees the manufacture and sale of defective tires in the B crime thriller, *Rubber Racketeers* (Monogram, 1942). From left to right: Rochelle Hudson, Cortez, and Kam Tong.

PRODUCTION NOTES, INTERESTING FACTS, AND TRIVIA:

1. The working titles for this film were *Tire Gangster* and *Hot Rubber*. Both Monogram and 20th Century Fox registered the title, *Hot Rubber*, but the latter studio never made the film they had planned.

TOMORROW WE LIVE (1942) (CRIME DRAMA)
ATLANTIS PICTURES CORPORATION
PRODUCER: Seymour Nebenzal
DIRECTOR: Edgar G. Ulmer
SCREENPLAY: Bert Lytton
LENGTH: 64 minutes.
STATUS: Exists. (DVD)

CAST: Ricardo Cortez (The Ghost), Jean Parker (Julie Bronson), Emmett Lynn (Pop Bronson), William Marshall (Lieutenant Bob Lord), Roseanne Stevens (Melba), Ray Miller (Chick), Frank S. Hagney (Kohler), Rex Lease (Shorty), Jack Ingram (Steve), and Barbara Slater (The Blonde).

SUMMARY: A master criminal known as "The Ghost" (Cortez) casts a spell over those around him, including an ex-convict café owner (Lynn) who does his bidding. The café owner's daughter (Parker), a recent college graduate, suspects her father's involvement with criminals, and with the help of her army lieutenant beau (Marshall), attempts to help her dad rid himself of "The Ghost" and rival gangs.

REVIEWS:
B Movies: "In *Tomorrow We Live*, it was Ricardo Cortez who played the slimy racketeer and Jean Parker the college girl in peril of his clutches. Bart Lytton wrote some pretentious flowery dialogue, which Edgar G. Ulmer poetically directed, but it was all out of place. Seymour Nebenzal produced it as if he had a combination of *M* and *Mayerling*. He didn't."

Chicago Daily Tribune: "Well, yawn your way thru this one if you want to. 'Ham and Eggs' reads a sign on the wall of the little desert restaurant where a considerable amount of the pictures' action takes place. You realize it is unintentionally symbolic. The players took care of the ham and the scenario writer the eggs."

PRODUCTION NOTES, INTERESTING FACTS, AND TRIVIA:
1. The working title for this film was *Remember the Day*.

2. *Tomorrow We Live* would be the first of 11 motion pictures director Ulmer would make for the poverty row studio, PRC. In a rare interview conducted by Peter Bogdanovich just prior to the veteran director's death, and published in Bogdanovich's 1997 book, *Who the Devil Made It*, Ulmer said, although he had no long term contract with the studio, they gave him great creative control, and referred to him as "The Capra of PRC."

3. Although Jean Parker enjoyed working with Ricardo Cortez, whose professionalism she appreciated, she disliked the direction of Ulmer, with whom she worked on two motion pictures: *Tomorrow We Live* (1943) and *Bluebeard* (1944). In a 1997 interview with the author, published in *Films of the Golden Age* magazine, she recalled the director.

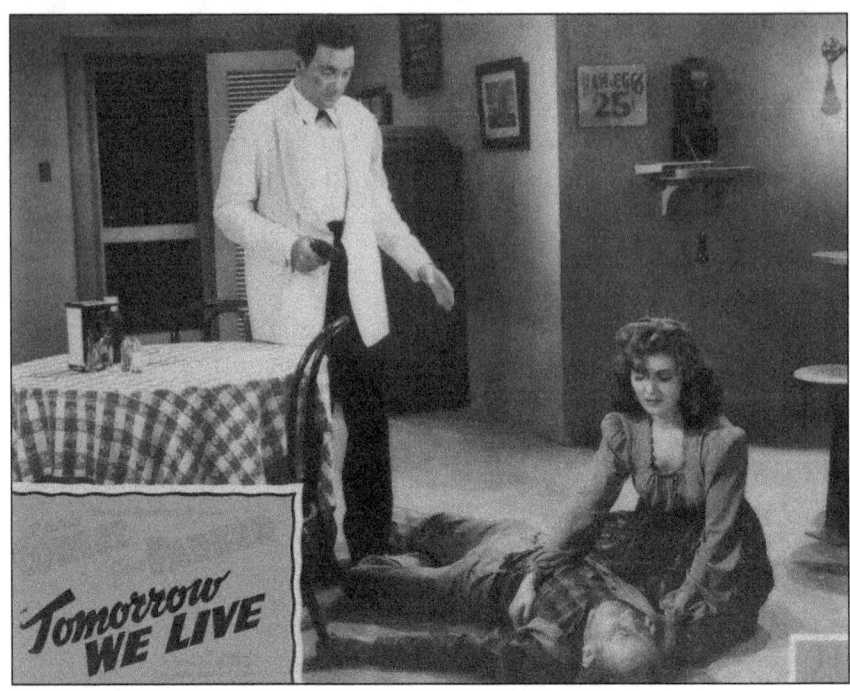

Ricardo and Jean Parker in *Tomorrow We Live* (1942), directed by Edgar G. Ulmer. Photo courtesy of Jan Taylor Garfield.

"I didn't like Ulmer. He would say 'Miss Parker come up a little bit back!' He threw his vowels around making it almost impossible to understand him. Then he'd repeat himself as if I was deaf. I was so furious! He was a fine director though, I must admit!"

MAKE YOUR OWN BED (1944) (COMEDY)
WARNER BROTHERS
PRODUCER: Alex Gottlieb
DIRECTOR: Peter Godfrey
SCREENPLAY: Francis Swann, Edmund Joseph (script), Richard Weil (adaptation)
LENGTH: 80 minutes
TAGLINE: "Riot this way folks!"
STATUS: Exists.

CAST: Jack Carson (Jerry Curtis), Jane Wyman (Susan Courtney), Irene Manning (Vivian Whirtle), Alan Hale (Walter Whirtle), George Tobias (Boris Murphy), Robert Shayne (Lester Knight),

Tala Birell ((Marie Gruber), Ricardo Cortez (Fritz Allen), Marjorie Hoshelle (Elsa Wehmer), and Kurt Katch (Paul Hassen).

SUMMARY: When a wealthy gun powder manufacturer (Hale) cannot find servants due to a wartime shortage, he invents a story of Nazi spies, and hires a bumbling detective (Carson) and his fiancé (Wyman) to pose as servants to protect him. When real spies show up at his home posing as actors, the detectives manage to deter them, in spite of themselves.

REVIEWS:
Saturday Spectator: "82 minutes of solid laughter and enjoyment are to be had these days, simply by seeing this hilarious new comedy..."

Variety: "*Make Your Own Bed* is a wacky farce sketched on broad lines to hit present audience requirements for light and fluffy screen fare... Picture will click for profitable biz in all bookings."

PRODUCTION NOTES, INTERESTING FACTS, AND TRIVIA:
1. Based on the play, *On the Hiring* (1919), by Harvey J. O'Higgins and Harriet Ford.

2. Warner Bros. archival records (at U.S.C.) indicate some scenes were filmed at the W.K. Jewett estate in Pasadena, California.

3. Columnist Hedda Hopper reported the cast and crew had a small party on the set of *Make Your Own Bed*, to celebrate Ricardo Cortez's 21-year anniversary in the movies.

4. Warner Bros. billed *Make Your Own Bed* as Jack Carson's first starring comic role.

THE INNER CIRCLE (1946) (MYSTERY)
REPUBLIC PICTURES CORPORATION
PRODUCER: William J. O'Sullivan
DIRECTOR: Phil Ford
SCREENPLAY: Dorrell McGowan, Stuart E. McGowan
LENGTH: 57 minutes
STATUS: Exists. (DVD)

CAST: Adele Mara (Geraldine Travis a.k.a. Geraldine Smith), Warren Douglas (Johnny Strange), William Frawley (Webb), Ricardo Cortez (Duke York), Virginia Christine (Rhoda Roberts), Ken Niles (announcer), Will Wright (Henry Boggs), Dorothy Adams (Mrs. Wilson), and Martha Montgomery (Anne Lowe).

SUMMARY: In order to protect her younger sister, a beautiful and mysterious woman (Mara) sets up a private investigator (Douglas) to take the rap for a murder.

REVIEWS:
Variety: "The Inner Circle hasn't much to recommend it. Even whodunit addicts will turn a quizzical eyebrow at the tangled, illogical, and crudely put-together story . . . Vet actors William Frawley and Ricardo Cortez, police detective and nightclub menace respectively, give big assists . . ."

PRODUCTION NOTES, INTERESTING FACTS, AND TRIVIA:
1. Original title of the film was *The Twisted Circle*.

2. Born in Portland, Maine, director Phil Ford (1902-76) was a former actor who became an assistant director and second-unit director before being promoted in 1945. For the next seven years (1945-52) he helmed over 40 low budget movies (mostly westerns) before turning his attention to television during the 1950's, directing over 50 episodes of the classic series, *Lassie*. He was the son of actor/director Francis Ford, and the nephew of legendary director, John Ford.

3. An article published in the *Medicine Hat News* stated that one

of the famed "Goldwyn Girls," 25-year-old screen starlet Martha Montgomery (1920-2005) told reporters her role as the suspected murderess in *The Inner Circle* was a distinct change of pace. She said before doing this part she had been playing "pleasant, happy girls in Hollywood musical comedies."

THE LOCKET (1946) (DRAMA)
RKO RADIO PICTURES
PRODUCER: Bert Granet
DIRECTOR: John Brahm
SCREENPLAY: Sheridan Gibney
LENGTH: 85 minutes
TAGLINE: "Men took their lives in their hands when they took her in their arms!"
STATUS: Exists. (DVD)

CAST: Laraine Day (Nancy Monks Blair a.k.a. Nancy Patton), Brian Aherne (Dr. Harry S. Blair), Robert Mitchum (Norman Clyde), Gene Raymond (John Willis), Sharyn Moffett (Nancy age 10), Ricardo Cortez (Mr. Andrew Bonner), Henry Stephenson (Lord Windham), Katherine Emery (Mrs. Willis), Reginald Denny (Mr. Arthur Wendell), Fay Helm (Mrs. Bonner), Helene Thimig (Mrs. Monks), Nella Walker (Mrs. Louise Wendell), Queenie Leonard (lady singer), Lilian Fontaine (Lady Wyndham), Myrna Dell (Thelma), and Johnny Clark (Donald).

SUMMARY: Minutes before his wedding, a millionaire (Raymond) receives a visit from a psychiatrist (Aherne) who says he is the ex-husband of the bride-to-be (Day). The psychiatrist says she is mentally unstable, and proceeds to relate her story in flashback.

REVIEWS:
Motion Picture Guide: "They should have named this picture, 'Flashback' because that's what it is, one flashback after another with the tale told in the style of Akira Kurosawa from several points of view . . . A good cast in a diffuse film."

Variety: "Interestingly told, carefully produced, pic measures up as a neat entry in the psycho field, able to carry off top position in any situation. Vehicle is a strong one for Laraine Day, and she does much with the role of Nancy . . . Ricardo Cortez, seen too seldom in films of late, is excellent as the murder victim . . ."

PRODUCTION NOTES, INTERESTING FACTS, AND TRIVIA:

1. The film is unusual because it utilizes multi-layered flashbacks to relate the story.

2. Director John Brahm was borrowed from 20th Century Fox, and Miss Day from Paramount.

3. *The Locket* marked the screen return of Gene Raymond after a five-year stint in the military, and the debut of actress Martha Hyer, who portrayed one of Day's bridesmaids.

4. According to RKO archival records (at U.C.L.A.), production costs (both direct and indirect) for *The Locket* totaled $906,523. Of the cast members, Brian Aherne was by far the highest paid, netting $75,000 as compared to lead Laraine Day who made just $37,500. Interestingly, the third highest paid actor in the cast was not Robert Mitchum but supporting actress Katherine Emery who was paid $15,000 for her work, in comparison to Mitchum's $12,000. Ricardo Cortez received $3,333.33 for 1 2/6 weeks of work on the picture.

5. Publicity items for the picture indicated the set used for the house of Mrs. Willis (Katherine Emery), was the same one utilized for the house of Alex Sebastian (Claude Rains) in *Notorious* (1946).

6. The distinguished-looking lady who portrayed Lady Wyndham, whose jewelry is stolen in *The Locket*, was Lilian Fontaine, the mother of actresses Olivia de Havilland and Joan Fontaine.

7. According to the *American Film Institute Catalog*, after the completion of the picture, both Miss Day and Mr. Brahm embarked on a twelve city promotion tour. On the tour, they

explained how certain scenes were filmed, utilizing actors to impersonate the various crew members.

8. According to the *American Film Institute Catalog*, Laraine Day designed the spun-glass fabric used for her wedding dress in the picture.

Blackmail (1947) (CRIME DRAMA)
REPUBLIC PICTURES CORPORATION
PRODUCER: William J. O'Sullivan
DIRECTOR: Lesley Selander
SCREENPLAY: Royal K. Cole (script), Robert Leslie Bellem (original story), Albert DeMond (additional dialogue)
LENGTH: 67 minutes
TAGLINE: "Murder, mystery! A private eye…On the hunt for a disappearing corpse!"
STATUS: Exists.

CAST: William Marshall (Daniel Turner), Adele Mara (Sylvia Duane), Ricardo Cortez (Ziggy Cranston), Grant Withers (Inspector Donaldson), Stephanie Bachelor (Carla), Richard Fraser (Antoine le Blanc), Roy Barcroft (Spice Kelloway), George J. Lewis ("Blue Chip" Winslow), Gregory Gay (Jervis), and Tristram Coffin (Pinky).

SUMMARY: When a night club singer (Bachelor) who was blackmailing him is found dead, a wealthy businessman (Cortez) engages the services of a young private eye (Marshall) for protection, and to find out who was responsible. Collecting the true facts proves both psychologically and physically challenging for the young investigator, who must contend with the millionaire's violent chauffeur, his unscrupulous business associates (Barcroft, Coffin), and his beautiful and dangerous mistress (Mara).

REVIEWS:
Variety: "Blackmail never proves as exciting as its title would indicate. Actionless motion and dull talk keep interest at a minimum. Production dress is good but physical quality fails to make up for

lack of punch . . ."

PRODUCTION NOTES, INTERESTING FACTS, AND TRIVIA:
1. The script for *Blackmail* was based on a short story entitled, *Stock Shot*, by noted pulp writer Robert Leslie Bellem, published in *Hollywood Detective* magazine in June, 1944. The working title of the film was, *Lightning Strikes Twice*.

2. During his prolific career, pulp fiction writer Robert Leslie Bellem (1902-68) was said to have penned over 3000 short stories which were published in various magazines, including *Hollywood Dectective*, which Bellem created in 1942. The magazine was published for eight years until October, 1950. Bellem's most famous creation was hardboiled private detective Dan Turner, depicted in *Blackmail* by actor William Marshall.

MYSTERY IN MEXICO (1948) (CRIME DRAMA)
RKO RADIO PICTURES
PRODUCER: Sid Rogell
DIRECTOR: Robert Wise
SCREENPLAY: Lawrence Kimble (script), Muriel Roy Bolton (story)
LENGTH: 66 minutes
TAGLINE: "A night of tropic terror—in a city made for romance!"
STATUS: Exists. (DVD)

CAST: William Lundigan (Steve Hastings), Jacqueline White (Victoria Ames), Ricardo Cortez (Joe Norcross), Tony Barrett (Carlos), Jacqueline Dalya (Dolores Fernandez), Walter Reed (Glenn Ames), Jose Torvay (Swigart), Jaime Jimenez (Pancho Gomez), and Antonio Frausto (Mr. Gomez).

SUMMARY: In Mexico City, an insurance investigator (Reed) disappears with a diamond necklace. In pursuit are another investigator (Lundigan), the man's sister (White), and a gangster.

REVIEWS:

Motion Picture Guide: "The actual Mexico City locations are well used with some good performances . . . There is nothing out of the ordinary, but it's well handled, harmless fun."

Variety: "Ok program material . . . Robert Wise's direction has given the piece a good pace and develops sufficient thrills to maintain casual interest in the script . . ."

PRODUCTION NOTES, INTERESTING FACTS, AND TRIVIA:

1. In the book *Conversaions With Directors*, edited by Elsie M. Walker and David T. Johnson, director Robert Wise said that *Mystery in Mexico* was one of the films he regretted doing while under contract to RKO during the early years of his career.

2. In January, 1947, the *Hollywood Reporter* announced RKO would make *Mystery In Mexico* a "bilingual release," but the *American Film Institute Catalog* reported a Spanish version has never been found.

3. According to RKO archival records housed at U.C.L.A, production costs on *Mystery in Mexico* totaled $257,420. Some exterior scenes were filmed at RKO's Churubusco Studios in Mexico City. The scenes cost the studio $88,274. Of the actors, William Lundigan was highest paid at $15,000 for 6 1/6 weeks of work. Ricardo Cortez was paid $3,500 for 2 1/6 weeks of work.

4. In his book, *The Films of Robert Wise*, author Richard C. Keenan said when Mexican actor Juan Garcia failed to show up for work on *Mystery in Mexico*, the key supporting role of Carlos, the double-dealing taxi driver, was given to Tony Barrett. Ironically, Mr Barrett ended up winning the lion's share of the film's acting honors for his charismatic performance.

5. Actor Tony Barrett (1916-74) was a character player who made over 30 motion pictures before turning his attentions to television, where he became a successful television producer and writer.

Among his writing credits were episodes of such memorable television series as: *Peter Gunn, The Untouchables, 77 Sunset Strip, Honey West,* and *The Mod Squad.* He was nominated for an Emmy in 1970 as co-producer of *The Mod Squad.*

6. *Mexico City News* gossip columnist Pepe Romero served as a technical advisor on the film.

BUNCO SQUAD (1950) (CRIME DRAMA)
RKO RADIO PICTURES
PRODUCER: Lewis J. Rachmil
DIRECTOR: Herbert I. Leeds
SCREENPLAY: George Callahan
LENGTH: 67 minutes
TAGLINE: "The blazing, amazing truth! About the world's cruelest racket!"
STATUS: Exists. (DVD)

CAST: Robert Sterling (Sgt. Steve Johnson), Joan Dixon (Grace Bradshaw), Ricardo Cortez (Anthony Wells), Douglas Fowley (Sgt McManus), Elizabeth Risdon (Jessica Royce), Marguerite Churchill (Barbara Madison), John Kellogg (Frederick Reed), Bernadene Hayes (Liane Hill), Robert Bice (Drake), Vivian Oakland (Annie Cobb), Dante (Dante), Kathleen Ellis (Julie), Rand Brooks (Robert), Frank Wilcox (Dr. Largo a.k. a. Mike Finlayson), and Dick Elliott (Thurman).

SUMMARY: Two police sergeants (Sterling, Fowley) of Los Angeles' bunco squad are assigned to investigate a phony fortune telling ring headed by a suave confidence man (Cortez).

REVIEWS:
Variety: "As a programmer for lowercase bookings, *Bunco Squad* will get by. There's nothing out of the ordinary in its makeup, being a melodrama based on how phony fortune tellers and mediums operate. It has enough general interest to see it through play dates . . . Cortez's master crook is smooth. . ."

Production notes, interesting facts, and trivia:

1. Based on an unpublished novel, *Fortuneer* by Reginald Tavener, and the 1938 RKO film melodrama, *Crime Ring*. The latter, directed by Leslie Goodwins, starred Allan Lane.

2. The *Bunco Squad* file in the RKO Archives (stored at U.C.L.A.) indicates material was added to the script to reflect the contents of actual files from the Los Angeles Police Department. Also, in an effort to promote realism, fortune tellers were consulted, who provided insights regarding their trade.

3. Records stored in the RKO Arhives also reveal total production costs on *Bunco Squad* were $219,728. Of the cast, lead actor Robert Sterling was the highest paid, taking home $3,543 for his role as police sergeant. Second highest paid was Cortez at $2,916.67 for 2 2/6 weeks of work.

4. *Bunco Squad* marked the last film appearance of Marguerite Churchill (1910-2000), who made a name for herself as a leading lady in both A and B productions during the 1930's and 1940's. She was the ex-wife of Ricardo's best actor friend, George O'Brien, and had worked with Cortez twice, in *Man Hunt* and *The Walking Dead*, both made in 1936.

5. Producer Lewis J. Rachmil (1908-84) was an Oscar-nominated art director before turning his attention to production during the mid-1940's, when he worked on multiple entries of William Boyd's *Hopalong Cassidy* series. During the 1950's he branched out into television while still making movies, including *The Violent Men* (1955) and *Gidget* (1959). In the 1960's, he produced several motion pictures for Mirisch Films in England.

6. Leading man Robert Sterling (1917-2006) told the press he liked his role in *Bunco Squad*. In a self-penned article for *Screenland* magazine, published to coincide with the film's release in August 1950, he said he enjoyed playing diverse parts. "In RKO's *Bunco Squad*, I'm a young cop who goes after racketeers who prey on the people with a belief in, or a fear of the

Ricardo's last cinematic foray into crime came in RKO's low budget crime drama, *Bunco Squad* (1950). From left to right: Elizabeth Risdon, Bernadene Hayes, Cortez, John Kellogg, and Robert Bice.

Bernadene Hayes and Cortez in *Bunco Squad* (RKO, 1950).

supernatural. It isn't a big picture, but it's different, and I think exciting . . ."

THE LAST HURRAH (1958) (DRAMA)
COLUMBIA PICTURES CORPORATION
PRODUCER: John Ford
DIRECTOR: John Ford
SCREENPLAY: Frank Nugent
LENGTH: 121 minutes
TAGLINE: "Hurrah for the big book, the big cast, the big picture!"
STATUS: Exists. (DVD)

CAST: Spencer Tracy (Frank Skeffington), Jeffrey Hunter (Adam Caulfield), Dianne Foster (Maeve Segrue Caulfield), Pat O'Brien (John Gorman), Basil Rathbone (Norman Cass Sr.), Donald Crisp (Cardinal Martin Burke), James Gleason ("Cuke" Gillin), Edward Brophy ("Ditto" Boland), John Carradine (Amos Force), Willis Bouchey (Roger Segrue), Basil Ruysdael (Bishop Gardner), Ricardo Cortez (Sam Weinberg), Wallace Ford (Charles J. Hennessey), Frank McHugh (Festus Garvey), Anna Lee (Gert Minihan), Jane Darwell (Delia Boylan), Frank Albertson (Jack Mangan), Charles FitzSimons (Kevin McCluskey), Carleton Young (Winslow), Bob Sweeney (Johnny Degnan), Edmund Lowe (Johnny Byrne), O.Z Whitehead (Norman Cass Jr.), Arthur Walsh (Frank Skeffington Jr.), Helen Westcott, Ruth Warren, and James Flavin.

SUMMARY: When a veteran Irish-American mayor and old-time political boss of an eastern city (Tracy) decides to run for another term, he receives an unexpectedly stiff challenge from a novice backed by a dedicated group of his opponents. His nephew (Hunter), who works for a newspaper which opposes him, chronicles the events of the campaign.

REVIEWS:
Motion Picture Daily: "The virtuosity with which producer-director John Ford handles actors, camera, and film to achieve a particular effect has seldom had so wide a range as in this delightful, absorbing,

warm, and human study of a politician of the old school and the ould sod. Combined with the Ford magic is a Spencer Tracy performance perfect in spirit and letter . . . The subordinates are sketched in a lower key, but each is a gem of characterization with Pat O'Brien and Ricardo Cortez as John Gorman and Sam Weinberg, principal lieutenants . . ."

New York Times: "Now that all key districts have been heard from, including Hollywood, it is safe to expect that Edwin O'Connor's highly touted political character, Skeffington, will repeat in an overwhelming landslide as the People's Choice this year . . . Mr. Tracy is at his best in the leading role . . . Edward Brophy as a dopey idolator, Pat O'Brien as a sane strategist, James Gleason as a fast finagler, and Ricardo Cortez as the guardian of the 'Jewish vote' make things as merry for the audience as they do for Skeffington."

Production notes, interesting facts, and trivia:
1. Although several articles indicated both James Cagney and Spencer Tracy had been mentioned as leading candidates to play the lead character, Frank Skeffington, Orson Welles claimed he was Ford's first choice. Welles said he was filming on location at the time of the offer, and unbeknownst to him, one of his attorneys turned the part down.

2. Actor Jeffrey Hunter was borrowed from 20th Century Fox to play the key role of Skeffington's nephew, Adam Caulfield.

3. The film reunited Tracy with his old Irish drinking buddies: O'Brien, Gleason, Brophy, and McHugh, and veteran director John Ford, who helmed Tracy's 1930 melodrama, *Up the River*.

4. During the filming, Tracy told the press, the movie might well be his last, but Tracy would make six more motion pictures after *The Last Hurrah*, until his death in 1967.

5. Archival records indicate that, although the film was made for $2.5 million, $200,000 less than budgeted, it was a box office loser to the tune of $1.4 million.

Frank Skeffington and his trusted deputies. From left to right: Ricardo, Edward Brophy, James Gleason, Spencer Tracy, and Pat O'Brien in *The Last Hurrah* (1958). Photo courtesy of Jan Taylor Garfield.

6. In his volume, *Searching for John Ford*, author Joseph McBride said on the fourth day of filming, news reached the set of *The Last Hurrah* of the death of Columbia boss, Harry Cohn. Director Ford admired Cohn, and dismissed the company for the day. He also took time away from the production to attend Cohn's funeral held on adjoining Columbia soundstages. He sat in the front row.

7. Author Ronald L. Davis in his book, *John Ford, Hollywood's Old Master*, stated Spencer Tracy's longtime companion Katharine Hepburn, was instrumental in helping director Ford convince Tracy to take the role of Frank Skeffington.

8. In an article by Thomas Pryor in *The New York Times*, it was reported Ford lined up over 400 extras to film the torchlight election parade seen in the picture. Each was paid $22 for the evening. Eight assistant directors rode herd over them. The master property man on the film, Charles Grannuci, was

responsible for purchasing and supervising the many props, including 200 torches, 500 blue campaign sashes, campaign buttons, cream colored dusters, and hats.

FILMS (AS A DIRECTOR)

INSIDE STORY (1939) (CRIME DRAMA)
20TH CENTURY FOX FILM CORPORATION
DIRECTOR: Ricardo Cortez
SCREENPLAY: Jerry Cady, Herbert Lewis
LENGTH: 61 minutes
TAGLINE: "The story a girl dared to tell! The headline a reporter would not write!"
STATUS: Exists

CAST: Michael Whalen (Barney Callahan), Jean Rogers (June White), Chick Chandler (Snapper Doolin), Douglas Fowley (Gus Brawley), John King (Paul Randall), Jane Darwell (Aunt Mary Perkins), June Gale (Eunice), Spencer Charters (Uncle Ben Perkins), Theodore Von Eltz (Whitey Walker), Charles D. Brown (J. B. Douglas), Cliff Clark (Collins), Charles Lane (district attorney), Louise Carter (Dora), and Bert Roach (Hopkins).

SUMMARY: While drunk, a lonely reporter (Whalen) pens a column in which he attempts to locate the loneliest girl in New York. He eventually finds a young clip joint hostess (Rogers) who fills the bill, but she is mixed up with gangsters, and the reporter soon gets more than he bargained for.

REVIEWS:
B Movies: "As a director, Cortez gave the same quality found in his screen performances—smooth, workmanlike, steady, eschewing flamboyance, but making certain everything was in place, all details attended to in good order."

Variety: "Mystery murder and newspaper yarn sets well as a vehicle for Whalen and his comedy stooge. Picture has added distinction of Ricardo Cortez's name as director, his first effort along these lines after 16 years before the cameras. Howard J. Greene and Cortez have given their leads strong support . . ."

PRODUCTION NOTES, INTERESTING FACTS, AND TRIVIA:
1. Based on the short story, *A Very Practical Joke*, by Ben Ames Williams, published in *The Saturday Evening Post* in 1925.

2. The third and last in 20th Century Fox's *Roving Reporter* series. The other films were *The Truth About Murder* (1938) and *While New York Sleeps* (1938), both starring Whalen and Chandler (as his sidekick).

3. The Fox Film Corporation filmed the Williams story before, in 1930 as *Man Trouble*, starring Dorothy Mackaill and Milton Sills.

CHASING DANGER (1939) (ADVENTURE)
20TH CENTURY FOX FILM CORPORATION
PRODUCER: Sol M. Wurtzel
DIRECTOR: Ricardo Cortez
SCREENPLAY: Richard Ellis, Helen Logan, Leonardo Bercovici (original story)
LENGTH: 60 minutes
TAGLINE: "While the world sits on a powder keg...They chase a dame!"
STATUS: Exists.

CAST: Preston Foster (Steve Mitchell), Lynn Bari (Renee Claire), Wally Vernon (Waldo Rohrbeck), Henry Wilcoxen (Andre Duvac), Joan Woodbury (Hazila), Harold Huber (Carlos Demitri), Judy Gilbert (Teeda), Pedro De Cordoba (Gurra Din), Stanley Fields (Captain Fontaine), and Roy D'Arcy (Corbin).

SUMMARY: While in the Middle East covering an Arab revolt, a pair of newsreel cameramen (Foster, Vernon) become endangered when they try to help a clip joint hostess (Bari).

REVIEWS:
B Movies: "This one involved revolt of Arab tribes against France, and Cortez guided it through excitingly enough . . ."

Variety: "Average comic-melodrama only fairly diverting. . . Failure of script is somewhat offset by director Ricardo Cortez's expert handling of a pair of harum-scarum scamps who talk their way in and out of tight situations and numerous jails . . ."

PRODUCTION NOTES, INTERESTING FACTS, AND TRIVIA:
1. Working titles for this film were *Dangerous Cargo* and *Camera Daredevils No. 2*.

2. *Chasing Danger* was the second of only two films in 20th Century Fox's short-lived *Camera Daredevils* series about the adventures of two newsreel cameramen. The first, *Sharpshooters* (1938), starred Brian Donlevy and Wally Vernon. In *Chasing Danger*, veteran actor Preston Foster replaced Donlevy, and Cortez replaced director James Tinling.

3. Whether inadvertent or not, Ricardo Cortez was a cupid of sorts. Actors Joan Woodbury and Henry Wilcoxen met and fell in love while making *Chasing Danger*. They were wed shortly after shooting wrapped in December 1938. Lynn Bari also married her boyfriend agent Walter Kane shortly after completing this movie.

4. Ironically, actor Brian Donlevy, who played the lead character, Steve Mitchell, in the first *Camera Daredevils* feature, *Sharpshooters*, played a character with the same name in his long running espionage television series, *Dangerous Assignment*.

5. Leading lady, Lynn Bari (1913-89), took French and Arabic lessons for her role in *Chasing Danger*. According to a *Uniontown News Standard* article, her Arabic progressed so well, so quickly, it became challenging to her instructor. "I'll be glad when we're finished with these lessons," her teacher confessed. "Every time I come in and say, 'Good afternoon, Miss Bari, how are you?'

she lets loose a flood of Arabic back at me in such a rush I hardly know what she's saying. I'm taking a post-graduate course in Arabic just to check on her!"

THE ESCAPE (1939) (CRIME DRAMA)
20TH CENTURY FOX FILM CORPORATION
PRODUCER: Sol M. Wurtzel
DIRECTOR: Ricardo Cortez
SCREENPLAY: Robert Ellis, Helen Logan
LENGTH: 62 minutes
STATUS: Exists. (DVD)

CAST: Kane Richmond (Eddie Farrell), Amanda Duff (Judy Peronni), June Gale (Annie Qualen), Edward Norris (Louie Peronni), Henry Armetta (Guiseppi Peronni), Frank Reicher (Dr. Shumaker), Scotty Beckett (Willie Rogers), Leona Roberts (Aunt Mamie Qualen), Rex Downing (Tommy Rogers), Jimmy Butler (Jim Rogers), Roger McGee (Swat), Richard Lane (David Clifford), Jack Carson (Chet Warren), Matt McHugh (Pete), Helen Ericson (Helen Gardner), and Robert Scott (Mickey).

SUMMARY: At a gangster's (Norris) funeral, a doctor recalls the sad tale of his life of crime, which ended when his gang kidnapped his daughter, and he loses his life saving her.

REVIEWS:
The Film Daily: "Gangster story told in narrative form will serve neatly as program offering . . . The cast is capable and hard-working and Ricardo Cortez does a workmanlike job of direction. . ."

Variety: "An unusual and novel technique of celluloid story unraveling has been employed by writers Robert Ellis and Helen Logan to make *The Escape* a refreshing retreat from the ordinary . . . Ricardo Cortez' direction is almost uniformly excellent. To the extent of the limited ability of some of the players, he keeps them all working in a subdued key."

The tale of a young man (Edward Norris) from a good family who falls into a life of crime was the storyline of *The Escape* (20th Century Fox, 1939), directed by Ricardo Cortez. From left to right: Amanda Duff, Edward Norris, Henry Armetta, and Kane Richmond.

PRODUCTION NOTES, INTERESTING FACTS, AND TRIVIA:

1. The working title was *East Side, West Side*.

2. Robert Ellis (1892-1974), who co-wrote the script of *The Escape*, was formerly a movie actor and director who helmed Ricardo Cortez's official film acting debut, *The Imp*, in 1919.

3. A *Hollywood Reporter* item from July, 1939, noted scenes involving reporter Chet Warren (played by Jack Carson) were added to the film after production wrapped. Ricardo Cortez and Mr. Carson initiated a friendship while making the picture, which endured.

4. A report published in the *Panama City News Herald*, stated leading man, Kane Richmond (who portrayed a policeman), had problems filming some of the action scenes in *The Escape*. After a strenuous night of bowling, his hands were so severely

calloused, he had trouble shooting scenes requiring him to draw and fire his pistol in pursuit of desperate criminals. According to the reports, Richmond was in so much pain, he groaned "I wished this story was set in London." When director Cortez asked why, Richmond replied "Because then I'd be playing a London bobby—and they don't carry guns!"

HEAVEN WITH A BARBED WIRE FENCE (1939) (DRAMA)
20TH CENTURY FOX FILM CORPORATION
PRODUCER: Sol M. Wurtzel
DIRECTOR: Ricardo Cortez
SCREENPLAY: Dalton Trumbo, Leonard Hoffman, Ben Grauman Kohn (script), Dalton Trumbo (original story), Sam Duncan (contribution to script construction)
LENGTH: 65 minutes
TAGLINE: "You've heard about kids like these! You'll like them!"
STATUS: Exists. (DVD)

CAST: Jean Rogers (Anita Santos), Raymond Walburn ("The Professor" Townsend Thayer), Marjorie Rambeau (Mamie), Glenn Ford (Joe Riley), Nicholas Conte (Tony Casselli), Eddie Collins (Bili), Ward Bond (Hunk), Irving Bacon (Sheriff Clem Diggers), Kay Linaker (Nurse), and Paul Hurst (Guard).

SUMMARY: A department store clerk (Ford) in New York buys a tract of land in Arizona and hitchhikes out West to farm it. Along the way he meets a young hobo (Conte), an illegal alien (Rogers), and an eccentric college professor (Walburn).

REVIEWS:
Hollywood Reporter: "A fine example of a well-made low budget picture. Its story is wholesome and leaves one with the kind of feeling you have after a cold shower bath on a hot day."

Leonard Maltin's Movie & Video Guide: "Spunky little road movie with Rogers, Ford, and Conte linking up and riding the rails to California . . ."

Lima News: "*Heaven with a Barbed Wire Fence* boasts no big names, no expensive budget, but it is expertly directed by Ricardo Cortez and emerges as a wholesome and keenly satisfying little film . . ."

Syracuse Herald Journal: "Once in a while an unpretentious little film like *Heaven with a Barbed Wire Fence* comes along to break the monotony of Hollywood's repetitive string of B pictures, with a breath of freshness and originality . . . Director Ricardo Cortez has told the story simply and effectively without resorting to the usual melodramatic tricks. He receives good support from a cast of unknowns . . ."

PRODUCTION NOTES, INTERESTING FACTS, AND TRIVIA:

1. The film was partially shot on location in Thousand Oaks, Newhall, and Saugus, California.

2. According to the *American Film Institute Catalog*, young Nicholas Conte (1914-75) was signed for his part in *Heaven* based on a 20th Century Fox screentest for the lead in *Golden Boy* (1939), which he lost to William Holden. Eventually, Nicholas, who adopted the name Richard Conte, went on to have a substantive acting career both in films and on television, often playing flawed tough guy heroes or world-weary criminals.

3. Hardworking B movie players like actress Jean Rogers (1916-91) were often required to play multiple roles at the same time. During the making of *Heaven*, she was also filming the 20th Century Fox comedy, *Stop, Look, and Love*, costarring William Frawley and Robert Kellard.

4. Former newspaperman turned scriptwriter, Dalton Trumbo (1905-76), was responsible for the story and for co-writing the script of *Heaven with a Barbed Wire Fence*. He would eventually make a name for himself, writing several acclaimed screenplays including *Kitty Foyle* (1940), *A Guy Named Joe* (1943), *Thirty Seconds Over Tokyo* (1944), and *Our Vines Have Tender Grapes* (1945). He would also become famous as one of the Hollywood Ten, a group of filmmakers sentenced to a prison term for

contempt of Congress for refusing to testify before the House Un-American Activities Committee about his alleged Communist party membership. He was subsequently blacklisted for many years, during which he wrote scripts under assumed names and won an Oscar in 1956 (as Robert Rich) for his screenplay *The Brave One*. With the help of director Otto Preminger and actor Kirk Douglas, who both insisted he be credited for the screenplays for their films, *Exodus* (1960) and *Spartacus* (1960), Trumbo was finally able to emerge from the shadows.

5. In their book, *Dalton Trumbo: Blacklisted Hollywood Radical*, writers Larry Ceplair and Christopher Trumbo stated Trumbo was paid $10,000 for the script of *Heaven with a Barbed Wire Fence* (based on one of his stories). Although the screenplay was later reworked by writers Leonard Hoffman, and Ben Grauman Kohn, Trumbo shared screenwriting credits with them.

6. Ricardo Cortez worked on material penned by co-scriptwriter Ben Grauman Kohn (1908-61) three times. In addition to *Heaven with a Barbed Wire Fence*, Kohn wrote the story for *Ladies of the Night Club* (1928), and the script for *Manhattan Moon* (1935).

CITY OF CHANCE (1940) (CRIME DRAMA)
20TH CENTURY FOX FILM CORPORATION
PRODUCER: Sol M. Wurtzel
DIRECTOR: Ricardo Cortez
SCREENPLAY: John Larkin, Barry Trivers
LENGTH: 58 minutes
TAGLINE: "She wanted thrills—And she found them in the dangerous hours before dawn!"
STATUS: Exists.

CAST: Lynn Bari (Julie Reynolds), C. Aubrey Smith (The Judge), Donald Woods (Steve Walker), Amanda Duff (Lois Carlyle Blaine), June Gale (Molly), Richard Lane (Mattie Connors), Robert Lowery (Ted Blaine), Alexander D'Arcy (Baron Joseph), George Douglas

(Muscles), Harry Shannon (Passline), Edward Marr (Charlie Nevins), Robert Allen (Fred Walcott), Charlotte Wynters (Mrs. Helen Walcott), and Nora Lane (Mrs. Dorothy Grainger).

SUMMARY: A Texas girl (Bari) gets a job as a newspaper reporter in New York. In order to get her boyfriend (Woods), who runs a gambling house, to come back to Texas with her, she does a story about his casino, and tips off the police who raid the establishment and arrest him.

REVIEWS:
The Film Daily: "Well paced action meller with able cast will serve nicely on any bill . . . Ricardo Cortez gives the film a snappy pace. . . ."

Variety: "*City of Chance* unquestionably was put into the hopper as a program production, but it has turned out stronger than some of those intended 'A' films. Ricardo Cortez has turned in a craftsman-like assignment in directing this film, which is hindered only by lack of names."

PRODUCTION NOTES, INTERESTING FACTS, AND TRIVIA:
1. Working title was *The City*.

2. Ricardo Cortez was originally slated to direct and star in *City of Chance*. His acting role was eventually played by Donald Woods who ironically had replaced him in the role of Perry Mason just three years earlier.

FREE, BLONDE, AND 21 (1940) (DRAMA)
20TH CENTURY FOX FILM CORPORATION
PRODUCER: Sol M. Wurtzel
DIRECTOR: Ricardo Cortez
SCREENPLAY: Frances Hyland (script), M. Clay Adams, George Wright (contributing writers)
LENGTH: 67 minutes
STATUS: Exists.

CAST: Lynn Bari (Carol Northrup), Mary Beth Hughes (Jerry Daily), Joan Davis (Nellie), Henry Wilcoxon (Dr. Hugh Mayberry), Robert Lowery (Dr. Stephen Greig), Alan Baxter (Mickey Ryan), Kay Aldridge (Adelaide Sinclair), Helen Ericson (Amy McCall), Chick Chandler (Gus), Joan Valerie (Vicki), Elise Knox (Marjorie), Dorothy Dearing (Linda), Herbert Rawlinson (Mr. Crane), Kay Linaker (Mrs. Crane), Thomas Jackson (Inspector Saunders), and Richard Lane (Lieutenant Lake).

SUMMARY: At a hotel for women, two young friends (Bari, Hughes) end up on opposite sides of the law. Bari marries a kindly doctor (Wilcoxon), while Hughes ends up in prison when she gets mixed up with gangsters.

REVIEWS:
The Film Daily: "As a frothy concoction of comedy and drama, with a murder thrown in for good measure, the offering should amuse audiences, generally . . . Director Ricardo Cortez did a good job . . ."

Variety: "A programmer that is strictly for the double bills but may be considered to deserve more than being hooked to a major top-bracketer . . . Ricardo Cortez, who directed, didn't have so much to work with . . ."

PRODUCTION NOTES, INTERESTING FACTS, AND TRIVIA:
1. Working titles were: *The Girl from Kansas City* and *Hotel for Women #2*.

2. The film was first billed as a sequel to Fox's *Elsa Maxwell's Hotel for Women* (1939), but there were almost no similarities between these films except the New York City hotel named the Sherrington.

3. 20th Century Fox remade *Free, Blonde, and 21* in 1944 as *Ladies of Washington*, starring Trudy Marshall and Anthony Quinn.

4. Critics generally liked the picture, but many thought it odd that it was shown on double bills with the heavily dramatic grade A drama, *The Grapes of Wrath*.

5. A *Massillon Evening Independent* article chronicled a humorous anecdote which occurred on the set of *Free, Blonde and 21*, when director Cortez was forced to do a fourth take of a particular scene. The first three had been spoiled by the backfire of a car, a low flying plane, and an overturned lamp. This one was ruined by the rattling of suspended catwalks. According to the report, when the frustrated director screamed "Quiet," instead of solitude, he was greeted by peels of laughter. There had been an earthquake.

GIRL IN 313 (1940) (CRIME DRAMA)
20TH CENTURY FOX FILM CORPORATION

PRODUCER:	Sol M. Wurtzel
DIRECTOR:	Ricardo Cortez
SCREENPLAY:	Barry Trivers, M. Clay Adams (script), Hilda Stone (original story)
LENGTH:	56 minutes
TAGLINE:	"She's lovely! Mysterious! Exciting!"
STATUS:	Exists. (DVD)

CAST: Florence Rice (Joan Matthews), Kent Taylor (Gregg Dunn), Lionel Atwill (Rusell Woodruff), Kay Aldridge (Sarah Sorrell), Mary Treen (Jenny), Jack Carson (Pat O'Farrell), Elyse Knox (Judith Wilson), Joan Valerie (Francine Edwards), Dorothy Dearing (Emmy Lou Bentley), Dorothy Moore (Happy), Julie Bishop a.k.a. Jacqueline Wells (Lorna), Charles D. Wilson (Brady), and William B. Davidson (Grayson).

SUMMARY: Major challenges arise for a young policewoman (Rice) when she goes undercover to break up a jewel smuggling ring and ends up developing romantic feelings for a smuggler (Taylor).

REVIEWS:
The Film Daily: "What makes *Girl in 313* solid pop entertainment

is a dual factor—the smooth and skillful manner in which the story is handled and the contributions made by the girl who has the title role . . . Ricardo Cortez has done a good job of directing and the technical ends of the photoplay are firmly fashioned . . . ."

New York Times: "Light and swiftly paced, the plot may point to the death of the hero, but the plot itself is too improbable to ask for a probable solution . . ."

PRODUCTION NOTES, INTERESTING FACTS, AND TRIVIA:
1. Working titles were *Hotel for Women #3*, and *Million Dollar Diamond*.

2. A 1940 article in *The Motion Picture Herald*, noted fictional characters from two 20th Century Fox films: *I Was an Adventure* and *Free, Blonde, and 21* appeared in the film as secondary characters.

3. Actress Florence Rice was borrowed from MGM to play the lead in *Girl in 313*.

4. Columnist Jimmie Fidler reported a series of entertaining mishaps which occurred one day during the production of *Girl in 313*. While filming a scene which required him to drive a new car with a trick gear shift, actor Kent Taylor accidentally backed into an arc light that set in motion a chain reaction. When the arc light toppled, it upset a ladder on which an electrician was perched. According to Fidler "the electrician upset the script girl's stool and the script clerk, clawing for balance, pulled down another lamp. Ricardo Cortez emitted a roar of wrath. 'Who the devil is directing this scene, Rube Goldberg?'"

5 Scriptwriters Barry Trivers (1907-81) and M. Clay Adams (1909-2008) had more than just the screenplay of *Girl in 313* in common. Although both worked in the film industry beginning in the 1930's, both would achieve their greatest fame for their television work. Mr. Trivers contributed scripts for such noted series as *The Millionaire, Perry Mason, Have Gun Will*

Travel, Rawhide, and *Kojak,* but is best remembered for penning the original episode of *Star Trek,* entitled *The Conscience of the King.* Adams won fame on the small screen as the director of the 26 episode NBC television documentary, *Victory at Sea,* and as a production executive and producer of such early hit series as *The Sergeant Bilko Show.* In 1961 he formed his own production company in New York City, and was in charge of the production of such series as *The Defenders, The Doctors,* and episodes of *Bell Telephone Hour,* and *Hallmark Theater.*

THE SHORT FILMS OF RICARDO CORTEZ

THIMBLE, THIMBLE (1920) (DRAMA) (SHORT FILM)
VITAGRAPH COMPANY OF AMERICA
DIRECTOR: Edward H. Griffith
SCREENPLAY: Paul M. Bryan (script), O. Henry (story)
STATUS: Believed Lost.

CAST: Johnnie Walker, Rod La Rocque, Jack Crane (a.k.a. Ricardo Cortez)

SUMMARY: Two look-a-like cousins try to fool an old man who is delivering a family heirloom to one of them.

PRODUCTION NOTES, INTERESTING FACTS, AND TRIVIA:
1. In a 1931 interview with *The Film Daily,* actor Johnnie Walker said he recommended young Jack Crane (Cortez) for the role of the brother in this O'Henry adaptation, because he looked like Rod La Rocque, who was to play the other main role.

2. Several published reports indicated Crane (Cortez) received $200 for two weeks' work on this film.

3. Edward H. Griffith (1894-1975) was a Virginia-born newspaper reporter and magazine writer before becoming involved in theatre and film. His work in the cinema began in 1915 when he was hired as a screenwriter and actor for the Edison company.

By 1917 he was directing both shorts and feature films. His feature film directing credits include *Holiday* (1930), *The Animal Kingdom* (1932), *Another Language* (1932), *No More Ladies* (1935), and *The Sky's the Limit* (1943).

SCREEN SNAPSHOTS SERIES 10, NO. 8 (1931)
(PROMOTIONAL SHORT FILM)
COLUMBIA PICTURES
DIRECTOR: Ralph Staub
SCREENPLAY: Ralph Staub
LENGTH: 9 minutes
STATUS: Exists.

CAST: As themselves: Pola Negri, Bebe Daniels, Mitzi Green, Polly Moran, Mack Sennett, Barbara Stanwyck, Ricardo Cortez, Joe E. Brown, Harold Lloyd, June Clyde, George Bancroft, Max Sennett, William Wellman, Laura LaPlante, and Neil Hamilton, etc.

SUMMARY: Multiple Hollywood stars are seen enjoying themselves in and around Hollywood.

PRODUCTION NOTES, INTERESTING FACTS, AND TRIVIA:
1. According to a June 14, 1931 item in *The Film Daily*, Barbara Stanwyck and Ricardo Cortez were costarring in the drama, *Ten Cents a Dance*, when they appeared in *Screen Snapshots*. In their brief yet entertaining segment, Cortez is seen attempting to teach Stanwyck how to swing a golf club at a Palm Springs resort. When she drives her ball into a nearby brook, Stanwyck quips "I hope it drowns!"

HOLLYWOOD NEWSREEL (1934) (STUDIO PROMOTIONAL SHORT)
WARNER BROTHERS
DIRECTOR: George Bilson
SCREENPLAY: George Bilson
LENGTH: 9 minutes
STATUS: Exists.

CAST: As themselves: Busby Berkeley, Joan Blondell, Joe E. Brown,

Ricardo Cortez, Patricia Ellis, Sammy Fain, Hugh Herbert, Guy Kibbee, Hal LeRoy, Margaret Lindsay, Frank McHugh, Jean Muir, Dick Powell, Ginger Rogers, and Donald Woods, etc.

SUMMARY: A behind-the-scenes look at Hollywood at Warner Bros. Studio.

PRODUCTION NOTES, INTERESTING FACTS, AND TRIVIA:
1. Filmed to coincide with the release of the Warner Bros. mega musical, *Wonder Bar*.

2. Cortez is seen briefly with the Rose Bowl winning Columbia football team's captain, Cliff Montgomery.

3. Hal Leroy performs and Patricia Ellis sings music composed for the Warner Bros. production, *Harold Teen*, in the short.

BREAKDOWNS OF 1936 (STUDIO PROMOTIONAL FILM)
WARNER BROTHERS
LENGTH: 9 minutes
STATUS: Exists.

CAST: As themselves: Ross Alexander, Humphrey Bogart, George Brent, Joe E. Brown, James Cagney, Ricardo Cortez, Bette Davis, Ann Dvorak, Kay Francis, Leslie Howard, Paul Lukas, Fredric March, Paul Muni, Pat O'Brien, Claude Rains, Edward G. Robinson, Warren William, and many others.

SUMMARY: Humorous flubs and outtakes from various Warner Bros. films being produced at the time.

PRODUCTION NOTES, INTERESTING FACTS, AND TRIVIA:
1. In his 15 second segment, Cortez flubs one of his lines from *The White Cockatoo*.

2. Among the films which have outtakes featured are *A Midsummer Night's Dream* (1935), *Bullets or Ballots* (1936), and *The Petrified Forest* (1936).

Sunkist Stars at Palm Springs (1936) (MUSICAL)
METRO-GOLDWYN-MAYER
PRODUCER: Lewis Lewyn
DIRECTOR: Roy Rowland
SCREENPLAY: John W. Kraft
LENGTH: 20 minutes
STATUS: Exists.

CAST: As themselves: Edmund Lowe, The Fanchonettes, The Downey Sisters, Peter Lind Hayes, Robert Benchley, Betty Grable, Walter Huston, Buster Keaton, Frances Langford, Claire Trevor, Dick Foran, Betty Furness, Ricardo Cortez, Johnny Weismuller, Vince Barnett, Hugh Herbert, and Fuzzy Knight, etc.

SUMMARY: Winners of the Lucky Stars National Dance Contest (a woman from each state) are welcomed to Palm Springs and introduced to a bevy of motion picture stars who are involved in various recreational activities.

Breakdowns of 1937 (PROMOTIONAL FILM)
WARNER BROTHERS
LENGTH: 7 minutes
STATUS: Exists.

CAST: As themselves: Humphrey Bogart, George Brent, Ricardo Cortez, Bette Davis, Claire Dodd, Glenda Farrell, Errol Flynn, Kay Francis, Alan Hale Hugh Herbert, Allen Jenkins, Boris Karloff, Pat O'Brien, Dick Powell, Claude Rains, Jane Wyman, and many others.

SUMMARY: Humorous flubs and outtakes from various Warner Bros. films being produced at the time.

PRODUCTION NOTES, INTERESTING FACTS, AND TRIVIA:
1. Warner Bros. introduced the film by saying, "It may not pay to be crazy, but it helps. If you don't believe us—WATCH."

2. Cortez is seen for a few seconds with Boris Karloff in a scene from *West of Shanghai*. Karloff flubs one of his lines.

TV APPEARANCES OF RICARDO CORTEZ

All Star Review — Season 2, Episode 2 (1951) — Jack Carson (host) with guests as themselves: Lola Albright, Ricardo Cortez, James Dunn, Jack Durant, the Honey Brothers, Hal March, Jack Norton, and Billy Sands. (1 hr. NBC)

The Jack Carson Show — Season 1, Episode 1(1954) — Jack Carson (host) with guests as themselves: Kay Brown, Ricardo Cortez, George Gobel, Dennis O'Keefe, Constance Towers, Claire Trevor, Zsa Zsa Gabor, Sheilah Graham, and Jon Hall. (NBC)

This is Your Life — Gloria Swanson (1957) — Ralph Edwards (host) guests included, as themselves: Gloria Swanson, Rod La Rocque, Francis X. Bushman, Mack Sennett, Lois Wilson, Raymond Hatton, Monte Blue, Julia Faye, Ricardo Cortez, Edmund Burns, Allan Dwan, Jesse Lasky, and Wally Albright. (30 min. NBC)

Bonanza — episode "El Toro Grande" (1960) — The Cartwrights (Hoss and Little Joe) face unexpected challenges when they attempt to purchase a prize winning seed bull from a wealthy Spanish landowner (Cortez) in California. Cast: Lorne Greene, Michael Landon, Dan Blocker, Pernell Roberts, Ricardo Cortez, Barbara Luna, Armand Alzamora, Alma Beltran, and Jose Gonzales-Gonzales. (1 hr. NBC)

Hedda Hopper's Hollywood — Rexall Television Special (1960) — Host Hedda Hopper looks back over her long career as a columnist, interviews celebrities, and visits them at their studios and homes. Guests as themselves: Lucille Ball, Gary Cooper, Ricardo Cortez, Bob Cummings, Marion Davies, Janet Gaynor, Bob Hope, Harold Lloyd, Liza Minnelli, Ramon Novarro, Anthony Perkins, Debbie Reynolds, James Steward, Gloria Swanson, and King Vidor. (1 hr. NBC)

RADIO APPEARANCES OF RICARDO CORTEZ

Guy Lombardo's Pleasure Cruise (*Guy Lombardo Show*) (NBC). Cortez filled in for the regular announcer. February through May, 1935.

Shell Chateau (NBC) September 21, 1935.

The Fleishman's Yeast Hour (NBC) August 6, 1936 (Cortez acts in a playlet, "Belief," about the Spanish Civil War).

Red Cross Flood Relief (Rally) (NBC) February 1, 1937.

Your Hollywood Parade (NBC) January 12, 1938. Cortez and Madeleine Carroll enact the playlet, "War News, Exclusive," written by Arch Obeler.

The Treasury Hour (Blue Network) October 21, 1941.

Your Movietown Radio Theater (ZIV SYNDICATION) 1947

Hollywood Theater (WGN) November 26, 1948. Cortez appears in the title role of "The Doctor Is a Wolf."

The First Hundred Years (ABC) September 8, 1949–September 29, 1949.

Hedda Hopper's Hollywood (NBC) January 10, 1960. Radio broadcast of television special.

SELECTED BIBLIOGRAPHY
(PARTS I & II)

BOOKS

Aliperti, Cliff. *Helen Twelvetrees, Perfect Ingenue.* CreateSpace Independent Publishing Platform, 2015.

American Film Institute Catalog of Motion Pictures Produced in the United States, Feature Films, 1921-1930. Berkeley: University of California Press, 1999.

American Film Institute Catalog of Motion Pictures Produced in the United States, Feature Films, 1931-1940. Berkeley: University of California Press, 1999.

American Film Institute Catalog of Motion Pictures Produced in the United States, Feature Films, 1941-1950. Berkeley: University of California Press, 1999.

Balio, Tino. *Grand Design: Hollywood as a Modern Business Enterprise 1930-1939.* Berkeley: University of California Press, 1996.

Basinger, Jeanine. *Silent Stars.* New York, Alfred A. Knopf, 1999.

Beauchamp, Cari. *Without Lying Down, Frances Marion and the Powerful Women of Early Hollywood.* Berkeley: University of California Press, 1998.

Behlmer, Rudy. *Inside Warner Brothers (1935-1951)*. New York: Simon & Schuster, 1987.

Berlin, Howard M. *The Complete Mr. Moto Film Phile: A Casebook*. Rockville, MD: Wildside Press, 2005.

Birchard, Robert. *Cecil B. DeMille's Hollywood*. Lexington, KY: University of Kentucky Press, 2004.

Blake, Michael Francis. *Lon Chaney: The Man Behind the Thousand Faces*. Vestal Press, 1993.

Bogdanovich, Peter. *Who The Devil Made It*. New York: Ballantine Publishing Group, 1997.

Brownlow, Kevin. *The Parade's Gone By*. Berkeley: University of California Press, 1968.

Bubbeo, Daniel. *The Women of Warner Brothers*. Jefferson, NC: McFarland & Company, 2001.

Burton, Alan & Steve Chibnall, *The Historical Dictionary of British Cinema*. Lanham, MD: Scarecrow Press, 2013.

Cagney, James. *Cagney By Cagney*. New York: Doubleday & Company Inc., 1976.

Capra, Frank. *The Name Above The Title*. New York: The MacMillan Company, 1971.

Ceplair, Larry & Christopher Trumbo. *Dalton Trumbo: Blacklisted Hollywood Radical*. Lexington, KY: University Press of Kentucky, 2014.

Chaney, Raymond. *American Vision: The Films of Frank Capra*. New York: Cambridge University Press, 1986.

Clarens, Carlos & Foster Hirsch. *Crime Movies.* Cambridge, MA: Da Capo Press, 1980.

Cox, Jim. *The Daytime Serials of Television 1946-60.* Jefferson, NC: McFarland & Company, 2006.

Curtis, James. *Spencer Tracy: a Biography.* New York: Alfred A. Knopf, 2011.

Davis, Ronald L. *John Ford, Hollywood's Old Master.* Norman, OK: University of Oklahoma Press, 1995.

DeMille, Cecil. B. *The Autobiography of Cecil B. DeMille.* New York: Prentice Hall, 1959.

Dick, Bernard F. *Engulfed, The Death of Paramount Pictures and the Birth of Corporate Hollywood.* Lexington, KY: University Press of Kentucky, 2001.

Dickens, Homer. *The Films of James Cagney.* New York: Citadel Press, 1972.

DiOrio, Al. *Barbara Stanwyck A Biography.* New York: Penguin, 1985.

Eames, John Douglas. *The Paramount Story.* Portland: Octopus Books Limited, 1985.

Edwards, Kyle Dawson. *Corporate Fictions: Film Adaptation and Authorship in Classic Hollywood Era.* Austin: University of Texas, Austin Press, 2006.

Eyman, Scott. *Print the Legend: The Life and Times of John Ford.* New York: Simon & Schuster, 1999.

Finler, Joel Waldo. *The Hollywood Story.* New York: Wallflower Press, 2003.

Ford, Peter. *Glenn Ford, A Life*. Madison, WI: University of Wisconsin Press, 2011.

Funk, Edward J. *Eavesdropping: Loretta Young Talks about her Movie Years*. New York: Edward Funk, 2015.

Garnett, Tay & Fredda Dudley Balling. *Light Up Your Torches And Pull Up Your Tights*. New York: Arlington House, 1973.

Golden, Eve. *Golden Images 41 Essays on Silent Film Stars*. Jefferson, NC: McFarland & Company, 2001.

Grey, Pearl Zane and Lina Elise Grey. *Dolly and Zane Grey: Letters From a Marriage*. Reno: University of Nevada Press, 2008.

Hamann, G.D. *Ricardo Cortez In the 30's*. Los Angeles: Filming Today Press, 2012.

Hann, Christopher & Paul Robert Magocsi. *Galicia A Multi-Cultured Land*. Toronto: University of Toronto Press, 2005.

Holston, Kim. *A History and Filmography of Reserved Seat Limited Showings 1911-1973*. Jefferson, NC: McFarland & Company, 2013.

Jewell, Richard. *RKO Radio Pictures, A Titan is Born*. Berkeley: University of California, 2012.

Jewell, Richard & Vernon Harbin. *The RKO Story*. New York: Arlington House, 1982.

Katz, Ephraim. *The Film Encyclopedia, 3rd Edition*. New York: Harper Collins, 1998.

Keenan, Richard C. *The Films of Robert Wise*. Lanham, MD: Scarecrow Press, 2007.

Kiszely, Philip. *Hollywood Through Private Eyes*. New York: Peter Lang, 2006.

Kulik, Karol. *Alexander Korda, The Man Who Could Work Miracles*. New York: Arlington House Publishers, 1975.

Lankevich, George J. *American Metropolis, A History of New York City*. New York: New York University Press, 1998.

LaSalle, Mick. *Complicated Women: Sex and Power in Pre-Code Hollywood*. New York: Thomas Dunne Books, 2000.

Lasky, Betty. *RKO The Biggest Little Major Of Them All*. Jacksonville: Roundtable Publishing, 1989.

Lawrence, Danny. *The Making of Stan Laurel: Echoes of a British Boyhood*. Jefferson, NC: McFarland & Company, 2011.

Leider, Emily. *Dark Lover, The Life and Death of Rudolph Valentino*. London: Faber & Faber Incorporated, 2003

Louvish, Simon. *Cecil B. DeMille: A Life in Art*. Thomas Dunne Books. New York: 2008.

Maltin, Leonard. *Leonard Maltin's Classic Movie Guide*, Third Edition. New York: Penguin Books, 2015.

Mank, Gregory W. *Bela Lugosi and Boris Karloff: The Expanded Story of a Haunting Collaboration*. Jefferson, NC: McFarland & Company, 2009.

Mank, Gregory William. *Hollywood Cauldron*. Jefferson, NC: McFarland & Company, 1994.

Mank, Gregory William. *The Very Witching Time of Night*. Jefferson, NC: McFarland & Company, 2014.

Mann, William J. *Wisecracker, The Life and Times of William Haines.* New York: Penguin, 1998.

Marks, Ruby. *Jane Withers, 61 Success Facts.* Aspley, Australia: Emereo Publishing, 2014.

McBride, Joseph. *Searching for John Ford.* Jackson, MS: University of Mississippi Press, 2001.

McCabe, John. *Cagney.* New York: Alfred A. Knopf, 1997.

McClelland, Doug. *Forties Film Talk.* Jefferson, NC: McFarland & Company, 1992.

Mendelsohn, Joyce. *The Lower East Side Remembered & Revisited.* New York: The Lower East Side Press, 2001.

Menjou, Adolphe. *It Took Nine Tailors.* New York: McGraw-Hill, 1948.

Miller, Don. *B Movies.* New York: Ballantine Books, 1973.

Morrison, Michael A. *John Barrymore, Shakespearean Actor.* New York: Cambridge University Press, 1997.

Nash, Jay Robert & Stanley Ralph Ross. *The Motion Picture Guide.* Canterbury, UK: Cinebooks, 1986.

Nollen, Scott Allen. *Boris Karloff—A Critical Account of His Screen, Stage, Radio, Television, and Recording Work.* Jefferson, NC: McFarland & Company, 1991.

O'Brien, Scott. *Kay Francis I Can't Wait to be Forgotten.* Albany, GA: BearManor Media, 2007.

Parish, James Robert and Michael R. Pitts. *The Great Science Fiction Pictures.* Lanham, MD: Scarecrow Press, 1977.

Parish, James Robert and Michael R. Pitts. *The Great Gangster Pictures.* Lanham, MD: Scarecrow Press, 1976.

Quinlan, David. *The Film Lover's Companion, 4th Edition.* Secaucus, NJ: Carol Publishing Group, 1997.

Rhodes, Gary. *Edgar G. Ulmer: Detour on Poverty Row.* Lanham, MD: Rowman & Littlefield Publishers, 2008.

Rhodes, Gary D. and Alexander Webb. *Alma Rubens, Silent Snowbird.* Jefferson, NC: McFarland & Company, 2006.

Ringgold, Gene & DeWitt Bodeen. *The Films of Cecil B. DeMille.* Cadillac Publishing, 1969.

Robertson, James C. *The Casablanca Man, The Cinema of Michael Curtiz.* New York: Routledge, 1993.

Robinson, Edward G. and Leonard Spigelgass. *All My Yesterdays.* New York: New American Library Inc., 1973.

Rubens, Alma. *Alma Rubens, Silent Snowbird.* Jefferson, NC: McFarland & Company, 2006.

Scherle, Victor & William Turner Levy, *The Complete Films of Frank Capra.* New York: Citadel, 1977.

Schickel, Richard. *D.W. Griffith, An American Life.* New York: Simon and Schuster, 1984.

Schickel, Richard. *The Men Who Made the Movies.* New York: Atheneum, 1975.

Schulberg, Budd. *Moving Pictures, Memories of a Hollywood Prince.* Ivan R. Dee, 2003.

Schultz, Margie. *Irene Dunne: A Bio-Bilbliography.* Westport, CT: Greenwood Press, 1991.

Shearer, Stephen Michael. *Gloria Swanson, The Ultimate Star.* New York: Thomas Dunne Books, 2013.

Sikov, Ed. *Dark Victory, The Life of Bette Davis.* New York: Henry Holt And Company, 2007.

Silver, Alain & Elizabeth Ward. *Film Noir, An Encyclopedia Reference to the American Style.* New York: The Overlook Press, 1979.

Slide, Anthony. *Silent Players: A Biographical and Autobiographical Study of 100 Silent Film Actors and Actresses.* Lexington: University of Kentucky Press, 2002.

Slide, Anthony. *The Encyclopedia of Vaudeville.* Westport, CT: Greenwood Press, 1994.

Soister, John T. *Up From the Vault: Rare Thrillers of the 1920's and 1930's.* Jefferson, NC: McFarland & Company, 2004.

Solomon, Aubrey. *Twentieth Century Fox, A Corporate and Financial History.* Lanham, MD: Scarecrow Press, 1988.

Stevens Jr., George. *Conversations with Great Moviemakers of Hollywood's Golden Age at the American Film Institute.* New York: Random House, 2006.

Swanson, Gloria. *Swanson on Swanson.* New York: Random House, 1980.

Swenson, Karen. *Greta Garbo, A Life Apart.* New York: Scribner, 1997.

Swindell, Larry. *Spencer Tracy.* New York: New American Library, 1969.

Talbot, Margaret. *The Entertainer: Movies, Magic, and My Father's Twentieth Century.* New York: Riverhead Books, 2012.

Taves, Brian. *Robert Florey, The French Expressionist.* Lanham, MD: The Scarecrow Press, 1987.

Thomas, Bob. *Joan Crawford.* New York: Simon and Schuster, 1978.

Thomas, Bob. *Selznick.* New York: Doubleday & Company, 1970.

Thomas, Tony & Aubrey Solomon. *The Films of 20th Century Fox.* New York: Citadel Press, 1979.

Tuska, Jon. *The Detective in Hollywood.* New York: Doubleday & Company, 1978.

Walker, Elsie M. & David T. Johnson, editors. *Conversations With Directors: An Anthology of Interviews from Literature/Film Quarterly.* Lanham, MD: Scarecrow Press, 2008.

Welles, Orson & Peter Bogdanovich. *This Is Orson Welles.* Cambridge, MA: Da Capo Press, 1998,

Wellman Jr., William. *William A. Wellman and the Making of the First Best Picture.* Westport, CT: Greenwood Publishing, 2006.

Wilson, Victoria. *The Life of Barbara Stanwyck: Steel True 1907-1940.* New York: Simon & Schuster, 2013.

Zeruk, James Jr. *Peg Entwistle and the Hollywood Sign Suicide: A Biography.* Jefferson, NC: McFarland & Company, 2014.

ARTICLES

Bodeen, Dewitt. "Ricardo Cortez." *Films in Review*, 1984.

Bosquet, Jean. "Movie Idol Cortez Returns." *Los Angeles Examiner*, March, 1958.

Burke, Gerald F. "James Michael Curley: A Lasting Hurrah." *Jamaica Plains Bulletin*, November, 2006.

Busby, Marquis. "Ricardo Cortez." *Los Angeles Examiner*, 1931.

Clynton, Lionel. "The Last of the Latins." *Film Weekly*, June, 1932.

Cortez, Ricardo. "What They Want to Do When They're Fifty." *Motion Picture Magazine*, October, 1925.

Grant, Jack. "Ricardo Cortez Reveals Who He Really Is!" *Movie Classic*, April, 1932.

Haynes, Marjorie. "Cortez The Conqueror." *Movie Mirror*, 1937.

Kohl, Leonard Jr. "Formerly Kay Linaker." *Scarlet Street*, 2004.

Lang, Harry. "I'm Just A Big Bluff." *Hollywood*, 1932.

Lederer, Josie R. "Regarding Ricardo." *The Picturegoer*, May, 1926.

Leiber, Evaline. "The Comeback Champ." *Photoplay*, December, 1931.

Leiber, Evaline. "Ricardo is a Riddle." *Photoplay*, November, 1932.

Martin, Jerry. "Hollywood's Most Sensitive Actor." *The New Movie Magazine*, September, 1934.

Morin, Relman. "Cinematters." *The Los Angeles Post-Record*, 1933.

Morley, Dickson. "Tragedy is His Teacher." *Picture Play*, 1934.

Quirk, James R. "Hollywood's Greatest." *Photoplay*, April, 1930.

Ramsey, Walter. "The True Story of Ricardo Cortez." *Modern Screen*, July, 1932.

Reid, Margaret. "His Face Is His Misfortune." *Photoplay*, June, 1929.

Rosen, James. "Dianne Foster: Something of My Own." *Films of the Golden Age*, 2009.

Rubens-Cortez, Alma. "How They Popped the Question." *Photoplay*, October, 1926.

St. Johns, Adela Rogers. "The Star with the Broken Heart." *The New Movie Magazine*, July, 1932.

Shaffer, George. "Shunted Twice, Ricardo Cortez Reaches Goal." *Chicago Daily Tribune*, June, 12, 1932.

Skolsky, Sidney. "Tintypes." *Los Angeles Herald*, June, 1934.

Soanes, Wood. "Ricardo Cortez Utilizes Wall Street Training with Talent for Films." *Oakland Tribune*, October, 2, 1932.

Spensley, Dorothy. "Ricardo—the First." *Photoplay*, September, 1925.

Talley, Alma. "The Sorrows of Ricardo." *Photoplay*, 1927.

Van Neste, Dan. "An Interview with Jean Parker." *Films of the Golden Age*, 1997

Whitely Fletcher, Adele. "How Ten Stars Overcame." *Photoplay*, October, 1931.

Wilson, Harry D. "Made Great by Tragedy." *Modern Screen*, 1931.

ONLINE RESOURCES

American Film Institute Database
http://wwwafi.com/members/catalog/

American Silent Feature Film Survival Database
Library of Congress
https://www.loc.gov/

Ancestry.com
http://www.ancestry.com/

Classic Images
http://.classicimages.com/

Family History Library, L.D. S. Church
http://www.familysearch.org/

Filmreference.com
http://www.filmreference.com/

Garbo Forever website
http://www.garbofoever.com/

Glamour Girls of the Silver Screen
http://www.glamourgirlsofsilverscreen.com/

Golden Silents
http://.www.goldensilents.com/

Hollywood Walk of Fame website
http://www.walkoffame.com/

Internet Broadway Database
http://www.ibdb.com/

Internet Movie Database
http://www.imdb.com/

Immortal Ephemera
http://www.immortalephemera.com/

Irene Dunne website
http://www.irenedunnesite.com/

Jerry Haedinges' Vintage Radio Logs
http://www.otrsite.com/radiolog/

Joancrawfordbest.com
http://www.joancrawfordbest.com/

Legendary Greta Garbo website
http://legendarygretagarbo.com/

Library of Congress websites
http://www.loc.gov/library-digital.html

Media History Digital Library
http://mediahistoryproject.org/

Nitrateville website
http://www.nitrateville.com/

Official Greta Garbo website
http://www.gretagarbo.com/

Old Time Radio website
http://www.otr.net/

Pre-code.com
http://www.pre-.code.com/

Radio Goldindex
http://www.radiogoldindex.com/

Rudolph Valentino Homepage
http://www.rudolph-valentino.com/

Self Styled Siren Blog
http://selfstyledsiren.blogspot.com/

Silent Era website
http://silentera.com/

Silent Film website
http://www.silentfilm.org/

Silents Are Golden website
http://silentsaregolden.com/

Smithsonian Magazine website
http://www.smithsonianmag.com/

Turner Classic Movies website
http://www.tcm.com/

U.C.L.A. Archives website
http://www.cinema.ucla.edu/

END NOTES

PART I

CHAPTER ONE
"BIG DREAMS IN LITTLE HUNGARY" (1900–22)

[1] Lankevich, George J. *American Metropolis, A History of New York City.* New York: New York University Press, c. 1998, pgs 127-128.

[2] Mendelsohn, Joyce. *Lower East Side Remembered & Revisited.* New York: The Lower East Side Press, c. 2001, pgs 12-14.

[3] Hann, Christopher and Paul Robert Magocsi. *Galicia A Multicultured Land.* Toronto: University of Toronto Press, c. 2005, pgs 3, 6-7, 27-30.

[4] The main sources for birthdates and birthplaces of Morris Krantz, Sarah Lefkowitz Krantz, their respective families, and their children, Jacob, Malvina, Bernard, Helene, and Stanley, were the United States Census records, 1900, 1910, 1920, New York State Census, 1905, 1915, and Morris Krantz draft registration taken from online records obtained on Ancestry.com. Additional records were located and or on the website of Family History Library of the Church of Latter Day Saints LDS in Salt Lake City, Utah.

[5] Ricardo spoke of his parents, siblings, and early history many times in interviews, particularly during the early 1930's. Notable articles include: "The True Story of Ricardo Cortez by Ramsey,

Walter" (*Modern Screen*, 1932), "I'm a Big Bluff" by Lang, Harry (*Hollywood* magazine, 1932), "Ricardo Cortez Reveals Who He Really Is" by Grant, Jack (*Movie Classic*, 1932), "Cortez the Conqueror" by Haynes, Marjorie (*Movie Mirror*, 1937), "Shunted Twice, Ricardo Cortez Reaches Goal," by Shaffer, George (*Chicago Daily Tribune*, 1932), "Ricardo Cortez Utilizes Wall Street Training With Talent For Films" by Soanes, Wood (*Oakland Tribune*, October 2, 1932, Columbia Studio Biograhy, 1958).

[6] Shaffer, George. "Shunted Twice, Ricardo Cortez Reaches Goal." *Chicago Daily Tribune*, June 12, 1932, pg F9; and Grant, Jack, "Ricardo Cortez Reveals Who He Really Is, *Movie Classic*, April, 1932, pg 58.

[7] Ramsey, Walter. "The True Story of Ricardo Cortez, Part One." *Modern Screen*, July, 1932, pg 38.

[8] Ramsey, Walter. "The True Story of Ricardo Cortez, Part One." *Modern Screen*, July, 1932, pg 39.

[9] Ramsey, Walter. "The True Story of Ricardo Cortez, Part One." *Modern Screen*, July 1932, pg 40.

[10] Haynes, Marjorie. "Cortez, the Conqueror." *Movie Mirror*, February 1937, pg 70.

[11] Soanes, Wood. "Ricardo Cortez Utilizes Wall Street Training With Talent for Films." *Oakland Tribune*, October 2, 1932, pg 18; and Ramsey, Walter, "The True Story of Ricardo Cortez." *Modern Screen*, July 1932, pg 40.

[12] New York State Census Records, 1915, Ancestry.com.

[13] Shaffer, George. "Shunted Twice, Ricardo Cortez Reaches Goal." *Chicago Daily Tribune*, June 12, 1932, pg F9; and Ramsey, Walter. "The True Story of Ricardo Cortez." *Modern Screen*, July 1932, pg 40.

14 Fletcher, Adele Whitley. "How Ten Stars Overcame Self Consciousness." *Photoplay*, October 1931.

15 Lang, Harry. "I'm a Big Bluff." *Hollywood Magazine*, April 1932, pg 50.

16 Bosquet, Jean. "Movie Idol Cortez Returns." *Los Angeles Examiner*, March 1958, pg. 10; and Soanes, Wood. "Ricardo Cortez Utilizes Wall Street Training with Talent for Films." *Oakland Tribune*, October 2, 1932, pg. 18.

17 Soanes, Wood. "Ricardo Cortez Utilizes Wall Street Training With Talent for Films." *Oakland Tribune*, October 2, 1932, pg 18.

18 Paramount Studio biography, Ricardo Cortez files, A.M.P.A.S. library; and Ramsey, Walter. "The True Story of Ricardo Cortez." *Modern Screen*, July 1932.

19 Columbia Studio Biography, 1958, Ricardo Cortez file, A.M.P.A.S. Library; and Grant, Jack. "Ricardo Cortez Reveals Who He Really Is." *Movie Classic*, April 1932, pg 114.

20 Bosquet, Jean. "Movie Idol Cortez Returns." *Los Angeles Examiner*, March 1958, pg. 10; and Morin, Relman. "Cinematters." Los Angeles Post-Record, November 17, 1933.

21 Skolsky, Sidney. "Tintypes." *Los Angeles Herald*, June 20, 1934; and Ramsey, Walter. "The True Story of Ricardo Cortez." *Modern Screen*, July 1932.

22 Bosquet, Jean. "Movie Idol Cortez Return." *Los Angeles Examiner*, March 1958, pg 10; and Ramsey, Walter. "The True Story of Ricardo Cortez." *Modern Screen*, July 1932, pg 40.

23 Lang, Harry. "I'm a Big Bluff." *Hollywood Magazine*, April 1932 pg 50.

[24] Bodeen, Dewitt. "Ricardo Cortez." *Films in Review*, 1984, pg 323.

[25] Death records, Family History Library, L.D.S. Church, Ancestry.com.

[26] Shaffer, George. "Shunted Twice, Ricardo Cortez Reaches Goal." *Chicago Daily Tribune*, June 12, 1932, pg F9.

[27] Death records, Ancestry.com and Family History Library, LDS Church.

[28] Haynes, Marjorie. "Cortez, the Conqueror." *Movie Mirror*, February 1937, pg 70.

[29] Lederer, Josie A. "Regarding Ricardo." *The Picturegoer*, May 1926, pg 33.

[30] *L.A. Telegram* article, May 10, 1926.

[31] Talley, Alma. "The Sorrows of Ricardo." *Movie Mirror*, 1927, pg 22.

[32] Charles Furthman interview, *Los Angeles Examiner*, January 25, 1934.

[33] Bodeen, Dewitt. "Ricardo Cortez." *Films in Review*, 1984 pg 323; and Ramsey, Walter. "The True Story of Ricardo Cortez." *Modern Screen*, July 1932, pg 114.

[34] Ramsey, Walter. "The True Story of Ricardo Cortez." *Modern Screen*, July 1932, pg 58.

[35] Skolsky, Sidney. "Tintypes." *Los Angeles Herald*, June 20, 1934; and Ramsey, Walter. "The True Story of Ricardo Cortez." *Modern Screen*, July 1932, pg 58.

[36] Bodeen, Dewitt. "Ricardo Cortez." *Films in Review*, 1984 pg 323; and Ramsey, Walter. "The True Story of Ricardo Cortez." *Modern Screen*, July 1932, pg 58.

[37] Ramsey, Walter. "The True Story of Ricardo Cortez." *Modern Screen*, July 1932, pg 58.

[38] Ramsey, Walter. "The True Story of Ricardo Cortez." *Modern Screen*, July 1932, pg 99.

CHAPTER TWO
THE LATIN FROM MANHATTAN (1923–24)

[39] Grant, Jack. "Ricardo Cortez Reveals Who He Really Is." *Movie Classic*, April 1932, pg 58.

[40] There are several versions of how Ricardo Cortez got his stage name. The most famous of these had him being named after two cigar brands. This fanciful bit of Hollywood lore was repeated so many times it took on a life of its own and is still being repeated to this day. Among the many notable articles to mention it is Allen Doll's 1981 *New York Times* piece, "How Hollywood Has Portrayed Hispanics." Other versions were provided by Grant, Jack in his article, "Ricardo Cortez Reveals Who He Really Is," *Movie Classic*, April 1932, pg 58, and by Ricardo's first wife, Alma, whose memoirs were published in book form, *Silent Snowbird*, by Rhodes, Gary D. and Alexander Webb, pg 88.

[41] Skolsky, Sidney column, June 30, 1934; Grant, Jack. "Ricardo Cortez Reveals Who He Really Is." *Movie Classic*, April 1932; and Morin, Relman. "Cinematters." *Los Angeles Post-Record*, November 17, 1933.

[42] Ramsey, Walter. "The True Story of Ricardo Cortez." *Modern Screen*, July 1932, pg 99.

[43] Katz, Ephraim. *The Film Encyclopedia*, 3rd Edition. Harper Collins, c. 1998, pgs 893-894, and John Douglas Eames. *The Paramount Story*. Octopus Books Limited, c. 1985, pgs 7-26.

[44] Katz, Ephraim. *The Film Encyclopedia*, 3rd Edition. Harper Collins, c. 1998, pg. 1182.

[45] Leider, Emily W. *Dark Lover, The Life and Death of Rudolph Valentino*. Faber & Faber Incorporated, c. 2003, pgs 232-243.

[46] Paramount Studio Biography—A.M.P.A.S. (Academy of Motion Picture Arts and Sciences—Margaret Herrick) Library, and *Chicago Daily Tribune*, January 21, 1923 pg D11.

[47] *Lima News*, May 9, 1923, pg 9.

[48] *Motion Picture*, February 1925, pg 101.

[49] Lang, Harry. "I'm Just a Big Bluff." *Hollywood Magazine*, April 1932, pg 50.

[50] Ricardo Cortez silent film scrapbook clipping—*Call of the Canyon*.

[51] Spain, Mildred. "Stars of Today" column. *Chicago Daily Tribune*, May 20, 1923, and Ricardo Cortez scrapbook clipping.

[52] Cortez mentioned his ostracism by fellow Paramount employees and the underground campaign of lies and innuendo during his early months as a studio contract employee in several interviews, in both the 1920's and early 1930's. Various authors also wrote about it in multiple newspaper articles. Among them are: Lang, Harry, "I'm a Big Bluff," *Hollywood Magazine*, June 1932; Grant, Jack, "Ricardo Cortez Reveals Who He Really Is!" *Movie Classic*, April 1932; Talley, Alma, "The Sorrows of Ricardo," *Movie Mirror*, 1927; and Ramsey, Walter, "The True Story of Ricardo Cortez," *Modern Screen*, July 1932.

[53] Shaffer, George. "Shunted Twice, Ricardo Cortez Reaches Goal." *Chicago Daily Tribune*, June 12, 1932, pg F9.

[54] Several Clippings in Cortez's silent film scrapbook highlight press coverage of his "romance" with Agnes Ayres, and Julia Harpman, "Inside Dope on the Movie Stars," *Chicago Daily Tribune* (undated clipping from *Chicago Daily Tribune* from 1923).

[55] Stephen Michael Shearer. *Swanson, Gloria, The Ultimate Star.* Thomas Dunne Books, c. 2013, pgs 111-112.

[56] Swanson, Gloria. *Swanson on Swanson.* New York: Random House, c. 1980, pg 212.

[57] Swanson, Gloria. *Swanson on Swanson.* New York: Random House, c. 1980, pgs 213-214.

[58] "Inside Stuff on Pictures." *Variety*, January 17, 1924, pg 20.

[59] Louvish, Simon. *Cecil B. DeMille, A Life in Art.* New York: Thomas Dunne Books, c. 2008, pg 233.

[60] *Feet of Clay* clippings — Ricardo Cortez silent film scrapbook.

[61] Birchard, Robert. *Cecil B. DeMille's Hollywood.* Lexington: University of Kentucky Press, c. 2004, pg 47.

[62] Lane, Tamar. "That's Out." *Motion Picture*, March 1924, pg 60.

[63] Lane, Tamar. "That's Out." *Motion Picture*, January 1925, pg 107.

[64] *Variety.* March 19, 1924 pg. 22, and Ricardo Cortez silent film scrapbook clipping.

[65] "Battered Hat Brings Luck to Ricardo Cortez." *Los Angeles Examiner*, May 15, 1932.

[66] *The Swan* clippings — Ricardo Cortez silent film scrapbook.

CHAPTER THREE
FLYING WITH THE SNOWBIRD (1925–26)

[67] Rhodes, Gary D. and Alexander Webb. *Alma Rubens, Silent Snowbird*. Jefferson, NC: McFarland & Company Inc., c. 2006, pgs 8-12.

[68] Rhodes, Gary D. and Alexander Webb. *Alma Rubens, Silent Snowbird*. Jefferson, NC: McFarland & Company Inc., c. 2006, pg 42.

[69] Spensley, Dorothy. "Ricardo—the First." *Photoplay*, September 1925, pgs 63, 112.

[70] Rhodes, Gary D. and Alexander Webb. *Alma Rubens, Silent Snowbird*. Jefferson, NC: McFarland & Company Inc., c. 2006, pg 87.

[71] Kingsley, Grace. "Heart Affairs Hold the Ear of Hollywood." *Chicago Daily Tribune*, 8-17-24.

[72] *Bakersfield Morning Echo*, April, 23, 1925, pg 6.

[73] "Sheik contest" — Cortez silent film scrapbook clipping.

[74] "He Stars After Dropping Sheik Roles." *Charleston Daily Mail*, October 25, 1925, pg. 23.

[75] Rhodes, Gary D. and Alexander Webb. *Alma Rubens, Silent Snowbird*. Jefferson, NC: McFarland & Company Inc., c. 2006, pg 6.

[76] Rhodes, Gary D. and Alexander Webb. *Alma Rubens, Silent Snowbird*. Jefferson, NC: McFarland & Company Inc., c. 2006, pg 6.

[77] *Chicago Daily Tribune*, March 2, 1925.

[78] *Los Angeles Times*, April 4, 1925.

[79] *Oakland Tribune*, August 9, 1925, pg 14.

[80] *Jefferson City Tribune*, November 6, 1925, pg 2.

[81] "Movies Rebuild City." *Oakland Tribune*, August 5, 1925, pg. 8; and *Oakland Tribune*, September 13, 1925, pg 60.

[82] *Oakland Tribune*, August 5, 1925, pg 8.

[83] Myrtil Gebhardt column, *Ogden Standard Examiner*, August 16, 1925.

[84] *Jefferson City Tribune*, November 6, 1925, pg 2, and Cortez silent film scrapbook, *The Pony Express* clipping.

[85] *Variety*, September 14, 1925, pg 42.

[86] *Davenport Democrat & Leader*, October 25, 1925, pg 1.

[87] *Steubenville Herald Star*, October, 22, 1925, pg 9.

[88] *Fresno Bee*, September 27, 1925, pg 12.

[89] *The American Film Institute Catalog, Feature Films 1921-30*, pg 609.

[90] *Variety*, October 7, 1925.

[91] *Chicago Daily Tribune*, October 11, 1925.

[92] Russell Birdwell column, *Steubenville Herald Star*, October 19, 1925, pg 1.

[93] Swenson, Karen. *Greta Garbo, A Life Apart*. Scribner, c. 1997, pg 95.

[94] Swenson, Karen. *Greta Garbo, A Life Apart.* Scribner, c. 1997, pg 96.

[95] *Chicago Daily Tribune*, June, 1932.

[96] *Chicago Daily Tribune*, January 19, 1926.

[97] Rhodes, Gary D. and Alexander Webb. *Alma Rubens, Silent Snowbird.* Jefferson, NC: McFarland & Company Inc., c. 2006, pg 87.

[98] "Validity of Actress' Marriage Probed." *Cumberland Evening Tribune*, February 2, 1926.

[99] *Salt Lake Tribune*, February 2, 1926, pg 18.

[100] *Oakland Tribune*, February 9, 1926, pg 24.

[101] Rhodes, Gary D. and Alexander Webb. *Alma Rubens, Silent Snowbird.* Jefferson, NC: McFarland & Company Inc., c. 2006, pg 89.

[102] *Volcano* pressbook and Ricardo Cortez silent film scrapbook clipping.

[103] *Port Arthur News*, August 18, 1926, pg 7.

[104] *San Antonio Express*, August 5, 1926, pg 59.

[105] DeMille, Cecil B. *The Autobiography of Cecil B. DeMille.* New York: Prentice Hall, c. 1959, pgs 264-265.

[106] Schickel, Richard. *D.W. Griffith, An American Life.* New York: Simon & Schuster, c. 1984, pg 519-520.

[107] *The Sorrows of Satan* files, A.M.P.A.S. Library.

108 Menjou, Adolphe *It Took Nine Tailors.* New York: McGraw-Hill, c. 1948, pgs 176-177.

109 Stanley Cortez Obituary, *Los Angeles Times*, December 28, 1997 and George Stevens Jr. *Conversations with Great Moviemakers of Hollywood's Golden Age at the American Film Institute.* Random House, c. 2006, pg 446.

110 *Chicago Daily Tribune*, March 31, 1926.

111 Schickel, Richard. *D. W. Griffith, An American Life.* Simon & Schuster, c. 1984, pg 522.

112 The Eagle of the Sea, *Lima News*, November 7, 1926, pg 3.

113 Rhodes, Gary D. and Alexander Webb. *Alma Rubens, Silent Snowbird.* Jefferson, NC: McFarland & Company Inc., c. 2006, Silent Snowbird, pg 90.

114 "Famous of Films Express Regret at Valentino Passing." *Los Angeles Record*, August 23, 1926.

115 Brownlow, Kevin. *The Parade's Gone By.* Berkeley: University of California Press, c. 1968, pg 104.

116 Schickel, Richard. *D. W. Griffith, An American Life.* New York: Simon & Schuster, c. 1984, pg 524.

117 Reid, Margaret. "His Face is His Misfortune." *Photoplay*, June 1929.

118 *Los Angeles Examiner*, March, 31, 1927.

119 *Los Angeles Examiner*, January 5, 1927.

120 *Kokomo Tribune*, December 9, 1926, pg 16.

CHAPTER FOUR
CRASH AND BURN (1927–29)

[121] *Variety*, February 6, 1927, pg 12.

[122] *Abilene Morning News*, February 22, 1927 pg 10, and *The Film Daily*, March 4, 1927, pg 60.

[123] Leiber, Evaline. "The Comeback Champ." *Photoplay*, December 1931, pg 43.

[124] *Motion Picture*, January 21, 1927.

[125] Louella Parsons column, *Los Angeles Examiner*, February 22, 1927.

[126] Greer, Elizabeth. "News of the Camera." *Motion Picture*, June, 1927, pg 102.

[127] *Abilene Morning News*. February, 22, 1927, pg 10 and Louella Parsons column, *Los Angeles Examiner*, February 26, 1927, pg 5.

[128] Leiber, Evaline. "The Comeback Champ." *Photoplay*, December 1931, pg 45.

[129] Untitled article on the production of *Anna Karenina* retitled *Love* from Ricardo Cortez silent film scrapbook.

[130] Swenson, Karen. *Greta Garbo, A Life Apart*. Scribner, c. 1997, pg 152.

[131] Swenson, Karen. *Greta Garbo, A Life Apart*. Scribner, c. 1997, pg 153 and *Motion Picture News*, June 10, 1927.

[132] Rhodes, Gary D. and Alexander Webb. *Alma Rubens, Silent Snowbird*. Jefferson, NC: McFarland & Company, c. 2006, pg 90.

[133] *Huntingdon Daily News*, June 4, 1927, pg 4.

[134] *Mansfield News*, October 16, 1927, pg 24.

[135] Rhodes, Gary D. and Alexander Webb. *Alma Rubens, Silent Snowbird*. Jefferson, NC: McFarland & Company, c. 2006, pg 90.

[136] Rhodes, Gary D. and Alexander Webb. *Alma Rubens, Silent Snowbird*. Jefferson, NC: McFarland & Company, c. 2006, pg 91.

[137] Rhodes, Gary D. and Alexander Webb. *Alma Rubens, Silent Snowbird*. Jefferson, NC: McFarland & Company, c. 2006, pg 24.

[138] Beauchamp, Cari. *Without Lying Down, Frances Marion and the Powerful Women of Early Hollywood*. Berkeley: University of California Press, c. 1998, pg 223.

[139] *The Film Daily*, October 17, 1927.

[140] Ramsey, Walter. "The True Story of Ricardo Cortez." *Motion Picture*, pg 101.

[141] Rhodes, Gary D. and Alexander Webb. *Alma Rubens, Silent Snowbird*. Jefferson, NC: McFarland & Company, c. 2006, pg 91.

[142] Soister, John T. *Up From the Vault, Rare Thrillers of the 1920's and 1930's*. Jefferson, NC: McFarland & Company, c. 2004, pg 393.

[143] Haynes, Marjorie. "Cortez the Conqueror." *Movie Mirror*, February 1937, pgs 70, 72.

[144] Haynes, Marjorie. "Cortez the Conqueror." *Movie Mirror*, February 1937, pgs 70, 72.

[145] *Oelwein Daily Register*, August 30, 1928 pg 8.

146 *Mason City Globe Gazette*, August 30, 1928, pg 2.

147 *Woodland Democrat*, September 1, 1928, pg 1.

148 Raymond Chaney. *American Vision: The Films of Frank Capra*. Cambridge University Press, 1986, pgs 201-203.

149 Basquette, Lina. *Lina, DeMille's Godless Girl*. Denlingers Pub. Ltd., c. 1990.

150 Victor Scherle & William Turner Levy. *The Complete Films of Frank Capra*. New York: Citadel, c. 1977, pg 74.

151 *Salt Lake Tribune*, October 21, 1928, pg 10.

152 *Muscatine Journal*, November 22, 1928, pgs 1, 4, and *Lowell Sun*, November 22, 1928, pg 12.

153 *Appleton Post Crescent*, December 1, 1928, pg 5.

154 *Danville Bee*, January 1, 1929, pg 7.

155 *Wichita Daily Times*, January 1, 1929, pg 1.

156 Wilson, Harry D. "Made Great by Tragedy." *Modern Screen*, 1931, pg 127.

157 Rhodes, Gary D. and Alexander Webb. *Alma Rubens, Silent Snowbird*. Jefferson, NC: McFarland & Company, c. 2006, pg 98.

158 *Decatur Daily Review*, January 26, 1929, pg 1.

159 *The Star* Rhodes, Gary D. and Alexander Webb, *Alma Rubens, Silent Snowbird*, McFarland Journal, Sandusky, Ohio, January 26, 1929, pg 1.

[160] Rhodes, Gary D. and Alexander Webb. *Alma Rubens, Silent Snowbird*. Jefferson, NC: McFarland & Company. c. 2006, pg 98.

[161] Rhodes, Gary D. and Alexander Webb. *Alma Rubens, Silent Snowbird*. Jefferson, NC: McFarland & Company, c. 2006, pg 104.

[162] *Waterloo Evening Courier*, February 26, 1929, pg 2.

[163] *Olean Times*, February, 16, 1929, pg 1.

[164] Rhodes, Gary D. and Alexander Webb. *Alma Rubens, Silent Snowbird*. Jefferson, NC: McFarland & Company, c. 2006, pg 112

[165] *Oakland Tribune*, April 16, 1929, pg 1.

[166] *Biloxi Daily Herald*, May 16, 1928, pg 6.

[167] Rhodes, Gary D. and Alexander Webb. *Alma Rubens, Silent Snowbird*. Jefferson, NC: McFarland & Company, c. 2006, pg 104.

[168] Ramsey, Walter. "The True Story of Ricardo Cortez." *Modern Screen*, pg 10, and *Joplin Globe*, July 30, 1933, pg 14.

CHAPTER FIVE
ENDINGS AND BEGINNINGS (1930–31)

[169] Slide, Anthony. *The Encyclopedia of Vaudeville*. Westport, CT: Greenwood, c. 1994, pgs 181-182.

[170] *Hattiesburg American*, December 21, 1929, pg 1.

[171] Rhodes, Gary D. and Alexander Webb. *Alma Rubens, Silent Snowbird*. Kefferson, NC: McFarland & Company, c. 2006, pg 153.

[172] Seale, George H. "Alma Rubens Is Victor Over Foe." *The Bakersfield Californian*, January 30, 1930, pgs 2, 17.

[173] Articles and clippings from Ricardo Cortez's vaudeville scrapbook.

[174] Rhodes, Gary D. and Alexander Webb, *Alma Rubens, Silent Snowbird*, McFarland & Company, c. 2006, pg 156.

[175] Louella Parsons column, *San Antonio Light*, January 13, 1930, pg 11-A; and "Alma Rubens Will Rejoin Her Husband." *The Bakersfield Californian*, February 7, 1930, pg 3.

[176] *Los Angeles Times*, May 7, 1930.

[177] *Providence Journal* clipping, March 10, 1930 — Cortez's vaudeville scrapbook.

[178] *Boston Globe*, March 3, 1930 clipping — Cortez's vaudeville scrapbook.

[179] Davidson, Grace. "Ricardo Cortez, No Movie Ham." *Boston Post*, March 3, 1930.

[180] Soanes, Wood. "Ricardo Cortez Utilizes Wall Street Training With Talent for Films." *Oakland Tribune*, October 2, 1932, pg 18.

[181] Ramsey, Walter. "The True Story of Ricardo Cortez." *Modern Screen*, August 1932, pg 102.

[182] Ramsey, Walter. "The True Story of Ricardo Cortez." *Modern Screen*, August 1932, pg 102.

[183] *San Antonio Express*, May 7, 1930, pg 11

[184] Ramsey, Walter. "The True Story of Ricardo Cortez." *Modern Screen*, August, 1932, pg 102.

185 *The Film Daily*, August 4, 1930, pg 5.

186 Evaline Lieber. "I Haven't Had a Comeback." *Photoplay*, December, 1931.

187 *Her Man* files — A.M.P.A.S. Library.

188 *Her Man* files — A.M.P.A.S. Library.

189 Evaline Lieber. "I Haven't Had a Comeback." *Photoplay*, December 1931.

190 Evaline Lieber. "I Haven't Had a Comeback." *Photoplay*, December 1931 and *Her Man* files — A.M.P.A.S. Library.

191 Beauchamp, Cari. *Without Lying Down, Frances Marion and the Powerful Women of Early Hollywood.* Berkeley: University of California Press, c. 1998, pg 310.

192 Memos in *Her Man* files — A.M.P.A.S. Library.

193 Rhodes, Gary D. and Alexander Webb. *Alma Rubens, Silent Snowbird.* Jefferson, NC: McFarland & Company, c. 2006, pg 156.

194 *Syracuse Herald*, September 23, 1930, pg 2.

195 "Alma's Suit Puts Cortez in Strange Enigma Role." *The Nevada State Journal*, October 8, 1930 pg 3.

196 RKO Studio Records Collection, U.C.L.A Library Special Collections, Young Research Library.

197 Rhodes, Gary D. and Alexander Webb. *Alma Rubens, Silent Snowbird.* Jefferson, NC: McFarland & Company, c. 2006, pgs 31-32.

198 *Syracuse Herald*, November 9, 1930. pg 15.

[199] Rhodes, Gary D. and Alexander Webb. *Alma Rubens, Silent Snowbird.* Jefferson, NC: McFarland & Company, c. 2006, pg 170.

[200] Rhodes, Gary D. and Alexander Webb. *Alma Rubens, Silent Snowbird.* Jefferson, NC: McFarland & Company, c. 2006, pg 198.

[201] Rhodes, Gary D. and Alexander Webb. *Alma Rubens, Silent Snowbird.* Jefferson, NC: McFarland & Company, c. 2006, pg 37.

[202] *Syracuse Herald*, December 7, 1930, pg 13.

[203] Wilson, Harry D. "Made Great by Tragedy." *Modern Screen*, 1931, pg 55.

[204] *Chicago Daily Tribune*, January 6, 1931. pg 7.

[205] "Former Film Star Held On Narcotics Charges." *Billings Gazette*, January 5, 1931, pg 9.

[206] "Alma Rubens Must Face Quiz on Dope." *Bakersfield Californian*, January 13, 1931, pg 2.

[207] "Alma Rubens is Critically Ill." *Olean Times*, January 21, 1931, pg 1.

[208] "Alma Rubens Dies of Pneumonia in House of Doctor." *Oshkosh Daily Northwestern*, January 22, 1931.

[209] "Alma Rubens, Movie Star, Dies Suddenly." *Chicago Daily Tribune*, January 22, 1931 pg 1.

[210] *Chicago Daily Tribune*, January 23, 1931, pg 23.

[211] "2000 Movie Folk, Fans at Rubens Rites." *Oakland Tribune*, January 25, 1931, pg 63.

[212] "2000 Movie Folk, Fans at Rubens Rites." *Oakland Tribune*, January 25, 1931, pg 63.

[213] York, Cal. "Hollywood Going's On" column, *Photoplay*, April 1931, pg 108.

[214] *Berkeley Daily Gazette*, August 6, 1931, pg 2.

[215] Rhodes, Gary D. and Alexander Webb. *Alma Rubens, Silent Snowbird*. Jefferson, NC: McFarland & Company, c. 2006, pg 90.

CHAPTER SIX
UP FROM THE ASHES (1931–32)

[216] *Illicit* file, RKO Archives, Charles E. Young Researh Library, University of California, Los Angeles.

[217] DiOrio, Al. *Barbara Stanwyck, a Biography*. New York: Penguin, c. 1985, pg 69.

[218] Edwards, Kyle Dawson. *Corporate Fictions: Film Adaptations and Authorship in Classic Hollywood Era*. Austin: University of Texas, Austin Press, c. 2006, pg 305.

[219] *The Maltese Falcon* file, Warner Bros. Archives, University of Southern California.

[220] Edwards, Kyle Dawson. *Corporate Fictions: Film Adaptations and Authorship in Classic Hollywood Era*. Austin: University of Texas, Austin Press, c. 2006, pgs 306-307.

[221] *The Maltese Falcon* file, Warner Bros. Archives, University of Southern California.

[222] Undated Memo from Darryl Zanuck to Roy Del Ruth — *The Maltese Falcon* file, Warner Bros. Archives, University of Southern California.

223 "Ricardo Cortez, No Spik Spanish." *El Paso Times*, May 30, 1931, pg 7.

224 *The New York Times*, March 1, 1931 pg X5.

225 *The New York Times* review of *The Maltese Falcon*, May 22, 1931, pg 26.

226 Copy of letter from Col. Jason Joy of M.P.A.A. to Warner Bros. objecting to certain aspects of *The Maltese Falcon* dated January, 16, 1931, *The Maltese Falcon* file, A.M.P.A.S. Library.

227 Louella Parsons column, *Los Angeles Examiner*, June, 6, 1931.

228 Elizabeth Yeaman column, *Hollywood Daily Citizen*, March 16, 1931.

229 Dashiell Hammett quote, *The Maltese Falcon* file, Warner Bros. Archives, University of Southern California.

230 Jewell, Richard and Vernon Harbin. *The RKO Story.* New York: Arlington House, c. 1982, pgs 9-11.

231 *Berkeley Daily Gazette*, August, 6, 1931, pg 2.

232 Soanes, Wood. "Ricardo Cortez Utilizes Wall Street Training with Talent for Films." *Oakland Tribune*, October 2, 1932, pg 18.

233 Wilson, Harry D. "Made Great by Tragedy." *Modern Screen*, June 1931, pgs 54-55, 127-128.

234 Wilson, Harry D. "Made Great by Tragedy." *Modern Screen*, June 1931, pg 127.

235 Wilson, Harry D. "Made Great by Tragedy." *Modern Screen*, June 1931, pg 127.

[236] Wilson, Harry D. "Made Great by Tragedy." *Modern Screen*, June 1931, pg 55.

[237] Wilson, Harry D. "Made Great by Tragedy." *Modern Screen*, June 1931, pg 55.

[238] "Cortez to Make Put on the Spot." *The Film Daily*, February 12. 1931; and Elizabeth Yeaman. *Hollywood Daily Citizen*, May 27, 1931.

[239] Marquis Busby column, *Los Angeles Examiner*, July 5, 1931; and Tay Garnett & Freddie Dudley Balling. *Light Up the Torches And Pull Up Your Tights*. New York: Arlington House, c. 1973, pg 118.

[240] Lasky, Betty. RKO, *The Biggest Little Major of Them All*. Highland Park, IL: Roundtable Publishing, c. 1989, pgs 75-76.

[241] "Ricardo Cortez Utilizes Wall Street Training With Talent for Films." *Oakland Tribune*, October 2, 1932, pg 18; and Adela Rogers St. Johns. "The Star With the Broken Heart." *New Movie Magazine*, July 1932, pgs 96-97; and Shaffer, George. "Movie Gossip from Hollywood." *Chicago Daily Tribune*, February 9, 1932.

[242] *Los Angeles Evening Herald Express*, January 12, 1932.

[243] "Who's Who This Week in Pictures." *The New York Times*, April 10, 1932, pg x5.

[244] *Symphony of Six Million* file, RKO Archives, Charles E Young Research Library, U.C.L.A.; and Variety review, April 19, 1932; and Lasky, Betty. *RKO, The Biggest Little Major of Them All*. Highland Park, IL: Roundtable Publishing, c. 1989, pgs 75-76.

[245] Leiber, Evaline. "Ricardo is a Riddle." *Photoplay*, November 1932, pgs 45, 117.

[246] John S. Cohen Jr. review of *Symphony of Six Million* in *New York Sun*.

[247] Holston, Kim. *A History and Filmography of Reserved Seat Limited Showings 1911-1973*. Jefferson, NC: McFarland & Company, c. 2013, pg 74.

[248] Aliperti, Cliff. *Helen Twelvetrees, Perfect Ingenue*. CreateSpace Independent Publishing Platform, c. 2015, pg 201.

[249] *Variety* review of *Symphony of Six Million*, April 19, 1932.

[250] Grant, Jack. "Ricardo Cortez Reveals Who He Really Is!" *Movie Classic*, April 1932, pg 56.

[251] Lang, Harry. "I'm a Big Bluff." *Hollywood Magazine*, June 1932, pg 41.

[252] Lang, Harry. "I'm a Big Bluff." *Hollywood Magazine*, June 1932, pg 41.

[253] Lang, Harry. "I'm a Big Bluff." *Hollywood Magazine*, June 1932, pg 50.

[254] Shaffer, George. "Shunted Twice, Ricardo Cortez Reaches Goal." *Chicago Daily Tribune*, June 12, 1932 pg F9.

[255] "Ricardo Cortez Divorce Testimony Aids Quirk's Defense." *Illustrated Daily News*, June 24, 1932.

[256] *The Phantom of Crestwood* file, RKO Archives, Charles E. Young Research Library, U.C.L.A.

[257] *The Phantom of Crestwood* file, RKO Archives, Charles E. Young Research Library, U.C.L.A.

²⁵⁸ *Thirteen Women* file, RKO Archives, Charles E. Young Research Library, U.C.L.A.; and James Zeruk Jr. *Peg Entwistle and the Hollywood Sign Suicide: A Biography.* c. 2013, pgs 178-182.

²⁵⁹ *Hollywood Citizen News* item, August 22, 1932.

²⁶⁰ Richard Jewell. *RKO Radio Pictures, A Titan is Born.* Berkeley: University of California Press, c. 2012, pgs 46-47.

²⁶¹ Richard Jewell. *RKO Radio Pictures, A Titan is Born.* Berkeley: University of California Press, c. 2012, pg 47.

²⁶² "Radio Will Not Take Up Ricardo Cortez's Option." *Variety*, August 30, 1932, pg 3.

²⁶³ Richard Jewell. *RKO Radio Pictures, A Titan is Born.* Berkeley: University of California Press, c. 2012, pgs 61-62, 65; and Lasky, Betty. RKO, *The Biggest Little Major of Them All.* Highland Park, IL: Roundtable Publishing, c. 1989, pgs 79-83.

²⁶⁴ Elizabeth Yeaman column, *Hollywood Citizen News*, September 27, 1932.

²⁶⁵ MGM contract to employ Cortez, document dated October 15, 1932, found for sale on Amazon.com, and Cortez sound scrapbook clipping.

²⁶⁶ Clippings from file on *Flesh*—A.M.P.A.S. library.

²⁶⁷ *Variety*, October 3, 1932.

²⁶⁸ Eyman, Scott. *Print the Legend: The Life and Times of John Ford.* New York: Simon & Schuster, c. 1999, pgs 135-136.

²⁶⁹ Eyman, Scott. *Print the Legend, The Life and Times of John Ford.* New York: Simon & Schuster, c. 1999, pg 135.

270 Karen Morley taped interview with Dan Van Neste, 1999.

271 "Cortez Returns to Paramount." *Variety*, September 27, 1932, pg 3.

272 RKO Archives, Charles E. Young Research Library, U.C.L.A.

273 *Hollywood Citizen News*, December 2, 1932.

CHAPTER SEVEN
PROFESSIONAL SCOUNDREL (1933–35)

274 Shaffer, Rebecca. "Fairbanks and Crawford Rift Was Inevitable." *Chicago Daily Tribune*, April 2, 1933, pg NW6.

275 Thomas, Dan. "What's a Good Fellow." *Rhinelander Daily News*, August 14, 1933, pg 4.

276 *San Mateo Times*, February 7, 1933, pg 2.

277 Elizabeth Yeaman column, *Hollywood Citizen News*, February 7, 1933.

278 Louella Parsons column, *Los Angeles Examiner*, March 16, 1933.

279 Elizabeth Yeaman column, *Hollywood Citizen News*, March 15, 1933.

280 Louella Parsons column, *Los Angeles Examiner*, March 16, 1933.

281 Morley, Dickson. "Tragedy Is His Teacher." *Picture Play*, 1934.

282 Martin, Jerry. "Hollywood's Most Sensitive Actor." *New Movie Magazine*, September, 1934, pgs 64, 93.

283 Ship's records, May 1933, Ancestry.com; and Harrison Carroll. "Behind the Scenes in Hollywood." June 21, 1933, pg 4.

284 Harrison Carroll column, *Los Angeles Evening Herald Express*, May 16, 1933.

285 *Torch Song* entry, *American Film Institute Catalog 1931-40*, and *Torch Singer* pressbook.

286 Morley, Dickson. "Tragedy is His Teacher." *Picture Play*, 1934.

287 Ancestry records, IMDB, Frank Coniff Obituary, *Kansas City Times*, May 27, 1971.

288 Author's 2013 interview with Diedra Hart and Divorce Records, Ancestry.com.

289 Morley, Dickson. "Tragedy Is His Teacher." *Picture Play*, 1934, pgs 16-17, 61.

290 *The Film Daily*, August 1, 1933.

291 Cortez's Warner Bros. contract, dated August 25, 1933, pg 7, Cortez file, Warner Bros. Archives, University of Southern California.

292 *The New York Times*, February 15, 1934.

293 IBDB.com (Internet Broadway Database).

294 "Tons of Temperament Near Explosion in Wonder Bar" article, *Wonder Bar* file, Warner Bros. Archives, U.S.C.; and O'Brien, Scott. Kay Francis, *I Can't Wait to Be Forgotten*. Albany, GA: Bearmanor Media, c. 2007, pg 129-130.

295 "Ricardo Cortez to Marry." *The New York Times*, December 7, 1933, pg 27.

[296] Louella Parsons column, *Charleston Gazette*, January 28, 1934, pg 8.

[297] *Wonder Bar* file, Warner Bros. Archives, University of Southern California.

[298] "Wonder Bar Will Open at Sheboygan Theatre on Saturday." *Sheboygan Press*, March 29, 1934, pgs 22-23.

[299] Hal Wallis Memorandum to Busby Berkeley, dated January 6, 1934, *Wonder Bar* file, Warner Bros. Archives, University of Southern California.

[300] O'Brien, Scott. Kay Francis, *I Can't Wait to Be Forgotten*. Albany, GA: Bearmanor Media, c. 2007, pg 128.

[301] *Variety*, March 8, 1934.

[302] *Los Angeles Times*, January 5, 1934.

[303] *Los Angeles Times*, January 8, 1934.

[304] *The Man with Two Faces* file, A.M.P.A.S. Library; and Robb Nixon, "The Man With Two Faces" article, tcm.com.

[305] Gene Markey February 21, 1934 memo to Hal Wallis regarding *A Lost Lady*, Warner Bros. Archives, University of Southern California.

[306] Wilson, Victoria. *Barbara Stanwyck Steel-True 1907-1940*. New York: Simon & Schuster, c. 2013, pg 404.

[307] Reine Davies article, *Los Angeles Examiner*, July 16, 1934.

[308] Morrison, Michael. *John Barrymore, Shakespearean Actor*. New York: Cambridge University Press, c. 1997, pg. 275, and *American Film Institute Catalog* (1931-40).

309 James Francis Crow review of *Hat, Coat, and Glove, Hollywood Citizen News*, July 24, 1934.

310 Ricardo Cortez sound film scrapbook.

311 "Mate Tells of Marriage Woes." *Los Angeles Examiner*, June 15, 1940.

312 *Los Angeles Herald*, June 14, 1940.

313 Explanation of the Production Code came from articles in A.M.P.A.S. library.

314 Contract for loan of Cortez's services to MGM dated, Warner Bros. Archives, University of Southern California.

315 McCabe, John. *Cagney*. New York: Alfred A. Knopf, c. 1997, pg 144.

316 *The White Cockatoo* file, Warner Bros. Archives, University of Southern California.

317 *Uniontown Morning Herald*, June 5, 1935, pg 2

318 Warner Brothers inter-office memos March 1, 1935 involving Hal Wallis and Roy Obringer, Warner Bros. Archives, University of Southern California.

319 *The New York Times*, November 3, 1934, pg 20.

320 *The New York Times*, June 24, 1934, pg X3; and Shaffer, George. "Pirate Yarn's the Thing Now in Hollywood." *Chicago Daily Tribune*, June 5, 1934, pg 20.

321 *Chicago Daily Tribune*, January 26, 1935, pg 22.

[322] Several studio produced Ricardo Cortez articles regarding mens' attire and jewelry are included in the Cortez file at A.M.P.A.S. Library.

[323] *San Antonio Light*, May 30, 1935 pg 12 and *Oakland Tribune*, June 6, 1935, pg 16.

[324] *The Film Daily*, August 26, 1935, pg 12.

[325] Mank, Gregory William. *Hollywood Cauldron*. Jefferson, NC: McFarland & Company, c. 1997, pgs. 189, 194; and Redman, Emily. "To Save His Dying Sister-In-Law, Charles Lindbergh Invented a Medical Device." Smithsonianmag.com, September 9, 2015.

[326] Mank, Gregory William. *Hollywood Cauldron*. Jefferson, NC: McFarland & Company, c. 1997 pgs. 188-201.

[327] *Oakland Tribune*, March 15, 1936, pg 78.

[328] *The Walking Dead* files, Warner Bros. Archives, University of Southern California.

CHAPTER EIGHT
VON STROHEIM OF THE B'S (1936–40)

[329] *Tyrone Daily Herald*, February, 26, 1936, pg 20.

[330] Cortez's Warner Bros. contract dated May 14, 1936, Cortez file, Warner Bros. Archives, University of Southern California.

[331] *The Case of the Black Cat* file, Warner Bros. Archives, University of Southern California.

[332] *The New York Times* review of *The Case of the Black Cat*, December 26, 1936, pg 15.

[333] *Syracuse Herald*, November 14, 1936.

[334] Tuska, Jon. *The Detective in Hollywood*, pg 99.

[335] Alan Burton and Steve Chibnal. *The Historical Dictionary of British Cinema*. Lanham, MD: Scarecrow Press, c. 2013, pgs 329-330, and www.pinewoodstudios.com/.

[336] September 8, 1936 contract between Warner Bros. and Dominions Film Corporation (Great Britian) to lend Cortez services for *Talk of the Devil*, Cortez file, Warner Bros. Archives, University of Southern California.

[337] *The New York Times*, September 16, 1936, pg 23.

[338] *The New York Times*, October 1, 1936.

[339] Memos and contract dated December 10, 1936 between Warner Bros. and Paramount to lend Cortez's services for the film, *Her Husband Lies*, Cortez file, Warner Bros. Archives, University of Southern California.

[340] Lay-off notice, 1937, Cortez file, Warner Bros. Archives, University of Southern California.

[341] Letter dated March 20, 1937 sent to Warner Bros. from Chinese Consulate, *West of Shanghai* file, Warner Bros. Archives, University of Southern California.

[342] Termination agreement between Ricardo Cortez and Warner Bros. dated April 9, 1937, Ricardo Cortez file, Warner Bros. Archives, University of Southern California.

[343] Los Angeles Herald, September 13, 1937, and *Los Angeles Examiner*, September 13, 1937.

[344] *Los Angeles Examiner*, October 8, 1937.

[345] *The Film Daily*, August 27, 1937, pg 4.

[346] *The Portsmouth Times*, April 3, 1938, pg 20.

[347] Katz, Ephraim. *The Film Encyclopedia*. pgs, 1156-1157, New York: Harper Collins, c. 1998; and Tony Thomas and Aubrey Solomon. *The Films of 20th Century-Fox*. New York: Citadel Press, c. 1979, pgs 11-14.

[348] Thomas, Tony and Aubrey Solomon. *The Films of 20th Century-Fox*. New York: Citadel Press, c. 1979, pgs 13-16.

[349] Thomas, Tony and Aubrey Solomon. *The Films of 20th Century-Fox*. New York: Citadel Press, c. 1979, pgs 16-18.

[350] Thomas, Tony and Aubrey Solomon. *The Films of 20th Century-Fox*. New York: Citadel Press, c. 1979, pg 18.

[351] Balio, Tino. *Grand Design: Hollywood as a Modern Business Enterprise 1930-1939*. Berkeley: University of California Press, c. 1996, pg 326.

[352] Bud Schulberg. *Moving Pictures, Memories of a Hollywood Prince*. Ivan R. Dee, c. 2003. pg 449.

[353] *Tyrone Daily Herald*, April 8, 1938, pg 4.

[354] Louella Parsons column, *Los Angeles Examiner*, August 1, 1938.

[355] Louella Parsons column, *Los Angeles Examiner*, August 5, 1938.

[356] Louells Parsons column, *Los Angeles Examiner*, August 5, 1938.

[357] Johnson, Erskine. "Behind the Make-Up" column. *Los Angeles Examiner*, November 19, 1938.

[358] Johnson, Erskine. "Behind the Make-Up" column. *Los Angeles Examiner*, December 15, 1938.

[359] *Variety* review of *The Escape*. November, 8, 1939, pg 14.

[360] Edward Norris interviews with Dan Van Neste, 1999, 2000.

[361] Ford, Peter. *Glenn Ford, A Life.* Madison: University of Wisconsin Press, c. 2011, pgs 25-26.

[362] *Oakland Tribune*, July 11, 1939, pg 23.

[363] *Santa Barbara News*, December 26, 1939.

CHAPTER NINE
ONE A HEEL, ALWAYS A HEEL (1941–49)

[364] Louella Parsons column. *Syracuse Herald Journal*, November 29, 1939, pg 12.

[365] Louella Parsons column. *Syracuse Herald Journal*, November 30, 1939, pg 15.

[366] *Lowell Sun*, July 17, 1941.

[367] *Los Angeles Herald*, June 14, 1940.

[368] *Los Angeles Herald*, June 14, 1940.

[369] "Mate Tells of Marriage Woes." *Los Angeles Examiner*, June 15, 1940.

[370] Jean Parker interviews with Dan Van Neste, 1996, 1997.

[371] Louella Parsons column. *Los Angeles Examiner*, August 27, 1941.

[372] *Yuma Daily News*, September 20, 1941, pg 1.

[373] *The New York Times*, September, 22, 1941.

[374] Christine Cortez obituary, *Hartford Courant*, September 25, 1941.

375 Dorothy Kilgallen column. *Lowell Sun*, June 10, 1943, pg 23.

376 Louella Parsons column. *Lowell Sun*, September 1, 1943, pg 18.

377 *The New York Times*, May 15, 1944.

378 *The New York Times*, July 18, 1944.

379 *The Billboard*, August 5, 1944, pg 23.

380 *The New York Times*, April 27, 1945; and *The New York Times*, May, 4, 1945.

381 *The New York Times*, July, 28, 1945.

382 *The New York Times*, September 26, 1945.

383 *Madison State Journal*, November 9, 1945, pg 6.

384 *Berkeley Daily Gazette*, July 15, 1946, pg 16.

385 *The New York Times*, November 11, 1946.

386 *The Locket* files, A.M.P.A.S. Library, RKO Studio Records Collection, Special Collections, Charles E. Young Research Library U.C.L.A.; and Laraine Day Oral History, A.M.P.A.S. Library.

387 Laraine Day Oral History, *The Locket* file, A.M.P.A.S. Library.

388 Among the many articles which detail Cortez's sporting activities, interests, and attendance at various sporting events, are: Adela Rogers St. Johns. "The Star with the Broken Heart." *New Movie Magazine*, July 1932.

389 Shaffer, George. "Cortez Keeps News Clips of Movie Career." *Chicago Daily Tribune*, January 7, 1937, pg 15.

[390] "Prince of Wales Omitted in Selection of 10 Best Dressed Men in Universe." *Moorhead Daily News*, December 29, 1933, pg 8.

[391] Donald Kranze interview with Dan Van Neste, 2013.

[392] Ricardo Cortez files, A.M.P.A.S. library.

[393] *Joplin Globe*, June 15, 1945 and *Burlington Daily Times-News*, August 1, 1945, pg 4.

[394] "Theatre News." *The Sandusky Register-Star News*, December 31, 1948.

[395] Donald Kranze interview with Dan Van Neste, 2013.

[396] Thomas, Bob. "Cortez Calm in Crisis—Fewer but Better Movies Predicted." *Long Beach Press Telegram*, March 24, 1958, pg 24.

[397] Ricardo Cortez's A.F.T.R.A. contract dated, September 1, 1949.

[398] Cox, Jim. *The Daytime Serials of Television*, 1946-60. Jefferson, NC: McFarland & Company, c. 2006, pg 29; and "Sweetness Rules Roles on Video's Batch of Soapers." *The Billboard*, December 16, 1950, pg 11.

CHAPTER TEN
A LAST HURRAH (1950-59)

[399] "What They Want to Do When They're Fifty." *Motion Picture*, October, 1925.

[400] *Oakland Tribune*, February 20, 1950, pg 15.

[401] *Los Angeles Examiner*, August 24, 1950.

[402] State of California Marriage Index 1949-1950, Ancestry.com.

403 Honolulu, Hawaii Passenger Records and Crew Lists 1900-59, Ancestry.com.

404 Birth records, Margarette Belle Cortez, Family Research Library, L.D.S. church and Ancestry.com.

405 Author's Interview with Donald Kranze, 2013.

406 Ricardo Cortez page, Internet Movie Database.

407 Columbia Pictures Studio bio, 1958, Ricardo Cortez file, A.M.P.A.S. Library.

408 "In Memoriam, Stanley Cortez." *American Cinematographer*, March, 1998, pg 126; and *Variety* Obituary, December 29, 1997; and Biography of Stanley Cortez, filmreference.com.

409 Katz, Ephraim. *The Film Encyclopedia 3rd Edition*. New York: Harper Collins, c. 1998, pg 242.

410 Author's interview with Donald Kranze, 2013, and Donald Kranze page, Internet Movie Database.

411 *Los Angeles Times*, October 30, 1959.

412 *Lima News*, April 1, 1956, pg 10.

413 *This Is Your Life, Swanson*, Gloria guest list, Internet Movie Database.

414 Erskine Johnson column. *Humboldt Standard* (Eureka, CA), November 13, 1954, pg 2.

415 Louella Parsons column. "Ricardo Cortez Back", *Milwaukee Sentinel*, February 8, 1958, pg 4.

[416] Orson Welles and Peter Bogdanovich. *This Is Orson Welles*. Boston: Da Capo Press, c. 1998, pg. 28, and Internet Movie Database—IMDB.com.

[417] Swindell, Larry. *Spencer Tracy*. New York: New American Library, c. 1969, pg 209.

[418] Erskine Johnson column. *Lawton Constitution Morning Press*, March 23, 1958, pg 10.

[419] Tutarra, Paul. *The Last Hurrah*. tcm.com.

[420] Curtis, James. *Spencer Tracy, A Biography*. New York: Alfred A. Knopf, c. 2011, pg 743.

[421] Rosen, James. "Dianne Foster: Something of My Own." *Films of the Golden Age*, 2009.

[422] *Motion Picture Daily* review of *The Last Hurrah*, September, 1958.

[423] "Old Timers Will Tour for The Last Hurrah." *Motion Picture Daily*, September 28, 1958, pg 2.

[424] McBride, Joseph. *Searching for John Ford*. Jackson: University of Mississippi Press, c. 2001, pg 593.

[425] Burke, Gerald F. "James Michael Curley: A Lasting Hurrah." *Jamaica Plains Bulletin*, November, 2006.

[426] Toro, Marie. "Television Today" column. *Cedar Rapids Gazette*, May 28, 1958, pg 9.

[427] Bacon, James. "Inside Hollywood" column. *Independent Start News*, October 25, 1959, pg 56.

CHAPTER ELEVEN
A COMFORTABLE PLACE (1960–77)

428 *Chicago Daily Tribune*, January 6, 1960, pg A8.

429 The date of the award and location of Cortez's star on the Hollywood Walk of Fame via walkoffame.com.

430 Throughout the 1960's, Ric and Margarette Cortez's names appeared in articles noting their involvement in various charities, fundraisers, and other philanthropic endeavors in New York. Among *The New York Times* articles detailing their work are: "U.S. Committee on Mental Health Planning Dinner," November 28, 1961, pg 33.; "Benefit Concert By Olga Coelho Listed on Feb. 15," February 11, 1962, pg 92.; "Hospital Will Gain by Debut of Leningrad Philharmonic." July 22, 1962, pg 61.; "Dutch Health Unit Honored at Dinner." May 16, 1963, pg 29.; "Alps Springtime To Be the Theme Of May 13 Party." May 3, 1964, pg 99.

431 Obituary for Sarah Kranze, *The New York Times*, February 23, 1965, pg 33.

432 2013 interview with Don Kranze by Dan Van Neste.

433 Obituary for Bernard G. Kranze, *The New York Times*, January 19, 1968, pg 47.

434 Winchell, Walter. "Of Broadway" column. *Lebanon Daily News*, May 1, 1965, pg 12; and Jack O'Brien. "Voice of Broadway" column. *Dunkirk Evening Observer*, February 4, 1967, pg 23.

435 O'Brien, Jack. "Voice of Broadway" column. *Dunkirk Evening Observer*, September 9, 1969, pg 11.

436 2013 interview with Don Kranze by Dan Van Neste.

[437] Various sightings of Cortez between 1965 and 1975 were noted by columnists Walter Winchell, Jack O'Brien, Earl Wilson, Hy Gardner, and Bob Polonsky. Among the articles mentioning him were: "At Random with Hy Gardner" column. *Jonesville Daily Gazette*, April 21, 1966, pg 16; "Earl Wilson Says" column. *Syracuse Herald*, April 24, 1968; O'Brien's, "Voice of Broadway" columns: *Glen Falls Times*. December 22, 1967; *The Bradford Era*, July 26, 1968, *Anderson Herald Bulletin*, May 17, 1972, pg. 5, *Lebanon Daily Press*, December 15, 1972, pg. 24. *Logansport Pharos Tribune,* June 6, 1973, pg 4; and Polonsky's "Flicker Footnotes." *San Antonio Light*, December 6, 1970, pg 262.

[438] O'Brien, Jack. "Voice of Broadway" column. *Lebanon Daily Press*, January 29, 1974.

[439] The last passport of Ricardo Cortez issued in 1975, lists his employer as David Greene & Company.

[440] Allan, John R. "Hope Found in Market Momentum." *The New York Times*, September 4, 1975, pg. 50; and *Independent Press Telegram*, September 6, 1975, pg 17.

[441] O'Brien, Jack. "Voice of Broadway" column. *The Bradford Era*, January 30, 1974, pg 20.

[442] "Actor Has Operation." *Nevada State Journal*, April 15, 1934, pg 1.

[443] Obituaries varied in length from two or three sentences to several paragraphs. Perhaps the most thorough was offered in *Variety* on April 29, 1977 (eight paragraphs). Almost all of the obituaries list his birthdate as 1899 and his birthplace as Vienna, Austria.

[444] O'Brien, Jack. "Saying So Long to a Fine Old Friend." *Anderson Herald Bulletin*, May 9, 1977, pg 10.

[445] O'Brien, Jack. "Voice of Broadway" column. *Anderson Herald Bulletin*, June 8, 1977.

[446] Death Records for Helene Kranze, Mildred Rehn Cortez, and Stanley Cortez— Ancestry.com and L.D.S. Library.

[447] Death Record for Margarette Cortez — Ancestry.com and LDS Library archives.

[448] 2016 interview with Carol Bell by Dan Van Neste.

CHAPTER TWELVE
RICARDO CORTEZ — ONE AUTHOR'S VIEW

[449] *Chicago Daily Tribune*, May 1940.

[450] Carmie Amata. "Cortez, First Garbo Co-star in U.S." *Cleveland Plain Dealer*, May 17, 1977, pg 9.

[451] 2013 interview with Don Kranze by Dan Van Neste.

END NOTES
(PART II)

Genre, studio, cast, credits, and length of each film was taken from *American Film Institute Catalog of Motion Pictures Produced in the United States. Feature Films*—Three Volumes: 1921-30; 1931-40; 1941-50.

The plots are summaries of the various synopses found in the A.F.I. catalogs and by viewing the films.

Film review excerpts were taken from the following newspapers, film journals, books, and online resources:

Alt Film Guide.com
Altoona Herald
Bangor Commercial
Billings Gazette
The Chicago Daily Tribune
Cleveland Plain Dealer
Conference of Catholic Bishops
Denton Record-Chronicle
The Film Daily
Hamilton Evening-Journal
Harrison Reports
Hollywood Citizen News
Hollywood Daily Citizen
Hollywood Reporter
Illustrated Daily News
Kansas City Star
Leonard Maltin's Movie & Video Guide
Lima News
Los Angeles Evening Herald
Los Angeles Examiner
Los Angeles Evening Express
Los Angeles Record
Los Angeles Times
Medicine Hat News
Mexico City News
Minneapolis Star

Modern Screen
Motion Picture
Motion Picture Daily
Motion Picture Guide
Motion Picture News
Moviefone.com
Movie Weekly
Murphysboro Daily Independent
National Board of Review
New York Evening Post
The New York Times
Oakland Tribune
San Francisco Chronicle
Saturday Spectator
Screenland
Silentsaregolden.com
Syracuse Herald
Time Magazine
Uniontown Morning Herald
Variety

The primary sources for information regarding the status section of Cortez's silent and sound films and their availability on dvd is:
American Silent Feature Survival Database
Library of Congress http://www.loc.gov/.

In addition to the literary sources listed in the bibliography and online resource sections, trivia, production notes, and interesting facts items were also taken from the following sources:

ARCHIVES:

Academy of Arts and Sciences Library (Margaret Herrick Library)
Brigham Young University
New York Public Library
Museum of Modern Art
RKO Archives, University of California at Los Angeles (Charles E. Young Library)

Warner Brothers Archives, University of Southern California
Wisconsin Center for Film & Theater Research

NEWSPAPERS, MAGAZINES, JOURNALS:

Ada Evening News
Altoona Herald
Berkeley Daily Gazette
Box Office
Charleston Daily Mail
Chicago Daily Tribune
Classic Images
Connersville Daily Courier
Cumberland Evening Times
Elmira Chronicle Telegram
The Film Daily
Galveston Daily News
Gastonia Daily Gazette
Hattiesburg American
Hollywood Citizen News
Hollywood Daily Citizen
Hollywood Reporter
International Photographer
Joplin Globe
Kansas City Star
Laredo Times
Las Cruzes Sun-News
Lima News
Lincoln Star
Los Angeles Evening Herald Express
Los Angeles Examiner
Los Angeles Record
Lowell Sun
Manitowoc Herald News
Massillon Evening Independent
Medicine Bay Daily News
Medicine Hat News

Middlesboro Daily News
Modern Screen
Monroe News Star
Montana Butte Standard
Moorhead Daily News
Motion Picture
Motion Picture Herald
Murphysboro Daily Independent
Muscatine Journal and News Tribune
Nevada State Journal
New Castle News
New York Evening Post
The New York Sun
The New York Times
Oakland Tribune
Panama City News-Herald
Photoplay
The Reel Journal
Riverside Daily Press
Rushville Republican
Salt Lake Tribune
San Antonio Light
San Marino Tribune
Sandusky Register
Sandusky Star Journal
Scarlet Street
Screenland
Sheboygan Press
Sunday Times Signal
Syracuse Herald
Tyrone Daily Herald
Uniontown News Standard
Washington Post
Waterloo Daily Courier
Variety

PHOTO CREDITS

All reasonable effort has been made to trace the copyright holders of the photos featured in this book, but if any have been overlooked, the author and publisher will make all necessary adjustments.

All Paramount & Republic photos © Paramount Pictures. All Rights Reserved

All RKO photos © RKO Pictures LLC. All Rights Reserved

All Warner Bros/First National photos © Warner Bros. Entertainment Inc. Co. All Rights Reserved

All Columbia photos © Columbia Pictures/Sony Entertainment. All Rights Reserve

All MGM photos © Metro-Goldwyn-Mayer Studios Inc. All Rights Reserved

All 20th Century-Fox photos © 20th Century-Fox Film Corporation All Rights Reserved

The remaining photos are from the author's personal collection unless noted.

ABOUT THE AUTHOR

A native of Michigan, Dan Van Neste was a nationally known recording artist and a rehabilitation counselor prior to becoming an author and biographer. During the last three decades he has penned over 50 major classic movie-related articles for various magazines, newspapers, and film journals. Best known for his star profiles in *Classic Images* and *Films of the Golden Age*, his work has merited seven cover stories and often included original interviews with vintage filmmakers. His acclaimed book *The Whistler: Stepping Into the Shadows* is a salute to the influential, groundbreaking suspense film series produced by Columbia Pictures (1944-48).

For more information visit http://www.danvanneste.com/

INDEX

A

Adams, M. Clay – 499-500
Adamson, Ewart – 205, 443-444
Adler, Luther – 247
Affairs of Anatol, The (1921) – 41
Aherne, Brian – 478
All Star Revue (1951) tv – 504
Alvarado, Don – 28, 381
Amata, Carmie – 287-288
Americano, The (1917) – 53
Ames, Robert – 373
Anderson, Bronco Billy – 52
Anthony Adverse (1936) – 202, 441
Appel, Anna – 150, 152p, 153p, 154, 388
Arbuckle, Roscoe "Fatty" – 38, 302
Argentine Love (1924) – 46-48, 47p, 136, 316-318, 317p
Arlen, Richard – 284p, 453
Arliss, George – 224
Armetta, Henry – 192p, 230p
Armstrong, Robert – 154, 284p
Arthur, Jean – 218
Astor, Mary – 132, 133, 139, 141, 142p, 150, 192, 194, 194p, 202, 288, 372-373, 374-375, 422-423, 427, 438

Atwill, Lionel – 238
Aylsworth, Merlin – 163
Ayres, Agnes – 33, 40, 43, 45-46, 47, 54, 56, 110
Ayres, Lew – 156

B

Bacon, Lloyd – 182-184, 200, 417
Bad Company (1931) – 145-147, 147p, 148p, 149p, 166, 286, 382-385, 384p
Baker, Melville – 48, 319
Bancroft, George – 60
Banks, Polan – 203
Banky, Vilma
Bara, Theda
Barbary Coast (1935) – 199, 200
Bari, Lynn – 228, 234, 490-491
Barker, Reginald – 362
Barnes, George – 403
Barrett, Tony – 481
Barrymore, Ethel – 41
Barrymore, John – 135, 179, 194, 195, 243, 288, 419, 467, 468
Barrymore, Lionel – 86, 87p, 133, 371
Barzman, Norma – 248
Basquette, Lina – 100, 291

Bawden, James – 294
Baxter, Warner – 419, 464
Beach, Rex – 374
Beal, John – 195, 196p
Beauchamp, Cari – 94, 119
Beaumont, Harry – 424
Bedroom Window, The (1924) – 43, 310-311
Beery, Wallace – 24, 60, 64p, 164, 165, 224, 326p, 397, 457
Beggars Are Coming to Town (1945) play – 247-248
Behind Office Doors (1931) – 133, 372-373
Behlmer, Rudy – 412-413
Bel Geddes, Norman – 75
Bell, Carol – 277, 279, 280-281
Bell, Monta – 65, 67p
Bell, Margarette (Mrs. Ricardo Cortez) – 256, 260-264, 262p, 263p, 273-275, 274p, 276, 277, 278-279, 280-281
Bellem, Robert Leslie – 480
Benadaret, Bea – 257,
Bennett, Alma – 358, 358p
Bennett, Constance – 141, 394
Berkeley, Busby – 182, 184-185, 188, 218, 415-416
Berlin, Howard M. – 460
Berman, Pandro – 150, 388-389
Bice, Robert – 484p
Big Business Girl (1931) -133, 134, 378-379
Big Executive (1933) – 176, 406, 407-408
Big Shakedown, The (1934) – 181, 410-411
Birchard, Robert – 314

Birth of a Nation, The (1915) – 16
Bishoff, Sam – 434
Blackmail (1947) – 255-256, 479-480
Blake, Michael F. – 342
Blessed Event (1932) – 154, 156
Blocker, Dan – 271-272
Blondell, Joan – 167, 188, 370, 403
Blood and Sand (1922) – 33, 35, 37p, 46
Blythe, Betty – 374
Bogart, Humphrey – 139, 287, 288
Bogdanovich, Peter – 473
Boles, John – 284p, 403
Bolger, Ray – 421
Bonanza (1960) tv – 271-272, 273, 504
Bond, Lilian – 243
Boot, Charles – 214
Borzage, Frank – 418
Bow, Clara – 315, 316, 411
Boyd, William – 407
Brahm, John – 248, 249, 478-479
Breakdowns of 1936 – 502
Breakdowns of 1937 – 503
Breen, Joseph – 198-199, 421, 443, 447-448
Brent, George – 200, 203, 412, 428
Briskin, Irving – 351
Broadway Bad (1933) – 167, 402-403
Bronson, Betty – 332-333, 334
Brook, Clive – 309
Brooks, Phyllis – 222, 225
Brophy, Edward – 266, 268, 269p, 271, 466, 486, 487p
Brown, Harry Joe – 145
Brown, Joe E. – 191p, 265
Brown, Johnny Mack – 364

Brown, Melville – 374-375
Brown, Porter Emerson – 219, 455
Brown, Tom – 218
Browning, Tod – 24, 382
Brownlow, Kevin – 77-78, 314, 336
Bruce, Virginia – 199, 243, 431, 459-460
Bryan, Jane – 448
Bubbeo, Daniel – 414
Buchowetski, Dmitri – 48, 49, 85, 86, 288
Buckingham, Tom – 145, 367
Bunco Squad (1950) – 260-261, 261p, 482-485, 484p
Burgess, Dorothy – 195
Burke, Edwin – 18, 110
Burnett, W.R. – 167
Busby, Marquis – 146
Busch, Niven – 192, 411, 422
Bushman, Francis X. – 266
By Whose Hand? (1927) – 89, 343-344

C

Cabanne, William "Christy" – 371
Caesar, Irving – 182
Cagney, James – 146, 199, 200, 201, 201p, 267, 436, 486
Calhern, Louis – 192
Californian, The (1937) – 220-221, 221p, 452-454, 454p
Call of the Canyon, The (1923) – 38, 304-306, 306p
Camille (1921) – 35
Capra, Frank – 100, 150, 288, 356-357, 467
Captain Blood (1935) – 202, 393
Carewe, Rita – 102

Carradine, John – 226, 266
Carrel, Dr. Alexis – 205, 442
Carroll, Harrison – 497
Carroll, Nancy – 167, 170
Carson, Jack – 245, 475, 492
Case of the Black Cat, The (1936) – 212-214, 214p, 446-448
Case of the Stuttering Bishop, The (1937) – 217, 218
Cashy, Milton L. – 221
Castle, William – 443
Cather, Willa – 192
Cat's Pajamas, The (1926) – 71-72, 71p, 174, 332-334
Cavanaugh, Paul – 141, 307
Ceplair, Larry – 495
Chadwick, Helene – 435
Chandler, Chick – 225, 489
Chaney, Lon – 85, 86, 89, 308, 342, 381
Chaplin, Charlie – 16
Charlie Chan in Reno (1939) – 230-231, 382, 460-462
Chasing Danger (1939) – 227-229, 489-491
Chatterton, Ruth – 178, 309, 412
Chevret, Lita – 151, 152p
Children of Jazz (1923) – 38, 303-304
Christiensen, Benjamin – 89, 288, 342-343
Churchill, Marguerite – 440, 483
Cimarron (1931) – 162
Citron, Dr. L. Jesse – 103-104, 105, 142
City Girl (1938) – 222, 286, 457-458
City of Chance (1940) – 234, 495-496

City That Never Sleeps, The (1924) – 43, 311-312, 353
Clarens, Carlos – 384
Clarke, Mae – 145
Clemens, William – 440
Clive, Colin – 426
Clurman, Harold – 247
Cody, Lew – 25
Cohen, John S. – 153
Cohen, Octavius Roy – 265
Cohn, Harry – 270-271, 487
Colbert, Claudette – 132, 288, 406-407
Colbert, Norman – 233
Collier, Buster – 100, 358p
Collier, Constance – 199, 431-432
Colman, Ronald – 224
Comingore, Dorothy – 247
Compson, Betty – 33, 60, 62p, 265, 325, 326
Confession (1927) a.k.a. *Woman on Trial* – 84-85
Conklin, Chester – 265
Conn, Maurice – 222
Conniff, Andrew – 177, 183
Conniff Lee, Christine (Mrs. Ricardo Cortez) – 176-178, 183, 184-185, 189-191, 190p, 195, 197, 203, 209, 210, 215, 216, 217p, 221-222, 231, 237-238, 241-242, 244-245, 246, 291, 417, 469
Conniff, Frank – 177
Conniff, Lucy – 177, 183
Conniff, Vincent – 177, 221, 241
Conquering Power, The (1921) – 35
Conroy, Frank – 145, 146
Conte, Nicholas a.k.a. Richard Conte – 231, 232-233, 234p, 494

Conway, Morgan – 461-462
Conway, Tom – 420
Cornish, Dr. Robert – 442
Cooper, Jackie – 202
Corda, Maria – 72, 90, 345-347, 346p
Corelli, Marie – 335
Cormack, Bartlett – 160
Cortez, Ricardo
  Birth & Early Childhood – 9-16, 289
  Death – 278-279
  Directorial career – 222-239
  Early bit roles – 20-25, 39
  Grooming & Appearance – 18, 19, 203, 204p, 251-254, 290
  Hobbies – 12, 57p, 142-143, 249-254, 263p 263-264, 290
  Investments – 107, 203, 250, 290
  Later years – 273-279
  Marriages – Alma – 70-129; Christine – 189-242; Margarette – 260-280
  Paramount years – 31-85, 34p, 167-179
  Personality – 10, 12-15, 39-40, 156-159, 289-290, 291
  Radio appearances – 203, 204p, 505
  RKO years – 122-163
  Romances – 40, 43, 45-46, 47, 142-143, 169-170, 174-175, 243-244, 245-246
  Stage appearances – 15, 20, 110-111, 114-116, 209-210, 210p
  Television appearances – 262, 271-272, 273, 504
  Tiffany-Stahl years – 95-101

20th Century Fox years – 222-239
Vaudeville – 110-111, 114-116
Warner Bros. years – 179-220
Cortez, Stanley a.k.a. Stanislaus Krantz – 8, 10, 74, 117, 125, 127, 146, 149p, 159, 264, 280, 294, 394
Covered Wagon, The (1923) – 58, 60
Crawford, Joan – 106, 170, 171p, 266, 288, 364
Crisp, Donald – 266, 270
Cronjager, Eddie – 233, 238
Cronyn, Hume – 248
Crosby, Bing – 252p, 406, 407
Crosland, Alan – 213, 288, 318, 429, 447
Crow, John Francis – 195
Cruze, James – 43, 58, 60, 61, 99, 288, 325-327, 353
Curley, James – 266, 271
Curtiz, Michael – 181, 205-206, 288, 413, 435
Cytheria (1924) – 54

D

Dale, Bill – 435
Dale, Margaret – 422
Damita, Lili – 145, 436
Daniels, Bebe – 33, 46, 47p, 48, 71, 135, 136, 139, 288, 305, 317p, 318, 376, 377
Daniels, William H. – 86, 329
Dare, Dorothy – 170
Darwell, Jane – 266, 270, 270p
Davidson, Grace – 114
Davies, Marion – 67p, 111, 124, 125, 127
Davies, Reine – 111, 127, 192

Davis, Bette – 132, 139, 181, 199, 200, 201p, 222, 369, 411, 449-450
Davis, Ronald L. – 487
Daw, Marjorie – 305
Day, Laraine – 248, 249, 249p, 250p, 478-479
Dean, Priscilla – 24
De Havilland, Olivia – 478
Delmont, Gene – 338
Del Rio, Dolores – 141, 182, 184, 185, 186, 187p, 416, 417, 418p
Del Ruth, Roy – 136, 138, 140, 224, 377
Dempster, Carol – 72, 335
DeMille, Cecil B. – 33, 43, 44, 45, 49, 72, 288, 313, 314, 435
DeMille, William – 43
DePutti, Lya – 72
Desti, Xenia – 94, 348
Dieterle, William – 193, 435
Difani, L. J. – 70
Digges, Dudley – 136, 427
Dillon, John Francis – 411
Di Orio, Al – 369. 371
Dix, Richard – 38, 141, 160,
Donlevy, Brian – 490
Donnelly, Ruth – 185, 186, 429
Douglas, Kirk – 495
Doyle, Laird – 200
Dr. Jekyll and Mr. Hyde (1920) – 33
Dressler, Marie – 16, 431
Dubin, Al – 182, 415
Duer Miller, Alice – 408
Duff, Amanda – 492p
Duffy, Gerald C. – 345
Dunn, James – 172
Dunne, Irene – 132, 141, 151, 152p, 161, 266, 288, 379, 390, 399

Dvorak, Ann – 410, 417, 427
Dwan, Allan – 41, 46, 49, 266, 309, 318

E

Eagle of the Sea, The (1926) – 75-77, 76p, 203, 336-338, 338p, 457
East, Weston – 431
Eddy, Helen Jerome – 97p
Edwards, Kyle Dawson – 135
Edwards, Ralph – 266
Edwards, Sam – 257
Eiler, Barbara – 257
Eilers, Sally – 216
Eldredge, John – 424
Elliott, Frank – 315
Elliott, Gordon "Bill" – 448
Elliott, Robert – 136, 229, 377
Ellis, Patricia – 445-446, 502
Ellis, Robert – 20, 21, 492
Emery, Katherine – 478
Engle, Billy – 394
Entwistle, Peg – 162
Erskine, John – 90, 345
Escape, The (1939) – 229-230, 230p, 245, 287, 491-493, 492p
Estabrook, Howard – 374
Etting, Ruth – 371
Evans, Madge – 164
Excess Baggage (1928) – 99, 352-353
Eyman, Scott – 165

F

Fain, Sammy – 413
Fair, Elinor – 407
Fairbanks, Douglas – 33
Fairbanks Jr., Douglas – 170, 171
Farkus, Karl – 182
Farmer, Frances – 243, 244, 244p
Farnum, Dustin – 16
Farnum, Franklyn – 53, 88
Farnum, William – 24
Farrell, Charles – 181
Farrell, Glenda – 411, 466
Faye, Julia – 314
Fazenda, Louise – 185, 186
Feet of Clay (1924) – 43-45, 44p, 45p, 49, 312-315, 314p
Ferber, Edna – 98
Ferguson, Elsie – 319
Fidler, Jimmy – 499
Fields, Joseph – 205
Fine Clothes (1925) – 59
Finkel, Abem – 200
Firebird, The (1934) – 193, 193p, 425-426
First Hundred Years, The (1949) radio – 257
Fitzgerald, Edith – 132, 369
Fitzmaurice, George – 54, 345
Fleming, Victor – 38
Flesh, (1932) – 163-165, 166p, 400-402
Flood, James – 96
Florey, Robert – 178, 194, 409-410, 427
Fontaine, Joan – 478
Fontaine, Lilian – 478
Ford, Albert – 70
Ford, Glenn – 231-232, 233, 234p, 291
Ford, John – 164, 165, 166, 266, 267-268, 269, 288, 402, 476, 487-488
Ford, Peter – 231-232, 233, 291
Ford, Phil – 476

Ford, Wallace – 270
Forman, Henry James – 60, 325
Foster, Dianne – 268
Foster, Norman – 145, 226, 230-231, 382, 462
Foster, Preston – 227-229, 469, 490
Four Horsemen of the Apocalypse, The (1921) – 35, 46
Four Star Revue (1951) tv – 262
Fowley, Douglas – 225
Fox, William – 223
Foy, Bryan – 200, 213, 440
Francis, Kay – 132, 141, 178, 180p, 181, 182, 185, 186, 218, 288, 307, 381, 412-414, 424, 451
Frawley, William – 494
Frederick, Pauline – 397
Free, Blonde, and 21 (1940) – 234, 496-498
Fringe of Society, The (1917) – 20-21
Frisco Kid, (1935) – 199-200, 434-436
Frye, Dwight – 136
Fuller, Frances – 421
Fulton, Maud – 135
Fulton, Reed – 265
Funk, Edward – 405
Furthman, Charles – 24-25

G

Gable, Clark – 215p, 404
Gambling Ship (1933) – 172
Garbo, Greta – 2, 65, 66, 67p, 68, 176, 329-330, 330p
Gardner, Erle Stanley – 199, 211-214
Garfield, John – 247
Garmes, Lee – 74, 90
Garnett, Tay – 118-119, 145, 146, 147, 148, 366-367, 384
Garrett, Oliver H. P. – 218, 451
Garrett, Otis – 467
Garrick, John – 145
Gebhardt, Myrtle – 60
Gemora, Charley – 384
Gentleman from America, The (1923) – 27, 298-299, 457
Gerstad, Merritt – 85
Ghost Flower, The (1918) – 53
Gibbons, Cedric – 85, 199
Gibson, Hoot – 16, 27, 299
Gilbert, Eugenia – 343-344
Gilbert, John – 86, 94
Girl in 313 (1940) – 238-239, 239p, 245, 287, 498-500
Girl in 419, The (1933) – 172, 235
Gish, Dorothy – 33
Gish, Lillian – 23, 319
Gleason, James – 118, 119, 266, 268, 269p, 271, 367, 486, 487p
Go-Getter, The (1937) – 216, 217
Godfrey, Peter – 245
Goldstein, Emanuel "Manny" – 25-26, 27
Goldwyn, Sam – 319
Gombell, Minna – 429
Goodman, Daniel Carson – 53, 54, 58, 59, 88
Goodwins, Leslie – 483
Goudal, Jetta – 56, 321p, 429
Goulding, Edmund – 86, 164
Grain of Dust, The (1928) – 96, 351-352
Grant, Cary – 175, 176, 215p, 406, 408
Grant, Jack – 157

Graves, Ralph – 110
Green, Alfred E. – 192
Greene, Lorne – 272
Greenstreet, Sydney – 139
Grey, Zane – 305, 306
Griffith, D.W. – 16, 23-24, 53, 72-75, 74p, 77-78, 288, 301, 333, 335-336, 431
Griffith, E. W.
Guinness, Alec – 48, 319
Gun Runner, The (1928) – 96, 220, 354,
Gunning, Wid – 61
Gwenn, Edmund – 441-442

H

Half Breed, The (1916) – 53
Half Naked Truth, The (1932) – 160, 162
Haines, William – 99, 353
Hall, Alexander – 406
Hall, Mordaunt – 61
Hallelujah I'm a Bum, (1933) – 182, 415
Haller, Ernest – 410
Halliday, John – 150
Hamilton, Hale – 377
Hammerstein, Oscar – 98
Hammett, Dashiell – 134-135, 138, 139, 140, 288-289, 376
Hanson, Einar – 84, 85
Harding, Ann – 141, 373
Hardy, Sam – 397-398
Harlow, Jean – 404
Harolde, Orville – 17
Harris, Jed – 246-247
Harrison, P.S. – 96
Hart, Diedre – 177

Hart, Moss – 402
Hart, William S. – 33
Hat, Coat, and Glove (1934) – 194-197, 196p, 286, 418-421, 420p
Hayes, Bernadene – 261p, 484p
Hayes, Will – 132, 197, 376-377, 394
Hearst, William Randolph – 53, 104
Heart of Salome, The (1927) – 89
Heaven With a Barbed Wire Fence (1939) – 231-234, 234p, 287, 493-495
Hecht, Ben – 199
Hedda Hopper's Hollywood (1960) tv – 273, 504
Hell's Highway (1932) – 160, 162
Hepburn, Katharine – 421
Herbert, Hugh (actor) – 185, 186, 416
Herbert, Hugh (screenwriter) – 188, 213, 448
Herczog, Geza – 182
Her Husband Lies (1937) – 195, 218, 286, 450-452
Her Man (1930) – 117-120, 120p, 121, 129, 132, 154, 166, 271, 286, 365-368, 367p
Hersholt, Jean – 357
Hiers, Walter – 38, 300-301, 301p
Higgin, Howard – 118, 324
Hip! Hip! Hooray (1915) (stage musical) – 15-17
Hirsch, Foster – 384
Hoffman, Leonard – 231, 495
Hoffman, Maurice – 95
Holden, William – 494
Holloway, Nancy – 257

Hollywood (1923) – 38, 301-302, 353
Hollywood Newsreel (1934) – 501
Holmes, Brown – 135
Holmes, Phillips – 118, 119, 367
Holt, Jack – 374
Honors Are Even (1924) play – 203
Hoover, J. Edgar – 210, 211
Hopper, Hedda – 248, 273, 475
House on 56th Street, The (1933) – 178, 180, 180p, 194, 286, 408-410
Howard, Frances – 48, 319
Howe, James Wong – 305
Hubbard, Lucien -135, 136
Hudson, Rochelle – 472p
Hughes, John – 200, 436
Humberstone, H. Bruce – 225
Humoresque (1920) – 53
Hunter, Jeffrey – 268, 271, 486
Hurst, Fannie – 99, 147, 355, 388
Hurst, Paul – 233
Huston, John – 139-140, 288-289
Huston, Walter – 288, 457
Hutchinson, Josephine – 428
Hyer, Martha – 478

I

I Am a Thief (1934) – 193-194, 194p, 426-427
I Killed That Man (1941) – 243, 244, 468-469
I Love That Man (1933) – 170, 172
Ibanez, Vincente Blasco – 35, 46, 65, 66, 318, 329
Illicit (1931) – 120, 132, 133, 140, 368-370
Immerman, Dr. Stanley – 173

Imp, The (1919) – 21p, 22, 24, 295-297, 492
Ince, Thomas – 53
Inner Circle, The (1946) – 248, 476-477
Inside Story (1939) – 226, 228, 488-489
In the Name of Love (1925) – 58, 323-324
Intolerance (1916) – 53
Is My Face Red? (1932) – 1, 154-156, 155p, 195, 286, 379, 392-395, 395p

J

Jack Carson Show, The (1954) tv – 262, 504
Jackson, Charles Tenney – 75, 337
Jagger, Dean – 367
Janis, Elsie – 21p, 296, 297
Jazz Singer, The (1927) – 95, 150
Johann, Zita – 399
Johnny Get Your Gun (1917) play – 18, 20
Johnson, Erskine – 266, 267-268
Jolson, Al – 182, 183, 184, 186, 187-188, 415, 417
Jourdan, Louis – 48, 319
Joy, Colonel Jason S. – 133, 139, 161, 366, 376, 390, 394, 399
Judge, Arline – 154, 155p

K

Kahal, Irving – 413
Kahane, B. B. – 163
Kandel, Aben – 182
Kane, Walter – 490
Kanin, Garson – 248

Karloff, Boris – 205-206, 219, 220, 299, 337, 441-442, 444p, 456, 457, 503
Katz, Ephraim – 35
Katzman, Sam – 351
Kaufman, George S. – 191, 422-423
Kearns, Joseph – 257
Keaton, Buster – 265
Keenan, Richard C. – 481
Kellogg, John – 261p, 484p
Kelly, Grace – 48, 319
Kelly, Paul – 247
Kent, Larry – 362
Kent, Sidney – 223
Kennedy, Joseph P. – 141
Kennedy, Merna – 416
Kenton, Erle, C. – 176
Kern, Jerome – 98
Kerry, Norman – 16, 25-27, 26p, 35, 86
Kibbee, Guy 185, 186, 416
Kilgallen, Dorothy – 246
Kingsford, Walter – 429
Kingsley, Grace – 56
Kohl, Leonard – 438
Kohn, Ben Grauman – 231, 495
Korda, Alexander – 90, 345-347, 393
Kosloff, Theodore – 38, 303-304
Krantz, Helene – 10, 280
Krantz, Herman – 8, 23
Krantz, Malvina – 10, 22
Krantz, Max – 9
Krantz, Morris – 8-10, 14, 15, 22-23, 88
Krantz, Yetta – 8
Kranze, Arthur Barry – 265, 280
Kranze, Bernard a.k.a, Bernard Krantz – 10, 264-265, 275, 421
Kranze, Daisy – 265
Kranze, Don – 256, 261, 265, 275, 276, 280, 291
Kranze, Sarah Lefkowitz a.k.a. Sarah Krantz – 9-10, 12-15, 22-23, 24, 88, 264, 275
Kruger, Otto – 419

L

La Cava, Gregory – 149, 150, 151-152, 224, 389-390
La Grange, Louise – 94
La Rocque, Rod – 22, 43, 266, 309, 314p, 319, 336, 500
Ladies of the Night Club (1928) – 96, 348-350, 349p, 495
Lait, Jack – 145
Lake, Alice – 435
Landon, Michael – 271-272
Lane, Allan – 483
Lane, Tamar – 44-45
Lanfield, Sidney – 167
Lang, Harry – 157
Lasky, Jesse – 28, 32, 75, 266, 305
Last Hurrah, The (1958) – 181, 266-271, 269p, 273, 280, 287, 485-488, 487p
Le Baron, William – 75, 150
Le Gallienne, Eva – 48
Le Roy, Hal – 186, 416, 502
Le Roy, Mervyn – 305
Lee, Rowland – 224
Leeds, Herbert I. – 260
Leonard, Barbara – 349p, 350
Leonard, Robert Z. – 95, 164
Levy, William Turner – 100

Lights of New York (1928) – 95
Linaker, Kay – 291, 438
Lindbergh, Charles – 205, 442
Lindsay, Margaret – 428, 436
Lloyd, Harold – 265
Lloyd, Frank – 75-76, 288, 337-338
Locket, The (1946) – 248-250, 255, 287, 477-479
Loesser, Frank – 446
Logan, Helen – 229
Logan, Jacqueline – 38
Lombard, Carole – 132, 149-150, 203, 215p, 288, 387
Lombardo, Guy – 203, 204
London, Jack – 350
Loos, Anita – 173, 404
Lorelei Madonna (1916) – 53
Lorre, Peter – 139, 226, 227p, 460
Lost Lady, A (1934) – 192, 423-424, 469
Lost Zeppelin, The (1929) – 96-97, 361-362, 362p
Louise, Anita – 193p
Louvish, Simon – 43, 313
Love (1927) – 84-87, 87p
Loves of Pharaoh, The (1922) – 33
Lowe, Edmund – 266
Lowery, Robert – 461
Loy, Myrna – 161, 399
Ludwig, Edward – 218
Lugosi, Bela – 445
Lukas, Paul – 149, 246, 419
Lundigan, William – 466, 481

M

MacArthur, Charles – 199
Mackaill, Dorothy – 381, 489
Madison, Noel – 151, 152p, 389

Major, Henry – 294
Make Your Own Bed (1944) – 245, 474-475
Male and Female (1916) – 41
Maltese Falcon (1931) a.k.a. *Dangerous Female* – 134-140, 137p, 138p, 143, 195, 283, 288-289, 375-378, 427
Maltese Falcon, The (1941) – 139-140, 288-289, 427
Mandalay (1934) – 181, 411-414, 417
Manhattan Moon (1935) – 199, 432-433, 495
Man Hunt (1936) – 200, 439-440, 483
Man With Two Faces, The (1934)
Mank, Gregory – 441, 442, 445
Mankiewicz, Joseph L. – 176, 408
Mann, William J. – 353
Manners, David – 172
Marchal, Arlette – 324
Marion, Frances – 94
Markey, Gene – 192
Markson, Ben – 154, 393-394
Marshall, Herbert – 203, 242
Marshall, Trudy – 497
Marshall, William – 480
Martin, Duke – 362p
Masks of the Devil, The (1928) – 91, 94
Mason, LeRoy – 102
Mathieson, Otto – 136
Mayer, Louis B. – 164, 199
Mayo, Archie – 369-370, 435
McBride, Joseph – 487
McCarthy, Cormac – 131
McCrea, Joel – 141, 329

McDonald, Frank – 437-438
McGann, William – 213, 447, 448
McHugh, Frank – 266, 270, 486
McKee, Nat T. – 189, 190p
Megrue, Roy Cooper – 203
Meins, Gus – 453, 454
Men of Chance (1931) – 150, 385-386
Menjou, Adolphe – 64p, 72, 73, 73p, 74p, 178, 409, 412, 419, 424
Merkel, Una – 136, 138p, 170, 173, 174-175
Merrick, Mollie – 397
Merry-Go-Round, The (1923) – 25
Mersereau, Violet – 462
Midnight Mary (1933) – 1, 173-175, 174p, 286, 403-405
Midstream (1929) – 96-97, 97p, 110, 286, 358-360
Miller, Arthur C. – 74, 145-146, 148
Miner, Worthington – 195, 421
Mitchum, Robert – 249, 249p, 478
Mix, Tom – 16, 110
Mockery (1927) – 86-87, 89, 308, 341-343
Mohr, Hal – 74, 206, 442
Molnar, Ferenc – 48, 319
Monsieur Beaucaire (1924) – 46
Montana Moon (1930) – 106, 170, 363-364
Montgomery, Martha – 476-477
Mooney, Martin – 200, 434
Moore, Carlyle – 448
Moore, Colleen – 164
Moran, Lee – 349p
Morgan, Frank – 424

Morgan, Ralph – 167
Morison, Patricia – 464
Morley, Karen – 160, 164, 165, 166p, 397
Morosco, Walter – 20
Moskovitch, Maurice – 388-389
Mouthpiece, The (1932) – 96
Mower, Arthur C. – 189, 190p
Mr. Moto's Last Warning (1939) – 226-228, 227p, 228p, 382, 459-460
Muir, Jean – 437
Muni, Paul – 437
Murder of Dr. Harrigan, The (1936) – 200, 437-438
Murder Over New York (1940) – 238, 462-463
Murray, Mae – 28, 95
Musuraca, Nicholas – 248
Mysterious Mr. Moto, The (1938) – 225
Mystery in Mexico (1948) – 256, 480-481

N

Nagel, Conrad – 319
Nebel, Frederick – 465, 466
Negri, Pola – 33, 48, 84-85
Neilan, Marshall – 33
Neufield, Sigmund – 222
Newell, Gordon – 453
New Orleans (1929) – 96, 100, 357-358, 358p
New York (1927) – 80-81, 83, 339-341, 340p, 435
New York World – 15
Next Corner, The (1924) – 38, 141, 307-308, 381

Nissen, Greta – 324
Niven, David – 269
No One Man (1932) 149-150, 386-387
Norris, Edward – 229-230, 230p, 492p
Not So Long Ago (1925) – 58, 322-323
Nugent, Frank S. – 267

O

O'Brien, George – 24-25, 440, 483
O'Brien, Jack – 276, 277, 279, 280
O'Brien, Pat – 266, 268, 269p, 270, 382, 467, 486, 487p
O'Brien, Scott – 414
O'Brien, Tom – 27, 299
Obringer, Roy – 202
O'Connor, Edwin – 266
Okay America (1932) – 156
Oland, Warner – 463
Old Man and the Sea, The (1958) – 267, 268, 269
Oleson, George – 341
Oliver, Edna May – 431
Oliver Twist (1916) – 33
Olmstead, Gertrude – 329
One Romantic Night (1930) – 319
Orchid Dancer, The (1928) a.k.a. *Woman of Destiny* – 90, 94, 107, 347-348
Outside the Law (1921) – 24-25
Owsley, Monroe – 133, 371

P

Parish, James Robert – 376
Parker, Jean – 242-243, 473, 474p
Parsons, Louella – 84, 139, 172, 184, 225, 238, 244, 246
Patrick, Gail – 218, 451
Pendleton, Nat – 309, 402
Percy, Eileen – 38, 304
Perils of Pauline, The (1914) -16
Perjury (1921) – 24, 297-298
Perret, Leonce – 89-90, 347-348
Phantom in the House, The (1929) – 107, 360-361, 469
Phantom of Crestwood, The (1932) – 160-161, 161p, 393, 396-397
Phleuger, Dr. Charles F. – 124, 126, 143-144
Pickford, Mary – 16, 33, 265
Pierson, Liz – 243
Pitts, Michael – 376
Pitts, ZaSu – 154
Pollard, Harry – 98
Pollard, Snub – 110
Pomeroy, Roy – 313
Pony Express, The (1925) – 58-64, 62p, 63p, 181, 195, 286, 324-327, 326p, 327p, 353
Postal Inspector (1936) – 210, 212, 444-446
Powell, Dick – 182, 184, 185, 186, 416
Powell, William – 80, 218, 451
Power, Tyrone – 457
Praskins, Leonard – 402
Preminger, Otto – 495
Private Life of Helen of Troy, The (1927) – 90-93, 92p, 93p, 344-347, 346p, 393
Probert, Constance – 243
Prowlers of the Sea, The (1928) – 96, 350-351
Pryor, Thomas – 487
Public Wedding (1937) – 217

Q

Queen Christina (1933) – 176
Quinn, Anthony – 497
Quirk, James R. – 159-160

R

Rachmil, Lewis – 260, 483
Raft, George – 167, 172, 176, 284p
Rainger, Ralph – 406
Rains, Claude – 478
Rambeau, Marjorie – 118, 119, 233
Rambova, Natacha – 35
Rank, J. Arthur – 214
Rathbone, Basil – 48, 266
Ratoff, Gregory – 150, 152p, 154, 388-389
Raymond, Gene – 369, 478
Reachi, Manuel – 56
Rebecca of Sunnybrook Farm (1917) – 33
Reckless Living (1931) – 145, 230, 381-382
Ree, Max – 345
Reed, Carol – 216, 450
Reed, Luther – 80
Reed, Tom – 192, 422
Regenerates, The (1917) – 53
Reichenbach, Harry – 159
Reid, Wallace – 33
Reisner, Charles – 431
Renaud, Jean-Joseph – 347
Rennie, James – 46, 132
Reticker, Hugh – 205, 442
Reynolds, Ben – 356
Reynolds, Craig – 448
Reynolds, Gene – 453-454
Reynolds, Vera – 43, 44p, 313, 314p, 315

Rhodes, Gary D. – 52, 123
Rice, Florence – 238, 239p, 499
Rich, Irene – 424
Richmond, Kane – 492-493, 492p
Risdon, Elizabeth – 484
Riskin, Robert – 132, 369
Rivkin, Allen -154
Robbins, Barbara – 195, 420-421, 420p
Roberti, Lyda – 406
Roberts, Roy – 247
Roberts, Theodore – 71p, 72, 333
Robinson, Casey – 154, 393
Robinson, Edward G. – 192, 288, 423
Roche, Arthur Somers – 199, 430-431
Rogers, Buddy – 265
Rogers, Charles R. – 117, 141, 165-166, 172, 210, 216, 382
Rogers, Jean – 225, 231, 233, 234p, 494
Roland, Gilbert – 464
Roland, Ruth – 20
Romance of the Rio Grande (1941) – 238, 463-464
Romero, Cesar – 464
Rosen, James – 268
Rosen, Phil – 43, 469
Rothstein, Arthur – 218, 451
Rubber Racketeers (1942) – 242, 471-472, 472p
Rubens, Alma – 8, 32, 46, 51-56, 55p, 58-59, 61, 65-66, 69-70, 75, 81, 87-89, 90-91, 94, 98-99, 100-106, 110-111, 112p, 113, 117, 120-129, 142, 143-144, 158-160, 190, 242, 245, 286, 291, 323, 379

Rubens, Theresa – 52, 58, 69, 70, 101-106, 125-127, 142, 159-160
Rubin, Benny – 284
Rubin, J. Walter – 150, 160, 162, 397
Ruebens, John B. a.k.a. John B. Rubens – 52
Russell, Rosalind – 431

S

Sanders, George – 226, 460
Sarnoff, David – 141
Satan Met a Lady (1936) – 139
Savage, Juanita – 56, 321
Schafer, Rosalind – 431
Schenk, Joe – 101, 223, 341
Scherle, Victor – 100
Schickel, Richard – 72, 333, 335
Schubert, Bernard – 150
Schulberg, B.P. – 218
Schultz, Margie – 399
Scola, Kathryn – 192
Screen Snapshots Series 10, No. 8 (1931) – 501
Seastrom, Victor – 94
Seiter, William A. – 389
Selwyn, Arch – 203
Selznick, David O. – 149, 150, 152, 162, 163, 164, 388-389, 393-394
Sennett, Mack – 53, 266
Sennwald, Andre – 138, 139, 181
Serlin, Oscar – 247
Seven Keys to Baldpate (1917) – 33
Seward, Billie – 245, 246, 256
Shadow of Doubt (1935) – 189, 430-432
Shaffer, George – 159

Shannon, Peggy – 469
She Went to War (1929) – 101, 102, 144
Sheehan, Winfield -223
Sheik, The (1922) – 33, 35
Sherman, Lowell – 435
Shores, Lynn – 150, 388
Shot in the Dark, A (1941) – 242, 465-466
Show Boat (1929) – 98, 99, 102, 144
Siberia (1926) – 70
Sikov, Ed – 449
Sills, Milton – 16, 20-21, 489
Silva, Henry – 460
Sixty Cents an Hour (1923) – 38, 300-301, 301p
Skolsky, Sidney – 32
Slide, Anthony – 329
Sloman, Edward – 362
Small, Lillian – 266
Smarty (1934) – 188-189
Smith, Wallace – 452
Snow White (1916) – 33
Snyder, Eddie – 118, 367
Soanes, Wood – 115, 260
Society Scandal, A (1924) – 41-43, 42p, 49, 308-309
Soister, John T. – 336
Somborn, Herbert – 28
Sorrows of Satan, The (1895) book – 72
Sorrows of Satan, The (1926) – 72-75, 73p, 77-78, 181, 286, 333, 334-336
Sousa, John Phillip -17
Spaniard, The (1925) – 37p, 56-57, 57p, 321-322, 321p

Special Agent (1935) – 200-201, 201p, 210, 211, 433-434
Stahl, John M. – 95
Stanwyck, Barbara – 132, 133, 134p, 192, 288, 369, 371, 424, 501
Starrett, Charles – 466
St. Clair, Leonard – 248
Stedman, Vera – 435
Steiner, Max – 152
Stengel, Anton – 472
Sterling, Robert – 483
Stiller, Mauritz – 65-66, 84-85
Stone, George E. – 201p
Stravinsky, Igor – 424
Stringer, Arthur – 354
Stuart, Gloria – 172
Sturgeon, Roland – 52
Summerville, Slim – 462
Sunkist Stars at Palm Springs (1936) – 503
Supernatural (1933) – 172
Swan, The (1925) – 48-49, 85, 318-319, 320p
Swan, The (1956) – 48, 319
Swan, The (1920) play – 48
Swanson, Gloria – 28, 33, 41-43, 42p, 49, 51, 266, 309, 319, 334
Sweet, Harry – 118, 367
Swenson, Karen – 66, 86
Sydney, Basil – 216
Symphony of Six Million (1932) – 147, 149-154, 156, 181, 195, 286, 387-391, 391p, 393

T

Talbot, Lyle – 181, 412-413, 424
Talbot, Margaret – 413
Talk of the Devil (1936) – 216-217, 449-450
Tallent, Jane – 435
Tandy, Jessica – 248
Taves, Brian – 409-410, 427
Taviner, Reginald – 260, 483
Taylor, Estelle – 80p, 305, 315, 341, 435-436
Taylor, Kent – 238, 239, 499
Taylor, Lawrence – 248,
Tearle, Conway – 381
Tearle, Godfrey – 362p
Teasdale, Veree – 424
Temple, Shirley – 224
Ten Cents a Dance (1931) – 132-133, 134p, 140, 370-371
Ten Commandments, The (1923) – 313
Tetzlaff, Ted – 467
Thalberg, Irving – 27, 86, 199, 364
Thalberg, Sylvia – 364
Thayer, Tiffany – 161
Thimble Thimble (1920) – 22-23, 500-501
Thirteen Women (1932) – 160-162, 393, 398-399
This Is Your Life (1957) tv – 266, 504
This Woman (1924) – 43, 315-316. 469
Thomas, Dan – 415
Time Out for Murder (1938) – 225
Tinling, James – 490
Tillie's Punctured Romance (1914) – 16
Tobin, Genevieve – 417
Todd, Thelma – 118, 119, 136
Toler, Sidney – 230, 461, 463

Tomorrow We Live (1942) – 242-243, 472-474, 474p
Tone, Franchot – 173
Tong, Kam – 472p
Toomey, Regis – 466
Torch Singer (1933) – 175-176, 405-407
Torrence, Ernest – 60
Torrent (1926) – 65-69, 67p, 96, 286, 32-330, 330p
Tover, Leo – 151, 161
Tracy, Lee – 156, 160
Tracy, Spencer – 266-269, 269p, 271, 288, 486, 487, 487p
Transgression (1931) – 141, 307, 380-381
Travis, June – 214p, 448
Treasure Island (1920) – 33
Trivers, Barry – 499-500
Trumbo, Christopher – 495
Trumbo, Dalton – 231, 494-495
Trumpet Blows, The (1934) – 176
Tucker's People (1943) book – 246-247
Tuska, Jon – 213, 460
Twelvetrees, Helen – 118, 119, 120p, 132, 141, 145, 147p, 154, 156, 176, 367-368, 367p, 384p, 408

U
Ulmer, Edgar – 473
Uncle Tom's Cabin (1918) – 33
Underworld (1927) – 84, 85

V
Vadja, Erno – 84, 324
Valentino, Rudolph – 32, 33-36, 37p, 39, 43, 46, 56, 77, 127, 286, 288

Vallee, Rudy – 243
Valli, Virginia – 362
Vane, Sutton – 313
Van Trees, James – 173- 405
Velez, Lupe – 169
Vernon, Wally – 227-229, 490
Vidor, Florence – 75
Volcano (1926) – 71, 136, 331-332
Von Stroheim, Erich – 25, 27, 232

W
Walburn, Raymond – 233
Walker, Johnny – 22, 500
Walking Dead, The (1936) – 1, 205-206, 212, 287, 440-444, 444p, 457, 483
Wallis, Hal – 182, 184, 188, 205, 219, 412-413
Walsh, Raoul – 56, 57, 61, 164
Wanger, Walter – 75
Wanted (1930) playlet – 110-111, 114-116, 115p, 116p
Warburton, John – 162
Warner, Doris – 170
Warner, Jack – 135, 178, 180p, 188, 199, 210-212, 219, 456
Warren, Harry – 182, 415
Way Down East (1920) – 23
Weaver, Marjorie – 454p
Webb, Alexander – 52, 123
Wetzenkorn, Louis – 386
Wells, H.G. – 443
Welles, Orson – 267, 486
Wellman, William – 72, 173-175, 288, 333, 334, 405
Werker, Alfred – 222
West of Shanghai (1937) – 1, 219-220, 455-457

Whale, James – 170
Whalen, Michael – 225, 489
While New York Sleeps (1920) – 225
White Cockatoo, The (1935) – 194, 428-429, 502
White Shoulders (1931) – 141-142, 142p, 373-375
Who is Hope Schuyler? (1942) – 242, 469-470
Wilbur, Crane – 219, 457
Wilcoxen, Henry – 490
Wilkerson, William – 245
William, Warren – 139, 189, 211-212, 447
Wilson, Carey – 345
Wilson, Harry D. – 143
Wilson, Lois – 38, 80, 266, 306p
Wilson, Victoria – 369, 371
Winchell, Walter – 154, 221
Windsor, Claire – 96, 97, 110, 127, 360, 362
Wise, Robert – 256, 481
Wolfert, Ira – 246-247
Wonder Bar (1934) – 181-188, 186p, 187p, 200, 414-418, 418p, 502
Woodbury, Joan – 490
Woods, Donald – 412, 496

Woody, Jack – 368
Woolcott, Alexander – 191, 422
World Premiere (1941) – 243-244, 466-468
Wurtzel, Ben – 225
Wurtzel, Sol – 222, 223, 224-225, 226, 231, 239
Wyman, Jane – 245
Wynn, Nan – 466

Y

Yeaman, Elizabeth – 162, 164, 170, 424
Young, Elizabeth – 176, 408
Young, Loretta – 132, 134, 158, 173-175, 174p, 244, 288, 405
Younger Generation, The (1929) – 99-100, 102, 150, 355-357, 467
Young Rajah, The (1922) – 35

Z

Zanuck, Darryl – 74p, 134, 135-136, 139, 220, 222, 223-224, 239, 376
Zbysko, Wladak – 402
Zeffrin, Lester – 458
Ziegler, Jules – 246
Zukor, Adolphe – 33, 75, 78, 339

www.ingramcontent.com/pod-product-compliance
Lightning Source LLC
Chambersburg PA
CBHW060310230426
43663CB00009B/1650